AUSPICIOUS THOUGHTS, PROPITIOUS MIND

Published under licence by Brown Dog Books and The Self-Publishing Partnership, 7 Green Park Station, Bath BA1 1JB

www.selfpublishingpartnership.co.uk

ISBN printed book: 978-1-83952-057-0
ISBN e-book: 978-1-83952-058-7

Cover design by Kevin Rylands
Internal design by Andrew Easton

Printed and bound in the UK

This book is printed on FSC certified paper

MIX
Paper from
responsible sources
FSC® C013604

AUSPICIOUS THOUGHTS, PROPITIOUS MIND – THE PARTS AND THEIR CHAPTERS

PREFACE

To have a disposition means a person's inherent qualities of mind and character. Our character is determined by our inner moral values, and our personality reflects what we're like as an individual, and the positive or negative way we view the world. If we are cheerful, we're often said to have a sunny disposition, which, when taken in the best sense, needs a sound mind; and a sound mind is that state of a person's mind which is adequate to reason and comes to a judgement upon ordinary subjects, like other rational people. In law, our sound mind is the state of mind of a person which is sufficient to reason and reach a judgement upon ordinary subjects, like other rational persons. There is a presumption of law that every person who has acquired full age is of sound mind, and therefore is competent to make contracts and perform all civil duties.

It is difficult to say whom this book is for, or indeed, if it is for anyone specifically at all; or perhaps more grammatically expressed, we should say, for whom this book is written, whereby it is implied, as sine qua non, that they would read it. One may write a book with the intention that others, even many others, will want to read it; or a book may be written just to get something down on paper, to get it off one's chest, so to speak. In a way, this book is written as if the words could be contemporaneous notes, a record for what any man or woman of today may be saying.

As sentient creatures, we all are capable of some useful degree of perceptiveness, and that degree can be heightened by informed contemplation; informed perhaps by some of the aspects within these writings. And those who become experts at informed contemplation may even find their curiosity can be somewhat requited and so add that to their perception.

The book's title was chosen because it suggests aspects of **eudaemonia (Aristotle),** meaning achieving the best conditions possible for us, in every sense – not only happiness, but also virtue, morality, and a meaningful life; and also aspects of a practical philosophy that can encourage an adroit and practical worldliness, a certain 'savoir faire' in matters of the heart and mind. Some thoughts are expressed here, some opinions mooted, some questions posed; some provoking questions as well as provoking answers are offered, as well as some generally held attitudes and beliefs challenged. Some readers may see a touch of satire and what may be accepted as wit.

It can be both evocative and provocative; can appeal to any philosophical turn of mind in us, perhaps even question the psychology of our thoughts, our way of thinking, our beliefs and those subsequent actions, not only as individuals, but also for groups and nations. It can interest the secular, the humanists and the believers. Having read, some may think, 'Yes, I agree with that,' or 'No, I don't,' or 'I didn't know that,' and 'I wonder if this author is right about that?' It may also serve as peripheral reading for students of psychology and philosophy, but if the professors didn't like that, and in despite of that, the students could still go and read it.

This book can be viewed as a study, a treatise, to be considered with some degree of serious application. Some apology is made for using unusual words, even words with scientific origin. The English language has very many words that lie unused as unpopular, not taught in schools, not spoken on TV or in films, in case the viewers and readers are left in some bemusement or some ignorance of the meaning of the script or text, and so feel cheated in the pocket for what they have paid out for some entertainment. These days it is easy to 'Google' a word whilst reading, to get the full depth of the meaning an author wishes to convey, and that is so here, with this book.

The author uses the full range of words at an author's command, be it English, French or Latin or whatever, believing that words can give a text a more full meaning to the reader if used as they should be, else why else are they there, in the vocabulary, and yeah, even in the dictionary, else they will be lost to the language? Readers may get more from this book, then, if they have a tablet alongside and search online dictionaries for their interpretation of words found unfamiliar in meaning. Or, if keen still, but struggling, the tablet alongside could also be a paracetamol, to be taken with a glass of water.

Is this a book to read and then give to the Scouts' used book sale? If that is to be inevitable, then before that, it is hoped a reader will find within its pages something to chew on, to ponder over, before rushing, or perhaps wearily plodding, onto the next chapter; but then at least one would be able to say honestly at dinner parties, 'Yes, I have read it.' As a collection of interrelated, correlated thoughts with some non sequiturs thrown in, some might want to discuss it. Some never seem to want to discuss what they have read, unless pushed, and there are others who find stimulation in almost everything they read and are often very ready, keen even, to discuss the book with someone, usually someone of a similar intellect.

The thoughts that began the process towards this book began to be compiled in the late 1950s, when 'A penny for them', meant 'A penny for your thoughts' – an often used expression – that you wanted to engage in conversation with someone who was obviously deep in thought, but you didn't want to intrude to any great degree; so you offered just a penny, and not ten pounds. Which prompts the question of what price do we put on peace of mind, or on knowledge and wisdom; and it will become the reader's choice to say whether there is any of that in these pages.

There will be many instances in these chapters where the word 'man' is taken to mean mankind, and it is hoped that the intelligent female reader will not endeavour to deny the history in which men were, by some sort of evolution, probably due to physical strength and brutish roughness, due to testosterone, the first, the prime, if we are allowed that word, movers and shakers of history; the rulers, for the most part, and yet, when it suited man, they fell back on their undenied acknowledgement that when a man wasn't available, such as a king, a woman could do the job just as well, and there are many examples to illustrate that. No, it's mainly a biological thing: women bore and raised the children, for their confinement at term took them out of the loop, and so men generally held the reins of power, at the top and in all the seams through society.

But today things are very different, and women assume their rightful place alongside men, taking it in turns to hold the reins, and society is the better for it. However, history pops up and it is that history that is inevitably alluded to here, in these chapters, from time to time. And of course, if the word 'man' is written specifically to refer to the male sex, that will be made clear, otherwise man and mankind means men and women and humankind. There is no need for anyone to get upset, certainly no need to start stuttering and spluttering imprecations, if there seems to be any bias to one or the other; that just isn't meant, just isn't there.

The learned with their erudition may read and regard all these lines from their magisterial height as just a homespun philosophy, and so, in saying that, aim to prove their worth, to earn their keep. For the clergy there are certain aspects in some chapters that they could well dismiss as 'wrong thinking' and throw it away, burn it, even wouldn't want it in the church jumble sale raising money for the leaking roof.

The young? It could well be for them, but they're too busy finding out about life for themselves, freed from parental and scholastic restraints, making friends, wining and dining in bijou bistros, drinking too much, making love, and making mistakes. No time at all to read; too busy texting and Facebook, Twitter, Instagram, gigs and making friends, perhaps meeting a future life partner. Can't neglect that earnest search for a mate to read a book; or else off seeing the world (good thing), preferring finding out for themselves, making up their own minds, and making their own mistakes. It's a pity because so much of this book could potentially be of wholesome benefit for them: the millennials and the snowflake generation.

The parents of the young? No time to read; too busy working, hard-working earning to sustain the household income, and then too tired to read, just too, too busy. As parents, they are responding to their responsibility for a family home raising children, and so working, like the seven dwarfs singing, 'I owe, I owe so off to work I go.' We must keep up the mortgage payments, the maintenance payments to the WW1 (Was Wife One) and the payments on the car. Comes in from work, reads the kids a story, eats the reheated supper and falls asleep in front of the telly. No time for reading. And the weekends? Where do they go? Liking weekend lie-ins, brunches, some footie with the kids, the Sunday papers, Sunday evening glued to the hypnotic, shallow, predicable TV dramas, hoping to see a frisson of sexy flesh, and with that moment, feel alive, young once more. And then it's Monday, bloody Monday. Shame, as this book is also for them.

The elderly? Old dogs? 'New tricks.' Too late? Too challenging of their long-established thinking. Too late: schmuck. The surfers? They'd prefer to find it on the net, or a screen, not a book.

Adults, having been young adults once themselves, can suppose after some observation, that the young adults of today are, in all reality, probably only a little different from the way young adults have always been. Some of these young people admit they didn't pay much attention in class, or reckon the teachers were rubbish, only later, a few years down the line, find they have developed a quest for information or opinion; a desire to rack up their street cred. And yet, it is more than just a matter of street cred; many find on reaching true maturity, for men around 30 and for women around 25 years of age, that they now have an awareness of their sensibilities. It is that awareness of their sensibilities that this book seeks to arouse and expand, a kindly, just and proud sensibility, one that can come to balance the two factors we all have to deal with, to face up to and resolve, the factors that all issues subsume to, boil down to, and they are money and ethics, or a mixture of both. And we can include sex in with ethics, if we must.

Agree or disagree with what is written here has then, at least, stimulated something. One could say it is written from experience, 'Pour encourager les autres', but that is not completely true, and yet there is an element of truth there. Only an element, because after 20 years in the writing, it is not thought possible for anyone to be so smart, so good, so correct as being able to put into practice all the hints and nuances meted out in these chapters.

The nature of the deity as described in these pages is that of 'In Omnibus Deum,' that translates as meaning 'a god for all.' In Latin so that it has that terrific impact in the language of the great Roman Empire that presaged the early Christian Church. Presented here is a plausible understanding of the nature of God, like a fact, a fact of life and the expression of that explanation may or may not be uniquely new. If it is not entirely new, then those earlier or pre-existing explanations are very rarely heard, certainly not in modern times. And so now, perhaps for many people, the theme running through this book can come as a new concept for the reader to think about. In the following chapters, words and phrases occur from time to time that can be heard, albeit in different contexts, in the marketplace of life, and so they have no special identity that is attached to them. This author has listened to wise and less wise words of many of those who are always ready to tell us how to think, and how to be, and as a result has come, through the years, to a way of thinking now set out in these chapters that anyone picking up these thoughts, and then reasoning them, may derive and acquire some peace of mind. Here also, many questions are posed, and not so much the suggested answers, but a pathway offered for some self-reasoning to find an answer that fits, for the while.

Reading and devouring books written by a range of authors and thus their different types of books over a lifetime will inevitably leave their mark; and of those authors most notably are such as Andrew Roberts, Robert Harris, Margaret MacMillan, Ian Kershaw, A. J. P. Taylor, Max Hastings, Leo Tolstoy, Mikhail Sholokhov, Pushkin and Dostoyevsky, Anthony Trollope, Jane Austen, S. S.

Montefiore, Alexander McKee, R. Knight, James Holland, John Steinbeck, Harper Lee, Somerset Maugham, J. B. Priestley, Ernest Hemingway, Walter Macken and many others. Rather too many perhaps to set down here, all of whom who have enhanced the author's life, by taking from each book at least one learned fact or some facet, some aspect of human existence to add to the pieces of the puzzle, the picture and then, in a way, to produce a sort of distillate that is this book with its so many garnered observations, inferences, ideas and reflections on society, as society is now, or as it was in their time; that time, those days that have helped shaped us as we are today.

The author uses the term 'we,' as if in some sort of illusion, the reader might think it is an allusion to the royal 'We'. The use of 'we' is deliberate as it carries with it the notion that, at least, it is the recognition and appreciation of the collective effort that has brought this book about. We start with, as hopefully the reader here will move on and read later, about our two minds, Mind A and Mind B, that 'alter ego,' that when in accord, in agreement, if both could speak simultaneously, they would say 'we.' Please note, we are not talking of 'bipolar' here, or even schizophrenia, for those unfortunates suffer from a deeper malfunction of the duality of our minds.

The 'we' also includes the ever-understanding tolerance of a very intelligent and gifted spouse who feigned indifference during the time 'in utero' of this book, patiently waiting for the parturition. The 'we' also includes the long-'suffering' dedication to the cause of Clare Backshell, by whose friendly support, frustratingly struggled to read the author's appalling handwritten manuscripts and set them into digital format so vital these days for any real hope of progress, hope of getting anything done. The 'we' includes the proofreader: what patience, tolerance and single-mindedness sorting out errors from intentions.

The 'we' includes the publisher, whose art and skill in making decisions that can have far-reaching effects on those with their interest in the publishing house, including that interest being a livelihood. And the final 'we' can include you, the reader. Many pleasures, sentiments, paragraphs and chapters are waiting with the air of taking you along with the author, a sort of 'cruise in company,' both in the same boat, looking out, where it's going, and looking within, for all that the boat has to keep you afloat, and nurture you, secure you, moving on to the next waypoint. This may seem an obscure analogy, but as Mr Bennet says to Lizzy, his daughter, to the good news from Mr. Gardiner, in his brother-in-law's letter,

'Read on, Lizzy, read on!'

The author makes some apology to the grammatical purists who take issue with his starting a sentence with a conjunction, or a co-ordinating conjunction. The prose is written in many places as if being spoken direct to a willing listener, viva voce.

On occasion, the author's observations, remarks and thinking have been set down as intentionally oblique, not deliberately to obfuscate, but to endeavour to initiate a thought-process leading to a thought-chain, a questioning, not only what the reader reads, but the reader questioning their own previously held concepts, beliefs and understandings. To chew things over; to agree, or to disagree, to research further towards, perhaps, an enlightenment.

The book endeavours to impart two ideals, similar in a way to the Gospels' record of what Jesus advised of us, 'To render unto God, that which is God's, and to render unto man, that which is man's. Which is also to say, to know what are 'God's Rules' and 'Man's Rules.' And before the atheists say 'Pish' to that, let's hope they will read on, and then ask themselves, 'Pish?'

The author arrived at retirement after a working lifetime of experiences of meeting and 'dealing with people,' business associates, employees, friends, clients and those no longer clients as having sought the services of another more to their liking (inevitably, but hopefully they were only a handful). Succumbing almost, but not mentally, only physically, to life's stresses, the author sought out as if led by an automaton, or unbeknowingly, his angels, the advice and help needed to look at life differently, in a better, more relaxed and fulfilling way, certainly a more philosophical way. It is those very thoughts, curious perceptions and understandings that form the basis, nay, the excuse for this book.

Some of these lines here are hardly likely to go down well with those who unreasonably love formal ritual, and religious ritual for its own sake. Pomp and circumstance are fine for the military. They need it for their 'esprit de corps,' to go to war, and we like to see their ordered disciplines. We need them to help us know they are there, and we feel just that bit more secure. But religious vestments lined up like troops with their generalissimo. No, thank you; man's vanity, vainglorious reasoning. In royalty? Yes; the monarch is still notionally head of the armed forces. In Great Britain the monarch is there by the will and consent of the majority of the subjects and stands as the keystone that holds up the arch of our state, based on parliamentary and judicial law, the law of the land.

Most of us have bleated plaintively at one time or other, 'I just didn't think.' These chapters are aimed to encourage a practical thinking, based on a practical philosophy, and an everyday psychology. Psychology is a science, whereas philosophy is an art, and where the two range alongside each other, the edges become blurred. And in that blurring, counselling can be found. Counselling is probably the most useful of the three disciplines.

The London, England, bus route 88 takes passengers between Camden Town and Clapham Common, and has done since the late-19th century. It was in effect then an omnibus for commuters, and horse-drawn, for those working in the city but living in the then rather unremarkable suburbs of Clapham.

There is this notion, a concept, of a bald-headed man on the back of the Clapham omnibus, that has been and still is used today in law and elsewhere, but today in that notion that 'man' could just as equally be a woman or another of indeterminate sex. The 'Man on the Clapham Omnibus' is a hypothetical person, regarded and accepted as very ordinary and rather nondescript. He is a reasonable person, reasonably intelligent and educated. It is he against whom all our conduct can be and has been measured, as a norm, that middle road we, in all generality, come to know as acceptable and safe, with no heads above the parapet. Public opinion … is the opinion of the bald man at the back of the Clapham omnibus. Oh, would that it were still. And so it might be, if it were not for Facebook and Twitter etc.

Why bald-headed? It is said men shed either tears or hair. It depends. And why at the back of the bus? There he can observe the others or just choose to ignore and continue to ponder and muse. And being bald we can could assume he is a man in command of his feelings, and so of note, a thinking, philosophical man of some sound judgement as he considers his values, his opinions and his preferences in all things. But, equally, he could be very hirsute and not ever easily given to tears.

A legal fiction is a fact assumed or created by the courts which is then used in order to help reach a decision or to apply a legal rule. The concept goes way back into history. In Roman law, the term, 'bonus paterfamilias' (good family father) refers to a standard of care, analogous to that of the reasonable man in English law. The French term, 'bon père de famille,' conveys the sense of a reasonably cautious person, and a man of ordinary prudence in managing his own affairs.

In this zany, crazy unstable world, is there place for the 'man on the Clapham omnibus?' Most certainly not only a place, but also he is needed, and badly, not as an embellishment on society, but as a cornerstone, and at the foundation of any and all good society, a certain common sense, that is the reality of that Clapham man.

There is a certain logic in the order of presentation of the chapters, but it may not be the reader's preferred order, assuming there is enough there to like in the first place to want to shuffle them around, like the scholastic mullahs do with their Koran.

Yes, it's a bit like that: chapters arranged with the author's own idea of a logical order. That wouldn't ever do for a thriller. And this is certainly no thriller. And, although it may not be a page-turner either, as we said earlier, it is hoped to be a good read, for someone.

Read on, Lizzy, read on, is the encouragement of Mr Bennet.

INTRODUCTION

Within these chapters is an introduction to a line of thinking of a practical and useful nature, that can lead towards a self-awareness, and a path, if chosen, towards some peace of mind. The reader may come to think and accept this as an example of a useful practical philosophy; a pocket philosophy. Not a pocket in the usual sense but that pocket of the mind, so not literally weighing us down as an inside jacket pocket or hiding in a handbag. Here is a philosophy that can actually be practised, while other philosophies may be just studied. Practised in the sense that it is a rehearsal that can be repeatedly rehearsed until the performance is just right, and right enough to be happy with it, with little risk of 'first night' nerves when the time comes; but also practised in the sense when doctors practise medicine, delivering daily of their skills, not as an automaton, but as a course of action that is expeditiously reckoned and chosen through training and experience.

If we have a philosophy in our life, we have a theory towards adopting an attitude that acts as a guiding principle for our behaviour, and then our having or showing a calm attitude towards disappointments or difficulties that may come from our actions or from those of others.

This book is presented in seven parts. Each part has its chapters, and each chapter mostly has some correlation with its preceding chapter and to that part's chosen title. The seven parts are titled with a phrase chosen to convey a meaning to its chapters. The first part deals with something of the forces in life that daily act upon us, whereas the second and third parts look at our existing together, as individuals, as groups and as nations. From there, the reader is taken on to a theme of how certain numbers can feature and have an influence our lives, while the next part, the fifth, looks at when things go wrong. The sixth ponders how our imaginations have worked to bring us to where we are today and how our minds can create some adopted beliefs, some troublesome. The final part, the seventh, presents chapters that offer a concept of a life of worth.

Possibly the most striking idea set down is that which challenges our commonly held notion of God, and of the gods that people have 'identified' as something they felt they needed in their lives since early man; the ideas challenge the feeling of there being a final arbiter, and that's no bad thing, but when we grant human characteristics to our chosen god and give that chosen god daily power over us and all our actions, thinking all the while of God as a person, a sort of all-powerful but real person, up there in the clouds, or Heaven, whatever that is, then this is a matter worthy of closer scrutiny.

Here presented is an explanation, an answer, a response to that notion of God people hold, such as the bereaved for an unexplained loss, demanding, 'Why did God let this happen?' The answer offered here turns a common concept of God on its head and puts to the reader that God, yes, is truly there all the time, always has been, but has been sadly only as the unknown god in us, Deus Incognitus. And this book seeks to unveil the concept 'In Omnibus Deum,' meaning 'A god for all' the unknown 'good' in us, in the world, too, so we may have a chance at a better understanding; one that even atheists cannot reasonably deny. But getting anyone to change their fundamental beliefs, one may as well stand fully clothed under a cold shower tearing up £20 notes.

We can choose to acknowledge and accept the power of goodness in our lives. Goodliness directs all our decisions, our thinking and our feelings, our finer feelings. There are some very simple 'one-liners' to chew over in the TV commercial breaks; one-liners such as, 'Why we really should eschew anthropomorphisation of the deity.' And 'No one is with you constantly; no one is completely on your side.' Thinking about that one, this follows only too well, 'When we sign, we are signing as the MD of our life.' And we are always the MD of 'Me Incorporated,' unless we have a Power of Attorney appointed, who then becomes our MD; and that's tough.

We know that 'God' is not the property of any one religion or set of beliefs; God is all goodliness and so is all-embracing and whilst the Trinity, the Beatitudes, the Commandments and the twelve disciples have been adopted and are most pertinent to the Christian faith, anyone of any race can 'pick up and run' with the message of love in these 'fundamentals' that represent expressions of love. For anyone at the bus stop, when the bus arrives, the omnibus, can get on the bus, there's always room, and if we don't get on, the omnibus goes on. There's always room, as Jesus said: 'In my Father's house, there are many mansions.' Something of a TARDIS, then.

This book looks closely at some words we use, everyday, yes, used literally every day, without thinking about their true meaning, and also those words that crop up when we are being earnest, used again without thinking, or knowing almost anything of their true or reckoned as generally accepted meanings; but also words in the scriptures and beliefs, particularly from the point of view of their etymological derivation. The writer likes words, likes people to 'mean what they say, and say what they mean,' and to look at the motivations we have, if any, for those phrases we trot out in conversation, in meetings, in seriousness and in jest. Such as, 'With respect, I think…' and 'Have a nice day.'

Within the following chapters there is much focus placed on our animal origins and the animal within us today, that many would rush to deny. We live in a highly sexualised society, but society may well always have been so; but hardly the same degree at all as now, for modern communications and the general liberal attitudes to dress and vulgar behaviour, with so much flaunting among both sexes demonstrating the obviousness in that sexualisation, for many, it is the high spot of their life. 'What else is it there for, but to take and enjoy?' they ask. And they may well ask. After all, one cannot have sex without getting 'anatomical' and anatomy is biology and biology is animals. And the whole business is commercialised; businesses making a living because they know that sex sells; anything that appeals to our basic inner self, from dresses to undress, to our conviviality as the purpose, the raison d'être of living a life, or should we say, 'living the life.'

And yet, almost as if we are all born with dual natures, we have a dichotomy, that other side to our characters, our higher side suggestive of less animal, less base. It involves keeping our clothes on and using our brains, either to be creative, or simply to earn a living, but hopefully both. In the duality of that challenge to our lives lies the eternal conflict between ethics and money. There is more written on this intriguing mix that follows inside the chapters.

This book is about us, today, not in history, yet, and so seeks to present some questions about human life in this, the early years of the second millennium of the Common Era (aka AD). The term Anno Domini is usually translated or understood to be 'the year of our Lord' or, in other words, the date taken to be the year of the birth of Jesus Christ. It is our arbitrary date, worked out by our astronomers to be the nearest reckonable time by, and in, the movement of the cosmos. If we are going to count the years, we need to give them an identifying number as they go by, and we need a start point, and that point was chosen and adopted by the Western, mostly Christian world, and now the world generally, for the sake of agreeing and accepting something common, as common ground so we, the world, can move on. Of course, ancient civilisations, Chinese, Japanese, and Egyptians etc., have their own 'start date', but for the purpose of 'getting on' today, they seem mostly to have gone along with the Western notation.

The term Anno Domini does not sit well with many who, not being Christian, or un-Christian and an 'I deny Christ,' have pressured for the term 'Common Era' (CE) instead. BC (before Christ, so becomes BCE – Before Common Era). The start point is still the same, though; namely, the most closely reckoned year of birth of Jesus Christ. Odd, that! So, they don't mind the start date, just the term applied to it, as was. When it comes down to the bedrock of what is logical in people's beliefs, there are very many absolutely illogical-illogicalities in so-called 'religious faiths,' religious thinking.

That a life can be led with peace of mind is something we all seek, if only we knew it, and that is the peace of God, which is said to pass all understanding. We can and should strive to reach that understanding, and the life with peace of mind will be a worthwhile life, led by a worthy person, of integrity. To go a whole life so, would be a wonderful thing; and literally a thing to fill us full of wonder. Frankly most of us would 'give our eye-teeth' (as it were, so to speak, but not literally) for a week or even a day, and perhaps even for a full hour with complete peace of mind.

If we can get control of our thoughts, we can learn how to tame and live with our feelings. We can choose what we think, with practice, and we can choose to some degree how we feel about things – with practice. We can elect to move towards more peace of mind. All our life means making choices; mostly choices for making a living, for money, in all its aspects, and choices for an ethical life. Both mean making a quality choice; making the best choice for us, in line with our adopted values.

We focus quite a lot in these chapters on our thoughts and ideas and also on kamikaze attitudes and beliefs. Thoughts are what we consciously range our mind over as in meditation, e.g. 'Thinking about things.' Ideas come to us spontaneously as in our imagination and as creative, inventive thoughts.

Ideas that get into our heads can be false thoughts and unwise or unhealthy for us to dwell on; thoughts that go against the grain of accepted principles and culture. There is a saying in the world of computers, 'Garbage in, equals garbage out.' In short, if we make an input error, we get out a false result out. And yet, we never hear it said about possibly the finest commuter of all, the human brain, and yet it is so true. And then think of some of the trite efforts on TV, or the poisonous hate spouted to rain down of the heads of susceptible young Muslims by an evil imam. Is there such a thing as a duty of care not to fill our brains with garbage? And if so, who is to say, who is to know, what is garbage and what is not?

Ideas come anytime, spontaneously, either out of the 'blue' or as a result of something heard, seen or read. Most need writing down there and then as they may not occur again. More than one idea, notions written down become a list and lists are so very good; they stop us being 'listless.' Worthy ideas are then worked on in our minds to become worthy goals, ready to be submitted to the goal-setting process.

We very much need to be aware of our thoughts, as in beware of what becomes a 'passionate belief.' Thoughts that become 'passionate beliefs' evoke emotion, liberate adrenalin, fire up the heart and muscles for action, and when there's no action, just raises the blood pressure and 'stresses' the mind and guts into discomfort. Sir Humphrey in 'Yes, Prime Minister' once protested he'd never believed in anything passionately in all his life, and this raised a hearty laugh, but on reflection, unless it is for a truly worthy cause, one of goodliness towards mankind (er, sorry, humankind), he was wise.

Also, thoughts can come into our minds put there by others; by what we hear and read, and sometimes by what we see. If we stop to consider how a film is made based on a book, some read the book and never see the film, suspecting they will be disappointed. Some just see the film, for speed, like Japanese or American tourists 'doing England in four days,' or just don't make or just take the time for reading, and probably mostly this can be said of those who spend much time chattering.

We can 'force' ourselves to think about something, perhaps an issue, or an opportunity. Take time out and banish other matters pressing to be attended to and to 'think.' But, 'I didn't think,' is so often heard. Pity. To take time each day to meditate, to think, is so good for us, to be less of an automaton, instead more directionally driven, is better. We need to make ourselves think about the important things in our lives, what's both the 'urgent and important,' and the 'urgent but not important.' That done, we can move to the 'important and not urgent,' and then our recreation, when we endeavour to re-create ourselves, as a person, as an intellect, as a skilled person, even one of renown, but someone to ourselves, someone worthy and worthwhile to spend time with. And only then, finally, to the not-important-not-urgent, the trivia, the fanciful. Categorising and knowing what is important to us, and also what is or should be urgent: these are worthy thoughts.

So, what makes a cause worthy? Any cause that is filled with the love of God is worthy. It is in line with our adopted values, eschews the Seven Deadly Sins, reflects the messages of the Ten Commandments, and acknowledges a discipline: the discipline of accepting constraints.

Reading is to the mind what exercise is to the body. Reading exercises our imagination and worthy reading is healthy because the mind is being led constructively, and not aimlessly, for an aimless imagination is something that could then be a danger. Too vivid and too purposeless an imagination is not good. Such imaginations are fanciful and potentially harmful if taken literally, taken on-board, to lead as far as a kamikaze pilot.

The point about imagination and reading is that, and here we are talking of fiction, an author has to create characters, who then have features and characteristics, who move through their scenery, all of which is imagined by that author, and then skilfully written down in such a way that the reader in turn is able to imagine, with their own interpretation what it is the author is describing. It will be similar, but never the same, and no two readers ever have quite the same imagination from reading the same text.

Unfortunately, the young, those young with minds so potentially capable, minds that are 'brainwashed' by the many false 'earthly' beliefs that they become so obsessed and controlled by their elders that they are prepared to follow, to obey and to sacrifice their lives to idolatrous beliefs, like the kamikaze pilots dying for their Emperor, the suicide bombers dying for Allah and others for other half-brained causes, not one 'of God,' not of the good that tries to live within us, that spark of light that is snuffed out by the flood of inappropriate 'dark' thoughts that have been allowed to take root and grow into a 'passionate obsession'. Parents could better teach us always to beware our thoughts.

Often children are educated into one religion; how much better when they are educated into the vast variety of 'faiths' and beliefs in the world; the world's religions, for they form an integral part of history, and through that comes geography, which leads to today's 'humanities and politics.' They would then have an adequate education by the time they leave school to choose to go out into the world and find out more about the religions for themselves. But at the same time, it would be prudent to infuse the young minds with a better understanding of the natural 'love' within us, and how different are the feelings between us all; and to respect that, to observe, to ponder and to accept the actions of others and their reasons for them. If only there could be enough time for schoolchildren to stand and watch a herd of cattle, or a flock of sheep and then poultry, then pens of pigs; seeing how they behave, when grazing, or at 'feeding time,' and even some of their 'courtship' and mating rituals. And when the children become adults, they could see so much parallel animal behaviour in the human adult world. Few agree, as they are so very reluctant to think we can be likened to animals, it would be beneath their dignity. And that's a pity, their chosen loss.

We are so bad at keeping a tight rein on our thoughts. How many times a day, or in a week, perhaps at work, do we speak without thinking? That is to say, we must have had the thought to speak it in the first place, but we didn't think enough, in advance or be smart enough at the time, to realise what we were about to say, and then said without enough thought, enough consideration, enough sensitivity, which is the same as saying without enough feeling, enough sensibility for the sensibility of others.

Also, we frequently act without thinking. 'I didn't think,' we bleat. We do something wrong, or we break something, or we borrow something that in doing so, hurts the owner; we crash the car; all put down to 'we weren't thinking.' No, we were not, and this book seeks to awaken our awareness. What is the time? The time is now. Where are you? I am here. The 'here and now.' As we say, 'There's a time and place for everything.' We do no harm at all to ourselves, or to anyone, if we are truly alert to the now, this moment. So often our minds are 'miles away,' while doing other things, like slicing vegetables and we slice our finger as well. The here, the place, where we are and the now, right now, this moment. What is life but a series of moments?

And so, we live with our thoughts, and we have plenty of them all day long, and some are plagued with them in a restless attempt to get away from them in dreamless sleep. Dreams are our thoughts and imaginations working when we are asleep, the sleep that's recharging our body systems. Dreams are a sort of 'defrag' processing of the mind (defragmentation – as per computer speak) when we are categorising similar or linked thoughts, events and emotions we have either experienced, or we anticipated experiencing, or feared we might experience. Dreams may be pleasant or unpleasant; we don't have much choice in the matter. Or do we? Much depends on what's been on our mind during the day or previous days, or more precisely, how we deal with what's on our mind.

And there are those dreams we speak of, often lightly, as in, 'Oh, that's my dream car,' or 'That's my dream holiday.' Lightly by most, as what they say is not often a serious objective, but if their fortunes in life turn, then those dreams could come true. Oddly, through the waiting period and when the happy day of affordability comes, those items desired previously as a 'dream' no longer hold the interest. No serious goal then, because we should not speak to others of our serious goals unless relevant and related to our goal researching. We write down our serious goals to help progress them to reality because serious goals are only reached on a step-by-step process.

But there are also 'daydreams' and daydreaming, when some dreamers are found hardly conscious, not in a state of alert awareness of what they are about, but obviously awake. Our mind has wandered off on a trip, usually as trip of fancy, into a fantasy world sometimes, or perhaps a glorious trip down memory lane. And while going down the lane, we improve the dream as in edit the 'memory' to include something fanciful, some pleasing embellishment that it would appear to be like a lost opportunity retaken. And that adjusted dreamlike reality, so fulsome in the mind of our imagination, we daydream in our subconscious state until someone 'rudely' wakes us up and returns us to the hard, cruel true reality of the day, our day at the workplace, the workbench as the boss, the supervisor is bearing down on us. Who hasn't ever indulged in some 'daydreaming?'

Some say they have a constant 'noise' in their minds from ever-occurring thoughts, most of them very random, emotionally driven, good and not so good, that either delight or trouble us each waking day. We say 'waking' as what goes on in our minds at night may be something we might recall in the day, but maybe we can recall nothing, as if our minds were truly switched off, recharging perhaps. We wish each other 'Goodnight,' and mostly without thinking. It is habit, but hardly meant, not genuinely deep down meant, as if we had a concern; as in, are we actually thinking we wish someone a good night's sleep, so that they may wake joyfully in the morning?

But the noise is another issue. How can we stop the noise, or at least control and reduce the noise? Do we accept that the noise has to be there at all? Perhaps the noise is what some 'suffer,' but others, being more mindful of their minds, through genetic luck, through a fortunate upbringing and education, or through a learned skill can say truthfully that they are not aware of this 'noise' others say they are afflicted with.

Reporters present at calamities where someone has just survived, eased out of the tangled mess that was once their pride and joy Porsche, shake a microphone in your face and ask you, 'How do you feel?' Idiot: how do you think? We are supposed today to be so 'in touch' with our 'feelings' as if we have an HR compliance department in our head, monitoring, recording our every event and our every feeling. And as if any particular feeling felt is one of very many available from a collection as numerous as there are words in the dictionary, and allowed to reign at random, for a duration. It's nonsense.

On the other hand, how convenient it would be always to have a contemporaneous record of our feelings. Every decision we ever make, however logical we think we are being, even the biggest, or especially the biggest decisions we ever make, are, at bedrock, emotionally driven. Not meaning histrionics, of course, but the emotions driven by our self-concept and our self-image that together make up our self-esteem, and other factors that bear upon our personality at that time. We may well come to doubt our memory, the memory of our feelings at the time; and it is sensible to record the reasons for our important decisions, for a down-the-line record.

Just look at how confused some of us are after being in a car accident. Later the smoke of shock clears, and we marshal our thoughts into reason, a sequence, even a justification. Who can be so in touch with their feelings that they can say accurately what their feelings were at any given precise moment, even in times much shorter than 20 years ago? It would have helped had we made a record at the time, contemporaneously, but how many keep a diary these days? Politicians do, so as to justify themselves in their book published after they have fallen from grace, as they all seem to, eventually, and write hopefully to add to their pension.

Why are some so keen to accept some books as fact, when on investigation it has been found that the so-called facts were not contemporaneously recorded, but are copies, translations of writings made many years after the events took place and possibly may be the first writing down of anecdotes told as fireside or bedtime stories, 'pour encourager les autres'. After all, they had no TV to fill their time.

Reading. Ah yes. All sorts of novels, thrillers, travel, history, science fiction, or just science. Few are interested in hearing others' acerbic views on life unless they come from someone already famous, smart and preferably witty. But to the bore at the yacht club bar, that would mean listening and then having to tell what our experiences, our opinions are. It's good to talk, so very good, and laugh. Yes, we can laugh a lot. But one can hardly talk back to a book, but we can laugh at it, but right here, to laugh preferably with it.

But it's maybe too late, not too late at night, but too late in life unless we are really interested to read a book like this. We may defiantly mumble, 'The young should read this.' And perhaps they might, because the young of today are different somehow with respect to their approach to life, wanting their work-life balance to be just so; and to their reactions to life, to their experiences, their concerns, and in particular to their care and concern for others, especially friends and family. We have stress counselling, marriage guidance, charities who offer trained counsellors to the young from fourteen years of age. We have post-traumatic stress disorders and a whole tranche of neuroses that can be 'helped' by psychotherapy and psychotherapeutic drugs, psychiatrists and clinical psychologists. In the First World War if a man on the front lines had a nervous breakdown and was sent home, he was cold-shouldered as 'not brave,' and 'not made of the right stuff,' or 'coward,' even. If you refused an order to 'go over the top' and attack the Germans, you were shot; so, your choice was a near-certain chance of dying by a German bullet or a certainty of dying from your officer's British bullet, if he could shoot straight.

Some things have been written in the chapters that follow, along the lines of the aphorism that, 'What we dwell on in our minds with feeling, becomes our reality.' That reality may be a worthy reality as perceived in the greater scheme of things, that notional 'mainstream' accepted in our life, in our environment, our 'little world,' or that reality could sadly be a muddy backwater, lurking 'out of kilter,' probably a 'fish out of water' here, where we are now, but would not be so in another culture, in another country, or who knows, even another world, if there is someone out there somewhere in space for them. And for him or her, this is sad, as there'd be no conviviality and no compelling urge to be part of the community, the village communities of our existence.

The reality is what's on our mind, the rationalising of our thoughts, and such things, such challenges, lead to many words expressed, both spoken and written, as we try to fathom the human mind, living in the world, dominated by one species, the human animal.

PART ONE

A FORCEFUL LIFE

CHAPTER 1
A MEANING AND
PURPOSE TO LIFE

Sometimes we hear people say, 'What is life all about?' Or more likely, 'I just don't understand what life all is about!' Voicing that question in times of anxiety, confusion and bewilderment is very natural and so often no answer is forthcoming. So, we have another beer, or glass of wine, another cigarette, pop another pill. Some turn to religion and some find an answer there.

Does life have to be 'all about' something? Does there have to be a meaning to life, a purpose to life? Surely, we can accept that life is just there? We know inanimate objects are just there, like hills and mountains, and lakes and seas, and stones and rocks, and winds, and fire and earth. They are just there. Do they have a meaning, a purpose? Hardly, because they are not alive.

Ah! So, it's because we are alive we have to think there must be a meaning, and a purpose. Well, how is it that live things are alive, and dead things are dead, and all live things finish up dead, anyway, only then to disintegrate and disappear? Is it because we have no permanency, unlike the inanimate things, we are just here temporarily, and that as we are here, alive, then surely we must be here for a purpose? And if we are here for a purpose, that purpose must necessarily mean something, amount to something.

There must be some special ingredient that makes us alive. And what is more, all living things can reproduce themselves, bringing more live versions of themselves into the world, inevitably ever since that first life started, and the special ingredient is passed on, like great-grandma's secret favourite recipe, from generation to generation.

Once life was started, created or evolved, way, way back beyond our imaginations in time, did that life form just start as one cell, one organism, that then by mutations and evolution subsequently produced all the multitudinously wide variations in plant and animal life, including all those weird insects and not forgetting bacteria, fungi, yeasts and viruses. All life reproduces itself. If it didn't, the species would die out and become extinct, kaput.

Isn't that enough purpose in life? To keep life going, and in doing so, do it successfully? Life has to be able to adapt to the environment, and the environment is for ever changing, mostly due to the challenges brought about by all the other life forms on earth, but also by the climate with its ever-changing sea levels and the advancing and retreating ice ages, and volcanoes. All life itself affects the environment as living things feed on the environment, and, in dying, degrade, leaving chemical detritus that itself is absorbed into and contributes to the changes in the environment.

The initial life, that first cell, or more likely those first cells were probably bacteria or yeasts in the nutrient soup that is the sea. Even they were biologically and biochemically complex, but we can only theorise on how life first started. The irresistible temptation is to conclude that life evolved in the first place, as a result of the chance meeting and then a synergism between carbohydrates, amino acids, natural oils and high energy-containing molecular bonds, and life was started with the catalytic effects of sunlight and other electromagnetic radiations from space; and then miraculously evolved to be able to reproduce itself, asexually primitively, then advancing to sexual reproduction.

Whatever sort of mind could have invented such a phenomenon as sexual reproduction to advance the genetic mix so that some of the offspring faced a better chance of conquering the environment, to survive against the competition of all the other life forms on earth, including its own? All those anatomical, physiological, behavioural, hormonally driven requirements for sexual reproduction now so successful in mankind, especially for it to become such a pre-eminent occupation as to endanger the species itself, by sheer weight of numbers breeding, that the planet runs out of ingredients to sustain the species, water, food and space to move. Could we become the architects of our own demise, the environment turning against us to kill vast numbers by disease, or will the universe that brought life deliver some cataclysmic event? Such thoughts only aggravate our morbid fears.

From this conjecture, a question always arises: 'Was there any intelligent force from space, around earth acting to influence the creation and development of life, developing progressively through all those many millennia until life on earth becoming as we know it today?' And if so, has that intelligence a purpose in doing so?

It is very commonplace among the peoples of the world to believe that that outside influence was God, our God, or their God, and it's God's world and all living things are God's, as a result of God's creation, and therefore God must have a purpose for us all. But what is God's purpose, assuming there is one? The only one theologians can come up with is that God wants us, God's chosen life forms on earth, seeing that all other life forms in some way seem to be there to serve mankind's existence (does that include wasps, then?), God wants us to go to Heaven, presumably to join God, and all those who have gone before us. But we know our bodies die, and are left behind, so therefore we must gather that the spark of life that is in us, leaves us, like a bolus of invisible energy that must go somewhere, because we know energy cannot be destroyed, and so it goes to Heaven, presumably. That spark we have always referred to, until recent times, as our soul.

So, there we have it, the two options to consider. Either we are just here because life started as an accident, or more correctly perhaps better described as an event, and life then just grew and grew, or there was a divine intervention. But this is not a particularly satisfactory answer to the question and in such situations it helps to turn the question on its head.

We humans are a highly intelligent and sentient species of animal. We have too many attributes that distinguish us from the animals to list here, but the most pertinent ones are those to do with our feelings, our sensitivities and our sensibilities. We have very powerful capabilities to survive and thrive, despite all the challenges thrown at us. Such challenges as natural disasters, violent storms, earthquakes, tsunami and floods, volcanoes and forest fires, besides all the man-made disasters such as wars and failures of man-made constructions, such as collapsing bridges and tunnels, crashing trains, planes and cars, and fires that are destructive of life and property as well as accidents in the homes, in the shops, offices and factories. On top of that we have disease and pestilence and famine, all to contend with.

All of those things, life's exigencies, need to be faced, accepted and dealt with by our sensibilities, and so this life, as described above, is surely a reason big enough for anyone to admit it ranks as a powerful 'purpose to life.' In short, it is to live, to survive and to thrive as best we can, using what we have. It was Darwin who said that it is not the strongest or the most intelligent who will survive, but those who can manage change.

But what about a meaning, as in 'the' meaning? Our feelings have to do with the meaning of life. Although we generally live our lives quite unconsciously most of the time of the deep-rooted awareness within us of the need to survive, we are very aware of our state of mind all the while during this process of surviving. That is to say, while we know we need food, shelter and warmth and most have a sort of built-in programmed desire to find a mate to continue the species, we have to deal with our emotions as they ebb and flow, as things go well and then things don't go so well.

We are here then, and we must get on with living our lives. We can best do that, we find, if our emotions are on an even keel, on a level mostly hovering around 'just reasonably content.' It is because we have the experience to know or have been guided to know that there is no such thing as 'living happily ever after,' because we all are subjected to life's vagaries, its eventualities, sooner or later.

And that is a meaning of life. It is the acquired art and science of achieving a state of mind that allows us to live our lives as best we can working towards the goal of being 'just reasonably content.'

We live in a continuum of change, in which life co-exists alongside death. That continuum of life means that where there is creation, birth, growth, synthesis, integration, building and organisation, there co-exists catabolism, disorganisation, disintegration, degradation, deterioration, damage, destruction, entropy, dying and death. Energy cannot be created or destroyed; but all the while energy is being captured and harnessed simultaneously as it is being released in this continuum of change.

We speak from time to time of being positive and sometimes, perhaps more often, we hear of people accused of being negative. We live so much of our lives with the options of two alternatives, two choices of things, positive versus negative, 'on' versus 'off,' up versus down, plus versus minus, do and not do, and so on. While the general understanding is that positive is one state, and negative is the opposite, when it comes to our understanding of good and evil, it is the case, in reality, that any sense of evil is just the absence of the good, the positive state, of goodness. Absent in the sense of there being 'nothing there.' Simply, just, 'not there.' It's just 'the negative state.' Emptiness. It's the same with right and wrong. Wrong is just the state of not being right and as darkness is just the absence of light. This is important when we come later to look closer at our decisions.

We can begin to think we may be getting somewhere near the truth of life, if we can accept these two energy states of good versus evil. Having accepted, we can move on to use the positive force so as to deal with tendencies towards the negative state in our lives, often looked upon as our negativity. When we are 'being negative,' it's just that we are not being positive, which is the preferred state, and hopefully to become, or at least, for us, the aimed-for 'default' state.

We know that life doesn't stand still and 'nothing is so good it lasts for ever, eternally,' as one lyricist has it. We know what is born must die. What grows also eventually dies. Whatever is made, manufactured, processed, eventually goes rotten or rusty, or crumbles. Even the most inert of materials eventually degenerate, although millennia may be involved in that. For centuries mankind has used its intelligence to find materials that last longer, degenerate less when built into the products man has made. Brick buildings outlast wooden ones, stainless steel outlasts iron, zinc and paint treatments delay rusting. Plastics are now stronger, more durable than decades ago.

Anything that is growing takes energy. The young eat food, which is converted to energy for growing bigger, taller, stronger and also stored in the body as glycogen and fat. Seeds germinate using energy stored in the seed. Young growing plants get their energy from sunlight, from nutrients in the soil and carry out synthesis in their leaves to create the ingredients for growth. We know of no intelligence yet that can make plants decide to continue to grow, or that can ordain that their 'offspring' must go and fend for themselves, as best as they can, as they do.

Anything that is created, made or manufactured by man takes energy in some form, be it heat, electricity or the physical force of a hammer, and it takes intelligence. Our human characteristic of organisation takes energy, and even down to the simplest event such as tidying our office. In our Western civilisation most of us live complying with the law. The law is decided by the rulers, hopefully by a democratically elected government and all this is to obtain a civil orderliness, because the opposite, when orderliness is absent, is a state of anarchy. The energy expended in the human organisation of government is tremendous, but it is much less obviously so compared to the energy requirements of a factory building 1000 tractors.

We can think about the less obvious creative energy when Sir Andrew Lloyd Webber writes a smash hit musical, and about the energy going into arranging and then printing the music for the orchestra to play it, the energy spent getting to rehearsals, and in rehearsing it again and again; the energy that went into making the instruments, the energy spent by the vocalist in training, and rehearsing. Energy is used in sending the performance over the radio waves to our audio, TV etc., and then finally to us, the energy stimulating the neural 'pleasure centre' in our brain, and the goodness within us creating a feeling of pleasure and contentment as we listen.

Once dead, our bodies are burnt or entombed, placed in the earth and left to decompose, to rot, and the remaining energy is released, just as iron rusts, our cars rust, the energy that was used in their 'creation' is being released. As a building goes up in smoke, tremendous energy in the form of heat is released. It is easier to demonstrate the release of energy than the harnessing of energy.

Human beings use their intelligence to harness energy to improve their lives. We are naturally goal-seeking organisms; we are never content with things as they are. We want to earn more, have more time off, more holidays, better cars, bigger houses and to that end we plan to move to a greater comfort zone from the one we are in. But this driven effort is hardly giving a meaning or purpose to our lives, or is it?

Each invention is a mixture of inspiration, planning and synthesis and each process requires energy, and each uses the positive force, as we are talking 'creative' here. Inspiration comes at the most unexpected times and places, and sometimes it's there, the answer full and complete. Quick – let's write it down before we forget. It can be anything from an idea for a new tool, a new surgical procedure, a new means of propulsion, a book, a business venture, any of which can result in a major change in the direction of our lives. Likewise each plan, each goal we have to improve our lives, needs the positive force because the positive force is creative. So, when we fail to plan, we are not using the positivity we are capable of, and that can be due to 'negative' thoughts, feelings and emotions. And if we fail to make plans for our life, we will seem to be going backwards, because life around us is always steadfastly moving on.

If we can recognise what positive thoughts and feelings are, we can use them to move to a new comfort zone. Our being positive when planning a new business is easy to recognise, but to create a new relationship is not so easy to see. Whilst in principle it's just the same, the skills are so very different. We can go to college to learn how to build and make things, to start a new business. We mostly have absolutely no training whatsoever in how to conduct a relationship, apart from the very rare influence from wise and prudent parents or relations. Otherwise it's all down to chance, what we may or may not have read in romantic fiction and some non-fiction, and our instinct.

We are so little knowing, have so little understanding of the deep nature of relationships, that can often be so fragile, especially when young, and relationships generally tend to be the code to our whole lives. But there are many opportunities for them to come off the rails, and when that happens, our feelings of hurt and disappointment are associated with being negative, exhibiting negative attitudes. We have moods, we blame others, we can lash out, both verbally and physically. Both in mind and in character we may be physically and mentally stooping, and in the worst instances we can become ill, and feel as if we are ageing, perhaps rapidly.

Positive emotions tend to be everything that is generally considered to make us justifiably and reasonably satisfied, happy and content. Love is, without doubt, the greatest of all positive emotions. As children we need love to grow and flourish and to become adults with high self-esteem and fully responsible for our own lives. As adults, loving relationships give us by far the greatest percentage of happiness in our lives, and we can realise the importance of this.

But what is love? So much has been written; the romantic, the idealistic, logical and even the scientific. To love something is to feel good when we see, touch, feel, hear, hold, gaze upon, and admire. Such concepts may relate to the abstract sense, e.g. a sunset, a log fire, or to the tangible and physical sense, e.g. a painting, a house or a car. Of course, these things can't love us back – and there's the rub.

Love between animals and man comes halfway between our love of things and our love for our fellow human beings. We know we feel love for our dog or cat. The dog obeys us (or doesn't), wags its tail in greeting, is always in a good mood, demands patting on the head, and clearly enjoys walkies. The dog may defend our property or our person from attack but does it 'love' us? Probably, but in the concept of human inter-love, it probably doesn't. 'Cupboard love' (as in food is its rewarding feature) probably features largely in it, but there are very many animal-related anecdotes that through their own demonstrations and proofs say something more is present in many cases.

So, what is love between humans? Love is a function of the subconscious mind to which the conscious mind is subsidiary. In summary, love is an instinctive subconscious desire for maximal self-actualisation in the person we love. What is meant by self-actualisation? For self-actualisation we can try reading self-fulfilment; it almost fits, but it includes our loved one living at the outer edge of his/her own ability, and believing this edge is indefinitely expandable. In other words, wanting 'no frustrated potential,' no untapped latent potential in the one we love.

We would obviously want our loved one's life to be as successful as possible. So, what do we mean by successful? Well, for a start we'd wish him/her to have peace of mind, to have a feeling of inner happiness, freedom from fear and anxiety, and free from negativity. We'd wish him/her to be free from disease and pain; and to have energy, enthusiasm with a positive outlook on life and all it brings. We'd want our loved one to be a positive, goal-orientated person, always enjoying the pursuit of a worthy goals. Also, we'd wish our loved one to be very aware of themselves, who they are, why they are and where they are going – a healthy self-awareness.

When the object of our love has achieved all those features, then he or she will be 'maximally self-actualised.' When we positively and, dare we say it, 'helplessly' and 'instinctively' wish and 'feel' that for a person, that is love.

Hopefully we ourselves are loved in the sense defined above, and not that selfish, consuming, demanding, devouring love so commonly seen. Our self-awareness will always help relationships to germinate and flourish. But it is perfectly possible for a single person to be maximally self-actualised.

The emphasis is mostly the 'self' in being 'self-actualised,' for we cannot 'actualise' someone else. We cannot make goals for someone else. We can help to bring about the best sort of environment and awareness of the options for self-improvement by which our loved ones can flourish and move towards maximal 'self'-actualisation. All the other positive emotions subsume to love. They include such feelings as:

Esteem
Confidence
Enthusiasm
Self-reliance, responsibility

37

Happiness
Contentment
Laughter
Appreciation, Valuing
Worthy desire
Optimism
Concentration

The roots of our feelings lie deep in our primordial brain and are generally thought to arise from our subconscious mind. Our emotions are learned starting as babies. There are only two fears, believed to be present in us from birth – they are the fear of falling and the fear of loud noises, and these two 'negative' emotions stay with us all our lives. They assume metaphoric identities on top of the literal meanings. For example, the fear of loud noises are the words heard only too clearly when the boss says, 'You're fired,' and the fear of falling is when we lose our job, that represents so much of what we have achieved for ourselves, falling back down the mountain we have climbed so hard to conquer.

Yes, fear is a negative emotion, and we would normally seek to avoid being frightened unless some particular goal we are pursuing is greater than our fear of what we may meet along the way. So what other 'negative' emotions are there? Negative emotions give rise to negative thoughts and we can list the most frequently occurring emotions given here:

Anger – the ultimate expression of negative emotions
Frustration
Disappointment
Fear of pain
Guilt
Fear of rejection
Anxiety
Doubt
Resentment
Envy
Jealousy
Irresponsibility
Hate.

For each of these negative feelings there is an answer. The answer will heal, plaster over and seal in our subconscious mind in such a way as to eliminate them from our daily existence. But some we can't eliminate from our subconscious mind completely, down to what we have experienced in our life. The answers start by recognising what those emotions are, and for those who may be overly concerned, they would need to really understand how their negative emotions came to be in their subconscious. Some may need some professional help with that. But for most of us, learning how to recognise and 'shut the door' on our negative feelings is enough. Can we? Really? Yes.

So here we go with the aphorisms. 'For every problem under the sun, there is a solution... or there is none.' And, 'what can't be cured must be endured,' and as far as enduring goes, this book aims to give some solutions, and how to endure with happiness and contentment those things we cannot change. In a word, the answer is attitude: how we 'look' at things. Even more, how we choose to look at things. The better we get at choosing the way we feel about things, our aptitude at attitude is improving – going up and up, so 'attitude plus aptitude equals altitude.' A positive mental attitude can overcome negative, self-limiting beliefs, and the 'It's not what we eat, but what's eating us,' syndrome.

In launching our children into life, we should aim simply to raise children with high self-esteem, accepting full responsibility for their lives from the age of eighteen years. Children (indeed anyone) will have high self-esteem if we refrain from criticising them. If we could only criticise their actions and not them. If only we could demonstrate our love for them more, particularly when they need it most, which is usually when they've done something to displease us. If only we could spend more time with them, small amounts of quality time are not really enough but large amounts of non-quality time are almost pointless. And children need to feel and see their parents loving each other.

Generally, most of us fail in so many ways. We have no training, no experience, no guidelines, no procedures, no protocols for parenthood. We may not even have wanted the child. What a mess! We can train a team of people to go to the moon and back, another team to give a perfect rendition of Handel's Messiah, but no one can tell us how to 'choose' a spouse, how to plan our lives, how to live our lives, stay out of debt, off drugs, fags, booze, prostitutes and mistresses, avoid unwanted kids, love the ones we've got! Just no one. At school, we learn the three 'Rs', reading, writing, 'rithmetic' and more, but less about real life.

As our population increases, as population densities increase, as techno-gadgets fill our lives, as our single-minded pursuance of materialism accelerates, we need more and more to develop as people, positive and loving, for if we don't, the structure of our society will break down. There will be a meltdown. There will be a breakdown in law and order, in health and happiness, and we will generally decline as a cultured, civilised species. Our best chance is if we address the young adults, the parents of tomorrow. Young adults unfortunately are the least receptive. Their natural way on reaching adolescent and adult life is 'I'm okay, I know what I'm doing,' and 'Yes, I'll think about it, but later not now,' and 'Why shouldn't I enjoy myself with my friends?' etc. etc. Or even, 'Leave me alone, I didn't ask to be born.'

The most receptive, useful age is 30-40 when people have burnt their fingers in unhappy marriages or been nipped in business. But by 30, many personalities have been formed out of the first twelve years of adult experiences, so it's harder to seal over the negative experiences, but not impossible. Now that society accepts divorce has no stigma, perhaps it doesn't matter that people have had negative experiences to deal with. But the pain, sadness, bitterness, resentment, cost and damage done to the children is definitely not okay. We most certainly do need to educate our children and young adults about relationships, but mostly we need to teach them about themselves. There is much that should be considered before starting a baby.

The meaning of life is a philosophical question many have laboured over. Many answers are offered. Some say, glibly, but with some accuracy, 'Life is just a series of events,' which is to say that there probably is no meaning, and if no meaning then in all probability there is no purpose, other than to survive as we have said earlier. If we believe in God and the afterlife, then that belief modifies our conduct here on earth, and it follows that we, being believers, all want to enter the afterlife, and, although we are not exactly in a rush to get there, we live our lives in such a way as to earn or maximise our chances for an eventual entry into that afterlife. So we believe.

If we do not believe in the afterlife, we choose not to believe in God as generally understood, and we also are not exactly in a rush to die, then there can only be two purposes here on earth. One is the biological, subconscious, automatic need or desire to breed, to have offspring, to raise children to follow on after us, after we have gone. Just like the animals. All they do is feed and breed, then die. We could say the same for us. We are here to feed and breed, but we also take the chance to have some fun along the way.

But as will be seen elsewhere in these chapters, the urge to breed is mostly cloaked as something quite unrelated to the intended ultimate delivery of a mewling, puking babe, as a famous author once billed it. No, the urge to breed comes as a psychosensual urge, and a most pleasurable psychophysical experience at that, that says it needs to be requited, similar in many physiological ways as when we need to eat to satisfy hunger, to drink to satisfy thirst, or answer the need to evacuate one's bladder or bowels. The urge defines and regulates and modifies our whole behaviour, as we move properly towards achieving a relationship with sex as the goal, but some more shamefully moving to take what a man wants, regardless of the feelings of his victim, and totally regardless of society and its laws. Not everyone experiences a desire to mate, due to biological variation, and the urge is stronger in some than in others.

The other purpose of the godless person's life is hardly a purpose at all, because it is a non-reason. It is just this – we are here so we might as well just have a good time. 'Why else are we here, on earth?' By this, we mean almost all other human activities apart from work and raising children. They include partying, holidaying, sport and culture, but this list is not prescriptive. Of course, to have a good time, one needs cash. To get cash, that means either work and more work, but some have that craft to make their cash starting with a little and make it make more. It can become such fun, that it becomes a wholly 'good time' in itself. Think here of 'playing' the stock market.

For many believers, the contention is that life here on earth is just a proving ground, where we prove our worth to God to be admitted to Heaven. But if we fail, do we go to Hell? And after Hell? If as it is taught, God is all forgiveness, our Hell will not be, cannot be, for ever; not that state of everlasting damnation as some preachers would have us believe. That's just too depressing a thought to live with. The whole point surely is that we are salvageable. Now that's a better thought. We can live with that.

It is possible, as some believe, that after our period in Hell, we come back to earth as someone else to have another go at life in the proving ground. We can wonder who Hitler is now. Perhaps Hitler might come back as a female. Would that be fair? To fail as a man, and have to come back as a woman. Isn't that harder still (having always to carry a handbag), or is it easier, on this second bash, easier to prove worthy, given the supposed general and more gentle nature of a woman compared to a man's? Isn't more crime committed by men and aren't the prisons more full of men than women?

So, the meaning and purpose of the proving ground is that we need to follow the tenets of the particular faith, that denomination that appeals to us most, and to get on with life being as kind and as loving and as law-abiding as we can be. And that's about it, in its most simplistic terms. For those who don't want to, or just can't bring themselves to believe in God, the answer to the meaning and purpose of life is a much harder one to answer. Why? Why harder? Because they have no tenets, no guidelines, at least not those guidelines that have been passed down through the centuries by the sages, the prophets, the priests and high priests and the saints, and their big book.

But they, the non-believers, can make their own tenets to follow, some guidelines to there being some meaning and purpose to their life. But why? Why bother? After all, aren't we only glorified animals? If we take away our soul, our spirit, all that is left is biological: meat, flesh, offal and blood (and bone, of course). Why would any animal have a meaning or purpose? So, why then are we here, alive, sentient, on earth, if there's no purpose? That we are sentient can be just a matter of evolution; evolution from our non-perceptive, arguably 'thick' atavistic ancestors. All right, then, so why are we here, just alive, ignoring the sentience? Alive, yes, we are alive, but what is being alive?

What is this thing called life? What makes us different from, say, a car? When we press start, it's as if the car comes to life; it has a purpose and its meaning is very simply to serve that purpose. We know that archaeologically and anthropologically speaking the sole purpose in life is to survive. All life emerges from a seed of one sort or another and then has to survive in the environment, which is nearly always very hostile, except episodically, when it isn't.

That is, and always was, the challenge, the competition. The environment to prehistoric man was both cruel and kind, in that it provided the essential ingredients and ambient temperature to support life. But those benefits came at the expense of the merciless invaders, collectively best called 'the germs.' Invaded not only by the germs, the bacteria, the viruses, the yeasts, the fungi, and the parasites, but also by any predators, including other examples of mankind as well. Are we the only species that regularly turns on itself and in large numbers to kill each other? Or is that just an evolutionary problem? We know some animals indulge in infanticide and even infantophagia. At mating times certain male animals will fight and sometimes fight to the death for the right to mate all the females in a group. And so, in a similar way, are we not, but surely we are not, just that phenomenon multiplied upwards thousands of steps in evolutionary terms, when we fight, and when we go to war?

Today, modern man's environment is mostly, but not always, much less cruel; we enjoy the food, clothing and housing we have provided for ourselves. Now much less cruel and we are more free from that competition with time to enjoy ourselves, have some fun, and, in more serious moments, we can ponder the purpose of life, and a non-believer can write some of those tenets. Having then written them, we can compare what they have written with the tenets of the believers. And what do we find? We find that apart from the requirement to go to church and to pray, the tenets on conduct, our purpose of living together without harming or killing each other, without stealing, lying and cheating to put 'one over' someone, without fornicating and causing someone some misery and causing miserable children, or even spreading venereal disease, we see that the tenets are very much the same. How extraordinary is that? Holders of each type of tenet could face each other, sheepishly.

Okay – we know we can bring a car to life by pressing start, but that life, of course, is 'not a life as we know it,' but a life that is subservient to the will of the driver, who to a very large extent controls the fate of the car. To those who believe in fate, theirs is a lost cause because they can never best guess the will of the driver. We are more like a driverless car and we, like that car, are dependent on our internal navigator and all our safety sensors and built-in safety response mechanisms. There is no start button. Alive means the battery arrives charged, and then maintained mostly by food. All it needs, all we require, is to be given a destination, and that is the purpose of life – a destination.

We need a destination, but not necessarily a place. If we believe in God, then that place is Heaven. If we do not believe in God, then the destination is a state, a state of metaphysical existence, peaceful, loving co-existence with the rest of humanity. But hang on a minute. Isn't this what believers aim to emulate here on earth, so to be worthy of more of the same in Heaven, that state of peaceful, loving co-existence? Don't we believe in God because we accept that that state of peaceful co-existence is not achievable on earth to either the believers or the non-believers, because embodied mankind is so weak, so frail, as to be always erring? But both believers and non-believers have to try?

Who or what pressed the start button that created and brought about the life of all living things? Living things seem to be rather like the scientists' dream of a 'perpetual motion machine,' in the way living things continually and perpetually reproduce themselves. Their machine doesn't exist because they can't eliminate friction. Friction is to the machine what the cruel, limiting environment is to life. When anything that is alive reproduces itself, that 'spark' of life, that essential something that keeps the metabolism going every day until death, passes perpetually from generation to generation. It is truly something to marvel at, to wonder at all the 'sparks' of life all around us, everything that is alive, both animals, which includes us, and all plant life. No wonder people just feel they want to celebrate 'Life.'

If life was not due to that chance meeting and interaction of molecules in the sea, we can reasonably conclude that life came as a result of an influence from the universe, perhaps a supra-natural intelligence like those electromagnetic radiations from space flowing over and embracing the earth. That intelligence that is there for us all to 'link and sync' with, and to download 'stuff' such as a positive attitude and energy, and to upgrade our hearts and minds with positivity. It is that life force, the force that sustains life, and then feeds all living things as the force of goodness, and that is our understanding of God.

When we have created robots that can then re-create themselves, will we have created life?

CHAPTER 2
FORCES VISIBLE AND INVISIBLE

How often do we pause in our routine hurly-burly to think about the forces that influence our daily lives? Those forces are invisible to our 'naked eyes' – and out of sight so often means out of mind, too. What are the forces? We will know what they are from schooldays; we may very well remember their principal features, the facts known about the nature of those forces. But what we are mostly subconsciously aware of is that we are very familiar with the effects of those forces, and also, sometimes, only too consciously.

We can take a quick overview of those forces, and re-state some very elementary physics. They are gravity, electricity, magnetism. We can include the energy sources of light, the solar radiations and, rather oddly, our weather for the purpose of these chapters, and ignore any fine quibble of the physicist by saying light and electromagnetic radiations are also forces. Each of these forces has an effect in some way on our lives, either consciously or subconsciously and it should be helpful to the ongoing reading if we can take a simplistic look at the way, the why and the how these forces act upon the world. Doubtless scientists and physicists may take a different and more profound and professionally technical view of those forces, with their specialist and highly academic recently gained knowledge, recent, that is, in the last 100 years, but that would make their input of little purposeful use here.

We learn about gravity at school, and then remain mostly unconsciously aware of it and its effects for the rest of our lives. We take it for granted. It is invisible, of course; it is still not widely or fully understood, but we accept it as being there; we can see the effects of it, and know that nothing on earth escapes its grip. Newton's apple fell from the tree to the ground instead of 'floating' upwards, as it might do, if ever there were a stronger force than gravity acting on it. We use the force of gravity in so many ways, but an everyday example of its hidden nature is the cold-water tank in the loft, where water is stored to remain there, and its potential energy lies in its height, waiting to be released only to travel of its own accord downwards, drawn towards our taps when opened, but in reality, downwards towards the bowels of the earth by gravity.

Again, we learn about magnetism at school, and this force has many features making it similar to gravity. It has polarity, meaning a plus and a minus, an 'in' and an 'out,' a north and a south, and only seems to affect certain iron-containing objects. It is invisible, but we understand it as we can demonstrate its effects. Some more detail on this force is about to follow.

Electricity is a force that is mostly invisible and is present in our world in two forms, dynamic electricity and static electricity. We can use magnetism to make dynamic electricity by harnessing stored energy in fossil fuels, and this electricity is a force that always has to be contained in its conductor wires as best as possible. We can store it in batteries, and store more in bigger and better batteries. It is invisible, but we know it is there, we can see its effects. We can see the posted prominent signs, and use our training, telling us 'where' it is, lurking in wires and cables, and flowing along the conductors, going about its business as planned by man, or until the conductors are damaged by accident, such as the weather blowing trees down, tearing cables apart, interfering with all man's plans for the containing of this powerful source of energy.

Static electricity is present in the form of charges that accumulate on the surface of just about everything around us that is non-conductive to dynamic electrical charges (e.g. non-metallic surfaces). If those charges can touch or reach the surface of the earth, those charges are released, neutralised. The charges are also in the air, on minute dust particles, and these are caught up in air convection currents and winds, and then taken up to the upper atmosphere to become an integral part of the clouds. The combined power of these charges in the clouds causes lightning, which occurs when the charge is released as the equalising charge from earth and cloud with an impressive flash of the rarely visible form of this awful power. Generally, this static form is invisible and mostly its presence is very much not thought about as we go about our daily lives. Its effects are subtle, except to the scientists and the technicians trained to consider the opportunities for utilising or dealing with this form of the force.

Both forms of electricity are thought to have a positive and a negative aspect. In the static form the opposite charges, negative and positive charges, can exist on a non-conductor apart, for a while but not in too great an accumulation of either positive or negative, as the force is so powerful, that the two opposite charges apart will flow to each other to discharge, to cancel each other out and there is a significant release of energy in some other form, such as the heat, sound and light, as in the case of a flash of lightning.

Light is an energy source that when directional or focused can behave as a force. By light we usually are referring to only part of the force, called visible or white light. Light is a whole spectrum of electromagnetic wavebands, and we should not doubt it is a force because they can bring about an effect. Each spectrum or band of wavelengths exhibit different features, and apart from visible light, there are infrared waves, ultraviolet waves and X-rays, to name the commonly known ones.

We have developed mechanisms for 'seeing' the other wavelengths of this pulsating energy, so we accept and believe they are there. However, it is really the case that we don't 'see' white light, we see the effects as white light falls on objects and what we are seeing is the 'reflected' wavelengths of light energy that fall upon the retinas of our eyes, turning that energy into nerve impulses that our brain interprets as sight, our ability to see. The animals and we, also being animal, need the ability to see to be able to hunt for food and to find a mate. Sadly, not all can see, and many others see not too well, and that means, in a caring society, humans can support those with impaired vision. For the animal kingdom, loss of sight means something much more tragic for those individuals.

Heat is a form of energy that is invisible, but it has the effect of heating all known matter, when it raises the temperature of that which has had the heat applied. We can make heat by the release of stored energy in certain fuels, and make heat by using electricity, and by electricity interacting with magnetism. Fuel energy, usually fossil fuel energy, was derived from the sun acting on plant life millennia ago to grow and then die. The effect of the subsequent layers of vegetation and gravity, through time, caused massive, compressive forces that led to the formation of molecules of high energy-containing carbon bonds, which are the 'fossil fuels' of coal, oil and 'natural' gas. When their energy is released by burning, usually in the presence of oxygen, the stored energy is given off as heat and light in various wavelengths. The force of heat itself is invisible, but its effects are often very visible.

There is no opposite force to heat. The opposite of 'hot' is 'cold,' but there is no opposite to heat. When heat is absent, it is cold. This is important concept to take on-board for later, when we talk about good and evil.

Sound is a form of energy or force occurring in the form of waves of air pressure. Our ears can detect many of the wavelengths of sound, but there are many wavelengths inaudible to the human ear; some of those are audible to animals but many are inaudible to all ears, known as ultrasonic. Again, a force we cannot see, but we know it is there when we can hear it, and we can demonstrate the effects of ultrasonic sound waves, that can be impressively powerful. The effect of the force of sound is to bring about a vibration in the molecules of the substance that the sound falls on. That vibration can have dramatic effects, usually by its temperature being raised. A gas medium such as air is needed to transmit the sound waves. Where there is no gas, as in space, sound doesn't travel.

It has already been said that we are born with an innate fear of loud noises. It is interesting to note that we are unable to 'turn off' our noise receptors, our ears, and our hearing is working 24 hours a day for us; whereas we can close our eyes, or turn away. However, it is also interesting to note that hearing loss comes for very many people in early old age, becoming progressively worse. The causation is both physical and behavioural. Physical, in that the delicate mechanisms within the hearing apparatus become less efficient, and behavioural, because some of us become poor listeners as we go through life, being only too ready to say what we think and want, and spend inadequate time listening to the opinions and desires of others. On the basis of having two ears and only one mouth, it is said we should do twice as much listening as talking. People who don't interrupt are mostly really good listeners.

The point about sound is that it is the main means by which we communicate, and it represents thus a powerful force that we can use to influence others.

The weather is not strictly speaking a force of its own but occurs due to the interaction between some of other forces mentioned above. There seems to be two systems at work, one associated with high pressure in the atmosphere, and one associated with low pressure. Although not usually referred to as such, we can look on the high-pressure systems as positive and the low pressure as negative. This is reasonable since the air flows from the positive to the negative, from high to low, like the water in the loft water tank, and in general terms fine, settled weather is associated with high pressure, and unstable, overcast and violent weather with low pressure.

The weather seems to be a system of dynamic forces that gain their energy from the sun's heat of the day and the cooling lack of sun at night, and the ever-turning effect of the earth's rotation, as the layers of air closest to the surface of the earth get dragged along with that surface, and the outer layers of air dragged much less so, in a sort of laminar flow. The end results are a kind of well-stirred mix of hot and cold air masses that are being swirled continuously by the spinning earth, changing its axis from one part on the earth's surface being on its closest orbit to the sun in summer, and therefore its warmest, to six months later being furthest from the sun, so at its coldest. It's the wonder of the seasons at work.

And then there are things like volcanic eruptions spewing carbon dioxide and all sorts of effluvia into the atmosphere than can make certain influences felt by the weather for quite a period before those effects wither and die for a return to the normal almost unpredictability of the weather. Unpredictable, except in general terms for the seasons and for the next few days' or weeks' weather forecasting. There are other weather phenomena that are known about, such as the 'El Niño' effect.

That other invisible force – The Power of Goodness
There is a force acting on and in our lives, that we are seldom taught to get to know as a force, which is a pity. It is omnipresent. We can feel it, especially when young and growing up, when our emotions are being developed from their innate rawness to something that we can experience and enjoy in adult life. Sadly, we may be denied that experience and enjoyment if we are brought up denied of love in childhood. We can call the force the 'power of good,' but possibly and preferably just 'goodness,' and providing we are receptive individuals, that goodness can bring about a state of mind, the condition in our thoughts and actions, and in our heart that we can justly say is what constitutes goodliness.

Would that we could all agree once and for all on a simple name, like to other forces. No-one argues with the term 'electricity,' for example. They are all nouns, so to come up with something suitable it has to be a noun. Some will suggest 'love,' but that is too non-specific, so misused. For the ancient Greek philosophers, there were the three main types of love: Eros, Agape and Philos. No. No. That's no good. Frankly, the noun, the word 'Goodness,' is just the ticket. It says it all. Everyone knows or at least has a reasonable idea, the same essential idea of what Goodness is, even if it means different things to some, depending

49

on their diverted attitude, or any mistaken ideas that this book could help to dispel. And what is more, if we come to think of it, we already acknowledge in the vague depths of our consciousness that there exists a metaphysical state of something we already call Goodness, a concept that is difficult to grasp as it seems to want to be evasive against definition. It is as if already within our subconscious cognisance and awareness some sort of intelligence is there, in the ether, as it were, watching over our lives. We admit this every time we utter such phrases as, 'Goodness only knows,' and 'Thank goodness for that...' And 'Goodness gracious me!'

So, it is a key feature of this book to introduce the acceptance of Goodness as a force like all the other energy forces listed above, for if we can re-adjust our view on this, we get so much nearer to the meaning and purpose of life itself. We can't see, hear, smell, or touch goodness. But we can all, well mostly all (not too sure about Hitler and his like), see, hear and touch the effects of Goodness at some point in or lives, and possibly sometimes even smell the effects of Goodness, and we are not referring to incense-swinging here. The big question is, as it always was, throughout history: how can we recognise Goodness and its effects for what it is?

It seems the opportune moment now to introduce the concept that it is no coincidence that *god* is spelled with only one 'o' and *good* had two 'o's.' That is to say, in terms of the evolution of language from prehistoric man, it is possible the monosyllabic grunts that were the earliest attempts at meaningful vocal communications were used for the same meaning. But this is so for many words we still use today: one small change in the inflection in the voice, the spoken word and the meaning has changed. Sailors sometimes argue over the words 'fake' and 'flake' used for the coiling down on deck of a warp, a rope. Originally most sailors had little or no education and language was picked up by rote.

So, is it a coincidence that the additional 'o' in *good* came from a common source of the word used for an understanding of *god*? Or is it that the notion of *god* came about and thereon became always to be associated with whatever was identified as *good*? There is a force for good(-ness), the force for good(-ness) is identical to God. And there now, it's been said. The force for Goodness is identical to God.

How often do we exclaim, 'Good God!' without thinking? Consider the following statements, chosen colloquialisms that are still often used in conversation. 'He's a no-good. And I bet he's up to no good at this very moment, and in the end, he'll end up a no-good.' Compare that with the following constructed variant, dropping an 'o.' 'He's a no-god, and I bet he's up to no god at this very moment, and in the end, he'll end up a no-god.' And there we have it, 'he' not only is a 'no-good' on earth, but also, for believers in Heaven, he ain't going to get there; well, not straight away, anyway. He'll go somewhere very hot first for a time, is the belief, and we are not talking Benidorm here. And for the humanists and for Christians also, he'll have little peace of mind here on earth and will end up a deeply, deeply unhappy person in old age. Perhaps this is why it is so often said, only the good die young. And for believers in the afterlife, they could always hope to get to Heaven early, the proving over and done with, but they don't, and like a humanist, who also wants as long 'on this mortal' as they can get.

We can aim to truly recognise and appreciate what is good by having a more sensitive but acute awareness of what is good, of that which has an aura of goodness, the positive, bringing to us good and just feelings, a state of continually recognising the goodness in life, and the goodliness in others.

In considering and accepting today the contention of there being a force for goodness, we may be coming back to that early primitive understanding, prehistoric man's philosophy of the good in life. In effect what they said then and we can say now is, 'All that is good is of God.' It would also follow from this that God was not then at that prehistoric time an object or of any substance whatsoever, but more precisely a pleasant feeling of a warm, peaceful contentment of 'rightness' within each person, a state of goodliness, or the power of goodness and the 'force for good,' within.

Goodness is that state that brings and invokes in susceptible beings, qualities and behaviour of rightness, righteousness, honesty, friendliness, generosity, virtue, kindness, integrity, grace, morality, graciousness, kindliness, mercy, probity, beneficence, uprightness, and merit. It includes the state or quality of being good, that moral excellence, virtue, of kindly feeling and kindness; of generosity and excellence of quality; the best part of anything; the essence and strength. A euphemism for God.

If only we could be all those things just for a short while, let alone always, consistently and permanently. Is it possible that by the power of our own like-minded, well-meaning imaginations, we can create, meaning we can generate, that force for goodness, a goodliness emanating outwards from us, as a life force, to transmit to others, in varying degrees, at varying times, depending on our 'moods.' Is that how some became saints, like those early apostles, Matthew, Mark, Luke and John? Is it comparable to say, downloading an app, enhancing its functionality, and then sending it out to be useful to others?

All those defining positive words synonymous with good imply the attributes and features of goodness, and goodliness. And the message propounded here in these lines is exactly the concept of what God is. Goodness fits the bill as the unique permanent example of this perfection. It is not helpful for believers to refer in the prayers, hymns, chants and sermons to refer to God as Him. How did it come about that we continually anthropomorphise God, calling God 'Him' and asking for things? It is so very disappointing to see how, through all the ages, the Church and the people have resorted to ascribing humanesque qualities to God as their means, their quest of coming to their understanding of the nature of God.

One reason could be is that while accepting that God is the force for goodness, omnipresent and available at anytime for us to experience goodness and goodliness, we always feel, do we not, that there has to be a purpose, a plan for us, for our lives and an expectation that we should aspire to fulfil, and then ask for help to achieve that. And to ask for forgiveness, when we stray from the objective, the straight and narrow. Can we accept that a force for goodness is without a concomitant intelligence like ours, but is still in overall control? And one day the whistle will blow for the end of play, and the trumpet will sound that the Day of Judgement has arrived. And we have to live with this morbid fear.

Much depends on how we view the effect that other forces have on their susceptible substrates. Has gravity a design for us and for everything, drawing everything towards the centre of earth? Does magnetism design to put pressure on ferrous objects to move, or those objects themselves to become magnetised? Is there an intent? Does electricity know that at the earliest opportunity it will send its charges through a medium to offload its pent-up energy and design to bring about light and heat or other effects it is capable of? These may seem very extraordinary questions to pose. But no more extraordinary than to say that there is a super-being in Heaven with a design for us all.

Somehow we have never been able to think anything other than that we, here, alive on earth, are not the only intelligent life-form in the universe. We cannot accept that we are alone. And if there are other intelligent life-forms out there, somewhere, perhaps with a skill and knowledge of the mysteries of the universe far in advance of ours, one such could be God. This is easily believable. It is for each of us as an individual to decide which we think the more credible – that we believe in God as a super-powerful capable being out there somewhere, with a design of harvesting souls, or that the force of goodness has a design for us with its type of intelligence that we as yet do not understand but we know it's good, good for us all, potentially, if only we will allow it.

Christians believe that Christ was God Incarnate, made man, to live and to suffer as mankind suffers. He is referred to as the Son of God, and sometimes rather oddly as the Lamb of God, like a lamb to the slaughter, 'Father, forgive them for they know not what they do,' as He went to the slaughter as an innocent; innocent of anything at all, except to tell the truth against the wrongdoing in the world. Was He man or God? He was undeniably to everyone, except the most perversely minded, a man of God.

Jesus was the most perfectly, permanently positive person the world has ever known. He had all the good attributes listed above. But was he being perfect or 'good' at the time when he upset the money-handlers' tables in the temple? Didn't he rather lose his cool then? If so, is this the one and only time? Or was he completely calm and in control and knew very well exactly what he was doing in the name of the 'Father?' Almost certainly, the latter was the case, because losing his cool, even however briefly, rather goes to prove his humanity here on earth, for a duration of some 34 years?

Scientists often have a problem with the question of the virgin birth. Even some high-ranking churchmen have had a problem with this. We want to know, believe and understand how this thing could come about. We can assume that as Jesus was a man, he came with the usual XY chromosome complement. Mary had only X chromosomes, and therefore a parthenogenetic birth like worker bees (reproduction without sex) or a cloning, like Dolly the sheep, was not the answer. Somehow, the Y chromosome was introduced. It is possible that Mary, although manifestly female, had a chromosome complement of XY, but came with a complete set of female reproductive organs. In which case, she could have reproduced by parthenogenesis, like cloning.

It is a more likely explanation that one or more of the forces that act on us, for example an electromagnetic wave force, caused a mutation on the chromosome with the net result of the production of a Y chromosome in place of one of the pairs of X chromosomes. Mutations can alter our DNA and trigger cancer – for example, those living under pylons and their force-field of electromagnetic radiations. If such a force altered an ovum X-chromosome and produced a Y chromosome, could it then be the explanation of the virgin birth? In 2018, scientists found that certain wavelength energy from light-emitting diodes (LEDs) can alter DNA of certain cell systems; in this case found to be in the breast of women and prostate of men with the result of the cells becoming cancerous, i.e. causing their DNA to persistently and purposelessly proliferate, in other words to become the malign growth that is cancer.

It follows, then, that certain wavelengths can alter genes, and it is assumed even an X-chromosome to become a 'Y'. And for the form of those waves of DNA-altering energy, as far as with Mary was concerned, was this 'visitation' of a bundle, bolus or bolt of energy the 'Holy Ghost?' Later in these chapters an explanation of the Holy Ghost as a force of goodness is offered, and could such a force have been capable of achieving the chromosomal change? If so, then the powerful, focused beam of the force of Goodness, acting, drawing towards its ultimate and inevitable outcome surely must have been by an intelligent design or a focused force-field of goodness in a love-starved world. Surely not by a random chance event? Yes, that is the big question. There is much to swallow.

Supposing this was all mythology, that instead, Joseph and Mary created Jesus and the rest is all a story – and Jesus was a godly inspired person who was able to lead out his life and act out the scriptures that predict much about the life and death of the Messiah the Jews so badly hungered for. That he was a healer seems very wholly to be true, and this led to his crucifixion, which act is fact, as it was recorded by the Romans. Does it matter? Does it alter the concept of the Trinity? Well, no, not really – not in essence – just some long-held preconceptions.

All the major faiths seem to have a problem in the way in which their concept of God is put across to their faithful. Through the centuries and even up to today, there has always been and still is this anthropomorphisation element in the way that the god of that faith is referred to. That is to say, that the only way the faiths seem to be able to put their idea of God across is by bringing in an element of human-like qualities so that we can relate better to the idea of God. Writers of science fiction nearly always give the other life forms encountered in space a humanesque shape, a head with eyes (but sometimes only one), a mouth that speaks and usually a nose to breathe, but with all usually depicted in very grotesque designs. The contention is that we need to get away from any references expressed as God having a 'humanesque' quality but having an omnipresence and omnipotence. From early childhood we instil in our youngsters a mistaken concept of God, thinking and believing that we are doing the right and best thing.

When we pray, to whom are we praying? The traditional answer is to our idea of the 'humanesque' idea we have of God. The other answer is and mostly without knowing it, we are praying to ourselves, our innermost persona. What we are expressing is a feeling that, if we have been sufficiently introduced to prayers when young, we are tapping into, 'syncing' with, the force for goodness. We may be expressing appreciation or stating a positive goal that requires the force of goodness. We may be crystallising our thoughts, along the lines of a reversal of a situation that exists, such as an absence of goodness, and, for example, when we pray for a visitation of goodness to help bring about someone's delivery from a state of illness. Even atheists could pray if they accepted this.

Why, then, should we believe in the power of prayer? When a group of people are gathered together, each with a common purpose in prayer, the conjoining of the emanating goodliness can influence towards the desired result. The power of millions of people praying for the same good and worthwhile happening, praying with sincerity and a firm conviction that their efforts will succeed, with 'faith,' will and often do succeed, at some time in the future – not necessarily when most desired, but it may well happen. We may all pray that a people may be released from the cruelty of a despotic dictator. They will be, at some time, and the more sincere prayer there is, the sooner the common good will prevail. It just takes the simultaneous combined 'will' of thousands or even millions earnestly believing in the force for goodness, to pray for something, and it will happen. Prayers need to practically achievable in human terms. The most successful prayers are those that aim to bring about a state of goodliness in people's hearts and minds, and the overcoming of illness.

Prayers for peace are very worthwhile, as are prayers for reaching better understandings between nations. Prayers for honesty, integrity and selfless statesmanship in our political leaders are worthwhile, as are prayers for fair and just conduct in business-people – for a fairness, as in quality and quantities when trading, in buying and selling; and being just, in matters of mark-ups and profit margins in business. A justness, in settling disputes between parties in conflict resorting to the law. Financial compensation is not the answer for all matters before the courts, but we are ridden in the concept that money assuages all things. The culture that money assuages all ills and wrongs is no way forward towards a just society, and simply accentuates the feeling of society that money is the answer to all our problems. Far from it, it is mostly the excessive and greedy pursuit of money that is the cancer eating away at the core of society today.

As living creatures, we have been given receptors that register pain and we have been given the ability to move away from pain. Pain comes in all degrees, but in reality, traumatic pain is that with which we most readily identify. It may be the most obvious pain, for example, we feel when being bitten by a dog. We instinctively move away or act to stop any further bites! But pain can also come as psychic pain, but we may only register the pain as a feeling of disappointment or sorrow. In these cases, we seek to act to limit the causes of such feelings if we can, and if only we knew how to. Often our interactions with fellow humans are so inexpert that the 'pain' worsens instead of improving!

For example, we may have an argument with our sister: tempers are raised and we both declare we hate each other. Subconsciously, we know this is not true and we feel miserable, so we try to make it up, but in doing so, the cause of the row is touched on, and because neither of us has addressed that main question and still neither of us is prepared to give ground, the row flares up again!

Similarly, rows between husband and wife may brood on for months and even years where a sensible understanding of the fundamental issues between them has never been resolved, and frequently old 'negative attitudes' arise, such as the loathing of the wife's mother!

Excepting for a few perverse humans on this planet, we, the rest, together with all animal life, live our lives with a conscious but subconsciously driven goal of wanting to move 'to a greater comfort zone.' Here we are referring to a greater physical comfort zone for our body's needs. And some of us also for our 'psychic' needs for a greater peace of mind, being a freedom from fear and from negativity. These moves to a greater comfort zone manifest in all sorts of ways. For our physical needs, most simplistically, we need a suitable roof to live and sleep under, we need the warmth of clothing and we need nourishment for the body.

For our 'psychic' needs we need to love and be loved. We also need good company, and then opportunities for intellectual expression. We study to get a job, then a better job, to earn more pay to move to our desired greater comfort zones. We work and plan to achieve these things progressively, each according to his or her own ability and motivation. Unfortunately, with modern materialism and the acquisitive society, many have become distracted from what is a necessary or reasonable comfort zone for us to aim for, and we become obsessed with an excess of self-indulgence. But 'toys and goodies' make the world go round, make the economy work, they say. True, but wealth that is fairly and justly earned is a valid commodity; but trampling on one's fellows for material gain is often what detracts from the justification for that wealth.

What is it, then, that stops and delays the achievement of our desires, our move to a greater comfort zone? Those desires need to be realistically achievable and proportionate to our current abilities, and to the springboard that we currently are standing on. Proportionate in that all journeys begin with the first step. If we can identify and pursue only that which is good, and by acknowledging the force of goodness, we can shape our lives for the better.

No religion or faith is worthy of the name if it seeks the advance of its followers to the detriment of the rest of mankind. Any religion or faith that sets its followers apart or above those who do not follow it, is necessarily not only not worthy to be called a religion or religious faith, but merely a sect or cult of people, who unfortunately are misguided, and so can never know truly loving peace of mind. Some of these sects or cults in the world today are large and have great influence over their followers and even the host country government's decisions, as the government tries to achieve a peaceful, practical balance and tolerance in society. There are such religious faiths in the world, intolerant of other faiths, and they can grow more powerful, usually by the indoctrination of a not-so-subtle fear, and, so spread in a society like a cancer, that risks overrunning a host culture.

The great faiths that have evolved in the world have an indoctrination policy that theirs is the one true great faith. That is to say usually that their 'god' is the god above all gods. Consequently, the rivalry between faiths is real, and many of the wars throughout history have been caused by differing underlying religious beliefs. Clearly, if the world is ever going to advance to a state of true world peace, we need a much greater understanding of the way the human mind works; and come to some sort of consensus as to the meaning and purpose of human life. Whether we can ever bring true atheists on-board is a challenge, as they are pragmatists, throughout their lives, and if they ever get to Heaven, they then may change their opinion! Fortunately, most atheists believe in a moral code of behaviour that nicely coincides with the aim of moving to a greater comfort zone. Persuading them to accept the power of Goodness is the first step to bringing them on-board and should not be too difficult.

So, we can come to a consensus that sees a need for a policy of pursuing that which is very likely to help most people to move to a greater comfort zone. But isn't this what all governments do for their people anyway? The answer is that yes, governments do seek to look after our physical needs within the strictures of their underlying political beliefs. The last century taught the world that communism doesn't work, because it doesn't free its people to flourish. The previous century to that taught the world that unbridled capitalism doesn't work because of the natural selfishness and greed of mankind. The last century and this century will teach the world that socialism doesn't work either as, like communism, it doesn't free the people to flourish and have peace of mind. The European Union will fail unless just and fair private ownership and personal initiative policies are vigorously pursued. Governments could more readily bring in policies to monitor and control the wrongs of the excesses of capitalism, than ever to expect socialist policies to be efficient and provide contentment for the majority of the people. Such action will then bring about ultimately a better federal state of Europe and able to relate happily to Asia, the Far Eastern bloc, China and the Americas, even Russia.

But apart from tending the physical needs of the people, governments will need to start promoting in society those requirements of behaviour that conform to a programme for mutual understanding and acceptance between its various groups. This refers to not only religious and racial groups, but also differing socio-economic groups. One person may support dog racing and another horse racing. There is usually no friction between them. They co-exist, and their followers hardly want to change society and its government. Another person may support tennis and another rugby football. There is no friction between them, and they hardly act in such a way as to change society in the way government runs the country. But the religions and their denominations are seen as divisive. There is a mutual suspicion, and instinctive dislike for another person's different beliefs. And they want to interfere with the way the country is run, to interfere with schools, and the operation of the law, and they clone themselves to amass and live in whole streets, and colonise rows of shops. It's divisive behaviour arising from divisive theologies. Not at all of the sort of goodliness that flows from the force of goodness, if allowed.

Many people accept that there is within us something that departs when we die, that it leaves our body and goes somewhere. Those who do not believe this, mostly don't believe because there is no rational explanation of what this thing within us might be; so therefore, they say, it doesn't exist. We have conjectured that there is something that keeps all life going, and whatever that life force is, it is passed from each generation to the next. If all living things share this life-force, it is absolutely impossible for us to imagine that on the death of all living things that spark goes to Heaven. We pull up a lettuce, it dies, its spark of life goes to Heaven? Can that possibly be so? And if so, what is the nature of Heaven? Is it our concept of Heaven, those sunlit hills far away, warmth, shady glades and babbling brooks where we are young again and happy with peace of mind? With lettuces?

There is within us a centre that, rather like a light bulb that glows, or a flame that flickers, is fed by the life-force within us, our cell systems, all micro-throbbing away quietly with their machinery of cellular metabolism and producing its own source of life-force keeping the bulb just glowing, the flame just flickering. Let's give it a name, let's call it the soul. That soul thrives and glows more when absorbing the life-force from the ever-present power of goodness in the world and can be made to glow more brightly by being loved by others and by having others pray for us. Wise and appropriate meditation makes it glow more brightly, as will being in a place of beauty, or around art or music. When glowing more brightly we have more peace of mind, feel happy and content and are creative. When we die, the bolus of energy in the light bulb, our soul, leaves our body, but is not lost to the universe.

The power of goodness is like visible light, which we know comes from the sun, or reflected from the moon or from the conversion of some form of stored energy into light. The sun's rays radiate throughout the universe, indeed there are many suns. Earth is bathed in our sun's rays, day in and day out, and at night we are aware of the sun's reflected rays by the moon. True, cloud masks some parts of the earth's surface from the sun's and moon's rays at times, but there is always somewhere where it is shining, and it is still daylight even under the cloud. And similarly, in this analogy, the earth is bathed in this force field, the power of goodness, and is received by all living things for their good, stimulating and energising the growth and life of each living thing. Humans have evolved to have this centre within us, our soul, that responds to that power, and the bulb glows more brightly.

Unfortunately, just as tall buildings block out the sun and cast a deep shade, so, too, there are features that cast a shadow blocking us from the power of goodness, so that the light bulb is deprived of its need for succour to help it glow brightly to be able to see our way better. These shading features are mostly the negative experiences and poor attitude that are the causative problems for many people; negative experiences from painful incidents in their past and poor attitude is learned or, should we say, acquired as we go through life. The identification and treatment of negative attitudes can be the work of highly skilled people, and theirs will be the most important role for the society we live in today. With success in this field, we can expect an advancement of society and the acceptance of some of the ideas expressed here in these chapters that may leave an impression.

If there is little or no light, as when in the shade, it means an absence of that munificent influence, the power of goodness. It does not mean we are in the presence of evil, a force for evil. There is no 'force for evil,' only the absence of goodness. It's the same as something cold; it's just without heat. We have considered how the earth is bathed not only in sunlight, but also by the encompassing power of goodness. The question of the afterlife is best explained by the analogy that the power of goodness in the universe is rather like a steep, high waterfall and ever-ongoing, tumbling rapids, bathed in sunshine, and with much spray going in all directions and each droplet of spray holding a sparkle of light. Our spark of life that was in each of us, is like a fine droplet that is sparkling from the sun's rays, in a splash flying high then gradually falling until we hit the surface of the water and merge with the water, scattering with a burst of light. And like merging with the water, we release our life-energy to contribute to the great force field of goodness, that super-natural intelligence that 'surrounds' the earth. The water continually sends its spray as sparkling life forms that repeat the life event, not as ourselves of course, but as an entirely new droplet, in the stream ever flowing on.

Is goodness so invisible? An invisible force? Like gravity, electricity and magnetism? Their effects are relatively easy to see, to witness. The effects of goodness, we may not be so readily able to recognise, and we often need some discernment, some consideration. Our 'eyes' may become blinkered. It is likely that the good see more goodness than the rest of us. It takes practice, positive attitudes, an abandonment of prejudice to allow acceptance to climb on-board. None of these are easy; but a small first step helps. Good God, madam, sir, is it that so hard to swallow?

CHAPTER 3
LIFE FORCE

Most of us are already acquainted with some biology of our body's cell systems. The cells have a continual dependence on oxygen from the lungs and brought by the blood, which is a nutrient soup of life-sustaining ingredients, albumins and globulins, vitamins, hormones, glucose, salts, amino and fatty acids. And the blood carries the waste metabolites away to the kidneys and liver. This goes on from the moment life starts and for a very short while after death ensues.

If we consider a car being built in a factory: when it's finished, some oil lubricant is put in the engine. Some fuel in the tank, some 'juice' in the battery, all systems now complete and ready to go. Someone turns the key, the engine starts, the systems all work, including the exhaust, and it will keep running and running at tick-over revs until the fuel runs dry or something breaks, or someone switches it off.

What is it that starts us? Are we a self-running machine, self-running and running once started? An outside force? It cannot have been a human action, turning the key and pressing the start button, releasing everything from a biological battery to start our heart, like an engine that springs into life? Is there a comparison with human life here? So, what kick-started us? What pressed the start button of our life? We should say no-one, because the energy for life was already in the live eggs and the live sperm which fused to form us, the new live offspring. That egg and sperm life-force is a continuation from generation to generation and the initial kick-start must have happened now so long ago we've forgotten about it, if indeed we have ever known what that force was. Is that life-force a fantasy or a reality? We know our body's cells are alive with their continuous metabolism, but when we die, is it just that we've broken down, some part 'busted' and the engine stops?

But aren't we more than a machine? How we love to laugh and cry, and enjoy beauty? Machines don't do that. Those human features may be no more than some very complex needs of our highly developed brain working. Or is there really that something that we call a soul? We are something more than a very highly complex piece of machinery; being alive, we are self-determining, once born, and a potential power of goodness, in us, giving us, our sentience and purpose? Or is all this just so much idle pondering, when all the time we are no more than just such very complicated machines we can't possibly understand ourselves? We can't seem to reckon it all out? Do we hide in the notion of God, that all-powerful life force, life-giving and sustaining life-force, and the power of goodness? Think of that baby experiment, deprived of love and laughter that had to be cancelled because the babies weren't thriving. Without the power of goodness, the life-force, the love of God, we seem not to thrive. And the 'experiment' continues in some sad households today, yielding up to make young adolescents who are beyond any real hope of becoming well adjusted, content and useful people in society.

It's interesting to think then about hermits and how they thrive. It's a matter of attitude. Either hermits chose to live that way, or, if forced to live their way, then the hermit has survived because of his/her attitude to their predicament: a positive mental attitude. They have learned to nurture the life-force within them. They have peace of mind, freedom from fear and freedom from negativity. These things nurture and secure the soul which, like poking a fire and smouldering ashes, bursts into life. This then is the nature of our souls, and the nature and power of goodness, the power of God.

Let's consider the cells in our body, all the different types. There are those that are the original cells we were born with, the neurons in our brain and spinal cord. They are as old as the body they are in. And yet they are probably the only ones, seemingly incapable of replicating themselves as far as is known, and they don't die off for their place to be taken by their 'offspring' or replicate to replace a neighbouring neurone which has 'died' for some reason, usually as a result of a deprivation of oxygen or nutrients, or an injury, such as a bullet, or compression from a fracture of the skull, or spinal fracture, or a compression of the nerve tissue caused by a pooling of blood or a thrombus.

Other specialised cells are doing a specific job, cells like liver cells, 'filtering' the blood of unwanted and unnatural substances and denaturing them ready to be exported into the bile or sent to the kidneys for elimination from the body by the alternative route, the bladder. Liver cells perform at least twelve 'services' to the body, but this is not that sort of biology book, so they are not listed here, and the kidneys are busy filtering the blood of unwanted stuff, excreting into the ureter as urine, but not before the 'renal tubules,' those prolongations of the nephrons that deal with our electrolytes, keeping the 'salt' balances in the body right, and to keep it continue functioning. Nephrons, once come, stay or die, and like the neurone that is for life. But they can increase in size if the workload increases by the inactivity or death of a neighbouring nephron, like some sort of work ethic.

So, what we are saying here is that, of the vast complexity of different types of cells, some are born to die, like skin cells, their parents busy replicating and shoving their 'offspring' off to progressively die as they form squames so that with millions of others form our skin, and the finally dead squames being sloughed off as we go through the day, and night, where they are eaten by house dust mites and other minute creatures, too, probably.

Are the neurons and nephrons the leaders of the cellular community, the king and queen who rule over us? Other cells, serfs, servicing functions, labouring away until death through overwork comes and the gap filled by their progeny; like the goblet cells lining the gut, the mucous cells lining the lungs, and perhaps the glial cells in the brain and spinal cord producing a jelly and support for the all-important neurons and their ever-so delicate interneuronal connections, the synapses. And then there are other serfs, servant-cells so hungrily specialised they perform together to make a tube, named the Schwann-cell sheath, down which the dendron of the neurone finds its way to its receptors or to its motor-end plates to kick-start the muscles.

Who or what designed all these cells? Their design 'template' is in the DNA, in the genes sitting in the chromosomes. Yes, yes, but who or what designed the template? Many will want to answer God. God did the designing of the template. And many will say but who or what designed God? And there many come unstuck.

Others say that it has all come about, chemically and biochemically over many, many millennia driven by the chance development of chlorophyll, turning the sun's energy and CO_2 and the nutrient soup of chemicals that forms the sea, into a chemical reaction that we have come to know as life, the life-force within each of us, all animal and plant life, all the wide diversity of plants on earth and the just as wide diversity of animal life on earth. And the basic difference between animals and plants? Well, in essence, animals move about to be able to feed and breed, and plants stay put to feed and breed, with the exception – yes, there's always, in life, the exception – of those aquatic plants that just float about.

To re-phrase the famous quip from *Star Trek*, 'It's life, Jim, but not as we know it.' No, it's not. Not that we know it, well, not yet, anyway. Not quite, because, for we humans, there's something else, something extra. And this has to do with our being 'sentient beings.' This special feature is not exclusive to humans, as other animals, most notably mammals, have a degree of 'sentience' about them.

So, what does this sentience amount to? Ideologically, it amounts to complex behaviour patterns that are driven by ideals higher than just the physical need to respond to an environmental situation. Animals fleeing a forest fire are not an example of 'sentience,' but it certainly shows a strong will for self-preservation. A mother turning aggressive to defend her children, in either animals or in man, is not sentience. It is a biological instinct, as instinctive as the urges to breed that spawned the children in the first place. But the devotion of a dog to its master, and the horse that senses its fallen rider, its owner, its keeper, feeder, groomer, its bonded person: both of these examples exhibit sentience of a type, which we can simply call love.

But true sentience is different. Maslow's Hierarchy of Needs starts at the bottom with basic functional biological needs for survival and existence. When those needs are met, and as we go up the hierarchy, we see that at the top there are activities of mankind, humankind, that is where sentience is best exhibited. There the scientists are ever developing the world's understanding of the world, its physics, its chemistry and yes, its biology.

Sentience includes constructive dreams, designing and creating new things for our advancement as a society, as a species, for our comfort and yes, even our means of destroying our enemies, should they ever seek to destroy us. Sentience is not only in the realms of science, but also in the realms of art and music. The concert pianist playing a concerto, learned note for note, complete and correct, lasting 40 minutes and played for the sheer enjoyment and inestimable pleasure of the audience.

The wonderful world of art, ancient and modern, so different, so varied, there's something for everyone to admire and appreciate, to derive a warm glow of pleasure enough for the beholder to create a sigh; and that art can and should include the art of the natural world, the beauty that is planet earth, sometimes a raw, savage beauty, as in storm waves crashing on the rocks, to the calm, serene, peaceful scene of a babbling brook or a sunlight vale, with dancing shadows as leaves rustle in the afternoon breeze and shadows lengthen.

This is sentience. And it is so much more. Our sensibilities include so many forms that we accept every day. It is an emotional response, not a life-needing response, not a response that is vital to our survival. No, it's a response to do ultimately with pleasure, either for ourselves, which is always the prime mover, but for pleasure in others, however indirectly this is desired to come about. It can be viewed as a direct 'care and concern' for others, not necessarily unrelated to their need for a physical survival, but care for their pleasure and comfort, brokering a little peace of mind. In short, it's all a 'kind of loving,' and the 'kindness of a stranger' as we pause to allow a driver to pull out in front of us from a side road – an act of kindness – to a stranger.

We have defined 'love' in another chapter and have even used the word 'instinctive' in that definition. But it is used only in the connection with our being 'sentient beings.' Love is a set of very highly complex emotional processes primordially based on the 'need to breed,' but that is mostly absent from our thoughts when falling in love, a desire to make love, and yes, as the expression of love, but the outcome nine months later is not usually high in anyone's mind at that initial time. It's dissociative thinking, if any 'thinking' at all is involved, which mostly it isn't.

So, if this loving is not for self-preservation, preservation of the species, why would we bother with love, after all we are just an animal, are we not? It is because what we have evolved to be, although love does help humanity in its basic need, the animal in us 'needs to feed and breed.' So, why is love brought into it when we can breed like the animals, without us being dependent on any love being vital to the transaction? Where does love come into Maslow's Hierarchy, if at all?

The expression of love is a basic human achievement in itself and for itself, for the mind's comfort, pleasure and satisfaction; and besides that, it is good for our sought-after peace of mind, it also happens to be good for the continuity of the species.

The feeling of peace of mind is ever the greatest and mostly admirable personal objective; it needs love and needs to give love to achieve that. That ability to receive and to give love starts with the life-force we were born with. The degree to which we give and receive love is an ability that comes as part of our sentience, and that sentience means it is very much open to us to make our choices in life.

The life-force has the power of goodness that brings our soul alive. It drives our sentience, and can promote in us, if sufficiently susceptible, a state of goodliness, that is of God.

CHAPTER 4
'THERE ISN'T A GOD'

This chapter title may please atheists, possibly comfort agnostics, and infuriate followers of one of the monotheistic faiths. How can someone not agree with this statement, when offered the alternative statement, 'There is God,' meaning not at all in the sense, 'Look see, there is God, standing over there, watching us,' but in the sense we have, when we say, 'There is life,' or 'There is love?'

So, how can we say on the one hand, 'There isn't a God,' and on the other hand, turn around and say, 'There is God?' However, some might suggest the other way of saying there isn't a God is 'There is no God.' Likewise, we imagine that atheists, agnostics and those followers will react in the same way. But this time how can we possibly agree with this statement? This is something we would like to explain.

The problem derives from mankind's inordinate desire, and habit and enduring practice of anthropomorphisation – the ascribing of human-like characteristics to other things. As sentient creatures of high intelligence, our thinking seems, for most of us, still to be restricted to amusing ourselves or at least desiring some satisfaction from ascribing to all sorts of the animate, and the inanimate, the human characteristic of a name, firstly, and then human emotions. There was a TV advertisement for a lawn feeder. Oozing up out of the lawn is a bear-like creature with emotions fleeting across its human-like face first in rain and then in sunshine, and happiness when the feeder is applied. The little girl from the house runs out and hugs the bear. Little girls should know better.

Pet animals and wild animals are given human characteristics and emotions, and there have even been films made about cars with humanistic characters. Yes, hilarious and very enjoyable, but the whole underlying business smacks of something quite serious, too.

There are many fields of human creativeness, intelligent people motivated and pursuing an interest, an idea for development and improvement. But why? From where does this intellect come, the inspiration come? Almost every invention has been for the good of mankind in some way, to some degree, greater or lesser, directly or indirectly. Developments in medicine, and in particular surgery, are very good examples of the power of goodness working in us.

There are only two vices: so Leo Tolstoy writes in *War and Peace*, spoken by one of his main characters, Prince Bolkonsky, the Senior. He would muse: 'There are only two evils, superstition and idleness'; curiously he says there are only two virtues – intelligence and energy.

There is much sense in these simple statements. Much of what we choose to believe can and perhaps should be relegated to the category of superstition – a term generally regarded as having negative connotations. But many of the great so-called 'faiths' revolve around much that can be construed as superstition.

We should be happy and at ease believing in certain facts that are pretty well undisputable. For example, that there was a king called Henry VIII, but much of what is written about his reign, his court and other than the bare facts, we can be less certain. So it goes with history, and especially the books of the two great faiths, the Bible and Koran. Their stories have been around so long that, whether true or not, what matters is the perceived good that comes out of them. Working out what is good takes just a little bit of thought, of intelligent thought and a goodly dose of an understanding of 'goodness.'

There are the major religions – each using a 'book of rules' for behaviour and beliefs written centuries ago – by men. These books contain messages which are deliberated upon by the followers of the religion, and often the reasoning or interpretation put forward by intellectual theologians is beyond the comprehension of us ordinary folk.

So, we need to be wary of diktats arising in this way, ideas and so-called guidelines originating from the past, and be fully aware they are just the product of men writing about events and stories handed down often through centuries of time, but not written contemporaneously. These men in all probability were 'good men,' writing about goodness and evil, and perhaps 'divinely' inspired, but perhaps not. We say wary, because we may only be able to understand truly their message when the foundation of our perception of goodliness and evil are more realistic. 'Read on,' Lizzy.

In each of the great religions the deity is 'personified' to a greater or lesser degree, ascribed with quasi-human nature as in their God is open to supplications, called upon to respond with favours for the 'devoted' and to the detriment of the 'non-believers' (as in 'Please, God, confound my enemies and send a plague on both his houses'). Imagined and personified, as a fatherly God, who is seen in the subconscious of an adult as he or she remembered their father when they were very young, as all-powerful, dominant, seemingly all-knowing, awe-inspiring, capable of great love and affection; but capable, too, of wrath and punishment.

For many, too, the Devil is also personified, but into a 'deity-like' figure, but only ever capable of bringing about chaos (aka evil), with horns, fangs, cloven hooves and carrying a spear and permanent leer on his face. Satan is assumed to be male – but we needn't think that to be necessarily so – if we at all are tempted to believe in Eve, tempting Adam.

In some ways, we may be nearer the realistic understanding of good and evil if we start by looking at the way we think and speak about the Devil. For example, the often used phrase, 'The devil you will, I'll see you in Hell first before I let you…' And expressions like, 'Good God' or 'God help us,' and even 'Oh my God.' We never speak or think of, 'Oh! It's God in me that just makes me want to …' which would be a better understanding if we did.

Each of the four great religions claims theirs to be 'the one true religion' with their one true God. They can't all be right. Or could they all be right? Are there sufficient areas of understanding of goodliness and evil that the differences are merely derivations arising from man's propensity for evil whilst believing that 'God' is being served. What we are saying is that these 'differences' may be construed by some as the 'Devil' at work, but more properly by the reasoning of these chapters is that it is more likely to be man's poor understanding of the true nature of God as written in their scriptures.

It becomes a problem when religious followers are too keen to follow the rules of their religion, their book of rules, while at the same time giving way to their natural instincts, and here we mean animal instincts, the law of the jungle, survival of the fittest, an eye for an eye, and resort to force or just the threat of it, to have their way. This means some of the religions may seek to exert their will over others by using their view of the words in their 'bible' to justify their actions.

We humans are very, very evolved and complicated animals, but we cannot deny we are, in essence, an animal. In its most relevant respect, we spend our lives seeking to move to a greater physical, mental or pleasurable comfort zone, and avoiding physical or mental pain as we feed and breed and then die.

It is in the nature of man to seek to understand and then control the world we live in. What we can't understand is usually relegated to the realms of mystique, religion, suspicion, magic or the occult. The seeking out and turning to religion is to seek to move to a greater mental comfort zone – we want a power to sustain us, provide for us, including a life hereafter, to thank when things go well, but also to minimise pain in our lives now, and even a power to keep our enemies at bay and visit that 'plague on both his houses.'

There is a power of goodness, but it is not derived from God or Allah, in the sense most usually believe. We need to stop thinking of God as a person, 'God wants us…' and 'God is…' and 'God made the world…' and 'Dear God…' The best way to change our thinking, or perception, is to stop referring to God as such. The word is too synonymous with the history of the world with each race having its gods, the Greek Gods, Roman Gods, and Egyptian Gods etc. We need a new word – but not for now. Let's just try to understand the situation.

We know there is a force for goodness or goodliness. We also have been conditioned to think there is a force for evil. 'But do we know?' you might say. 'What do you mean by a force?' What we do know is that we cannot make anything material, and indeed nothing material grows in this world without the use of energy. Most of the energy used becomes stored in what has been made by man or stored in what has grown. The energy comes from what was previously stored in materials used to make an item, and its source of energy was from the sun. Energy can be neither created nor destroyed, it can only be changed from one form to another (Einstein).

From the moment a man-made item is completed, in its showroom condition, if you like, it starts to degrade. This degeneration process can take many years, or even centuries, for some materials. The degeneration process can be delayed by cleaning, polishing, recoating, oiling etc., but ultimately all things made, degrade, and in doing so, much of the inbuilt energy becomes dissipated. This process is also known as entropy and is the opposite of anabolism, by which things are made or grown.

We can contemplate the design and planning stage of construction and manufacture. These early stages take thoughts by men and women, often much thought, often by a team of people all working towards the same goal. We know therefore that these thought-processes consume much mental energy, which can leave us either 'mentally exhausted' or on a mental high (until we collapse) as we search for an idea, 'rack our brains' as we say, for the best answer required for the design or plan.

Frequently the idea comes in a flash at a time quite unrelated to work time, even sometimes when we are on holiday. This is creativeness, and all creativeness derives from one basic need to move to a greater comfort zone. Even though those designs which are later misappropriated by the evil aspirations of some, e.g. Hitler, Stalin, the underlying belief is that the designing and inventing person would move to a greater comfort zone.

The power of goodness is like a worldwide web surrounding the surface of the earth as a positive psychic-electro-magnetic force, there and available for any one of us to tap into, to sync with, and to download positive thoughts and actions. For the power of goodness we can read the power of God; the terms are synonymous.

There is no counter-force as generally supposed, as generally taught and like in a children's comic story, an evil 'black hole' in space that draws everything and everyone into its grip only to be suspended there in space or to be decimated into millions of particles. In reality there is only the absence of that force of good; there is no force of evil, no Devil, no Satan, no Beelzebub, as is so frequently assumed, or any force that could negate that worldwide web of super-intellect, and the power of God. That state of absence is present in us in a small way, in all of us all the time, like a void, as we are not capable of being perfectly persistently positive. That state can, in the absence of positivity, lead us to a state of chaos, when temptations, 'miscreative' thoughts, to be a miscreant, and leads us to behave in a way this is not of God, and, in so doing, this is when we are most commonly thought of as evil.

But the really clever miscreant thinking can be smart and can delude us, so that they masquerade as having a 'goodliness.' That type of miscreant thinking seeds its own kind and grows, denying the power of goodness; hence dictators and all their evil works. Every few years nations go to war, the aggressor, to further their pernicious aims, and other nations go to war to resolve inequities perpetrated. It is said that the most common causes, rather than reasons, for war throughout history have been down to religion, rather than for territorial gain, but when religions identify with certain geographical locations, their 'Holy places,' and want to occupy them, war usually ensues sooner or later.

If we are to advance, that is the human race is to advance, then we need to accept that scientific advances provide us with all the technological benefits we enjoy today: homes with insulation and heat, cars, planes, trains, tunnels and bridges, mobile phones, visual and audio entertainment, medical diagnostic procedures and treatment, to name just a few. They do not in themselves go any way towards bringing about any tolerable degree of peaceful cohabitability here on this earth.

It is undeniable that we have not progressed one iota in any ability to live together in peace, and consequently prosperity suffers. There is always some war, civil war, guerrilla or partisan war going on at any one time, to the extreme detriment of those affected locally and the perpetrators can enjoy no peace of mind, however justified in their thinking they may feel.

Even away from the national level, we don't live in peace with our work colleagues or neighbours or our families. Negative attitudes are often rife in us as parents, and any strife witnessed by our young children, can 'mould' and 'shape' them, 'chips off the old block,' for their own adult life. And yet surely, one of the prime roles of parenthood is to enable the child to develop a conscience, an awareness of good and bad, right and wrong, and the awareness of the effects of choices they will make, that is the responsibility for their actions. From an early age we need to teach them: 'Beware your thoughts because they become words, beware your words because they become your actions, beware your actions because they become your habits, and beware your habits because they become you.'

A developed conscience will tell us that we don't want to do or say anything which would have the effect of detracting from another person's ability to move to a greater 'comfort zone' or lead to a feeling of mental or physical pain. We will naturally be aware that, due to the pressure of the numbers of the humans on this planet, competition in all things is strong, and it is not necessary for the developed conscience to step back from the competition for fear of doing or saying something to the others' detriment. But it is vital that we always act within our adopted values, which are our signposts for conduct.

What are these adopted values? We have a duty as parents to live our lives as well as we can, if only as role models for our children. We need to adopt values by which we will live our lives in future and talk to our children about these, so they can in turn adopt their chosen values.

A value is an abstract sense, a characteristic of a positive nature. There are core values, and supplementary values, for example. Integrity is a core value.

Honesty is a supplementary value. We can list all the values we can think of and then choose five favourite values as those we'd like to adopt and to become known by. As useful exercise we can ask ourselves is: 'What would I like people to say about me at my funeral?' If we then adopt values, they become our signposts of conduct and behaviour towards others, in all our dealings.

It is our conscience that will hurt when we fail to live by our values, when we have to accept the responsibility for our actions. It's no good blaming others ... until we accept that it was what we said, or did, that caused us the disappointment, the aggravation or pain. And until we acknowledge that, we cannot truly begin to reconcile our self with our conscience and our values. By 'reconcile' here is meant to move on in our life without burdening our self with our past mistakes. We have to forgive our self. And if we reach a point where we can only justly and fairly conclude the fault lies with another, then we have to learn to forgive that person, and in that forgiveness there is comfort, which, in a way, becomes for us something good, like a perverse but worthy selfishness.

We mostly emerge from childhood and adolescence with a bruised and scarred innocence. We became bruised and scarred as a result of our parents 'doing their best' to bring us up well. The problem is, as always, we have been exposed to our parents' negative experiences of their life, their pain, in trying to cope with all the demands they had placed upon them, keeping up mortgage payments, keeping a job, keeping looking slim, young, fantastic, fun-loving – and above all, determined their children will be at least as successful as they were, if they were, goading them to more and make something better of their lives; and we, in turn, want our children to succeed in those things we couldn't. And we are young and resilient, or were. We can use this resilience to advance, to our advantage, to shrug off the bruising and scaring and any sense of an inevitability of fate, and to grow in stature, of personality, not girth.

The interminable and undeterminable question is, 'Is there such a thing as fate?' As always, we should first define what is meant by the words used in the question. Generally, we think of there being a set plan of our life, sketched out by someone or something, probably at the time we were born, and try how we may, we cannot deviate from it. He wanted to be an airline pilot, tried and tried but each time was rejected in the selection process. Fate, they say. They may say that to many 'big' eventualities in life, as if we are reduced by fate to hardly more than a leaf being blown about in the wind, or a twig floating downstream to the sea, where we die. So, is there any point in wanting, planning, striving too hard? We get what we get – don't we? Let's not think too much about it, let's go and have a pint down the local. Sad that he then got drunk and was stabbed in a fight. But it was fate, wasn't it?

No. No. This simply won't do. We cannot live our lives thinking that we are mostly helpless to direct them. Smart alecs say that whatever we achieve, by determination, by learning and application of skills and endeavour, and all that we have had to reach for, and gained, was our fate. But the point here, in this book, is that we should not concern ourselves with a 'Which came first, the chicken or the egg?' type of question, and 'Is there such a thing as fate?' is one such question. Some may see it as a rhetorical question, in the sense that either everyone knows an answer, or perhaps there is no answer.

However, it is by far and away the best thing for us, for us all, if we say, 'There is no such thing as fate.' To absolutely deny it, refuse to believe it, to refute its existence, not give the thought house-room. And then we can then get on with our lives, the now become unhindered, unimpeded job of 'running' our lives, drawing on the power of goodness and of God, the worldwide web of super-intellect, to live our lives to their full potential, and not reach the age of 80 thinking, 'too late, smuk.' Just keep the unanswerable question to a conversation over dinner, where it makes good sport. There is more written about fate elsewhere in these chapters.

We need to have faith in the process of thinking and becoming and being positive, as much as we are capable; confident that the process of thinking positively and the power of goodness that is God, and of all goodliness, will assist us as we stretch the envelope of our worthy and wholesome self-fulfilment.

PART TWO

IN THE MOOD

CHAPTER 5
MORBID FEARS

We may think today we can rightly have our own 'morbid fears,' fears generated by the popular newspapers and the news and news commentary programmes on radio and TV, when people of very articulate capability spout their theories endlessly as they are paid their 'crust' to keep the wolf from the door. And we like mutts soak up most of it, while the morbid fears play on our mind and churn our stomachs into dyspeptic spasms and sore heads from rising blood pressure, as we are left helpless like a stranded whale on a beach – hopelessly powerless to do anything about – yes – our morbid fears.

Was it better to be medieval man? Certainly not medieval woman, who were regarded as chattels, and were very likely to die in childbirth, if not that, then to give birth to thirteen children to see only half of them survive beyond ten years of age.

So, without morbid fears generated by newspapers, TV etc., did they have morbid fears? We know they lived in a very uncertain world, like us, but no thoughts of atomic bombs or the cutting of gas or oil pipelines or cyber rape of the system. Their own world most definitely will have had their morbid fears, of assassination if famous at all, or just plain murder for a crust, or to die or be maimed from a fall off a horse, having to go to fight for the Lord of the Manor. Better to die than to be permanently maimed and unable to work, to die in penury. For them, so much was down to fate. Oh, yes. They believed in fate, big time, and in God; God gave the good bits, and fate gave the bad bits. So, their morbid fears were that God would forsake them and fate would play its hand, deserved or not deserved. Most will have felt underserved, no doubt, just like us today, especially those festering in prison; they mostly never feel their 'fate' was deserved.

Disease, pestilence and an early death were all so commonplace that it is likely that an individual's expectations were not high, and the average philosophical outlook was one of acceptance of their likely lot. Not quite so. History shows that optimism and ambition were in abundance, loved bloomed, both where it should and where it shouldn't, as always.

In short, were things of the nature of morbid fears so very different then to nowadays? Oh. Yes? The details have changed, of course, but the reasonableness of those fears, the rationalising, the expectations and thoughts for the future, both optimistic and pessimistic, the basis for them, is probably much the same as it always was. There's much less belief in God, the Christian God, and sadly more so than of the God of the Jews and the God of the Muslims. And for the non-believers, do they believe at all in fate? Do they believe in anything, anything worthwhile, that is? Is theirs the way to avoid 'morbid fears,' to go through life like a leaf floating on the surface of a stream, swept along in the current of life, being bumped and buffeted by all the slings and arrows of fortune and misfortune, until ditched out to sea to lie on the seabed, decaying alongside 'Davy Jones' Locker?

What can we do if we find we are of that sort of nature, that sort of persona that finds those morbid fears keep coming back to bother or even to haunt us as we endeavour to lead a reasonably sensible, worthwhile life, with some practical optimism for the future of mankind, the human race?

Perhaps our morbid fears need rationalising. We could apply the worry buster. Write down our worst fears and their worst possible outcome, worst for us, that is. Oddly enough, just doing that alone, honestly and frankly, many of the fears then shrink, even disappear. For those concerns we can influence, we feed them into our goal-setting machine and take a first step, one of many, like making a list, steps towards fulfilling a worthy goal, a goal that grants us another slice of our well-earned contentment, that essential aliquot, an integer of our 'peace of mind.' But for those whose morbid fears don't shrink? What then?

The mantra 'For every problem under the sun, there is a solution, or there is none,' is a philosophy worthy of serious consideration, especially by those weighed down by their morbid fears. And so, having considered the matter, we can then embolden ourselves to become a little like the non-believers. Their 'ça ne fait rien' attitude to life, and with the frequent shrugging of their shoulders to concerns they can't influence, carries them through life, and so our rather more delicate sensibilities become just that little bit less brittle, and that's no bad thing. A little less of a snowflake?

Some people are deep – some shallow – most middling – what makes us so? The genes, our upbringing, life's experiences? Who can say if one of those factors is more than the others? Certainly, our biological pain receptors, both the physical pain, and to our brains the psychological pain, give most of us a prod to use our intelligence to avoid that particular pain again, if we can. That more or less is the definition of intelligence; nothing to do with most teachers' idea of intelligence, how much or how well we can do mental arithmetic, learn our tables etc., do sums and the like. No. It's our ability to learn from our environment and our experiences to move on to a greater comfort zone. A zone with more food, more shelter, more security, more clothing to our backs, more warmth and then when we have all that, move to greater enjoyment from relationships and matters of the higher mind, thoughts and pleasures, of sport, arts and music and freedom of thought and expression, towards the beauty in life, and creativity.

Cynicism is a character trait that can be transitory at times. The opportunistic cynic can earn a living as a 'commentator' in the media. Cynics' feelings often stem from feelings of inferiority with or without a concomitant ignorance and envy. One of their favourites is to say that the more 'intelligent' you are, the less happy you are. But as we have just seen, and this goes for just about every 'statement' of such a nature, we need to be sure that we have a certainty in the meaning of the words used. Here, we'd say, 'How do you define being happy?' or, 'How do you define intelligence?' It's prudent always to check on the meaning of words people use before falling into their trap of going along on their own peculiar 'bus ride,' their eager cynicism feeding their unhappy ego.

It is a practised art – especially for those column writers who earn a living by being cynical – never saying enough to be sued, just enough to irritate, amuse or titillate. They prey upon the innocent, those sincerely trying to be upright, and they also prey upon the vain and insecure, as it is not often easy to distinguish between. The writers feel intellectually superior but suspect themselves of being morally wrong and, being so, knowingly inferior with their conduct. Should they feel so? They, at least, get the rest of us thinking about them, but mostly about the objects of their cynicism.

What is it, in essence, that separates us from the animals? It surely is, in all essence, 'the gift of imagination and the means to communicate it.' We say this in all essence as there are so many differences that separate us from animals. But, truly, what do all the others subsume from? Of course, there are very many differences: getting down to the minutiae, and identifying them can make for good sport over dinner, or indeed last most of the evening.

We began to evolve from prehistoric man when we developed an imagination and so became creative; creative of all the things that we need to improve our lot here on earth. All the inventions that ever were, are the result of imagination. And here we are not just referring to the mechanical gadgets so beloved of inventors and 'mad' professors, but almost any institution we can think of has come about as a result of our gift of imagination. The law, our political institutions, our democratic government system, trains and railroads, cars and lorries, aircraft, and ships, computers and 3D printers, surgical operations and prostheses etc., and so on. All have come about due to mankind's ability to imagine, and much of those imaginings are directly as a result of our ideas. We have ideas all the time. Yes, animals build nests and lairs, but that's about all. Yes, they hunt in packs for their own good and support, but fundamentally, they are the same as they have been for centuries, even millennia. And what is perhaps the most significant for us, even though they can at times form huge colonies, with thousands or even millions of their own kind, they never go to war against their own kind, to kill and maim their own kind. Odd, that. They leave that to us humans.

There are other aspects, contrasts, worthwhile mentioning. Above all, there is that imagination which enables us to create abstract things, such as companies or organisations for a purpose of orderliness and to make a profit for a livelihood. No longer can we survive by going hunting and leaving the woman at the cave tending the children and trying to grow a plant for food, and we wear clothes (mostly) but usually take most, if not all, of them off for our primordial activities that include Bacchanalian parties and mating behaviour. We have a high degree of communications through language(s) to facilitate the spread of ideas, thoughts and feelings, although it isn't always wise to try to share our feelings with anyone, even anyone at all. There can be too much wearing of our heart on our sleeve.

We have that vital willingness (mostly) to live under a rule of law, and we have evolved with an ever-increasing understanding and achievement of some mastery of the world around us – the physics, chemistry, biology and less obviously the mathematics that operate between those 'disciplines.' This leads to our connivance as intelligent animals of high development to live voluntarily under the rule of law, which then governs all our lives, but only by and with our common consent. Those who don't accept that, that which is for the greater good, for the good of all, are cast out (or rather cast into prison!).

The other aspect of our difference from animals is the art of communication, between ourselves for the good, ultimately, of us all, or at least we hope so. 'Jaw-Jaw is better than War-War' was the saying. In short, we expect all our communicative skills so to be able to influence and to persuade that peace and trade will reign. Sadly, not always so. Hotheads and people of limited articular skills in oratory and in limited comprehension after listening, coupled with the dangers of differing languages and the vagaries of our leaders, lead us to wars. Either that or there is an inbuilt tendency to malignity in man that makes wars inevitable. Oddly, the people who make the wars are not usually the people who have to go and fight them, nor be one of the many to be maimed or to die.

So much depends on good and proper communication. It starts with clear thinking – on being 'right-minded.' Chatting over ideas with a friend or colleague, wondering minds collectively seeking an answer to a challenge, a conundrum, is acceptable communication when sharing and developing ideas. But in most other transactions of thoughts, feelings and principles held dear, we need to be clear-headed, right-minded even before attempting to communicate. Whether of differing social rank or the same, if something worthwhile is to be achieved, then we need to be clear in thought and in word.

A character from Jane Austen's famous *Pride and Prejudice*, Lady Catherine de Bourgh, said, and with some force to her junior by social rank, Elizabeth Bennet, 'Let me be rightly understood.' Perhaps we should use that phrase more often, but it is regarded as rather abrasive these days.

And there is the rub, as we endeavour to communicate our thoughts, our instructions, wishes and ideas. There are several 'mind-to-mind' problems en route. We can set these out; the hurdles that need to be surmounted when they tend to get in the way of clearly understood communications.

In wishing to transfer a clear thought, created and held in our mind, we select some well-chosen words to speak that are reckoned to be within the vocabulary of the listener. We need to be sure of the meaning of the words we use and hopefully sure the listener has the same understanding. From there on, the communication has these hurdles to surmount:

1. Be sure that we have the attention of the person we want to speak to, and preferably within comfortable earshot, and preferably in the same room. Eye contact helps hold the attention.

2. Articulation of those chosen words with clear elocution – well spoken, head up, no mumbling, brought up to look at the person we are speaking to, minimal accent and minimal dialect, no food in the mouth, no chewing gum, false teeth that fit, and so on.

3. Words can become 'distorted' as they travel through the 'ether' and especially where and when there are extraneous competing noises. Little imagination is needed here to see what is meant by this. Crowded, noisy restaurants, echoing walls, no soft furnishings to absorb sound, factories, machinery, piped music in hotel bars etc. etc., and not forgetting in high winds that can whip our words away, lost and gone to leeward at a fast rate of knots. Stand to windward if we can.

4. The quality of the auditory apparatus of the receiving person. Not only the elderly can suffer from hearing loss. Even the young frequently have defective hearing due to damage to their hearing by excessively loud music, but also from childhood ear infections. Some are born deaf. Our hearing is a very precious asset, and it should be valued as such. This step may well be the biggest impediment to clear communications. That being so, if all the other factors listed here are paid sufficient attention, then the listener will stand a better chance of understanding what he/she is hearing. And he/she for their part should be as diligent as funds or the National Health Service will allow to obtain and use the best aids to improving hearing that are available.

5. Finally, the spoken words have landed up in the brain of the listener, their final destination for reception and processing into some sort of sense. Here there are massive influences that are ready to help or to obfuscate the interpretation and understanding of the received message, or should we say the perceived message. Take the famous joke about the First World War message passed along the trenches from soldier to soldier all with ears ringing from a vast succession of explosions all around them. The command message started, 'Send reinforcements, we are going to advance' only to be received by the ears of the final listener as, 'Send three and fourpence, we are going to a dance.'

Occasionally, and perhaps rather more frequently than one could guess at, we experience communication difficulties that have caused a misunderstanding through the assumed meaning of words by the two or more parties involved.

Despite dictionaries, people can use the same word but to each it can mean something slightly different. Meanings generally in society can vary with generations as they come and go, and words drop into disuse. Who uses the word 'dissemble' today? Very few and yet it is such a useful word, and we can impart a comment or thought with some single word that would otherwise take two or three or even more.

When being posed a question, we can and perhaps we should, instead of jumping to our own assumptions, ask the questioner what he/she means by a word or words they used in the question. This would reduce misunderstandings.

Much communication involves the expression of ideas, thoughts, wishing to influence the other person, often to persuade them to our way of thinking. We may as well speak to a blank wall as try to speak in such a way as to convert a Jew to Christianity, or a Muslim to the Jewish faith. To both are anathemata. That is to say, the listener may hear our words, even comprehend them, but their own ideas, preferences, prejudices and bigotry perhaps, as viewed by others, prevent them from fully understanding the reasoning behind the heard words of the speaker. We can see this all the time in political exchanges. We know the listener is not 'listening;' as he/she is constantly interrupting the speaker before he/she has even finished one sentence. This is a complete travesty of the art of communication. So rude, so narrow-minded, so dim-witted; no true intelligence at all. And we all know, or at least those who have been victims of not being listened to, know the types of people when we are just 'wasting our time' speaking to them.

This wilful resistance to the ideas, as in the ideology, of the other person – deliberately 'not understanding' is a psychic block, brought about by the antipathy, nay, the hatred perhaps, of the speaker and what he/she 'stands for' or is 'identifying with.' The worst form of deliberate misunderstanding can be brought about by a pre-existing cynical objection to and a resentment of the speaker, bordering on hatred, certainly prejudice, which is to say that's how they cramp 'free speech.' Sadly, such attitudes of denying others freedom of expression come more frequently today as a gathering force of friends, relatives and associates feel they have to adopt the same prejudice in order to continue to be accepted as 'one of them,' one of the 'Rent-a-Mob.' In their clone, their esoteric coterie where, to get along, they feel they have to 'go along.' The best example of these 'crowd behaviours' is trade unions, immature student gatherings, and unhappy people frequently of a leftish persuasion, gatherings of those whose lot in life, so far, has been one of disappointment and of frustrated endeavours, many with much justification. Like the French paysans, who are the experts.

It can be disappointing to experience a failure by someone we are communicating with to find that they just seem unable or unwilling to grasp the idea or concept being pointed out to them.

Open-mindedness, open to new or different ideas, different attitudes and beliefs, often goes with an inquiring open mind, eager to be informed, educated, made wiser. Such people often read a lot; several books about the same subject to glean others' points of view. As the saying goes, 'To read one book is to copy, to read two books is to do research.' A person with an open personality is usually willing to be instructed, to engage in debate, and probably has little in the way of preconceptions or prejudice or, if any, then is still ready and willing to learn, to be influenced in his/her thinking based on the wisdom and experience of others, yet still knowing that he/she remains the final arbiter, the final judge of what his/her opinions and attitudes will be.

However, whenever we meet a closed mind, or even one narrowly open, the closed mind can be a sign of insecurity; as in an insecurity of job, of status at work and in society, in relationships especially close relationships, an uncertainly or even a fear as to his/her financial position, solvent or greatly in debt. Therein lies an inferiority complex, and that may be anxious to prove itself of worth, but sadly often there can be too little justification at that time. Other signs can be prejudice, sure of its own rightness, anxious to be proved correct, even denying of self when wrong. This is a sad character; and is difficult to befriend.

Winston Churchill, that great Prime Minister and statesman, said many things that have been so frequently repeated and, in this context, here he said, 'Democracy is a bad system, but it is the best we have' (or words to that effect). It is bad in many ways, mostly due to the vanity and vagaries of man, the verminous jealousies, the spiteful vindictiveness with which politicians seek to scrabble over each other for promotion and the 'top job.' One could imagine just about all the most undesirable characteristics of human nature bottled up in one building, the Palace of Westminster.

But where the politicians fail us is in the way that they never clearly elucidate for us the major and most significant of the ideologies separating the main parties. They always seek to enumerate so-called policies on tax and all things to do with the pound in our pocket, treating us like schoolchildren, as if the only thing we can understand, especially at the time of the hustings, is how much better off we will be with one party, and how much worse off we will be with the other party, and vice versa. It's pathetic: the same lack of sound argument, the basis of sensible discussion and intercommunication failed to appear in the Brexit Referendum campaign.

When it comes to voting, we tend to make our choices for a particular party like this. One is that we believe in what the party stands for (that's good), and the other is that we vote for that party for no other rational reason than we like a certain politician or politicians (sort of okay); the other being that we loathe and hate the politicians of the other side, more (excellent). Go hang their policies!

If we can discern what the principles of the party wanting our vote are, they need to be clear what and who they represent (as in from 'whom' their main core of support derives and why). We need to choose, make an informed decision, but we may possibly make it on peripheral policies, if not on core principles.

For example, we can only exist and thrive by trade, and by that we really mean trade with other nations. It is trade that brings us our income, even wealth, and the means to survive and hopefully to improve our nation's lot. Trade is always competitive, but it is also intellectually stimulating and so brings forth innovations from our creative natures, that in themselves evoke a presupposition of a high degree of education.

The point is that we can only trade if the products and the prices are right. We get those right by having a reasonably tight control over our costs, and that essentially means labour costs as well as raw materials and the costs of plant, research and development.

If we get the labour costs out of proportion, then businesses become unprofitable and the country starts to sink into debt. Some parties massage their followers into a hatred of the privately owned businesses; they think the state should be the only mechanism for holding and appropriating capital for business use. Yet they have seen, or would have seen had they looked, been open-minded enough to see that those communist experiments have failed and failed big time. Of course, there are bad sides to capitalism, abuses of the 'system' due to man's inordinate greed; but think of the small shop on the corner. How did he or she get their stock to sell in the first place? By capital, either already owned or borrowed. Would we take that away from them? They work hard and provide a service and are free to make their own decisions: capitalism at its most innocent.

We need to be as much aware of the evils of big business as a power game and the corruption of massively overpaid directors as much as we need to be on the lookout for the forces working, mostly through hard left-wing trade unionists, working towards their undeclared ambition to throw society into anarchy out of which their beloved idealistic state of communism would emerge, with everyone as well off (or more likely as poor) as the next, all directed by the officials of the state (themselves in power, of course, in the back seat of the chauffeured Rolls-Royce).

There is the concept of the professional as in one who works to a standard of professionalism, that is either self-imposed or more usually to an imposed and qualified standard set by a 'professional' body. Fundamentally, the term belonged to the learned professions, bodies set up to regulate and to train, assess suitability to 'practise' by examination and approve membership of the professional body by the granting of documented qualifications, all to set a standard of works that the 'public' could rely upon, for quality and value for money.

These learned professions became so mostly by 'book learning' in the original concept, of course, and it's so very different today, but still only by extensive and hard study do we ever reach the 'professional' standard required. And once there, arrived, clutching the paper that shows we have achieved the required standard, it doesn't end there. Today's professions all are required to undergo continuing professional development, because the knowledge base and required standards of the work performed are continually evolving. Not only that, but the professions have a set of ethical standards for conduct of their members, those rules that were drawn up by upright leaders of the profession who knew that we are all subject to temptation to earn a quick buck, or to give way to earthly desires that are verboten in a professional – the client or patient relationship. To drive this home to the new graduate, he or she is required to take an oath, usually spoken in the company of others, witnesses to the commitment to uphold the standards of the profession. The professional body also takes it upon itself to police the activities of its members and has the power to remove a member's 'permit to practise' either temporarily as punishment or permanently so as to deprive its errant member from earning a living anymore by that profession. Serious stuff.

The point of all this is to ask ourselves: is there any professionalism outside of the professions?

There is a much-misused term – a 'professional' job, such as when a plumber of four months' study mends a dripping cistern. But is it misused? What is wrong with comparing the standards that are supposed and generally expected of doctors, solicitors, architects etc., with another's set of skills usefully employed, to work to a set of standards? Builders and the building trade are the most commented upon, for their work, whether it is good work or rather too frequently shoddy work. When the job is well done, and done to last, using high-quality materials and to a high-quality finish, is that not also deserving of the praise, a 'professional job?'

Is there any professionalism in commerce and industry? Commerce, often so vilified for their machinations to sell their wares with all the conniving schemes they can get to persuade us to buy their goods, a process that starts with creating a sort of desire, a desire to own, to have, to hold and to use. Something that hadn't occurred to us that we couldn't get by in life until now, now that we have their product. And when we have had it a while, why suddenly there's the super new, improved version that equally we shouldn't attempt to live without. Any professionalism? Hardly, but an art form certainly.

But can it be that there is a certain skill, perhaps come about via study and experience that the leaders of commerce know the best route to profits, to survival of the company amongst fierce competition, to job retention for themselves and their employees, yet remaining within the law. Is there not justification for comparing those efforts with those of the professions? Or is it that professions earn their living by levelling 'fees,' and in commerce one earns a living out of margins, profit margins. Room for some snobbery here, if ever one should be so minded, as of old, of the sobriquet of 'New Money.'

It is easier to say there is professionalism in industry. Industry making and creating inevitably involve engineers, and the engineering profession is not at all to be regarded as the Cinderella profession, because without it, so much of our society would still be in the Dark Ages. And what is more, we are so fortunate to have professional engineers who have standards, of their professional body, their training, their ongoing study and a set of ethics that, if not adhered to, could mean the collapse of a building, or a bridge or whatever else, 'goodness only knows.' (an obscure but commonplace expression and there's more debate on this elsewhere in these chapters).

Of all the professions, the most bewildering is the legal profession. Hardly the 'oldest profession' (Ha! ha!) but certainly one of the oldest, having evolved almost as mankind itself evolved from Homo erectus into Homo sapiens. Lawyers are good with words, saying what they mean, and not always meaning what they say; often not necessarily meaning, as in believing what they say. What the original American Red Indians came to be associated with by repeating the phrase in 'western' films, 'White man speak with forked tongue.' This is because lawyers are trained in adversarial practice, that is to say, to every point of view there is an opposing point of view, and their art is to see both sides of an issue, being prepared for all the eventualities they can think of and some they can't. They are quick to tell us we have 'a good case.' They mean as a good fee earner for them, and not what we want to hear, with unfounded optimism, which is that our case is likely to be successful.

Lawyers compile documents and agreements, even laws, often writing very long sentences with no punctuation where and when the meaning is not always obvious to laypeople, and this cunningly leaves more room for interpretation by other lawyers, often at some great expense, in order to obtain a judgement, an opinion or an interpretation of the 'intention' of the writer, hopefully. Either that or even more obfuscation, at least to the man in the street, who despairs.

The law regulates the conduct of people, and that, once laid down, is not optional. The laws are made in parliament by politicians, who in the 19th century were referred to as the 'law-makers.' It is a pity, perhaps, that not all politicians are not lawyers, being bound by their ethical codes of honesty and probity. Ethics regulates conduct of people by voluntary means, that are optional. That is to say, we can take ethics or leave them, or take sometimes, and not others. They may have an effect on our life, as to our job, keeping it or losing it, and to the keeping or losing of friends.

Unlike those in commerce, state employees are mostly working at applying the law – and, as such, they are very keen to work 'by the book.' And in this way, not to 'blot their copybook' too, and risk losing out on a lovely inflation-proofed pension, in time.

In Tolstoy's *War and Peace*, General Nikolai Bolkonsky, a father with some philosophy on life, saw life as a challenge to recognise the choices between acting with intelligence and energy, or whether to allow suspicion and sloth to reign over us. There was a once-well-regarded, a one-time popular middle 'road' not too left- or too right-wing Prime Minister, who went on to say from his retirement about the Brexit Referendum in words that in effect meant, 'Don't concern yourself about the question of any democracy in Europe, in our lives: all you need to think about is how you will be so much better off you'll be staying in Europe.' And this is the nub of just about all man's deliberations here on earth; we come up against it all the time and constitutes what are our morbid fears. Wherever we look, whatever we see, hear and read about or learn even, it boils down to the essence facing mankind throughout history, even to today and tomorrow, and that is the hard, sometimes cruel balancing act we have to perform, the balancing of choosing to go with what is ethical, moral and of humanity's highest ambitions and on the other arm of the scales, money, wealth and what is most simply expressed as man's love of 'gold' and all it represents, what it can buy, including power, power over other people. The clash between ethics and money.

As we go through life, we are swimming in a sea of humanity's evolutionary achievements, and if we stop to think how those achievements have come about, no doubt they will have sprung out of minds driven by a desire for more 'gold,' but many will have come about as a result of man's inordinate creativity, for improvement of someone's lot, and not at all out of any sense of gain. For example, let's think of a surgeon developing a new technique for faster, quicker healing. Or, for example, the painter, the artist, creating just because it is a wish to set down on canvas what he/she sees in their mind. For gold? Most artists die poor and their paintings do better after their death. What for the NHS surgeon?

But in the development of the theme of our morbid fears, it is not the issue of earning a living that is in the balancing arm of the scales. Earning a living is that very worthwhile activity of us all, or should be, if our politicians and economists can arrange matters so that all who want to work, can. Earning a living by work, a good living, very good living or just a living is not the 'gold' we are talking about here. The gold is the excess above and beyond what we earn through honest labours for our living.

What is being referred to here is the 'moral' issue that arises for most at some time in our life and that is the issue of balancing ethics today, with honesty and probity, with the unslakeable thirst most have of us have for more 'gold.' Of course, our world would diminish if men and women didn't strive to earn some more 'gold.' It's just that we need to balance the desire, that is to say to keep it in check and be aware, conscious of the ethical and moral side to situations that arise, mostly for businessmen and businesswomen, that any profit at all is good, but too much? Where does the excess come from? Who is it hurting to make or take so much profit? Will it 'profit' him/her in soul or in spirit to become so very wealthy, by so much greed or dishonesty. Honesty? Can't our alter ego speak clearly enough at the time of temptation to help us rationalise that what we are about to do for gold is justified, in some way, that only alter egos can?

Not that anyone making money should be overly bothered by the siren calls of the anti-capitalists. To give it all away; to suddenly be overcome by the misplaced moral only to see the contract being lost to you and going to a slicker, less honest person. And that's where the morbid fear comes in. To keep our head above water as we swim in that sea. The question is profoundly complex, balancing ethics with our want of gold. So complex as to want to shrug the shoulders and, just as that PM implied, to think what concerns us only should be the matter of gold because the ethics question just complicates matters too much. And if we do that, what are we left with? Why, our morbid fears, of course.

Should we let our morbid fears prey on our minds and make us fret too much? To do so would become one of our shortcomings, and should we be overly concerned about any of our shortcomings? Surely the way to look at shortcomings is with equanimity; and if we do that, we can be sure that we will be in plenty of good company, won't we, Mr ex-PM?

We should not, indeed we must not, ever have morbid fears that allow our imaginations to run riot.

If we feel some things that evince in us or lead to a tendency for us to change in some way, then we must be sure that the evidence is there – evidence of a need for that change, and that that change will bring good for others in the first place, and when that condition is satisfied then good for us, too. That is to say the change is not just a selfish change. Selfish feelings such as these are often harmful to others, especially our loved ones.

An imagination 'running riot' is in no way comparable to the inspiration we receive when meditating, daydreaming or even asleep, dreaming. Something that is correctly termed as inspirational is automatically creative of something good, almost always good for others, at least in the first place.

To imagine falsely, or imagine on a whim of a current, trendy, fashionable way of thinking or behaving as people are prone to do, are today's greatest sadnesses, even evil (in the sense of lacking goodness), and it's right to label those imaginings as 'morbid fears.'

Remember 'a man is a man when a man is needed, else he remains a child,' (and this ancient encouragement to ward off our morbid fears is of course, all gender-inclusive). But to get to grips with this we need, especially in these times, to be clear what is meant by being a man, and of course in being a woman. It is more, oh so much more, than one's sexual apparatus, although that is the denoting feature, the bedrock of our being, our biological justification for asserting our sex, as opposed to our sexuality. But the expression has much a deeper meaning than that to the contemplative mind, and to the inquiring intelligence. It will prompt much musing; and provide even more grist to the mill of our minds as they churn over such phrases, and there is help, both of a direct nature and also indirectly in the following chapters here, as we read who we are, what we are, why we are and what we can be, as we deal with our morbid fears.

Read on, Lizzy ....

CHAPTER 6
THE NATIONAL MOOD

Instead of 'The National Mood' this chapter could just as easily have the title of 'The Nation's Well Being,' which for many of us can be brought to mean our nation's mental health.

In the run-up to the millennium 2000, everyone was worried that all the world's computers would crash at midnight on Dec 31st/Jan 1st, 1999/2000, unless readied beforehand and 'millennium bug'-free, millennium-compliant. Where will computers be at the start of the next millennium, 3000? Where will human life be, if any is left? Will the world be ruled by a despot based in North Korea?

In that run-up, all sorts of conjectures were put forward, optimistically that the 'brave new' millennium would bring, indeed would 'spring' out of mankind's bosom, new hopes, new wonderful happenings, a new nirvana. Some hope. But what was said along with many other things, and with some more realism, was that medical advances were becoming so good, so 'achieving,' that in the new millennium it wasn't physical illness that would be the major problem, the major challenge, but mental illness.

Psychologists have mooted that we are all either neurotic or psychotic, to a degree, in most of our life. If we assume they are right, then the mood swings of the neurotic are characteristic of the majority of us, not the psychotics fortunately, for they seem to be in the minority. For simplicity's sake we can define psychotics as those 'being out of touch with reality.'

But, ah! You say, 'who's to say what reality is?' And there's the rub, the issue that holds back the nation's mental welfare. We just cannot, and do not want to, 'define' what is our 'reality,' the 'normal.' A reality, if not 'the' reality is that each of us should have freedom; to have, to breathe, to experience and to be free to think, to express ourselves and to live our lives in all freedom. But with one condition, which is that we are free to enjoy our freedom to the exact degree that our freedom does not impinge on anyone else's freedom.

Out of this basic principle, if we can accept it as an understanding of the reality of life, comes an order that aims for us each to achieve as much of that desired freedom as possible. And that order means we have 'the law,' the law 'of the land.' We say, 'of the land' because that phrase carries the implied sense that the law is of the people, wanted by the people; formed and created and observed by the people – the 'law of the land.'

The law balances our freedoms, restrains our selfish inconsiderate ambitions, and brings a 'normality' to the conduct of the many, so that law-complying conduct becomes 'the reality.' The law is a wonderful thing. In essence, the law is an abstract idea, derived from the imagination of man, developed over many millennia, from the earliest times of the evolution from Homo erectus, our direct ancestry to Homo sapiens. It is the willingness, the consent of mankind to live in peace under the law that separates us from the animals. Animals have only their law of force. The strongest and fiercest rules, okay? Step out of line and you are 'cuffed' one, possibly injured, maimed or killed in a fight. The law of the jungle.

When enough people, in a land, in a country, the citizens, become unhappy with their 'law of the land,' and if their rulers, who are the legislators, who are there as elected representatives, but can also be and frequently are despots, rulers by birth or by an assumption, a grasping of power through force, then the 'law of the land' is disregarded, overthrown and the people return to, resort to, the law of the jungle. That means revolution and removal of the legislators from 'power,' and replacing them with new legislators, the new oligarch. Sadly, the new legislators so relish and enjoy their new role, their new power, that they want to cling onto what they have assumed to: the authority, the comfort, the wealth, and the obsequiousness of their servants. If they can keep the people happy and comfortable, living in peace and prosperity, then they are in for the long haul. But mostly it happens the people are not kept happy, and so to maintain the authority, their freedoms are impinged upon to keep the people subservient, keep them down. How long is it before they rebel? The history of the Romanovs gives some idea of the very long years and years before despotic rule was overthrown, only to be replaced by a worse regime.

So, what is the reality? The reality would seem to be that state of living, that behaviour of us, that behaviour that is modified, regulated, and for the most part complying with the rule of law applying to the society for the time being. And if we deny that reality, ignore it, as if it didn't exist, and live in 'our own world', 'cloud-cuckoo-land,' 'La-la land,' that is something like a psychosis. And from this, we can conjecture that the psychotic may be a 'happier' person than the rest of us, the neurotics; we, who live with our worries or concerns, living out a life of successes and failures, ups and downs.

The something of the animal in us very much likes routine and is 'phased,' possibly phased into a dislike of change, until the imposed change becomes habitual, and then we accept it as 'routine,' the new 'normal' and then we get to like it. The essence of life is that we are beset by change. Much change is driven by demand, and much of that demand comes as a direct result of population increase and the balance demanded as a result of the natural evolution of the new diseases. Our innate intelligence drives the intellectual inventiveness and it's the demands of population growth and disease evolution that drive our inventiveness. We are creative creatures, teleological organisms, ever wanting to move to a greater comfort zone. Goal-creating and goal-seeking, sentient beings, moving higher and higher up Maslow's Hierarchy of Needs.

Much of our happiness comes from the pursuit of a worthy goal. Much more comes from 'peace of mind,' but that is so elusive. Primitive man, clad in animal skins, would go hunting for food, he hunted, killed, disentrailed what he could catch, and then cooked on the campfire: the original BBQ. She, also clad, picked berries and fruits, scratched around the cave mouth trying to grow something that had been found to be edible. She, no less fierce, but kept that in reserve for protecting her offspring. They had no books to read, no films to watch, no mobile phones to talk to their friends or post pictures on Facebook and Snapchat, no guided holidays, cruises on liners or no restaurants to save the cooking and the washing-up. Did they have peace of mind?

If you watch a bird land on the lawn in its hope of finding a juicy, fat worm, does it have peace of mind? Why doesn't it just get on with it, scratching and pecking? Because it needs to keep an eye open, constantly always, always alert for predators. The constant, ever-present fear of the neighbourhood tomcat, and also from the sparrowhawk, and others of similar need and intent, suddenly swooping out of the sky. Peace of mind? Certainly not. They lived with it, as did prehistoric man, his fear was of the sabre-toothed tiger and other wild beasts, but also a fear of fellow man. That fellow man, who being hungry, unsuccessful in a day's hunting, 'covets' his neighbour's food and seeks to deprive him of it. Furthermore, his 'wife' died in childbirth, and he wants his neighbour's mate and seeks to procure her as well. Peace of mind? We think not.

So, peace of mind is a concept, born of modern civilisation, and a hoped-for sequel to a society willing to live under the law of the land. Peace of mind probably comes from freedom from fear, freedom from anxiety and freedom from negativity. The three emotions, causes and effects are interrelated. For example, anxiety feeds fear – fear can be said to be just very extreme anxiety. It is a heightened emotional state. Does the bird scratching on the lawn feel fear as it does so, or is it so accustomed to being alert to danger that it faces danger bravely, as an exercise, an everyday exercise in order to eat? The bird may not even feel anxious. Perhaps being very brave, anxiety and fear can be controlled, minimised, relegated to a reduced state of awareness, through training and mental preparation and an ordering of the emotions – what used to be called 'self-control.' And, to a certain extent, this can give a degree of 'peace of mind.'

Negativity, however, is a different issue, a different matter entirely. Most of us learn and carry out negative thinking at some time in our lives. Some seem to live their whole lives manifesting negative attitudes. So being negative comes with adopting negative attitudes, and by adopt, we mean it is a choice. We always have a choice on our attitudes, and being negative about something or someone, or indeed just about everything, especially when life seems hopeless, hopelessly muddled, disappointing and desperate, can become something of a habit. Bad.

There are some from whom we never hear a negative word spoken about anything or anyone. What's more, these people seem to be the happiest people we ever meet. In education, especially a university's traditional education, one is brought up to think. Think analytically, comparatively and critically. Indeed, some go on to earn their living by being a critic. And critics have their ability to discern what they like and dislike, approve and disapprove, honed to a fine degree. In criticising, we are making a judgement, an opinion, and being judgemental, and inevitably we are being negative, about something in the decision process, if dislike of something happens. And yet, what the critic dislikes, we may like, even like a lot; and the same applies vice versa. The critic here is paid to be negative, or positive about the object he/she is asked to judge, to appraise. We are not, so why would forming an adverse opinion about a play, a painting or a book or a speech be frowned upon as being negative about something?

95

The answer is that, rather strangely, we can get into a rut, a way of thinking, a way of feeling and responding, to just about everything. The extreme form of this rut is the dislike of just about everyone and even everything. And a rut is a no more than a grave with the ends dug out.

What we are saying here is that it can too easily come about that we become too quick, too ready to find fault, to criticise, to be too clever, by half. Too lacking in understanding. We apply negative labels to groups and things, as in 'all politicians are liars' and 'Bloggs' products are all rubbish, 'car traders are all crooks,' and so on. Not good. Making these sweeping negative generalisations. Not good. Why? Well, for a start, it doesn't leave us feeling good; that is to say, feeling good about our self. Saying these negative things leaves a 'nasty taste in our mouth' because we know we have not been fair, just been 'venting' something. So often we exaggerate, just to 'prove a point' as in 'all politicians are liars' meaning really, more fairly, that 'some politicians are liars' or more likely to mean that as a 'type' we find politicians and their obfuscations untrustworthy.

And there is another rub. Often we make sweeping negative generalisations because we can't find the words to express adequately the diverse thoughts and opinions we have and would like to express. Sometimes, time and place restrict us, as in a crowded, noisy restaurant: it's too much effort to communicate sensibly. Sometimes, we know that to say more, more explicitly, with more erudition would either bore or disinterest those in the party we are talking with. A quidnunc.

So, beware trotting out negative opinions. It is a complex issue, and it is said, 'You can't really like and approve of anyone, if you don't really like and approve of yourself.' To have a worthy, justifiable self-esteem is a precious gift, and it is a gift that can be acquired; acquired through practice. Close studies here in these writings and many others elsewhere can help show us how to develop, practise and become someone with appropriate, justifiable self-esteem and that is a worthy goal towards a happier existence. We are not talking overinflated egos here; more someone who is at peace with him/herself and others. Not all others, of course, but at least those with whom we are related, our friends and acquaintances and in our workplace. And to know that we are liked as much as we like them. It is worth working at. It takes time: the younger we start the better.

Knowing about negativity, recognising negativity and eschewing it, is an expertise that is not too difficult a skill to acquire. Adjusting our attitudes is a little tougher. If we aim to be more fair, we'll be being more fair to ourselves. There are always at least two ways to look at things. One advertisement on TV may bore and irritate us, especially as it is so often 'repeated' and how odd, we may think when told, that someone, someone we know and like, loves the advert, and watches it in contented amusement, possibly even buys the products. And so it is; there's always another viewpoint. We tend to make 'judgement calls' based on our own priorities, preferences, our own experiences. To be in the mindset of always being aware that the other person's priorities and experiences are very different, helps us make allowances for a behaviour that we would otherwise criticise, be negative about.

The harm in negativity, the true reality in negativity, is not just having a negative opinion about something or someone, it is the emotion and the degree and depth of emotion, of feelings even, to go so far as hate, that are bad and need to be avoided. By thinking, remembering, recognising and allowing that others are being more fair, more positive in their opinions, more circumspect, helps to reduce the errant, deep intensity of our negative feelings.

The gathering and then delivery of news to an audience should be a matter of the highest integrity, to be as accurate as possible, to be as fair as possible, so that the audience can be well informed of the truth. Sadly, this high ideal is not always found. Reporters and editors, even the owners and high masters of the news media, have their own agendas, and so peddle out the news day after day, night after night, as if seen through a coloured filter, and the filters in the UK are mostly red or yellow, with only a little blue. And why the filter? Because they are 'selling' their product for their livelihoods to their favourite audience who know what they like, what suits their palate. And as for the BBC, supposedly independent, not 'selling' its news, regrettably is seen still as putting their own 'slant' on matters of news, frequently acting as the 'official' opposition to the government, anti-Tory when the Tories are in power and anti-Labour when they are in power, but then there is just news with an obliquity that is 'anti' in the way as a school report says, 'Could do better.'

Television was a great invention, and like all great inventions, humankind finds both good and worthy uses for inventions, as well as evil uses. We 'discover' the science of flying machines for transport and travel. Wonderful. Oh! Look! We can use them to drop bombs. We discover the power of the atom; we can generate electricity; we need so much. Oh! Look! We can make an atomic bomb to kill our enemies. Yes, there's a downside to just about every splendid invention, not intrinsic but extrinsic by the machinations and perversions of mankind. And the same goes for television and the internet.

If we walk the dog in the evening, and see, without peering, into people's living rooms, they may well be sitting watching TV. Watching what? At first there was no choice, but then not many had invested in this new gadget in the house. Then, some choice, a second channel, still no adverts. Oh! Joy! No adverts. Then adverts and more and more channels giving slightly more choice, and then recorders, catch-up and box sets, anything to escape the too-long intervals of adverts.

At first there was a fear of 'man's hypnotism,' man's indoctrination, but fortunately the additional channels and 'box sets' viewing widened the choice enough to take some of that concern away. The problem now is that there is so much screen time needing to be filled every day and evening, 365 days per year that the quality of programmes suffers, and many repeats are screened, and we watch repeats, repeatedly. Why? Through boredom, and through not wanting to risk watching something new and being disappointed, bored. And an evening's viewing on commercial channels can be, and usually is, so boring as they, the adverts, are repeated and repeated, the crass and the vulgar together and so long in duration as to try a saint's patience. Those brief clips advertising a programme always seem to show the only good bit in the programme we are being encouraged to view. Wait until we see the reviews and then go to iPlayer? Reviews? Aren't they just 'One man's meat…?'

Are we too dangerously 'hooked' onto watching TV, meaning that small screen in the corner (or bit bigger now and mounted on the wall above the mantelpiece, replacing the Hockney print). If TV's programmes are not 'of quality' as to news and entertainment and if sport has little appeal, what then? Are we as a nation's people in danger of risking our 'mental health' with this invention? And how can it be unreasonable to conjecture that a nation's people, most anyway, watching so much TV, spending so much time looking at screens, can possibly be 'harming' our mental health, the nation's mental health?

On the plus side, and to be fair, as we must be, there are very many good programmes screened. Programmes that stimulate the intellect, that inform and broaden the mind, about travel, about the world of nature, revealing opinions, valid and bizarre on some issue or other. No, it's certainly not all boring repeats, and so we endeavour to be selective, and the competing channels play spy on each other and screen their best programmes often at the same time, competing for viewers. Thankfully those are not lost into the ether nowadays due to catch-up TV: a sort of nah-nah-nan-nah-nah to the programmers.

Whilst watching TV and looking at screens we are taking in information, be it fact or fiction, just taking it in, and it goes into our 'temporary download files,' which our emotional centre continuously is scanning and reacting in a way to send certain subconscious messages to the higher brain, messages of pleasure, dislike, shock, horror, disgust, disbelief, and so on.

In doing this, we are in a 'world' of our own, just us, our eyes seeing, our ears hearing, at one with our reactions to what we are looking at on this screen. If we accept that 90% of our happiness comes from loving relationships, then we have a powerful need to spend time within those relationships, and that means talking to, talking with, listening to, being out and about with, and laughing with others. By loving relationships, we don't only mean spouse, children, parents, we mean any relationship built because we have a love of goodness, of goodliness, of God. Those 'loving relationships' include friends, neighbours and work colleagues, just about everyone we spend time with, although always accepting that many will not share the same advanced understanding and a perception of the 'power of goodness,' of God. No matter. It works one-sided, but eschew the pigs.

The point is that whilst screen watching, in the psychic insularism, we are not fully into a loving relationship; for that is put on hold for the duration. When the TV pause or off button is pressed, it's time for catch-up, talking to and with, laughing with our loving relationship people, either erasing the 'temporary downloads,' or filing them in our memory bank's files, hoping each is appropriately classified to be stored as something of worth, and not unworthy. Bin the unworthy, the rubbish.

It is risky, risky to our minds, to our mental health, to be absorbing information, fact and fiction and then doing little or nothing with it. We could be, and perhaps should be, talking it 'out' or writing something down, something analytical or competitive, something creative based on the screen viewing done. Loneliness inhibits this talking out and it's good to have a pet we can talk to, a dog or cat, or even a budgie to talk to. Or even, although perhaps only one-sided, an Alexa or her mate Siri. Hardly interactive, but better than nothing to talk to. One can talk to oneself, but is anyone listening? Be sure to listen to yourself, if you are going to talk to yourself.

Modern education seems to have produced a strain of Homo sapiens well able to criticise and appraise the world they are in and make judgements; and sometimes we feel that that is about all they have been educated to do; but that would be grossly unfair. Sadly, these judgements are often irrational and unjustifiable, especially when it comes to a decision to align with a certain religious grouping or in a particular 'political' sect.

The other malaise seen frequently is a lack of an understanding or even an experience of any form of self-discipline. Self-discipline certainly comes from within, but how did it get there? Self-discipline is different to ritualistic habitualism, which is either mostly copied or mimicked, but can be self-generated, self-imposed, and so can often be an irrational behaviour, but by its nature usually harmless, as in an obsession, such as with the arrangement of the neatly folded towels on the towel rail.

Discipline as taught, for example, in school, or later in the armed forces, and to a degree at work, can be both good and bad. Also, it can be mild or extreme. Much depends on the teacher and on the ready compliance of the pupil, the object. Bad discipline does harm to the young mind and builds resentment, even hatred. Naïve, unthinking and cruel parents inflict their authority through their size and physical force on a child to get the child to succumb to their will; and the child's recalcitrant behaviour brings on even more stern discipline until some form of compliant behaviour is obtained.

As humans, living under the law of the land, we have developed the notion of rights and privileges. 'I know my rights,' we often hear expletively expressed. No, they don't. They don't, because they have never been taught the difference between rights and privileges. Even some modern internet dictionaries fail to make it fully clear, so it's hardly surprising that there is confusion. One internet dictionary describes a privilege as a special 'right.' What nonsense. So confusing.

In fact, there is clear water between these two human benefits created for us. A right is a benefit defined in law, meaning parliamentary law as in a Bill of Rights, but also those rights that are created as in given and afforded by local government and even in another way, by contract law. Rights, once given, created in law, are a basic and fundamental protection of each of us and so almost never, and certainly intentionally never to be taken away, removed. That is to say a right is not revocable. Whereas a privilege is a benefit awarded by an authority or an authoritative figure or body, to be enjoyed, as in 'privileged,' possibly over another who does not have the privilege; but that privilege is revocable. This can be as a result of changes that have come about in the application of a policy variation or as a result of the unsatisfactory conduct of the privileged person.

Privileges are used as sweeteners to the young undergoing disciplinary training. Many, perhaps most of us, grow to appreciate and even enjoy good discipline with the sense of orderliness and security it can bring. Neat, tidy habits; freshly showered; clean, uncrumpled clothes; brushed hair; clean finger- and toenails; clean, polished shoes not broken at the heel; an orderly table laid, with napkins; clean, uncluttered kitchen sink and work surfaces; papers in order on a desk. We can see the benefit of good discipline readily becoming a healthy self-discipline as we grow up, as we grow up to adulthood.

Far more difficult to bring about is the self-discipline of our thinking. We are not referring here to the learning of subjects and their facts, that trotting them out well is what gets us through exams, but to the development of some sort of control over what we think, what we think of things, and of people, and their groups, but also, what we think about, allow our minds to range over, and more deeply considering, more deeply rationalising those thoughts. And then also, from time to time, possibly for a brief ten minutes or so each day, to deliberately have no thoughts at all, to deliberately banish all those thoughts, however 'minor and unimportant' and how 'urgent and important.' Just to be able to literally go into pause mode, press the pause button. It is not easy to achieve this. For most of us our minds are bubbling away like a stew on the hob and we have seldom sat down, banished all outside influences, turned the TV off, taken the phone off the hook and closed our eyes and meditated. Meditate but not cogitate. Blank mind. A thought pops up. Bang it on the head and push it back down. Just for even five minutes would be better than none, and it's okay to put the timer on.

There are times when things make us cross, angry or just downright disgruntled as in the vernacular we say, 'pissed off.' Everyone knows what that means (including The Queen) and has experienced the feeling – very often the cause is something we can do nothing about. It's there, or it's done, and we can do nothing about it except feel pissed off. Are we enjoying feeling like this? It's like banging our head against a wall. Do we enjoy doing that? No, of course not, so we make up our mind to stop banging our head on the wall. Ah! That's better. That banging really hurt. And the same applies to stopping feeling pissed off:

we just make up our mind to stop feeling that way. 'What do you mean? "Stop feeling that way"? They're emotions, it's how I feel, I can't help that, feeling pissed off, can I?'

Yes, we can, but it takes practice. If we can switch off successfully for five minutes when we want, we can switch off unwanted, unhelpful even destructive thoughts and emotions. Some people imagine a railway control box in their mind, the junction box as described elsewhere in these chapters, the box high up with a viewpoint of the rails, points and trains, an overview, perhaps of life, to see what's going on with banks of levers controlling the signals and the points that can change a direction. A control box, that the operator inside controls everything that is within his/her domain to control.

Imagine that and we go into our control box, find the lever marked 'feeling pissed off' and literally pull it to its off position. And if we want to be thoroughly modern about it, the control room will be all buttons and switches, even little sliders on mobile phone settings to activate or deactivate. We can imagine anything we like as long as it serves its purpose of the 'control' part of self-control. Sceptics and the unpractised may never acquire the knack of resorting to this method of 'self-control:' so be it. If the bus, the omnibus, arrives at the stop and they don't want to get on, that's their choice. It's their decision.

The methods by which self-control is acquired are diverse and any one method has no special merits over another. Discipline taught, good discipline leads to self-discipline, and self-discipline is an adjunct, a corollary of self-control. Marshalling our thoughts, our thinking processes, which are just trains of thought, is an exercise requiring practice. Like physical fitness, exercising at a specified time, possibly a special place, is a good guide for mental exercises. We move from five minutes of mental 'blankness'-like meditation, to five minutes of thinking about anything that crops up in our minds, or something we deliberately want to think about. Not just any old think, but a positively minded, analytical thinking about the subject, be it an issue, a concern, or pleasant events, both in planning and also in recollection. Our choice entirely, no random thoughts. If random creative thoughts pop up to distract from our choice, then have a pencil and paper handy and log them to be thought about when you choose, not let that other mind, lurking in your subconscious, choose.

Yes, that other mind. Our second mind. How often do we hear the expression, 'I am in two minds to ...' do or to say something? We also hear, 'I've half a mind to ...' do or say something. So, what's going on?

In the first case, the 'two minds' refers to what goes on, for example, in our processes when making a difficult decision. One mind identifies the pros; the other, that doubting mind, the cons. We hesitate to reach a decision. This is a toughie. We vacillate, but eventually we decide on a course of action. And then, within moments or perhaps later, sometimes much later, before the decision has been fully implemented, we question the decision, or more precisely, the other mind questions the decision, throwing up all sorts of doubts, underscores the cons, and adding a general thought of 'Have I done the right thing?' 'Have I made the 'right' (sic) decision?'

Now, as we have elaborated elsewhere in these writings it is best not to think in terms of such a thing as a right decision, mostly because we just cannot make a decision at the time, or at anytime, believing it to be the wrong decision. We can only ever make any decision, believing it to be the best decision, best for us, at that time. The other options, the alternative decisions, are the second or third or fourth etc., in rank to the best decision. We make the best decision after weighing up all the factors that we can identify that are brought to bear. Consequently, there is no such thing as the wrong decision, one that turned out poorly; just a decision that worked out to be 'not such a good decision.'

So, we have two minds, each mostly doing their own job, but with overlap, and with an agreed position on which mind overrules the other, when needs must. For example: we wish to cross the road, but we are also thinking about what to buy in the butcher's for lunch that day, as in what the kids may prefer. We emerge between two parked cars and step into the road into the path of a bus. Do we carry on thinking about the butcher's choices or do we stop to think, 'Shall I step back to avoid being run over?' Of course, we step back, unthinkingly, automatically, as an automaton, with much well-honed self-preservation reflexes. It is our second mind that takes over control, to save us. No questioning, no 'Shall I?' from the first mind: the second mind is suddenly dominant and controlling everything. The first mind then says, 'Wow! That was a close thing, I wasn't fully concentrating!'

We do this all the time, with only 'half a mind' on the job, and if we can do a job, and think about something else at the same time, we may say that's multitasking. But is it? How many of us drive our cars along a very familiar route, say the way home every day, arrive home and realise we can't remember any part of the journey, because we have gone all the way along and been thinking about something, some issue of concern, or some event that has happened? It brings 'a cold realisation' of how dangerous a situation we have created, yet come through. We could have killed someone by not concentrating. 'We didn't think,' we say. Oh! Yes, we did think but we weren't thinking about the driving, and so we were driving 'without due care and attention,' as they say.

It was Mind B that 'drove' us home, while Mind A was preoccupied. Mind A is really the supra-controlling mind, but occasionally slacks off, and allows Mind B to 'play along.' Mind B stores all the emotions, good and bad, and can think a thousand times faster than Mind A. Think of 'B' response to the bus about to squash us flat. That response from 'B' was made in a nanosecond. 'A' catches up and B follows up by releasing mechanisms for 'shock'. 'A' starts thinking by 'thanking his lucky stars.' Luck didn't come into it, or fate. We were saved by Mind B, the self-preservation controlling centre that controls all our emotions, including negative thoughts.

In essence what we are saying here is that Mind A needs some training, some discipline, applied initially from without, until it comes from within. Like dog training. Like military training. Many other people in society bemoan the stopping of National Service, that compulsory two-year military training for all male youths over eighteen. Nowadays it would include females, too. Why National Service? Because of the enforced discipline it gives (that becomes self-discipline to last a lifetime) such as personal hygiene, personal presentation, punctuality, respect for authority, even if not for the personages, more that there has to be 'authority,' respect the democracy we live in, and so on.

So without that, we, the country, gets along as best it can, with whole swathes of people only having a vague idea of what it would actually mean if we had to 'turn to,' to defend 'our liberty,' fight to defend it, or even any serious understanding that we are 'free,' as in we live in a 'free' country, but only as free as our collective need, our government's decision that we are all needed to defend that freedom. It's an understanding we need to come to.

So disciplined thinking is for Mind A, that gets us to have a concentration appropriate to what is being done at the time. She asks, 'What's the time?' The disciplined mind should answer, 'The time is now.' Drag those other thoughts away and concentrate. An older person, but potentially anyone, concentrates while going downstairs, not wanting to fall. He/she is 'Here, now, going carefully down the stairs.' No question of 'I wasn't thinking.'

Similarly, Mind A must concentrate when driving, especially that familiar route home. Somehow, we need to control all those other thoughts, and really, really concentrate on what we are doing, from peeling onions with a very sharp knife, to cutting logs with the chainsaw. And many other things, like, for example, accidentally clicking 'send,' when we meant to click 'paste.' So easily done, and when done, we have either made ourself look rather foolish sending half a message, or an email sent in too much haste, to too many people and then we regret it. Best to keep all emotion out of emails?

It is Mind A that, when disciplined and trained, that says to itself 'go into the junction box, the control box (over Mind B) and switch off those thoughts, those feelings.' For example, Mind B says you are grieving, grieving for a lost loved one. Mind A says, Yes, grieving is right and proper and natural, but I will decide how much and how intense that grieving will be, and at some point, down the road of time, I will decide when to stop grieving. I will enter the junction box and switch off grieving, and throw the switch for 'recovering from grieving, picking up the traces of a life.' Conscious, disciplined thinking. Not easy, seldom easy, even to the trained, disciplined mind. So, a period of Mind B in predominance, showing our emotions, is good and natural. But the degree, the extent, the duration, the intensity, always belongs to Mind A, which should only ever hover in the background at the initial shock.

Best develop Mind A. Train it like a puppy. There is real joy in a well-trained dog. A loving, respectful master-servant relationship. Mind B is a sort of munificent alter ego; munificent, thank goodness, but only if it is not allowed to run rampant.

When we are young children we have no 'mood-enhancing substances' in our lives, apart from food and sweets; the former vital and necessary in essence, but both can be to excess, either products of self-indulgence or sought-after love replacements. Moods come and go, up and down, but as young children we have no responsibilities, so we are carefree, free of any need to be earning a living, to look after ourselves, to survive in the big, wide world. It's not seen like that, as children look forward to becoming an adult. 'What are you going to be when you are grown up?' is the frequent question. Learning to ride a bike, often the first 'liberating' experience, we are away, out of sight (and control) of our parents. But we see adults, behaving, well, like adults. They drink coffee, tea and alcohol.

Some smoke. They drive cars. The child thinks, 'To be adult I must take up these things,' and with little or no asking ourselves, as adolescents impatient for adulthood, why adults do these things. The adolescent implies to his/her friends, 'Look at me, how grown up I am, smoking and drinking, wearing make-up, and mum's (or elder sister's) clothes.'

We gradually get into the adult world, the world of work, and then play. Work has its demanding myths, and obligations, eased by that morning coffee or tea, a break for a cigarette, even if 'vaped'; it brings the end of the week, with its 'must go out Saturday night,' and 'let's get pissed and go for an Indian (curry, that is).' But why deliberately 'get pissed,' as in drink so much alcohol, initially uplifting, then mindlessness sets in, to leave a mood of hopelessness on Sunday morning and a 'thumping' headache, and short of money, too. So, we brag about how good it was, kidding ourselves that we were always in control of ourselves, making good choices for our lives, having fun, and going along with our mates (all caught in the same mindset).

On any occasion, that first drink, that first smoke, even, changes the mood. It relaxes us, or is it that the physical process of lighting up, pouring and taking the first sip and knowing that for a few minutes, at least, we are stepping off the 'roundabout' of our life for a period? Can we get the same mood effect by stepping off the roundabout without the cigarette, be it nicotine or 'vapour' or without the alcohol? The answer is yes for many. Many who can relax and 'muse mood' without substances.

The problem with substances is that they all become addictive, and many to the detriment of the individual as a person, to his/her finances and most importantly, to their relationships. Youths, students at parties, away from home, at university probably, like to party. A party is a noun. We all know what the words 'a party' means. They are usually qualified with some descriptive adjective, as in birthday party. To youths and adolescents, the word takes on a different meaning, a more significant meaning. Afterwards, people talk of a 'great party' but what makes a 'great party?' Often it's not great for everyone there. People go with an expectation of a good time, a great time even. As we leave we thank the hosts, if they are anywhere still to be found, and not in a stupor, or in an inappropriate clinch in the bedroom, we leave, saying thanks for a great party. Great as in good food, drink and good company, hopefully. For many a party is an opportunity to flirt and be fanciful, to lose inhibitions for a while, a snog, a grope, possibly further, only to be regretted tomorrow perhaps, or just perhaps sometimes, as we vow to behave better, next time out, if there is one. Is that what 'to party,' the verb, means? But do we not come to expect too much of this social gathering?

To party well, one needs to be in a party mood. And there are substances that help that mood. It starts with alcohol and nicotine, enough to remove some inhibitions, some shyness perhaps, to flirt. Other substances can more effectively increase the party mood, a sniff, a spliff, Captain Jack and all his friends and relations. And so the dangerous rot sets in. All sorts of untoward sequelae from substances trying to ensure it's a great party for us, at the end of a hard, long week at work: 'Go on, you deserve it' attitude. Deserve what? Addiction to the point of total degradation and death? Deserve loss of family, friends, job, be raped on the way home; deserve even death? Is that so?

The tendency, the temptation, is to think, as a young person wanting to experience all that, 'I can control myself, I know what I am doing, I won't let myself become addicted.' Each thinks himself or herself somehow 'better' than others. It's mistaken, of course, even plain vanity. And then there's the cruelty of one's peers, often jealous or envious peers. There you are, young, beautiful, too, with many admirers, would-be lovers, intelligent, with '10 straight 'A's,' summa cum laude, and victor ludorum, with a rich daddy, and now at medical school, soon to be qualified to become a doctor, brain surgeon-to-be. Equally it could be an airline pilot, or a Queen's Councillor or budding distinguished high diplomat. In fact, everything going for you, but have never experienced ecstasy. No, not the ecstasy felt inside when your results are announced, but the oh-so-promising mental thrill from the tablet offered you by them, your so-called friends, but jealous, envious friends, goading you to be 'one of them' have fun, take the pill. Within half an hour you are in a coma, being rushed to hospital ICU for six hours and then, dead. Who needs chemical extrinsic mood-enhancers? Why do people do it? What's wrong that they feel they have to do it? Isn't alcohol enough? Of course, sudden collapse and death like that described are rare, so it's a question of risk, a risk that is overlooked at the time, another case of 'I didn't think.' No, they didn't, and no, the person, that very highly gifted person, the one they secretly admired but also envied and were jealous of, has gone. Let's all get seriously shocked, saddened, and display those 'feelings' – big time.

The national mood is definitely affected by the news, shocking terrorists' bombings affects us all. Other news gives the national mood a bipartisan division. When a political party 'gets in' then usually about half the country are pleased, full of optimism; the other half disappointed, often to the point of desperation. These moods can last, sometimes right up to the next election. And the moods can also affect things like the stock market, and trade union meetings.

The weather also definitely affects the national mood. A long spell of fine weather uplifts us all. Out come the shorts, more flesh is exposed, drop-top cars drop their tops, and out come the BBQs. It's party time, big time. And the reverse happens in winter, a long spell of cold, wet and windy weather, we've not seen the sun now for a week, it's all so very 'depressing,' if we let it. Likewise, extreme weather, floods, storm damage, homelessness, no power for days, food rotting in freezers. This news is 'depressing,' and even stressful to some, certainly to those directly involved.

It's an awareness, a collective awareness that most of us feel, for others, while thankfully safe ourselves, a feeling of sympathy and an empathy for others; the national mood. When Princess Diana was lost to 'us,' the national mood of mourning was self-evident.

To what degree, as a nation's people, are we collectively affected by news-filmed scenes of violence, gratuitous violence, rioting, destruction, harming, maiming and killing? Affected by uncouth, inarticulate, uneducated bigotry? By obscene grotesqueness, and by vulgar, overly suggestive crudeness, mostly loin-instigated? By on-screen presentations so completely lacking in any aesthetic or artistic taste. Yes, and most of those descriptions can be applied to the twelve minutes of advertisements several times an hour to crash into our lives, our homes, our families, so intrusively night after night, offending us, with the danger of turning us into simple-minded automatons. National mood? Certainly, it's as if the advertisement makers can only dream up the worst of their outputs after themselves taking an LSD tablet. Crazy.

TV soaps, same night after night, others week after week, presenting little for thought but the irrational and bizarre, let's say 'out of control' emotional behaviour of the cast in the plot, scenes of foul-mouthed slanging matches as producers vie for a TV plaudit and try to make a strong storyline. Viewers with any sense will shout at the screen as if to make the scriptwriters and actors see some sense; other viewers may be subclinically or, more likely, subconsciously influenced by the seeming drivel being spouted, and unknowingly learned as we are trot out similar behaviour patterns ourselves. National mood? To some degree, yes, very probably.

Better to find and read a good book. Something that bears a worthwhile thought, broadening the mind, not narrowing it. Beware 'the national mood.' Is it real? Lead or follow? Is it imaginary or real? It is both, almost certainly, both at different times, and yet it can be at all times.

CHAPTER 7
MAN IS AN ISLAND...

It was John Donne in 1624 whose thinking pronounced, and summarised here with some paraphrasing, that, 'Man is not an island, entire of itself... anything that diminishes mankind diminishes me also, for I am involved in mankind.' And, of course, we can accept that philosophy but not in totality, as there is always the other side of the coin, to consider, if we have the will.

Considering for a moment the make-up of living things, we see the anatomy, the physiology and cellular biology present in all living organisms and yet immediately upon its death, all those physical structures are still present, but their biochemistry stops working, bit by bit and rapidly. So we can reasonably ask, and ponder, 'What is the driving force, the life force, once gone, although the body, the bones, muscles, heart, lungs, brain and those millions of cells and their biosystems, are essentially the same in structure and microstructure are dead. That 'magical,' spiritual, ethereal package of energy (dare we suppose to describe it so?) has gone. Gone? Gone where? I never saw it go. 'And the light in his eyes went out,' is a phrase used in literature, as he/she gasped their last breath.

We have expounded in another chapter on the matter of senses. We should consider, as well, what or from where, are the origins of our thoughts; and what are the influences on our thoughts, and also how our thoughts then influence us, our actions and words.

We often act or speak without thinking, which is to say thoughtlessly. If we accidentally touch something very hot in the kitchen, we let go immediately, in a nanosecond. That took no thought at all. The sensory nerves in our fingers sent the message ultra-fast to the brain and the brain responded ultra-fast to the muscles to say 'Let go' to the fingers, and in a nanosecond later the brain registers a pain reaction, so we rush to the cold tap and souse the burnt fingers in cold water.

This little event creates thoughts, or should do, to the tune of, 'We need to beware of hot things in the kitchen in future.' It takes our sense of self-awareness to create that thought. Not a thought that takes the brain of an Einstein to formulate, but an innate sense of learning within each of us, for if we don't learn like this, our life will be one long hazard after another.

So, it is clear that external influences, in our environment, stimulate one or more of our eight 'God-given' senses, the sense we were born with, that creates and influences our thoughts. And yet, we are also very capable of having thoughts quite remote, quite uninfluenced by the environment. And an easy way to go about this is to 'meditate,' in a quiet, cool, comfortable place where we won't be disturbed, and either have a think about something that is 'on our mind' or just let our thoughts ramble, to think whatever 'pops up,' so to speak.

Not all our thoughts are worthy, and our learning as we travel through life influences other thoughts to 'judge' our unworthy thoughts, so we can elect to adjust the unworthy thoughts to be more charitable or more kindly disposed to those who might otherwise have been criticised, or dealt with unkindly. There is the mantra, quoted elsewhere and here again because it is so vital. 'Beware our thoughts, because they become our words, and beware our words because they become our actions, and beware our actions because they become our habits, and beware our habits, because they become us.'

So what, if anything, is the connection between thoughts and learning? As seen above, life's experiences, both good and bad, can leave us with a new learned behaviour pattern, as in, 'We'll be more careful of hot things in the kitchen in future.' If we don't 'learn' that lesson, then our lives won't change much, won't develop, and certainly won't improve. Hence the oft-quoted phrase we hear, 'Some people never learn,' but we are talking here about much more complex behaviour patterns than burnt fingers in the kitchen.

We can conjecture what it is that facilitates learning and what obstructs learning. However, these are very complex matters and are addressed by many professionals, especially those in the field of education, so only a simplistic overview will be attempted here.

A definition of intelligence is that ability to adapt to our environment. That is to say, not the green environment, but in most cases, we mean the brick and concrete environment, where, if we learn well to adapt, to survive and to thrive, we are known as 'streetwise.' Does this take 'book learning?' Formal classes in school or other departments of education? Is this a case of 'survival of the fittest?'

The answer probably lies in looking more into what goes on in class learning. It may be totally boring to hear about Henry VIII when we are ten, but by the very being in school, being fed information that may or may not stick, our brains are receiving information, and much will get stored, to be regurgitated later, either at an exam, or at some time when suddenly we find to our delight we can expound and impress others with our knowledge.

So, schooling can condition our minds into the 'learning' mode, and that is the merit. To carry this principle to a more extreme example is the learning of Latin. Now Latin is a dead language, no one communicates, speaks in Latin anymore, so why learn a dead language? It's boring. No, it's not. And it's not really dead, as it lives on as a medium for training the brain in logical deduction. Jostling with the translation of this archaic language just happens to be a form of training, and analytical training that is rare in education today. It is a pity that that is not better understood by those who organise and fund 'state education,' but with so many other subjects to learn, something has to be chopped.

Admittedly, it is not easy to stimulate the interest in many aspects of 'subject' learning by children in school these days, if it ever was. Most professionals develop a knack of achieving the awakening of their charges' intellect. One issue that can crop up is to do with the child's attitude, and not only is this a concern for the adolescent, but the attitude can live on into adult life as well. Our attitude to learning can be well adjusted, keen with enthusiasm, or it can be distracted by challenges to our life as a whole, by our not being 'well adjusted' at that time, by there being some unhappiness, breeding negativity, blocking out any prospect of any learning going on, on that day or, sadly, on any day.

As children and youngsters, we can learn either by accepting the process where we are put under a formal education, and as well we learn in an unconscious way merely by living, by watching others succeed or fail, in real life, or in stories in books or films viewed. It is perhaps incorrect to say just the young. We can continue that 'learning' by living all our lives, and learning by living happens so subtly, we are often unaware until we find ourselves drawing on a copied behaviour spoken or acted in response to a situation.

A significant and dominant factor in the bringing about of an attitude to learning is that of the influence of our self-image: the person we'd like to be like. Our hero, someone we admire. We emulate their dress, their composure, their style of speaking and behaving. But do we have their book learning, their command of language and their style of leadership? Many youngsters dream on until the phase passes, but for some it leads into an awareness that to do better, we have to go about the business of learning about so much more, the so much 'everything,' if there is a desire to become something in this world.

However, despite our enthusiasm for learning facts and figures for self-improvement, and the desire to get a good job, we can sometimes find out that, of the people we have come across, some turn out to be unprincipled scoundrels, lying and cheating for a quick buck. Also, we may have been deceived, drawn away from our previously good conduct and character, and turned into an unworthy person by being taken in. Perhaps more accurately, we have taken up with someone because of some physical attraction, and a lust for sex. Perhaps we're only just becoming involved on the fringes of some unseemly types of people, who then evoke in us the sense that 'this is not for us.' Our natural instinct can instead be to seek out and go for something, someone, and to be in the company of people of higher ideals of honesty and integrity. They may not have so much ready money and may be less 'flauntingly attractive,' and less interested in accepting shallow relationships, such as sleeping around. But from this we realise that we have developed some sort of 'moral compass.'

It is hoped that, in general, children will grow up with firm ideas of what is generally regarded as right and wrong, good and bad, such as honesty versus false witness. More abstract virtues such as honour, respect and generosity, and that special notion of honour as in 'honour thy father or mother,' (hopefully they will be around to be honoured).

It is very good that these ideals are also taught in schools, but the many 'natural and instinctive' undesirable interactions between children, such as squabbling over who owns which toy, who damaged it, who hit who first etc., make it a tough job. The teaching helps make them 'civilised' and with the inculcation of 'ideals' they can be fit for adult life and for them to become someone.

As well as all that, the metaphorical 'throwing his/her toys out of the pram' is a rage reaction by most children at some stage, only to develop into the same kind of behaviour in adults as a moral blackmail, where we see, in essence, 'If I can't have my way, I won't contribute any more, and I will leave this organisation etc.,' or resort to tears to get one's way in a shaky relationship, or just take a sicky.

It is a reaction that sometimes persists into adulthood. It emanates from vanity. It was well evidenced by some French leaders by their reaction to Britain voting to leave the EU. Some EU leaders were clearly falling to the temptation to 'throw their toys out of the pram,' and their ultimata aimed towards the British were clearly spiteful and vindictive, as were the words spoken (as reported by the press), their reactions, particularly their body language, when meeting our representatives and in particular when meeting our Prime Minister – how childish!

Chivalry is another high ideal that still but barely persists from a bygone era; but what does it mean in this day and age? On a sinking ship it has always been women and children first (to the lifeboats or rescue vessels) then the elderly. Leaving the fit and strong males to last and so with the risk of being still on-board when the ship goes down, and the lifeboats are all full and can take no more. In this situation it implies not only an 'obligatory' sense of chivalry, but also sacrifice, to be prepared to sacrifice one's life for others – possibly the highest ideal of all, but to some it is no ideal at all, just a ridiculous notion. These days would the women take offence at being hustled into the lifeboats with this sexual discrimination? What about LGBT? How would any life-saving priority be made? Would it be the sex we are in our heads or the sex we are between our legs? Would it be, 'After you, sir.' 'No, after you, madam. You are a madam, aren't you?'? What would a cross-dressing male do in this situation? Would he save his skin as a man in women's clothes, or would he 'come clean,' be a man and state his true sex, and stay on-board to drown, like a man, as the women and children row away to salvation?

If chivalry is a ridiculous notion as an ideal, to some, it is a sensible notion then to question all ideals. If it is an ideal to be truthful then we need to look at what is and what isn't true. If we witness an event, such as a car crash, we know what we saw, and say what we saw. Another person, perhaps on the other side of the road, also saw the crash and he/she will say what they saw. The two reports of exactly what happened may not be the same. For example, if a cyclist was involved one might say the cyclist wobbled into the path of the car, the other may say the cyclist didn't wobble.

To both observers they believe their versions the truth, the truth of what happened. Feelings become involved in influencing the two versions. The one, a vain person, proud of his good eyesight, confident always in his opinions, becomes arrogant if his opinions are challenged. The other, a less assertive person, disliking altercations, given to self-doubt, wavers in his opinions: did his spectacled-assisted eyesight 'deceive' him? He relents and so a conclusion is reached on a version of the 'truth.' So, if truth can come in many 'shades,' many degrees of reliability, as an ideal, do other ideals come similarly by degree, and do they interact or are they influenced, can they be influenced, by other emotions?

The straight answer is yes. We all have different notions of what is true, honourable, what respect is and of course, generosity. So, as it is obviously complex, we aim for an easy understanding – the theme of these writings – we endeavour towards what is generally understood by these terms, these ideals, and apply them with a modest confidence in their worth. In this sense, in their broad adoption, we are not alone, as an island, but among many such islands, and so we know we can acknowledge readily that we are involved in mankind, and so we are not an island entire of itself.

Jesus said (so we believe from the scriptures, but they were written by the hand of man, very many years later): 'No one can come to the Father except through me' and 'Do this in remembrance of me.' But who and what was Jesus? What did He mean by Me? Surely it is undeniable and so axiomatic that He was the embodiment of all that is good. Total and complete goodness! Is that what He meant, could have meant, by saying 'Me' He meant 'my' example, 'what I am,' 'how I am,' 'who I am,' ' what I do,' and 'what I say.' The 'Me,' the total 'Me.' And 'Me.com?'

If we can follow and lead our lives by His good example, do and say as He does, then we are or will be going 'through the Him' to that state of all goodness. Of course we fail, miserably, so in need of spiritual nourishment at communion, with the mass of fellow believers, the bread is taken as the 'body' of the Church, and that sip of wine to acknowledge that lifeblood, the spirit of goodness among us all on earth, and we pray that that goodliness will be with us until we come to communion again.

As we think more about His 'way,' what He represented, what He was, He becomes less human in our minds – by 'human' we mean as in flesh and blood – and He becomes more the concept of 'the Christ,' the 'Redeemer,' more a godly figure, a god on earth, walking among us; well, among them, actually, among the Jews, the Hebrews, His kinfolk (and the odd Roman), ostensibly at that time, in those days, and for ever after spurned and rejected as 'one of them.' Could this be the bedrock, the rock-bottom, nitty-gritty, subconscious reason that some have feelings deep down of something against the Jews? If so, it can't be logical.

Let's think less about his human life; his eating, for nourishment of his human body, his clothes for warmth and modesty, his daily habits, and think more about his ethereal spirit, that concentration of goodness, here on earth, in that place, that location of all earth, where he was, those co-ordinates, that 'lat and long.' What is the reason, or perhaps there's no reason that has ever been clear to us mortals, why Jesus came when he did and where he did, at that time in the history of mankind? For a reason or no reason. It happened; something happened. Something incredibly good happened. Surely that is what is important? He came. He lived. He held the Ten Commandments to be worthy, He gave us the Beatitudes, and His prayer. He healed. He was crucified, by a world that 'received' him not.

He became like the victim of a tsunami – He was flooded, sunk and washed away, to survive under the surface, but physically lost and gone; but, like the lost city of Atlantis, we still believe He existed, and that, if sought, He can be found.

Who built the universe? Who owns the universe? Is there more than one universe? What is time – an ever-rolling stream, like an ever-advancing army of a trillion trillion ants, like an ever- and ever-rising tide, never going into ebb? Can we go through a door and re-enter life as it was 10, 20, 70 years ago and see ourselves as we were then? Could we ever be ourselves again as we were then, or can we only ever imagine being that older, invisible non-participant, just an observer, like in a film?

If we think of the universe, new stars being born, new solar systems, the universe ever expanding into space. How is that space contained? Is it, say, in the pocket of some supergiant? If the smallest molecule that exists looks out on its world, its world around it, the universe for that molecule will be 'proportionately small.' Is it possible in our imagination to think of the universe so small as that molecule sees, and so, in only the tiniest part of some even bigger universe, or bigger universes?

These questions, the universe and time, are beyond our simple comprehension. Yet we comprehend ourselves, as flesh and blood and character and intelligence and willpower. We seem to want and feel that we are here for a purpose and that being so, someone, somebody, something, some God must have arranged for us to be alive, else why else would we be so certain we are here for a purpose? Some regard that purpose as fate.

The concept of God, and hence the perception of God is that God has a purpose, a design for us and in so assuming, conclude that God has those human characteristics of intelligence and character but with omnipotence, too. Polytheistic Gods may or may not have a purpose for us, but each is believed to have human type of thinking, of intelligence and character, with motives as well as with certain powers.

The unseen forces in our world, like magnetism, gravity and electricity, in the universe, too, surely do not have any intelligence and human-type character. We have seen their powers, but they are generally considered to be without design or purpose, at least any purpose, any intent for us, we humans on earth. But who knows? We have to admit that our understanding of those forces and any interaction, any 'collaboration' between them for a design on the lives of plants and animals here on earth is way beyond us at this stage of science in the world.

Take away any notion of these unseen forces having any human characteristics such as intelligence and character to have a design for us, or indeed for themselves. But wait. Each force produces an effect – on the animate and inanimate objects within its force field. And that effect takes up the object of that particular force. For example, the apple on the tree is within the force field of earth's gravity – when free to move by the breaking of the stalk, the apple moves under the effect of the force field. In fact everything on earth is held by the effect of the gravitational force field, including sand on the beach, water in the lake. If gravity had intelligence, we would think it has a design on all those objects within its powers, to draw in and to hold everything possible in its clutches, until a greater force comes along?

The same process of thinking can be applied to magnetism and electricity. Magnetism always trying to draw in certain metallic objects, while repelling or ignoring others. Similarly for electricity; always trying to move, to flow and to deliver its powerful source of energy until, spent and exhausted, the energy dissipates into other forms.

The same applies to the power of goodness, of God. A force field acting on us all, affecting us all to a greater or lesser extent. The force field can become immensely focused, as laser light is light intensely focused, and goodness, so focused, produces wondrous effects on certain people whose alert receptors are capable of absorbing and benefiting from this focused 'goodness.' Jesus was one such.

Born of a woman, a virgin, under the effect of intense force of goodness. The force of goodness is present everywhere, on earth at least, in our solar system probably, but a force that is constantly washing over us, as we move through its force-field, its field of energy, of goodness, stimulating our receptors, which we can respond to, or switch to low or very low receptivity, but we cannot ever turn off completely, all the while we are alive. And that applied to you, too, Mr Hitler.

Why do we say things like 'it was meant to be?' The silent, unspoken acceptance that 'there is a fate that is running our lives that we cannot control.' Surely, many can be readily forgiven for thinking that their life could be as if it were ordained by God, or the Devil. Many believe we are 'free' to do what we want but only within certain limits, but if we try to step outside these limits, set by our 'fate,' then fate takes over and prevents us from doing whatever we were about to do.

Someone who didn't get on a plane at the last moment, either overcome by an 'irrational' urge to change their plans or perhaps just a sudden, unaccountable sense of fear! Someone who drove a different route on the 'flimsiest' of whims, and like the plane not boarded, which crashed, and so avoided a certain calamity. Fate had a hand, we say. It was meant to be.

For others, less inclined deep down to believe in fate, may still say 'it was meant to be,' as it is a cliché, something we say of habit, or it's what many habitually say and we just join in, to blend in. To get along we go along – as it were. That is to mean, when we say, 'it was meant to be,' it's more as in a way of accepting what has happened, perhaps as a thought of consolation rather than literally believing it was the hand of fate. And when Saddam's stadium collapsed, killing very many, he just said, 'It's the will of Allah.'

So, if it was not fate, what was it? Planes crash, always for a reason, a technical failure, a human failure or meteorological event, all of which 'happen.' Being on that particular plane, on that particular flight, on that particular day, was our choice, our decision, rationally made in the expectation of being safely delivered. Likewise, that car trip, that route, that time, our chosen speed, all our decisions, however subconsciously and innocently made.

In health and safety terms, climbing into a metal tube with many others that we know will be loaded with high-octane fuel and the tube on its wings will be self-projected thousands of feet above the earth at hundreds of miles an hour has to have an implicit hazard of an ability to blow up or crash. Likewise sitting in a metal box on wheels self-propelling at significant speed along roads crowded with boxes all doing the same, the roads often bendy, bumpy or slippery, has to have an implicit hazard that the box may crash and injure us and others.

Technical humans have spent vast hours with their skills over and over again designing and making planes and vehicles as 'fail-safe' as possible. With the aim of making as sure as possible that those implicit hazards do not come about; and if they must come about by some mathematical calculation, then their frequency of occurrence must be as rare as possible, as small a 'chance' of that statistic arising as infinitesimally small as they can make it. They develop the risk control procedures to reduce the risks as much as is humanly possible within the knowledge and skill base at the time.

All the procedures set in place are there to reduce the risk of the implicit hazards occurring. But these 'crashes' do still occur, and always for a reason, as we have said. Mostly these days they happen, not because of a single failure of a single item, but because of a sequence of a series of unrelated events, failures; most individually would not cause the catastrophe, but when coinciding, do. Like dominoes.

Is this fate, then? Or is it all down to chance? The answer here is that it has to be 'chance'. There can be no question of any system or actuality of fate so cruel that it 'takes out,' kills hundreds of people in one go in a plane crash, or wipes out whole families in a car crash. There can be no question of, 'Why did God let this happen?' or even, 'Why did God make this happen?' For those unfortunates who experience events in their lives and whose thinking of God makes them ask those questions, mostly turn away from God, to one of godlessness for the rest of their lives. They actually 'blame' God.

'Chance' is that unfortunate sequence of events in our lives that brings together events, things happening, either good or bad. The 'crossings of paths,' the chance meetings, the chance of overhearing, the chance of reading an article are random, have to be random considering the millions in our country, billions in the world and the multiplicity of things we get up to as an intelligent species.

And so it happens that we accept our decisions made to get on the plane, to accept that all has been done to contain the risk, as the 'chance' of a crash is so small that it is an acceptable risk. Today that risk is so small that few bother to think about it. It has become 'subconscious,' it's rather like the risk of childbirth. How many people know of or even acknowledge that childbirth carries an implicit hazard of death to the mother and also to the child? Many risk-control procedures are in place to reduce the risks. But the implicit hazard is still there.

We can note here as a convenient point on the matter of risks that it is unfortunate that in general parlance the terms 'hazard' and 'risk' have for so long been virtually synonymous, but in health and safety terms, in 'Risk Assessment' terms, the hazard is one thing, the risk is another.

To explain – a mountain road with sheer precipice on one side, the precipice is the hazard. The degree of risk depends on how frequently we drive along it. If we drive along once a year, the risk is low. If every day, the risk in higher. With the construction of crash barriers, they reduce the risk, done after the risk assessment. The first barriers prove too weak as the 10-ton lorry crashes through into the ravine below, and death of the driver ensues. Following a further 'assessment,' the barriers are extended or modified to strengthen them, even though the crashed, now dead, driver was found to be drunk at the time. Even so, we feel the decision has to be made that we must make this hazardous road safe even for drunken drivers. So, the decision is made, and the result is further risk assessment. If the road is made one way, the risk is reduced even further; a Swiss-style arrangement, when vehicles can go up and along one way, and the other way at other, certain defined times of the day.

Another approach is to remove the hazard. The above example hardly applies, but some overzealous so-called health and safety nuts, er, sorry, persons with some small skill but perhaps big authority seem to think that removal of hazards is the only way, and in so doing, remove some of the features we have come to love and enjoy in life, whereas a proper assessment of the risks and lowering the risks would be a better and acceptable answer to deal with the identified hazards. In Sheffield, the removal of 6,000 trees in the city was open to better assessment; removal of some, but 6,000 all presenting as a hazard? We wonder.

There seems to be little we can do about the non-valid, so-called 'risk assessments' and H & S zealots. Their attitude, their policy, blandly seeks to remove all hazards to sterilise life, to make us risk-averse. We go to sea. The sea is a hazard. The smaller the boat, the greater the risk. Really? What about the *Titanic*? She was huge. She was reckoned to be unsinkable. The ice hazard was known, was it not? But was it known by the decision-takers, the captain and senior officers? The captain decides the course and speed and makes his risk assessment accordingly based on the known factors at the time.

So, the job is to identify as many of the hazards down to the smallest detail, and once identified we can set about assessing the likelihood, the risk of those hazards operating so to bring about their effects. And those risks can be reckoned by degree, the amount of chance of the identified hazards 'operating' to bring about their effects. And then there's the 'risk' of unprotected sex, the chance of pregnancy ensuing, or VD and AIDS. Some enjoy ignoring risks, and when all goes well, it's 'Yee-hah!'

In many cases a degree of 'risk,' is accepted, if thought about. We still get on the plane, still drive the car. Some won't get on the plane at all because they are not the 'driver,' they won't delegate 'control' over their destiny to another driver. It's their way of reducing risk. So, no holidays abroad, unless we go by car and ferry. Ferry? Who's driving that?

And so we see we are most definitely not an island entire of itself. John Donne was right. But, in reality, we are more like a grain of sand on the shore, similar to, but not the same, definitely not the same as all or any of the other grains.

CHAPTER 8
TAKEN IN DRINK

We humans have an aquatic heritage: in fact we believe all life on land originated in the sea. Our way-way back ancestors, many millennia ago, were aquatic creatures, marine creatures of the sea; fishlike along with many other early fishlike, living organisms in the salty, nutrient soup we call the sea. We say nutrient soup because all that was needed to sustain that life was there, in a constant re-creative process by the interaction of bacteria growing and thriving on the detritus of dead and dying creatures, dying from age and infection. And the sun and the rotation of the earth played their part: the sun variously heating equatorial seas and the rotation of the earth stirring and stirring by its interaction with gravity and the moon's gravity, all acting like a huge, giant soup cauldron. Other nutrients feed continuously into the sea, from the land masses, those far back in the seeds of time, ancient eruptions from a seabed, and bringing with them their rivers pouring their gifts of vegetable matter, an effluvial mixed with more solid grains of the earth, minute particles of sand and grit, like an ever-running effluent into the sea.

In time, as we know, humans evolved into what we are today, a very highly intellectually developed animal. For millennia, successive offspring variants that thrived and survived better in their environments, and by means of that defining process have brought us from those early, fishlike creatures to what we are today. From creatures extracting their much-needed oxygen from the nutrient soup via the intricate filtering of their gills, it is, or was, a big step to absorbing oxygen from the air via lungs; formed by the chance downward out-pouching of our pharynx to form an organ destined to become our lungs, taking up the chest cavity and wrapped around the heart. It was a more obvious step seeing how our ancestors first became amphibians, waddling up the beach, the pectoral and pelvic fins eventually being replaced by evolution into fore- and hindlimbs. The whole process of this evolution is so miraculous it is hard not to think that some designer, some architect, wasn't involved, making us, and all the other animals and plants. And to imagine this 'person,' this being, this force was God, the God of all, all-powerful on another planet, somewhere, ever-everlasting. Well, He'd (or She'd) have to be to be around all those millennia since our fishlike creature days of our origins. (As an aside, it is of course a ridiculous notion, is it not, to think that God has a sex? The dear-old Church of England has spoken in muted tones that it has a problem with the question outsiders have posed, 'Is God male or female?' Of course, God is neutral, as God is without a physical form, and as has been said elsewhere in these writings that it is misguided to anthropomorphise God; and anyway, the angels are believed to be smooth 'down there,' in the genital area, if that helps.)

The point of all this evolutionary stuff here is to say that fish never go thirsty, that is as long as they are in water. It is not supposed even that they drink for their needs of hydration. But we, in common with virtually all land animals and plants, need water, because the water we have in us is always and continuously being lost to the environment, either as a necessity of our metabolism, or because we are built in such a way, what we are 'made' of, composed of such tissues that they are incapable of preventing water molecules escaping into the atmosphere.

It is a complicated field of study as to how plants conserve their water, which is drawn up through their delicate root hairs in the earth and, to a degree, absorbed from the rain by the leaves. But when it's not raining, and even when it is raining, plants lose water from the pores on the undersides of their leaves by a process called transpiration. The wind is very drying, as we know from hanging washing on the line, and many plants are able to tap into their water supplies in the earth's deeper layers, and in times of drought, they close the pores, the stomata in their leaves, to reduce the loss to the wind and hot, dry atmosphere.

Of importance to us is to note how cacti in the desert ever survive. Many species of these plants have evolved to have a fairly thick outer skin, a 'cuticle,' that is their trunk, their stem, and their leaves are mostly rudimentary spines, sharp, prickly thorns to stop animals eating the fleshy, moist trunk. The cuticle resists water loss by evaporation, very effectively allowing the cactus to thrive in the desert, and its roots grow deep down to get some water.

At the other end of the scale is where we are. We have skin, a complex organ serving particularly to keep water evaporating from our underlying organs and tissues, like a film of semi-porous polythene around a joint of meat; and a second function of keeping infection out. Imagine an unwrapped joint of meat left on the patio table. It would soon dry out, desiccate and harden, and become infected with bacteria and moulds ever present in the air, as well as an attraction for all sorts of insects, birds, and any passing Labrador, drawn by the smell of flesh, raw flesh.

The sweating process by which our skin loses water is well known, and some people sweat more freely than others, especially the unfortunate women sweating their way bravely through the menopause. Basically, sweat is designed to run freely on the surface of our skin, and by the phenomenon of the 'latent heat of vaporisation' to cool us. Horses do this well, when allowed by their grooms. Dogs can't sweat, so they lose heat via their tongues, which give off water to lose heat in the same way. It's not very efficient and dogs easily get to overheat and collapse, called 'heatstroke'.

What is less well known is that our bodies are continually losing water over our whole-body surfaces by a process called 'cutaneous insensible water loss' (insensible because we are just not aware of it). And where does this water go? Mostly, it goes into our clothes, our underclothes firstly, if worn, and traditionally these are made of cotton or wool as these fibres can absorb water, whereas the synthetic materials cannot and the water molecules pass straight through to the next layer of garments worn, and later to become stinky if not cleaned.

This 'soaking' of our clothes includes our stockinged feet and into our shoes. And if it were just water, pure water, the process wouldn't be as problematic as it is; problematic because water isn't the only product of our skin going into our clothes. Our skins are continually 'exfoliating', shedding and sloughing off the dead skin cells, the 'squames' of keratin as new cells are created deeper on the thin outer layers of cells that form our skin. It's a constantly rejuvenating process; our skin cells; just like many cell systems in our bodies, like red blood cells, for example, with their lifespan of just over three months.

The other ingredient soaking into our clothing is skin grease, from the grease glands in our skins, there to coat our skin hairs, and called sebum. Less proficient in humans compared to the fur- and hair-covered animals, but there, nonetheless. And this admixture now in our clothes of moisture, skin flakes and grease is an ideal medium for the multiplication of certain bacteria, having a heyday and giving off much malodorous 'pong,' often evident in a crowd of the 'great unwashed'.

When gathered in churches of medieval times the pong of gentry and peasantry collectively was overwhelming, and the priesthood would go down the aisle and around the church swinging the incense, just like a modern so-called 'fresh-air' aerosol, and that is biggish business. Eau de Cologne helped greatly, on those that could afford it.

People who sleep 'starkers' are often proud of it, and why not if they are sleeping in their own beds where they no doubt change their sheets and undersheets and mattress covers regularly and throw away their soiled mattresses of skin exudates and skin sloughs, every five years. Notice the shop that delivers our new mattress and takes away the old one, for a fee: the shop's agents wear rubber gloves and put the old mattress in a huge polythene bag to avoid spreading 'goodness only knows what' contamination. (How does this popular phrase relate to our earlier definition of goodness?) And for Pete's sake (who, for Heaven's sake, is Pete? Heaven's sake?), when visiting and sleeping as a guest in some one else's bed, wear nightclothes, preferably jim-jams, and take them home and launder them yourself.

The problem of 'body odour' is that we can't smell our own stink, especially halitosis. It usually takes someone, perhaps a spouse or kind friend, and no matter from whom it comes, we always feel it's an affront to be 'criticised' in this way. Bloody cheek etc. But we know we are grateful, really. The other way of being aware of body odour and halitosis is by not having it in the first place. Regular showers, regular clean clothes, dental brushing and flossing with an antiseptic mouthwash, and regular trips to the dentist. Be true to our teeth, or they will be false to us!

So much for a potted biochemistry of our skin, and it seems appropriate here to say a few words about the biophysics of our feet. Many believe, with much justification, that how we feel, feel in ourselves, starts with our feet, and that means shoes. It is disconcerting to see so many walking with a limp or a 'rolling gait,' a kind of forward movement that says I walk like this because my back, hips and knees hurt as I walk.

We are better if we buy the best shoes, and that includes trainers and deck shoes, that we can afford to buy. Shoes on sale are deceiving – the cheap ones look the same as the higher-priced ones, and even feel as good trying them on. But the price difference is hidden in the making, the materials that don't stretch and give, and lose shape and fail to continue to give the intended and needed support to the instep and ankle. Avoid cheap shoes wherever possible. Mrs Thatcher didn't, and did you notice her gait?

We do need to have a care for our feet. The biophysics are complicated. Our evolution has brought us from four-legged creatures to two-legged so that, being freed from weight bearing, our forelimbs, our arms, now with hands are free to do all that we do. Essentially free to advance humankind.

With four-legged animals, horses, cattle, dogs etc., approximately 60% of the body weight is taken on the front limbs, and only 40% on the hind limbs. The hind limbs are predominantly used for forward thrust. Think of horse showjumping. Lifting a ton of equine flesh over a five-bar gate, all that power comes from the back legs.

Now to consider us, poor humans, evolved by surviving better from our less able forebears, by our intellect and use of our forelimbs for manipulation, our hind limbs, our legs, have to bear 100% of our weight and provide the forward thrust. It is no wonder that the hips, knees and feet groan. And what do we do? We eat so much more than we need, like Labradors, eating anything anytime and anywhere, in the street, or the train, on the bus, always eating and getting fatter and fatter as a species generally.

So buy the best shoes we can afford, a higher-priced shoe but not expensive necessarily, but more than as generally spent. If we ignore fashions' malign influences, the higher-priced shoe will have a higher, built-in value, they will hold their shape, give support in the right places and they will help take care of our feet. If our feet feel good, we will walk better, 'hold ourselves' better, be in a better mood, and enjoy the day. And who knows, in that contentment, what we save by eating less, that may pay the extra cost of the good shoes.

Today washing facilities are more readily available, but laundry can still be a concern. Laundry has implicit costs: water, heat, soap and detergents, time is involved, someone's time that may have to be paid for, drying facilities and then ironing and airing. Laundry also requires at least one set of alternative clothes to wear, and preferably a third set as well. So being clean and sweet-smelling doesn't come cheap. But it's necessary; well, generally regarded as necessary, and important, more important than that summer holiday? 'You mean I can't go smelly all year because I want my week in the sun?'

We lose water inevitably from our bodies in other ways. We need to excrete waste metabolites, end products of metabolism, and we do this via our urine and faeces. Prolonged diarrhoea, very fluid bowel 'movements.' can lead to dehydration. Our kidneys have several complex functions, but they exist primarily to see that, by our evolution from the early fishlike creature, we can retain that original salinity in our tissue fluids and our saline cellular systems so to continue to exist on the land that we have evolved to accept as our natural environment. That is to say, the kidneys monitor and control our body's salt and water balance, and as the circulating blood passes through the kidneys they can adjust the salt and water content of the exiting blood that returns to the rest of the body as a distributing medium for salt and water balance for the body as a whole.

They also filter out under pressure much of the unwanted metabolites; the blood pressure being so necessary for the filtering process to work. The kidneys excrete much of the waste products, most noticeably urea, the by-product of proteins used, no longer wanted, and broken down into smaller molecules. One such protein is the haemoglobin of red blood cells, breaking down to orangey-green bilirubins and biliverdins to be excreted in urine, and colouring it.

The kidneys need water to work. They drive us to drink by sending messages via the blood to our brain, our hypothalamus and pituitary gland beneath, saying to the body, 'This body needs water.' And the cerebral cortex usually does something about it. All that loss of water needs to be supplemented by a concomitant water intake, frequently by the imbibition of water at the meal, or by drinks before, during and after the meal.

Physiologists are a bit divided on just how much water we should drink each day, and it's hardly surprising seeing that we are all so different, different in size, in degrees of metabolic activity, as in our metabolic rate, but also our physical activity. The very act of digestion, following mostly in the two-three hours of starting eating, the digestion of food requires water. Volumes of digestive juices are poured out of our bodies into that enclosed, entrapped tubular system like a set of underground caves that form our 'bowels,' mouth, throat, stomach, small and large intestine, colon, and rectum. In reality, we, our bodies are wrapped around the food eaten. All the food and drink contents of us, but not actually in us. Like Winston's idea for Europe – us of Europe, but not in Europe. That's GB.

So, we hope by a somewhat lengthy preamble, to have established adequately that we need to drink water. And frankly, that's all we need. Certainly it's all the other animals need: water, just water. Preferably, or perhaps, we should say essentially, clean, healthy water. Many animals can get by, by drinking less than clean water, but we are now so removed in resistance terms that we soon get ill and probably die from drinking contaminated water. In disaster zones, when sewage and water systems all fail, disease, mostly cholera, soon breaks out. Cholera kills mostly by causing excessive diarrhoea and the subjects die from dehydration, and so hydrating a patient as a first aid attention can save many of these. Giving wholesome water to the peoples of the world is a very worthy aim – if only fighting factions in those localities could be dealt with at the same time.

So how long can we go without water, or come to that how long can we do without food? We have had, as a civilised people, much opportunity to have more data on these parameters. From those who 'go on starvation' in prison, and from Hitler's concentration camps, it seems we can go for about three weeks without eating, depending on our fat reserves in the first place, but not entirely as the obese can then suffer from 'ketoacidosis,' caused by the faulty breakdown of the fat deposits. We need certain ingredients from food after three weeks, vitamins, protein and trace elements to stave off illness that otherwise soon develops.

But we can only survive five days without water. Again this depends on the ambient temperature, our physical activity and doubtless other factors. So we need to keep drinking, and to drink water is very okay, but our ingenuity through the centuries has wanted to liven up and embellish the otherwise boring (that sounds ungrateful) imbibition of just plain water.

There are only so many ways we can 'liven up' water, to make it 'tasty' and interesting, and it has come about that we don't necessarily always drink to slake our thirst, we drink as a social exercise, a social experience that has become a custom and habit of just about all civilised peoples in the world.

Grapes, grain, flower and fruit, leaves and beans, and that is about it. Mankind has successfully experimented over time with all of those 'fruits of the earth' and made a whole range of drinks, from brandy to beer, from pop to lemonade, a wide range of teas, coffee and cocoa, these latter known as beverages. Each drink contains a varied amount of water, as the essential ingredient. Each has a large commercial backing of research into flavour, branding and promotion.

If we think in terms of the largest volume of water society consumes in these flavoured drinks, it could be tea, with coffee second, but beer may win the day, seeing that it's drunk in pints and litres rather than tea in cups, and coffee in mugs.

A lot is attached to 'having a drink.' On greeting a visitor, no matter if friend, relative or stranger arriving at our house, expected or not, it's good manners to say, 'Come in, can I take your coat, please have a seat and would you like a drink?' and then go into tea, coffee, alcohol or soft drink. Our visitor may or may not realise she or he is thirsty until it's mentioned. It's good manners to consider the degree of hydration of another (and the need for a pee). 'I was thirsty, and he wet my lips with vinegar on a sponge.' Poor Jesus, why so cruel to him? The crowd, the malevolent crowd? Today's Facebook trolls?

These days so much more emphasis is placed on keeping ourselves well 'hydrated.' With free water in the dentist's, there's something to do while nervously waiting? Schoolchildren, each at their desk with a plastic bottle (sic) of mineral water to sip from as a legitimate distraction from the teacher's boring monologue.

The list of habitualised drinking customs is very long, but it is fascinating to note how the need for water intake has become such a 'fashionable' feature of our lives, and includes 'champagne' receptions, beer fests, wine and cheese parties, wine tasting sessions, aperitifs before dinner, wine and water with the meal, port afterwards, then coffee and liqueurs, and of course not forgetting the soup course, after the hors d'oeuvres and before fish.

Soup is a delightful way to take in water. So many options, and not all hot: think of gazpacho. In the 1960s a book was published about the psychology of advertising and packaging. How our preferences, our choices of products were made based on our personalities, our fears, our vanities. The book claimed that people who like soup were basically insecure, and drank soup so as to feel again the security they felt when a foetus in their mother's womb. What a load of rubbish, absolute tosh. For a start, babies don't think in the womb: they would need to have experiences to draw upon to think. Babies 'float' like our primeval, fishlike ancestors in a 'pond' of amniotic fluid, which itself floats in an outer supportive liquid of allanto-chorionic fluid, like a water-filled balloon within a water-filled balloon, and it's dark in there. Unlike fish they are entirely dependent of the mother's circulation to bring oxygen, nutrients for sustenance and maintenance of life and to remove unwanted metabolites.

And here is the point, that in the embryonic phases as we pass through in development from the fertilised egg to a new, whole human baby, the foetus in the early phases develops a vestigial set of gills that mostly soon fade to leave, but one remains as our Eustachian tube, from the pharynx to our middle ear, then to our outer ear that was once the outer opening of the gill. Likewise, the human early foetal kidney develops like a fish kidney, a mesonephros, only to fade and then develop into the more specialised 'land-orientated existence' of the mammalian kidney, the metanephros.

One remnant of this process, dubbed 'embryology repeats phylogeny,' is that part that has been left over from the lamprey. At some time in evolution, the multicellular organisms floating and swarming in the sea developed to have a primitive stiffening of their body shape by a form of a rod running the length of the body. This was a fluid-filled rod that by osmotic pressure was stuffed stiff, like a long, thin, rigid, sausage-shaped balloon. Later their off-spring reinforced this stiffening and gave more shape to the body by developing semi-stiff cartilage around the rod, something for muscles to attach to, and muscles meant fins to move and a tail to flap to progress in search of food and a mate. Then the cartilage around the rod became bone, much stronger bone, and so able to stand the additional gravitational and muscle forces on the limbs of its terrestrial existence. Today the remains of our ancestral lamprey are the discs between our vertebrae, the discs that 'slip' (what a misnomer – 'squidge' would be a better word).

Our bodies are made up of over 80% water. Our bodies are continually losing water. In the ways described, and to stay well we need to drink water, continually in some form or another. Too much and we need a 'pee'. Thank goodness for that. Some 'beverages' have chemicals that have effects we are aware of, but hardly consciously, of their pharmacological effects.

Both tea and coffee, as well as cocoa, contain caffeine, theophylline and theobromine. Caffeine is a cerebrocortical stimulant – wakes us 'up', stimulates mental processes and is also found, but less so, in tea and cocoa. Theophylline is mostly active on the heart muscle, increasing rate and strength of beat, both only weakly so, unless taken to excess. Tea has more theophylline than coffee and cocoa. Theobromine's actions are more towards the kidneys, stimulating more production of urine. So, tea, coffee and cocoa have all three ingredients, but in variable proportions. Cocoa is a night-time drink, promoting sleep because it's mostly made with milk and thus a food. Its kidney action can lead to a night-time visit to the loo.

The alcoholic drinks have a commonality in the pharmacological actions, varying only by the degree of alcohol taken in, and depending on the alcoholic content. It is probable that alcoholic drinks soon became popular for their effects on us, rather than their flavour. Whereas tea and coffee are drunk more for their flavour. Beers are drunk very much for the flavour, and with wines and spirits for flavour, yes, but possibly more for their predictable effects on our mood, as mood-enhancers.

All we need to know about alcohol is this. Alcohol at first stimulates, and then depresses. Depresses our mood, our minds. The stimulation phase is good, we feel good, friendly, less shy, cheeky and perhaps flirty, and we shrug off the cares and toils of the day.

'The sun's over the yardarm; time for a horse's neck.' The effect is almost immediate, that first drink such as a long draught of beer, gulped down as if desperation were the king of the moment; but the immediacy is probably a learned behaviour pattern. 'Ah! That's better,' as we 'smack our lips' and put the beer down on the bar and begin to socialise.

The problem of alcohol is that the passing phase from stimulant to depressant is hidden, occult; there's no warning. The only way we know, get to know, how much to drink, is by experience. It's personal: some can continue to drink and remain very sober, when another is sliding under the table.

The depressant stage is sad, sad to see and sad to recover from the next day. So let's be clear. By depressant in these pharmacological terms, we don't mean 'a depressed psyche,' we mean depressed abilities: ability to balance, to speak properly, to see straight, to think and reason straight and to walk straight or drive safely. All our normal abilities are 'depressed'.

There is one vital final thing we need to acknowledge about alcohol that we all know. It is addictive. It takes a hold on our mind, our personality. We need a drink. We need that feeling it gives us. Not the good feeling we used to know, when we were something, somebody good, somebody worthwhile, worth knowing. No, it gives us a different feeling, a sudden calming of the high state of nervous tension that had built up since our last drink, that last mouthful. Someone says or was it Mind B, 'Have another.' And then it's not long in time before it's a case of, 'Oh! Damn, my glass is empty, so go hang convention, I'm going to drink it straight from the bottle – it's quicker that way.' A quicker way to be taking a drink.

And sooner or later, we get know from a relative or a friend, but possibly the vicar, or even a stranger, when one of them tells us, 'we are taken in drink.'

—•—

131

CHAPTER 9
THE VOYAGE OF LIFE

Jesus was fond of using parables to get his messages across to a gathering of 'everyday folk,' villagers, artisans, 'les paysans,' the man on the 'Clapham omnibus,' and not necessarily intellectuals, pseudo-intellectuals and would-be intellectuals, for they could work out 'the message' for themselves without any allegory to help them.

In these chapters from time to time reference has been made to the comparison between life and making a passage, voyaging by sailing on a small cruising yacht. Anyone who has read any biographies by such yachting people will know sailing is certainly not all glamour and romance, blue skies, light winds and gentle waves, all in perfect harmony, all systems on-board working well, and fresh bread in the boat's oven. For those are the rare days, the days that make the tough, hard, sea-cruel days worth it. And why this comparison with small boat cruising? Well, we are all individualists, our own skipper, 'Master under God,' and the world's surface is two-thirds sea.

Many passages are made with a small crew, often just the skipper and, but not necessarily, a current life partner or spouse. But many small yacht passages are made single-handed, when the skipper is 'Master under God' of the vessel and its non-existent crew. The skipper is responsible for the safe passage of the yacht towards and until its next arrival at a port or an anchorage, when the skipper can rest up a while.

The skipper has many responsibilities on passage, but many have had to be considered at the outset, the preparations, such as victualling for the expected duration of being at sea, fresh water for drinking and cooking, fuel for the engine that is used just for entering and leaving harbour and charging batteries, any fuel for lighting including navigation lights at night, spares for the engine, care of the sails, rigging and spars, condition of the ground tackle, anchor and warps and lifelines; life jackets and life-raft for emergencies, flares, up-to-date charts (maps for the sea), working and efficient instruments, for speed, depth, wind speed and direction; VHF and shortwave radio communications, first aid kit and other minor but necessary equipment. All this the skipper has trained for even before setting out. The similarity here, for us, is our professional and technical training for the world of work, and where applicable, all the multifacets of setting up and running our own business. For the skipper, much of his or her responsibilities come from an attitude, and an attitude of being prepared, and prepared for as many eventualities that might arise. Concentration and planning. Preparedness gives peace of mind and confidence.

The comparison continues. We have plotted our course to steer, avoiding rocks and rough overfalls. We set off and adjust the sails so as to be able to steer our desired course. We find the wind 'heads' us, pushes us off the course desired, and so we adjust steering and sails to 'tack' towards our next waypoint, a point in life, a goal, where we have to change direction, tack on to a new course. It could be a qualification reached, a marriage, a new job, house move, all waypoints (stages) of significant course changes. Struggling to sell our house, the difficulties 'heading' us like the wind, so we tack, seemingly deviating from where we want to go but getting there with patience and moving obliquely, first this 'tack' then that 'tack' until the next waypoint (steppingstone) is reached.

The prudent skipper, on the helm, steering the vessel, is always on the lookout for potential obstructions, a collision course with another vessel, sees it coming and by rules of the road reckons who has 'right of way,' but there is no right of way; in the last resort even if the rules say 'stand on,' hold our course, as in a close discourse with another person with tension, in the last resort we give way to avoid a collision, a fight verbal or even physical. Prudent action in time. Both wind and tide can set us off our desired course, both non-human influences on our lives. Illness can strike us, or our loved ones, and that means we have to change our plans. The puncture in the car tyre, the massive hold-up on the motorway en route to the airport. We cannot always steer the course intended. We have to replot, plot a new course, reckoning always on the safety, the safe arrival of our vessel at the next waypoint. Each night is a waypoint, an anchorage, we 'drop the hook' and rest and sleep and plan tomorrow. And write our logbook, for the relevant and interesting points in passage of that day. Ordering our thoughts of the day, marshalling them in causes and effects. Brief notes, little or no emotion. Wallowing in our mistakes, wallowing in self-pity – are both big no-no's.

Another merit that the yachting skipper, indeed any yachting person, comes to learn, to appreciate, is this. Apart from it becoming second nature that we know instinctively when it's time to relax on-board when underway, the weather is fine and warm, the sea calm, the wind fair, little other 'traffic' about, no need for safety harnesses and the decks are stable, we also know when it's rough to reduce sail area to make the craft manageable, to close the ports (windows) to keep spray and water out of the vessel, to wear protective clothing, life jackets and harnesses to keep us on-board and to maintain the course steered and logged half-hourly. Apart from these things, passage making at sea teaches us patience. A small yacht will only average 4 or 5 knots, which is to say five or six miles per hour (very approximately). The novice experiences the eerie feeling of being out of the sight of land for the first time. It is often unsettling. The 'land' is a fixed point, a known familiar and 'safe' point in our lives, like our home, or parental home, our job, our brother, sister or other dearly loved one, always nearby. Out of sight of land at first is eerie, a weird feeling, but also adventurous, a new experience. Some say we never truly grow up until our parents are dead, out of sight; of land. The yachting humourist answers the novice's question, 'How far is it to the nearest land?' and the reply is, 'About 15 metres below us.'

Soon, in the distant haze, the vague notion that that shadow on the horizon, may be, could it be? Is it? Yes, it is – land; we can see land. Land Ho! A frisson of excitement in the novice, a smidgeon of comfort in that. As in life, we can sense that that feeling of hope and expectation, the fruition of our planning, is at last beginning to take shape, to be realised, yielded, achieved.

And then the wait. As children ask, from the back of the car, on a long journey, 'Are we nearly there yet?' So, the skipper and crew, if any, must wait and be patient, often for many hours as the yacht slowly approaches the coast: it is this long-since-seen land that can take many hours yet of patient sailing on passage before landfall yields up the entrance to the planned harbour, the final waypoint on this particular part of the voyage. Thus, some learned patience, that experience, that calm mental approach to 'confined' actively on-board, that the seasoned traveller successfully adopts, be it on a coach or in an aeroplane. Our Mind A, in control, suppressing impatience and anxiety, banishing them below decks, and closing the hatch, in the 'hold' of our vessel, where they are best stowed for life's journey, life's passage.

The last example of this analogy of a life with that of the small boat skipper is that the skipper allocates almost all of this time and concentration on where the boat, where he or she, is going, and with a smaller amount of time to look back, back on life, as it were; and here in this analogy. The boat leaves a wake, an indication of the course steered, be it straight with a steady helm, or wavering through an uncertain or inexperienced helm. The angle of the wake to the craft can indicate any deflection from the course steered to the course achieved. The wake is soon lost as the water settles again, just as the wake we leave in life, we leave impressions behind us. They are fresh, fresh impressions on people wherever we go. Many will not be remembered in much detail. The angle of the wake to our course can vary too much and can indicate how we are being set apart from our intended destination by offsets such as wind and tide. We tend to be affected by offsets all the time. The distractions from what we truly wanted to do, at that moment, in that day, with our life, even. Offsets such as the demands of a spouse with their own priorities, from children demanding attention, a co-worker who needs help or guidance, from incidents such as accidents to others that we are bound to assist with. All life's offsets. We realise we need to adjust our desires back onto our preferred course as soon as we can, else, if not, not notice the angle of our wake: we can be set onto rocks or run aground. Too late, 'smuk,' meaning we only achieved half today of what we intended.

Psychiatrists love to get their patients, their subjects, talking about their upbringing, be it remembered as good or bad. This is not the wake of our vessel at sea, this is the post-build survey of the vessel's construction and hence its seaworthiness. If the individual components are of good quality and strong (aka the boat's scantlings) then the vessel will be good for life.

But a well-cared-for craft of lesser scantlings can be strengthened in parts, the parts most needed, where life does its best to damage the weaker vessel, wind and wave, wear and tear. That is, if we look back at our construction, the sensible skipper will accept matters, and then do what he/she can to put matters right as best he/she can. It's no use one bleating about one's defective, love-deficient upbringing, being built with weak scantlings; a skipper looks forward with good preparation and good positive maintenance to 'refit' and strengthen his vessel.

There is the continual need for economy, economy in everything. Careful not to waste battery power, wasting electricity leaving unnecessary lights on, likewise the paraffin lamp; we need the oil for the anchor light. Economy with the gas for the cooker; we're on the second and last gas cylinder already. Ration the drinking water to make it last until we make harbour. And so on, always economy of the ship's stores of energy and potential energy, and foodstuffs.

That economy becomes a habit, a lifestyle, and with the crew person, it's a shared and enjoyed common purpose. Each day brings a new challenge, but no one thinks like that; it's just another day, another 'milestone' along the 'intended track.' Who, on land, thinks like that, as we get up, get washed and dressed and head off for work? On the boat, it's free time, answering to no one but ourselves and Neptune, we're 'Master under God.' But tide tables do have an influence on the matter, because as well as going up and down, tides go horizontally; and we mostly aim not to have to buck the tide; it's generally better to go with the flow. And yet, we check the course being steered, and the course steered in the last hour, take our position nowadays by GPS, record the position in the log in case the GPS 'goes down,' or the Americans decide to turn it off for a while – chaos. We check 'are we on our plotted course' our desired course, and replot if we are off course due to currents, windage and sloppy steering, or even a previous miscalculation.

Surely there is an allegorical connection with life here? A planned, considered life, a life where goals, imagined, or dreamed of, written down to empower the mind and character, to go about achieving, advancing, albeit slowly, on a day-by-day basis, to the next harbour, rest-up holiday, rest and 're-create' ourselves, our boat shaken down, tidied up and restored, our 'make-and-mend' time that always was and hopefully will mostly remain on our … traditional Sundays.

We helm our way through the day, enjoying each wave, each interaction with our colleagues, clients and customers. There's the occasional wave, the mythical one in seven, that threatens to send water over the bows and give us a drenching; yes, we got a soaking but swing the boat back on course, drying out in the wind and sun, we promise to try harder next time to get 'taking the wave' just right, anticipating its arrival, and avoid too much drenching. 'I suppose I deserved that rebuff, it hurt me.'

We get to know where the overfalls are, those nasty patches of water and waves that toss the boat violently and can cause damage to our unsecured items on-board and 'down below' in the cabins. We get to avoid saying 'the wrong thing' to the wrong person, the disgruntled client, and to avoid driving carelessly in the rush hour and to steer a careful course through the peopled day, avoiding the pigs.

If we have been fortunate enough to be introduced to sailing as a child, it usually begins, for us, as Daddy or Mummy takes us out for the first time in a small dinghy that is intended to be for us, ours, when we get 'the hang of it.' Up to four or five years of age, we mostly have Mum or Dad looking after us. The first launching on our own, adrift from Mum and Dad, is like our first schoolday. There are other dinghies around, and a rescue boat called a teacher. And we're off. Growing up comes next, bigger dinghies, we learn to race, the class tests, who comes top?

After school and college, we are like getting our cruising yacht. The major difference is the yacht has a ballast keel firstly to keep us upright, and secondly to deflect sideways drift, off course. Just like our spouse, or partner, the person who enters our life, the keel that helps keep us upright, and helps steer the best we can, to windward. It's metaphorical but a sailing boat cannot go directly into the wind but achieves its goal by going on an angled course, an angle of 'attack' seemingly away, not directly but indirectly, towards the 'target,' and then 'tacking' to go on the other diagonal.

Youngsters often see their goal and are drawn to its attraction in their mind. When it's explained that to be a spaceman, brain surgeon, airline pilot or conductor of an orchestra, that these things aren't just reached and 'taken' or grabbed! They are worked towards first, like a yacht, tacking into the wind.

And then there are those incidents that happen; as in going aground, stuck on a shallow seabed, perhaps we thought or miscalculated the rise of tide over a shallow bank as we negotiate a contract with a customer, without just that degree of care and calculation and lose the customer. When aground, a soft grounding, we can wait for the next tide to float us off, praying the weather remains mild, but rough weather rising while still aground can damage and even sink the boat. Losing that contract, the rough weather may come in retribution from the boss, may lead to demotion in some way or even loss of our job. A hard grounding as on rocks can sink the boat quite quickly. A rough passage knowing the firm is losing business, customers and staff leaving, the rough weather and then we're on the rocks, driven almost helplessly into the notice of redundancy. It can take some time to rescue what you can from the wrecked yacht and repair it or build another, get another job or another career, and begin cruising our life again.

137

Those moments in life, an accident, a severe illness of self or loved one, the serious falling out with an offspring that gets to look irreversible, the shock of discovering spousal infidelity, and so on; all these analogies occur at sea, hence the expression, 'worse things happen at sea.'

The point is that when at sea, either single-handed or short-handed, we are solely responsible for every single aspect of our safety. We naturally do not want to drown, to suffer concussion with a headbang on the yacht's boom, or break an arm in a tumble down the steps of the companionway or fall overboard, tripping over a line that should have been stowed away tidy-like, seaman-like. It is regarded as 'bad form' to have a 'careless, carefree attitude' and then bleat and expect others to come to your rescue because you are aground, or run out of fuel on a windless day, or shredded your old sails in strong winds, sails that should have been renewed years ago with money that instead was used high-jinxing on holidays in the sun.

The rescue teams of the Coastguard and Lifeboats are there for those true real happenings and disasters like a dismasting, or fracture of a skin fitting, allowing water to flood in then sink the boat. Our ambulance service, our medical teams and firefighters are there for all, but many of us could have either foreseen the yacht is at risk, and through anticipation, that includes education, we can manage to stay at sea, on passage, with our own resources, our own self-help and a great sense of self-fulfilment. No introspective, depressed navel-gazing; but a firm chin, tucked in, and head up; shoulders squared, not drooped, eyes into the distance and we are cruising. A well-found, well-trimmed 'ship;' the feeling is unbeatable, incomparable. An achievement.

A worthy achievement. Life can be like that.

PART THREE

ALL THAT WE ARE

CHAPTER 10
OUR RELATIONSHIPS

It is said that relationships boil down to one of three types, namely:
- Symbiosis – the living together in a relationship that is mutually beneficial.
- Commensalism – when living organisms cohabit and there is an interrelationship that is neither beneficial nor detrimental to either; one could say a relationship of mutual indifference.
- Parasitism – when one organism thrives at the expense of or to the detriment of the other.

And so we look at marriage and cohabiting as 'partners' to see which category applies, and we find all three types in various marriages, various pair-bonds. Furthermore, we can find each of the three categories in the same marriage from time to time, but not necessarily. When observing a cohabiting couple, it doesn't take a great deal of imagination to work out what's going on.

For some couples, from the beginning, they believe in a total merging of mind, body and spirit into one; doing everything together, never apart, asleep or awake. The realities of life, work or war get in the way until retirement comes and then they are 'together' again. But as they live their lives, any difference in a choice to be made, any straying from the 'joint' everything can be explosive, until one or the other begs forgiveness. For other couples, soon after coming together it becomes established who it is who always owns the 'majority' of shares in this business, who always has the chair, and is the CEO and finance director, all-in-one becomes apparent, the other being the worker bee.

And then there's the 'respectful' relationship, respectful of the other's persona, as an individual, their absolute right to make their own decisions, have their own money to spend, their freedom of choice, what they do and how they think, what to wear, where to go, what to choose to support, and yet always listening to each other, taking soundings on matters before making a choice, respecting the other's opinions, a loving relationship that is truly symbiotic.

Children need love, but they also need feeding and clothing, training and protecting. Raising children is a job, because they can't do it for themselves, and it can be hard work, but mostly it's a pleasure and rewarding if the raw ingredients are forthcoming: the food, the clothes, the warmth and the roof over their little heads.

The inverse of this is what does the child feel? They certainly feel their needs, to have food to eat, clothes to keep warm, and protection from a 'grown-up.' They hardly feel 'the need' to receive an education, but through discipline, implied or real, they know which 'side their bread is buttered' and comply by going off to school where, once there, they find some interest, some enjoyment and sometimes a good dose of angst.

Once grown up, the umbilical cord nurturing the child from infancy is cut, by one side or the other, or by both. And yet, many will return to the parent for a transfusion from time to time of love or money or both. The saying is, 'To a mother, a son is hers until he marries; her daughter is hers for life.' There seems to be much truth is that. The parents frequently wonder how the children are faring, even their adult children; the children about their parents less so, until the parents fall ill, when mostly some concern is felt, either out of love, or duty or both.

'Getting old is not much fun,' say some, and there is a dilemma here for parents and their children. Should the young, the middle-age children, grown up with a family of their own, be introduced to and be made so well aware of the realities of being 80 or 90? Is it fair to make their horizon dark with cloud, instead of a 'sunlit uplands?' We are goal-seeking organisms, always motivated to achieve something, some epicurean or other pleasure, some comfort for ourselves, steering a steady course we have planned to navigate to, a new harbour to experience a sybaritic hedonism perhaps, before setting out again. All sorts of restrictions, mostly unimaginable to the young, come to bear on those in their eighties and nineties, so that that life of goal-seeking and achieving shrinks and shrinks. Attitudinal adjustments become imperative if one is to live at these great ages with peace of mind, as much as one can muster after a lifetime of fun and laughter, of freedom from pain, and freedom from the fear of 'losing one's marbles.' Freedom from fear of losing one's life 'partner-in-love,' to who knows where. Best not trouble the young with it. Why spoil their fun, they will come to it, in time, and it will come soon enough, sooner than they 'deserve' perhaps.

The use of the word 'deserve' could be more closely and appropriately used, as being what we get or should get out of our service to others. Those relationships that nicely fit into one of those categories have an element of service and disservice, from the extreme domination of the type 'A' personality over the timorous, submissive, subjugated cohabitee, even down to physical means, or to the less obvious but equally cruel interrelationship of the et-epimeletic (sympathy eliciting) wife (shall we say wife here, just for example) with the pusillanimous, uxorious husband. Even worse in the case of the 'shrike', where a perfectly sound personality seeks counselling and psychiatric help only for it to be found that (let's say it is he) he is living with a seriously ill partner, bipolar or schizophrenic, and has driven the spouse to believe he is the one who is mentally ill. She is the shrike. So hard to recognise and possibly more commonplace than generally thought.

All relationships need nurturing, especially loving relationships, even those across the seas that distance separates, and they must be raked and fanned into a brief and transient flame from the dormant, glowing ashes of familial love at home, or like any house plant, needing watering, wiping down, rotating so all parts get their share of the sun. We should groom our partners, pander, but only proportionately, to their needs and whims. Husbandry is an archaic term that refers to the management and care of that which is husbanded. Today the term is used mostly for care of livestock, but it is clear that the word has its origins in husband. From this it is easy to imagine what a husband's duties are. Let's hope those duties come readily out a genuine love. There seems to be no comparable word for the wife but 'wifely' will do, but it also leaves much to the imagination, and that can be good.

Most of us are lazy and selfish when it comes to our need to feel loved, to be loved, and this goes especially to men who are often poor at being demonstrably affectionate to their partner, especially once the first flush of physical attraction and physical need has cooled due to everyday matters and an allowed degree of boredom has settled in. We need to make an effort, regularly, and if that's so awkward or alien then try harder, being careful to be sincere, or certainly not insincere, so then to 'fake it' until we make it! In time, being more appreciative, more helpful, more loving in small ways becomes a habit and that's good.

The too smart person will often ask 'what is love anyway?' Even any sort of smart person will ask it occasionally. It's like the smart question, 'What is the meaning and purpose of life?' Love is difficult to define in simple terms and many have tried. The Greeks divided love into three types, eros, agape and philia. Eros was the physical sex-involved love between couples, either hetero- or homo-, of courting and marriage, while agape was the familial love for one's parents and fellow siblings. Philia was that abstract love as in a love of beauty, art, literature, music: a love of life. This may or may not be a fair way of looking at love, as almost certainly our feelings, the nature of our feelings, and the degree of our intensity of our feelings will be different in each of us, person to person, man to woman, woman to man, man to man, woman to woman and man and woman to children.

Then there is the love of God; not God's love this time, but our love for God, which as propounded in these writings means the love of goodness and goodliness, a love of loving, of being upright, rectus, principled and fair. Not in an extrovert way, not in a vain, proud way, but quietly gaining comfort and a certain peace of mind from our modest, unassuming, quiet love of goodness, goodliness and God.

As said previously, there is a concept of love that is probably the most powerful, and certainly for many is the most thought-provoking, and possibly the most apposite definition of all. It is that love is that feeling that develops spontaneously by which there is a wanting, a willing, a wishful desire, an expectant hope for the loved person to become maximally self-actualised, a kind of self-fulfilment, functioning at the outer edge of their own ability, which is infinitely expandable. We are mostly not used to thinking of love in this way, and it can take some thinking about.

One of the greatest achievements we can gain for ourselves is peace of mind, which comes with freedom from fear, freedom from anxiety and freedom from negativity: marshalling the whole of one's life to achieve those three things is a very worthy objective. With peace of mind comes a feeling of inner happiness, which is a natural state. Along with peace of mind come health and energy. 'Hello, how are you?' This, our habitual, kindly greeting implies the thought which could be more expressly put as, 'I hope you are well?' We naturally wish this, of course for those we love, it is part of love, the peace of mind that comes from being healthy and having energy. And we can include our friends here.

It is thought that much joy in our lives comes from loving relationships, perhaps as much as 85%, if we want to put a figure on it; often measured by the amount of laughter, and conversation. But laughter tends to lessen when problems come, and likewise conversation. Both the quality and quantity of loving relationships are important. Love grows, flourishes when frequently together. When apart, less so; much depends on contact. The armed forces know this, and mail and voice contact between those away from home, and loved ones at home, is addressed as much as conditions will allow. Absence makes the heart grow fonder; yes, but beware our expectations on the returning home of the loved one. They will have had experiences afresh in the meanwhile that may need to be reckoned with, in time, when the time is right. Beware those expectations that have mounted up during the absence.

Subconsciously, we also wish 'financial freedom' in our loved one. Few are without money worries, although the term 'worries' is probably overdone, but without going into detail, money worries can come about through mismanagement or misfortune. We have virtually no guidance or education into the management of our money. We may have prudently advising parents, or elder siblings, but the adolescent with the first tranche of earned or given cash has their own objectives for it, mostly some fun. Wise management is mostly learned, the hard way. Misfortune with money is usually outside our control and can come unexpectedly, such as redundancy, or inability to earn through illness or accident. 'When poverty comes in the door, love flies out of the window.' A tough, old idiom, inevitably some truth in it, sadly.

Also, we wish for our loved one's freedom from the fear of the loss of their home, for example, freedom from anxiety as to how they can feed their family. And we wish them freedom from negativity; as in a resentment of the employer issuing redundancies or going bust, for example.

We want to feel the person we love has worthy goals and ideals. We are teleological organisms, always seeking out something for ourselves, so let it be worthy. To many, it's the meaning and purpose of life, the progressive realisation of worthy goals: aiming for 'A' levels,' university place, good degree, good job, good holiday, good marriage, and perhaps a good family.

Isn't a truly loving relationship a worthy goal? Can we work at looking for that, for love? Yes, we can; and not allow our heart to rule our head, rushing into sudden, life-changing, impulsive and ultimately decimating actions; a sudden tempestuous relationship that ends in abandonment with the unplanned and 'unfunded' baby arriving. 'Worthy goal?' Hardly a goal. It was all too compulsive, as if drunk, and probably was aided by drink. Be 'cool' is the intonation, but to think cool under pressure, even being accused of being 'a cool one,' takes preparation and practice. Mostly we are not programmed that way when young. The folly of the young. It's no wonder many do not want to be young again.

The final wish for our loved ones is a fair degree of 'self-knowledge' or 'self-awareness' that comes from having an 'intrapersonal' intelligence that comes with the experiences of life; an awareness of the 'conditioning' coming from our previous experiences that can give rise to a better self-concept, self-image and self-esteem, and freedom from negativity. It needs us to use our eighth sense.

With all the above, that is what love is. Yes, as stated at the start, the definition isn't easy, and on thinking about it, it's quite complex, when analysed.

And so what about family relationships? The obvious thing to say is that no two families are alike, but having said that, there are certain similarities and certain 'pitfalls' that trap many of the unwary. The business of running a family is best looked upon as just that – a business; and like all businesses it starts with two common facets, the job of promoting that business and then the management of the assets of that business.

The promotion of the business will much depend on what the agreed aspirations are for the couple, the partners, the husband and wife, the 'key persons' hopefully with key person insurance, heading up the 'family' business. Here we are referring to any cohabiting couple drawn together by mutual attraction and hopefully by love, with or without children.

Those common aspirations can be generally set down as 'living a life' and living the life, the sort of life they want, together. They agree how to go about moving towards their common and their individual goals for their lives. It's like the company with its business plan.

The working out of business relationship between the partners, between them, can either take some time or readily slip into roles that derive from their innate or adopted attitudes to the relationship. For example, a couple may be so in tune together in their thinking that being observed could be likened to a dance routine of two tap-dancers with top hats and canes. Each step is the mirror of the other, totally syncopated. For another couple, it can be like a man and his dog (or woman and her dog). The dog is obedient to its owner's commands, adores its owner, always anxious to please, readily greeting, and looks forward to treats and walkies when the owner is so minded. And then there's the couple who are orbiting planets. Each is a self-sustained system, going along in its own orbit and that orbit crossing its partner's orbital path, as in the evenings and nights; happily together, but also happily their own 'persons.'

The asset management of the 'family business' is vital to its survival and ideally should be openly shared between them, both being, or should want to be, aware of and partly responsible for those assets. Each business or family will need financial assets, money either brought into the family, or borrowed as in a mortgage. The main financial assets are usually vested in the house or flat, the car or cars, the fixtures, fittings and equipment.

When it comes to divorce, the enforced division of these physical assets can be the first realisation of the true nature and true worth of the 'family assets,' most acquired jointly through the 'marriage' by one means, as in salaries, or the 'dowry,' as brought-in capital, at the outset. The starting point for negotiations to divide those joint 'family assets' is 50/50, if there are no children to consider.

Partners and husbands and wives are not always completely open and honest about their earnings, and indeed their capital, and there are some very good reasons for this. Gone are the days when the wage earner would hand his wage packet over to the wife, who would then hand him his week's beer money, and she uses the rest to run the house and family. Life and literature is full of dramas: we hear and read about drunken gamblers and reckless spendthrifts letting money run through their fingers like a handful of sharp sand. There is a very good case for the family business having three accounts, the general account that runs 'all aspects of the business,' and then the partners' own 'private accounts,' private in that they have sole charge over. The feeding into of those 'partners' accounts should be open and honestly agreed and adhered to. This arrangement carries many practical 'relationship-nurturing' benefits.

The third and final assets of the family business are the human resources, the other assets being property and financial, as already considered. As to human resources, these are initially the 'key persons,' the partners, meaning so often the husband and wife. They have come into the business with certain attributes, skills, valued experience and certain qualifications.

It is these attributes that drive the success of the business, as to its size, the quality of its other assets acquired, and in particular the method and style of the 'promotion of the business,' the living of their lives. If both partners are diligent, hard-working and energetic, the business will be more successful. Here, hard-working need not necessarily be taken to mean income earning, it can just as well mean income-saving, working hard at prudent spending, always. Such skills can be worth a wage.

In young couples, the skills and attributes of both parties may not readily come to the fore. Often thinking there are no undiscovered skills can be a mistake. The degree of fortitude and resourcefulness can often not be manifested until the occasion, when the need arises; when the previously regarded epicurean, sybaritic less than diligent partner suddenly changes and rises to the occasion. But they may not, and what then?

Love and understanding bring out the full attributes, and conversation is the medium for this. It is often said that as we have two ears and only one mouth we should do twice as much listening as speaking. This is probably very true, best in conversational styles between loving couples, and equal balance between listening and speaking is more respectful and relationship nurturing. So, for the voluble, loquacious partner, he or she should do more listening. And for the reticent partners, make an effort to meet his/her partner halfway in their conversations. Thinking before we speak was a clever style adopted by pipe smokers. To keep the pipe going, a regular puff was needed. While puffing, one had time to think.

The quick tongue, smart alec, sharpshooting repartee that some can indulge in is best tempered down, as raw, exposed feelings can be sincerely damaged by harsh, impromptu remarks, too readily thrown by the sharp tongue. Think how the mighty ship, with its heavy but valuable cargo steaming happily through life, is steered by its relatively small rudder; the rudder decides its course, and, of course, then its fate. And so it is with our tongue, such a small organ, relative to the rest of our body, yet with our tongue we steer the course of our life, and even when we write, our tongue is all but saying it. Beware our thoughts, because they become words, and our actions, that can become our habits, by which we can become known.

Best avoid the garrulous chatter, and certainly avoid anything that clearly is going to be an altercation; and avoid that someone, so ready to argue to the point of making it a row. Theirs is almost an art form. The moral is, 'Don't fight with pigs. They enjoy it and you get dirty.' If sucked into a row with your spouse or partner, do not bring either partner's mother into it! Just answer back, 'I love you', 'Yes, I know, but I love you,' then 'I am sorry you're upset but I've always loved you.' You'll either calm the savage beast, or get a saucepan thrown at your head. Sometimes you just can't win. Win? Is it ever a matter of winning?

It is a truly wonderful thing to live with someone you love, who knows you love them, who loves you and knows you know they love you, so that you can have peace of mind, freedom from demands upon you, pressure, recriminations, guilt thrown at you, expectations, unrealistic hopes and imagined anxieties and concerns and knowing that those same traits are reciprocated. And loved with the definition we have offered here. But we still have to say it, those three little words, every now and then.

The only time in life we are truly our 'whole' selves is for those few years when adolescence is over, and we become adult, adult singles, completely free to be totally selfish as in developing our personalities, who we are, who we are becoming. We said 'few years,' because in the scheme of things, of life and looking back, those years seem brief, short and brought abruptly to an end by the 'choosing' of a partner, a spouse, to 'pair-bond' with, and so end our 'sole proprietor of my life' status. Then the new business of partnership, the family business, starts with responsibilities to each other to make the 'family' business work. In the childless state, this is fine, perhaps better than 'sole proprietor' with more certainty of the love and understanding from your partner than uneasy dating or evenings and nights on your own. Many will have a period of time before having children, 'starting a family,' while, in the common parlance, 'building the nest,' ready for the brood. But many also will bear a child before they have truly settled into their relationship of living together. Whilst usually a bundle of joy, the rapid changes in status and responsibilities can unsettle many newly come-together couples. That can be so unsettling sometimes to the immature, who hasn't slaked his/her thirst of selfishness in some years of sole proprietorship, that the only recently formed pair-bond can break down, with tragic consequences.

The relationships between parents and their children are so very, very varied one really should not even try to generalise. The broad types of relationships are well documented, though. Those who deal with the matter of caring for the very elderly will be able to relate the surprisingly high number of elderly who have no relationship with their now adult children, having all fallen out with each other over something or other, years ago. As a consequence, the elderly person has no visitors to speak of, but still register their son or daughter as their next of kin. Only when the elderly person is ill and in danger of dying does the 'family' suddenly gather, like a gathering of the clan, or more likely a flock of vultures waiting for the rich pickings out of the will.

Often the child, son or daughter falls out with their parents because the parents are seen as at fault, which may or may not be fair. On the parents' side, we have had no training in parenthood, no chance to gain a qualification, no advice, no NVQ, no previous experience and we are also very preoccupied with the business of keeping our own body and soul together. We go to court to prove grounds for divorce. It would be better if we had to go to court to prove grounds for marriage and then parenthood.

A common failing is to have one favourite child over another. Although genetically very similar, each child is different and can be very different indeed from its other siblings. There is a commonality with first-born children, the way their character develops being there first and alone, for a while alone and always with no older brother or sister to turn to, to copy or to play with, whereas successive children have their older siblings. And there is a noticeable difference, too, between the first-born females followed by brothers and first-born sons followed by sisters. Despite their genetic similarities, the differences can be so dramatic as to wonder how has this come about. It could mean a studious, budding genius, perhaps in brainpower, or some musical art. Alternatively, it could be a troublesome, lying, cheating, bullying, sneaking underhand thief.

And so it is tempting and so easy to have favourites, but we should never compare one child, to its face, to another child. That can lead to so serious a problem that harm could result. It follows then never to declare any favourite and to eschew any temptation to favouritism. And if, however hard we try, say at present-giving time, birthdays and Christmas, we are unable to give each child requested presents, a degree of envy or jealousy can result. Yes, it's hard! Blessed are the peacemakers!

Children can sense if one parent favours its brother or sister. The other parent may favour a different child. Even if unspoken, and even if untrue, a non-valid assumption by the child, it can lead to prejudices. Living closely together breeds a familiarity amongst children, who then can be so innocently frank with each, to such a degree that will never be experienced in their adult relationships. What does survive into adulthood is a rivalry that can lead to a weakening and often a severing of that bond, the immutable bond between siblings, between brothers and brothers, sisters and sisters, and so on. Their individual successes and fortunes in life should be accepted, no need for any open acknowledgement, or resentment; just 'Get over it.'

Loving relationships are best nurtured by time spent together, time in conversation and laughter. To an extent all loving relationships depend on this. But for the remote relationships, family members moving far away from one another for work reasons, or just for a preference to live somewhere else, the relationship is nurtured by communication, phone chatting, emails, Skype. But what do you talk about? Q: 'How are you?' Ans: 'Fine.' Of course you are! Why not tell your brother or sister/cousin/parent how you really are? You would probably tell them if they lived in the next street. It's just to friends and acquaintances you say, 'Fine, thank you.' 'What have you been up to?' is often a good one but chatting about offspring is easier than chatting about our self. The point is, the simple, uncomplicated contact is made; diligently very regularly, if possible. If not in the habit, it's hard to make the first contact, to break the silence. But if she or he as sister or brother has no time for this, and will not get on the bus, the omnibus, it drives on. What's new? Probably a quidnunc.

We never really truly get to know another person, even our spouse of 40 or 50 years. Knowing every thought, every emotion, whim, their 'ponders,' their fantasies, anxieties even. And why should we expect to? Loving them is enough. Their planet orbiting around ours is enough; seeing they are reaching for the infinitely expanded boundary of their abilities, with no frustrated potential, towards becoming maximally self-actualised. Loved, generously so. Not at all selfish love, not a 'wanting,' needing kind of love, but just there, simple, uncompromised, uncomplicated, instinctive love.

How much distinction is there between love and need? Infants and children need their parents, or a substitute to feed, clothe and shelter them; and as they grow, if treated right, if treated with love, they grow to love the parents. On reaching adolescence, there's a weaning off of the need for support, but it is supplied anyway by the parents, who may feel they should give overt practical, emotional and pastoral support in spades. It can be resented by the young adult. And love as a demonstrable, physical feature of hugging and kissing, hello and goodbye, can be quietly dropped by the young adult as too much, even too sissyish. What is being said here is that parents constructively loved the wee, defenceless baby that is theirs, and loved nurturing it. That love changes as the child grows, and changes into a less 'mooning', less 'adoring' love as the child needs instruction, guidance, teaching and rescuing.

In this the second decade of the second millennium, it would be an omission if little acknowledgement were made of the arrival of LGBT as a prominent drumbeat in those who are focused on their perception of unfairness and discriminations in our society, our urbane society with its sophisticated, discerning, chattering classes, although often scruffy.

It is important to say immediately that much of this book is about the power of goodness, of goodliness, meaning God and godliness, and the spirit within; and that is our soul. We are as grains of sand on the shore, or indeed anywhere. No one grain of sand needs to be regarded as identical to its neighbouring grain of sand, or to any other grain of sand, and there are so many, many grains of sand.

As an evolved mankind, and of a fair degree of civilised conduct exhibited by most of us, we have, that is to say most of us have, collectively chosen to live in peace with each other, under the law, the law of the land that defines how we arrange and manage in our society, the ownership of property, as in 'goods and chattels,' and the conduct of relationships between us to 'keep the peace.' Furthermore, providing we all live within the law, then we accept those differences between one and another as natural fact. For centuries, 'Man's Rules' tried to define a set of behavioural patterns for us all, in society, and to suppress or even banish any behaviour that didn't fit the 'standard' design or concept of the 'right' or the 'normal' conduct, the mainstream and the orthodox, that we were all expected to conform to.

In this 21st century, there has come about a greater understanding of the varieties of behavioural conduct in people, and as long as any conduct acts within the law, then that conduct should be accepted by all. The point is that the law often lags, in its development, behind the social changes, and certain pressure groups emerge to bring 'pressure to bear' on parliament to 'update' the law in these LGBT and other matters. Often those pressure groups, the 'agonists' for change, are opposed by antagonists, very often religious groupings: quoting from their Holy Book they draw on and allow to dictate their lives, their thinking and their beliefs.

God, as the power of goodness, draws only on the spirit within us. That goodliness has no 'concern' as to someone's body, only the mind, their soul, their spirit. How anyone dresses, dressing as either a male or a female, these are only 'earthly things' and as long as the motivation and conduct is all good, with no wrongdoing, not setting out to deceive, then only good should prevail.

Similarly, as we know that everything we ever do is for love, or to make up for the lack of it, then that natural expression of love we are drawn to does not distinguish between the sexes. Not all grains are the same, as none of us are the same. If love draws a man to a man, or a woman to a woman, then if that comes about through all goodliness, then it is as it is, and not for others, for anyone, for no one to judge, to criticise, to pooh-pooh.

It helps to bear in mind, all the while, when we hear people speaking in a discriminatory, divisive way about sexual orientation or indeed about race, that those of other racial or sexual persuasion didn't ask to be born that way, to be born white, or black, or brown, or yellow. And neither did they ask to be born with a certain sexual orientation that would give way to societal discrimination. We are as our genes made us in these things. But creed is another matter: we do have choice there; perhaps not initially, if we were force-fed a diet of a certain creed when we were young, but later when we can discern for ourselves, if we have the wit to.

Furthermore, it helps to recall that people 'didn't ask' to be born into a poor family, or a rich family, and whichever the case, is it imprudent that society and governments sometimes want to pick one or the other, either, to deride or to patronise, to discriminate for one against the other?

Is it prudent for our governments, pushed by activists, to positively prioritise to promote a situation, so that employers have to discriminate in favour of a child's background and education or for the lack of it? And to consider the education and careers of the parents of the applicant, 'the jobseeker,' in such a way that the children of the rich should be discriminated against? And how would an orphan answer questions about his or her parents' education and career?

Wouldn't it be better, more fair, more reasonable, or shall we simply say just more sensible, not to ask at interview which school an applicant went to? We would want to know about their educational qualifications, certainly. We are already not 'allowed' to ask all sorts of questions that used to be used by an employer needing to form an opinion as to the person's likelihood of being an employee of ability, reliability and compatibility with the workforce.

Now we have to use other means. We can dispense with their school and certainly not at all interested in their parents, and anyway, an applicant may lie.

One applicant may say his dad's in prison. Should we think, 'Quick, give him the job.' And then think, 'Can he do the job?' and then think, 'Who cares, we are doing what HMG wants.' But if we employ lots of incompetents and misfits the company will go downhill. Er – yes, we need to think of that. There are evils associated with wealth, when it buys privilege and there's always the risk of nepotism. Surely it's better if we aim to root out the wrong, rather than set one section of society against the other, the young who didn't ask to be born what they were born into.

All one hopes for, as indeed we hope for all of us, is a good, godly, spiritual, loving relationship – a relationship that expresses itself in a way that observes the law, only ever seeks what is good, and acknowledges the wonder of the gift of all the best of human attributes, avoiding the Seven Deadly Sins, being very aware of the power of goodness, strengthening our values, and anyone, anyone at all, can choose, if so minded being guided by the Beatitudes, with observance of the Commandments and aware of the Trinity.

We shall need to be mindful of our basic biological animal make-up. There can be no escape from the biological view that LGBT's predilections are a denial of the fundamental precepts of our biological existence. From time to time we read in the papers news of how fish are 'changing sex,' in particular that males are becoming infertile and other male fish are producing eggs. This phenomenon is being attributed to certain persisting chemicals accumulating in the water as by-products of man's society. In the recent past, articles about the persistence of molecules called oestrones, which are the by-products of the metabolism of sex hormones, mostly notably from the birth pill that enters into water systems, via sewerage, that is treated, and the water recycled. The molecule is not filterable. It has been said that London water has been drunk three times, but this is probably untrue. What is known is that the oestrone molecule is very stable, passes through micro-filters, and has feminising actions in our bodies. In females oestrone can enhance the secondary sexual characteristics, such as breast development and hips, and even sexual behaviour may be altered. Whereas males may appear less obviously male with some loss of male characteristics as in physique, voice, body hair, and behaviour such as a 'softening of conduct,' and also a loss of fertility.

In animals, where overpopulation in a given space as in overcrowding occurs, there develops changes in the behaviour patterns. Pens crammed with only young boars and no gilts, indulge in simulated mating patterns with other males.

Is it because overcrowding is felt so totally subconsciously that some humans are not breeding, in that they have a natural disinclination of doing so, and so subconsciously may be diverting their sex drive to homosexuality? An upsetting notion indeed. One can understand an instinct to limit the size of a family, but there's little real evidence of this. Fecundity is as rife as ever. But it's true some do feel that, and some choose to have no children at all, but it is seldom attributed to overcrowding.

This is not to say that LGBT is as a result of overcrowding, or of any question of build-up of feminising molecular radicles in our environment because it is recorded that these behavioural varieties have been present in human societies for some many centuries. Throughout history variants have been 'forbidden' and persecuted, yet in times of ancient Greece, for example, homosexuality was accepted as the highest sought-after ideal state. Others put the rise of homosexuality as the cause of downfall of some of the great empires. Today these varieties of conduct are accepted and hopefully understood without passing judgement. It is what goes on in our mind, and in our heart, that matters. If we have peace of mind, and a loving heart, who could wish for anything more?

Infidelity is being unfaithful – unfaithful to a certain promise made, spoken or written, a handshake, an exchange of rings, but also often not; often it's just an unspoken understanding as in it shouldn't be necessary, it is assumed, as a 'sine qua non.' We all should know instinctively from our upbringing, our culture, our honour, to say what we mean, and then to mean what we say, or say nothing at all.

The term 'infidelity' is most usually used to refer to the loss of fidelity in a relationship or marriage. The ceremony of marriage is a public statement made before family, relatives and friends of a promise of fidelity, to resist the temptations of life's vicissitudes and be 'faithful.' This is a deeply emotional matter, deeply committing one to another, however tempted to stray in a lustful desire or in revenge for being dealt a dose of partner's rank behaviour, unloving.

It is, for most, absolutely impossible to get over a partner's first bout of infidelity. A drunken 'one-night stand' at a party may be easier to forgive and forget than a partner's first affair, a sequence of clandestine meetings for sex, until either appetites are slaked, or the affair discovered. 'Men can't be trusted' is the mantra, but it would be more fair, more accurate to say, 'some men can't be trusted' or even 'many men can't be trusted.' Those who can, they may be naturally monogamous, having found an ideal partner, honourably never feel the urge to stray, or perhaps their 'sex drive' is less than some 'randy old goat' that may be his friend, divorced three times; just can't keep it zipped up.

So, there is most likely here an interaction going on between our genetic make-up, our 'innate' personality, our fortune or misfortune in forming a 'permanent' bond, a link, a promise, a commitment to be faithful to someone. A bond possibly made early in life, too early in life for the many who later stray in what has quickly become an unhappy marriage, or unhappy relationship. And even more unhappily, if the unhappiness arrives after spawning children, those so innocent, helpless, love-hungry young beings, instinctively knowing Mummy and Daddy should love each other, and cry, yes cry terribly, when Mummy and Daddy shout at each other and throw things.

To the adolescent and young adults, love is all about kissing, cuddling and sex, but we can take note of the words of the idiom glazed into the pottery of the ashtray, 'Kissing don't last – cooking do!' So we say, 'Hello, darling. Had a hard day? Slip your shoes off, sit on the sofa while I pour you a glass of wine. I've lit the fire, and I know it's not my turn to cook but I'll go and cook us supper. I've prepared a surprise for you.' It's in these things that caring, supportive giving endures. Sex is a traumatic tumble, messy business, so great at the time, and so keeps the world turning, but in the end, sex doesn't endure, but the world does keep turning. For the great majority, that primordial physiological need fades, withers even, as it has served its biological purpose.

Love endures, and improves with age, like a good claret, it mellows, its flavour improves, its colour and bouquet improve and yet unlike a bottle of good claret that there is only so much of it to enjoy, love endures. And like good claret, it is something to thirst after, something to have and appreciate. Worth working for, looking for.

———•———

CHAPTER 11
ON BONDING

Cartoonists and the like have often amused their readers with pictures of the Neanderthal caveman, with long hair, unshaven, clad only in a loincloth of animal skin, with a stone mace in one hand, striding out and with his other hand dragging a cavewoman along by her hair along the ground. His 'kill.' He's hunted and 'gotten' himself a mate. And somehow for some reason, this is funny. It denotes something of the early relationship between man and woman, and yet, there is no real evidence of this was how things were.

It could just as well have been the scene of a cavewoman, clad in skins around her waist, standing at the mouth of a cave, her lips deep red from eating red berries, her long hair brought forward to cover most but not all of the cleavage, and thrusting one alluring thigh naked through a gap in the loin furs, when the caveman hunter running by, chasing a rabbit or a dodo bird, hesitates as his loins stir at the invitation of this vision of loveliness distracting him.

Either way, those scenes promote the idea of man's, as in mankind's, early pair-bonding. Such pair-bonding, as we know it today, is rare in animals, and here we are mostly talking mammals. Most mammals live in some sort of colony – be it herd, pack or flock, and their continuity comes about by the most potent male having secured through his fighting strength the 'right' to mate all the females. Thank goodness mankind is not the same!

The males fight for dominance until the weaker is either subdued or killed. In being subdued he loses his 'mating rights.' Is this what human wars are all about? We know our civilisation has evolved to be so very complex it is hard to see the fundamental motivations anymore, but is this what wars are really, as in fundamentally and biologically, about? We no longer expect our nation's leaders to be at the head of the legion, leading the charge into battle: that stopped with Richard III. Others do the fighting and killing, the subduing, for our leader.

156

Note, then, that the spoils of war for the soldiers used to be the 'right' to take their pleasure of the women of the defeated, caveman-style.

Humans go in for pair-bonding, big time. And this bonding behaviour can be seen very early on in a young person's life. There is some sort of attraction between two, that can be seen in children as young as five. Boy and girl preferring to talk to and be in the company of each other in preference to any others. They may hold hands when the class is 'walking out' somewhere. And when encouraged by adults, and sometimes needing no encouragement, it is usually the girl who will give the boy a kiss on the cheek. How sweet. 'Ah!' we all go. The boy often pulls a face – thinking kissing is soppy.

Such early bonding rarely lasts, and the attraction fades, and sometimes moves on to another, but more frequently such early bonding is just an innocent phase in development. But the attractions can continue into early teenhood, but then shyness sets in and he may admire her (not the same her as at five years old) or she admire him, all from an unspoken distance.

These early teens' mutual attractions can manifest bizarrely as teasing each other, not meant as insults, and done as if to be ready to deny any attraction. It's there, but blushingly hidden, afraid in case it is detected, only to be rejected. That's how unsure of ourselves we are at that age. Let a girl know how we are attracted to her, and be snubbed? Such a snubbing could kill the attraction stone-dead. We'd rather die! What a thing, a difficult, challenging thing, growing up is. The phase passes, and 'Hell, if I don't ask her out soon, I'll never get to date her and someone else, probably that jerk who keeps chatting her up, will get to date her.'

It starts with a date, agreeing to go together to the school dance, and if it goes well, you are an 'item' together. For a while. Testing the waters, finding out about each other, who each of us are, in the many ways, and possibly every way, in bonding terms.

Some breeds of birds pair-bond for life. He helps build the nest, and even sits for a while on the eggs, incubating. We joke about the 'birds and the bees', and joke about explaining life and sex to our children when the moment is right, about 'the facts of life.' Most of us do a rotten job; so embarrassing trying to tell our children what our parents failed to tell us. Where do you start? With the birds and bees? Birds yes, bees no. With birds, there's a good analogy, pair-bonding, nest building, incubation, feeding the young and fending off predators. Bees no, no comparison at all – one queen laying all the eggs, workers doing nothing in their lives but work, and drones doing nothing at all, except the odd one if he's lucky mating the queen occasionally. No comparison.

Many humans bond, like the bullfinch, for life. This can be founded on the good fortune for each to have found each other, in love when young, grow fond of each other with a deep, enduring mutual fondness, admiring and accepting each other's idiosyncrasies, with spoken and mostly unspoken love for them, those idiosyncrasies, that is. This is true symbiosis, a mutually beneficial relationship.

For others, not quite so fortunate, their life-long pair-bond, sticking together in a sort of once-in-love-when-young, lovingly raising the children, but then going into old age together, out of habit, and not really happily, a sort of mutual irritation with each other, but never seriously considered any other alternative. A 'going along, to get along.' Split? Why? What for? Together we are better off – financially and in the end, that's what counts, isn't it? This is commensalism; a sort of mutual indifference with mutually incomplete, very incomplete, tolerance, and in a generous light, a not particularly mutually beneficial or mutually detrimental relationship.

There is the joke along the lines of 'she marries the man of her dreams, her Mr Right, and spends the rest of her life improving him.' It's a joke, but with an underlying message, that living together means mutually adopting or tolerating each other's habits and personalities. Either one can be the 'stayer,' the one who identifies with the understanding that living together usually requires some effort of selflessness to make it succeed. There is, perversely, more pleasure in giving than receiving.

It is a genetic trait that men tend to have a 'roving eye,' genetically programmed to spread his genes as in 'sowing his wild oats,' as it used to be spoken of, in the philandering days of youth, the first era of sexual maturity. Each experience of these dalliances he regards as an adventure, and many remain thirsting for more and more adventures of this ilk throughout their whole life.

The concept of fidelity in pair-bonding is instinctive, at least, it virtually always is at first. It is fundamental in that it is reinforced by both our religious upbringing into the marriage service, 'keep thee only unto him/her,' and reinforced by our deepest feelings of the continuing need for self- and social approbation and security. When those feelings are continually reciprocated throughout the life of the pair-bond, they are accompanied by a concomitant fidelity.

Polygamy does not come at all to the Western civilisation, and in those other cultures and individuals that can afford it, there seems to be nothing of the depth of mutuality of love and binding passion between the man and any one of his wives. But this kind of society is so foreign to ours, we will say little more.

If we have applied the word polygamy at all in our Western culture, and if used, it is likely to be misused to describe the individual who has had more than two spouses in the lifetime. The term would not be used to denote someone who'd lost two spouses through illness or accident. It would mean the individual who, being amazingly optimistic, has gone through two or more divorces and insists on trying their hand again at getting married. Analyses of people who have been divorced, show that the more you have been divorced the more you are likely to be! As if it were all down to some defect or deficiency of character. Conversely, there are reckoned to be more truly happy second marriages than first marriages. It's as if we have to go through the first pain, to gain.

That love overrules everything is pretty much mostly true for just about everyone. Princess Diana felt unloved in her marriage. No amount of position, wealth, societal admiration, two lovely sons, none of this could compensate her for her feeling of not being loved as she would have it. Such a tragedy, all round.

Our response to being unloved is very individual. For many, a suspicion that all is not well in the pair-bond becomes evident in small ways at first. Changes in the mutual participating, what used to be so pleasurable. For some, the bad news, usually of 'infidelity,' as in found another 'mate,' to mate with, comes as a bolt out of the blue, because we have so much been seeing the bond relationship with a tunnel vision that failed to read the signs.

But deep down, how many of us can say we know we are truly loved, respected, honoured; liked – even? Not a question to ask your partner, just a question to ask ourselves and if the answer is no, we can start to do something about it, if we, our selves, are 'enough,' can raise the energy, kick enough habits or even be bothered.

The interrelationship, the interdependence, the mutuality between two people in a pair-bond varies between couples, but there are enough similarities to draw some conclusions as to types of relationships found commonly. Rather like the relationship that exists in chemistry between certain molecules of different chemicals as in, for example, a bond between carbon and hydrogen that can be a relatively simple, 'low-energy' bond as in methane, then a higher-energy bond in propane, higher still in butane, and very high indeed in acetylene. People in pair-bonds can be similarly linked. Without reflecting on the quality of the love between them, one pair may do everything together, always acting in harmony; often wear the same colour clothing, matched even, in 'perfect' harmony, these days we might say, 'fully synced.'

At the other end of the spectrum, there is the couple who, like planets in their own orbit, 'meet up' in mind, in body and in spirit, perhaps only at bedtime, or only at the weekends, or perhaps only when home 'on leave.'

There is a thinking that to share love, as in to actively love someone, we have to be 'in the company' of the one we love. That is to say, they need to be there, with us, in effect, daily, nightly. When our loved one is absent, away, out of sight, out of earshot, we know we love them, as we know our ten times table, instinctive memory recall of familiarity, we love them, but are not 'loving them' at that moment, because they are not here, with us, to be loved; to see, to look at, to speak with, to laugh with, to hug; to everything, the act of loving.

This is why modern communications are so brilliant at keeping the momentum of loving; emails, voice calls, Skype, Facebook with photos etc. etc. Absence makes the heart grow fonder – they say – what rubbish, except that by saying it, we are supposed to feel better about any being apart. Being together, metaphorically hand-in-hand, going down the pathway of life with all life-changing experiences thrown at us, means that life changes us both, mutually, but not both in the same way; and as we change, grow older, we can either become more loving, nicer to love or less so. Less so leads to unhappiness by both, and possibly ends in divorce. A man away at work for some years, perhaps a soldier, not seen his wife in all that time comes home a 'different man,' a changed man, to find a changed wife. Life-changed. They know they are supposed to love each other still, as they did when parted, but they will not know how the 'cookie will crumble' until some more time has passed, together.

They say that a woman's love is more deep, more enduring, more given to monogamy than a man's. That may be so; it is written in enough fictional literature. The saying was, 'To a woman, marriage is her whole life; to a man, it is something apart.' Perhaps it was true to certain wealthy classes of people in Victorian and Edwardian times, but it's hard to feel it is valid in this second millennium. Men still bear the bigger responsibility for the numbers of divorces coming about, due to their infidelity, which could mean his primordial and genetic impulses drag him to break a vow of monogamy, that state of being faithful to one wife, one at a time.

Many couples stay together for the children's sake. It seems axiomatic that a child needs a mother and a father, their progenitors in their life, in their upbringing. A preferred ideal is the undeniable benefit to the child to receive unconditional love in childhood from two parents. Why? So they can grow up into a well-rounded character, free from negativity, and with high self-esteem, ever mindful of what manhood is, and what womanhood is. And yet many children do not have the benefit of an unconditional love from two parents, but from only one for various reasons, such as the father killed at war, the mother dead in childbirth, or single parenthood from divorce. Are these children disadvantaged for life? Much depends on the remaining parent. Much depends on the individuality of the child, especially on becoming an adult. But an unbalanced upbringing can lead to an unbalanced adult. But disadvantages of childhood can be overcome, dealt with, and be helped into a mindset to develop wisely, and acquire a desire for self-improvement; sadly that potential for self-improvement can only begin with an awareness of the opportunity. Hopefully, this awareness can come from the parent, the uncle or aunt, grandparent, schooling, chance reading, chancing on browsing the internet.

The father or mother who abandons a child, leaving the child to be brought up by the remaining parent, may be departing in a desperate need to remain sane by leaving a tragically unhappy marriage. The leaving parent comes to feel, and hope, as the dust settles from a journey of separation of spirit and perhaps of geography, too, that in their neglect, and despite their neglect, the child may yet come to be a whole person, positive in outlook; and the now adult child has reckoned, reasoned out the absent parent's neglect, dealt with it, put it in the hold and battened the hatches on any negative thoughts, the thoughts of that parent's neglect. If not, if this doesn't come about as hoped, there will be a need by the 'child as was' for some sound counselling to begin an improved self-awareness.

We each of us are a planet in our self. Even in a marriage, a pair-bond, with another planet, orbiting either in parallel or only occasionally 'meeting' or coinciding orbits, in the last resort, we are alone. All alone, with our minds, our hearts, our feelings, and our choice what to feel, our decisions, all those decisions we choose to make.

While our partner in our pair-bond is sufficiently 'like-minded,' the bond stays, strengthens even. If we have any doubt on the 'issue' that we are alone, our own planet, think about the moment as an adult, in a marriage or deep pair-bonding relationship with or without a family of loving children, the moment when we are about to have an operation, a life-threatening, life-risking operation, and we are asked to give our signed consent. No one else can sign – we are responsible for our life. It's our decision, our choice. We may listen to the doctors, and to our loved ones, but it's still the case we are alone. An individual grain of sand on the shore, our decision. And in all our life, in all things, the same applies. Never inappropriately should we divest ourselves for the responsibility for ourselves. Even in the most, almost incredibly deeply loving pair-bond, we ultimately are alone. Yes. The skipper of our own vessel, 'Master under God.'

Pair-bonding in humans can be heterosexual and homosexual. Homosexuality is rarely seen in mammals. Their sexual behaviour is mostly driven by sexual pheromones and acute olfactory senses. In the countryside, the natural state on earth (not cities, they being all of mankind's needful yearning for civic domain), in the countryside, when a bitch is on heat, say, on one farmstead, male dogs will cover some miles from other farmsteads, the scent of her being 'in season' travels on the wind. She is 'on heat' for ten days before she is ready to mate. By then, there is usually a sizeable gathering of males eager to mate with her. There may be some fighting for the pole position. When she is ready to mate, she accepts her chosen male, mates with him, and then resists for a brief while as the other suitors anticipate. The next day, she will mate again, or perhaps the day after. It may be with a different male. The first one, slaked, weakened even, may have gone home.

In tomcats, the union seems a very painful process, with much yowling. With cornified barbs in his penis, to keep the tom in coital union for long enough, then when spent, the queen may turn on the tom, fiercely and in certain circumstances, if he is trapped, she could even kill him. A sort of 'Wham-bam, impregnated-me-thank-you-man, now you die.' Bit rough, that.

Humans' sex drive seems very much less down to 'seasonal' influences of pheromones. No packs of dogs roaming the city streets following a bitch on heat, as in days of yore. We have other gatherings called parties, time to flaunt ourselves as best we can with perfumes and exposed flesh, desires raised by 'inhibition-quelling' alcohol, and maybe other recreational substances (that disgusting euphemism for potentially lethal, sooner or later toxic indulgences).

As Homo sapiens evolved at some point, from a fundamental 'instinctive-animal-mating-behaviour' to the selective choosing of a mate and became much more orientated towards the pre-mating relationship; the attraction and fascination of one for the other, as in physique, physiognomy and character as expressed by this newly evolved 'sentient' being, of early culture. And, in all probability, with that development came the early law, an agreed 'code' of conduct for the human grouping, the primeval village; no creeping into another's hut and stealing a fur, and the tethering of the guard dog to the wall of the hut, by the door, known then as the 'dog of the ninth pole.' And no doubt, if there was any tendency towards misplaced mating behaviour with another man's 'woman,' or indeed, with another man, that was probably outlawed. Outlawed because we know at some point in history homosexuality, at least between males, became an issue for many societies, disordering them with what would have been seen as dysfunctional behaviour.

For whatever reason, it was seen as unwanted, unnatural, unhealthy even to the mind, to the proper order of society, to the fragile structure of orderliness that separates us from the animals (despite, as said here, that homosexuality is rare in mammals). The behaviour was seen as 'without reason' and 'bestial' even. Bestial? Well, we know that when deprived of society of the opposite sex, mammals indulge, at mating time, which is usually seasonal, in going through mating movements with others of the same sex. Young boars with no females around have been seen to occupy themselves, when not eating, by jumping on the back of another boar and making copulating thrusts with the hips. Some even mounted facing the 'wrong' way round. Animal-like, because they were animals, they were acting mindlessly, just full of male hormones, doing what comes 'naturally.' Five- and six-month-old puppies, in excitement of play then sometimes in the rough-and-tumble, find themselves in the mating position on another and begin the copulatory-thrusting movements. Owners, shocked, rush to the vet to get 'him' castrated. No need, this is innocent, very innocent, and not sexually driven at all, being too immature. Some reflexes are spinal reflexes, involuntary, like the knee-jerk when the doctor taps our knee, and with very little or no connection to our higher brain. There are built in sensory-neuronal-motor-muscle reflexes, in readiness for sexual maturity; they rely solely on the contact of sensors in the forearms (front legs) and chest on the proprioceptive (positional) reflexes. The human hug is near to this, and can even on rare occasions, if the presenting conditions predispose, a hug can often be the precursor to further moves along the 'precoital' pathway. A man may tumesce as not being in control of his groin. When this happens in hospital, meaning a spontaneous tumescence (not meaning from hugging a nurse), the nurse just taps it with her pencil, and it goes down.

Bonding between men is seen in at least two, but possibly more, types of relationship. Traditionally, adult males frequently find a friend, a chum, a buddy, someone they relate particularly well with. They may have a similar temperament, similar in attitude to and tolerance of life, often both are married, with families. Their friendship is just that, no more. They help each other when help is needed, to mend the car, fell a tree, renew the guttering etc. They are mates, best mates even. Very many men have or had 'a mate.'

Sadly in modern society, 'prised-open' minds now assume something else. In this highly, overtly overly sexualised society, people ponder, even snigger, at two men being best mates. Yachting is a hobby often enjoyed by husbands, and their wives possibly less so, preferring gardening or horses or shopping. So, the hubby takes a mate of his sailing as his crew. It's innocent, totally innocent, and yet, today our too hasty, even nasty minds question. Just because homosexuality is now legalised, so much now featured on TV and films, so rammed down our throats, to accept and banish all previous prejudices, that a man is afraid of having a best mate, a 'crewman,' when arriving in harbour. So what? We can never ordain what people think, never could, never will. Shame we couldn't be colour-coded to show our sexual predilections, if it matters that much to people. Only a few homosexual men mince.

Homosexual relationships between men have been around for centuries, and an issue for some societies. For centuries men ruled nations, fought its wars, in disciplined ranks of military hierarchy. And that hierarchy was an orderliness that homosexuality could or would perhaps threaten.

Homosexuality between women is and has been much seen to be much less of an issue. Society more or less says, 'So what?' Unless that bond breaks marriages or perversely leads to crime, no one seems to care much. What is more, it is much more understandable, more readily tolerated, indeed if it is to be an issue at all.

Understandable, because by many women's reckonings, and some men's, women get the raw end of the deal out of heterosexual relationships, mostly meaning marriage. As already implied, when a woman loves a man, her first real love, it is deep and abiding, her whole life revolves around it. This notion, so popular a belief by past literary authors of both sexes, becomes the key part of literature, as previously said. However, times have changed: the birth pill has given women so much more freedom, and with that their justifiable claims for more equality with men, in all ways, have 'changed the nature of the beast' (so to speak).

But having said all that, it is still the women who bear the children, shoulder the bigger share of the responsibility for rearing the children because their innate feelings readily render them more capable, a capability arising from a mother's instinct. But bearing children and rearing them takes it out of a woman and she becomes totally reliant, reliant but not necessarily totally dependent, on her man being there supporting her and the children and what's more, being faithful. Faithful in body and mind. And yet, so often, how very sadly, women are 'let down' by men. Men who go philandering, adulterating what could and should have been a beautiful relationship of the family, and sadly, too, men who decide to eschew love for a woman, or even love of women, and go out to bond with a male. Yes, women get the raw end of the deal, especially when the bond turns out, later, to be a 'lavender marriage,' and we haven't even mentioned the physical and metabolic illnesses of pregnancy, the psychological illness of post-natal depression, and childbirth still carries a risk of death. Yes, women get the raw end of the deal. She needs a bullfinch, to build the nest, to sit on the eggs from time to time, to bring the young their food, daily, day in and day out until the fledglings can 'flee the nest.' No going off with a floosy or to play with another man's bits, as she, his distraught wife, could see it.

It is tempting to think that now homosexuality is recognised and legalised even to reach a state called a marriage, it is on the increase. That may be so. If so, why? Theories have been put forward. Theories like overcrowding. We don't yet know, and few seem worried about the physiological and sociological effects of human overcrowding. Overcrowding in animals is known to lead to more searching and struggling for food, and when food is not found then the weak are one of the first to flounder. But overcrowding with or without food, for the time being anyway, also leads to bullying, sexual perversions, as in attempted cross-mating with the same sex, and leads to the pecking order (including feather pecking) with self-mutilation and to self-harming, as in deranged behaviour, and perhaps most importantly, to infanticide and infertility. That is to say that collectively in animals these aberrations are self-limiting tendencies. But we see most of these problems, too, in the cities of our human overcrowded culture, but also sometimes in the countryside, where it is less crowded.

In both human and some animal behaviour, new behaviour patterns 'appear' through mimicry. We may mimic what has been seen on TV, or the big screen or read in a book. People get ideas, and, if the mood or the urge takes them, they copy it, because it's okay. It's okay to 'come out,' to be AC/DC, to be transvestite, to have thoughts real or imaginary that you are a woman inside a man's body, and so on. Where does all this come from? Can it be due to the 'evolution' of society, of mankind? Or is society mindlessly declining into a morass of moral decrepitude? Who can say? There was a time in the 1960s when it was thought harmless and innocent fun to depict actors as camp on comedy shows. In the light of modern understanding and tolerance that may have been meant to be innocent, but almost certainly was not harmless, as those who were truly gay must have felt it badly.

If all this were a modern phenomenon, we could ask questions like, is it something in the drinking water? Why are the fish in the sea 'changing sex' more these days? Why are we all so welcoming of the sexualisation of society today, of sexualising young children, their clothes, what they see and hear on TV, in films and the internet? Do more sixteen-year-old girls really have bigger breasts than sixteen-year-olds had 50 years ago? Certainly there is much more physical expression of female secondary sexual characteristics than 50 years ago. Sexually maturing males have much more encouragement towards an almost totally distracting preoccupation of the mind by the constant sexual overtness of human conduct today for it to become, for some, an obsession that can lead to the violence of rape.

Not all homosexual relationships become relationships built around the sexual practices, and the psychic and physical pleasure that is thought to derive from their particular sexual practices. Some homosexual relationships are 'asexual'. That is to say that the attraction between the two is an attraction; a form of loving develops that never needs, never wants, never even considers, moving onto the intimacy of the physical sexual relationship. The Church of England expects this asexual bonding between its 'outed' clergy, bishops and all.

Some claimed compliance with this code. Others decried it.

The level of sex drive is different in all of us, and is also different at different stages of our lives. Some seem never to have any sex drive at all. If known, that may become ridiculed. But the ridicule could just as well be directed against those whose sex drive is 'out of control' and tends to wreak havoc wherever they go. It is possible the truly asexual but deeply emotional, as in a loving, relationship is found more in women than men. As said, it's probably more understandable in women than men.

In terms of the evolution of mankind from Homo erectus to Homo sapiens, homosexuality is probably a relatively recent thing, seeing as we have moved from the very, very early Homo sapiens still with marked 'animal-like' mating habits, and a sole purpose, a well-understood and accepted purpose, their almost sole concentration on staying alive; fed, bred, safe and warm. Not much scope for so-called higher human ideals, higher up Maslow's Hierarchy, where homosexuality sits. It's in modern times, say the last five thousand years, where homosexuality in men, at least, has become a more 'modern' and understood practice that is now accepted as a physiologically and psychologically driven need.

At the time of ancient Greeks, at the time of ancient Greek philosophers, homosexuality was somehow idealised as a way of organised societal life. Young men would pray to the goddess 'Iphimedeia' that they might be favoured with the advances of a high senator or other such person of high rank and nobility. The philosopher Plato would have had all the women removed to what in effect would be a baby farm. His theory of best society was that once a year there would be something like a Bacchanalian orgy at the 'farm,' where the men would go, mate with the women and get them pregnant, and the women would then stay at the farm rearing and raising the children to early adulthood. Plato's thinking was that this is what women were best at, designed for, as it were. The rest of the year the men would be 'free' to carry out the lives of homosexuality whilst running and governing the country. These days the term 'a platonic relationship' is taken to be a friendship usually between a man and a woman that is without even any hint of a romantic and sexual relationship, even though it might not persist and become sexual later. A platonic relationship. But all those years ago, in Plato's own terms, a platonic relationship meant a 'one-night stand.' Odd, that!

For centuries Western culture has been predominantly Christian, but always with a fair smattering of Judaism. The Christian has had a very difficult time in this second millennium AD (CE, now 'Common Era'), struggling to know how to view and how to respond to the 'rise' in the movement to legalise, even to popularise homosexuality. The issue seems to be mostly male-directed. As a society, the 'chattering society,' news items, magazines, pundits spouting, we are told next to nothing about what the more rigidly disciplined faiths think and say, preach and rule on the matter of homosexuality. Doubtless such relationships occur in Islam, in Judaism, in Buddhism and Hinduism. How do they react? Tolerantly? Quietly – as in 'brushed under the table,' a sort of quiet acceptance. No brandishing, no 'washing of the dirty linen in public,' as the secular society does?

It is not certain if the Bible is clear on this point. We are intoned to 'love one another'. So what's the problem? The variation in sexual practices, the deviation from the 'animal' or 'biological' use of genitalia from breeding, is set aside, but didn't the 'deviation' from that start with contraception? What one does with one's 'bits', or with another's 'bits,' is it of any concern to anyone else? How can a basic physiological practice come to be so controversial? If we itch, we scratch. If our bladder's full, we go and empty it. If hungry we eat, if thirsty we drink, if feeling randy, we rand. The difference is when feeling randy it usually involves some sort of build-up, the amuse-bouche, then the aperitif and the starter before the main course. Practised lovers enjoy the five-course meal, inclusive of soup and fish, in no hurry for the main course, before gently leading into the dessert, the cheese and then the coffee and petits fours, all the while seeing that your partner enjoys most of the meal as well.

And it is this involvement of the second person that becomes the problem for the 'Church.' All they want is to define for us a code of practice, based on the Bible, that is deemed worthy and good, so as to facilitate our ultimate acceptance into Heaven. If we can't believe in Heaven, we can presumably wham, bam and rand as much and with as many folk as we like. But can we? Even atheists and agnostics have a social conscience. They can believe that fidelity in a pair-bond is an essential component to happiness and peace of mind (and freedom from STDs).

The intrusion of a third person, or the breaking of the mutual cohabiting to stray and experience another person's physical and perhaps personal attributes causes doubt, suspicion and jealousy. Or is it those things? Isn't it just as likely to be the case that, being used to the love and approbation, continual and unquestioned, we 'bathe' in the glow and warmth of the up-to-now exclusivity of our pair-bond. Our partner's affection now seems suddenly diluted, dimmed, and then questioned. And we question ourself as to, 'What have I done?' and, 'What have I not done to keep my lover happy, content and safe?' Sadly, it's none of those things, it's more likely the feral wanderlust operating, the almost everlasting and enduring, animal-like need to spread our genes. To that extent, we do lose a degree of our being civilised. Sadly, too, that the flowers having bloomed and borne their fruit, what so often is left is less than attractive as the years take their toll.

The Church, the Christian Church, can be or should be happy to preach and encourage true loving relationships between pair-bonding couples. If the Church sets out what a loving relationship brings, what it has as its merits, without doubt it would need to include all loving relationships. Marriage is a toughie for the Church. Due to history, the legal conjoining of two people can be licensed, in Church or in secular locations. This is something of a pity because there is a fundamental difference between a 'state' marriage and a religious marriage, that is to say the religious marriage comes with more.

In general, we are so bad about how we enter into what can later become a legal relationship or arrangement. Simple things, often generous, kind gestures of support and generosity, can go sour. The most common example is when we lend a friend in need our car, something often done by the young on impulse; they feel good about being easy-going and 'cool' about it. 'No problem, mate,' kind of thing. The mate crashes the car and it's unquestionably his fault and the car's a 'write off.' He's okay, but he wasn't insured to drive your car: a 'we didn't really think about it,' situation once again. So, we've lost our car, can't afford another, so we go to the Small Claims Court or Judge Rinder, and lose because there was nothing in writing.

Time and time again in life we do the same with other things, some with potentially big consequences, but mostly, when it comes to property and investments, we tend to wise up. Happily, there is a mandatory process that obliges us to have a written contract, so that we know, line by line, or have it 'spelled out' to us what we are entering into, e.g. 'If we don't keep up the mortgage payments, we will lose the house.'

However, the most vital financial commitment we enter into, the marriage contract, is seldom 'spelled out,' and the document we sign, the Marriage Certificate, has no contractual detail in it at all. In effect, by signing we are each giving half of our current assets, and our future ones, including a lien on our pension. The detail in the contract really only gets identified when the divorce happens, unless, as in America, we had 'a prenup;' but in principle, it was contractually established at law at the time of the wedding, but absolutely unwritten and it should be set out in print, and an opportunity to take advice on it beforehand. Would anyone call things off, if this written detail were to become mandatory?

Arguably there is no rationale, no sound reason other than custom, custom to do with the outmoded 'dowry' for any exchange of a liability to the pre-existing assets on getting married. Ideally these pre-existing assets should be declared and set out in the marriage contract as the enduring ownership by each, with a notional fixed interest rate that can be computed on an annual compound interest basis.

It is the growth on the assets during the lifetime of the marriage that should be split on divorce. However, the division of the 'growth in the assets' also needs to include the children of the marriage, and that means a proper home must continue to be provided when one existed before the divorce. In effect, this means that the 'divorce' settlement cannot be finalised until the last of the children in the marriage reaches maturity at the age of eighteen. It's a shame it isn't still 21.

All this legal 'rigmarole' is something the Church would prefer not to get involved in; these are matters secular, of the state and solely of this world. Therefore it follows that all marriages should be secular, held in the state's register office or other licensed places, but not churches.

Those who desire a religious marriage are then free to undergo the 'joining in Christ' as a second ceremony. Paradoxically, if an English (for example) married couple were to buy jointly a house in France, under French law, they would need to 'remarry' in France, as France doesn't recognise marriage contracts entered into in other countries for the purpose of registering title to French property. Well done, the French.

We often hear talk about, read about the oversexualised society of today, and we suppose we all know what is meant by that. If we consider the Muslim society, the most obvious by comparison is the dress. We see women, at least we assume they are women, clad in black, from head to toe, seeing only through a small slit – the hijab. Some less clad, but flowing robes or dress, down to the ankle, with the head covered with a scarf drawn down or demurely wrapped around her neck. 'A woman's hair is her crowning glory,' it is said. But this crown is not for all to see, only her family, once indoors. So, it's what's on view to the public is what matters; no perceived or reckoned inducement or encouragement of sexual attraction while the woman goes out and about her daily life. And this, then, is the rub, the kernel, the core of the matter. It's what's on view.

Whether it is known, understood or analytically considered, the change of relationship between the sexually immature boy, playing out, being friendly with, enjoying the innocent company of a sexually immature girl all changes as she, mostly, but he to a lesser extent, develops sexually and in so doing, they develop their explicit, overtly explicit 'secondary sexual characteristics'. She develops glamour, even without make-up or special clothes. She develops breasts, a waist and hips, lustrous hair, full lips, shapely legs and sensual skin. All these things the normal 'red-blooded' man comes to appreciate and be turned on by. That boy develops muscles, broad shoulders, strong forearms and biceps, powerful thighs, tight buttocks, strong chin and neck, and a deeper voice; and furthermore, she recognises these things as admirable and ponders his suitability for a relationship that could go places.

Neither sex can help or do much about the attributes they develop. Some have more than others. Our modern Western culture has developed a high degree of commercialisation in exploiting and emphasising these secondary sexual characteristics, with revealing as much of a woman's bodyparts as they and she can get away with, without being arrested for indecency. Such a contrast to Muslim society, and it's hardly surprising that the two cultures cannot live comfortably alongside each other.

The continual 'flaunting' of secondary sexual characteristics leads to a preoccupation with sex, sexual relationships, and any relationship that is intended or hoped will end up in bed sooner or later. The bull grazing in the field with his herd of cows has no thought of sex, until a cow 'comes on heat' (every three weeks until pregnant) and he scents her pheromones. Humans will mate anywhere, anytime, any place they have a fancy, anywhere that stands a reasonable chance they won't be caught 'in flagrante,' and these thoughts tend to be ever present in our over-sexualised society since the provocation, the 'inducements' are just about omnipresent, and ever present.

Furthermore, there is a continual stream of evocative images, in the papers and on the screens. But these visual delights can be just that, nothing more. We dress to look good, feel good. As to how revealing, that often is a matter of what is available in the shops. The culture has become more revealing, and will probably pass to become a more modest fashion in time. Women often complain

171

that 'there is nothing in the shops,' meaning nothing to suit the taste, perhaps even their desire to be more modest without appearing old and 'frumpy.'

Muslim women go out into society clad in a way that says, 'I am not interested or I have become conditioned not to be interested in sending a message (or simply just not allowed) that I am looking to 'pair-bond' with someone I may happen across.' Western semi-clad women send the message, 'I am a pretty woman, and you are welcome to look at me and that's all,' but also possibly, 'If a handsome hunk of a man comes by, then I just might fancy having his attentions, and even, but fancifully, his intentions.' Only by her behaviour would one be able to detect any further message.

If we watch TV soaps, they are all about relationships, all the time: virtually all their 'storylines' are about the meeting, the making of, the talking about and then the breaking up of relationships. Is there nothing else in life? They pretend to 'analyse' feelings, getting in touch with feelings, throw very amateurish relationship psychology at us as they seek to deliver their societal message to the viewers, the soap followers. Most of it is unimaginable nonsense, as in the 'no sense' equals nonsense.

If we say something is genetic, 'in the genes,' we mean that some physical characteristics and occasionally a behavioural characteristic are obviously inherited from one parent or the other, or even sometimes the characteristic is atavistic, inherited from ancestors, grandparents, or great-grandparents even, and so on. It could be any readily identifiable feature, such as the absence of earlobes.

If we use the term 'congenital' we mean a characteristic that is acquired 'in utero,' a development of the foetus, which could be a developmental accident. It applies for the whole process from the fusion of the two gametes, the successful sperm among many thousands of suitors, the merging its chromosomes with those of the opportune ovum to form, the new diploid zygote, the fertilised egg and from thence on to and through all the succeeding miraculous stages to the fully formed foetus ready to enter the 'brave new world.' It is so complex a unit that it can be regarded as a miracle of nature that more doesn't go wrong more often in the process of development. Apart from 'What sex is it?' The first thing parents used to want to know is, 'Is it all right?' meaning all the fingers and toes, eyes and ears and nose and more, including those important 'bits.'

Sadly, congenital mishaps occur due to external influences, most frequently due to ingested prescribed drugs during pregnancy. All drugs have side effects, that is to say an effect on the subject, the patient, apart from the intended pharmacological benefit that is assumed. Not everyone suffers all the side effects. Some of the 'people' feel some of the side effects, some of the time, and this is the phenomenon called 'biological variation.' The disastrous 'morning sickness' remedy thalidomide is the best-known example of congenital defects caused by a prescribed drug. Congenital defects do not go on to become 'genetic' or inherited defects, i.e. not 'passed on' as is often commonly thought.

The point for us is that some unfortunates are born with defects in the development of their 'sexual apparatus,' the both parts being the internal sexual organs and the external genitalia. These defects may or may not be correctable by surgery, to become the 'complete' male or 'complete' female. Some are born with a confusion between 'bits' male and bits female, known as an 'intersex.' On growing up, if some surgery has not yet been able to improve on matters, then as a young adult, he or she may find themselves needing to make life-affecting decisions to go for one sex or another, which 'loo to go in' for as much peace of mind as can ever possibly be achieved. Advances in surgery and hormone therapy arrive all the time to help these people.

But these days there is also a whole raft of people, whose internal sex organs and external genitalia are complete, who claim for some reason or another that 'they are in the wrong body,' meaning 'he' wants to be a 'she,' and 'she' wants to be a 'he'. As in 'wants,' claiming they should have been born the other sex because that sex is truly what they feel they 'are,' and have come to want to be that sex. For many, they seek to deny the sex they are born for a start, go on the road to 'cross-dressing,' and then hope for the chemical and surgical manipulations to bring about their desire, no longer to have to put up with the now disliked attributes of the sex they were born.

'They' even press for the sex of newborn children not to be registered, so the child to become adult one day can choose what sex they want to be, rather like changing one's name. 'Let's not give the baby a name,' so that it can choose its name when it's grown up. What tosh. Shall we just call it 'It?' And the second child, 'It2?' This is as bad and as sad as those unfortunate malcontents who obsess about wanting to get rid of one of their legs – Munchausen's syndrome.

Should society take these malcontents seriously – is there a justifiable case? Presumably the behaviour is a recognised behavioural 'condition,' a form of neurosis, or even potentially a psychosis, as in 'out of touch with reality.' Some suggest these unfortunates are 'failed' males, failed as a man, in all that a human male is generally reckoned to be; or a failed female, failed in all that a woman is reckoned to be. As in 'I'm no good at that, I'm a failure, so let me try something else.' Or is the condition a truly 'proper,' full-blown delusion, thinking it knows what it is to be of the other sex and obsessing about being 'trapped' inside the wrong body? It is a sadness that happens and how can such a person ever be happy? How can one ever derive any happiness in loving another, that love being relished in any reciprocation by a mind so ill at ease with itself? Would that a state of happiness can come about for these tested souls, where an easy acceptance of all the variants of human 'orientations' is acknowledged happily without prejudice. As the Memphis taxi driver says, 'Right on, brother!'

'Marriages are made in Heaven' is the saying once often heard. Some respond with, 'In which case Heaven is not working very hard!' 'Marriage is a lottery,' is the other saying, a lottery in which many thousands buy a ticket, but there are far fewer 'winners.' The childlike, fairy tale notion, 'And they lived happily ever after,' is something that in all reality, there is little reality. That is to say, that to a child, and to many adults, 'living happily ever after,' living a fate decreed by 'Heaven,' just happens. Just happens like the ongoing heart beating day and night, day in, day out until death, without any effort or input into seeing the marriage, the love affair, endures and endures. Oh, no! Some effort is needed. And if it is more effort than we can muster, and if our partner-spouse doesn't make anything like an effort, a similar effort, then all will fall apart, big time, and then there's a divorce.

The problem of 'mismatching' of couples starts with our sexual maturity arriving yonks before the maturity of our character, who we are, as adult human beings. For some, youth sex is just an early physical pleasure and delight, having sex with various others, usually of the opposite sex, as an adventure, exploring the difference between one 'sex' partner and another. Those relationships usually involved a degree, often a very fair degree of infatuation with the other person and so rarely a 'bonk' just for the sake of 'having a bonk.' Boys were accused of 'going after anything in a skirt,' and 'only out for one thing,' and for some, indeed for many, especially the adolescents, that's true.

For many, the infatuation is an intense psychological experience that can wrack the whole body, the whole life, whole existence of the adolescent. So that he or she can do nothing useful but think about, and dream about the object of their infatuation. It is such an intensely pleasurable experience, yet it's not just intense feelings, it's a state of mind.

It is when we are sure, so sure that the feeling, the state of mind, will go on for ever and ever, 'live happily ever after'-type of stuff. So, 'Let's get married' is the urge, and many will go on to ignore the advice of friends and the pleading of parents and relatives to wait, to be able to build the nest first, that these intense urges are transient at 'your age.' And, 'No,' we say, 'this love of ours is different; so different to anything anyone else has ever felt, we are meant for each other, we just know it!' And so, the wedding goes ahead, and soon the cracks appear. The first row, about money, then making up, but somehow not quite 100% made up, and soon another row, about money. She gets ill with cystitis after sex, and repeatedly so, and then the awful business of morning sickness comes. She feels wretched. They hadn't planned for a baby just yet; they need the money and she really loves her job. Life's a bit short on understanding and sympathy. The first child comes eventually, more expense, post-natal depression. And so on. We all know the story, and it's hard-going, the easy, carefree, exciting life changed for something different, not carefree, not exciting and love-lessening. The man is confused, bored and unrequited; so he strays.

Soon, it's, 'You are not the man I married!' and the riposte, 'You are not the woman I married!' Life, like the potter at his wheel, ever moulding us as if we are malleable like clay, only that we can also reach out and mould that potter of clay, the partner-spouse, in return. There need only be four ingredients for the recipe of existence: partner 1, partner 2, living together, and time masquerading as life. Ah! Yes! The reality that is life. How ill-prepared for it we are, at every stage, each of Shakespeare's 'seven stages.' And if someone were to try to prepare us, would it work, would we listen, would we remember? Do we ever, as individuals, as couples ever, or even as a tribe, as a nation, as a government, governing for our people, ever learn from history? Are we ever prepared for the next stage of life?

If we can ride out the storm of youthful emotions and land up in our twenties unmarried, is there a time when, on average, it's about the 'right time' to get married? All those fun things enjoyed since leaving home are becoming a bit mundane, a bit too routine, a bit dull.

We would like to 'settle down,' perhaps have children to focus our energies on, and at the end of the working day, the working week, for those times, the holidays when we are 'released' from the obligations of work, of earning a living, and now free to enjoy the reality of our life, be who we really, really are; not just the young executive clever in his/her own right, but interesting, funny, sporty, and entertaining, interested, too, in all life offers, especially in other people, what makes them 'tick'.

Gurus, those who ponder, study, conclude and pronounce on such matters generally reckon that a man's best age to enter into marriage is 30. By then his character is formed, settled. By then he should be at a stage in life when he's reasonably mature in his opinions and his objectives, his self-awareness, his career, and should make a reliable sensible husband and father.

For the women, they reckon on average it's best if she is about five years younger, becoming earlier more emotionally mature and her character more settled and suitable to settle down, to wed, to make a home together, to start a family together. More likely to succeed, him and her, if both characters are well formed, developed, crystallised before merging into a marriage, a marriage that stands the best chance of being a truly loving, mutually respecting, enduring togetherness, made in Heaven and winning the lottery. Should or could the government make a ruling on this? It wouldn't work.

Why the discrimination between the sexes? All that is fashionable in today's society revered. 'Here we are,' say the chattering PC classes, 'trying to eliminate and deny the difference between the sexes, treating them both the same in all things.' And, 'How dare we come along and rouse the spectre again of men being different from women and vice versa.' Oh! They do go on so.

It's best if it is rightly understood. Physically, in biological and anatomical terms there will always be a difference; wearing the same clothes, the same hairstyle, may mask matters, but as in all things, it's what's underneath that counts. And that includes the undeniable fact of life that for the foreseeable future, women will bear the children, and men will be their progenitors. Inescapable, apart from the experiments of the biological scientists working to control life itself. Furthermore, linked and almost inextricably so, are the functional biochemical, physiological differences between male and female, being mammalian, and of the biological genes, Homo sapiens. Still very animal. Can't deny it; can cloak it up with all sorts of fancy-pants PC metaphorical clothing, but underneath, animal.

What is more, instead of this 'dumbing down' of 'the male' and 'the female' into the 'identikit' unisex person, modern society should take on-board what it really is. By this, 'it' is meant that a man should identify as a man, pursue, follow and adopt all that is best in a man. For 'a man is a man when a man

176

is needed, if not, he remains a child.' To be justifiably proud in his maleness. Not 'lewd, lazy and lascivious,' as one actress put it. Not coarse, not vulgar, not flatulent, nor paunchy, shaven or bearded, not unshaven, but smart and showered, groomed hair, clean clothes, polished or clean shoes, not down at heel. But oh! So much more – of character, upright, prudent in all things, sober yet humorous, generous, honest and straight with money. Reliable. Hard-working and virtuous. Justifiable, proud, not 'strutting,' boastful or bragging, and not at all pusillanimous, but moderately uxorious, never excessively so. And then, as was always said, 'Such is the mark of the man.'

And a woman should be proud of being a member of the fair sex, for all that is best in womanhood. Well turned out, well groomed, well-chosen clothes that suit, no vulgar revealing at inappropriate times and places, hair cared for, honest above all things, intellect cared for, as in a wide general interest with or without some specific interest. And much more, of quality, with a sound sensibility. A good listener, no hogging the conversation, two ears and only one mouth. Modest and very honest, open but not too frank so as to offend; patient and tolerant of others, especially children. And so much more! It may be harder for a woman to excel at womanhood than a man to excel at manhood, but in general women seem to have been given those extra attributes to be able to cope and to deliver. And, as was always said, 'She was one such woman' (in the positive sense, to all but the mean-minded).

Sadly, in this rush for the practical aspects of social equality between men and women, as in opportunity at work, pay and benefits, which these are as they should be, the rush has detracted somewhat for some females, from a woman taking a pleasure and justifiable pride in being a woman. So, 'vivre la différence' can be the battle cry in response to the 'grey' people of the PC brigade, all wearing grey or black, with uncombed hair, but not meaning grey as in grey-haired, the result of advancing years, and when of early onset, too much worry.

We can coin a new phrase, 'My aim is to bond, and bond well, for double-oh-heaven!

CHAPTER 12
DECISIONS

How often do we hear someone say, 'I don't want to make the wrong decision.' In expressing ourselves in this way, such a phrase shows that we don't really feel 'in control' of our lives, and that we don't really understand the way life works; or it may be simply that we are very unaccustomed to making decisions that really count. Very unavoidably, the decisions that count, that matter to us and probably to others as well, are just the way life is, for it is frequently the case that some decisions are so hard to make, so neutrally equal in our mind, that either would be an acceptable decision.

The point is that we cannot live a day without making decisions. Decisions made after choices presented themselves to us. Most of the decisions are very minor. For example, what to choose to wear to work that day. If our choices are limited, the decision is easier. We may take other factors into account, which narrow the choices further. For example, if we get an interview with the boss, or an important client, we would probably choose to dress 'up' that day and we may only have one 'best' outfit, best suit. Or, it's no problem choosing which public school for our son because we can't afford it anyway.

However, when we come to consider some more important 'bigger' decisions, we may falter, hesitate and start asking others for advice. What do we do when one person's advice conflicts with that of someone else? Then we start wondering whose advice we should take, so we think our 'gut reaction' to the personality of each adviser and how we feel about these two people. For example, how we've always respected the first as a successful person, but we suspect he's never really liked us, while the second person's advice is like the person who gave it, easy-going, superficial, laid-back approach, as something which we admire in others but can't accept or come to terms with within our self.

And so the whole decision-making process becomes a pain, a worry, irritating, frustrating feeling of helplessness and confusion. Next, we're either smoking too much, or drinking too much, or eating too much or too little and not sleeping. What a bore it all is! No, it's not. We only have to make one decision and that is to take control (as we so like to call it) of our decisions, of our life. But what does that actually mean?

It's like this. Understand that any decision we make is a good decision, because when we make a decision we are taking control and moving forward. The essential element of life is change, it's unavoidable, so we need to accept it, accept it with good grace, even enthusiasm and determination to so influence those changes to see that they work out as well as possible for us and our loved ones.

So, it's good to make a decision. There is no such thing as 'the right decision' and no such thing as 'the wrong decision.' To think in such terms will restrict our ability to appraise life in a sufficiently flexible way and so to have that notion of being in control that helps us feel happy. We really ought to use the following words, as these will reinforce our new and correct attitude to the decisions we make, every day, by speaking of '*Really good decisions*,' which worked out well for us, and speak of the others as the '*Not so good decisions*,' the ones that didn't work out so well for us. We can say, 'That wasn't such a good decision.'

How can we best make decisions so that as many as possible prove to be 'really good ones,' and minimise the 'not so good' ones? We spoke earlier of choices, because awareness of these is vital.

We can and should only make a decision after we have identified, as best we can, all the possible choices. This is something we mostly fail to do, so it's no wonder things go wrong. Yes, we do identify choices, but frequently fail to identify all or enough of the choices, the significantly operating choices, the ones that will bring out the greatest effects as we evaluate them. Many of the major, most important decisions in our lives are made without properly evaluating all the options open to us. It takes time to think, plan and research all the choices. Often this research will cost us money, money which we think we'd rather not spend.

John and Jill are looking for a new house. They've seen two they like and are finding it difficult to choose. They write down all the points in favour and against for each house. They still find it difficult to choose. They briefly consider having each house surveyed but the cost is more than they want to spend, so should they have just one surveyed or neither? In the end, they choose neither and buy a house without researching all the available information. The cost of the repairs later found to be necessary turned out to be much more than the price of the two surveys.

So, it was not such a good decision not to have the house surveyed before purchase. They called it the wrong decision and fretted and felt moody and grumpy and upset about the inevitable belt-tightening budgeting to meet the cost of the repairs. Naturally, they were unhappy about it all.

What they should have said was: 'It is regrettable that we economised by not having a survey because then we either would not have bought this house, or we would have been expecting this extra expense of repairs. As it was our decision not to survey, we made a human error of judgement, that's all, it's not so bad, let's forgive each other (and ourselves) for our misjudgement. Now we will approach the challenge of putting the house right and enjoy the challenge of coping on a tighter budget until the repairs are paid for.

Life is here to be enjoyed, let's meet each situation as a challenge and meet it with good humour, optimism and forbearance. We can turn our back on feelings of guilt and inadequacy merely by adjusting the way we look at things. And this is one of the most fundamental decisions we can ever make. We can choose how we look at things. We can choose our attitudes. We can choose the way we feel about things and people. We can choose how we feel, and our moods, and we can choose what we think about.

There is a body of opinion which says that we should let our minds wander and roam at will. Few of us can afford such a 'luxury,' if indeed it is a luxury. We should regard it as something of a curse. To allow our minds to dwell on the past, and especially those aspects we view with regret, is to encourage our mood to be depressed, negative, forlorn and even desperate. To allow our minds to dwell on things that might 'go wrong' for us in the future is to cause ourselves worry and anxiety. To allow our minds to dwell on those aspects of our current life, which is less successful, or less perfect than we would wish, is to encourage an unhealthy attitude towards our life as a whole, lowering our self-esteem and tending to make us moody and even cynical. A good example of this is to wallpaper a room and then keep staring at the one small piece in the corner we didn't get right and become disproportionately focused on that one small mistake instead of standing back, looking at the room as a whole, admiring our work and discounting the small, now insignificant error.

That is to say, we have chosen to focus our attention on the room as a whole and we choose to look at our lives as a whole, those things we have, rather than have not. Most of us have two eyes, two hands, two legs. Most of us are housed, clothed, have a job, reasonably good health and good company. These are the things we can focus on. All those good things we take for granted, until they're gone. People recovering from heart attacks often approach the rest of their lives with a completely different outlook. They're glad to be alive and wished they'd recognised and valued their health before their heart attack.

So when someone next says to us that they meditate, we can ask them what they mediate about. They may not give an answer, other than to say, 'I just let my mind wander.' We could suggest to them that they could well choose positively and meditate about such as all those good things in our life. All the good, physical things, both our body that works as it should do, or at least as it has now adapted itself, or been adapted by medical or surgical help; and all the good, physical things in our life which support us and make us comfortable; food, clothing, shelter and food for the brain, a love of beauty, music and art; and also very vitally, all the good, worthy things which make us happy and fulfilled: friends, loved ones, success at work or sport. And we certainly don't want to give any pigs in our life house-room; no space to disrupt our meditating.

However, in the process of identifying all these good things, the overall picture of our life, we may well come to think about people less fortunate than our self. The cripple, we say, reminds us of our two healthy legs. There is so much suffering in the world that to reflect much and dwell upon it in our minds could frequently lead to feelings of sadness, depression and confusion about what we should do or how we should feel or think.

It is right we should be aware of such suffering and tragedies and we should choose how much we will allow them to affect us. We can decide to donate to a charity, or go and work for a charity, or offer to help a particular disabled person or even give up our jobs and go and work in some other country helping those working to relieve some situation or crisis. This would be a major decision in anyone's life, but for those who make it, often the decision-making process was easy because they just knew they had to give up their job and go and work in that foreign country. So, there was a strong element of desire, passion or emotion in the decision-making process, and provided as many as factors as possible having a bearing on the decision were identified and considered, then the element of emotion is approved.

We want to avoid the fraught recriminating situation where we have to blurt out, and for some even cry, possibly bucketsful, as we say, 'I am sorry. Sorry. I didn't think. I just didn't think; I never thought of that (or of them).' And likely as not, back will come the recrimination, 'No, you didn't think. You only ever thought of yourself, not of what you were doing to me, and to your children, yes, especially your children.' Avoid all this if we can. Whatever our passions, our desires, and the decisions they tempt us to, we need to work them through, as options for us, like we would on the chessboard, and as many of the optional ongoing moves and their consequences as our brains can take, or that we can fathom on our written-down list.

The emotional element is approved of because there is always an element of emotion in all our decisions. The emotional element must be identified, recognised and evaluated. The only way we lead our lives is by wanting and desiring to do, to have and to be. So, by thinking beforehand, well beforehand, preferably, what we want to do with our lives, what we want to do at work, at the weekend, with our holiday time, with our careers: and by thinking beforehand what we want to be, as in do we want to be fit, slim, healthy, attractive, married or single, be a father or mother, be a non-smoker, moderate drinker, be solvent, be rich, be clever, educated, well-read, be happy, content, cheerful? They become our 'adopted values.' By thinking, choosing and deciding beforehand, and imagining our achievement in advance that we are already being what we are aiming for, then we unleash our desire, passion and emotion in the daily decisions we make.

So, when meditating, that's what we need to be thinking. Only now there's a difference to the mystic guru's way of meditating: we do it on paper. When we are thinking and deciding what we want to do, to have, and to be, we need to write it down, again and again like 'lines at school' until it becomes driven into our subconscious. And then write the date. Why? Because, as we go through life, we will want to refer back to our lists, and we will want to revise the list. Why revise? Well, to be cruelly basic, it's no good any longer wanting to be a fighter pilot once over a certain age or if we've later found out that our vision is a bit defective. So, we revise our list. We could throw the old list away. That's our choice, but it's useful to keep old lists for a while, at least.

It is remarkable how often people ask for advice. Often other people are only too ready to give advice, even when it's not asked for. Often advice is not taken. Then those who give the advice are offended because their advice was not taken!

It's best if we don't give advice and never give advice and never ask for advice! If someone asks for our advice, we can politely decline, knowing we no longer believe in giving advice. So, what do we say? What we can say is, 'I will help you explore all your options. I will help you identify the possible outcome of each of your options. I will encourage and support you in you making your choice. I will help you identify your true wishes and desires, but I won't advise on what decision to make.'

When we adopt this approach, you may evoke a disapproving response. People often want to be told what to do, even though they may not do it. It's like, subconsciously, they want to shift the responsibility for the decision. For example, our teenage children may come to us for advice. We go all paternal or maternal, think how we messed up when we were young, think how lucky the kids are these days and tempted to tell them how they ought to behave. But we don't. We want our children to grow as self-responsible adults, so we offer to help them identify their options. But that takes time and kids just want a short, snappy answer; so they can go out with their mates and have a good time. We shouldn't fall for that, they'll come to respect us in time. In time, they'll make time to think about their options, talk them through with us, and love us for not being dictatorial, but truly helpful.

So, what about the 'not so good' decisions? Because it is impossible to know or predict how other people will act, how anything in life will turn out (e.g. a brand new car purchased, that was not affordable after all, and that we crashed): there will inevitably be many 'not so good decisions.'

So, we've laboured over identifying all the factors having a bearing on a decision which is now turning out to be 'not so good.' It's tempting to start doubting the decision. It's human nature in many of us, immediately to doubt a finely balanced decision very soon after it's made, and feel we should have made the other choice, but now it's too late. Yes, it is, and it's natural to doubt, and virtually immediately in the greater scheme of things, immediately to doubt, 'Have we done the 'right' thing?' Well, we really do need to reject those thoughts immediately, and be true to the reasons we made the decision. If it was that difficult a decision, we will have written the reasons down, so it's easy to remember and refer back to why we chose that decision. In olden times, some would write extensively daily in their diaries, including the reasoning in reaching a decision. Politicians and other 'top people' keep a diary of their thoughts and events in their lives, so when they retire they can write a book, hoping it will sell well, but at least publicise a justification for their actions when they were someone to be reckoned with.

So let's be true to the decision. Next, we need to make every reasonable effort to make it work. And then, if, after every effort has been made, it's still not working, we can re-evaluate the situation completely and set about making a fresh decision to improve on the matter, improve on our not so good decision that life has shown it to be and that's how it turned out.

Peace of mind comes from accepting we are responsible for the decisions we make; and from learning how to truly accept and forgive our self for all the decisions that do <u>not</u> turn out to be our better decisions. Some think that fate has a hand in the outcome of our decisions. It is not helpful to ponder and query if there is such a thing as fate. It is best to deny that fate exists at all. Only then we can accept full responsibility for our decisions.

Whether fate was or was not involved is immaterial. Planes fall out of the sky through the failure of some part or other, or human failure, or even rarely some or other meteorological event. Vehicles can crash for the same reasons. People get stabbed or shot by the maladjusted minds of the perps. To believe that there is someone controlling, some preordained life-plan for us to which we cannot help but adhere, like a tram on tracks, with no control over the points, is ridiculous, and it's called fate. So, we just made a bold decision that worked out well, and then people say to us, 'Well, that's fate.' That's why we say here, it's pointless arguing whether fate exists or not. Forget it, laugh at the notion. Just be sure we make the best decisions we can, and get to work on them as best we can.

Being older, we can reflect and say, 'I have wearily grown to live with and acknowledge all the damn fool stupid things I have ever done and even keep doing, well into old age and I have to forgive myself for them all, or well, nearly all, for the worst won't lie down, and keep recurring to haunt me, at times of reflection. But we don't necessarily have to accept that haunting. The art and skill of true self-forgiveness are hard-learned and are, like all skills, improving with practice. One of the best adjuncts to this self-forgiveness lies in the New

Testament, which states, in effect, 'if you truly repent you of your sin, then the sin is forgiven.' Very deep, very true. Hang onto that.

It's worthwhile noting, just to be sure that to achieve forgiveness of ourselves, that we do not, most emphatically do not need to make the often made mistake, made through a misunderstanding, that we need to make reparations with the person we have offended, the cause of our need to indulge in self-forgiveness. To attempt reparation can be so fraught that that pathway has to be very carefully trodden, with planning, tact and possibly with the help of a very understanding, most suitable and capable interlocutor; and they are pretty rare, hence the caution – and we suggest take a note of the thoughts written elsewhere in these lines, on the matter of trust.

However, we can gain some benefit and give help towards our peace of mind by writing 'the letter,' that letter where we would write to the person we offended so greatly. The damn fool stupid, even cruel thing we did, the one hugely great offence we have difficulty in forgiving our self for. That letter explaining and apologising for the genuine part, our part in the event, the happening that came about. And that letter, the letter, is the one that we have no intention of posting. No intention to post because to do so in many cases may very well be, may very well turn out to be, just another not so good decision. The writing of the letter, the setting in print, creates some orderliness in our mind; an orderliness of the coming to accept the realisation and the full responsibility for our wrong behaviour.

And that is why, if this letter-writing exercise is to be taken up, the draft 'I am sorry letter,' for Pete's sake (who is he?) do it in pen and ink on paper, and definitely not an email – it's far, far too easy to click 'Send.' No, sir, no, madam: absolutely best not sent by email ever. And not by post at all, ever, or not until we are as certain, as we can ever be, that it will do the recipient any good. And even then we must take no selfish account at all of how good we might feel in sending it, because however much the writing of it may salve our conscience, by sending it, that feeling could very likely soon be reversed.

There can be a habit in regularly making the same or similar decisions that can trap us into a complacency like we're on automatic pilot, a state of mind that says, 'We know what we are doing,' except that by life's distractions that are always popping up, we can slip up. Snap decisions can impress others, and even impress ourselves, when they work out well, and we can get to think we are better at this than others. Understanding and thinking about our decisions as routing choices for our life and sometimes the lives of others, yield the sense of a reasonably comfortable responsibility that is an essential ingredient of peace of mind.

CHAPTER 13
THAT BIG SIN, THOSE BIG SINS

One of the advantages of getting older, seriously older, in excess of the Biblical threescore years and ten, is that we have the option to look back and reflect on our lives, what has been, what could and might have been, and what should have been. What would we do differently if we could go back and do things differently? But what is the point? There's more chance of winning the lottery than going back and reliving our life as we would, if young again.

Of course we can all identify those silly stupid things we did, and if we can't because we can't remember them, then we'd have to rely on an old friend or acquaintance to remind us. That could be a cause of some embarrassment, even after all these years later, or perhaps we can't remember because we were never aware of those things we did, and said, that were taken as stupid in the first place. We must have been either very naïve, or arrogant.

And then our rambling thoughts remind us of our big sin. That big sin, that on recalling it makes our flesh creep. How bad that was and all its repercussions that hurt another, or more than one. Can we remember? It was obviously a major decision at the time. Did we ever write down the reasons we made that big, dramatic and painful step of one or more decisions? Write down the reasons why we jacked in that job, sacked that secretary, left our spouse, took that money we weren't entitled to. We can bet our bottom dollar that our big sins must have hurt someone else and yet here we are today, miles and miles further on in time, in our mind, from that or those events. That era in our life, when we just felt we had to do what had to be done, to move forward in our life, or as a person be bound thereafter to suffer and wither and shrink mentally; mentally frozen on the spot, unable to reach out for our full potential.

The way so-called big sins affect us when we are on the receiving end depends much on our resilience. If we are given the sack, whether justified or unjustified, and apart from any issues from a tribunal, we still have to get up after falling off the horse, and get riding again, get another job and put the sack from the old job down to experience.

Doing someone out of their money depends if they are aware of the loss and who they are. It all sounds very criminal, although some cases of fraud are so subtle that criminality is hard to prove. Money is important, but the degree of the importance varies so from one to another. To some, it's almost their whole life apart. And yet, some of the happiest, most pleasant and generous people we can ever meet in life are those whose income situation is not that good. Worshipping money never made anyone happy.

It's in the realm of personal relationships that the big sin, those big sins, endure. As implied we can get over, truly over, most things if we want, as said elsewhere in these chapters. And we can get over as in, 'I've got another job,' or 'I have another secretary.' We can work extra hard to restore any financial loss. But when it comes to the hurt of relationship breakdown, and if we stop to take the lid off the hatch where those unhappy memories, those negative experiences are stored, stored in the hold in the vessel of our life, it is then that the mayhem of bewilderment arises.

How did it come about that we did that? How did the marriage crash into the rocks and sink? We started the voyage okay. It's as one story in the book that starts with, 'It was damnable that Margaret had to get pregnant…' and so on. Who was Margaret? His wife? His mistress? His sister? The opening sentence is so telling and yet doesn't tell, but from the point of view of these writings, it's a human drama in the making and almost certainly a big sin is there somewhere.

And decades, later, musing in our armchair, we can ponder on those years ago and, if religious, we reckon on how we might fare on the Day of Reckoning, as the last trumpet sounds, all because of the skeleton in our cupboard. So, can we atone? Why should an issue that was 'dealt with' decades ago, a decision made, people hurt, people crying, people cursing us, still be unsettling? Did we feel a jerk then, a ratbag then, or were we resolute, firm in our resolve to justify our actions, and say, 'Sod them all?' And do we still feel like saying, 'Sod them all?' Or do we feel, now that most of our life has been led, as the school reports always say, 'Could have done better?'

Self-improvement gurus often say we should write the letter, the letter of apology, 'I am sorry for hurting you, for all the upset and unhappiness I caused.'

And then explain that which we didn't explain at the time, or explain then what appears to be our reasons now, our justifications as we feel them today, perhaps half a century later, in which case those reasons of today would have probably been rubbish then, nowhere near the real reasons that we had in our heart all those years ago. Just because we have written the letter doesn't mean we have to post it! And that's why it's best to sit down at the desk, table, dressing table, pub table, and not compose an email, because it's just too tempting to press send.

No, it's not always good, seldom, and even rarely good to actually send the letter, especially as long as 50 years later, 'I am sorry.' Of course, each case is different, but the exercise is deeply personal, specific to each sin. We need to be so fair, reasonable and introspective, balanced in our assessment of how 'the big sin' came about, for it is very rare that the 'blame' lies all on one side.

It's the same issue in a way as 'guilt throwers' and 'guilt catchers.' Surely, in our thirties that decade of our really growing up, becoming a really mature responsible adult, we really should have become responsible for our thoughts, words, actions and habits that we refuse to catch guilt thrown at us, and we certainly refrain from throwing guilt at others. We accept only that which we are responsible for; that for which, if appropriate, we are 'response' able, as in able to make a correcting response.

Now, at this time, looking back, we can muse and meditate, not exactly play a 'mind game,' but at least make a mental exercise and reckon on the guilt and its apportionment to our self and to another. Often we come out of this with the spine-chilling realisation that what we did then, for us, for us to move on and work towards a happier life we had to tread on someone, like an unwelcome spider. Except – that the spider 'bought' it and if we had to hurt someone, someone so vulnerable that they committed suicide, how could, how would we live with that, balance that in our mind for 50 years? Can it be done? 'If you leave me, I will hate you and hate you so much that I would rather die, so I will commit suicide.' Imagine having that said to you. And was then carried out, the deed done. Reckon that in our mind, then, and then, every now and then, when work or just our mind, is quiet.

Many may need counselling after such a sinister event, a huge event, and may eventually come to terms. We can put up a barrier of 'hardness,' rely on the cold reality of life that in the end, and probably from the beginning, we are responsible for our actions, our attitudes, what we say, think and do. We have choices, there are always choices. We see divorces and other extremely hurting situations within relationships are happening all the time, and that suicide is a rare outcome may reconcile us.

Just as people will find or make work for a livelihood, we need an income to live, the need drives us, so we have the need to get on with our lives, to live them as best we can, and as contentedly, even happily if we can. That is to say, we can't or shouldn't wallow in unemployment, although for some this is very hard indeed to get work, nor should we wallow in self-pity, or peevishness at the way we have been treated. And this is where the idea of 'sod them all' comes from; we get up, brush our self down and get back on that horse, then 'trot on,' and whilst tempted to blurt out, 'Cry havoc! And let slip the dogs of war,' we should preferably just shout, 'Sod them all!' and feel the better for it.

So that big sin is there, those big sins are there, but at our time in life, they are so far back they assume a 'story-like unreality,' and yet we know deep down we've done some hurt. It's so far back, and we don't know how it affected their subsequent life, for the worst, indifferently, or did a door to better things open for them? And when we look closely, very closely indeed into the detail of our life and our actions, motivations and options, we must know whether we would do the same or even 'have' to do the same again, perhaps even just to retain our sanity, we'd have to commit that big sin, tread on someone, just to move on, to be something living, and be our innate self, who we were, and who we had little or no choice, little or no other option to become.

But we cannot, should not, revel in the realisation that what we did, we had to. Rather, as age teaches us, acknowledging that those big sins are, 'It is life, Jim, and life, as we know it' (with apologies to Spock for misquoting him). And so there is the skeleton in the cupboard.

And with that acknowledgement comes, in our dotage, the knowledge that we can forgive ourselves for all the 'damn fool,' stupid, crass, cruel, wicked, thoughtless, selfish and for some regrettably necessary things we did, that hurt that person, those persons in our former life. The knowledge that we can, in the sense of 'le puissance,' (the power) for us to forgive ourselves, is rather different from being truly willing and so making us able to; but we do need to be able to and in a way that leaves us with the peace of mind we seek.

We can't just say, 'I forgive myself,' and walk away in an act that does nothing more than 'salve our conscience,' as in wipe a slate clean. No. We can never expunge our negative experiences in life. But we can relegate them to the vessel's hold and batten down the hatch. And that's what we do when we truly, skilfully, forgive ourselves for our errors. We accept responsibility, we acknowledge that responsibility, we know deep, deep down, we have done harm and we are truly sorry. We may even make reparations. Write the letter, we may even post it if we are sure, absolutely sure beforehand that it may do some good, undo some of the harm. But how would we know? Do some research? Clandestinely. Beware of reparations. We wish the Germans in 1871 and the French in 1919 had learned that lesson, to forgo reparations; rather more peace, (we can hope), would have supervened.

We don't forgive ourselves to 'salve our conscience'; we forgive ourselves only when fully contrite for our calumny. We can't prove our contrition to anyone, it's pointless and just as we should never share 'our goals' with anyone. Goals are deeply personal, and the art of self-forgiveness is a goal achieved. Frankly, the older we are, the more remote our great sin, those great sins, and the easier the self-forgiveness may come. But the enormity of the Big Sin is the same, and it has probably grown through the years. The more it grows, the more it bangs on the hatch that is battened down. And when sitting in the old armchair, we can let it out on a lead for exercise, go through it all, perhaps with a twinge of sadness, and add some more remorse, or rake over the ashes of the old remorse to rekindle it, and then pop the Big Sin back in the hold, and enjoy that peace of mind, now so well earned.

CHAPTER 14
UNCOMMON SENSE

Mothers of yore would often scold and shout at their early teenage children, before they grew too big, at their manifest lumbering and unco-ordinated clumsy attempts at life. Mothers scream with the words learned from their mothers and fathers, 'You haven't got the sense you were born with!'

Born with sense? What sense? We know the five senses, we learned them in biology at school. The senses of touch, smell, hearing, taste and sight. Yes, we were born with those, hopefully and hopefully still have them and are or should be very grateful for them; never take them for granted, they are so valuable to us.

But we don't always use them. And that's where the shouting and scolding come in. It's part of growing up. It's natural, so natural and commonplace that it's not that much worthy of distinction in these chapters. However, it is not really those five senses that Mum is shouting about. She is shouting about our lack of common sense, that evasive, hard-to-define quality of being streetwise. One can hardly teach it, but it can come from experience, often acquired the hard way through some pain; pain as in real pain, or pain in the pocket, or heart. Even pain as to one's undeserved pride, our false pride.

Common sense has much to do with reasoning and anticipation. Rather like a game of chess; our ability to work out quickly what the other side might do in response to our move, or our potential moves, just as there are almost always options on the chessboard, as in life. How to work them through in our mind, that's the skill. But if we go too far 'upfront,' we are getting away from common sense. The 'common' part applies, refers to everyday situations. Things like checking the cap is properly on the tomato sauce bottle before giving it a good shake; but not meaning the high wheeling and dealing in the boardrooms of companies engaged in mergers and acquisitions. That requires rather more than common sense.

We often hear of the sixth sense. It is associated with instinct. This instinct can visit us just once in a blue moon and by listening and reacting to it, it can save our life. Like the passengers who got off the *Titanic* at the last moment before she sailed because they sensed a feeling of something, very strongly, a foreboding with hairs standing up on the backs of their necks, or more likely an awkward, heavy feeling in the pit of the stomach with no rational cause? A 'gut reaction?'

This sense of instinct can be enduring in a way that some, the few, who are privileged to have this sense well developed, often listen to their instincts and set the course of their life after consulting it. They are not very numerous, but they are certainly the most charmed in life; but not always, for the worst of life's exigencies can still surround them as well as the rest of us. However, this sense of instinct coupled with 'common sense' go together as marvellous attributes. In fact, it is not very likely that anyone could usefully benefit from an acute sense of instinct without having developed a goodly dose of common sense while growing up. This is the sense that those who have it, hear it, listen to it, can be guided by it, refer to this sense as 'my angel' or 'my angels.' And they are virtually infallible. Their angels won't tell on which horse to put their last £100, but will guide them as to many of life's major choices and certain amazingly useful challenges in life, such as finding a car parking space. Yes, it's true, finding a parking space; believe it, some have it.

Little is said about the seventh sense. In the context of what has already just been said above, the seventh sense refers to the power of imagination and creativeness. It is what some have had through the ages, and they have advanced civilisation. Along with this sense, the innate imagination and creativeness can come solutions to the challenges in life, and can come to improve on what we already have. Part of this sense can come from never being content with what we have and so can use what we know and want, as more to advance humanity, its comfort on earth, freedom from pain, freedom from anxiety and hunger, but warm and so with a peace of mind and at peace with other people. A sense that drives us on, yes, and for fame and for fortune, too, for ourselves; but these are just the tangible fall-outs, the bi-products. It's the sense, the ideas, the inspirations that come, sometimes in the middle of the night, an idea that strikes as the answer to one's conundrum at work, or even not at work, perhaps nothing to do with work, an invention completely out of the blue. Like a concerto, there in the mind, every instrument, each note, each score. But then Mozart was a

193

genius, the extreme, the ultra-form of creative imagination in person. But then Brunel was a genius, too.

This inspiration, this seventh sense can be elusive. We may seek a solution to a challenge. Ponder and ponder. Strain hard to think, sketch and doodle and the answer still doesn't come; not even poor answers. The spouse says, 'Relax and forget about it for now, we are going out to dinner and don't you dare talk about work.' And there, bang, in between the soup and fish, the answer comes and what can you do but ask to be excused, leave the table, find a pencil and pad and write it down immediately? Inspired. Imagination. Seventh sense.

We can work on this, but gently. It is said all great men do their thinking on paper (and that includes women, too, of course). These days hardly anyone uses pencil and paper, but somehow it works, and is worth still giving it a go. Most of us need our other senses to be at rest while being 'creative,' meaning no distractions from family, loud music, cooking smells, alcohol and being uncomfortable.

But what this book really wants to talk about is the eighth sense. Yes, there is an eight sense. We know what it is, and yet it has never yet been referred to as the eighth sense. The eight sense is that sense of self, of self-awareness, of self-determination, eudaemonia (Aristotle). But it is more than that. It is the eighth sense that walks into the control room of our mind and pushes buttons and pulls levers that deal with the myriad of thoughts, both positive and negative, that keep coming, bubbling up from the saucepan of our subconscious mind and spilling over like boiling porridge, getting burnt.

We, that is us, our eighth sense, can, with training, pull the lever to cool the saucepan, to say, I reject those negative thoughts about that person. Another lever says I have mourned enough, now I must get on with my life. A button that says nothing is gained without some pain – I need to get some education to get a job to get an income, to get a life. Levers and buttons for all sorts of things, every decision, every feeling we ever have, we can learn to control our feelings and our thoughts by going into the control room, the old railway signal box, or if preferred go to the hamburger menu bars on-screen of our mind, go to settings, the setting of our feelings, scroll down our options and click to allow positive attitude or disallow negativity, hurt, blame, revenge, hopelessness etc.

Feelings bubble up from below, the subconscious, and they can run rife if we allow them an untrammelled existence. And they can take control of our conscious mind and interfere and misdirect our lives. We get sympathy and understanding from friends and family and antidepressants or Prozac from the Doc. No. No. No. It's not the way. We can meditate; quite calmly allow our minds into neutral, no drive; all peace and quiet to stop thoughts. Yes. Just stop. Each thought – stop it. Deny it time and space, so we can go into the control room. Ah! Here's a lever that says stop banging head on wall because it hurts too much. But we haven't been banging our head on the wall. No, not literally, but yes, metaphorically. Another 'make up our mind to be cheerful' lever. Yes, let's try that. Oh! But it's so hard to do.

But our eighth sense is so much more. 'He had the good sense to think things through before making his move.' The term 'good sense' is in common parlance, and we understand much by it. If we speak of someone having good sense, then he or she commands our respect, admiration and perhaps even esteem. And perhaps 'commands' is not the correct word, because there's no commanding here; we feel automatically, at least those of us with any willingness to accede and those of us with any sensibility to grant that we can have a higher regard for someone we think has good sense.

We need to be aware of our eight senses, to take care of them, to use, develop, value and appreciate them. Because they are worth it! Good heavens – whatever next?

CHAPTER 15
ON GENIUS

It is generally accepted that every now and then a genius appears amongst us, us as the human race, not just us, this family, this village, this city or even this country. The genius can be recognised worldwide. He or she is awarded the accolade for something done that is so excellent, so 'perfect,' so wonderful, so much better than the rest of us; for the rest of us. It could be in music, in physics, in surgery, science generally, but not forgetting civil engineering, and also the arts. Never in politics or statesmanship, but in military action sometimes, 'yes.'

Such people are inspired. A powerful visitation of their seventh sense. Their actions derive from inspiration they have received, inspiration that develops the wonderful skills, for example, through practice, practice and more practice of the expressive concert pianist. Inspiration that comes as a visitation to the creative super-mind of the composer of music, the designing engineer, the surgeon who seeks a better way, the nuclear physicist, the medical research worker, or even seasoned general, and even the unseasoned general, devising a warfare more designed to bring about as rapidly as possible the cessation of hostilities through victory, to return to, as Nelson 'coined it,' days of ease, and nights of pleasure.

Inspiration is of the power of good, the goodness within us, of God. All that is good is of God. There may seem to be inspirational actions that are basically evil, not of God. Hardly 'inspirational,' since inspirational literally should be taken to mean 'of or from the spirit that comes within us', that spirit meaning, the Holy Spirit, of God, of good. For Nazis to sit around a table brainstorming the question of what to do about the Jews when someone says, 'I know, let's kill them all in gas chambers.' Inspirational? Please, no, never. Genius? No, never. Pure evil? Yes. Pure? Yes, in this sense as in total absence of any goodness, a very, very dark place.

So, let's keep inspirational as a good word, for good only; let's not abuse and degrade the word with inappropriate usage for the negative thoughts of minds in the shade, in the darkness where the goodness has been blacked out.

Just as we accept that genius (in the plural 'genii' as was) exists amongst us, so we need to consider if simpletons also exist within humanity. We know the mind can be compared to a computer in many ways. The hardware being the basic neuronal structure, with the neuronal interconnections and nerve pathways; and the nerve impulses traversing the nerves and interneuronal synapses are the operating system. Do some have faster processing chips than others? Do some have more RAM than others? Very probably yes. But can these 'merits' or attributes be developed as an 'add-in' later, through education, training and experience and is it also automatically thus, as the software is loaded?

We may do well at maths and physics and go on to a career as an engineer. Others may do well in chemistry and zoology and go on to be a doctor. And so – loaded software – loaded as to what sits best, and suits the 'hardware' and the operating systems.

Unfortunately, the brain of the young develops so very fast, and in doing so, is fragile. This fragility renders it vulnerable to setbacks; setbacks that came from accidents of birth and as illness or injury, that can slow the brain, even disorder it. Other setbacks can come about from poor nutrition as to the proteins needed, the vitamins and minerals, all in balance, too much of one nutrient, too little of another. And setbacks from an inhibiting environment, negative conditioning from parents and rival siblings, 'bad' schooling from teachers and bullying peers.

Fortunately, the brain is phenomenally resilient and able to recover and go on to 'develop.' But it is not infinitely resilient and going on to develop does not necessarily mean to catch up. And so, in society we see a whole mix of 'minds,' of minds developed and developing, as in 'we learn something every day.' How true.

Where, then, should anyone pitch their message, their book? For very many centuries books have been the means of recording events and ideas. Some books have had profound effects on people, on whole groups of people, nations even. The Koran 'affects' millions and millions of people, perhaps as many as the Bible once did. Other books affect groups, such as Dr Spock's book affecting young parents bringing up children.

Books can become identified with a race or cult. The early Spaniards arriving in Mexico found a people with books, and in their fear and ignorance, the invading conquering Spaniards burnt all the books, every single one. Tragedy.

197

People go off people. A well-known fiction writer, sold many books, landed up in prison, and some people, including intelligent people like BBC managers, then burn all his books, as a sort of cleansing, ritualistic rejection of the author and, never mind the fiction that he wrote (it was really good and made him wealthy) but as a person, they said now we know he's a stinker, with an 'I deny that he is a successful, even inspired author and has given much pleasure to millions of readers!' How crass. What nonsense (as in no sense). Stupid. As if burning their books helps anyone. The same applies to the burning of flags. Also effete.

Books contain ideas and imagined stories, as well as lies. Hitler wrote *Mein Kampf,* which sold in millions and made him rich. Analysis later showed it contained mainly lies, so misleading readers, especially the innocent, naïve, and gullible, hungry and thirsty for some hope in their lives, their miserable lives, after the travesty of the Treaty of Versailles. What we are really saying here, is that in society, we have brains and minds (they are two different things) that vary widely, very widely, being at all stages of development, any one of them capable of developing something of a genius, potentially. If only.

If only what? If only our minds and our brains do not become dulled by boring, repetitive work, by alcohol, by nicotine, by 'substances,' by dull, boring, repetitive and crass TV programmes, and by dull, boring, repetitive and crass TV advertising. By the TV being on, inhibiting meditation time, or reading time, time for selective reading, intellectually selective. And, too, by the absence of an intellectual sparring partner or spouse. Someone to discuss, debate or argue a point with. As Austen's Darcy says, 'A mind improved through reading.' Not a mind dulled by non-use, misuse and by poor nutrition, dulled by lack of environmental stimulation, a change, a break or a holiday, or too much attention paid to social media, on smartphones. And a too inactive retirement.

The people Jesus wanted to reach were mostly the 'simple', everyday folk, villagers, crofters, carpenters, fishermen: in short, the artisans. He knew that the so-called intelligentsia of the Sanhedrin, the Pharisees, the Sadducees, the high priests, would all be too keen to hang onto their exalted positions, their influences on the people, their gold, their bigotry, their notions of what is religion, to hear what Jesus was saying. Just like the EU Commission, in a way, people whose opinions are their own, unchanging, like bigots.

No, Jesus's message was for us all and so it is simple. This book propounds a simple message, too, avoiding the highbrow, 'highfaluting' ideological expositions no one without a PhD can understand. If, at anytime, we find that we are 'blessed' or 'endowed' with a good brain, intelligent and perspicacious, and then 'crow' about it like a 'cockerel' on top of the hen-coop, then we'd better mind the farmer's wife or someone else doesn't take a pop shot at us and have us stuffed and roasted for Sunday lunch. Don't crow, even if you are or think you are a genius. We are not cockerels, and it will help if we recall that the deadliest sin of the Seven Deadly Sins is vanity. What sayeth the preacher? 'Vanity of vanities – All is vanity.'

Academics have traditionally rated their pupil's intelligence according to how easy, how quick the knowledge or skill they were trying to impart was picked up by the pupil. He or she is very 'bright,' they say. Bright pupils are easier to teach, and so make the teachers' day easier, their success as a teacher more easily reckoned. Fast learners can be held back by slower learners, hence streaming and segregation as in 'grammar schools,' then other schools. Bright children together collectively accelerate to a subject's progress. For political and for the perceived sociological difficulties of 'segregation,' streaming etc., has been slowed and rearranged to be as little divisive as possible, leading to massively impersonal 'comprehensive schools'. Correctness, perhaps, but isn't the end result nonetheless less than it could be? We now have a country 'staffed' mostly by people of a lesser education, with dumbed-down qualifications, second-rate 'First-Class' Honours degrees, and a country still vain, but struggling to find its way in the world. Happily its cultural mix is coming to the rescue.

It must be very tempting for academics to want to bring on the brightest students as fast as they can. On occasion we hear of a child of twelve or thirteen, already up to sitting 'A' levels. But is this at the cost of an all-round development? There is even a child genius competition. So refreshing.

However, there is a point. At anytime the brightness may fade, and also at anytime a child can become brighter, as if in an awakening. For them, there may be no real depth of knowledge, but knowledge and intelligence are two very different things. Many have knowledge, but lack the intelligence, especially to cope with life, or even use the knowledge they have. Each has their own intelligence. Many tests have been devised to 'test' so as to assess innate intelligence. That is to say, the supposed raw natural intelligence we were born with, that does not have and has not had the benefit from any form of education. Virtually all these 'tests' are flawed because, and this, surely is the point, education and life's experiences develop our intelligence. The two are inextricably mixed, they mutually interdepend almost. 'Give instruction to a wise man and he will yet be wiser' is the saying, and also 'reading is to the mind what exercise is to the body,' keeping it fit and active. This second idiom was coined in the days before TV, radio and the internet, but, considering the continuing high levels of book sales, reading is still very popular. For a start there are no 'adverts' to interrupt, and our eardrums are given a rest from the shouted advertisements and violent trailers.

The other problem with trying to assess intelligence is that there are different types of intelligence. Someone may be very good and 'clever' at school subjects, but hopeless in foreseeing that certain actions, say, in cooking, back at home, or in stacking crockery, something will inevitably happen, the food burns, the pile of crocks crash etc. So called 'barrow boys' in the East End of London markets have much street credibility and are more 'streetwise' than a cloistered academic, and they know far more ways to survive in a hard, sometimes cruel world filled with opportunistic villainy.

In a way, each of us has our own type of intelligence and that intelligence is not obvious, every day, as if hoist like a flag on a pole. Best just accept it's there. When interacting, or if suspecting a degree of obtuseness in someone, seemingly a dullard, have patience, my friend, have patience. Apparent obtuseness can be caused by language difficulties, a lack of vocabulary, hearing, shyness even, not an individual's fault, more of his or her upbringing, and whose parents themselves may have been disadvantaged by a deficient upbringing.

Difficulties in communication arise due to language itself, a shortage of word power, and the nation's language being attempted. They also arise from difficulties in expressiveness of thought, of articulation of that thought, through speech impediment, distortion of the reception of the spoken word through extraneous and competing sounds; through some lack of hearing ability by the listener's ears, deafness in other words; and finally through poor comprehension by the listening brain, interpreting the spoken word.

Any or all of these difficulties lead to misunderstandings, and yet intelligence has hardly become involved. Intelligence and education and life's experiences come into play when the listeners begin to make assumptions based on what he or she has heard, or thought they heard. Sometimes these assumptions lead to disastrous developments.

There is a very good case here for reintroducing elocution in education. For years, dialects have been accepted, encouraged even; for to criticise dialect is seen as too personal, too socially divisive, not inclusive enough for modern thinking. We are all supposed to be able to understand others' broad dialects, no more *send three and fourpence, we are going to a dance* (instead of *send reinforcements, we are going to advance*). People often assume that Nelson's dying were words were 'Kiss me, Hardy,' when it is just as likely that he actually said in his dying mind, either 'Kismet, Hardy' (Kismet meaning 'It is fate') or 'Kist me, Hardy,' (meaning 'Don't bury me at sea, put me in my sea-chest, my kist, and take me home'). Nelson could hardly be expected to enunciate clearly with a lung filling with blood, his system shutting down and every breath gasped and struggled for, from traumatic shock and pain, and we should not assume that the ears of those around listening were unaffected by all the roar and thunder of cannons repeatedly fired, and the screaming of orders, and the screams of dying, injured sailors. Ears were ringing, big time.

The story behind Shaw's Pygmalion typifies the ideal, when it comes to the matter of dialects and the vernacular. In the end, Miss Dolittle could speak 'posh' or speak 'cockney' where and when she chose, just as if she had thrown a switch. And this, then, is the point of elocution, and with it needs to go the vocabulary and the education to know that, in adult life, to succeed, and for the benefit of others, clear enunciation of speech will not only be advisable, it is also, arguably, very necessary.

However much some endeavour to achieve clear enunciation, some will have persistent difficulties, especially those of foreign extraction, whose native language from birth so formulates the tongue, the lips and the back of the throat to speak their own language that they can never 'get rid' of their 'accent' when trying to speak a new language. For example, it is said a Frenchman can never say the word 'whippet,' that much-loved diminutive greyhound, and pronounce it like an English person would. Many see a certain, even great, charm in the retained foreign accent in spoken English, and why not? Maurice Chevalier made a living out of his 'Franglais.'

Clearly, in this early second millennium, there is much not yet understood about intelligence and how it is 'shared out,' and how it operates within us, and how it manifests. We know, for example, that certain 'special needs' children, such as the young autistic, skilled at the piano, can have phenomenal powers of recall, to hear a piece of music for the first time, and then play it back on the piano immediately, note-perfect. Or take an artistic autistic child to a spot, say in the city, show the child a view of a handsome, ornate building, and the child will return home and draw what he or she has seen, perfect in every detail, as if a photograph, but, and here's the difference, the picture is 'reversed,' i.e. as if seen through a mirror. Miraculous? Yes. Genius? Yes. What is genius? This is genius. The amazing human mind. We can speak of being maximally self-actualised, with our capabilities reaching out to an ever-expanding 'envelope,' with us having no unfulfilled potential.

It is remarkable, totally remarkable, what some are capable of, and so we ask, can we do that? That we can do something, something more, that may turn out to be great, is accepted. For that something, whatever that is, when it comes about, if truly inspirational and great, we may be rated as 'genius,' in that one aspect; but most likely we will have to have departed this life before the accolade is awarded.

CHAPTER 16
CO-HABITING NATIONS

People treat history as if it were fiction, a novel without any message. They'd rather live their own lives, so to make their own history and thus their own mistakes.

Britain has for 300 years variously paid out, bribed and otherwise funded France, Prussia, Austria and even Russia and even fought so that no one nation would rule Europe and thus threaten and bully the British. The still newish, in historical terms, nation state of Germany has thrice trounced France in the 150 years since its creation 1871; she has smashed Poland more than once and even thought she could run over Russia; but then so did Napoleon.

Terrified of Germany now since 1945 the French have hoped their nation, once so proud, cultured and powerful, would do best if they 'cosied' up to Germany and by doing so has made Germany more powerful, and so to dominate the EU. She's like a boyhood gang leader who grows stronger and more of a bully by the fawning, frightened support of the followers in the gang.

Britain, as ever seeking peace after two world wars, joined the EU once de Gaulle was no longer there to oppose our entry. He opposed it because he knew we were too strong in personality to live compatibly in such a close relationship of business that joining the EU meant, and we drive on the left, think in pounds and ounces, and measure in feet and inches. Non, was always his reply, and he'd had a bellyful of Churchill during the war years, as we nurtured the French general in exile. These are the things that matter, fundamentally. Merging of political objectives means nothing when you drive on the wrong side of the road.

We joined in the belief that peace would be assured through the trade that would follow. History would have taught us that hostilities have arisen by the actions of politicians, not businesses in trade. Britain was still trading with Germany in 1914-15, even though we were at war with her. Once discovered, the trade was stopped.

It is NATO that has kept European peace since 1945 not the EU. When Balkan troubles came, the EU did nothing. NATO settled it, in 1995 and again in 1999. Germany is the powerhouse of Europe, the paymaster of the EU and probably always will be. That is why she has to be respected, but is also feared and hated by many who can put up only a token resistance. It is significant that the accounts of Germany and France have not been signed off by the EU auditors for years, because the accounts show the degree of disregard these top EU nations have, or rather the regard they have not got for the EU financial rules they themselves wrote. So it's do what I say, and not do as I do. Typical calumny.

So, what is the EU about? Peace? Trade? Or one nation-state socialism through a bureaucracy called federalism? The EU is certainly not democratic in the sense of British democracy. Its systems are not democratic, but big and clumsy and very costly as in 'expensive' (as in it costs more than it's worth) through different languages, economies, culture and aims.

For the majority of its citizens, the countries' peoples just want to go about their daily lives in as comfortable, peaceful and pleasant a way as possible. Politics is something that they really only turn their attention to at election time, for with them, once the election is over, there is nothing they can do politically speaking but accept their lot dished out until the next election.

Democracy only really stands a chance with smaller units, where voices can be heard and so make a difference. This is why so many Scots want to break from the UK, and why power has been devolved to them and to Wales and Northern Ireland, to further the interests of democracy.

We are essentially tribal animals. We like to live in villages like colonies. Even in cities, we live in villages. We form esoteric coteries to be a meaningful part of, where we know who people are and can interrelate with them. We can only absorb one or two new people, strangers, at a time. We are struggling to accept the very large number of immigrants, whether asylum seekers or economic migrants. It should not be overlooked that, however objectionable it may appear, several philosophers have mused that any large number of people acting together, bound by a religion, with alien cult practices, languages, dress and manners, can effectively be looked upon as a race of people, and large numbers of a race will affect and change the host nation's indigenous ethniculture.

Population density is an issue that is ignored when considering these matters and the immigrants are increasing their numbers yearly by the state's funded assistance, making for an easy fecundity that is childbirth. It is a little-known fact that the England is already the most densely populated country in Europe, measuring the known numbers of people against the areas of habitable land. Excessive densities of any species of mammals leads to disease, fighting, bullying, perversions, including sexual perversions, infertility and suicide, to name but a few of the evils of overcrowding.

It is the law that distinguishes us from the animals, that is to say we voluntarily choose to live within the law, set and varied from time to time by our lawmakers in parliament. With so many fundamental differences in basic law between EU countries, it is difficult to see how its peoples can live to be content. For example, in the UK we hold firmly to 'we are innocent until proven guilty,' but in other countries the way their laws are used and interpreted to achieve their justice varies country to country. Since devolution is so much an issue within the UK, i.e. to have more laws made by locally elected individuals, why would we expect remote people, unelected by UK voters, to be making laws that affect the people of the UK?

The EU Parliament is a sop to democracy. The real issues are managed by the nations' leaders, with Germany taking the dominant role. Those leaders are elected to govern their countries, not to govern the EU, and those leaders, unless they are themselves elected Euro MPs, should have no place in the EU Parliament debates and decisions. The Euro MPs are supposed to be doing that, but effectively they are toothless. The major policies as well as the pettifogging minutiae that run our daily lives are managed by the EU Commission, the EU Court of Human Rights and the EU Court of Justice, with their strings pulled by the founding big nations' leaders.

The EU Commission, the EU Court of Human Rights and the EU Court of Justice, all of them – every 'man jack' of them – are unelected in the British sense of these things, but more by a complex arrangement of committees composed of heads of governments and the European MPs. And they're well paid; the gravy train, snouts in the trough. Not that it's necessarily the fault of any individual. After all, if someone puts down a trough with food in it, hungry snouts will find it.

This is why the June 2016 UK Referendum was, is, so important. It is all about how we choose to be governed: return to the democratic government we know that has run the UK for many hundreds of years, or submit to the ever-increasing inevitable march towards a state that is a socialist, federal, bureaucratic oligarchy. Britain has been called the seat of modern democracy, the 'Mother of Parliaments.' Shame we ever were duped into thinking we were just opting to join a trading organisation.

That referendum and Brexit were not a question of being better off, or about immigrants or even about defence, as these issues all will be resolved according to the outcome of the referendum. It was about who governs us and how we wish to be governed. Brexit will be rather like marriage; you choose and then set about making it work on a 'for better or for worse' sentiment and it's best to say, 'You do it because of love.' And as they of the fair sex (are we still 'allowed' to call females that?) also say, 'Marriage is about finding Mr Right and then spending the rest of the time improving him.'

The question of Remain versus Brexit is not at all an easy one, and not at all as easy as just thinking about our view of democratic government. There's no reality in thinking of our 'Mother of Parliaments' as the ideal way of governing our own lives. One person, one vote sounds fine, but it's not quite that straightforward. In reality we live in a two-party parliamentary democracy, in which elected members, one from each constituency, align with one political party or another, and human nature being what it is, there are also a few oddments of so-called fringe parties, often looked on as either irrelevant cranks, or those who choose to dodge mainstream party voting and so dodge their responsibilities to the party system, as in 'it's a cop-out.'

The members of those two parties in general are 'supposed' to adhere to the official party line on issues, mostly decided by the party leader and sometimes by the inner cabal of favoured Ministers. Ah. Well, that's one person, one vote out of the window. Why? Because we have, by custom and practicalities, to rely on the judgement, not only of our elected representatives, but also especially the whims and determinations of the party leader, and, in the case of the ruling party, for the time being, the leader who also happens to be the Prime Minister. Mostly what he or she says, goes.

The committees of parliament do much good work grinding out clause by clause for new bills, and the committees are made up of members from 'both sides,' but many of the major issues that arise, world issues and defence or offence, land at the feet of the Prime Minister. At least he or she is our Prime Minister, for us, exclusively for the UK. Would we ever come to feel that the first elected President of the EU would be our President? Would we trust him or her on their judgement whether to go to war with Russia, or China, or the USA, or Saudi Arabia? Heaven forbid.

So, on the whole, we see our vote counts for so little, and what's more, we can never seem to agree with, or like, anything either of the two biggest parties want. Nor do we want any of the also-ran parties with their tiny-wee smattering of irrelevant members, elected on a 'by the way,' how about my odd-thinking party's representative, elected by a freak-thinking few, just to prove the system allows it.

Why vote, knowing this, why would anyone ever vote? That is a very silly notion. If we all thought like that, then there'd be no one elected at all, and chaos would take over and lead to the coming about of a despot, a dictator with a police state. To think our vote has to be important enough to influence the political conduct of the country is sheer vanity. Our vote is like a grain of sand on the shore. With enough grains of sand heaving against the breakwater we can shift it, realign it, the way we want it; we need every grain of sand we can get. Or we can align with all the other grains of sand and build up a headland, that then just grows and grows, like Dungeness that grows a metre a year and so the parties' need for all the grains of sand that can be had is just the same.

There is no excuse not to vote, unless stricken so ill at voting time. Our two-party parliamentary democracy's survival depends on everyone voting. There no real need for anyone to say, 'They don't know what the issues are: all parties seem the same, just out for their own,' and other such guff. Whatever our education, whatever intellect we have been born with, or have developed since, we can find out what it is that fundamentally divides the two main parties, and then make a choice. Ah! But how to find out? Should we listen to their promises made at election time, they call the hustings? Should we take any notice of their smiles, and their kissing of babies, their flamboyant posters and leaflets? Surely they should be able to summarise what they stand for in an easy sentence, or if not one, then just two; so we can see, at a glance, what we prefer, at least on this occasion, for this election. We can always change our mind at the next, having seen how our last choice worked out for us, and for the country. Surely, we could allot the same length of time to researching the parties' principles as we do to watching a commercial break on TV in the middle of our favourite programme?

It's for the good of the country, for the country. Is anyone really interested in how our vote worked out 'for the country?' Isn't the only thing that matters, 'how it worked out for us?' Us as in I, me, me-incorporated, and now 'Me.com,' running the business of my life? We may feel an empathy for our out-of-work neighbour and friend, but we are doing okay, had some good pay rises since the last election. Would we vote to change the government because our friend is out of work while we are doing okay?

So, there is no excuse not to vote, but plenty of excuses, sadly, for not knowing which party to vote for. Women in particular should always feel they should vote, for the sake of their forebears who fought and fought so hard for votes for women. Raising a family, while holding down a job, keeping the house clean and the children in order, while 'hubby' doesn't help much, it may not leave much time to listen to or read what are the current political issues of the day. And dare she vote in the opposite way to her husband: doesn't he mostly tell her what to think?

There really are only two elemental and fundamental issues that we face in our lives. They keep cropping up all the time, but we seldom recognise them as individual but opposing issues, opposing principles. They are ethics on the one hand, and finances on the other.

Money is the evolutionary result of collectivism. Collectivism is that feature of society that has come about by centuries and centuries of 'specialisation' of mankind's creativity; bringing us away from the caveman's need to provide all that he and she need to sustain their existence: the hunting daily for food, the disembowelling of the carcase prior to cooking on the fire that he or she has at last managed to relight, and then will later tan the hides and make them into clothes. All to get by, just to exist.

Nowadays, we use money as the means of exchange for each other's skills; each skill representing a small portion offered to society needed collectively for the many to exist. But collectively we needn't only exist, we can do more that exist; society has become so efficient in the 'essential providing,' for the exchange of some money, the bartering unit, and in such efficiency, that we have some spare time in our lives and some money left over for some fun.

On the other hand, ethics are to do with the matters of our love of life, and the notion that, in our love of life, we do not impinge upon someone else's love of life. Just as money has evolved as a bartering unit between us, and we exchange some of what we have for some of what we want, so ethics has evolved as the unit of behaviour that in effect is the courtesy we should always extend to each other, mutually to exchange for what we both want in order to get along. Just as the legal intricacies of money are governed by laws created in parliament, so is much of our conduct governed by laws similarly created and the observance of those laws is part of the code of behaviour that should govern our lives, so to get along.

But ethics are rather more than this. They involve not only the rightness, and the fairness between us, but also the consideration of the feelings of another, and involve altruism, granting another something ahead of granting it to our self. And in that potential to grant, we become torn between wanting it for ourselves, which can often involve money, but just as likely involve the concept of morality. Should the caveman go as far as to kill his neighbour to take that man's wife; should he go any way, any distance, in the conduct of his mind to seek to deprive another of what he wants for himself? Don't animals just take what they want, according to their courage and their physical strength and their position in the pecking order in their animal society, the herd, the pack and the flock? The possession of wealth imparts a position in our pecking order and a strength that can be used just to take what the rich person wants, not matter who it hurts. Money versus ethics.

Ethics become part of our love of life, and that love that implies we want others to be maximally self-actualised; a love for our self, yes, but more a love between us and others, including even the concept of a 'love' between nations; although the national leaders would hardly admit to that notion in their attempts at getting along. There should never be a rigid inflexibility, such as that exhibited by the EU leaders in the Brexit negotiations. Consideration of the long-term relationship that inevitably will happen as life rolls on, must be taken into account. Ethics, the love of life between the two parties, must take its place at the negotiating table. See how the male leaders of one country meet and greet the female leaders of another country with a kiss on the cheek, and in some cultures the male leaders embrace each other, even to the extent of a kiss on the cheek that's so 'foreign' to the stiff-upper-lipped British. Although all that so-called British 'reserve' is being corroded away, in our modern society, where seemingly now anything goes, such as 'think anything' and whatever it is, it's okay by the world, be it considered impolite, as in a mode of dress, or vulgar, as in mode of speech. No, we don't consider impropriety or vulgarity as anything much today. As long as everyone is happy and relaxed. Oh yeah?

It is a sad reflection that with the civilised lives we lead as individuals, as families and as a country, ethics and finances so frequently clash. The ideal versus the cost. As in changing our vote to give our out-of-work neighbour the better chance of employment, whilst risking our own pay rises, or even risking our job, and so our livelihood supporting our young growing family; or would we? Hardly.

And this is the rub, so clearly spelled out by an ex-PM, just before the Brexit Referendum, in his attempt to tell us what to think, what to prioritise from his point of view. In effect he said, 'Be better off if we stay in the EU, we shouldn't bother our heads about democracy.' Well, he would say that, wouldn't he, in his blatant disregard for parliamentary democracy in his time, but he did give greater democracy to the kilted warriors north of the border who still chant 'London is too remote'. Well, many think Brussels is too remote. The ex-PM doesn't hear that. So often we will hear the siren call, 'Be better off,' implying by fair means or foul, and even by questionable conduct, or by greed. So, it's a case of 'Let's not think about what's ethical, or think about what seems right, what's just, fair and of probity, or the dictates of our conscience.' Dare we hear it, in our heads?

And so, we agree to disagree, all those Brexit versus Remain. Be better off (they say) in Europe or be worse off with more and better democracy (which they don't say); more local decisions, being governed by people of our own upbringing, and don't brand people guilty merely by saying, 'J'accuse.' It's a judgement call.

In the end, we are but a grain of sand. We get what is dished out. What small influence have we, if any at all, over our national decision-takers? In truth, we have little enough, unless we can bang the drum loudly and with others, enough of others, to make a cause heard and felt.

We may or may not get the leaders we think we deserve, but they are the ones we have got, a heady mix of types and motives. We can only hope that a sense of honour and duty will prevail as their ethics, while they seek to improve our personal money. They are the law-makers, and they above all need to respect and observe the law, being always mindful that the laws of another land may conflict with those of ours.

PART FOUR

OUR NUMBER HAS
COME UP

CHAPTER 17
THREE IS A GOOD NUMBER

Most of us from childhood have a favourite colour and a favourite number. There may be no rational, valid reason why we choose such things, prefer such things. Colour is easier to reckon, but a favourite number? Do we go by some previous experience, a stroke of good luck, as in our number came up at the village fête raffle, as in ticket number 7 came up, and we got to choose our prize?

There is no rhyme or reason why we should stick at having just one favourite number: why not have several, we suggest as many as half a dozen? There are several numbers that can be brought to bear upon our sensibilities, as we carve a wake through life, en passage, cruising along to who knows where in the end, but we do believe it to be a worthwhile journey, and each number gives us the assistance we can best have on-board. We often adopt as a certain 'aide-mémoire' a word, a phrase or a number that can be associated with an idea, an aim, or a reminder of something more complex.

Offered here are a series of numbers that can be the basis for structured thinking, a way of living or trying to live to one's adopted guidelines, guidelines that we may want to set for ourselves towards a happier existence, towards more peace of mind. Let's call them our Cardinal Numbers. Cardinal after the Cardinal Points of the Compass, pointing in a direction. The numbers stand out from other numbers as chosen to represent something or other that leads us as an aide-mémoire, triggering thought-processes when we are under challenge or even when just meditating, helping us. The numbers are Three, Five, Seven, Eight, Ten and Twelve. We can describe the reasons behind each one, so here goes.

Three is a number.
The joke is that the best number for a committee is an odd number and three is too many. Three has tremendous influences on our everyday lives. The Romans

ruled with their triumvirate, three strong (as in strong-minded) men, ruling well for a while but then man's nature reverted to all the power vested in one. Britannia has her trident. Three is a very important number in our life.

Three is for the Trinity, the concept of God, Jesus, 'His son', and the Holy Spirit, 'His messenger.' One of the criticisms Islam throws at Christians is they believe Christians 'worship' three gods, which they say would be very wrong; there can only be one God. But sadly they, those Muslims, are mistaken, and quite wrong in their thinking or understanding. Even some Christians are uncertain how to look at the Trinity.

The answer is to think about the example of the three physical states of water. The water molecule denoted and known by almost everyone as H_2O, when frozen is called ice. Ice is hard, solid, rock-like; you can build hotels of ice, it can sink ships. That sense of the solid, the rock, the dependable, is like God of the Trinity. And, if you like, it represents the 'father of H_2O' because it is there solid over a wide range of temperatures, albeit all very cold ones, but it is tangible.

Liquid H_2O, we all know as water is the molten phase of ice. It flows, it seeps into almost anything, everywhere. It just seeks its own level, under the influence of gravity. It cannot be compressed but transmits applied pressure through itself to perform a purpose. We need it to live; it's a component part of our bodies, possibly as much as 65% or so. It refreshes us, both externally and internally. We enjoy it. Water is the Jesus of the Trinity, but it is still H_2O, the same molecules as ice.

Water evaporates at normal and raised temperatures into invisible steam. Steam is often identified as water vapour, which is visible, but steam is actually invisible. It is everywhere to a greater or lesser extent. We only think about it either when its molecular agitations slow down, it cools a little and becomes water vapour, which is visible, tiny droplets of liquid water we all call steam. And the engineers think about it very much and trap the energy in steam into a driving force. Steam is analogous to the Holy Spirit, invisible, charged with energy, everywhere, all around us. It is still H_2O.

And so, the Trinity is just God, that all-powerful, ever-seeing force of goodness, not only capable of appearing to us in three ways, but does so, all the time; the 'mystery' of the power of God, the power of goodness, of goodliness, and there, omnipresent, omnipotent, there, just waiting to be received and embraced; and adopted. No question of three Gods. Awe, shucks – huh! What a notion!

This book presents, even argues perhaps, that God is a life force for goodness. It is written in the Bible that God made man in 'His' own image. Certainly, we have evolved from more primitive creatures over many millennia, whatever brought that about, the origins of life, scientists may come close to understanding. Not for a moment, not even a second should we assume that God is a humanoid, a hominid, a being from space, green skin and strange wrinkles, anything like those creatures from outer space conjured up in the imaginations of the scriptwriters of *Star Trek* and *Star Wars*. No, the nearest we can currently be satisfied with is that by 'the same image,' is meant we can only exist and survive through goodness and love, and the love of goodness. It is who we are, and what we are. It makes us human, imaginative and creative. Not always are such thoughts, such awarenesses, at the forefront of our thinking, our daily lives, and as we habitually live them.

But is God a sentient force, with a plan for us, for the world and wider, creating our fate, individually and collectively? Does the force of electricity have a plan before next 'discharging its power' once released by the human throw of a switch? Does gravity have a design for us, or is it just that we, as in our physical bodies, are subject to its power? The answer is no, no and no. No design upon us.

God does not have a design for us and there is no fate that has been designed for us. But God does have a desire for us. We are free beings, with free will, with the free choice to accept God as a necessary force in our lives to grow and thrive. Beyond that there is mystery, and that is the attraction, the warm feeling of unexplained confidence, that which makes life. Consider a lettuce growing in the garden. It is growing, it is alive; it is composed of cells, alive with their metabolism. We pull it up; it dies, but slowly, as the cells gradually cease their metabolism. Removed from its source of water and nutrients, and from the daylight, from the power of the sun, the plant life dies.

Consider a spider: equally made up of cells busy with metabolism, structurally and anatomically wonderful in its way, alive. We stamp on it. Crush its anatomical architecture, destroying the interrelationship of the cell structures that make up a spider. And those cells, an instant before, were living, thriving, now rapidly dying, and then dead. Microscopically many cells may look unharmed by the crushing, but again their source of nutrients, mainly oxygen and glucose, will have stopped as the primitive circulation within the spider comes to an abrupt halt.

Consider us, alive and well. A bullet stops our heart, our 'nutrient lifeblood' source stops, and the cells within us slowly die as their eventual source of nutrients, like the spider, stops abruptly. A bullet through the brain has the same effect, as it is the brain which keeps the heart carrying on beating.

The point of all this is that the essential component of life, the process known as metabolism in all the cells that make up life in animals and man is fragile and totally dependent on that source of nutrients, oxygen and yes, sunlight. All those thousands of biochemical reactions going on in each cell, cells multiplying, dividing all the time. What is driving them? It is the mystery (as yet) of the life force. Scientists and others conjecture that early primitive life came about through the chance and admixture of certain complex molecules in a nutrient 'soup,' in a world many billions of millennia ago and they may be right. But look at man today, all that man has become, all that he has achieved, through science and all that man can create, things tangible and intangible through man's intelligence and imagination. Far, far superior to any other living thing, by evolution to a hyperintelligent, humanoid ape, sentient, in every sense of the word, with feelings, and feelings of love, in spades. Is this as a result of God's design for us? No, there is no design, as we have said, but we are susceptible, evolved only because we are susceptible to that force of goodness, that form of creative love.

Consider a surgeon in his/her work. How often do we hear that so-and-so surgeon has developed a new technique and new piece of equipment to achieve better surgery, quicker recovery, higher success rates? It took creative imagination, and that is the power of God within us. When Jesus healed, He said, go your way and tell no one, but they did tell, as He knew they would. So it is with our surgeon, being awarded accolades for his/her invention, who has to be aware of the option to be vain in that achievement or to opt for modesty. It is the case of going for one of the five values or one of the Seven Deadly Sins.

Of Jesus in the Trinity, matters are just as complex. We know the story of His life as recorded in the Gospels, and what a wonderful story. Born of a virgin: now that's a miracle to start with.

It is thought the Gospels were written some time after the death of Jesus, perhaps half a century. So, in the absence of any contemporaneous writings, we have to assume that much is anecdotal. At the time of that King Herod (there were several kings called Herod) and the Roman rule of Israel, there would have been chroniclers whose job it was to record events at court to do with matters of state.

How the details of Mary, her visit from the Holy Ghost and all that followed leading to her delivery of Jesus in the stable came to be set down in writing is not known. The flight to Egypt, Jesus's early life and then His baptism by John, the time in the wilderness, His temptation by 'the Devil',' His gathering of the twelve, His healing, the disciples healing etc. etc., up to His entry into Jerusalem on a pony or a donkey (opinion differs) – all of this is written in the Gospels, but how and where did the detail come from? How did it survive the 50-odd years from Jesus's life? Could there have been many letters written about Him, written contemporaneously or heard contemporaneously, perhaps freshly told anecdotes of His events, written by some literate elders in the society which ultimately were collated into the Gospels? Did Jesus come out of the desert and tell anyone who'd listen how He was tempted by the Devil, relating, 'Get thee behind me, Satan.' It's a good story, but is there any truth in it, and if so, where did the truth come from? Dare we accept such stories at face value? Could there have been such a thing as a weekly village news-sheet? On what would it have been written?

We know how people like to talk about events in their lives, to relate to others what they have seen, and then what they have been told others have seen or have told to them. We pass it on to our children and our grandchildren, sometimes in graphic details by those with a good eye and memory for detail; others whose story becomes 'send three and fourpence we are going to a dance', instead of the original story, 'send reinforcements we are going to advance'. Meaning that we should not necessarily believe all we read. So much can be lost in the period of time, in any translation, from first into one language and then from that language into a second and a third language and so on, through changes in the use of words through the centuries, despite the intense scrutiny of ancient scrolls by learned academics. A sort of Jesus 'suffered under a bunch of violets' situation.

The things to identify about Jesus are the miracle of His birth, the miracles of His healings, the miracle of His rising from the dead (but not in a form that He can be touched). These are the things we can believe or not. The one thing that is incontrovertible is His death upon the cross, because it was chronicled by Pontius Pilate's court recorder.

The Museum of Torture in Assisi, Italy, is a record of all the instruments of torture designed to break a person's silence and tell; there was no real thought or concern as to whether the person survived afterwards, having told what they knew, or told what they thought the torturer wanted to hear. But surely crucifixion was as cruel as any form of torture but with intention of causing death. To see that the victim could withstand the initial nailing through the hands and feet, the drink of strong herbal anodyne (pain-killing mixture) was administered – if only we knew what these herbs were because they certainly must have worked.

Without the drink many would faint and possibly die there and then while being nailed to the cross due merely to traumatic and 'surgical' shock. And that would defeat the object of those rulers who were condemning him, wanting their pound of flesh and yes, with the blood. The drink was so effective as to allow the crucified to hang by their nailed hands, pressure eased by their feet held against a block and some weight taken by the buttocks on another. They didn't want them to die too quickly; but after a few hours, and then bored by the spectacle, and certainly if not dead in time before the Sabbath 'started' at 6pm Friday, the legs were broken with clubs, which caused sufficient additional pain and then hypostatic shock (pooling of blood in the lower extremities) that the subject died. That is to say, the state had had its fun, provided the crowd with their ghoulish entertainment and/or its satisfaction, and now the party was over. Surely this is as cruel as any torture. But if we were to crucify a proven terrorist today, some would say it was justified, but surely not a completely innocent man? And that was Jesus, His miracles, His suffering, His message, He of the Trinity.

And now to the Holy Ghost, the third party to the Trinity. What do we understand by the Holy Ghost? In general, we tend to be frightened of ghosts as we are never sure whether we believe in them or not. If in doubt, we sometimes go looking for them in places, situations and circumstances where and when they are reckoned to roam. Graveyards on stormy nights at full moon, ancient buildings that creak in the night, usually where someone died an early, unfortunate or tragic death; was murdered, that epitome of evil unleashed. Ghosts are ethereal, can vanish into the 'ether', that supposed medium between the molecules of oxygen and nitrogen and the rare gases that make up the atmosphere. They show themselves by forming themselves into a 'plasma,' appearing like 'steam' (meaning water vapour), as a white, 'faintly' luminescent, almost opaque-like matter that moves effortlessly through walls, doors etc. – usually not floors or ceilings, so perhaps they, too, are subject to gravity? Are all these 'reports' emanating from the imaginations of the highly imaginative, or is there something in it?

Much reference is made to angels and archangels and all the company of

Heaven. If it is hard to understand what that, or they, might be, it is certainly much easier just to imagine there are such things and accept. If that that is our 'soul' is ethereal, then, like a ghost, it can exist, and in time join all the company of Heaven. There are people who are sufficiently psychic to be aware of 'their angel' or their 'angels' through whom, or through which, they lead much of their lives, drawing strength from listening to their angels. This is all crackers to some who haven't ever been in need of any sort of communion with his or her angels, mostly because they have never either experienced their presence, or known about such potential phenomena, or even pondered or thought of such things, or hearing of them, knowing what others think, they just deny their existence. Many others just marvel or stay in doubt. To so many of us, ghosts do exist, in one form or another, certainly never malignant, as is fantasised at Halloween. What a perverse thrill that is for those seeking some 'harmless' and banal fun. Let's be rightly understood here. There is no force for evil – there is only absence of goodness. Just as there is absence of light producing shade, shadow and darkness. Light is the good, shadow is the absence of good. The Holy Ghost is what transforms from the latent ethereal force for goodness, and being universal, omnipresent, is waiting and seeking out a receptor in us, and enters our soul, nourishing our spirit, our esprit de corps. *'Come Holy Ghost, our souls inspire and lighten with celestial fire,'* are the opening lines of a splendid hymn, so full of meaning, yet hard to sing, needing a very mobile 'Adam's apple,' as the notes go up and down like a yo-yo!

The Holy Ghost does its work. It doesn't take a form or shape. But angels may do, or do in our imagination: our minds can be tricked by imagination into seeing things, like our angels, so that in that sense they are real, but also *Noli me tangere,* see, but can't touch. How inspiring. How educating. How enlightening and how uplifting. Easy to those practised at logging in to their supra-conscious mind. Of course, the term 'ghost' for the Holy Ghost, in this day and age, of internet and sci-fi film-wise children and adolescents, and all that fun on Halloween, may well seem out of place in the context of God and Jesus, and all the serious stuff, discerning theology, and liturgy of the practised religious denominations in the Christian faith. Surely, for this third name in the Trinity, the Holy Trinity, it would be much better, so very much better today, if we and the Church only spoke of the Holy Spirit. No ghosts, thank you; they belong elsewhere in human imagination, another sphere of human beliefs.

Trinity means three and when we think of the number three, we may think 'two's company and three's a crowd, but for the message in this book for three, think of the Trinity: God the Father, God the Son, God the Holy Spirit. This is Cardinal Number Three we can always have in mind for number 3.

CHAPTER 18
AND SO IS NUMBER FIVE

It is thought-provoking when someone asks you: what would you like to be said about you at your funeral? If you are not a hero, or even had a chance to show you are, or if you are not a millionaire and so never given oodles to charity; if you have never invented anything of great note, or famous for a book or your career or work (and let's face it, most of us are none of these things), then what is left is the good points of your character, i.e. your values. And your values come about by your character, your good sense. But where did that come from? From your upbringing – very probably. But in the absence of that upbringing? From your innate (genetic) character very probably, too, in adulthood.

Most of us learn when quite young from a series of hard knocks in life, mishaps, misfortunes, from our mistakes and misdemeanours. Sometimes a person will accuse us of lying or even stealing. Perhaps we are guilty, and we find we are losing friends, society is shunning us, or we find ourselves tempted to mix with those we have previously considered lowlife.

So, what would we like to be said at our funeral? At funerals, the eulogy (meaning the 'study' of that which is 'good' about someone) means that we ignore the bad bits of someone's life. It is most likely that at some point in our lives we will benefit from pausing and taking time to think about what values we want to live our lives by, and to meditate on the issue, to cogitate, to ponder. It is generally said that of all those meritorious, abstract ideals and values, it is best to seek out five, to become our 'Five Adopted Values.' Five is enough. Five is a comfortable number to learn, remember, recall and grow into the habit of adopting, practising and 'becoming.'

What are these values generally considered to be? A list to chew the fat over, to choose from, just five? A list is offered here, but it is not exhaustive. Others exist for sure but of this list five 'worthwhiles,' as in worthy ideals or values, can be found. Note that some are very close in meaning to others, and so some are as subsidiaries of another. It is best to adopt five unrelated values, unrelated in aspect, when lived out.

Diligent – as in hard-working.

Polite – in all situations, turning the other cheek.

Generous – even to unknown persons.

Kind – as in alert to the needs of others.

Helpful – always ready to offer assistance.

Dignified – as in never crude or vulgar.

Friendly – readily accepting the approaches of strangers.

Fair – in dealing with others.

Professional – doing a job thoroughly well, to the best of our ability.

Solvent – managing our finances and living within our means.

Magnanimous – sharing the fruits of any 'victory' and not boastful.

Articulate – the practised art of saying what we mean and meaning what we say, clearly.

Cleanliness – in personal hygiene and in our living style.

Aesthetic – the appreciation of good design, and of beauty in life generally.

Prudent – as in careful, considered and well-judged decisions.

Integrity – truthful and honest in all our dealings, especially with matters of money.

Trustworthy – able to act and remain true to our word in all matters that are honourable and legal.

Self-esteem – the practised art of accepting responsibility for our actions and not speaking in a negative way or ill of ourself.

Cheerful – as in avoiding gloominess, understanding where that comes from, and looking at the bright side of life.

Cultured – a developed sense of awareness of the finer works of art and literature, of human and natural creation, and of geography and geology.

Informed – to keep abreast of what's going on in the world, as well as at home.

Fun-loving – a sense of fun, able to enjoy the fun of others and able to make others laugh.

Smart – in turnout, not always scruffy.

Positive – in attitude to all life's exigencies.

Having identified our five key values, we find that the others, or at least most of them follow in one's life. Beware of ever telling anyone what our 'five' are. They are highly personal and private to each of us. If we are to meet our ideal, it is essential that we keep them to our self. It's a matter of trust, to ourself, our personal objective. Don't tell anyone. Not even a spouse or love partner. Not for Facebook, Twitter, Linkedin or any of those things. For me only, just me, Me Inc., Me Ltd. Got it?

Having adopted our 'five' and rehearsed them in our mind, written them down, logged them in an encrypted file on our PC, it would be a miracle if we didn't soon find a need to have recourse to at least one of our values. Drawing on a value, it then acts as a moral guide, how we should be, behave, what decision to come to, and a warning to our self-appraisal to see the system working.

It is not the intention to deliver here a discussion on the merits of the values listed above. Internet definitions and debates abound on each. But we will enlarge a little of one or two, for interest's sake.

It need not always be the same five values. As life goes on, as experiences happen, we can and perhaps, should revisit the question of the 'adopted five' and go for an 'upgrade.' No harm in that, in fact it would be a good move. Refine our 'five'. Some may note that 'modest' and 'modesty' have been omitted from the list of values above. This is deliberate because of its questionable interpretation in today's world. The whole question of modesty today is complex.

There is modesty as applicable to our general conduct, and modesty as applied to our dress. With sportsmen and -women, top of their particular sport are mostly always modest in their magnificent performances and magnanimous to their opponents. Cassius Clay as Muhammad Ali did become immodest, claiming he was the greatest etc., but wasn't this all part of showmanship? If this was pride, it certainly led to his fall.

There is a saying that says, 'If you've got, flaunt it,' and this can apply to those who find they have become well off and are in a position to spend above their peers. The message seems vulgar and immodest, but the dictum implies also not to feel guilty in any financial success and, if we can, and wish to spend more than our friends and relations, it is difficult to see why one shouldn't. It's how one presents any new acquisitions that can upset others – the 'flaunting,' the showing off, monetary vulgarity, immodesty.

Modesty in dress is a very different and highly personal issue. There are such violent extremes. The Muslim creed, for example, does not allow any immodesty in dress by Muslim women in public and goes to extreme lengths to avoid any displays of physical attraction, and exposure of flesh. Many Western women feel no such constraints, and on occasion expose as much of their charms, with visible bodyparts as bare as possible. Does this count as immodesty? Who is to say? It seems the two extremes of conduct, the two ideologies, could hardly ever respect each other's way of life.

Clothes can be a fashion statement, i.e. we want to look good, feel good, even 'up to date,' otherwise, as in work or everyday wear, they are just functional, keeping us warm, with some protection and mostly dowdy, even scruffy. But when going out on the town, parties etc., dressing up is the thing and for some, that's where the 'undressing' tends to be done. The question is, is it immodest to display what can be seen as embarrassingly large amounts of flesh that even other women might condemn as undesirable and unwise? Women know their body is attractive to men and to some women. It is a case of subconsciously wanting to be more attractive but little conscious thought of what others may regard as immodest. What women find attractive in men does include certain aspects of male physique, and, whilst there is much chatter about a scene on TV when a male actor bears his chest, mostly what women find attractive in a man is his shape and conformation that can be seen without the baring of flesh. The same does apply to the female form, which is to say that whilst in today's world the exposure of so much flesh is accepted by many, it is unnecessary in the view of others who are uncomfortable with such immodesty. The phrase 'leave something to the imagination' used to be said and possibly applies today. So, to some it is okay to bare as much as they like, to others it is just not modest.

Integrity

Of all the values, the one that appeals to many to aspire to live by is integrity. 'He was a man of high integrity,' would be a great accolade for anyone. The use of the word 'high' here is interesting, implying that integrity comes in different degrees, different levels. Or is it that the word is slipped in to stress the word 'integrity?' Probably, because it seems difficult to think that we could deal with someone with integrity on one day and on the next day behave in a scurrilous way like a scoundrel. Surely you either have integrity or you haven't? Perhaps we didn't used to behave with integrity, but now choose to. In all situations? Probably not always. It could be very hard, superhuman even, always to conduct ourselves with high integrity. Perhaps integrity can be like the bar of soap in the bath; we can grasp it sometimes, but it often slips from our grip. But we can keep trying.

Diligence

Diligence is a value that may not have a ready appeal to some, as not particularly awe-inspiring, or something that carries much mettle. Our attention to detail goes along with being professional, capable. But not for all; especially the young, new to the world of work and its disciplines, its protocols.

There is, or should be, a moral dimension to paid employment. Our employer employs us to do a job, pays us either by the hour or by the job; mostly we all are paid by the hour. For that hour it is reasonable that we should work at the job we have been given to do. Depending on the nature of our work, our employer may say to us that he/she expects us to work diligently for say, 55 minutes of every hour, and the other five minutes do a less exacting job, such as tidying up, or just relax for five minutes before going back to 100% concentration on the work in hand.

Diligence is the voluntary self-application in the service of anyone who is either paying us to achieve an end result or a task we have accepted voluntarily to undertake. Messing around, chatting, daydreaming, running our social life while at work, all form no part of diligence. The selfless application to our work as in being diligent may be reduced by detractors, but diligence usually pays off in some way; by promotion, more responsibility, even a pay rise. Equal pay for equal work is the cry, but how often is equal work done? Not as often as is generally supposed.

Trustworthiness

Is an odd value because while we may choose it as an adopted value, it is not a quality that is immediately or even belatedly obvious, and because it relies on having a proven track record. Most of us like to think we can keep a secret, and most of us think that it does no harm to share it with someone else, someone we often feel we have a bond with, or would like to have a bond with. Either way, it's someone at that moment we want to trust, believe we can trust and so break our lightly given promise to someone else and share that secret.

'Can you keep a secret?' people often ask of their friend. Of course we all say

AUSPICIOUS THOUGHTS, PROPITIOUS MIND

yes, as we are dying to know the secret. And when we know it, we just have to share it, as a secret, of course. Not much trustworthiness there. When the giver of the secret later accuses us of breaking the secret which we have most definitely not shared, they are amazed and have to find out how else the secret came to be known. Not many can truly, trustfully, keep a secret when asked to.

The other aspect of trustworthiness is when we put ourselves or we are put by someone 'on trust,' meaning, we are put on 'our trust.' It is a matter of principle that we do and behave as expected. And there again, there is the concept of 'sacred' trust. When raised to the exalted position of a surgeon, or even an anaesthetist, we are on our honour to be very assiduously diligent, because the trust placed in us requires us to be 100% and intensely careful and skilful with the sacred life and tissues in our hands, and at our mercy. It is humbling. That job, and all that goes with it, can never be taken lightly, routinely, or for granted; no joking, no flirting with pretty nurses, no story-telling. Concentrate fully on the job in hand, even when closing the incision with fine suturing. It most definitely is not quite like a mechanic mending a car, for as it is said, 'we should never cry over anything that can't cry over us'; but the mechanic also needs to concentrate, for the lives of people in the vehicle or aircraft are just as sacred. And so the same applies to those who pilot and to those who look after our aircraft. Diligent in the operation of the sacred trust placed with them.

CHAPTER 19
THE DEADLY SEVEN

Seven is often given as a favourite personal number, and like a favourite colour, there is no special reason to it. That's to say there's nothing really special about having a favourite number, a lucky number perhaps. Of course, concepts of lucky numbers broach upon luck and fate and suspicions and imaginings; but not necessarily so, it can be a number chosen at random in a hurry when asked. Seven features very large in our lives, every week.

But for the purpose of this book, seven as a Cardinal Number means the seven of the 'Seven Deadly Sins.' Deadly because they are mostly pretty irresistible and if we succumb, the effects on our lives are deadly and deaden our soul, our chances in any afterlife. So, best avoided for a clean, successful life, but oh so tempting!: almost a too natural facet of human nature to resist! They are vanity, envy, gluttony, lust, anger, greed, and sloth.

VANITY is said to be the worst of the sins, driving all the other sins. To some it is synonymous with pride, but not to all. To Jane Austen, for example, she wrote of 'no improper pride,' implying that it's okay to have pride in certain things, certain attributes. Perhaps the matter presents a cascade starting at vanity, then improper pride, then to a just pride: like from an indifference to self-worth, or from humility to self-effacement and then to self-denigration. It seems true that upon deeper reflection, so much of what we say, what we feel and then what we do, can be boiled down to vanity, our assessment of who we are, who we see ourselves as, who we want to be seen as, and respected, valued as, even reckoned as held in certain high regard. A sort of unspoken 'Don't you know who I am!' Oh, so tempting to answer, sometimes.

The Bible, the Book of Ecclesiastes says, *And what sayeth the preacher? … Vanity of vanities! … All is vanity*. Written supposedly by a king, so he should

226

know. It was the old Bishop of Barchester's favourite quotation.

So, if vanity is the chief of the Seven Deadly Sins from which the other six flow, how can we keep it in check? Self-improvement gurus, self-improvement books and courses abound to help people of low self-esteem or those struggling to cope with life's stresses, those everyday pressures. Most preach and teach the worth of self-esteem, which is necessary and worthy. Can that be overdone and slip into vanity? Very probably. Possibly, like all the Seven Deadly Sins, but being aware of them, rehearsing the list, as a mantra, may be enough to keep us on the 'straight and narrow,' and let our physical and mental appetites burgeon.

ENVY in itself may not seem too terrible. We can be pleased for someone's achievements, possessions or promotion; but it could lead to serious wrong in wanting to act in some way to try to remove that person's achievement, that promotion so you don't have to envy it anymore. It's not too hard to be 'just pleased' for someone, but if we admit envy, it is a negative emotion; best rejected, suppressed. If given to envy, avoid saying, 'I envy you your ...' Instead, we can practise at thinking, saying and meaning, 'I am very pleased for you; well done, you.' It's no good thinking, 'Life isn't fair' with bitterness, because we should know, understand and accept from adolescence, that, yes, life is not fair, so we'd best get over it. If we allow any twinge of envy, then it should be there as a goad, a crack of our own whip, to strive more, better, to pursue our own goals, our own worthy goals, not try to detract others from theirs.

GLUTTONY is not necessarily easy to recognise. Those who lived through the World War II will know how little we actually 'need' to survive and do a day's work. Data was quickly calculated, and rations set for everyone in the country. Things like no more than 3 oz of first-class protein in a day. That means meat, or cheese or fish. People nowadays readily tuck into an 8 oz steak even 10 oz with gluttony, or perhaps need, if of very big frame and working out on over 3,000 calories per day.

Food is plentiful in the Western Europe, UK, USA and other parts, with a massive variety to suit all tastes and whims; there's not enough time in life to enjoy our favourite foods, dishes, and also try new flavours and textures. Or so it seems.

Eating is a pastime, hopefully an enjoyable one and sociable, preferably.

Some insist on silence and 'get it down you as fast as possible' approach. So be it. But gluttony is an obsession, in medicine 'polyphagia,' eating to satisfy a craving or a habit of craving. It can be pathological, that is to say driven by some disease process. More often, it has developed as a character trait, a defect in a personality to make up for some other deficiency. It is said that we do everything for love, or to make up for the lack of it.

Gluttony sounds extreme, and probably that is what is meant, but there are almost certainly degrees of gluttony as in 'somewhat gluttonous', and 'very gluttonous'. Mindfulness might help here; it's at the very time, at the table, that tempting menu, that offered 'second helping;' restaurants offering 'all you can eat for £x, $x or €x' and self-service bars where luscious breakfasts aplenty tempt us to fill our plates in a way we never would at home. Obesity, the outcome of gluttony, has developed into pandemic proportions in the USA, the UK and now some European countries. The French, with their worldwide reputation for excellent cuisine, redolent of a large plate with a seemingly small portion in the middle but delicious, are also seeing increasing numbers of obese people in their society.

So, has the glut of food produced gluttony, or is it anything to do with the type of foods commonly eaten these days in those countries mentioned? So-called 'fast food' may be making us all get fatter. For example, there has been a massive replacement of traditional fats such as butter and olive oil in prepared foods, both savoury and sweet products, with rapeseed oil, which contains a long chain fatty acid with some toxic side effects and called erucic acid (the healthy 'essential fatty acids' are short chain). It is conjectured this product could be harming our bodies' biomechanisms in which fats are stored and then broken down, i.e. fat metabolism, the balance and swing between white cells (the storage mode fat cells or adipocytes) and the 'brown and beige' cells, the good guys, who swing into action when we lose fat deposits and so lose weight. There may be something in this because surely people, as a mass, have not all injudiciously become victims of gluttony; or have we, and have they?

The self-control needed to eat only what we need is hard to come by. Those whose livelihoods depend on being slim find the willpower to control their calorie intake – e.g. actors and presenters on TV etc. Surgeons are often slim, or if not slim, not fat as they develop an abhorrence of body fat during the carrying out of surgery on fat people. As the operation gets underway, the first obstacle is an inches-thick layer of fat to be passed through. It is greasy, oily, and soon the gloved hands and instruments are coated in fatty slime mixed with blood. Once into the body cavity, everything has a fatty covering masking and delaying the progress of the operation. It is hardly surprising that we read every now and then that some 'patient' has had his/her surgery postponed until they lose weight.

But it is so hard to lose weight. The only diet that works is to eat very little food at all, but what little we do eat has to be balanced nutritionally or we risk illness. Prisoners of war on starvation rations and people who go on hunger strike lose weight, but very miserably. Mahatma Gandhi went on hunger strike several times, but less miserably because it was his choice. Going short of food will result in weight loss, but if to carried to excess and if no nutritional balance, our health can suffer.

What is often referred to as a stomach is meant as the abdomen. It is known that, as a rule, the size of the organ, our actual stomach, the bag-like receptacle that receives the food that is eaten, increases in size with the amounts of food eaten each day, at each meal. Happily, once eating less at each meal becomes habitual, our stomachs shrink over time to adjust to those smaller portions. There seems to be a contention between appetite, the amount of our appetite, and the size of our stomach. If we get our stomach size down through eating smaller portions, our appetite, our gluttony, reduces with it. The sensation of 'feeling full' is one of the main limiting factors of appetite at a meal. However, and sadly, generally feeling full only occurs when we have already eaten too much.

If we eat for pleasure, is it the taste we enjoy, as surely it can't be anything to do with chewing and then swallowing. And once swallowed we are unable to 'feel' the food anymore until the feeling of 'stuffed' arises. And if it's the taste that is the supreme pleasure in eating, then we can maximise the taste sensation by taking smaller 'mouthfuls,' smaller bite sizes and by eating more slowly. By deliberately chewing more slowly before swallowing, consciously enjoying what's in our mouth, increasing the sojourn of each mouthful before swallowing, we can gain more pleasure from less.

If we watch dogs eating, especially bigger dogs, like Labradors, they 'bolt' their food, that is the domesticated-animal dog food we give them. They bolt their food instinctively because they are programmed to assume another dog in the pack will steal it from them. Even though there's no other dog in the house they still bolt their food; it's instinctive and they're not bothered about table manners! And they can get fat, like their owners. We marvel at the speed which their food is eaten, and having eaten all, then immediately go on the search for more, the others' dog food or even ours. And we find it amusing, but make no comparison with ourselves. But do we, in our way, in our primitive, primeval mind, eat well now, and through the day, because tomorrow we may have to go without, if our hunting is unsuccessful? A deep, deep instinct in us, deep in our feral natures. We could dwell on that thought, and act.

Some seem quite unable to find the willpower to eat less and some of these have a gastric band fitted to 'shrink' their stomach so they cannot eat so much at one sitting. The process seems successful; it is better than having half of your stomach surgically removed. Surely we can get into the habit of eating less, just as it is the habit we get into eating more? Who knows? But what is generally accepted is that our thoughts do become our actions, and our actions become our habits, and our habits become us. Eating less could become so because we have become minded to, as in, 'I am minded to eat less.' An affirmation, in the present tense and a personal positive statement. A mantra.

There is also the moral angle. Our food is plentiful and reasonably cheap, and if it were not, would there be less obesity? But there is much starvation in the world, most notably Africa, sadly through famine and civil war. Surely the opulent West could do more to distribute food. Why are EU farmers paid <u>not</u> to produce food? It seems amoral. The earth is bountiful, it behoves those with food to see those without have food enough.

LUST has been defined accurately as an inordinate craving for the pleasures of the body, which seems a very good definition once we have looked at the key words more closely. The 'pleasures of the body' refer to the five senses of the body – sight, touch, smell, taste and hearing, and all of these senses come into play when considering the fulfilment of lust to a greater or lesser extent. To anyone who has experienced the act of physical union between two people, be it a natural or variant union, the same applies: the psychophysical experience is pleasurable, and if it were not so, then Homo sapiens as a species would die out for want of a need to reproduce itself.

Our sixth sense is instinct, intuition, imagination and includes love. It is this instinct, raw instinct, that drives the animals and essentially here the human animal to reproduce. If the act of mating were painful as, say, childbirth, there would be much less of it, very much less.

But as with all our pleasures, we can become 'obsessed' with any one of them to a point of it unbalancing our lives, our personality. Repeated actions for some sort of pleasure, be it physical pleasure 'of the body' or 'of the mind' become our habits and they become us. Lust then is that excessive, unbecoming obsession with the 'need' or more correctly the 'want' or 'desire' for the psychophysical pleasure of 'love-making' and similar related sexual pleasures. To say 'love-making,' as it is commonly spoken and written of, is inappropriate, because love doesn't come into it usually. Lust for sex with one's spouse or partner is not usually considered as lust. Lust is usually used for that action when one seeks sexual pleasures with others, often with those others with whom sex would be inappropriate, the breaking of marriage vows, breaking up relationships, distracting from duties, illegal with the underage, and other amoral or immoral relationships, inappropriate at work, and at many other activities in society. That is to say lust is not discriminating. By that is meant that it is selective in its objective, as in attraction applies, but in the condition of that objective, i.e. married or not, lust is not discriminatory.

To crave is a term used to imply a fair degree of want or desire, that is to say it is a relative term. We can wish for something, we can want something, or we can want it very much, and then 'want very badly!' Why do we say 'badly?' It implies that the want has become bad for us, as in it is distracting, even destructive, of some aspect or aspects to do with the balance of our lives. To want something very badly, and very, very badly (as we say) is to crave.

So fortunately for most of us who are aware since the age of maturity that there can be a physical attraction in others, usually through vision in the first sense, that attraction is natural, instinctive and is just an appreciation of that person's 'attraction,' their physique, their physiognomy and their presentation, as in their dress and her perfume, or even his perfume, but also and most importantly the person's personality. Just that alone can be so very attractive, the eyes, dancing, the smile, their way of holdings themselves when speaking and especially laughing. It is a big step from there to physically desiring that person, and an even bigger step to being driven to so act until that physical desire can be fulfilled. That attraction at once is the stuff of romance: 'Some enchanted evening, you can see a stranger across a crowded room and somehow you know, you know even then...' goes the song. But inappropriate, repeated seeking out, obsessively, with the intention of getting some 'illicit' sex is lustful.

Lust, then, is a deadly sin because of the harm it does to relationships of the lusting person and their 'victims.' Respect and self-respect are lost, careers ruined, and illegalities can end in jail. So far, we have only considered lust as a repetitive, habitual sin. Often it can be a single sin, applying to a relationship between two who shouldn't be in a relationship of a sexual nature, at least by common standards of behaviour, 'society's rules,' but that single act can slake a mutual lust, once and for all.

We are as a species, Homo sapiens, a highly developed mammalian animal, in that the degree of science we have developed has brought us so very far removed from the animals, which by our make-up of flesh and bone, blood, bowels, heart, brain and nerves we have so much in common that we tend to forget every day that we are, and always will be, basically animal. And when we design and build robotic humanoids as eventually will happen, no doubt, if we are foolish enough, we will be then capable of providing the raw materials they will need to reproduce themselves by a process, not manufacture, but by what may be called 'robo-facture.'

However highly developed our skills, our achievements in science, in art, in our performance of music, in making law and sociological organisation, as in politics and government, in warfare as in highly capable instruments of warfare, there is another side to our human nature. That side is that we need loving relationships, and, although these are not always the smooth path and rewarding experience we prefer, most manage somehow, and this is a most rewarding and worthy aspect. So, we have on the one hand a highly skilled person, achieving great things in his or her career, promotion, peer respect, a fine home, loving spouse and children, and then he or she throws it away, or at least, greatly risks throwing away all of that, just for a 'bit of fun,' for a sexual foray, a dalliance of the flesh. In short, a succumbing to lust, born out of desire, a human animal's subconscious becoming conscious drive to take a mate, that at times becomes the uncontrollable urge to 'spread one's genes' (lust in biological terms). So why does this mean risking 'all' for this? Much depends on the circumstances, but the loss of the secure, once loving home and family life probably hurts most. As to jobs, it seems those under the close scrutiny of the public, like politicians, tend to lose out most.

Such situations have in the past been described as a 'fall from grace.' The concept of grace is complex. The word 'graceful' is better understood for its simplicity. Dukes and duchesses are addressed as 'Your Grace,' a term that has evolved and remained as the word 'grace' has slipped from our everyday parlance. We could easily conjecture that someone we regard as having grace (full of grace) would be that ideal person whose life was lived free from the Seven Deadly Sins.

Certain aspects of sexual behaviour in society used to be referred to as dirty. Sex outside of marriage was often called dirty. And even sex before marriage was often so called. An adolescent female, and sometimes male, who is still living at home with the parents, would often be referred to as 'a dirty-little-stop-out-late.' And yet young men were encouraged by parents to go and 'sow their wild oats,' as if to get normal sexual desire requited and experience of varied sexual partners before settling down to marriage (and being faithful). Such hypocrisy, or was it? They knew 'nice girls' wouldn't oblige, nor most married women, but human nature being what it is, lustful, there would always be somewhere for wild oats to be sown, some innocent sowing done and escape harm, others would lead to unwanted pregnancy and in a married woman directly or indirectly very likely lead to divorce sooner or later.

So, the emphasis on lust seems to rely on the term 'inordinate,' in its definition – the excess of proper or normal desires. Inordinate implies immeasurable, and of course lust or even normal desire for sex is not really measurable. But we know what is proper and 'normal,' as it becomes the accepted conduct within society, within relationships, of grace. It is the undesired outcomes, the untoward sequelae, the irrational move of the chess piece that forfeits the queen, that brands lust as one of the Seven Deadly Sins.

The question is, 'Has society become too sexualised?' For years we have known that to have successful drama in films, or TV, in books there has to be a 'healthy' dose or a 'fix' of raunchy sex. It titillates, it excites, it's 'popular' because we 'identify' with the key players. Much comedy on TV includes frequent allusions to some form of sexual conduct, possibly wayward; and even sometimes the so-called 'kinky'; it gets a laugh.

What is surprising and much deprecated by right-thinking people, is the sexualising of young children, usually girls, in mature-style clothing that only mature women at their 'sexiest' would usually wear, including make-up. 'It removes the child's innocence,' they say. Certainly it is a modern phenomenon, that is to say, the encouragement of the parents, supposedly, mostly mothers with a father's connivance, or his objections are 'overruled,' dressing the child up

233

so 'precociously.' Young children have always played at dressing up, the same as they play at 'doctors and nurses' or 'cowboys and Indians,' but for the parent to buy these adult-style, so-called sexy clothes for young girls is very questionable. A similar question by parents, often arising, circles around the issue of sex education in school. That sex education is a sensible ideal is axiomatic, but what is questioned is 'what' is being taught, at what age is best, and do the teachers have the appropriate educational and balanced skills themselves to teach a fair reasonable and balanced attitude, the suitable approach to this complex issue? Many fear the answers are in the negative and children are becoming 'sexualised' at too young an age. For example, is it right to attempt to provide an education about sex and sexual conduct without the concomitant teaching of related moral and ethical issues?

Those old enough at this time of writing will recall the liberalisation of sexual conduct that came about as a direct consequence of the introduction of the 'birth control pill', and that includes the later development of the 'morning after' pill. The birth pill lead to 'Bacchanalian orgies' of Biblical proportions with 'wife-swapping parties' and 'car key parties'. It was society's sexual drive, having always been 'bottled up,' suddenly set free. Fortunately, things like that have settled down, because they led to many divorces, unhappy children of divorce and sexually transmitted diseases.

And then came the explosion of AIDS, of which the causes, its prevention and, to a certain extent, its treatment were fairly rapidly understood and largely overcome, after leading to surprising outcomes in some parts, such as the governments of some countries issuing free condoms!

It seems as if society and its governments have recognised or invented the notion and then accepted that all adults need frequent sexual activity for whatever benefit that activity brings. It's like saying something is building up inside and must be released or ... or what? This doesn't apply to all. Soldiers and sailors in a war situation, years sometimes, prisoners in jail go without regular sexual relief. If we look at the other mammals, their sex is purely procreative, never just recreational. They have their breeding seasons, the 'oestrus' cycles, and out of the breeding season neither male nor female has any interest in sex. Even during the breeding season, the male may be only attracted to the female for that brief period of her oestrus cycle when she is ovulating. But for humans we are blessed or cursed with a sex drive that has seldom any thought of creating a pregnancy, and the drive can be present virtually all the time with just a few off days, monthly, that are minimised when taking the 'birth pill'. So, is this 100% of the time sexually activeness a healthy physiological and psychological relief, or is it obsessive and destructive of a modest society of grace? Individuality of frequency of desire wears with age as other factors bring to bear, the raising of children, work responsibilities, sexual boredom within marriage or a relationship. Lust can also diminish, and does for most, with age; so that's good, isn't it?

Before moving on to the remaining Seven Deadly Sins let us consider how in human life sexual desire develops in the adolescent. Adolescence, a fairly drawn-out process of becoming a 'mature' human, is both a physical and a psychological process. It seems to begin to come about at different ages in different cultures, in different races. The reason for this difference may be part genetic, part climatic but may very well be influenced by the behaviour of overt sexism in their society and the general way of the upbringing of children as reflected in each parenting group, the family, and in society generally, including and especially psychosexual influences from the media, including the internet.

The genetic programming brings on the development of the physical changes to the body called the secondary sexual characteristics. We are born with our primary sexual characteristics which are the external genitalia. It is the first thing noticed at birth or was the first thing up to the time of pregnancy scans to determine sex, and in general those external genitalia determine our sex as either male or female, and those anatomical features reflect the different internal sex organs we cannot see. Biology being what it is, there are some born whose development of their sex organs, both internal and external, has 'got muddled' and no complete set of organs of either one sex or the other develops. These unfortunates are intersexes. These days surgeons do what they can later to try to reconstruct the anatomy, if not the associated physiology of full function, to be as completely one sex or the other. It is easier to construct the external genitalia of a female than a male human.

The features of the secondary sexual characteristics are different for each sex, with only one common feature, the development of pubic and axillary hair. In the human male there are changes in the general physique of bone and muscle size. This feature is better accentuated in some men than others, with the development of broad shoulders, thick necks, arm and leg muscles, facial hair, as beard and moustaches grown and the voice 'breaks,' eventually to settle down as bass, baritone or tenor. And with all this comes the experiences of sexual arousal, often initially spontaneous, then to settle down to a responsive arousal, responsive to sexual stimulation which can be visual, physical or just psychological, i.e. in response to thoughts. Visual stimuli are primordial mechanisms of sexual arousal and these processes are very well developed in humans of today. But women often say that it is also about 'his eyes,' or 'his lips,' or his voice and so on, and hence probably it is idiosyncratic, each having their own fascinations that for them are the attractions of a man.

The secondary sexual characteristics of the human female are quite specific so as to bring about the visual stimuli to the male, whose psychological adolescence has brought about the changes necessary for a boy to grow into a man and appreciate the visual shape and form of the mature female, who then brings about an urge in the male to find a mate, and 'mate' with her.

The anatomical changes of the development of breasts by local fat deposits as well as the development of mammary tissue, and fat deposits on the hips that with the retention of the child-like waist produces the 'hourglass' figure attractive to men. The child-like softness of the skin is retained, but the head hair mostly undergoes some changes that denote the more mature female.

To understand better the effects of visual stimuli, it helps to think about the shape of the face, and in particular, the shape of the nose. Visual stimuli pass from the retina, along the optic nerve to the hypothalamus, that part of the brain to do with our emotions, and then to the pituitary gland which releases hormones. It is the shape of the nose that presents often to the whole face of a newborn in many mammals, including humans, a concavity that evokes in us a response that recognises the defencelessness and helplessness of the newborn and the pre-adolescent. This 'care-eliciting' response in us, in both males and females, but rather more so in females, is a visually generated neuro-hormonal-psychological behavioural response.

This 'care-eliciting response' is an 'affectionate' response, is recognised by authors and film-makers who create creatures such as Bambi. It is mostly down to the concavity of the nose, omnipresent in children, and this feature is lost to maturing males and many females as adolescence ensues, to be replaced not by 'care eliciting' physical characteristics, but by secondary sexual characteristics that evoke sexual attraction.

Great swathes of features of modern living seem to revolve around the accentuation of secondary sexual characteristics. That is to say, we have developed set behavioural patterns that become important in our everyday lives, affect the economy, and have become important to us. Fashion and style, beauty care and cosmetics for both females and males are there to be taken advantage of, to enhance our visual appeal to others.

Sometimes carried to the extreme, fashion designers make clothes for women who expose and reveal as much of their bodies as they can get away with, i.e. women will buy, or have bought for them, and yet manage to escape, just, being arrested for 'indecent exposure.' In these cases, the visual stimuli being meted out are great, and sometimes too great, it is argued, for the safety of the individual concerned, in her state of relative 'undress.'

Of course, there will never ever be any defence of a male who attempts to force himself on a woman, the most base crude and animal instinct let loose and uncontrolled. This is a bit unfair to animals to imply that they rape. They do not, as a rule. The males are only interested in mating in the mating season, their own hormone levels peaking in response to the season of the year, the changes in daylight length, and the pheromones given off by the females. Any male mammalian animal attempting to force his attentions on a non-receptive female are dealt with by the female most ferociously. Even during the pre-mating phase of the oestrus cycle, the female either not quite ready to mate, or not prepared to mate with a male not of her choice, will be vigorously and violently dealt with. It's simply not worth the injury to the male, who mostly rapidly and early on gets the message. Prime stallions have had their 'delicate bits' badly injured by kicks from a mare not ready, which is why low-worth 'teaser' stallions are tentatively and temptingly offered, to find out if the mare is ready, but they are then not allowed to mount. That's tough for the substandard male.

Pheromones play a great part in animal sexual behaviour and in humans, too, to some extent. Having weaker olfactory senses, we use scents and perfumes to elaborate upon any pheromones we may have, and these are very effective in a part of our sexual arousal.

But it is important to understand about visual stimuli, about secondary sexual characteristics, why they are there, and their primordial biological purpose. Adolescence, that maturing process from the care eliciting child, into a 'full-blooded' adult comes about almost as a cascade of changes from eliciting care to desire, and then experience the full reality of sexual outcome, 'coupling,' making love, the full coital union as a 'pleasurable' experience. Then, as eating can become a pleasantly excessive desire that leads in the end on to unwanted obesity, so sex can become a pleasantly excessive desire that, with too much preoccupation in the pursuance of that pleasure, is lust that leads on to our degradation as a person. For a man is a man when a man is needed; if not, he remains a boy. We can reflect on the deep meaning of that not so commonly accepted statement.

The female sex is generally accepted as being the gentler and more caring of the two sexes. Unfortunately, at the hands of men, women frequently suffer greatly from many injustices both psychological and physical. Furthermore, many men fail to appreciate the special kind of love that a woman can have for a male partner, which is usually instinctive, and it is regretful to have to acknowledge that many men fail to appreciate the special gift that as a woman she can bring to a heterosexual relationship. The upshot of this is that many women can get to feel a more natural attraction to a member of their own sex, especially those who have suffered at the hands of a man or men, for a mutually common understanding and empathy that becomes a kind of loving.

Before leaving this subject we should mention the unmentionable to most of society and here we refer to self-relief, or the act of relieving each other as an alternative to sexual intercourse, that of masturbation. If phenothiazine can be abbreviated to PTZ, and phenylbutazone PBZ, then we can abbreviate masturbation for the convenience of the few words here on the matter to MTB. The act of MTB comes along with the onset of sexual maturity, and can be said to be an automatic relief of one's sexual urges, needs or frustrations. MTB does not seem to be practised in animals, so it's for humans only, and one could say it's a 'jolly good thing, too,' seeing that we have no 'mating season' like the animals but an 'all-year-round' mating season, ready to try to make it with the opposite sex, or for some, the same sex. Is this another example of nature's compensating mechanisms?

In the 18th century MTB was thought a sin. It was known that the brain and spinal cord were made up of a soft, white, semi-fluid nature, and at the base of the spine, around the corner, so to speak, was a man's penis. On ejaculation the white seminal fluid was thought to be brain matter and so it was concluded that excessive draining away one's brain matter would drive the perpetrator of MTB mad, and so MTB was condemned as a sin. And that act continued to be regarded as a sin right through up to the era after the Second World War.

238

Prior to the liberalisation of sexual 'morals' following the development of the birth pill, courting couples would often indulge in what was termed 'heavy petting,' the act of giving each other mutual sexual relief, giving each other an orgasm by digital means or perhaps if really, really heavy, lingual and oral MTB (note here the 'original' meaning of the word digital – the fingers and little to do with computers etc.). The dangers here were that passions would just take over and 'penetration' would take place, and perhaps a pregnancy follow. Mothers and fathers would fret severely for their daughters, courting heavily. But nature takes its course. So, whether MTB is a good thing, or when can it be a bad thing is debatable. Being too ready to develop fantasies bound up in MTB can lead to a character who never develops into a mature, sociable, confident in mixed company, and all-round 'well-balanced personality.' Too much MTB can become a cop-out from developing social skills that can lead to meaningful relationships with the opposite sex; instead, just living in a fantasy dreamworld wound around the secret of self-relief, certain of that pleasure, at least, rather than risk a put-down by a member of the opposite sex we are attracted to.

The answer, probably like so many things, may well lie in moderation. There are times, already alluded to above, when the sexes are separated for long durations by war, or by the nature of one's employment, and, although the subject is virtually never spoken of in 'good society,' it is there 'underground.' There is in cockney rhyming slang a word used that rhymes with the once world-famous stellar observatory at Jodrell Bank. And private it must be, because it is illegal to be seen carrying out indecent exposure and an act of indecency, a sex act in public. To be caught in a pole-dancing club in the act of MTB, where there are notices forbidding such things and to be thrown out by the club bouncer, must rate as one of the most humiliating experiences that sort of man could ever experience. So, too much MTB is also here regarded as a form of lust, which then rates easily as one of the Seven Deadly Sins.

ANGER: surely everyone, except the most angelic, is familiar with experiencing anger. One definition is anger is that response manifested by and in an individual who, at that moment, spurns love and instead opts for rage. So, as implied, the angelic one is so full of love for the world that they never manifest anger; it hardly seems possible.

Anger can be described as that automatic, instinctive uncontrollable (initially at least) response evoked in us when things happen or are said or are written that go against our wishes, desires and instincts.

Looking at things that happen that can make us angry, they can be human instigated, i.e. brought about by the actions or words of another being, either innocently or sometimes deliberately to upset someone else. The amount of and complexity of human interactions in life are such that we are almost bound to upset someone, somewhere, sometime, however hard we try to avoid it. But other things happen that are not directly humanly attributable. For example, the car breaking down or refusing to start when you are in a hurry, late for an appointment, often evokes a furious condemnation of the vehicle or of 'the Gods' who 'run our fate.'

Some get into the habit of too readily losing their temper; it is said they have a short fuse. It may be genetic. It is demonstrable in infants, those who readily 'throw their toys out of the pram'.

So why is anger reckoned as a 'deadly sin?' For a start it is hardly conducive to healthy interrelationships and because it is destructive of one's self. When angry, we cannot think constructively or objectively, or listen to our affirmations. We become harder to love, we throw things, and we break things often treasured and possibly things of value to someone. We break chairs and tables and kick in door panels, and even worse we drive fast and dangerously, perhaps knocking a cyclist over, hitting, perhaps killing a pedestrian, crashing the car or motorbike. Anger can be so destructive.

And then we say things in anger, things we mean at the time to hurt, to offend, to get 'our own back.' Things we often come to regret later; regret because it meant it lost us our job, or promotion, or a good friend, even a loved one. Sometimes we slow down in anger, come 'off the boil' and scheme to hurt back, to get revenge, to assert ourselves, show 'them' who 'we' are, by letter, by word or by a devised action. The saying is, 'Don't get mad; get even.' So wrong. As said, beware our thoughts, etc.etc., and our words because they can become our actions. Beware.

We have said that anger is an automatic, instinctive response and that probably is true to the extent that it is part of our biological make-up, significant in that part of survival mechanisms associated with 'fight or flight,' which is when several physiological changes suddenly come about within us, to immediately prepare and enable us to fight on being attacked, and to run or climb from danger when it arises. Adrenaline release increases blood to the muscles, makes the heart beat faster, getting oxygen round to the muscles and stimulating the brain to a wide-awake alertness. To a degree, our bodies undergo the same changes when we get angry, and our super 'empowered bodies' respond with action and ready to do damage in some way. If there's no action, all that change in us is unspent, and in some way it is ultimately harmful to our bodies when 'unreleased' energy is repeatedly bottled up. We suffer high blood pressure, and risk a heart attack, or a burst blood vessel. So destructive.

So, if it is inevitable that we are going to get angry, what's to be done? To some extent we can avoid getting angry in the first place by developing the art of understanding why others do (or don't do) things or say or write things. We all have our own self-image, who we are, what we are, even who we think we are, and therefore people should recognise that and respect it. But they have their own personalities, too, and often these personas 'clash!' 'Who does she think she is?' or 'I thought she was my best friend, how could she...?'

If we can be more accepting, more forgiving, that helps, but equally should we reward bad behaviour by 'turning our back?' People will 'challenge' us virtually all the time in so many situations, work and social, like chickens sorting out a 'pecking order' – they want to be the top cockerel and will subtly and even overtly try to put others down to enhance themselves. Sometimes it is just as simple a fact as we like to have our own way! So, if it's automatic we are going to get angry at things or people in life, then seeing it's so deadly, how can we cope with the inevitable?

Gurus say it's okay to get angry at times and deal with it. Some say, 'don't get mad, get even!' This is rubbish. It involves a chronic, slow-burning, scheming, subliminal anger that is as destructive as any outburst of rage. Don't do it! Act to preserve our self, yes, but to 'get even,' no.

Sometimes we are aware of being angry as a result of some interaction earlier in the day, at work. We know we are angry but because we have been so busy that day we can't recall who or what it was that made us angry in the first place. It is important to take time out as soon as possible, to go and think quietly about our day, going right back to the start of work and we at some point then remember what it was that made us so angry. Somehow just remembering who (yes, it's almost always 'who' that makes us so cross) and then we can arrange our thoughts to deal with it. This can be as simple as, in our mind, thinking, labelling, the person a fool, or other similar put-downs, that soothe away the anger.

The saying goes, 'Never let the sun go down on your wrath,' and this is so true. We have to deal with our rage, in our minds as soon after the annoying event as possible, and if not then certainly by bedtime. The saying that goes with it is, 'Hope makes a good breakfast, but a poor supper;' it has a deep meaning for most of us, and is worth working out, working through both sayings from time to time, especially when we are seeking some peace of mind, peace from our anger. Wrath is an archaic term, but today can also imply that simmering, long, drawn-out anger that persists after the first fulminating rage has been spent.

'He is an angry man' is a judgement passed by some against someone who always seems cross and angry with everything and everyone in his life. Nothing is ever right in his view, nothing is ever done right, the government is corrupt, councillors are useless, his boss is lazy, there's never a parking place, this meal is disgusting etc., etc. He is to be pitied. He needs counselling, but he'd fly into a rage at the mere suggestion; persevere, by all means, but not at the expense of our own happiness. Often these people are quite intelligent. It's just that their thinking has gone off-track. Women can also suffer from the same malaise of mind, and then, when older, risk being referred to as a harridan.

So, it can be said with some fairness that it is okay to get cross and angry, momentarily, because we are made that way. But only momentarily. And then reject those angry, destructive thoughts and feelings. How do we do that? Well, probably each will find and use their own remedy but a common one is to ask our self, 'Am I enjoying feeling this way?' Only the most perverse would say yes, so of course the answer is 'no'; and we make up our mind to feel better, to relax, to stop feeling angry. This becomes a practised art form. It usually works. The same applies if we ask ourselves if we enjoy banging our head on the wall? No, that hurts. Well, so, stop banging it then, eh? Meercat simple?

There is an analogy that says that in our head, there is a control room. In our mind we can go into that control room through a door and see all the switches there, and they are labelled. We can find the switch for anger and switch it off. And bingo! The anger goes away. Originally the analogy depicted a railway signal box with massive mechanical levers that are pulled and swing from the position 'ON' to the other, the 'OFF.' But these days all the train signals are electronically manipulated and that's much less dramatic to imagine. We can imagine the 'settings' on our phone and 'disable' undesirable features, like anger, that despite being switched off last time we got angry, has somehow, as phones tend to do, got switched back on again. Is 'On' the default position?

We can also deal with anger by linking its control with forgiveness. We shouldn't rush unthinkingly to forgive people who have done or said something that has made us angry. It is written in the New Testament that Jesus said, from the cross, 'Father, forgive them, for they know not what they do.' In essence this applies to most situations that provoke anger in someone. What we did or said to provoke someone's anger was done, or said, perhaps thoughtlessly, not ever a thought by a kind person that it could 'put someone out.' And, 'Oh, I never thought of that,' is our response, and, 'I didn't mean to offend you' – the defence when we are told how we have upset someone. We can't always work out, as in anticipate, if our actions will upset someone. Consequently, when someone upsets us, does or says something that makes us angry, then we can think about why or how this has come about and be understanding, or to a good degree at least 'forgive' them. And this is the beauty of forgiveness: if we can genuinely forgive others then that is so good, such goodness manifesting in us, but also, if we can forgive ourselves for our own stupidity or thoughtlessness, we come out of it with our self-esteem not too damaged and with a goal to do better next time. We can gain some satisfaction from being forgiving, because we also benefit from doing that, by ridding our self from some guilt.

If we can strain to search for the reasons for someone's behaviour we are very near to coming to terms with theirs and our anger. As Tolstoy's Prince General Nikolai Bolkonsky in 'War and Peace' said, 'Tout comprendre, c'est tout pardoner.'

GREED can be said to be a desire for material wealth or gain, ignoring our spiritual side, and goes with avarice and covetousness.

One of the things that helps bring us peace of mind is freedom from fear of financial hardship. It is also natural to want to move to a more comfortable place, and once our basic needs as in Maslow's Hierarchy of Needs have been met, to be able to enjoy the intellectual stimulation that we can rise up to in life.

Set against these natural and worthy attributes is the 'deadly sin' of greed. As we acquire something, usually money or what money represents, e.g. prosperity, we can become 'obsessed,' as in obsessively fascinated by the feelings of satisfaction when we look at our bank balance growing and growing; in all probability as a result of our efforts coupled with good fortune; here meant as a good dose of luck, as in being in the right place, at the right time and knowing the right people. The feeling is so good it becomes addictive, that is to say, for example, 'now I have a million, I want a second million in case something goes wrong, and I lose the first million,' and so it goes on. So, not only is it addictive, but also there is this fear of loss that drives us on and on; it's a development of our newborn fear of falling. Also, there is the competitive streak, of wanting to do better than so-and-so, have more than so-and-so, or even more than anyone at all, more than everyone.

And we don't obtain material wealth by giving it away. No; if greedy, we need every single penny. 'Look after the pennies and the pounds will look after themselves,' is the mantra of the thrifty, and, as such, is very worthwhile. But to the greedy it is then avarice. We hear it claimed often boastfully, 'I never give tips,' or, 'I never give to charities.' It is so often said by those who could comfortably afford to ease a person's life by giving a tip, or help a worthy charitable cause.

So, greed interferes with our ability to show some love, some concern and consideration of others: whether they are less well off or not, is not really material. It is the disproportionate desire for wealth or gain, the obsession that is destructive of our personality. Greed is often not obvious in otherwise pleasant, seemingly well-balanced people. But appropriate generosity is a quality that completes the good character, whereas greed, avarice and envy detract from the whole person.

Covetousness is an adjunct to greed, as is envy. Never envy but be genuinely pleased for someone who has something we can admire. Never covet what it is they have, just to make it yours, not theirs. It is a development of greed.

Greed then becomes like a habit, a way of thinking that drives us on, and drives us apart. Remember, what we have, what we have gained, means someone else cannot have; it represents their loss. When greed goes to excessiveness, then it is definitely depriving of others. It is written that Jesus said, 'It is easier for a camel to pass through the eye of a needle, than for a rich man to enter the Kingdom of Heaven.' One can become well off by hard work and fair dealing without being greedy. What is meant by being 'rich' is a term open to very different interpretations. To someone with virtually nothing, everyone will seem rich. To someone with a total worth of a million, someone with 20 million will seem rich.

Many 'rich' people are not so rich as thought or to be supposed; they are often heavily in debt and are using other people's money, e.g. the 'investors' and the banks, to enjoy the 'good life' while they go along, always hoping their schemes work out and that they can get out of debt.

But is it right to suppose that by having some wealth, some property and money you are depriving others? Let's look at this.

A man has two adult married sons with a wife and young children to support. He gives each son a cow. One kills the cow and eats the beef with his family. The other goes in search of someone with a bull that he uses to get his cow pregnant. Soon the second son has two cows, and, in time, a whole herd, enough to have some beef for himself, his family and to use the milk for butter and cheese. He sells the hide to a tanner to make leather for shoes and bones to a farmer for bone meal fertiliser. He becomes rich, his brother remains poor. In time, much time, the two brothers pass away, leaving their sons and grandsons. Then the grandsons become adult, one rich, the other poor but neither knows how the difference in their fortunes came about. One having inherited money and property, the other inherited nothing. Is it right to say the rich man is depriving the poor one? The man with the herds and the farms that support his wife and children and also employs labour, houses his staff on the estate, is giving a livelihood to many. It is hardly greed that motivates his life.

But there are many opportunities for greed. The wages he pays could be so low, the housing marginal and in bad repair, just so the boss can be 'better off;' now that's greed through avarice. Greed is the obsessive and excessive acquisitional desire for gain. It is deadly in its effects as it changes us from a whole, loving person to become unloving, ungiving to the point of uncaring for others, even those close to us. It is therefore a deadly sin; as in dead to others and dead to God.

The poor relation covets the other's wealth, his house, his car, his everything, and plots schemes how he can defraud his relation of his wealth. The mere wanting is then covetousness and it is the drive to action that is evil, the end result of a deadly sin.

SLOTH: the final sin of the Seven Deadly Sins to look at is sloth. Another archaic term, but still so full of meaning, of implication.

Delving straight into one of the worst forms of sloth is the unfortunate person whose personality has led to a cycle that is hard to reverse, and that is when a worker loses his job and goes onto long-term benefits. Job applications become neglected as interviews are unsuccessful, and with state benefits life struggles on. Acceptance of this depressing state leads in some to a 'what's the point?' attitude and this leads to a 'I can't be bothered to try' attitude and this leads to sloth. Understandable, but not commendable.

Being the adaptable humans we are, we can grow, even tend to grow to accept a life on benefits and get to prefer it to the self-discipline necessarily found in a working person. Sloth sets in and becomes difficult to shift. It's the attitude, 'I'd rather lie in than get up,' and 'I'd rather watch TV than go and take a walk'. Sloth, then, is a mental state, an attitude, it's laziness in its worst form. A slothful person is unhealthy through lazing around, not eating properly, not seeking out health-promoting foods and is unhygienic neglecting to bathe regularly, and launder their clothes.

There are other forms of sloth that should be considered. To a working person, the weekends present an opportunity to be slothful. Any why not? Haven't we earned it? Don't we deserve it? We have worked hard all week and deserve to 'flop.' Deserve? Yes, deserve. The word 'deserve' breaks down in its origins to 'de' meaning 'from,' or 'or out of.' Serve is 'service' i.e. 'out of service rendered.' So, all week we have been in the service of self and others and now 'deserve' to be slothful. Perhaps; but time out of work is not a time for going into a state of 'suspended animation,' the inactivity of laziness, of sloth; it is better to reserve non-working time for recreation, in all its senses.

Work is defined as that voluntary activity in which we submit the quality and quantity of our outputs to the scrutiny of others in return for a livelihood.

Voluntary, because we have a choice – to work or not to work (or, in the case of some very unfortunates, to work and work at finding or making work). The outcomes of what we do at work are the 'quality and quantity' of our outputs, which we should always endeavour to achieve the best we can in these things, these things done in the service of others. For them, and for our self-esteem; i.e. we go to work to work, not to mess about, to be inefficient, to be paid for doing very little. Where's the pride in that? Where is the self-worth? 'The scrutiny of others?' Those others could be our line manager, our boss, or bosses, quality control, and most importantly the 'end-users,' the customers. We go to work to serve others; we are always serving others. Some think: 'I'll go self-employed, be my own boss, so I can please myself.' No, we cannot please our self, if we want an income, to continue to have an income, we will have to be of service to our customers. Our success will be exactly proportional to the degree to which we please our customers – And who are our customers? They are the whole world. Please one and potentially we can please many, many more, just through recommendation. Offend one (as in 'Go and take your business somewhere else') and we automatically offend several or even many others, their friends and relatives, and so lose their custom. We are 'of service' all the time at work, and 'deserve' a break, a restful period, a little each evening, each weekend, perhaps a little sloth, but plenty of recreation.

People talk of 'work-life' balance and this is a sensible approach, but it needs to be an 'informed' approach. Ideally our lives as adolescents and adults are in three parts that we should aim to observe and to keep in balance, with the emphasis on 'balance' being proportional, relevant and appropriate to the stage of life we are in. To explain: the three parts of anyone's life are work, training and recreation. We train to obtain and gain in work, to advance at work, and we work to provide the livelihood that funds our recreation.

Recreation literally means and comes from 're' and 'create'; 're' as in 'again' and 'create' as in become, to make and 'restore.' In recreation, we can become again who we are, and what we want our lives to be. We can truly become ourselves in our non-work time. We can spend time with our loved ones, our friends, our families, playing sport or enjoying hobbies. Life is about loving, spending quality time with the people we love, who love us.

Recreation restores us ready for work, and work should be viewed as enjoyable and as fulfilling as possible. Much depends on our work experiences and they can influence our attitude. Or can they, do they? Or does our attitude influence our work experiences? It should be the latter.

Training is basically our education, getting more qualifications to be able to do the job we really would like to do, to earn more so that our time in recreation is enhanced; training, and ongoing training, always throughout a whole career, is important. Every job has a job-related journal, however remotely unconnected it might appear to one's role, especially if a menial role, if that's what it seems. For example, if our job is as a riveter building a ship, we can seek out information, periodicals, the internet about the whole process that we are just a small part of; we can take an interest and see where that can take us, even if we find we have to couple that with much patience.

This work-life balance often varies as we go through life. The young spend a greater proportion of their time in training. In tertiary education, work may be only a small part, such as a Saturday job, or holiday work. In our twenties and thirties, we work hard to earn as much as we can to get our lives, our families, established with somewhere to live and to furnish the home. In training, when young with minimal work, recreation plays a big part in our life, with sport, travel and socialising. As families come along, those activities reduce to spend more time working, and more family time. The rugger boots and cricket bat get put in the attic with the rucksack, with a vague notion that they will be used again, sometime, somewhere in the future.

The saying goes, 'All work and no play makes Jack a dull boy.' Boy here means 'man.' The saying is almost archaic, but it denotes the value of recreation. In the work-life balance there is no room for sloth! Or is there? Scientists and biologists have worked out that, for a man (or a woman) doing eight hours of hard, physical labour such as working in the fields or building houses or roads, it takes two hours of rest for the body to recuperate from all that exercise. So that person may come home at 6pm, and just eat his 'tea' or 'dinner' or 'supper' (named according to local custom or upbringing) and then 'flop' (in front of the box) for two hours. So, at 8.30pm he or she should become active again, in some form of recreation. But how many of us become slothful and spend the whole of the rest of the evening as a 'couch potato' in front of the 'goggle-box'?

For the person whose work is mostly involved in using their brain, their intelligence, to carry out their work for eight hours with no real physical exercise during the work period, it has been worked out to need just half an hour to recuperate, which hardly seems anytime at all before he/she can take up some active recreation time or time in further training, but to be physically active would mostly be the healthier option.

So, sloth comes about because of attitude, which may come about from genetic influences, from our upbringing, from influences of peer groups, friends or relatives, from misfortunes in finding and seeking work, from those disappointments. It also comes about sequentially from being unfit. The less exercise we take, the less we want, the less we can manage. It is known that exercise stimulates the brain, by releasing substances called endorphins and serotonin, and these invoke a feeling of well-being, and feelings perhaps of being more optimistic or at least more realistic.

Sloth can have associations with listlessness. Many of us feel listless occasionally. When so affected it helps if we just 'make a list,' of 'Things To Do.' Our moods are seldom on an even keel all day of every waking day. The fairy tale 'They lived happily ever after' is an unrealistic, childlike notion. But it is true that for some they wake up each morning almost smiling, and smile their way through the day. To have such a happy, positive countenance is a blessing. And they smile even into old age. The creases in their faces are so different to so many of the aged whose usual facial creases and wrinkles reflect the care-worn worries and disappointing frustrations of a lifetime. When driving in slow-moving, heavy traffic, catch a glimpse of the facial expressions of the drivers coming in the opposite direction. The natural, relaxed facial expression of many is one of grim glumness.

The attitude responsible for sloth can be worked on. Like just about every 'attitude' we hold, it can be improved upon, to recognise 'sloth,' true 'sloth' as a deadly sin, derailing our lives, for ourselves and for our loved ones. The saying goes, 'attitude plus aptitude equals altitude.' The attitude we improve upon by willpower and any outside help. Aptitude comes from our natural skills and training. Together the altitude reached in our lives, as a whole, is higher, improved, and of greater worth.

INDULGENCE: whilst not one of the recognised Seven Deadly Sins (if it were that would make eight), we feel it fits in well here to say a few words about indulgence, or, to be more precise, 'self-indulgence.'

In the 1960s and 70s, in the armed forces, a specific example looked at here is the WRAF, the Women's Royal Air Force. The women all serving in this force were volunteers who had 'signed up' to serve for specific periods of time, usually three years and upwards. They had entered into a contract with the RAF to serve. However, the contract could be broken by the RAF for certain misdemeanours, and for pregnancy. There were no pregnant women allowed to serve in those days: whether the pregnancy was intended or not was immaterial, or whether married or single.

On each camp, each RAF station, there would be a weekly news-sheet for the camp's personnel to read. It included such things as personnel leaving the service on retirement or through ill health, although no actual medical details were included, of course. But for a woman, being discharged the service, the appropriate extract from Queen's Regulations and Air Council Instructions would be stated very briefly with an extracted wording without any mention at all of pregnancy: 'WRAF So-and-So name and rank, discharged the service …

free as an indulgence.' Everyone knew what it meant, 'up the duff, pudding club, family way, bun in the oven,' and so on. All pretty disreputable comments these days, thank goodness – literally.

That is to say free of her contract to the RAF, free to indulge herself in whatever took her fancy or as life proposed and offered, almost to say that, as she had indulged herself, sexually, she knew that she would be discharged, set free if pregnant. Free as an indulgence. But today, so grossly unfair; offensive even.

We are always indulging ourselves in so many ways. Even eating breakfast or lunch or supper, or be it just a snack bar, or a mug of tea, we are indulging ourselves. But are we? Are we, really? Surely the term doesn't mean those everyday 'essential,' life-supporting actions of eating, drinking, keeping warm and dry? Those aren't indulgences. No. Indulgence carries a degree of excess; more that we need, more than of anything that we need, above our needs. So, one mug of tea can quench our thirst, but a second starts the indulgence, possibly. Three, straight off, definitely, unless recovering from shock. The one ginger nut biscuit with it takes the edge off our appetite, but a second? Is that necessary? Is it indulgence? With the third and fourth definitely. It could depend on whether we need to slim down or not.

So generally, indulgence is the taking to excess, more than we need, or do we 'need' any of it at all? Take smoking. It's an indulgence; we don't 'need' to smoke, never have. Sure, it is just pleasurable, at first, and then becomes addictive, so then, we do 'need' it, to calm our nerves, to stave off our hunger when either there's no food to eat, as in war situations, or no food in the house, but we do have ciggy or two.

From this we get the picture that anything pleasurable taken to excess is an indulgence. So far we have only alluded to food, but of course there's drink, alcohol. That gives us pleasure, but taken to a greater degree is definitely an indulgence, and then more than that and we become a dependent alcoholic, all from indulging ourselves. Free as an indulgence – except the alcohol is not free.

There are more examples of how we indulge ourselves and in ways that can be bad for our health and for our personal finances, bad for our peace of mind and friends drifting away, and the family grows to disrespect us. That these indulgences become 'addictive' is axiomatic, and many are known as evils in society, ruining people's lives, such as all forms of gambling and 'recreational drug-taking.'

We all start, mostly when young, when we are very full of confidence, confident in ourselves and say, 'I can handle it, I will keep it in control, I won't let it rule me, I know what I am doing.' Oh, yeah? We've heard it all before, bravado, bragging it out, even bluffing it out, and then, later, the lying starts, and the lies get bigger and bigger until one day they are discovered.

No, they, the gamblers, and the drug users, all succumb to a greater or lesser degree; every man jack of them. And this is down to vanity, the 'master sin' of the Seven Deadly Sins. It's vanity that weakens our resolve and we indulge too much. Oh, but it's so pleasurable, 'I feel so good,' indulging; my friends all say it's good for me, I am nicer person when I give way and indulge like they do, every Saturday night. Eating and indulge to gluttony. It's a case of, 'I am feeling fine eating, I am enjoying it, it makes me feel good, I can forget my cares and woes when enjoying myself eating.' But look how many deny themselves food when in grief, with an 'I am just not hungry,' for days on end in bereavement. No vanity there, then.

It's a sort of vanity to feel good from our greed for money and other possessions, and so this can become an indulgence, because, as already said above, greed is an excessive term in itself. Similarly, so can lust, with its drive to an excessive desire for a certain kind of physical pleasure, sins of the flesh, also be doubtless down to vanity, at 'conquering' another subject, another victim. 'I knew I could get him or her to be unfaithful, and so ha-ha.' A victim to the object of their lust, for just the once, or for the time being, a torrid and probably tawdry affair.

So, the word 'indulgence' carries with it a kind of warning, a flag raised as an alert; do we actually need this, or need this much of this? Is this good for me, neutral for me, or if most definitely not good for me, then why am I bothering with it?

We've said several times in the lines in these chapters, 'Beware our thoughts etc.,' but now we can add and with good cause, 'Beware our indulgences,' or better still, 'Beware of indulgence.' Full stop.

CHAPTER 20
EIGHT IS A BEAUTIFUL NUMBER

The next most important 'Cardinal Number' for us is eight. It refers to the eight 'Beatitudes of Jesus' delivered by Jesus to a congregation of his countrymen, presumably mostly Hebrews of the Jewish faith on a hillside (possibly Mount Eremos) and nowadays known as the Sermon on the Mount but also possibly as his 'Sermon on the Plain.' They had gathered to hear Jesus speak, keenly waiting to hear his message, their message of hope. To many, they had always been expecting a Messiah, a leader who would lead them out from under the yoke of the Romans, which inevitably would involve fighting battles, killing and bloodshed.

Their lives had no 'mod cons,' without which our lives today would be hellish to the point of being unliveable. But if any of us have never had 'mod cons,' cars, phones, TVs, washing machines, dishwashers, fridges, freezers, electricity, ample running water, hot and cold, flushing toilets, broadband etc. etc. then we wouldn't miss them. We adapt to the circumstances we find ourselves in, that we have grown up with, to accept as normal. Their main concern was to have a better life without the taxes imposed by the Romans, and enjoy more of their own produce instead of it being mostly taken by the bullying Roman soldiers. Their spiritual lives would have been very much of a secondary importance. Remember there are only two aspects that religions concern themselves with: convincing us there is a life hereafter, and that our behaviour on earth buys the ticket to the afterlife. So killing someone would be a definite 'black mark,' possibly to even killing a Roman soldier. So to that extent, in those put-down societies, subservient to their masters, the Hebrews would have had, through their religion, which was pretty rigid, an awareness of the 'need' to lead a good life, a better life, for the next life. After all, they already had the Ten Commandments.

And so they came to hear what Jesus had to say. Perhaps they might have been expecting some form of 'rabble-rousing' invective, similar to that which we see or hear of so often today, a small crowd of unhappy people gathering in response to messages via Facebook and other social media connections, to lead a protest, a demonstration, even 'Rent-a-Mob,' hell-bent on 'violence' either to further their cause, or just out to 'enjoy' themselves with their twisted minds, and twisted hearts, and twisted lips.

But Jesus never had that sort of reputation; it's impossible. In a world devoid of medicines, disease was rife, and word spread rapidly that Jesus was a healer, healing the sick, the maimed and the disabled. Word spread like wildfire (meaning as fast as a donkey could go) and that gift of healing they believed could only have come from God, so Jesus became that 'Man of God,' and a 'Man of God' could only be a prophet, but, perhaps, even the Messiah. But if the Messiah, how could He lead the nation to defeat all its foes? And as we now know, the Jews rejected Jesus as their Messiah, murdered Him and two thousand years later, they are still waiting for their Messiah. What a hoot! Why? Because any 'Messiah' is Biblically predicted to enter Jerusalem through its East Gate, which now being in Muslim hands, the Muslims bricked it up! In that last week of his life Jesus entered Jerusalem through its East Gate, and we still have Jewish denials all-round the place.

The reluctance of some religions to deny history and proven facts is breathtakingly stubborn to the point of idiocy. Take Jewish ritual slaughter and take Muslim halal meat. For once the two opposing religions agree on something and that is that their followers shall only eat meat that has been slaughtered according to their now archaic rules. Their rules dictate that the animal shall have its throat cut only after a prayer by the appointed 'Holy' person authorised to make the cut. Originally, two thousand years ago this made good hygiene sense, that is to say, not to eat meat from an animal which had died, e.g. from disease, injury or old age, because it had not been 'bled out.' Bleeding out removes much of the blood from the tissues, which in those days, and now, helps keep the meat more free from the inevitable decomposition, especially in the Mediterranean heat, and with no means of refrigeration. Not only decomposition, but an animal alive is presumed healthy since it's not dead. Coming across a dead animal, dead from some unknown cause was often, if eaten, fatal to humans; for example, anthrax. So ritual slaughter made good sense then.

These days the animal is first stunned electrically to render it unconscious and then killed by the bleeding-out process of cutting its throat. But not for

Jews: they still insist on cutting the throat of the fully conscious, absolutely terrified animal, either cow or sheep as it is forced into a crate to have its throat cut or a revolving crate that is rotated until the animal is upside down. Upside down is the most unnatural and dreaded position for these animals. They have never been upside down in their lives (except for the occasional sheep which accidentally rolls upside down into a furrow in the land, and can't get up, and that's when the crows come and peck its eyes out). The neck of this unhappy beast is then extended by the 'priest' who feels his long-bladed knife, saying his spiritual words of prayer, and slits its throat expertly, it is hoped, to sever both jugular veins and both carotid arteries. It is the severing of the carotid arteries that renders unconsciousness and death, brain death, ensues in some several seconds, because the brain is also fed by an artery that can't be included in the cut, the intervertebral artery, and so its oxygen continues to go to the brain.

These days there is an ante-mortem and post-mortem inspection to rule out diseased animals. Slaughter without pre-stunning is cruel and unnecessary. Ritual throat-cutting with prayer is an unnecessary intrusion dictated by a blind, illogical following of archaic rules, followed so the religious leaders can maintain their grip over the malleable minds of their 'cult' members. They daren't let anyone question the rule book of their religion. Where would it end?

This is an example of the mindset that the Hebrews had of their faith at the time of Jesus. They believed they were 'God's chosen people' (chosen for what? For God to send Jesus, His Son, with a new covenant, a new promise?). They were instructed in their faith and effectively their minds were ruled over by the high priests and their underlings. So what was the attraction of the man Jesus, known to be a healer, a worker of miracles that healed people? Had the word got around that he also had some cheering and philosophical words, a preacher, a prophet? Most probably. It is written that Jesus spoke at length to his disciples, by way of instruction, gave them some healing powers, and they went out as his healing missionaries.

So it is likely that the crowd gathered for both reasons to see, to be near and hear comforting words from Jesus, that 'Sermon on the Mount.' Jesus's approach was similar to, and a variant of, that method adopted by lecturers even today, and that is to *Tell them what you are going to tell them, tell them, and then tell them what you have told them,* as the reader here will soon find out.

Each of Jesus's recorded sayings in the sermon began his sentence with

'Blessed are…' so, before looking at each of the eight individually, it's sensible to look at this word, as written, now for centuries, 'Blessed.' We feel we know almost instinctively what it means, what it implies, but can we express the meaning suitably in one or two synonyms?

For a start, is it something that has been blessed? That is to say 'blessed' is in the passive tense. Something or someone has done the blessing. To bless; what does that mean? To impart, to donate, to give, to render something, in this case something good, something worthy, something upright, something Holy, of God, God's blessings as in 'may all goodness be upon you,' be in you, be with you. To bless.

Those, then, who have received this blessing of having 'all goodness' delivered to and within them become those who are blessed.

The problem is that there is no certainty that this translation and this word 'blessed' actually impart the sense of the full meaning of Jesus's words. Almost certainly there were no contemporaneous notes taken down. Memories were relied upon for years and years until these events came to be chronicled. And when eventually they were, it is inevitable that the memories failed to recall the exact words Jesus spoke. There may even have been differences of opinion, even arguments over it. But the chronicler had a job to do and wrote what seemed most likely, in his language, and then centuries later that language is translated into modern languages and again the translation of the New Testament will seek to – nay – have to come up with a translation that is most like the nearest, in all imagination, to what Jesus was most likely to have said and meant.

So 'blessed' is a good word, appropriate in the sense of these 'Beatitudes' but of very deep meaning. We have to decide whether the word was meant in the passive sense, i.e. they have been blessed, as in already 'blessed,' or is it in the subjective sense, 'May God's blessings be upon them,' and even in the future tense, 'God will bless those who are…?' Moot points perhaps, but worth pondering upon as we look at each of the eight.

'Blessed are the poor in spirit for theirs is the Kingdom of Heaven'

We have elsewhere discussed such terms as 'Kingdom' and 'Heaven'. Heaven is that state of total ideal, perfect and enduring goodness, and Kingdom as being that state of a 'concentration' of the force for goodness, so powerful, and as an entity. In this sense, Kingdom and Heaven can be taken as being effectively tautological, synonymous.

To understand what is meant by the poor in spirit is more challenging. We know what 'poor' means, as in 'without,' especially used to denote physical wealth, but less specifically used to apply to any lowered, reduced or diminished state of something. If we are not poor in spirit, then perhaps we can be said to be 'rich in spirit,' but such a phrase is never used. Our first interpretation is likely to be someone feeling low, 'down in the dumps,' 'fed up,' 'not in a good place,' or even in a 'bad place,' or 'a dark place' with no sunshine in a life at that moment. Someone without any 'get up and go' or any 'joie de vivre,' the joy of being alive, but more a life of 'bonjour, tristesse.'

It could mean any of these unfortunate 'souls,' and the Beatitude implies for feeling like that, they will be able to walk straight into the 'Kingdom of Heaven.' Clearly none of this makes sense. Have the words spoken by Jesus reached us with the meaning he meant? Possibly not. Poor in spirit most likely means unloved. Those who are victims of poor parenting, and unhappy childhood, and unfaithful spouse, or having to live with a cruel and no longer loving family. These are the poor in spirit, the unloved and in Heaven there is love. They want to give and receive love, to others, despite their inner unhappiness, they experience all the warmth and feelings of goodness whenever given an opportunity to show and be loving to someone. We need to bless them, with God's help.

'Blessed are they who mourn, for they shall be comforted'
Fortunately, to mourn is a natural response to the loss of a loved one from this life. Here Jesus is saying that if we are genuine in our mourning then that is 'of God.'

There are degrees of mourning, meaning various proportions of depths of feelings, of disturbed emotional well-being. We tend to mourn the loss of the young very much more than someone who has led their whole life up to a 'ripe old age' and death has been long expected. It is said, 'No one should live longer than their children,' and the loss of a child hits us tragically. Some never get over it. Their mourning, their grief, is so real as to make them so poor in spirit that there is no comforting them. But they will be comforted, by the love of God. To be so full of grief, ongoing and enduring can mean the ultimate extreme form of mourning, but to mourn can, and perhaps should be a conscious choice, and this is where the love of God can come in.

The royal family has a 'period of mourning,' a defined state of conduct for a period of time. If we mourn so much, too much, it can and does disorder our lives. And this is in all probability a correct and appropriate response to the loss of a loved one, including the loss of a much-loved pet. The 'shock or realisation' that we have lost a loved one is an instinctive emotional response. There is nothing unhealthy in that. What is unhealthy is when the grief and mourning are so extreme that it can so harm our life as to cost us our job and our health through not eating, neglecting our personal hygiene etc. So we are free and able to choose the degree to which we mourn, and for how long, not allowing our emotions to run riot, indulging in self-pity. We can learn 'to go into the control room' and slide the button down to lower the degree of mourning from the 'danger' level to the safe level, and set the timer to auto switch off mourning in so many days, weeks or months. Pity Queen Victoria didn't do this.

So for how long and why can we do this? Because we are blessed by being 'in mourning.' That goodness, that love that flows from us as we mourn is reciprocated and reinforced by the love of God, that all-powerful force in the universe. And how do we know this? Because Jesus left us His message, 'Blessed are those who mourn,' and by His message alone we are comforted, knowing love is there to open our hearts, to reassure us when we are low in spirit. Just to know, as in to be told, or to be reminded that as we mourn, we are blessed. It usually takes a God-fearing person to tell us, someone who is a good Christian, certainly in that act, anyway.

'Blessed are the meek, for they shall inherit the earth'
So here we have Jesus referring to the future of the earth, to life on earth. Not the Kingdom of Heaven but to earth. Again we wonder here if something has been lost in translation, lost in meaning through the centuries. Or is it just a 'figure of speech,' for Jesus was fond of parables? Meek is harder to define than someone who is not meek; someone who is not meek is someone who is proud, and vain, brash. We have addressed inappropriately proud, improper pride and vanity as the 'worst' of the 'Seven Deadly Sins,' the chief sin that drives the other six. It would seem to make sense, then, if someone is not vain in any way at all, they could correctly be described as meek.

Unfortunately, in modern words' parlance, the term 'meek' is mostly used in a derogatory sense to mean weak and feeble, someone who is pusillanimous or wet. This is unfortunate because we can hardly think Jesus would be extolling this as a virtue; 'feeble-mindedness.' He is more likely to mean those who have resisted vanity in all its forms. For nearly all of us are given to vanity in some way, some aspect of our lives, some aspect of our characters, so much so that, until we indulge in a fair self-critique, we are not aware of it. Any challenge to our self-image and our self-concept, who we believe we are, and who we think we are seen as, can evoke a response driven by some degree of vanity.

Oh! To be free of all vanity, to be virtuous, and virtue is its own reward, and the reward of those free of vanity, the meek, is the joy of an untrammelled life here on earth. It's become our 'makarios,' our own 'nirvana,' we have 'inherited' it. It's as if life here on earth becomes as if a blessed existence, here on earth. Oh! To be meek! But it's so hard! And yet, there are many who are meek; those less fortunate than ourselves. Those who sadly are afflicted with chronic ill health, those who are maimed through accident of birth or accident in life, those who depend upon the physical support of others, most frequently of loved ones, but also depend on the state. Are not these the meek, the disadvantaged in some way, the potentially if not actually 'poor is spirit'? To some degree or other they suffer as we haven't known it, theirs is a true meekness, the acceptance of their being, their humility. They deserve 'peace of mind' and love, and loving care.

Jesus is saying they will be blessed, become blessed, and in so doing come to that state of Heaven on earth; that concept that tends to be so elusive at times like this. To many, 'inherit the earth' probably means after God has got rid of all the bad guys, after Armageddon, after life on the earth has been decimated by a collision with a mega-meteorite-cum-asteroid. Either that or God will have brought it about that the government of earth's peoples will be given solely to the meek, to rule over the unmeek, the vain. Hardly.

Certainly 'shall inherit' is a reference to the future and the scriptures (written by man, remember, but probably by 'Holy', well-intentioned, even 'blessed' men) foretell of God's Day of Judgement; as if a whistle is blown to signify the end of the game, the end of the match, and God comes to judge the 'quick and the dead' – 'quick' as in currently alive, and the dead, meaning all the dead there ever was – and that will run into billions even trillions since man became man, the spiritual man, whenever that was. It is a concept that seems irrational, at least to the philosophy of this book. If we believe the scriptures, there is, in effect, an ongoing judgement, of us, our souls, upon death, a judgement that is understanding and forgiving, and that, that which is in us, which is our soul, becomes part of the universal force for good, ever flowing, ever present, ever enveloping the world, the great universal intelligence that we know is there, as in we 'just know,' uncannily.

Us. There. It's like this. Imagine a molecule of carbohydrate that was bound up with others in St. Peter's body. On his death, the body buried in the earth decomposes, and the molecules are released so that a molecule of carbon eventually lands up in a plant that is then eaten. And then that molecule lands up in someone else's body. And so on. Who knows where that same carbon molecule is two thousand years later. It could be within any one of us. Imagine that, part of St Peter within someone today. Yes, some huge jump in imagination, but not impossible. And so it is with the subatomic constituent of forces, of electricity, of magnetism, of gravity, of the force of goodness. It's not too hard to imagine where that force of goodness within us now will ultimately land up, inheriting the earth, to roam at large, to influence and to be a guide to others; that love-force of goodness.

'Blessed are those who hunger and thirst for righteousness, for they shall be satisfied'

It is not easy for us to be clear here on what is the full meaning is of Jesus's words, as they have been written down, translated and written again, down through the centuries.

The phrase 'hunger and thirst' can literally mean to fast oneself to bring out the desired response in others who are perceived to be acting in no good way. Like Gandhi did. Like Emmeline Pankhurst. And does it mean that the fasting person will be spiritually 'fed and watered' by being blessed, for the duration of the fast, to the extent of being 'satisfied?' Was Gandhi so 'blessed?' And what about Ms E. Pankhurst?

Alternatively, we may choose to interpret the phrase to hunger and thirst too mean to go all out for, to work our hardest or, to do our 'darndest.' We often hunger after something. We seldom 'thirst' after something; but 'to hunger and thirst' is the superlative version, underscored, emphasised, empowered.

But if we have to 'bust a gut' to bring about a change of course in one or more from a pathway that was clearly not right, not of loving goodness, the Beatitude just says we will be 'satisfied.' No glory, no advance into a promise of Heaven on earth, just satisfied, with the desired outcome achieved.

More likely, perhaps more obviously, the hungering and thirsting is for righteousness in ourselves. It is ourselves we always need to work on. We always need to set goals for ourselves. We should never set goals for others. It is a complete waste of time and effort. We can only ever influence others by example. So what, then, is meant by this word 'righteousness?' It is hardly a word applied to an individual's qualities. We may say or think someone is righteous. We are hardly likely to say he or she exudes righteousness. The term 'self-righteous' is derogatory.

Righteousness would seem to be the state, the abstract concept of a state of rightness, of goodness, of upholding the Law of God as in the Commandments, the upholding the law of the land, of probity, of truth and honesty, straight dealing, faithful in body and mind to one's commitments, to one's duty.

Satisfied, just satisfied? No thanks – no reward? 'To give and not count the cost' and 'To labour and not to ask for any reward?' Yes, it's as the prayer goes. Yes, yes and yes; because that reward, expected or not, is not at all God's way. To be given pocket money as a child for helping to clear the table, the helpful act bringing a reward, is fine, in practical terms of service, but right thinking, finding the right way to think, to feel, to love others and oneself, is reward enough, enough in itself. It is the meekness referred to in the Beatitudes.

'Blessed are the merciful, for they shall obtain mercy'

This can make us think of the phrase, 'do as you would be done by.' If we are in a position whereby we can deliver some sort of decision, a judgement perhaps over another, perhaps the imposition of some fine, or punishment, but perhaps it's only a question of whether to drive home on someone their promise to do something, to return something, especially money or property, that, due to the unexpected exigencies of life, their misfortunes, even their stupidity, they can no longer fulfil their obligation. Or even possibly only meet an obligation with extreme hardship and suffering. In such cases one can be merciful. This does not mean one is expected to be absolute. It may not be wise to absolve someone completely. Granting mercy can be graded, the burden eased, made reasonable, fair and just. To get off 'scot-free' seldom does anyone any good. The quality of mercy is (or should be) most definitely 'strained' (with thanks to Balthazar, aka Portia, and to Shakespeare).

To be merciful, then, is a measured response to a situation, applying righteousness appropriately, proportionally to the situation. Being merciful when it is needed, appropriate, right, is something that we can do as an act of humanity, of kindness, of love and understanding, for our fellow mankind, something righteous and even godly. In the rich pageant of life we seldom consider enough our moves in the future, which is rather complex like a game of chess. Surely, we seldom, if ever, stop to think that, one day, we ourselves may be in the need of mercy. So, if we are to be merciful, we don't think, 'I'd better be merciful here, and so store up good points for when I need mercy myself.' No, we are satisfied with the righteousness of being merciful; that is all.

Can receiving mercy in return be in our time, here on earth? Possibly, but don't expect it. More likely, since these are God's words spoken through Jesus, mercy unto us will come from Heaven in its own way, in its own time, and when it comes, we will be able to recognise it for what it is, the love of God.

'Blessed are the pure of heart, for they shall see God'

Since Biblical times, people have wanted to see God, hoped, even expected that God would show "Himself" to prove "He" existed. They have never had their wishes met, and it is very unlikely in our current understanding that we will ever 'see God.' We and they should not make the mistake of thinking too literally. We can't see gravity, we can't see magnetism or electricity, we can only see the effects these forces bring about. As we have proposed and argued elsewhere, God is not a being in the sense we understand as humans, but a force, the force of goodness, of love. We could say that we can see God all the time, if we can see beauty in things, and if we can 'see' love being expressed and exchanged.

So why does this Beatitude say the pure in heart will see God? It's like this. In discussion, perhaps even in a disagreement we eventually manage to put our point, our case, our reasoning across to the other person, and then that other person, at last grasping the point, the principle we have argued, says, slowly and thoughtfully, 'Yes, I see what you mean. I see your point.' Negotiators today are trained not to see others' points of view, but be stubbornly determined their own objective must prevail.

So here we are saying 'see,' not with our eyes as in vision, but as an understanding in our minds. 'For they shall see God,' then means the pure in heart will understand the force of goodness, of love, and not only understand, but also know it, to be at one with it, and they themselves to be 'of God,' and in that, they will be both meek and righteous, and yes, mourn, too.

But 'pure of heart?' Pure is an absolute term, like unique. Something is either unique or it is not; you can't have something nearly unique. It is either unique or it is not. Something can become unique. Clarice Cliff may produce only ten matching pieces of china/pottery. They are sold to a retailer, on the way the lorry crashes, nine are broken, the remaining one, the sole survivor of that range, that batch has now become unique (unless Clarice makes another nine copies).

It is the same with pure. Chemically pure may be very difficult to find, or create; but creating pure will be easier. For liquids, repeated distillations of the distillate can eventually produce the 'pure' state of the chemical, if that is a liquid. Some say we are born pure, pure of heart; theologians say no, we are not born pure, we are born with 'original sin,' a concept they have cooked up, devised to drive us towards 'baptism,' the act that redeems us of our 'original sin.' What tosh! Of course, we are born pure of heart, and as we grow, and grow up and in response to all the situations we meet during that process, we 'learn' how to lie, to cheat, to scheme, to protect ourselves and defend our self-image, our persona. As young and then young adults we fall victim to all the seductions of easy money, a false life, in fact victim to all the Seven Deadly Sins.

And then can come an awakening, a revelation, perhaps a conversion on the road to Damascus, or was it the road to Bridlington, Bristol or Bridport or Brighton or Battersea? Or wherever? This distillation produces a distillate, and we develop something vaguely towards 'pure of heart.' We may even get, with time, to being somewhere near being pure of heart. But not pure, never pure. Never ever pure, because we are human and we fail, we always fail, and because we are frail, we err. Who can be 'pure of heart?'

'Of heart?' Why did Jesus, as it is written, say pure 'of heart?' Remember the heart is the seat of the emotion of love, to love, with love, loving. So, can we be perfectly loving, 100% of the time, ever? If that were possible, we would be as Jesus was, because to be 100% perfectly loving means to be 'of God,' godly, and godlike. We cannot, and therefore we shall not see God as the Beatitude says. But we can get nearly there. Not pure, not pure of heart, but sub-pure, less than pure; we can go on distilling the distillate. Eventually we shall see God, but in Heaven, in our afterlife, because that is the whole basis of the New Covenant of Jesus. His promise that, through Him, we shall enter the 'Kingdom of Heaven' and there all will be revealed, we will understand the nature, the being, the existence of God, God in the Trinity, and we can then say 'Yes, I see what you mean!' So,

Jesus said, 'Pure of heart' as a goal for us, as in 'If you want to see God, get pure of heart first.'

'Blessed are the peacemakers, for they shall be called the 'children of God'
Again we are aware that as with all the Beatitudes, they point to the future, perhaps even the 'future conditional,' as in, if you do and say this or that, then that or this will happen. Conditional. In this case, who will be doing the 'calling,' calling the peacemakers 'children of God?'

Studying Latin we learn that 'bellum gero' means 'I wage war,' and there was a lot of bellum gero-ing in those days. So, if someone becomes the aggressor, he or she automatically creates a defender. It's like buying and selling, oxidation and reduction. If someone buys, someone must do the selling, the buyer and the seller. If a chemical becomes oxidised, the donor chemical becomes reduced. The aggression creates a defender, even if we don't put up a fight and immediately sue for peace, as in we just roll over and submit. Whether we fight to defend or submit to losing to whenever the aggressor wants, we are a 'peacemaker' because we are bringing about, either by our success over the aggressor, or losing to the aggressor by submitting, we are bringing about peace. But is it a 'just' peace, or only temporary, or is it perhaps an enduring, lasting peace? On occasion, aggressors claim that by their successful pre-emptive strike, they have brought about peace. These situations arise through the progressive development of tension between peoples and between nations. War is the ultimate extension of foreign policy, a failure of diplomacy, a failure to resolve international disagreements. A failure of the peacemakers.

Chamberlain attempted to be a peacemaker, but was not called a 'child of God.' Up against Hitler his attempts, were well intentioned but misplaced, as history later showed. Anyone who either senses tense situations that can boil over into violence, anyone who chooses to work on behalf of a nation, to bring about the understandings and create goodwill to ease international tensions is working for peace. A peacemaker. They use diplomacy as their art, their means of making progress to resolve arguments; most are highly intelligent, well-educated people. But are they religious? We can imagine Christians on our side – other religions on their side? Or any at all? Does it matter? All that matters is that they are good people, of God, recognising the 'evil' that is war, ungodly war. People went to war for the furtherance of their misguided beliefs. The Crusades, all so mistaken, set Christian against Muslim and Muslim against Christian for centuries. In the First World War the German soldiers with 'Gott mit uns' stamped on their belt, claiming 'God is with them,' the aggressors, aiming a pre-emptive strike to reach Paris with their 'Schlieffen Plan,' subdued the French before the French could respond. Hardly 'of God.' So, so very mistaken. So evil, and it took four years for the peacemakers to bring about peace, a peace that was not to be enduring, as there was no just peace. Probably well intentioned at the time, the Paris Peace Conference of 1919 that lasted about three years to finalise the 'peace process,' only for it all to be undone in 1939. Nothing is ever settled, until it's settled right. (Thank you for that, Miss Marple.)

Perhaps we should revere our peacemakers more. We certainly do our brave soldiers, sailors and airmen, but our diplomats? Those striving behind the scenes to avoid disagreements, potential conflicts, those who work hard to see that any peace brought about, is right, fair and just. How about the peacemakers after the Falklands War? The Gulf War? Do we call them 'Children of God?' No, because we wait to see the outcome. The outcome may not be clear perhaps until the 'peacemakers' have retired or even passed on, dead.

So, it is most likely that in the Beatitude of Jesus, the peacemakers will receive their accolade, 'children of God' – after death. 'Children of God' implies the 'bringing into the fold,' the all-embracing, loving protection of God, the inheritance of God's grace, of all that is good. Pure goodness, as in pure of heart. So, it would seem Jesus, in saying peace-making is a 'meritorious' act, attempting to make peace, or striving to make peace, and if successful especially, is bringing one nearer to God. It is a God-like activity. If you try to bring about peace, but if you fail, are you worthy of being called a peacemaker? Now there is a question! Almost certainly yes, because attempting to make peace, to bring about the avoidance or the cessation of the evil of violence, the abuse of life that is war, is definitely a worthy activity. A Christian activity, loving thy neighbour, like the children of God do.

'Blessed are they who are persecuted for the sake of righteousness, for theirs is the Kingdom of Heaven'

Well, here we go again. This means they will join the poor in spirit, those whom we have already looked at in some small detail, and as to what might be meant in the concept of this book as 'the Kingdom of Heaven.' We have also set out what could well be interpreted as Jesus's expectation of the outcome of His use, His supposed use, of the word 'righteous.' And like a teacher, or even a politician, both of whom have the instinct or have learned the art and skill of oratory, whereby certain words and phrases used again can drive home the message, can stir in the listeners' hearts and minds.

But why persecution? Why would anyone want to be so antagonistic to a righteous person, or someone approaching a fair degree of righteousness, or come to that, any degree of righteousness at all, to be persecuting them? From history we know of the vast range of types and degrees of persecution of Christians, and of groups of so-called Christians persecuting other groups of so-called Christians. We say so-called, because some, purporting to be of the Christian faith, choose not to follow God's Rules and in preference, and by the ignorant persuasion of other so-called Christians choose to follow 'Man's Rules' for their conduct, their religious conduct, here on earth. These same distinctions are to be applied to other religions as well.

Let the message here be rightly understood. Faith is a belief. It is in the mind and it feeds the heart. There may be required practical demonstrations of that faith, such things as in the way of acts of worship, communal worship, and things like selective clothing and style of being hirsute, of eating and other behavioural idiosyncrasies, and other manifestations of the religion. Faith comes from God. Religion comes from man. We don't have to have anything to do with religion, it mostly means trouble. Trouble following their doctrinaire 'rules,' the eating only fish on Fridays mentality. Any self-discipline in our lives to identify with the life of Jesus should be entirely 'self-imposed,' as in it's our decision, our choice, without the obligation to feel we are 'going along' to 'get along' under pressure of some kind from others, from the expectations of their religion.

Any religion that does not believe in or preach peace, peaceful cohabitation on earth, and does not eschew evangelism of the pernicious kind, doesn't lead by good example but instead, by being doctrinaire, does not represent a true faith. And being driven by 'Man's Rules' that religion is then little more than a cult. Cults set themselves up on principle more akin to bigotry than a rational right and just thinking; setting themselves up as apart, as 'better,' as a distinct esoteric alignment of similarly persuaded groups, sometimes so big that they become more identified as a race of peoples, as with Jews, Muslims and Hindus. Some of these religious cults 'forbid' marriage outside of their cult in an attempt to keep their cult 'pure' and discreet. These are also known as, or can be described as, 'a religion of fear.' Its members become fearful of denying the cult's teachings and practices, and they even have their cult 'police,' who harry their victims into a nervous, frightened submission into being prosecuted for their straying from the fold.

Any religion that seeks to put down another religion, in order to advance its own, does not live 'at peace' in the world. This lack of tolerance, its bigotry, incites suspicion, fear and even the violent put-down of others, to further some aim, as in terrorism. Some believe, for example, that Islam could root out its terrorists, if it really wanted to.

To deny Christ is one thing. To persecute the followers of Christ is another. It becomes the actions of the Anti-Christ. To designate another religion, or indeed an individual or group of individuals as 'the Anti-Christ' is an extreme accusation that Christians are reluctant to use: the label is so deep and full of meaning. Perhaps the label could be more freely used. Those who deny Christ are anywhere and everywhere. Christians accept them, live alongside them, promote their interests, even. But do those in denial reciprocate? Do they aim to live with the Christians in peace, or are they, is their agenda, clandestinely, to seek to promote only their own kind; wheedle their way into our systems, our society, our governing so that they can have us all living in fear of their religion and then their law? Far-fetched? We think not. *The enemy shouteth. The Godless come fast. Iniquity, hatred, upon me they cast. Oh, where shall I fly? Oh, for the wings of a dove. Far away, far, far away would I fly.*

Righteousness is not to be confused with being religious. Many people lead a wholesome life avoiding the Seven Deadly Sins; following the principles identified in the Beatitudes, and most of God's Commandments, without necessarily giving a thought to their connection with the Christian faith. They may be naturally kind-spirited, loving people, probably mostly by having been given unconditional love when a child and growing up with that love. For many of us, we have received a good idea of what's right and what's wrong from our parents, from school, from reading and from observing what goes on in society, from the news.

But if we stand out, put our heads above the parapet and shout out, about being more righteous, is that a wise or prudent thing? Well, for a start, we risk accusations of being self-righteous, i.e. setting ourselves up as 'better.' No, we can only properly stand up for righteousness when we refuse to accept some form of wrongdoing, something we believe to be wrong, that is 'not good,' not of God's love for one another, and that's when we may well be persecuted. We may be criticised, made to feel tainted in some way, verbally abused, vilified, ejected from some group or other, or even subjected to violence. All because we know, or at least believe, that we should not 'go along to get along,' to get along with morally corrupt conduct, unbecoming behaviour. We would need to be pretty clear in our own minds what we believe is right, as in God's way, the way of love, and seeing the end result several moves ahead in life's game of chess. When Christ healed the sick, he bid them to go their way and say nothing. Few did, most put their heads above the parapet, as Jesus knew they would, with the ultimate end result of, and to bring about that Good Friday Agreement (note we are not meaning here the Northern Ireland-Irish Good Friday Agreement, but that other Good Friday Agreement, and not the one when Pontius Pilate agreed with the Jews, 'If I let you crucify this man and I let Barabbas go free, will you all now go away and shut up?' agreement). No. The Good Friday Agreement we mean is God's agreement that only by following the life teachings of Jesus can we enter Heaven.

So clearly, what is being said here is that many situations we find ourselves in, often become embroiled in, are complex, and to sort the right and wrong out from each other may not be as easy and straightforward as we would have liked them to be.

We can never get worse at anything for practising! That is to say, if we can practise and practise at the mindfulness and awareness of the power of goodness, of God, then we will find these tricky, difficult, testing situations somewhat easier to resolve in our hearts and in our minds. But beware, as our skills grow, the tests get harder, just like a digital game of chess on our tablet, a raised skill level.

Moving towards righteousness is worthy, but on the road, there will always be the roughness thrown at us by others, some degree of persecution or even 'unto death' for some, those of such grit, such stern constitution, such commitment to their belief in the faith of righteousness. We lesser mortals can only hope we are never put to that supreme test, for we know or suspect or fear, that to get along, we will go along.

Striving towards righteousness as we have said is worthy in itself because, being human, we cannot reach pure righteousness. The last Beatitude offers real hope, and, indeed, allows us to expect that, by striving towards righteousness, the pursuit of righteousness, the 'sake' of righteousness, we can become 'of the Kingdom of Heaven.'

CHAPTER 21
THE TEN COMMANDMENTS

Our next most important number in our lives, and most probably the most important is the Number 10. We count in multiples of ten and these multiples feature hugely in our everyday lives. Ideally all measurements would be in multiples of ten, and for many countries they have had the 'decimal' system for many decades, and the UK is getting there. UK money 'went' decimal nearly half a century ago now, and measurements of distance, in small things have been in 'metric' scale. But the UK has made no real effort for long distances, such as miles. Volume measures in the UK are mostly metric, except beer; we must have 'our pint!' Measurement of weight is half and half, and slowly decimal weights are being used with understanding without 'mentally converting.' Estate agents put the room sizes now in decimal measurements to hide the smallness of the rooms from the uninitiated.

So ten is an important number, but it is important not for the reasons given above. It is important in our everyday lives because there are the Ten Commandments of God.

A Commandment is a pretty strong word. It is an order. No quibbling. No doubt, no hesitation from authority. And where did the word come from? Who called this set of Rules for Conduct, this code of conduct, these guidelines, if you please, 'Commandments?' Yes, they are written in the imperative. Each as an order. Do this. Don't do that. Else…else what? In the military and to some extent, the police, they know what an order is. Most of society, from early days, but especially in the Victorian era and up to the end of the Second World War, knew what an order was, or so we believe. But these days, do they, after 70 years of peace, and half a century without National Service to train the young how to defend their democratic freedoms and in the process get to know what an order is, and what to do with it?

Did the name come from Biblical times, as in Moses came down the mountain and said, 'Hey, you lot, listen up. I have here a set of rules that God on the mountain had me write out on these tablets, one rule on each (the original tablets of very low storage, obviously), and this was in the days when an apple meant an apple and about which God said, 'Don't touch that apple. Those apples!' It is not known if God said to explain, 'Else you risk death of the good life as you know it.' All was well until someone, Eve it was, plucked an apple off the forbidden tree and told Adam to take a bite, and then he could see she was naked (more likely he saw that both were naked), and then all hell was let loose ever since: war, disease, poverty, pestilence, famine and plague, and the pox. That first original apple experience, and if we can Adam and Eve it (for they neither knew how to obey an order), led some very many years later to an 'outcome' on Mount Sinai, not Silicon valley, of a set of ten tablets, each with a message in writing, in a text, probably the first early SMS 'text' message.

But just a minute, this is an order, a Commandment, to be followed: we don't have any choice. All disciplined persons know it is our duty to obey lawful commands, at least as much as is humanly possible at the time. Obeying orders becomes automatic with training, with practice and with experience. The Germans are the best at it; it's probably in their genes.

So God's Commandments as written, as recorded from God, via Moses, at the Mount of Sinai, are not optional. God is not making it volitional to follow His Commandments, they are there, just like that, simple no quibble, so it's, 'Make it so, Mr Sulu,' and, 'Aye, aye, Captain;' is the response.

But then there is the view that because they serve to bring about certain sets of behaviour, certain standards of behaviour, aren't the Commandments (as so named) more a setting out of a 'code of conduct,' a list of expected behaviours, a set of guidelines. We know how civilians, as opposed to those in the military, hate anything that smacks of an 'order,' preferring to receive 'requests,' suggestions, not the imperative tense but the subjunctive or interrogative tense; a 'Would you stand to attention, please?' asks Sergeant Wilson. This way purports to allow individual discernment, discretion and some executive power that can lead towards the development of a fuller character, as in an optional choice; one is supposed to have been educated into making a good choice. Sadly, it's frequently no, not a good choice, that is, for a wide variety of reasons, mostly too libertarian in nature.

A plain simple command, to be carried out; not an invitation to debate, not a suggestion of any discussion, as is nowadays thought by the children of our modern educational systems, and by the universality of the media, TV and the internet. Question everything. Obey an order? Whatever do you mean? Whatever are you on about? Can we talk this through? Or can you send me an email? And so it has become, talking it through and risking an enemy bullet between the eyes in the meantime, waiting for the order to be obeyed. It's called free thinking, and could sink us all.

Companies large and small mostly have some form of a code of conduct. It tells us how we are to behave (when at work, and some codes try to include conduct out of work, too, lest any bad news report should reflect on the company). As if we need telling how to behave! We were taught how to behave by our parents, weren't we? We were taught how to behave at school, surely? We know instinctively how to behave, don't we? We can use our own nodle, if not drunk. The answers to most of those questions are, regrettably, no. We are not brought up, educated, never realised that at 'work' means 'being of service' to someone, and taught that, in just about all and any work situation we can think of, sensible, inoffensive and courteous conduct is required. And yet it is something more. A company's code of conduct is also about complying with and promoting the 'brand' that is the company. So, as well as requiring a good behaviour record, the code will set a standard for certain operational procedures, which could be practical but may be just verbal or presentational, e.g. how we look, how we deport ourselves, as in no slouching, no touch rules between employees that could be regarded as abusive or of a sexual nature.

These codes aim to cover as many aspects that might arise as the employer can think of at the time, and from time to time the codes are updated. The Ten Commandments of God endure since their inception and without needing updating, they are as they were and very adequately; no, more than adequately, let's say, ideally fulfil their role, their purpose. Or would do, if only we could follow them, obey them.

We can live our lives by them, on the one hand, we could be very mindful of the Ten Commandments, and on the other hand, be mindful of the Seven Deadly Sins. If only we could achieve that, we'd probably have reached a good degree of righteousness. But this is by no means an easy thing, and may we be forgiven for a feeling of being born to fail, at least in this respect.

The Commandments come in two parts, two types of order, two categories. The first group is to do with recognition, acknowledgement of the deity of God; that God exists. We know that this force for goodness exists. It has already been propounded elsewhere in these chapters. The problem for some is they want proof of everything before they can agree something exists. They can't see magnetism, but they agree it exists because its effects are demonstrable. Likewise for gravity, and even electricity. You can't see 'gravity' or electricity, or goodness. They accept all three exist, but we have difficulty interpreting goodness as God, as of God, as Godliness. Crazy! It's so easy. Why do agnostics, like the atheists who tried and gave up, insist on 'trying' to believe in the 'wrong' thing?

'Thou shalt have no other God before me'

Humans have 'invented' gods in just about every civilisation. Gods to appease, in some way, often through sacrificial offerings, and by the building of images and temples to worship. It is all a set of behavioural patterns arising from our fears and lack of understanding of the world of nature around us, over which we have no control, but the gods have, supposedly. And for all events that have a good outcome, or a bad outcome, those outcomes have been laid at the feet of the gods. Civilisations have 'invented' a god for this, another for that, indeed a god for everything imaginable. And for all those bad things, they invented the Devil. Satan aka Beelzebub. So, we have different gods for each of the things they did well, and hoped to go well, but only one to blame when they did bad things and offended the gods who'd turned their backs.

Well, at least that's mostly the case. We are acquisitive, goal-seeking creatures who can't help but feel there is some force acting to influence our lives, and that force has become for many civilisations and cultures the object of their worship and their supplications. If we truly understood the nature of God, of Goodness, complete righteousness and all goodliness, we would never 'ask' for anything, because 'asking prayers' are simply affirmations to do with goal setting. For example, a prayer for the complete peace of mind for a loved one sets the goal for us to help, as best we can, to bring that about. It's a good prayer because with that 'peace of mind' comes healing, the riddance of disease or its tolerance, when, if no healing is to happen, then for them, it's a case of 'God give me strength.'

'Before me' seems to imply that 'lesser gods' may be allowed. But what is a god? It seems hardly likely that any simple definition could be agreed upon in this context of 'lesser gods.' As we have said, cultures have invented gods for all sorts of things, mostly to pray to, to ask for things, and when those things come about, we thank God, that God, and ergo, that God must exist. Q.E.D.? We think not! What a crazy logic. We should have nothing else we pray to, because prayers are affirmations, born and brought about by our love of God and our love of all things good, as we draw strength from that force, the force for goodness. It's true that there is a sense, some sense of godliness, that God is there, listening and with us when we pray justly, sensibly and realistically. But to have it in our mindset that we are submitting our hopes and aspirations, however humbly, to an outside force to decide our fate is mistaken. Instead, the mindset needed is one of self-determination towards the desired worthy outcome. Asking, willing, out of a concern, for the force of goodness for another's sake is godliness.

To worship is to bow down in respect and even fear, to go down on our knees, either literally or metaphorically, to prostrate ourselves, to crouch in foetal submission, to beg forgiveness, to honour, to praise, to be joyful, to shout 'Hallelujah!' and bang drums, to sing chants and hymns of praise. It's all these things, and it is also the quiet thankfulness, that loving and admiring respect, a respite from the tumbling rush of our thoughts each day as we go about our lives, that pause. The pause when we stop and acknowledge, as we see, feel, hear, smell and even touch the wondrous thing that is life, born of God. That beautiful scenery, the wonder of the scented rose in full bloom, the competing chorus of birds in the morning, the beauty of a piece of hand-carved and polished wood we just can't help touching. What a wonderful way to worship. No building, no noise, no artificial smells, no chanting for its own sake. Let each worship according to his or her own style, accepting that it will always be personal, individual, but with a commonality with those of like mind.

Some tend to confuse, in the different denominations, as having almost a different God, or possibly just a different understanding of God, as to be 'almost' like a different God. There is a tendency to forget that the God of the Jewish faith is, supposedly, the same God as the Christians, Jehovah. It seems as if, when we give something a name, a pronoun, it personalises it, tending towards anthropomorphisation of the named things. For example, if we name our car, it gives some character to it, in our mind. It's no longer inanimate. It's half alive, we can love it, hate it, wash and polish it and kick it when it goes wrong and lets us down. And if we attempt to name God, the same happens. Do not go there.

So why, by this author, is collective worship so suspect as appropriate, or necessary at all, to be a faithful Christian? It is because collective worship leads to denominations and denominations are divisive; they lead to the adoption of more of 'Man's Rules' and less therefore, per se, of God's Rules.

But Jesus said, as it is written, 'where two or three are gathered together in His name there He is amongst them.' It is possible this has been interpreted as 'we must all get together for worship.' But does that necessarily follow? Getting together in His name surely means that He is not there when there is a gathering of two or three who are planning a robbery or other evil deed. So even amongst two or three good people when together at work, Jesus is there. It doesn't mean they have to worship.

'You shall not make idols'

So, if we accept and understand the nature of God as expounded in these chapters, there is no need of lesser gods, and we accept and understand then that there can only be one God in our lives, in us, doing good, for good, 'for goodness' sake.'

And because we cannot see God, feel God, touch God, hear or smell God, we cannot make an idol to God. And having and needing no lesser gods, we have no need of idols. And God's Second Commandment, 'You shall not make idols', falls into place. Plonk! Right there. Done.

'You shall not take the name of the Lord your God in vain'

This is the Third Commandment in this first category of the Commandments. The phrase 'taking something in vain' these days is a bit archaic. We sometimes read, 'in vain did I try this, and in vain did I try that, but to no avail, I just couldn't manage it.' Here 'in vain' implies a failure, something invalid, of negative outcome, despite the effort. It's not the same meaning as 'taking in vain,' which in this Commandment implies some deliberation of intent, either planned or spontaneous, whatever, most definitely of negative connotations, like something derogatory.

Here it surely means to denigrate, to talk down, to decry, abuse and defile. Surely it can also mean not to use God's name inappropriately. Just about everyone says the word 'God,' expressively, unthinkingly, as a descriptive underscoring superlative, at some time or other. Other expressions, some used like expletives such as the 'Oh my God' phrase, the so-called OMG phrase, or 'for God's sake' or 'for the love of God' or 'in the name of God, what is…?' Others of some vintage are 'Strewth,' meaning 'God's Truth' or 'Gor Blimey', meaning 'God blind me'. In the same category are exclamations like 'Good heavens,' and its opposite, 'Bloody hell.'

Should we be bandying the thought, the word 'God' about so freely, so unthinkingly, veering towards the disrespectful, and even 'in vain?' In this way, this Commandment is probably the most 'broken' of all. As our school reports used to say, regularly, 'could do better.'

If we are not to take 'in vain' the 'name of God' then we should take care not to 'take in vain' the revered prophets and Gods of other faiths. Cynical, atheistic intellectuals think it's smart and 'okay' to mock faiths and the tokens other people hold dear. Think of the 'Charlie Hebdo' event in Paris. So many condemned the violent retribution meted out by the 'extremists'; hardly a word criticising its causation, their motivation. 'Could do better.'

Okay, then, so they are not 'orders' as such, but a set of 'you *should* do this' or 'you *should not* do that'. All we know is that God's simple message is the only 'should' that needs to be borne in mind: 'we should love one another, as we would be loved' and don't take God's name in vain! Got it?

'Remember the Sabbath day, to keep it Holy'

Now this one really is a toughie. For years just about everyone, God-fearing and Jews alike, chose a special day of the week as their Sabbath day. The Jews chose Saturday; for Muslims it's Friday; and the Christians, Sunday. But the Jews chose theirs to start at 6pm on a Friday, and at the time of Jesus's crucifixion, He was still alive at the cross, as the start of the Sabbath day approached. The custom was, if the victim endured too long and the spectators got bored and if it's a Friday, then the victim had to be dead and off the cross before 6pm. How unholy and defiling to have a dead body of a criminal or otherwise nailed hanging, putrefying and decaying on a cross on the Sabbath. To ensure death then rapidly ensued in any crucified persons, the Jews would break the man's legs with clubs, the additional pain, traumatic shock and subsequent hypostasis, i.e. pooling of blood, would ensure death came quickly. It was recorded the Jews asked the Roman soldiers on guard for permission to break Jesus's legs, as they most definitely did not want Him still alive only to die on the Sabbath day, and then to have to do the 'God-forbidden-Sabbath-day-work' taking Him down off the cross and dealing with His body. Fortunately, Jesus died 'in time' and that final act of cruelty breaking

His legs was denied to the Jews, so they were free to indulge themselves in their idea of God's Sabbath day, their idea of keeping it Holy.

And their idea of keeping it Holy was to do no work on that day of any kind and since the exchange of their 'blessed' money was regarded as work, touching money was verboten, not allowed, at least not until 6pm on Saturday, cashing-up time. A day starts in the morning with sunrise, and ends with sunset. Starting notionally for the purpose of the clock and calendar dates, the next date starts at midnight and this is by Man's Rules. Starting the day at sunrise is the natural day, as governed by the movement of the earth around the sun, as earth spins. The day starts at sunrise and ends at sunset. Not Man's Rules, but God's.

If work is to be avoided on God's Holy day then we need to look at what is unholy about work. Surely there is nothing unholy about God's honest work, it's just that we are not free for recreation when working. As is remarked elsewhere in this book, we work, mostly, for our time later in recreation, and taking time to remember the Sabbath day and keeping it Holy is probably best if we are not working. It is Biblical that God created the world in six days, and rested on the seventh. We are not meant to believe these words literally, but allegorically, metaphorically; that we should work to create 'our world' and the world for others for six days a week, and rest on one day from our 'labours.' That was fine until the socialists came along and demanded two Sabbath days, a weekend, 'and if we don't get it, we are going to go on strike, so there, and we want the same pay as paid for the six days.' And the work output of the nation dropped by 12.5% per week, no doubt. Hitler actually believed we would not fight during the British weekend, it being so sacrosanct to us. The idiot.

It is inevitable and wholly unavoidable that some have to work on any individual religious chosen Sabbath, be it Saturday or Sunday. For example, firefighters, people working in hospitals, ambulance drivers, the police attending accidents. So how can they take 'the Sabbath day' off and not work?

Well, for a start, the 'official' Sabbath day is chosen by man, Man's Rules. In fairness, it's a day chosen to suit most, when most are not working, and for the religious it means a day attending a church service, which is, or should be, rewarding for the spirit and nutrition for the soul.

But for those working, how can they 'remember the Sabbath day?' Well, no one said the Sabbath day had to be universal, the same day for everyone. A hospital doctor may work six days out of seven, and that seventh day becomes his/her Sabbath day, and it may not necessarily be the same day of the week each week. So the seventh day, or to be exact, one day in seven, we should aim to be free of work, and free of the duties and obligations of earning a living and to remember our own individual Sabbath day and keep it Holy.

What does 'keep it Holy' really mean in practice? Many will say you have to go to church. Others say you should go to church. To go to church means choosing a denomination, which means choosing a style of worship that suits you. And maybe none suit you, which is regrettable but to some extent understandable.

But to keep the day Holy really means we can think of Holy as being of God, of God's love, the loving goodness that is God. So we endeavour to fill our day with loving thoughts and actions, we can visit or contact loved ones, family and friends, perhaps spend time with them, possibly enjoy a meal together, even begin the meal with a little bread, and a sip of fruit juice, the significance of both pointed out in another chapter.

Also, in the day, we can deliberately make time to 'commune with nature' to see some open green spaces, with grass and trees, with hills and valleys, and rivers and streams, and sky, the infinitely variable sky, with birds. If such treasures of 'God's creation' are nearby, then that would be very convenient, but to have to spend any time at all driving on today's congested roads, then it's not a good choice.

There are always treasures of God's creation all around us. Most urban areas have some open spaces, parks and the like. Or a nearby riverside or canalside walk, public gardens with plants and flowers. Open space.

And yet there is so much more to marvel in our environment. It depends how we look at things. We all see them, man-made. Buildings, factories, shopping arcades, and warehouses. Man-made maybe, but the architecture, the design, the layout, the choice of materials, the finish, the colours, the proportions and the settings were all inspirational. And that inspiration comes from God. The creativeness is God's, of God, working within us. 'Oh! No! It was my inspiration,' detractors from this philosophy will say. 'It is man's power to imagine,' they will say. But no, our creativeness comes from God, our love, our need, our impulsive inspiration to create is from our love of God, God's love within us. And this is the essence of faith, faith in God.

Our drives to adapt, to adopt and to improve are all inspirational. And so it is, that on our own special Sabbath day, we can spend time thinking about, spending time nearby visiting, seeing architecture in our buildings, our 'man-made' environment, appreciating the inspiration behind it all. L. S. Lowry and others had the skill and inspiration to be able to set down on canvas for us all to enjoy his view of beauty and God's 'work' in industrial scenes.

So remembering the Sabbath day becomes a matter of practice, a routine, a habit we can fall into. Keeping God's Commandment is a requirement expected of us, certainly for our own good. To begin with, it probably means some goal-setting and some list-making.

We should think about how to go about it. We can talk about it with a loved one, one we share our life with as he or she may become practically involved, hopefully sharing your Sabbath day with you. A very different Holy day, remembered each week, to be kept.

'Honour your father and your mother'
The final Commandment in this first grouping of Commandments is *honour your father and your mother*. We say this first group because all its Commandments are to do with the nature of God, God's loving nature, that power of goodness, and all godliness. And also of the one God, of God's name, of eschewing idolatry and of making a day each week a day of God. And yet added here is a Commandment to honour one's parents. And when we think of our parents, most of us instinctively assume the parents we have, our birth parents and for some others, hopefully perhaps their adoptive parents. It is written: 'The Kingdom of Heaven is like a child' and that Jesus said, 'suffer the little children…' Both of those writings denote the loving innocence of children. They need love to grow, to develop into whole adults. The degree to which an adult is a complete, warm, loving, content, even a happy individual, is directly proportional to the degree of the loving quality of their upbringing, that their parents poured out on the children. There's no escaping it. We become as adults how we were brought up. Brought up well or otherwise, the job was done, for the vast majority of us, by parents.

We do well to remember that those parents received no prior training, no qualifications on bringing up children. It's something most don't think about. We fall in love and say we'd like children. That's about it. Or we fall in love and a child is created, landed on your doorstep so to speak, to deal with, to 'bring up;' it's instinctive, it's biological. Some do it well, others not so well. And when our parents 'did it well,' it is easy to love and to honour them. But when they don't do it so well, or just one parent does it well, but not the other, it's harder, sometimes in really bad cases, it's hard to 'love and honour' one's parents at all. But as said, everywhere in these chapters, the nature of God, God's love, that love of goodness within us, if the flame is to be allowed to flourish, to glow warmly with all the love we can muster, we will forgive any shortcomings in our parents; their difficulties, their handicaps of their own upbringing, their sadness at the negative experiences in their lives. And in that understanding, that acknowledgement of the role situation of those disappointing parents, it hurts less and less as we practise the loving forgiveness of God that is honouring our parents.

And yet, having said all that, if someone still cannot find what it takes to honour his or her mother or father then there is another route to following this Commandment; and it is this. If we can't honour our mother or our father, we should not do, or say, or write anything to dishonour them, and eventually we can get to thinking nothing to dishonour them. And in that refusal, that rebuttal of any notion to dishonour them, there is honour. Bingo. Done.

We cannot leave this subject without considering the situation, even the plight of orphans and near-orphans. By definition an orphan is a child whose parents are both dead. But here we are bringing in the child whose parents have given up the child, mostly as a baby, for adoption, as if both parents are dead. There is also the semi-/demi-orphan, the child left to be brought up by one parent, the other having died, or 'gone off,' frequently with another man or woman and abandoning the remaining parent and the child. All of these situations represent the tragedies of life, the physical tragedy of death and the emotional tragedy of what was intended to be a loving and enduring relationship, or arose through the only too human biological behaviour associated with 'one-night stands,' and 'affairs.' Here the law requires maintenance of the child, but no law can make a wayward parent remain and bring up the child.

To the true orphan, it is hoped the child will have adoptive parents who will bring up the child, and to that child, the adoptive parents are the parents to be honoured. To bring up someone else's child, either to meet a longing desire but unable to have children of their own, or to bring up a child out of some sort of sense of duty to the dead parents, known or not, requires something that falls naturally to anyone bringing up a child, and that is to give that child love.

That we must love the child we have chosen to bring up for someone else is a kind of love that may well differ from the natural love we would have for a child born to us. Why is this so? Is it necessarily so? Considering the role situation of the adoptive parents, so much depends on those individuals, and their own kind of loving. To explain: we know the concept of 'tough love', meaning we are hard on the child for its own sake in the future; applying discipline for its own good. We want the child to grow up with a sense of right and wrong and even a sense of duty, but in doing so, we deliver the message, the training, the upbringing in such a manner that the child, while naturally wanting to love its adoptive parents, feels and resents their overbearing and their seemingly harsh 'rules.'

Bringing up children is not easy. It can impose a load on the parents, a physical load to provide the child or children with shelter and warmth, the home, with clothes, with food, and with the appropriate psychological needs of love, education and entertainment. A load can become a burden and yet a burden born so often 'manfully' by the single parent. One of the biggest supports, a lifeline to the single parent is to have a home and a regular income by which means to 'rear' the children. If the father dies, as in war, then hopefully there are means available, even if the circumstances are to be reduced, but the means available to provide a home, warmth and food. To the abandoned mother, for example, he who has 'gone off' with another woman cannot abjure himself in law or of all morality of obligation to support the children left behind. To the father or mother who just walks out of a marriage, a relationship, wishing 'to be free as an indulgence,' there needs to be found some degree of understanding. The child or children, when grown up, and indeed whilst growing up, will wonder, be bewildered, perhaps at a total loss to understand what drove the absconding parent to leave. 'But why?' they will ask, and 'What did I do wrong?' and 'Why didn't Daddy/Mummy love me enough to stay?' We are such deeply complex emotionally driven creatures that each can never hope to fully know and understand another. We just have to accept people as they are, and if a parent is unable to stay in a relationship and leaves the children of that relationship, we have to accept that, just then, at that time when it was what the leaving parent felt had to be done, for his or her sake. Remember, we are programmed only ever to make a decision that we feel is the 'right' decision at that moment. Whether a well-reasoned, well-thought-out, justifiable decision or a spontaneous knee-jerk immaturely made decision at that time, it would have had to have input from the final arbiter of all our decisions, our emotions, which come from our heart. Even the coolest calm, 'cerebral' decision-making we can indulge in, the final say-so, comes from our heart.

So, whatever it was that drove the leaving parent to go, we cannot fathom all the workings of the mind that played on the heart to say 'Go.' And for that reason, we need to forgive, an unconditional forgiveness, from the child who was, now an adult, of the 'wayward' parent, and with that forgiveness comes a sense of honour. Note the Commandment does not say 'love your mother and father,' and hopefully in the vast, vast majority there should never be a need for such an 'order,' but honour is something else, so complex, so variable in its definition, but always something positive, something worthwhile.

So, we have seen how the first five of the Ten Commandments of God are about the nature of God, God's love and towards godliness.

The second group are also of five that relate to our conduct here on earth, avoiding sins of action and sins of thoughts, as in avoiding the 'Seven Deadly Sins' and steering our lives towards the eight Beatitudes of Jesus, ably assisted by our 'five adopted values' and by the spirit of the Holy Trinity.

'Thou shalt do no murder'

Thou shalt do no murder is the first of the five and possibly the gravest injunction ever we could have imposed upon us. It is a simple, clear, unequivocal message, but becomes more complex at times. As civilised, sentient beings of highly developed intelligences, the human animal has developed for the good of its social group, a set of laws to live by, for orderliness in conduct, and for the acquisition and the holding of property. We live by the law of the land. Different countries have different laws, we may not like or agree with their laws, but they are their laws, and they live by them.

The law defines murder, and recognises there are different causations for murder, with appropriate punishments. Relevant to the Commandments is 'accidental' murder, a consequence, or unintended consequence, a 'collateral' of some other action, probably or possibly an action not born of love. The verdict of manslaughter may apply. So it behoves us to avoid situations and actions that may lead to murder. Straight, premeditated murder requires a motive, means and opportunity. Accidental murder is different, but is still murder.

The law of the land permits murder in times of war and we may have difficulty with that. Quite literally in an ideal world, if all nations agreed not to murder under the aegis of their nation's law, war would be abolished. But with war comes legalised murder. The objective, the motive, is to neutralise your enemy so he cannot murder you. So nations acquire the means, the tools of war, which have to be available and functionally capable and superior to the tools of war of the enemy. The opportunity in the first instance for war is when the opposing nation does something or some things which are beyond any further forbearance and the state of war is declared, and murder of the enemy becomes legalised, under 'Man's Rules'. But under God's Rules, no. So, where do we go from here? 'This isn't the way it was intended to be,' is the phrase Evita sang. Simply put, war is the failure of foreign policy, and enmity ensues to such a degree that if we don't kill our enemy, he will kill us. So whilst the fighting is going on we will endeavour to do two things; to stop the murder and come back as soon as we can to God's Commandment. The first is we aim to demolish the enemy's 'means' of making war, and his making his 'tools of war' and the second is to keep persevering to negotiate to a meaningful and worthwhile peace, an armistice. But often, once war is waged, the countries' leaders refuse to speak to each other of peace until one or the other has capitulated as beaten, and then the arguing starts all over again, arguing about borders and reparations. When war starts, ambassadors are withdrawn, frustrating any interlocution, and yet blessed are the peacemakers.

People argue that we can bring about peace by 'girding' ourselves with such powerful and dreadful, 'tools of war' that no one would dare declare war against us. The problem is the other side's tools are just as good. Both know that to let loose these weapons on the world would become so devastating that neither nation would be worth conquering; the world become so polluted that all life will be maimed. But does that stop the gesturing, the undiplomatic disrespect nations irritate others with. The 'vanity' of nations is the same as the vanity of its individuals, seen at its worst in adolescents, strutting their stuff, posing and posturing in their vain ignorance and naïvety in their human version of adolescent complex 'pre-mating rituals' that are designed to warn off, to eliminate the weak, so only the strong get to mate. Relationships deteriorate as objectives clash between nations until war becomes the only viable option – as they think. It should never be an option; one has to start it, their bellum gero attitude – so immature in some leaders, usually the despots, and then we have to go to war on a kill-or-be-killed basis. Look at the Prussians in the late-1860s leading to the formation of their new state of Germany, that development that the French in their vaingloriousness feared and fought to prevent in 1871, only to be humiliated. Can one ever humiliate a Frenchman? Annoy, yes, but humiliate that pride, mais c'est impossible, but that does have merits.

An accidental murder can come about as the result of an argument, a row, a dispute with another, especially in a domestic setting. Rows come about from a loss of temper, as one fights to put their point across to the other, shouting to thrash out their positions, their opinions. Sadly, tempers are lost and in a flash of desire to silence the 'opposition,' a knife is grabbed and plunged. Or a violent push, an attempt to push the 'opponent' out of the arena of the row, there is a struggle, a head hits a hard floor, or a corner and fatal brain damage is caused. 'Thou shalt do no murder,' and yet it is done, a row is a war, a war of words, a failure of foreign policy where the foreigner turns out to be your spouse, your friend, your partner, who suddenly turns into the enemy. This means using your arms and fists, even your feet and legs, and any other tool of war handy, a knife, an ordinary kitchen knife or a carving knife. The opportunity, the coming together, the 'party' that broke down became totally unreasonable, rigidly sticking to one's opinions, to not accepting responsibility for any transgressions, alleged or otherwise, especially not for the loss of temper. That flashpoint, that loss of self-control, who you are, who you want to be, what you would want to be known and loved as, all gone, for the while anyway, in that loss of temper that leads to violence, injury and a death. It is temper that is the key, and the key to temper is self-control. The same may go for statesmen, too.

Another accidental murder may arise out of mugging, a sequel to violent, physical abuse for theft, or just kicks, but possibly could be avoided by just handing money over. It is doubtful the matter is that simple. 'If he'd have given the money, I wouldn't have had to hit him' is their reasoning. Villains can always justify their actions. They are always blaming someone else for their criminal actions that put them in prison. They just never seem capable of accepting responsibility for their actions, so we are told; always too ready to blame others, anyone, for their predicament of being caught, guilty.

By far and away the most common and regrettable form of accidental murder happens daily on our roads. Do we ever get in our cars and think, 'Today, I could kill someone with this?' If we hold a knife or a gun, we are preconditioned by upbringing and training to know we are holding a murder weapon, but our cars, lorries and vans? No. It's a convenient means of getting us from A to B. But it is undeniably a potential murder weapon, and if we are not to commit murder, we need to be alert to the fact. Fortunately, the law prescribes mostly how we are expected to drive. Governments by their laws and by arranging road signs and markings all aim to stop us murdering someone, and less than murder, injuring someone. So far, so good, but we are expected to do more. There is a whole raft of driving offences we are aware of, or should be aware of, that require us to drive to a certain standard.

'Take care' and 'drive carefully' intone our parents when we first start to drive, and mostly we do. But we can 'multitask' as we drive, for we can drive, listen to music, hold a conversation and even 'be alone with our thoughts.' This is probably because much of the journey presents little in the way of hazards. Sadly, the 'accident' situation can arise in a split second, a nanosecond, and we rely on our innate reflexes, which, regrettably, can let us down if not wholly concentrating, 'multitasking,' distracted by loud music, the conversation, our thoughts.

If we have an accident and kill someone while 'breaking the speed limit,' how is that to be lived with? Thou shalt do no murder. Or have a skid and kill someone. 'Yes, I did know my tyres were illegal,' or 'Yes, I did know my brakes weren't working properly, I was going to get them fixed,' or 'Yes, I did know I needed to get my eyes tested.' How can we live with these condemnations?

Would we ever admit to the law-enforcing authorities that we weren't concentrating fully, that we were distracted by the argument we were having with our passenger? More likely we would try to blame the other driver, the weather, the lighting, the road surface. But in our hearts we know we could have avoided killing someone, had we taken just that bit more care, be just more alert to the fact that we were behind the wheel of a killing machine.

There is another way in which the law defines our lives on the subject of murder and legalised killing apart from war, and driving, and that is the delicate subject of abortion, the means of stopping another life entering this world.

'I'm going to have a baby,' may say a proud and happy mother-to-be, or 'I'm pregnant,' she may say, and those same words will be the words admitted by the woman for whom the world spells out the unexpected and, at that time, the undesired state, the unwanted state of her potential as a 'breeding female,' a sexually mature female who has indulged in making 'love,' the mating process, copulating or any other word that whilst factual, denigrates what is nothing more than a wholly natural and ultimate form of mutual self-expression of love, of passion, of physical and mental need, longing and desire, and fulfilment. That a baby could result is way, way, far away in the minds of the vast majority of love-making.

It's odd that we say, 'we're having a baby,' when what would be more appropriate is to say, 'we are creating a new person,' or 'an additional life,' because babies don't stay babies for long, and, although we love babies, the phase of babyhood soon passes and then the job of creating a new person begins and lasts for ever! Try it, next time, see how it goes, tell them, 'I'm having a new person!' 'You're what?'

The whole question around abortion revolves around the ethical and the biological. The best minds in the country have been consulted and come together to consider the issue of 'when does the foetus become a 'life,' in effect, a 'being,' a person in its own right? The foetus is wholly dependent on its mother for its continued existence, not yet breathing air for its oxygen but taking oxygen taken from its mother's blood. If the foetus is an individual life form, then by definition its relationship with its mother will be either commensal, symbiotic or parasitic. We could conjecture parasitism is the nearest, but this theme hardly applies, so in all reality, it is as always the exception that proves the rule. Scientific advancements with trained medical teams and their equipment have progressively meant that a foetus can survive as a baby born before 'term,' the natural ending of the pregnancy, either by natural birth per vaginam or by hysterotomy, the rarely heard of medical term for a Caesarean section. Most will know that Julius Caesar was taken by knife from his mother's womb as she died and was reared to become a great ruler of the Roman Empire. The attendants of his dying mother saw the foetal kicking movements and so, as far as is recorded, the first surgical opening of a womb, the first 'hysterotomy' was recorded. The Americans call it a caesarotomy. God bless America.

It is generally accepted that when the foetus is capable of a free existence, then life exists. Some argue that the new life is created when the two gametes, the egg and the sperm, meet and combine to form a new 'diploid' individual within a body cavity, the womb of the mother. Why say body cavity? Consider the food we eat, as we swallow, it leaves our mouth, the entrance to a long 'tunnel,' like a body cavity, that is really nothing more than an 'enclosed' part of the outside world. If you swallow a small, round stone or a marble, it will go on a journey along a tube, like a tube train, from beginning to end, and emerge in due course at the rectum. The stone has been 'in us,' but not 'of us.' (A bit like Churchill's concept for us and Europe, but back then we had an empire.)

Our intestines absorb into us what is takeable from the foodstuffs we have digested, to be 'of us' in our blood, then into our tissues, and what's not taken is left to pass on through. Imagine a cafeteria, we pass down a range of different food options, choosing and taking what we want. Imagine us standing still and the cafeteria options passing by us and us taking what we want, with the options moving on until the leftovers are tipped into the bin. The alimentary canal has always been an enclosed 'bit of the outside world', but the womb is different in that as it develops embryologically the womb forms itself into a potential cavity with a tract, a potential canal or passageway to the exterior, the vagina, guarded by the cervix, and then the vulva in the area known as the perineum. It is in that potential body cavity that the foetus sits and is attached to the lining of the womb for its sustenance, and the foetus grows in it.

Although of different genetic make-up from the mother, the new diploid being is not sentient at the early stages. It manifests many of the features of life but can only live in the 'parasitic' sense. So it is argued that, if we act to terminate a pregnancy prior to this onset of the 'free living' stage, then we are not killing a person, and so not committing murder. Many will argue that ethically by preventing that stage being reached it is morally murder, morally wrong. Roman Catholics have said that to deliberately avoid a pregnancy by contraception is the same as murder and so a sin. How can that be? If we abstain from any sex to avoid pregnancy, isn't that the same sin? Sins in the mind?

Of course, these are 'Man's Rules,' going by some predetermined date, set by parliament. We wonder what are 'God's Rules' in this situation? The whole point of these chapters is that by our joint endeavour we get to know God in all goodness, better. To be better able to work out for ourselves what is – so that we shouldn't need doctrinaire Man's Rules, but fathom for ourselves through striving, and striving to know the true meaning, the true worth of love. It's as if this were a test, but perhaps not, but it is certainly a testing issue, the issue of abortion, right at times, or never right.

Issues like the health of the mother, the hopeless prospect of survival of a deformed foetus, that 'accident' of nature, come to the fore. Calm, calculated, considered decisions need to be reached; can that be murder? Are we here to accept life, whatever it throws at us, or are we here to use our skills, our hearts and minds to deliver love, in the best way we can divine?

When a man gets a woman pregnant, he has created for himself an obligation, whether he likes it or not, whether he accepts it or not, to behave responsibly towards the mother-to-be. Hopefully, in a mutual, loving relationship to nurture and care for her, to build a nest in which to rear the young. And if he can't do that, then do what he can to see that friends and family support her and use, as in to give of his means, his resources, his income to provide her with what is necessary and vital. This is an emotionally charged field, but the obligation is biological and moral. It behoves God's love for one another, whatever distracting exigencies may prevail and interfere.

Some might say that it is the woman's absolute right to decide whether or not to carry her foetus to full term. The factors she may have to bring to bear are manifold and complex, but include her health, her mental health, her emotional state, especially if rape has been involved, and much more, including her personal beliefs regarding the retention or rejection of the potential of a life now within her.

In the end the question of abortion has two facets. Man's Rules dictate what is legal and they have been devised after the very best of brains have been applied to the scientific and ethical considerations. We can take some comfort from this. The other facet is to draw on the loving nature of goodness, that guides and helps us to resolve life's issues. We can only ever do what we believe is right for us at the time. Tough decisions made after identifying and weighing up all the factors that are relevant, the pros and cons, but in the end almost certainly with this decision, like so many, it will be our emotions, what we decide 'in our heart' to be the thing to do; such reasonings should be recorded as they are important, to be referred to after, perhaps long after, when memory fails, and doubt may set in. It is so vital that we are true to the decisions we make, to make the decisions work. And so, in this way, it becomes what we believe as to whether a personal decision for abortion was made in the knowledge of God's love, and the understanding that imparts. Sadly, many women come later to regret their action of having elected for an abortion. It takes some true grit to cope with this, and being true to our decisions is a vital element of coming to terms with the recrudescence of the issue that presented itself so long ago. And here's the value, the worth of writing down and storing those reasons when we make those major decisions in our life, as we go along.

As 'You shall do no murder' is the first of the second grouping of the Commandments, the group that is about how we conduct our everyday lives, can be first perhaps because since the time the Commandments were first committed to 'paper,' first written down, mankind has set up murder as the greatest and the worst that one human can do to another, here on earth; and a more important rule for our conduct than the remaining four 'rules.' But who can say? There is nothing that earmarks it as such. But to us, mankind, it is the most singularly difficult, even perhaps the most impossible sin to overcome, to set aside, to be forgiven for, by our fellow creatures. The notion, the act, should be so burnt into our minds, as in our upbringing and in adulthood that to murder is so, so very evil, so absolutely barren of anything of God. This is why the death penalty is so abhorrent.

And yet, the militia and the police are trained to kill, and isn't all killing murder? Not so. Man's Rules define in a justice that includes here justifiable killing. For example, we might think, 'Thank goodness,' when a gunman who has entered a schoolroom and murdered children. He is shot, and killed, but we don't say, 'murdered,' not in that sense. And so the death of a human brought about by the action of another can be understood as a killing for the relief of evil, as in war. But for many, an abortion to avoid an outcome of physical and mental aberrations in the child may not be so equally accepted.

People often muse upon whether animals have a soul and go to Heaven like us. It is very debatable. Aspiring to and reaching the heavenly state is, as we have seen, is arrived at as the result of a set of conscious choices, the love of goodness, the love of God, and all that that entails for us as sentient beings on earth. Animals are living things, and so are plants. Living things have life, and demonstrate the prerequisites of our definitions for life, and with animals those additional features of life that animals possess. But are they sentient beings? Can they make a conscious choice for good? Recognise and appreciate good? To be able to be said to be sentient, there has to be a creative imagination that is not a behaviour that is associated with survival (e.g. feeding) or procreation, e.g. mating, nesting, rearing young, or males fighting to be the one to spread its genes.

With this definition it is unlikely that animals will go to Heaven as a result of their behaviour, but when we hear of the spontaneous life-saving instances of dogs, horses and recently cats, who have acted in some way that has saved or rescued a human, usually a human whom they are particularly associated with, then it is very likely that that soul within the animal, will, in some form know God, and know Heaven.

With the rest of living things, their death must mean something. The lettuce plant pulled up to be eaten, the lamb slaughtered for its meat, their 'spark' of life, that bundle of life-energy surely enters the universal life force of 'intelligence' that surrounds earth and in the universe as it gives up its life. But pulling up a lettuce is not murder. Let's try to keep a clear, cool head on this matter.

'You shall not commit adultery'

As relatively rare as the committing of murder is, and so an easier Commandment to 'keep,' the committing of adultery is not a Commandment anything like so easy to 'keep.' The temptation to commit murder is rare or totally absent in most of us, most of the time, fortunately. But equally unfortunately the temptation to commit adultery is more commonplace. But what is adultery in reality? What is meant by the word in the Commandment, and has the meaning changed through the centuries?

As far as is known in these 'Biblical' times, the marriage of a man with a woman was the only accepted and allowed means of cohabiting; and sex before marriage may have gone on, but if pregnancy happened then so did marriage to 'legalise' the pair. And from then on, sex was intended to be confined to between husband and wife only. Adultery then became sex outside that marriage, which was either with another married person, or perhaps with an unmarried person. One was presumably breaking a vow, a promise, in so doing.

The question was, and still is, if a single person has sex with a married person, the married person commits adultery, but does the single person, seeing the single person is unmarried? Is that possible? If we 'entice' a married person to have sex with us, an unmarried person, is it wrong for us to encourage the married to commit adultery, and in so doing, partaking, do we not commit adultery, too, as it were, on moral grounds, like aiding and abetting!

Today couples live together, unmarried, have children just like married couples. Can they commit adultery, seeing that they are not married? Can they be unfaithful to their relationship? For some, yes; if their pair-bonding is one of a loving relationship which would regard any infidelity seriously damaging to their love match. But for others, no, theirs is a relationship of 'swingers,' who say to each other, yes, we will have sexual relationships with others and our pair-bonding will not be harmed, they say, they hope, they expect to work. Real swingers. Real 'Harry Hopefuls.' It may work for a bit, but it is unlikely a wholesome, loving relationship can exist and survive for them, their trendy inclinations will die in the end because people are just not made that way, playing fast and loose with love.

So, it is likely adultery applies more to a relationship between cohabiting adults who may or may not be married, and it becomes the harbinger of deterioration in that once loving relationship, possibly to its destruction. What we are saying here is that adultery may be the breaking of a bond of faith, whether spoken, implied or even written between a couple, who may or may not be married. And breaking that bond is described as 'being unfaithful.' Music-playing machines were once called 'Hi-Fi', short for High Fidelity, in sound reproduction. In that case, adultery must be 'Lo-Fi'.

The urge to have sex with someone we are attracted to is a very natural and basic biological function. We are programmed to 'spread our genes' with the objective of producing offspring who may be better genetically equipped to survive in the environment. There is a saying, 'men are naturally polygamous and women naturally monogamous.' It is not necessarily true, of either sex. It may be that some men are more inclined to seek sex 'elsewhere' outside marriage, a randy old goat or just a serially unfaithful liar, whilst their wife or the partner, more faithful, brings up the children. She frequently has no time, no opportunity, no real freedom to go and 'play' like the man has, while he is more out and about at work. It may be the woman's more of a natural tendency to 'pair-bond' for life, like bullfinches, and like the saying. But we have to beware such generalisations.

Children raised by a loving couple, sense and know that love is there, and they also sense and know when love is fading or gone, perhaps gone, in a flash. Gone because of adultery. Sexual 'pair-bonding' often, sex between a loving couple, signifying the mystical union, the biological 'animal' desire inextricably entwined with the love of the person, the love for the person, our spouse, our partner; belonging, totally committed, body and mind. And then suddenly, it's broken. That peace of mind, that surety, that confidence on which our life, our happiness, our whole happiness is built, is broken. Infidelity – why, why does it hurt so much? Can it be forgiven; this once, this once again, and even again? Accepting the physical closeness, the intimate proximity, the merging of the known and familiar worshipped body's most 'private' parts in coital ecstasy with another, that outsider? Forgive that? That once so very much loved, so blissfully happy life, secure in the marriage-partnership-togetherness, blindly trusting, so never-ever even crossed a mind, not even a merest hint at infidelity. Can we forgive that so as to start again, make a fresh start? Is that possible?

And then we hear from our confessing partner that the adultery committed has produced a pregnancy. Between 'them,' they have created a new life, a new person, the first of a new family, as well as the family already created. It's a huge shock. Huge, huge shock. Such unhappiness, such misery, so underserved. Really, 'undeserved' or deserved? 'De' meaning 'out of', and 'serve' meaning service, to others. Was there really a true wholly mutual, loving relationship here, now being broken by an adultery? Was he 'driven' to it? In that case, adultery will make it almost nigh well impossible to restore, re-create a 'wholly loving relationship' if one never existed in the first place. An early passionate infatuation in any relationship should never be a basis for a speedy marriage, especially when derived frantically due to a pregnancy from a fully consummated courtship in the first throes of joyous but premature sex.

Courtship came about as a social custom, a wise one as it happens, and courtship if reassured would then lead to an engagement that is best proceeded to marriage fairly soon, as soon as the arrangements can be made. Courtship is the 'finding out,' engagement is the commitment, reversible at this stage, like buying a house, we exchange contracts and put down the deposit that may be forfeited if we pull out, and then the completion some weeks later and we move in. Courtship, engagement and marriage should be the same. Courtship is the finding out, the house-surveying and approving stage, the engagement the exchange of contracts, and the marriage the completion and moving in. Long engagements are best avoided. It's like signing a contract, paying a big deposit, and then waiting and waiting for the goods to be delivered for the contract to be completed. Not a good contract. Yes, it may cut out the opposition, the competition, taking 'possession' of someone, for years, in some cases, perhaps 'right' for some, but not many; it's unnatural. It's unfair on both parties to expect to tie someone down to an agreement and then make them wait so long to fulfil the promise. We should take all the time we want getting to know someone before popping a ring on the finger.

Some, mostly the unmarried couples, say, 'Why get married? It's just a piece of paper,' and mostly they would be right these days. The state of living together 'in sin,' as it was once called, has come about to be accepted in society, especially due to the great society upheavals, the chaos of two world wars, when so much of the social order was swept aside and bringing with it the emancipation of women, so now banks and building societies lend and landlords rent to unmarried couples. It meant that their position in society was acceptable as a new social order, and then some legal rights of money and property were given to 'partners' cohabiting, the same as married couples, and at the same time tax advantages of being married were removed along with the state recognition of married women, indeed all working women, so having rights of their own, as individuals.

But marriage still matters as the LGBT groups have demonstrated, and this has brought about some difficulties for some churches, bound as they are by their 'Man's Rules' and seemingly unable to discern what 'God's Rules' are in these situations. Frankly, it would probably be better to review the state of marriage so we can see what it really represents. Firstly, there's the matter of money and property, as in wealth. Effectively on marriage there is a merger of joint assets and on divorce these assets are split 50/50, or at least that's the aim, as it tends to be applied to 'ordinary folk,' but not quite so for the super-millionaires. A man inherits his parents' house and then he marries a woman with no means at all. The marriage is childless, and they divorce after four years. She claims half of his house, as she is unskilled and has no real means of supporting herself anything like the standard he provided in the years of the marriage. He has to sell the house and is 'humbled' by the award and has to live in a lower-value house in a lower-value area because of the failure of his marriage. To many this is unacceptable, and if the roles had been reversed, would the same end result apply?

So the act of marriage is a business arrangement, and that, like any business, can succeed or fail, and the costs of failure can be very significant. Divorce settlements are even more complicated when children, young children up to the age of sixteen, are involved because there is the concept of the 'marital home' that the courts endeavour to retain on divorce for the sake of the children, and this is very right. It is still the case that it is the wife who bears the children, whose career is interrupted by childbirth, often more than once as she makes the family, and it is still so, that mostly the mother, of the two of them, is 'charged' with more time at home raising the children just like the caveman, and the basic biological divide of the father, the 'hunter-gatherer,' the nest is for the mother to rear the children. Today, roles can be exchanged once the children have arrived and this is very fair, but on divorce, some provision for the 'marital home' has to come about.

Unmarried couples 'divorce,' as in 'part' company, and have to sort out the difficulties with regard to the 'nest' in which the children are raised, and often there is much hardship all round as the 'leaving' person starts their new life often with a new 'partner' and starts a new family. Fortunately the law provides obligations for a man or a woman earning to send money to the remaining partner to raise his/her children, but it's never enough.

So, it's not 'just a piece of paper.' It represents a legal framework for the financial arrangements during the life of the participants and also upon death, the settlement of their affairs, which mostly the 'unmarried' couples do not get.

It could be said that a better arrangement would be if marriage, all marriages, had to take place in the government-licensed secular establishment. And then for those religious couples, they could have a second marriage service in church, the service of 'Holy Matrimony.' The first signifies the legal entity, the 'financial commitment' the couple are entering into, and then second, their marriage made 'in Heaven,' in God's love, their 'spiritual union.' So much better to clear the smoke, get rid of the romantic, unrealistic 'guff,' the fairy tale nonsense of 'living happily ever after,' without lifting a finger.

Others have said, having experienced the 'trauma' of a divorce court and an enforced settlement, that it would be better if we had to go to court, or at least a legal process, to prove our suitability and preparedness to go into marriage. It's so easy for the immature, the whimsical and the couples in the first throes of a whirlwind romance to get married. 'Marry in haste, repent at leisure' is the saying. But an unhappy marriage, that state where one or both conscientiously try to make it work before finally giving up is all so traumatic and can live with us the rest of our lives. It should not be so, and adultery is the biggest cause.

Others have said we should have to declare all assets before marriage. The fruits of those assets belong to the marriage, but on divorce the nominal value of the initially declared assets is returned to the two parties. Where a marital home is concerned that would have to be maintained and owned in the same way it was during the marriage until the last child reaches sixteen, when the assets shared are returned. The growth in the assets during the marriage would be split 50/50. So much better: no need for cheating husband or wife to 'hide' assets on divorce. We could have 'prenups' made on this basis.

'Thou shalt not steal'

Most of us instinctively revile the thought of being called a thief. The term 'thief' is so very nearly exclusively applied to one who goes on the prowl, looking to relieve others of their property or money, to live by the proceeds of their thieving, instead of doing 'a hard day's work.' Such people disgust us as the lowest of the low, and then there's the thief at work, caught 'red-handed, with their hand in the till'.

And yet, stealing of so many other kinds goes on in society, some so 'cloaked' in business manoeuvres as hardly to be seen to be 'stealing.' The deliberate cheating of an innocent person, perhaps a naïve person out of their property, their shares, their money by 'secret' underhand dealing, usually fraudulent, is stealing. This sort of active stealing has to be planned, thought out and meticulously devised to deprive someone, anyone, and mostly the faceless 'investors' of their money.

Passive stealing revolves around honesty and includes 'finders keepers.' A company 'under-bills' us, and we know it. We are given too much change, by mistake and we know it. Items are missed off our restaurant bill, and we know. We do nothing. We keep what should rightly go to another. It takes honesty and perhaps a little effort to correct what is not right.

At work, we help ourselves to all sorts of items readily, but not freely, available, like items of stationery, rolls of Sellotape, staplers, bulldog clips. 'They're only small items, the company won't miss them' or 'We all take them, it's the expected perks of the job!' Maybe, but it's still stealing. Petty thieving, that's what it is, such an easy temptation to fall into, so much so that it can easily become a habit and so doesn't trouble our conscience at all.

'I didn't take it,' not in that sense, 'I just borrowed it, but you weren't around to ask, and I did intend to return it, but forgot, and you didn't seem to miss it until now.' The usual disregard for the property of others, including cash 'left lying around' is very commonplace. It is odd that children often regard the property of their parents as 'there for the taking,' but when something of theirs is taken, often by a sibling, 'there's all hell to pay!' The way we look at property of others is very important, and extends into all of one's 'personal possessions,' including letters. A letter clearly addressed to a recipient should never ever be opened without the express consent of the addressee, and that goes for packets, addressed magazines through the post as well. Opening someone else's correspondence is tantamount to stealing their intellectual property, infringing their 'intellectual property rights' which also and primarily includes the theft of someone's artistic and intellectual creations. If one can breach the boundary of personal property in small respects, it is not hard to breach in other respects.

There is another form of stealing that hardly occurs to anyone as stealing. It happens all the time, and almost everyone is guilty of it much of the time. It is this. Our employers pay us to carry out tasks as conscientiously as we can, and we are paid for that service. If we fail to deliver of our best during working hours, diligently, and instead waste the time talking, or daydreaming but take home the same pay, that is a sort of theft, stealing from our employer. A kind of nebulous, intellectual theft, but a theft all the same.

Another form of theft that goes along with the notion of intellectual theft is fraud. High fraud by big companies is probably the worst kind, where directors and accountants set out deliberately to deceive the investors and the tax authorities to satisfy their greed. It is rank theft.

Total honesty, clear thinking, highly principled honesty is the aim. You shall not steal – not an option, but a clear Commandment of God, for the good of all of us.

'Thou shalt not bear false witness against thy neighbour'

How odd that 'against thy neighbour' is specified. Does that mean it's okay against anyone else, not your neighbour? Hardly! Who, in Biblical terms is 'our neighbour?' The man next door, the sweet old widow the other side, or the big man with his horrid, noisy dog opposite? Who is our neighbour? Someone who lives in the same Biblical village?

Does the Commandment mean everyone, or only those with whom we have an acquaintance? Or does it mean just about everyone. So, if it's everyone else, why specify? That only leaves us, our selves. So, is it okay to bear false witness against our self, to lie, to deceive our self? Hardly. So many great troubles start with a lie, to get us out of trouble or to gain something through deceit. But if we truly love good, goodness, goodliness, God and Godliness, then automatically we do not lie. We may not always be completely open, or be frank, because that then may cause embarrassment or trouble for someone else, as it were, 'to tell on them.' 'No one likes a telltale'. But we can just be quiet, not tell a lie, not be a 'telltale'.

Perhaps the words against our neighbour are put there as a form of emphasising, a hyperbole, to highlight and stress against whom we must not tell whoppers and land someone, anyone, falsely into deep water, which people often do to throw others off the scent of their own, or their friends' or relations' misdemeanours. It seems, then, neighbours are anyone other than those of our household.

The words 'false witness' then perhaps are chosen specifically to refer to situations where and when we are acting as a witness to some deed or other and so required to be absolutely straight, factual and honest. To state what we saw, what we heard. And in so doing we can only 'say it as we saw it.' It's up to the barristers to analyse what we say we saw from the position we were in; what angle, through any potential deluding screens, e.g. 'as seen' through the smoke, or through a trellis, or dazzled by bright sunlight. Our witness can only be 'Say it as you saw it' and likewise as we heard it, as we remember the words we heard. Did we write them down immediately? Almost certainly not, at least for most of us, we may not exactly recall the precise words, just the sense, the meaning of what we heard, according to the subjective understanding we placed on what we heard at the time.

So if we can only remember 'the gist' of what we heard we must be careful not to bear 'false witness.' It is not only the elderly whose memories can 'let them down.' Memory is odd; it plays odd tricks on us. One can either remember clearly and accurately on most occasions or not remember at all. It's best not to try too hard to recall 'some' name or place. Relax; move on, the name comes later, unrelated to the moved-on 'present' moment. The trickery comes when we remember with absolute certainty, as our persona tells us, only to find evidential proof that we have remembered incorrectly – even drastically incorrectly! It can be so humbling and even so humiliating. And so we do need to be cautious, circumspect about what we think we remember. So, it's 'Write it down,' the sooner, the better. Take a photo, factual, supporting, but not entirely immutable evidence – far more reliable than the fallibility of human 'memories' or shall we say, 'human fancies' or even 'human fantasies.'

At any hearing, at work, for example, or in a court of law, the presenting situation will be one where the outcome is potentially serious for the accused, the defendant, because it could lead to the loss of a job, the means of one's livelihood, or the loss of their liberty, in prison. And so any witness statement that can have a bearing on the issue must be true, and truly accurate, not vague. Vagueness is no good to anyone. We either 'had our wits about us' at the time, or we didn't. One should own up to that, if and when it happens, as in when we were daydreaming, however embarrassing to own up might be. It's best to be absolutely frank and clear about our evidence, firm and resolute in what we believe we saw or heard at the time. No false witness.

When do we first learn to lie? It's as children, certainly. But how young? How does the impulse to lie first occur? It will be either to avoid the 'loss of love' from a parent, as in to avoid a 'smack' for being naughty (isn't smacking banned?) or to gain something nice, like another sweet, 'No, Mummy, I've only eaten one sweet, so let me have another, please?' Most of the types of behaviour patterns are learned from others, from siblings and from our parents themselves. Children are close, mostly silent watchers and listeners, listening to conversations, dialogue between parents, and between parents and other siblings' little lies, first heard by the young child, realising that for some reason, whatever reason, parents and siblings don't always speak the truth, and by it, they either gain something, hang onto something, including 'peace' in the home, between people, or to avoid 'trouble,' a rebuke, a reprimand, a loss of some privilege or other. We learn by copying. We are acquisitive, we want things. We are comfort seeking, we want to avoid loss of 'comfort' even loss of liberty, by freedom of choice. 'Go to your room,' or 'Go and sit on the stairs and stay there until I say, and you will go without your supper!' Yes, definitely a loss of comfort! But as a species, we can only lie because we have the power of imagination. If dogs could speak, would they lie? Probably not, as it depends on an imagination.

And then we become practised, skilful liars, cunningly deceiving to advance our personal cause in life. Some go to the extreme, into a fantasy world, so obvious we all recognise it, and he's given the nickname 'Billy Liar.' The only one who believes what he says is Billy himself. He's mostly harmless, or should be. A distraction, an entertainment. Unfortunately, there are some 'almost Billy Liars,' who are or can be very convincing. They've convinced themselves in their sincerity, their earnest desire to be believed. Mostly, it's harmless stories about their past, relating anecdotes from their lives, their careers, promoting themselves to higher ranks, giving themselves more importance, more responsibility, or telling deeds of great experiences, with themselves as an important key player. Why do people exaggerate, aim to impress others with false stories of the activities, their influence, their status in life? To let others know 'who they are, what they are?' Perhaps a fear of not being accepted as someone worth knowing and associating with. Sometimes they 'wheedle' themselves into a coterie they wish to join, that they assume they would not be invited into without some 'bragging' about themselves.

'There are lies, damned lies, and statistics.' Such a true summary of the situation. 'Damned lies' do the real harm, the damaging to others; false witness; and we'll be damned for telling them. Statistics are data that depend on so many false scenarios, they often mislead. How was the data chosen, selected to be

297

chosen to be collected. How was it gathered; is it too selective? Is the number truly representative? Are the parameters truly applicable to the subject matter and to the conclusions. Mathematicians have devised good means of making statistics more meaningful, but sadly too often the conclusions are drawn by those who don't understand the true significance of the data presented. Statistics are used very often in the modern world. They are used to identify the safety of new drugs, and the Office for National Statistics to identify social trends. Often the data means we should be cautious in the reliance we place on statistics.

'All politicians are liars,' or so it is often said. They fail to answer direct, simple questions because to do so would be to admit some situation or other that would be harmful either to the government as a competent body, or to the true plan or ambition being developed, or perhaps damaging to our national security. There are so many reasons why politicians are 'economical with the truth'.

They are protected from prosecution for anything they say, 'in the House,' which is supposed then to let them be free to speak the truth 'in the House,' where it is regarded as a heinous sin to lie. It's not so much that they lie, they just don't speak the truth, the truth as we know it. And because of that, they have the knack of skirting around the subject, the question, by repeatedly putting their point, their argument, across. Even when asked, please answer just either yes or no, they don't. It's as if they're deaf to the 'yes or no' request. With them, lying is an art form they have to adopt to survive. 50% of the people they meet will be 'for' them and 50% 'against' and so they 'fence' questions, cautious and bland in their conversations, boastful of their and their party's achievements. It's all a sort of truth but a sort of lying, too.

'Thou shalt not covet'

Thou shalt not covet is the Tenth Commandment and possibly one of the easiest to keep, except for those rare individuals whose characteristic is to want for themselves something somebody else already has. Is envy anything to do with wanting to take away something, some piece of property or living creature that goes with someone else, like someone's dog, house, cat, or even a servant, employee or spouse?

To have a strong urge to have for yourself that which is another's can become a dangerous motive, will certainly lead, if carried out to a fulfilment, to a breakdown of relations between the two parties, to create rivalry and even hatred.

But how can the covetousness be carried out to fulfilment? If property is lusted after, then a straightforward option is to 'buy It' from the owner if he/she is willing to sell. Or one could steal it, but this risks criminality and punishment by the weight of law. Or one could so work on the mind of the owner by trickery so that he/she will part with it. A mind game, but a cruel deception. This could include getting the owner into a situation where he/she is indebted to you and you choose as your payment what you are coveting to 'settle the debt.'

If what is coveted is a person, say an employee or a spouse, then the route to fulfilment will vary with the objective, seeing that both of those 'objectives' are freely choosing individuals in their own right, and the coveting will involve persuasion that our grass is greener on our side of the fence.

Or is the coveting more about wanting to deprive another person of something they have? Possibly, and if so, it is a malicious intent, to be so deliberately harmful, and may be based just on twisted envy. It is more likely that from the Commandment's point of view, it is the feeling, the sensation, the lusting after, the act of wanting that which is owned by another; that longing, cerebrally and possibly obsessive thinking, that is the wrong. Say your neighbour has a fine new car. You like it a lot. You want one. Well, go and buy one! Can't afford it! So you get real, or you can work on the neighbour to derive a situation where he either sells you the car for what you can afford, or he somehow has to part with it to you. Sheer fantasy, most likely. So give up coveting: it does no good. But to covet, to desire his wife so as to covet her, is where the Commandment bears fully upon us.

In effect, this last Commandment recognises that we have property, stuff we acquire, and that includes living things, like dogs and cats, and horses, and in a way, persons. Although these days of no slave owning, we no longer can own a person. Historically even a wife was regarded as being owned by the husband, like property. But all we can ever enjoy as having, but not owning, is a person's loyalty and their commitment. We can lose that if we deserve to, but if coveted away when we don't deserve the loss, that could mean the loss of someone fickle, or less than worthwhile in the first place. We do tend to regard people as property in speech. We say, my wife, or my husband, or my manager, and my secretary. Supposedly one can say these things and loosely regard these people as ours, for now. And staff can be contracted to us or to our firm, as a business arrangement, but a spouse is contracted to us either by law in marriage, a contract made before witnesses, or as 'life partner,' just by implication but accepted as a 'custom and practice' commitment, by living together and raising a family together.

It is better to arrange our thinking so that we can become genuinely pleased for someone's acquisitions, their property. This is a practised art; it makes us nearer to being a whole, loving person. It is said that happiness lies in 'wanting what we have, not having what we want.' Following on from that is 'the expectation excels the event' and 'it is better to journey than arrive.' By all this we mean that there is something very perverse in us, that, having desperately wanted something, perhaps saved for, worked hard for, then eventually acquired, only to enjoy it perhaps briefly before losing the enthusiasm, the pride of ownership as our ever-acquisitive natures turn to desire, to lust after something anew. Apart from food, basic clothing, shelter and warmth, the whole of the rest of our economy depends upon our acquisitive natures, either acquiring the physical, the tangible, or the hedonistic, intangible but real enough pleasures that we seek.

We should never say, never admit the words to ourselves or to anyone, 'I envy you,' or 'I envy you your…' But it is often said, intending to be quite harmless. But it betrays a line of thought. Instead we should be pleased for someone in their acquisitions, admire it, whatever or whoever 'it' may be, and we can and should admit that admiration. With this 'practised art,' we avoid the guilt of coveting.

By far and away the most serious coveting in the whole world has been and still is the coveting of others' land by leaders of states. Throughout history various regimes have come and gone but all have been territorially ambitious, to 'own,' to rule over and to suppress indigenous peoples. Whole empires have been built on nothing more than a covetous greed, a covetous theft. And it still goes on today. Even after two world wars, the subsequent settlement of boundaries, leaders are not satisfied. It is as if they are playing a board game to acquire more property, for their childlike ambitions, their ego. The Tsars of Russia, a massive country, never satisfied, never felt secure, and yet believing in their anointed status by God, their thoughts, their actions could only be God-inspired. They lusted after territory such as control over the Dardanelles. Even the President of Russia today, and he is most certainly not 'divinely appointed,' spends his time festering on his ambitions to extend his influence, to have his way, his 'covetous way;' Crimea, Ukraine, the list is almost endless.

Similarly, the Jews, ejected from their historic lands by the waves of Islam, coveted back the lands of their forefathers, and the indigenes, the Palestinians, for so they had then become, were pushed aside as the modern State of Israel was 're-created' by Great Britain and others, and there has been no peace in the area since.

Great Britain was as guilty as any other of the imperialist countries, France, Germany and others. Expressed simply, it was, in those days, the thing to do. But would Christian leaders of Christian states go about coveting the land of others? And would it be acceptable to stand by and do nothing while the infidel forces succeeded in taking over and suppressing the rights of the indigenous peoples? Would America and Australia even have been developed to become the countries as we know them today? Surely it can't be wrong to 'immigrate' into and colonise a near-empty land occupied only by a small number of undeveloped native 'species?' But there are no such places like that left today except the deserts and if we found a way to make deserts habitable, would we covet the land to take it for our own? Each desert is already notably the 'property' of an existing state. Is it conceivable that we would allow an occupation by a country that has the skill and resources to develop a desert, to 'covet' the desert and take it away from its current owning state?

It would seem to be important for us all, including and especially the leaders of nations, to be aware of coveting the 'property' of other nations, not to indulge in coveting, and to be prepared to act to deter and to prevent the covetousness of other nations. Thou shalt not covet. It is written.

The Cardinal Numbers, three, five, seven, eight and ten, can be important to us because they form the whole basis for a foundation of character on which to build a wholesome life. There are, no doubt, other routes to the same objective, but if a 'working tool' is desired, an aide-mémoire, a yardstick, the five Numbers, once familiar with them, can and do 'fit the bill.' As the navigator learns his rules by which he guides his vessel through unfamiliar and unchartered waters, with all life's hazards along the way, the Cardinal Numbers are pointers that will fix his position at anytime along the voyage of life.

301

CHAPTER 22
THE DOZEN

Twelve is offered to be included as one of life's leading interest numbers. It can be the last of the 'Cardinal Numbers' that, by the reasoning put forward here, are the important signposts in our lives. Twelve is also charmingly referred to as 'a dozen,' in more than just English, and still features large in our lives, in measuring and packing. In the imperial measurement (note imperial as in 'of the empire') there are twelve inches to the foot. We can guess where the term 'foot' came from, but it's not so obvious how it became divided into twelve parts; especially when we have ten toes. In 'old' money there were twelve pennies in a shilling, but 20 shillings in the pound, so why twelve? Come to that why 20? Eggs are still packed and sold by the dozen, but just as often by the half a dozen – being a more conveniently sized package to handle. Bread rolls and similar were sold in twelves, but a 'baker's dozen' was usually taken as twelve plus one, as in buy twelve get one free, making thirteen; not buy twelve, pay for eleven. Juries have 'twelve just men and true' and now include 'true' women.

Jesus gathered around His twelve disciples. Twelve men who left their jobs, their livelihoods, their wives and families and their villages, to go around the countryside, listening to, learning from and marvelling at the words and works of Jesus, especially as He performed healings and other miracles. Why twelve disciples? Ten is a much more rounded figure. It's easy to do sums in tens. We have fingers and toes in tens. Jesus had His reasons. Twelve must have been a number of significance then to Him, even if not in general to the populace. However, the touring group was, including Jesus, thirteen. Unlucky thirteen?

The twelve names are listed in the Gospels, but few can remember each one's name, just the 'key players,' so to speak: Matthew, Mark, Luke and John just trips off the tongue. It is written in the Gospel that Jesus 'gave' His disciples some healing powers, and inculcated them with the confidence and to have the level of faith to use them. They were given the ability to speak foreign languages after the death of Jesus and His Ascension. It is understood, but with little or no detail, that they dispersed and went to preach the Gospel of Christ into other lands. Little of that is generally known or spoken of. Several were put to death for what they were preaching.

Judas Iscariot hanged himself after betraying Jesus, leaving eleven disciples, who then chose another to fill his place, so keeping the 'mystical' complement of twelve (why would they do that?), and from now on to be called 'Apostles.' Sets of spoons used to be sold right up to and including the 20th century called Apostle spoons, sold in twelves with the handles moulded into the vague likeness to man. Did Judas have a wife with children, or a job, a livelihood when he started to follow Jesus? Whatever happened to all those abandoned wives and children? It is not known if the 'chosen' were all bachelors or not. At that time, most adult men would have been married, and marriage mostly meant children. The Catholics' answer (usually) to any situation like this is 'The Lord will provide,' and they would mostly be right, and these days that may mean the state will provide, but not much.

We hear today of people being 'converted' to become followers and believers in 'weird' cults, mostly becoming obsessive. Most who join are single and it's hardly surprising to find a fair proportion of them are sons and daughters of rich people and give their money to the cult, or at least to the cult leader, who usually professes no interest in 'earthly riches.' The lying hound.

Knowing that this is what people do, that is, to 'throw up' their life, their upbringing, their family and friends, their job, to follow an idea, as in a Damascene conversion, then it's only a small step to understanding the disciples. There was no question of wealth, as none had money, or came from money, in that sense. Their conversion was mostly probably as mystical as the virgin birth; Jesus, that perfection of goodness personified, would have had that something special that, when inviting a man 'to follow' Him, gave an invitation that one could just not refuse. His presence would have drawn to Him anyone of a natural goodness of spirit, yearning, seeking a world that presages more of goodness than the chaos of the absence of God, the absence of goodness.

And so it is likely that twelve as a number became accepted as a number to be reckoned and revered as something special in our lives. A dozen, but not a dozen apostles, it's always spoken as twelve. The twelve days of Christmas, with twelve 'lords a-leaping': again that significant number.

Thinking way back to how it may have all started, this business of counting and measurement. Children begin by counting on their fingers, and with a total of ten, and then 20 if we are to include toes, then it is easy to reckon how the decimal system came into being, and so then the abacus, and mental multiplication and division became a cinch.

Someone, somewhere, however, must have proposed, and it was accepted, that a measure of distance should begin with a foot, the length of an average foot. It is generally thought that as a race, a species in those very early times, we were much shorter in height than nowadays, so it is reasonable to suppose that the average foot was shorter, too. But why three feet to a yard, is obscure. The penis of a stallion is called the 'yard,' because in its erect state it is a yard long. Presumably someone must have been at it with a tape measure at some time or other. But that would hardly have been taken as the yardstick. No: it is far more likely that the yard became the distance of an average step, a pace, and someone smart found that it just happened to be the distance of three feet. Where all this is leading to is how did the foot become divided into twelve inches and not into ten, which would have been logical, seeing that we have ten toes?

And then there's money, the early money that became pounds, shillings and pence. Whatever we may think these days of our relatives, those Europeans and their early ancestors, it seems we have to defer to their superiority of intellect in their choice of the decimal system over our Imperial system, so cumbersome, pounds, shillings and pence, pounds and ounces, inches, feet and yards. It's nonsense; but somehow it gave us the biggest empire the world has ever known – but so what? We can now say, perhaps with some justification, 'Was it worth it?' Are we, GB (UK Ltd) happy and successful as a nation? It's difficult at times to answer yes.

There seems to have been something of an obsession with twelve. Was it all down to Jesus and his disciples? Did our early fathers feel so devout that they had to make some recognition of the life of Christ in all that they did? Did they make it so that a shilling had twelve pence? If so, why were there not twelve shillings in a pound, or perhaps twelve florins in a pound? Why did they sell their eggs in dozens, and their rolls in dozens, but add one free one just for luck or was it 'Buy twelve, get one free?' For goodness' sake, we even sell wine by the dozen bottles. 'La cause de notre joie,' it says on the cork. We can get discount sometimes if we stretch to a case of 12 bottles.

Was it by the same principle that in our forefathers' quest to deliver justice, a sound justice, a just justice, that the jury system had 'Twelve good men and true?' Wouldn't ten have done just as well? Ten might have hanged a few more than twelve, or not let some innocents avoid the rope. On that basis was twelve ever enough? But twelve has that special quality.

So it seems that twelve can be associated not only with inches, eggs, and bread rolls, but also more importantly with the life of Christ, and his legacy, those fated men, the twelve Apostles of Jesus. So, by thus re-echoing, twelve is the due and proper 'Cardinal Number' to be included in our lives, in our thinking, in our meditating. Twelve, then, it is.

And so there are the six 'Cardinal Numbers' offered as the significant numbers and what they represent as the 'building blocks' of a life. As each is enumerated, what they are about comes to mind in greater or lesser detail, as a yardstick, a guideline, a 'moral compass' perhaps.

They are: three, for the Holy Trinity, five for our Five Adopted Values, seven for the Seven Deadly Sins, eight for Beatitudes of Jesus, ten for the Commandments of God, and twelve for the Twelve Apostles. The six Cardinal Numbers, to remember. Just half a dozen, if you like. Make it so, says Jean-Luc.

PART FIVE

WHAT HAPPENED ALONG
THE ROAD

CHAPTER 23
HATE

Where does hate come from? It's a 'common or garden' expression used daily, often without necessarily literally meaning we do actually hate something or someone.

We often say we hate things when we could say 'dislike,' more accurately. For example, we might say we hate spinach, when really we mean we dislike spinach. Or we could say we don't like it when 'he' leers at us that way, or 'we can't stand it,' instead of saying we hate it when he leers that way. We may say we hate 'this weather,' meaning we find inclement weather a nuisance, inconvenient or a disappointment, for spoiling some plans. And many hate spiders.

The way the word is used is here to stay, and it seems to be used as a superlative; used to emphasise or exaggerate our feeling about something, or someone. We have TV hates, for example: a certain personage or an advertisement, or even a whole programme for invoking in us dislike, disapproval and disgust; yes, but to the point of hate?

So what is hate, true hate, when we've got down to the bedrock? Real, proper, meaningful hate? Hate for a person, a group of people, a sect or followers of a creed, a hateful creed even, and hate for a nation, a nation's peoples.

We are not born with hate. We are often brought up to hate, or hate often comes with adolescence, that painful, drawn-out, fragile process over some years, and just as fragile in its way as the transient foetal first breath of air, and no longer the potential of 'drowning' in amniotic fluid; oxygen from the air not the mother's blood, that transient phase in parturition, in birth, balanced between dependency and independence, free living, with the cutting of the umbilical cord to become, then be, an adult. It soon passes.

But we are born with the ability to fear; fear just of only two things, fear of loud noises, and fear of falling. And this emotion of fear is our primordial negative emotion, based in the subconscious, most probably, in the part of our brains that's primitive, developmentally-wise, the hypothalamus, like the hold of a ship, below decks, not seen unless visited, where things like memories and undesired emotions are stored, whilst we enjoy the free air and sunlight on deck and steer the ship on its course. If an unworthy, undesirable thought pops up from below, we can push it back down and batten the hatches.

This is not a profound, deep explanation of the psychology of hate and hatred that an interested highbrow might want to read, but an everyman-in-the-street take, that anyone can reason, taking some, but only a little, of their time. Those two primordial fears become the bedrock of all our negative emotions, and negative emotional experiences, and negative emotional outbursts and negative actions as we grow up, and continue into adulthood.

As we grow up, we develop a strong sense of persona, who we are, often who we think we are and to some extent, know who we are on course to becoming. It is important to us; it carries a certain pride, mostly of worth, but sometimes false pride, but certainly pride in ourselves that we loath to have challenged. Challenging our persona brings an instant, ultra-split second, a nanosecond of fear, a fear of falling, not physically, as in infancy, but falling from the height our built pride has set us up on. And when that challenge comes, it comes often audibly, the spoken word, the machine-gun, rattled-out insult, loudly as any loud noise, because our auditory to hypothalamus neural pathway is primordially built to register 'loud noises,' it rings and registers as much as any high-decibel explosion would.

One of the first negative emotions the baby develops is that ability to perceive the difference between a smiling face of another human, and the frown and gloomy face of the unloving. If we frown at a baby, it's likely to cry. If we smile, it's likely to smile back, but it may be wind. Crying in the neonatal baby has, in the past, been put down to just 'exercising' its lungs. And how! It's an awfully loud noise from so small a scrap of humanity. Crying, of course, is about the baby's only means of communicating, in primordial terms, with its mother, an attention-grabbing manifestation of need of care, as in warmth, protection from the mother's arms, nutriment from her breasts, and removal of the chronic discomfort from soiled 'nether regions.' The crying indicates the baby's need for food, security and physical comfort and these early basic emotions build rapidly to add to the fear of falling and loud noises. Soon following these developments is the need for love, as expressed by the mother and others, in loving words, cuddles, stroking and smiles; the baby recognises the sweet tones of loving speech, baby language (ichy-ichy-coo language) and the feeling of pleasure, of happiness, those addictive emotional experiences, that later lead to complicated needs of an hedonistic life.

With our five senses, the baby, the infant, the child and then adolescent develops likes and dislikes, and likes and dislikes to degrees. We sense these with sight, hearing, taste, touch and smell. We don't all like and dislike the same things. Taste is possibly the best example of differential likes and dislikes, but the sight of 'art,' the sound of music, the odour of some fumes and the sensation, the feel of certain surfaces, we all can discern, so to differ and widely.

Just as we develop stronger preferences, a runny yolk to a cooked egg that's solid, so we develop stronger dislikes, things to be more widely avoided, more readily set aside, rejected. Being repeatedly exposed to the object increasingly disliked evokes dislike to a degree of disgust. Being 'forced' to eat something, say, tapioca as a child – 'Eat it, it will do you good, and you cannot get down from the table until it's all gone' – will get a reaction of disgust even to the extent of vomiting up the dreaded tapioca. We hate it so.

So that's where hate comes from: something that we dislike so much it evokes disgust to the degree that makes us hate it. It's an extreme form of dislike, with much disgust. How odd is it that, say, when asked to comment on a décor, a new décor, that we don't like, we can't take to or approve, we skirt round the bold truth, not wishing to hurt, and say, 'it's very nice, but it's not to my taste.' So, we have identified 'taste' as a word to be associated with likes and dislikes, at least for inanimate things like food, art, music, architecture and scenery; and things like activities, like 'gym' at school and cross-country runs. Here we are developing likes and dislikes for activities we are required to partake in by others, authority figures, even certain lesson subjects, and then for the teachers themselves. It may be their irritating habits; it may be their sneering, cajoling attitude.

As children, we are forced into a world, in term-time, away from the loving nest of home. Well, we have hoped it's a loving nest. Often it's not; a school can become a welcome escape from an unhappy home. What a disaster for the child, so young, so raw, so innocent, so needing love and stability, to have to experience parents arguing, shouting, throwing things; even hitting each other. Bewilderment sets in, then isolation, looking for a shield from the bruising witnessing of all this. It is such a shame, so sad, that this happens. Talk about royalty saying, 'Pas devant les domestiques,' it should also be 'Pas devant les enfants.'

Witnessing this, children often cry. They see their ideal, their experience of joint parental love flying out of the window, and a cold draught coming in the door. They don't like it, they very much don't like it, intensely dislike it so much they hate it, and shout at the parents to 'Stop rowing, we hate it, hate it,' and then cry their hearts out in all desperation and hopelessness.

As we learn more about the world, the things that went on in history, things like wars and such, we form some kind of judgement, often a common judgement, influenced by the teaching, the style of teaching, even the prejudices of the teachers. For example, we hear about 'Bad King John, and good King Richard,' about how the Jews murdered Jesus; Jesus who preached love and peace and healed the sick. They murdered Him, they bloody actually murdered Him. You hate them. And there we have it. Our childhood young, tender, delicate, emotional centre in our hypothalamus developing, deepening and strengthening the extent, the intensity, the strength of emotion, raising blood pressure and heart rate, tightening of the stomach, mouth going dry, pupils widening, nostrils flaring for more air; yes, you hate them, hate them for what the they did. But hang on a minute. This is history, in the past, two thousand years ago and look at you, it looks as if you are about to explode!

So here we have the potential for an idea bringing about a response so intense it becomes hate. The idea, the mistaken idea that the whole race; was it the whole race, or just some of the followers of Judaism who were responsible for the death of Jesus, or was it the leaders, who with paid agitators were able to stir up the bloodlust of the people, stir them up using their insulated ideas of the observance of the Sabbath and Holy Law, the scriptures, those questionably hallowed words?

The notion, the idea, even the principle of hating others, be they an individual, a group, a whole cult, a race or even a country, has to come from somewhere, something in our upbringing and something of a sort of reasoning, usually very misguided, acquired since, as we plough the long furrow of our life.

We like ourselves. Well, at least we know ourselves, we know what we like, all those things we approve of with our five senses, and to that extent we accept ourselves as the norm. We know our parents, brothers and sisters, all live under the same roof. We know them, they are real, they are life, or as life seems to the child, the adolescent, in fact we see them as 'normal,' or mostly so. Okay. So, we all think we are normal. That's good.

So, who is not normal? Isn't it just about everyone else? It's certainly those who don't do as we do, act as we do, go about their lives as we do, dress as we do, speak as we do and behave as we do.

And because they are not 'normal,' we have to ask ourselves, 'Do we approve of them, those being 'not normal?' Well, actually, we don't ask, our hypothalamus makes the judgement for us in a nanosecond. We call it 'first impressions' and it seems they seldom turn out to be wrong, wrong judgements.

The problem that arises with all this is that our experiences, what we have learned, what we have been told, or read, or seen on-screen become matters on which we make judgements. In fact we have become 'preconditioned.' Preconditioned, we hope, to identify good from evil, right from wrong, loving from unloving. But we mostly also become preconditioned by the teachings of others, by reading and screen-watching; a diet that can be either healthy for our minds, our attitudes, or unhealthy, as in building prejudices. And because artistic directors of films and plays are so clever at selecting actors whose facial features more readily fit the criminal part to act in their play, their film, we get, in real life, to identify those whose physiognomy has similar features of criminality, and without any other basis for making a judgement, we decide either we don't like them, or we don't trust them, or both. How unfair, being that judgemental. So misguided.

We need our opinions, like we need air to breathe. The man with no opinions isn't alive. Our opinions should be reasoned, informed judgements, seeing and coming to an understanding of others, others who may they think they are 'normal,' too. There is no such thing as 'normal;' it's a figment of our imagination. Forget normal. Only by working to come to an understanding of others, other cultures, other ideologies, is there any hope of getting on, and getting on means peace.

Look at the process of the major international diplomatic disagreements, such as the UK leaving the EU. Negotiations are finally left to the leaders, on each side, locking horns like two stags to put one over the other and get their way. But although the same species, these two are quite different animals, different in that they most definitely do not share the same understanding of logic, a common understanding of what is logical, what logic is, then there is no hope of them ever being seen as 'reasonable' together. That is to say, one cannot bring reason to bear. And then, eventually, emotions of dislike set in, and depending on the degree of self-control, that dislike can not only hinder the discussions, the arguments, the negotiations, but also can even turn to hate. It's time to change negotiators then; changing to negotiators for their different reasoning, their logic, often giving a different approach to otherwise what is seen as unsolvable challenges. But, of course, each has its political 'masters' driving the policy behind the negotiations and the two only have so much latitude.

The ability to hate, the propensity to hate, our readiness to turn on or turn off the hate switch in the control rooms of our brain, is an acquired function as our emotional 'power base' develops through childhood and adolescence, and then later becomes the learned functions of adults, arising out of a set of thought sequences that potentially can alter our behaviour.

We readily use the word 'hate' as a frequent expression but rarely, literally, do we mean we hate that something with any real intensity of emotion. For example, we might remark that we hate to see fully abled car owners using a disabled parking space, and with no disabled screen sticker. Don't you just hate that? How about when they interrupt and start introducing the next TV programme on-screen before the one you were watching has finished? Don't you just hate that? We mean, of course, dislike or disapproval. We should really reserve hate for what it truly is. We should always say what we mean, and mean what we say. Hyperbole is fine in its way, as long as everyone knows it's just that, hyperbole.

If we can develop the emotional ability to hate, by instinctive acquisition, under our own steam as children, we need no deliberate or unintentional incitement to hatred from anyone. But that is hard, very hard, in fact, to avoid.

Parents can pass on their prejudices to their children so easily. Family expressions of extreme dislike, distrust and disapproval of, say, certain political parties, certain religious groupings, certain ethnic groups, even whole nations, can lead to a form of 'hatred' in the young impressionable mind.

In fact, there can be a kind of perverse pleasure, self-satisfaction, in arriving at a judgemental decision to hate someone or some group. As in, 'We know now what to think, how to think, and this becomes part of our self-concept, who we are as in 'I hate smokers, gum chewers, Jews, Muslims, Sikhs, the Germans, the French; to hate anybody we decide to.' And then, 'Yes, I like this behavioural development, it makes me feel something. Is it something good?' No, it's not, but the feeling can be mistaken for something good, but only because we feel our vengeful decision somehow strikes a blow, a limiting constraint in our mind against the hated one or group. We want to spread the comforting thought, to get others on our side, in the battle to suppress the hated ones, and endorse our persona.

The deliberate turning of minds, often referred to as 'brainwashing,' is a skilled process. Turning towards hatred is easier than the reverse, turning to good, to goodness, to goodliness and so to God. The pressure, incitements and inducements are subtle, especially at first. The younger and less 'programmed' the mind, the easier it will be. Eventually, a hatred so intense is developed that terrorists will be prepared to sacrifice their lives in a terrorist bombing attack. Their love of their God as they have been brought to view their religion may have become inflated enough to serve that God in this way, to sacrifice their life and be rewarded with 76 virgins in Heaven. They don't understand they will not be taking their body with them to Heaven, and so the obsession of a list of virgins, ready willing and able to please the physical needs of the young man, is just so much rubbish (and they never seem to question what happens on the 77th night). To carry out their terrorist cause, to have that warped love for their God, has to be heavily supplemented by the development of that intense hatred of those they know will be maimed or murdered by their terrorist bomb.

And we in turn hate the terrorists: what they 'stand for,' what their thinking is, those who recruit and train them, and those who support their misguided, so severely mistaken cause. The words Jesus spoke from the cross apply today as much as then. 'Father, forgive them, for they know not what they do.' Hatred has so much to answer for and can only ever be overcome by love and understanding.

Reaching an understanding is an achievement that grants much more pleasure and sense of good feeling than adopting a judgemental position on hatred. People in commerce are often the best and more frequent group who can get to feel the good feeling of reaching an understanding. Both sides really only need to understand a few basics; what it is one is selling, its quality, its price and their ability to deliver. Get that understood on both sides and there's an agreement, a contract to do business.

It's trade that makes the world go around, not politicians, not soldiers etc. You have something to sell, you want to sell it. Get the price right. Get quality right and the delivery right, and the same applies when buying.

We don't have to like the people we are dealing with, although that helps.

Some in commerce will 'sup with the Devil' to trade, and that can surely only be good, breaking down prejudices, replacing suspicion and hatred with something better, building trust progressively, and some understanding.

We don't have to understand their logic. If they want to trade, then if tariff-free trade exists, we can get by and make agreements to trade without agreeing or understanding their logic. Of course, some contracts will be so complicated that lawyers on both sides will be involved, and the national law of some countries will be different to another's, and there their own 'logic' comes into play. Lawyers, commercial lawyers, are usually very smart and know how to ease an agreement along, understanding the other side's 'legal logic' but without necessarily agreeing with it. In this way, commerce eases and promotes international understandings, much, much more than any politicians can do. And this prompts the recurring idea that MPs should be over 50 years of age before thinking they are fit to become our legislators. Time enough for them to have acquired the experiences and qualifications for the job, and it's rather more than gaining a PPE degree. Just about every job, every worthwhile job, requires a structured ability based on a basic knowledge. Candidates for MP-ship, not always or even not often, have a broad experience of the world outside political theory, such as that which is acquired in commerce and industry and in the military. Politics, philosophy and economics degrees are all very well in their way, but alone are not enough, except that PPE can develop in one the art of being as slippery as grasping a fish for gutting.

Of course, very many trading contracts forged between peoples of two countries are frequently so much bigger and more complex than the eminently simple suggestion spoken of above. Many are major industrial agreements, and many are civil and military contracts that inevitably involve governments, then diplomats and politicians who, being involved, often have a 'what's in it for me?' approach, as in 'backhanders,' so frowned on in UK law, so loved by many other countries where the practice is part of their culture, and so are clandestinely arranged.

The other reality is that, as always, we are not the only fish in the sea, and other companies, and other countries, are competing for the business. Some will use unfair terms, underhand tactics, bigger backhanders, and even government subsidies to lower the price, to clinch the agreement. Perfidy, yes, but it's always there, greed, dishonesty, ambition to put one over your 'hated' competition, company or country. For decades, and even for at least one century Britain was referred to by European countries and probably elsewhere as 'Perfidious Albion.' Britain was regarded as untrustworthy and unreliable, seeming always to serve herself first, and Britain was hated for it. 'Give a dog a bad name' was the expression used to denote the labelling of someone, or some organisation or country, arising as a result of some disreputable behaviour. This is to say that a once-'hated' deed readily translates into the fear and anticipation of repeat behaviour, giving rise to 'a leopard doesn't change its spots.' This can be so unfair, but it may be deserved, when it can evoke a kind of subliminal hate, not actually hating but a hair trigger-precipitated readiness to hate again, possibly more fiercely next time.

'What is sauce for the goose is *not* sauce for the gander.' What we find to hate, another may be quite the opposite in opinion, in judgement. Opinions mostly come autonomously, but some only when provoked, requested by someone. In forming our opinions, reasoned opinions, we will want to avoid being too precipitate, too fast in coming to a conclusion before finding out as much as possible that may bring new facts to bear. We can have an initial provisional, as in a 'qualified opinion' in these cases.

The point is, once formed; we may want to hold onto that view. Who wants to dither and shilly-shally? If unsure, more research is possibly needed. Once held, we seem to have one of two routes to proceed. In looking at issues, say, situations created by people, we can adopt an opinion of that behaviour, that event. And that opinion may be judgemental either in a positive sense or in a negative sense, and that negative judgemental attitude can lead to prejudice, and that prejudice can lead to bigotry and hate.

The other route that can be taken, having formed an opinion in a more positive sense, on some behavioural issue, is that some allowance can be made, and that allowance can lead to an acceptance, and that acceptance can lead to tolerance, and worked-on tolerance can lead to understanding. From acceptance, tolerance and understanding can come more forgiveness of our fellow beings; forgiveness turns away hate and forgiveness is good, of goodness, and of God. But beware, and this is where so many 'do-gooders' go wrong. We can forgive in our hearts and minds, in our communion with the force of goodness, of God, within us, it is not necessary or wise to go about 'bragging' our forgiveness, even to the forgiven. What is more, there is no need to think we should make reparations; because with relationships, fresh attitudes about a person, a group, even a country need to be formed, based on experience, including allowing for any forgiveness. The old relationship has gone for ever, can never ever be the same again, and no amount of reparations can bring it back.

The errant spouse, probably adulterous, ruins the previous relationship. The offender pleads forgiveness and wants things to go back as they were. It's 'Get real. Any forgiveness will be silent, in the heart, and no going back. We'll work out a way to a new relationship as loving as possible on both sides; no more perfidy.' We will need to go into the control room, the railway junction box in our mind, and pull some pretty big leavers, and so plot a revised course to sail, with reduced canvas to repair that which is torn, our track more slowly progressing until the time comes, if ever, when we can hoist full sail again. But the new destination is not your favoured place; it is unlikely now that that wonderful, peaceful, lovely harbour, its waypoint first set out to reach, may not now ever be possible with the damaged vessel of your life; so a less than ideal harbour, less than ideal berth, but a berth for all that. Is it better at that stage in life to settle for a damaged, scarred relationship with a spouse, than to finish up a bitter single? Much will depend upon how well, how truly, we can forgive, and that depends upon love, the love in a heart that can forgive, and durst we say, forgive again, but hardly again and again. We can only bang our head on the wall so much.

Time heals all things! And that is mostly likely to be very true, but, like much healing, scars are always left, and some scars can be very sensitive; some remain vivid and most distort.

For a situation to come about where brothers hate each other is referred to in the Bible. It seems brothers, and sisters, can either be close (or even really close), or be indifferent to each other, or just plain hate each other. One wonders how and why such a hate situation can come about. There is nearly always some rivalry, perhaps, with jealousy between them when growing up. Skills and attributes develop differently, with every success in school, in club and societies, even parental adulation for the accolades heaped upon the successes of one, but not the other, the less gifted, less fortunate in the opportunities arising, as a 'coincidence' of life.

We know some people are clever and gifted and they become rich and possibly famous, but one's own brother or sister, who sadly, glowing with success and opulence, may no longer be modest, loving and sensitive, sensitive to the sensibilities of one's brothers and sisters. The challenge to the parents is to anticipate 'dangerous' situations developing, and they need to work hard to see that their sibling rivalries are mild, tolerated and acceptable. We have no training in parental skills, no qualifications and yet they are a skill set so vitally needed within families. Time often heals the gaps that have developed between brothers and sisters, as they age, as their fortunes, rich or poor, are decided by life's eventualities, but sadly, for some, the hate is taken to the grave, but not always to the graveside.

Hate for one's parents is tragic. Hate is usually, when it occurs, for only one parent, and an indifference to the other parent who supports, or cannot countermand, the hated parent, the spouse, who, because a life must be led, and be had, opts for as much miserable peace as can be tolerated.

Is it possible to both love and hate a parent? We know we have loved the parent, perhaps well-loved in childhood, but some thing or things happened along the line, when a major falling out occurred. Adolescence can be such a turbulent time and parents can be of so little understanding, short on patience, short on tolerance and short on forgiveness, short on love, the love of God. Parents often want and expect their children to grow into their own mould, that is the parents' mould, how they expect the children to be, to think, and eventually to live their lives, and to have identical self-concepts. And when the children don't fill the mould, have a different mindset, a mind set in teenagehood so different, even 'rebellious' that there is a major change in what was, even only five years ago, a loving family harmony.

Deep down one may feel that 'old' love for the parent, but superimposed on top are all the layers of angry, disappointed, frustrated emotions that in total leave a feeling of hate. The only thing to do then is to create a distance, and real or psychological distance, no contact, or a distance enforced by silence, leaving the emotions simmering on the back burner, ready to flare up if one parent or the other tries to make contact. We must honour our father and mother – as the Commandment has it. If we can't bring ourselves to honour, then let's do nothing, say nothing, and think nothing to dishonour them. And that's a good start.

So, can we bounce back, back from hate, hating someone, something, some group or other, some nation even? Can we, do we, get into a 'habit' of hating things, some people or other? Do we too readily think, or say, 'I hate.' As said earlier, it is common parlance, to say, 'I hate chocolate' or this or that, expressed almost unthinkingly, using and 'downgrading' the word hate, as in just so many soundbites.

Wouldn't it be better to try to adopt only using the word 'hate' for truly hating, blood pressure rising, heart pumping, nostrils flaring hate? Only say what we mean, and mean what we say. But how many people think like that? In a way, it's not so much the spoken word that matters. What matters is the emotion within us. Those emotions, almost involuntary, almost uncontrollable emotions, will tell us if we truly hate that something, or those someones.

Are those hate emotions controllable or shall we, should we, allow them to run riot in our heads, in our hearts and minds, guts, spleen and liver? Shall we allow ourselves to have the gall to vent our spleen to satisfy the hate down to our guts and in our hearts and minds?

Hate is so destructive to any peace of mind, and to any worthy conduct, any self-worth and in that, it can be destructive of a life, as a ship having been taken over by a mutinous crew, who know they've done wrong, can't help themselves but act up, act as if everything is okay. At some point the ship has to make port, and there, answer for itself, in judgement.

The game of chess of our life expects us to work out more than the next move, more than the next two moves, and what the effect, the responses, might be, if we can. Hate, adopting hate, allowing it to take seed and grow in our emotional centre, even to feed it with pernicious thoughts for a perverse satisfaction, even in its momentary pleasure, is not at all helpful to life's course. It can be a means of self-preservation, a shield, a defence, and perhaps a temporary self-survival mechanism, but is only a suitable short-term response. But to allow the hate to grow, to build, to become embedded? No.

Hate is bad enough to be one of the Seven Deadly Sins, making nine, if we included indulgence as number eight. One wonders how it was missed off the list. Being on the list then, we should eschew it. Go into the junction box, take the emotion lever from the 'Hate' position, and throw the lever onto the 'Disapprove' then 'Dislike' position, and prepare later to move it to the 'Indifference' then 'Tolerant' position, and ultimately to 'Acceptance.' It will be like easing the helm, coming off the wind, like reefing for a more pleasant, smoother, less stress on the boat and you; the helm, helming your life, in good and comfortable control again, the waves less hateful now you are not meeting them head on, each jarring the craft, testing its scantlings, its construction to the limits. It's rather like when we say, he (or she) is made of sterner stuff, but in a different sense, here.

Worst of all are the 'preachers of hate!' Those who preach and teach vulnerable and gullible minds from the pulpits of certain so-called religious groupings or sects, masquerading as a faith or at least a religious doctrine, when in true reality the term 'cult,' a religious cult, with jactitation as a religious faith, twistedly peddles their misguided, mistaken thinking that provokes violence, maiming and death. What for? For a cause. What cause? Their cause is against humanity, whilst part of humanity themselves. Their cause is taken up because life has dealt them or their parents a raw deal, even their grandparents, or great-grandparents, a raw deal. Cudgels taken up on their behalf, they just won't let it go. They should get over it. The sins of the fathers are not to be visited on the children. Hate achieves nothing, nothing worthwhile, nothing of good; only bad.

Hate, then, is like a 'deadly' sin when felt as meant, and if not meant, is best omitted from the daily vocabulary. And when meant, it does us and no one else any good, destroys lives, leaving little hope of peace of mind, and tests forgiveness and love to the limits. Let's get over it, as soon as we can, as soon as we can learn how to, identify the means and find the willpower. Is there a YouTube video clip on 'How to get on, to move away, and move on, from hate?'

It may mean some big steps, some big decisions, rather than live with this constant thorn, this irritant, which or who won't go away. We might even need to change jobs, but take care not to shoot ourselves in the foot in so doing. We might even move house, but with the same caveat. We might even have to work with the mantra, 'What can't be cured must be endured.' And, with the love of goodness in our heart, we can cure most things, especially that unreasonable hatred in our heart.

—•—

CHAPTER 24
VIOLENCE

Violence – it was Boris Yeltsin who said, in his wisdom, 'Any attempt to change life through violence is condemned to failure.' How true, but how often forgotten. It is often said older men make wars, but it's the young who fight them.' Bismarck said that 'Peace is that uncomfortable time between wars,' implying that peace was a hopeless, lost cause because humans gathered into nations would always only be ever to be able to settle their differences through violence. But then he was a pugilist by nature. Wars are fought over areas of land, the raw materials in that land and over trading disagreements, but also, and through history, more often than not, over religious beliefs, and the conduct those beliefs give rise to. We are, as a species, so smart, so clever, so intelligent, so 'developed,' so civilised, and cultured compared to the other animals on this planet, and yet we cannot stop war. We just cannot seem to live in peace with one another. There's always a war or wars going on in one part of the world or another, on and on sometimes, as the greater powers, who could stop them, don't, but instead keep feeding them the materials of war, and making a profit in so doing.

Somehow, almost mysteriously, we allow a cult leader to rise up and gain power over us. Someone who is unable to live in peace, someone who stirs up trouble between us and as we mostly want to get along, we find we have to go along. Such were Hitler and his Nazis, Stalin and his Communists, and many more the world over, throughout history. That is why democracy is so vitally important; a free press and regular independently monitored elections. This system may seem inefficient as one government undoes the changes of the previous government. But it is better by far than living under a dictatorship, a despot, with the fear of the secret police coming knocking on your door in the middle of the night, because your neighbour, who despises you, has lied about you to the authorities. Democracy – yeah! It is not a particularly good form of government, but it's the best we have, said Churchill.

War is the ultimate extension of a foreign policy; the result of its ultimate failure. If the world were a big United States of the World, would there be war, or would there be just local disturbances between rival groupings and so would just be called riots? If more and more countries merged to form continental blocks, as the United States of, say, Europe, and of Africa, and of South America; if the US merged with Canada and so on, would there still be wars? As ever, if bigger and bigger 'Super-National United States' went to war? It would have to be another world war, that's for certain.

Many put their faith in the development and the delivery potential of ever more dreadful weapons of mass destruction, more appropriately should be called weapons of massed murder. Both sides develop the same or similar dreadful weapons systems, and both fear going to a war that would lead only to a war of mutual annihilation. That mutual fear is what is called 'the balance of power.' And all sides are determined to develop more and more advanced weapons, so to maintain an advantage for a while, but to what purpose? Because we can? Because science and the men of science keep coming up with more ideas on how to subdue a potential enemy, more quickly, more efficiently? But will it be worth it? We know the other side still think the same, by spying, and are also carrying on working to develop and maintain that advantage, a sort of unspoken race, the undeclared arms race.

Many think that it's 'boots on the ground' that, in the end, resolve war. But when the ground is so deathly with radioactivity, there will be nothing left worth gaining. The original weapon was the clenched fist, occasionally aided and abetted by a kick or a bite. Ultimately, nowadays and in the future, weaponry will be delivered 'unmanned,' triggered by the flick of a switch, or the press of a button, from a fingertip.

We are still primeval enough to use the clenched fist, enough if only used by a tennis player, as at Wimbledon, as he or she raises the arm with a clenched fist as a vital point is scored. What does it mean, what does it signify? That the match is in effect a battle to win, to subjugate your opponent, and the necessary fight is the necessary game, set and match? It's vulgar.

There is a vicious streak running through society, that like a seam of gold in rock, rises every now and then to emerge and show itself as the most mindless, cruel perversity as to injure an innocent bystander, an innocent old lady, with her handbag, and her shopping, thinking lovingly of the impending visit of her much-loved grandson, when, wham, boom, she is knocked to the ground and is kicked and kicked needlessly by young thugs, and cheered on by a moll or two. And done for no other reason than it was a 'dare,' a kind of forfeit, for losing at a game of cards in a pub, now fuelled with alcohol and cocaine. It is impossible to comprehend this kind of incident, or those incidents where a man is killed by a stabbing, done in a split second of thoughtlessness, mindlessness, but not altogether unrehearsed, done because a lad has a knife and has idly pretended and practised how it would be, in front of the mirror in his bedroom, a fantasist, now acting it out for real, the split second gone, in a flash, a flash of blade, but too late, it is done, and there's the blood spurting as he, another young father collapses to the ground; just because he was trying to rescue his young son's bike from the taunting, teasing young tykes from the local estate.

Or is it understandable? We know that some breeds of dogs individually are as gentle and obedient a companion as anyone would want of a pet dog. But when the same dogs, either kept together with others of their type, say three of four and they are allowed to roam, or perhaps escape, turn into the most excitable and dangerous pack of beasts man ever has to encounter. A group of three or four Doberman Pinschers, or a group of three Rottweilers, loose in the park, or get into a stranger's garden, are very capable of killing a child and even an adult, as they go into a rampage, into their mindless, unprovoked attacking. These events have been known. There is something, like a sort of evil chemistry, perhaps by pheromones, the pack instinct, that flows between them when free of discipline and order, descending into that feral state of killing so to eat, except they are not hungry, and the killing is just exercising their killing prowess, ready for when the time comes, if it comes, when the law of the jungle rules again. So it is with these mindless thugs, fired up with testosterone, for, yes, sadly it is nearly always, always the males, the young males, who are the guilty, semi-feral beasts, their untrained brains, such a waste of human potential, incensed with the chemistry of the crowd, the rabble, and rabid, bloodthirsty crowd, and some molls. Bring back National Service.

Many derive a sort of perverse pleasure, a venal pleasure, out of watching violent sports such as boxing and wrestling. Throughout history, many have gathered to watch, to 'cheer on' and to revel in violence between two of our fellow 'civilised' human beings. This is an obscene pleasure, witnessing violence;

it is a depravity of body and soul. There have been public stonings, crucifixions, gladiators fighting lions, and bulls, and boxing and wrestling. Even duelling for 'honour,' and with 'seconds' duelling as well, only this time it's not done as a public spectacle to enthral and entertain, but without an audience and is a fight that may even kill, to settle a question of honour. Let's be rightly understood here, there is no such thing as an honour killing. In war, we kill to avoid being killed, and we fight hard to bring an end to the killing, and to bring about the peace, and as we say, the peace of God that passeth all understanding.

Not content with watching humans knock each other's brains out, people also derive pleasure out of watching animals fight – dogfights, bear-baiting, bull-baiting and cockfighting.

In an attempt to make boxing 'respectable,' there are rules and gloves. People still will flock to the thrill of a 'bare-knuckle fight,' seen as somehow having more primeval quality, more caveman primitiveness, as in 'this is how it should be,' a sort of 'primitive man against primitive man,' and like as not, it will soon be 'primitive woman against primitive woman' as they seem not to want to be left out of anything that men have always done, except to grow beards.

At war, at the 'front,' there is no cheering. Soldiers have been cheered by their home folk and other crowds as they go to war, and the victors are cheered on their way home after the war, but no cheering as the injured come home, or the bodies brought home, and there's definitely no cheering at the front where there's only death, blood and gore, bodies mutilated, brains and bowels blown open and spewed around, limbs shattered into fragments and blood-curdling screams of people in the most God-awful pain.

As a species, as a highly developed physically and mentally capable species, we are so shallow, so blind, so careless with the precious gift of the world, and the gift of life, and the gift of love. We are not worthy, worthy to inherit the earth, and what's more, will we ever be?

When the millennium year 2000 came there was such hope. Hope for a better start, a better life, a better world. And yet, although medicine has advanced so much, as to save so many to live and live onto a 'ripe old age,' we have made no progress with the mental health and stability that bring peace.

It is mental health that is needed, needed to help us realise what behaviour and beliefs are healthy and worthy, and enable us to live in peace and prosperity as a world. We have cults, masquerading as faiths, breeding discontent and ambition to take over the world. Weird 'Man's Rules' dividing us as we 'flag up' what we stand for, to be divisive in society, unwilling to accept fellow humans as of different opinions, different creeds, and different dress and behavioural patterns. We need to do better, as the school report says of its pupils.

Just as we have an independent judiciary (well, supposedly independent, but who appoints the judges, the High Court judges and the Attorney General and the official solicitors? Guess! Quis custodiet ipsos custodes?) We need an independent body of people trained and qualified in psychiatric profiling. Their objective would be to carry out psychiatric profiling on candidates for election to parliament, and then again for promotion to the government. And why not? Very many people are 'subjected' to these same examinations by companies before employing or promoting staff to key positions.

Although parliamentary party candidates are chosen usually by a committee upon interview, psychiatric proofing would be a useful tool. The system we have in the UK hardly allows an aggressive war leader to emerge and take over from democratic rule, but many would say that that was what very nearly happened in the Iraq War. By amassing, through the media, 'armies' of potentially violent supporters, like Hitler's 'Brown Shirts,' is the UK in danger of that happening under extreme-wing leaderships, who work the system we have, to their advantage, moving inch by inch towards an anarchic republic?

Of course, and sadly, psychiatric profiling of politicians is hardly a serious suggestion because it seems impossible that it could ever be brought about. It is only 'suggested' here to make a point. For a start, the profiling is fallible, and secondly, would all the nations, all the other nations follow suit? No.

They say the first duty of government is defence of the realm. What is wrong with leaders, both elected and despotic, that they cannot have as a modification added to that saying and 'not to seek to acquire another realm or part of one?' Or more simply and better, 'to live in peace with other nations.'

Leaders around the world are often unhappy with the 'status quo' they have risen to rule over. Northern Ireland and Éire, still hankering after unification, North and South Cyprus, a racially divided small island, North and South Korea, an ideologically divided small peninsula, Israel and Palestine, racially and religiously divided country of bitter feuds, hatred and intense unhappiness, both bent on vengeance and a 'right' to exist, to be there, Spain and Gibraltar, Argentina and the Falklands. All are 'coveting,' wanting what is currently 'not theirs,' although may have been at one time. Take Russia and the Ukraine, and Crimea – Putin carried out a successful sequester of Crimea because the United Nations had no stomach, no real mandate to do anything about it. Putin clearly wants the Ukraine back under Russia's (i.e. his) control and is prepared to divide the country of Ukraine and take it piecemeal if he can't get the whole. One would think Russia was big enough already without 'grabbing' more and more land, but the rulers of Russia, both the royalist Romanov Tsars and the common-bred rulers from Stalin to Putin, have all never been content, and use their 'bully boy' tactics to see what they can get away with.

'Don't mix politics with religion' is the mantra and it's so right, but politics can be mixed with the love of God. Blessed are the peacemakers, and we can presume that includes 'blessed are the peacekeepers.' Wanting and suing for peace too much can lead to appeasement, giving into 'bully boys' for the sake of peace. The United Nations has tried hard since its inception to keep world peace, but many countries are not adequately represented, and many do not pay their dues, to keep the UN afloat, or keep to agreed expenditure or arrangements so that at anytime a UN peacekeeping force can be brought into 'play,' when conflict arises. The UN needs revitalising, and that will include some means of seeing the 'big five' do not act subversively, as they do now, to support the anti-democratic satellite countries they have chosen almost clandestinely to champion.

The settling of issues between peoples doesn't dispel the attitudes and ambitions of the malcontents. In recent times in the UK, the people have shown themselves to be unwilling to accept and live by the result of an election or a referendum. Surely, a proper and suitable education should have produced a nation of subjects who, above all, respect the rule of law. The 'rule of law' requires under a democracy for there to be elections and referenda to decide who the lawmakers are to be for the next period, and what is the will of the majority of the people, at least the people who bother to vote.

To be working to thwart the result of an election or referendum is tantamount to treason, seeking to disrupt the rule of law, of democratic principles. People seem to seethe, to be consumed and eaten up with their loss at an election, and some invite a hate of the successful party to drive their every emotion and whim. How unhappy is that? If we vote as we have done to leave the EU, so be it. Respect the vote, however badly fought the process was, and it was, a travesty from a so-called educated, civilised people. If a political party rules with a very slim majority, then let it, and support that which it wants to deliver that is good, and only that. The country will go on, people will carry on with their lives, injustice will continue.

That's to say, a slowing of the pace of change, of improvements in our society may well be better done more slowly, but more knowingly, with a consensus in parliament. A big majority can bring about sweeping changes, that may or may not work out as planned for some, or for many, and people are fickle, voting a different way next time. Consensus politics with a minority government may well be a better way. Many countries get by with coalition governments, like Italy and Germany. UK's political observers denigrate and train us to pooh-pooh coalitions as if they were 'evil.' Nonsense.

Whatever we think of parliament, our parliaments and the parliaments of others, the democracies of the world should live together in peace, negotiating their differences, their different view or take on things, and remembering that the word 'parliament' derives from 'parler,' French, to speak, and remembering always that jaw-jaw, is better that war-war and how that all began with the clenching of the fist.

CHAPTER 25
IT'S ALL ABOUT SECTS

It seems we can't live without sects. Everyone seems to want sects. Sects make the world go round, been with us since time immemorial.

When the world was much less populated, and peoples lived in groups further apart, those early groupings, mostly family groupings, became established as villages, and with few opportunities for travel between villages, there inevitably came about a common custom, custom behaviour patterns, with intra-breeding (marrying within their own group) but also some inbreeding. Each village effectively was a sect, a group, together for mutual support, help and comfort. There was suspicion, and rivalry, with a good dose of fear of the next village along the valley or over the hill. Fear that they'd steal their cows, overnight, which did happen. So, sects went on the defensive, too.

And there we have the basic features of a sect. A grouping for a shared ideology involving mutual support and help, some comfort, especially sociologically speaking, and some interbreeding, with suspicion or fear of outsiders.

With population growth, villages became towns, towns became cities; and cities grew to become sprawling metropolises. And with these masses of population, it is no wonder we hunger for the primitive grouping of a 'sect,' a sect by any other name, be it tribe or clan. Hunger because we are still, at heart, that basic, semi-civilised, prehistoric early man inside us, and, when invited to join a privileged sect, oh, joy of joy. It may be the Masons, or a certain Masonic lodge, or the Ancient Order of Buffaloes, Round Table, Rotary, the Yacht Club, the Golf Club, the Labour Party, the Tory Party, the horticultural society who go on outings; it's never-ending. We are accepted, wanted even, and let's include the local church in that as well, be it synagogue, St. Mary's RC, 'All Saints' C of E, the local mosque, not forgetting the British Legion and the local working men's club, Mothers' Union, Women's Institute, and so on. To belong to something, with an ideology, gives that primitive feeling of the ancient village, governed by the village elders, the village 'fathers,' and those doctrines that inculcate the belief, the behaviour and our thinking; all that goes with being 'in the sect!'

There's nothing intrinsically wrong in belonging to a sect, as long as its purpose is good and worthy, for all, not just its members, and as long as we can avoid the 'fear' of outsiders, and avoid the straitjacketed, narrow-minded thinking that goes with some sects, most notably the so-called religious sects. Virtually all sects come with a price tag, what it will cost us to be 'accepted' as one of them. They need our money, often quite badly.

As for the intra-breeding, these days we tend to marry someone we have met at work, sometimes known from school or college days, work or sport. The old days of mother and father leading us into an advantageous marriage are all but gone; we tend to marry someone within our own sphere or sect. Many believe the coming together, 'perfectly matched,' is down to fate, but if you dally long enough somewhere, and move among the local grouping, the prospects, the 'chance' of meeting someone with whom there is a mutual attraction, albeit as it may turn out, only transient, is very high. It is nothing so much as to do with fate, then. But people do so love to believe in fate, that their life is mapped out already and they are walking the path of fate, with no choice. What tosh. While inbreeding is against the law, what about an intended spouse who has been adopted as a child, and who has no knowledge of their birth parents? What then? This happens in the aftermath of a war.

Some sects, particularly the older religions still try to maintain the 'intra-breeding.' This could be said of the Jews and the Islamists. The distinction between their 'faiths,' the religious creeds they follow, and their tribal origins, is often confused. Because of all the intra-breeding, the onlooker doesn't know whether he or she is dealing with a faith, a doctrinaire grouping, or a race of people. Would it matter? Does it matter?

In negotiating with, and getting along with, others, others who have 'coded' themselves as something readily identifiable in the crowd, we feel we need to understand, to 'get to know' who and what people are, what makes them 'tick.' But the tribal instinct is to close ranks, keep out 'outsiders' just to protect ourselves and gain strength and comfort from that.

There is still that fear of the tribe 'over the hill,' fear of 'stealing our cows' in the night. North Korea versus South Korea, Greek Cypriots versus Turkish

Cypriots, Éire versus Northern Ireland, and so on. Intertribal fear. No reasonable rationale. Primitive behaviour, still seen typically in children, and in grown-up children, adults who haven't yet 'grown up,' a primitive fear of the Ferengi, Johnny Foreigner, 'Don't like the look of him' and 'Wouldn't trust them as far as I could throw them, every man jack of them.' And so on: such awful unthinking prejudice, bigotry even, so wrong and unfair.

It is more than just 'a fear' of losing our cows, it's a case for hate. It is hate that is bred along with this fear, and the hate freezes the thinking process, 'blinding' the sect members to any reasoning, and to any persuasion to 'change' the doctrinaire rules of the sect, the tribe.

Nothing drives the fear more than the fear of the sect being 'overrun,' disturbed and annihilated. To protect themselves they either 'go secret' so that only members can be known to themselves through secret signs and 'magic handshakes,' or in the case of very large tribes, so big as to run a country, they adopt a defensive position with troops and weaponry, like the Ba'athists were in Iraq.

Part of the total primordial fear of being 'wiped out' is the sense of competition that grows between the sects. Stealing cows makes them richer, stronger; those who have lost cows, weaker and ready to be 'wiped out'. They adopt a doctrine that their sect must be the best, the strongest, to steal cows in the night, to go in for 'takeovers' of other competing companies, and if it's going to profit them, they go for mergers as well as acquisitions. Inter-company rivalry; it's tribal.

There. We've said it, companies are sects. They have most of, if not all, the features of sects. They provide social clubs for their workers, crèches and staff outings. They expect a certain code of conduct, and care for their members through Health and Safety policies (a sect in self-preservation mode) and company private health-care schemes, and a culture of 'Support the Company and Be True to It,' and it will support and be true to you; but only as long as your service to the company is profitable enough, in terms of more cows, that is.

But in general parlance, the term 'sect' is reserved for some sort of grouping that has a flavour of something 'radical,' errant from the mainstream thinking and behaviour, the thinking of zealot, fanatical types, generally disapproved of.

These sects are driven by an ideology, a set of thought-processes leading to convictions and beliefs not held valid by the vast majority of people, not mainstream thinking. That is to say their ideology is extreme in some way, so extreme as to be repugnant to the 'man in the street' or woman.

It is presumed that their new members – for they need new members as others die off or are maybe killed at war – that their new members come to join by committing to accept the ideology. And why would anyone do that? Have they been born with a mental capacity, a potential capacity to be willing to adopt a doctrinaire thinking that's blind to others' opinions, other ways of thinking, or, even if admitting to having considered other ideologies, prefer the one they have chosen, chosen to be convinced by, and chosen to live by, the rules of this ideology, the rules of this sect? Sometimes the indoctrination process can be so very subtle, expressed in a way gradually and subliminally to inculcate the sect's ideology. In such a way that outsiders say the new members have been 'brainwashed.'

Far more will become new members of the sect by virtue of their birth and upbringing. The necessary certain way of thinking of that sect's beliefs are inculcated in the young by the parents, and others of the sect, as the child grows up. Here we can refer to faith schools. The sagacious 'village' elders, drilling their 'warped and straitjacketed' thinking and opinions into the delicate, innocent, uncluttered minds, the as-yet-unprogrammed minds of young children. So wrong. Children should be brought up to know of the varieties of life, of the world and its peoples, the perceived merits and demerits of all forms of human activity, so that the young mind learns to make decisions based on researching as many factors that bear on the issue before deciding for themselves, choosing their options based on as wide an understanding of those options as possible. Those elders know exactly what they are doing, seeking to strengthen the sect, the 'village,' the cult, then better prepared to fend off outsiders, to be blind and deaf, and reject any outside, 'foreign' thinking.

We may view the ideology of a sect or cult with disdain, disapproving of what 'it stands for,' which is often not for the general good, but exclusively for the good of its members. Whilst we may dislike their thinking, their beliefs, it doesn't automatically follow that we have to 'dislike' or disapprove of the individual cult members. On their own, in life, in society, at work, any one of 'them' may seem perfectly likeable, even appear to be 'well-balanced' individuals. Unless they wear a 'uniform' or some sort of 'branding,' a badge, like a skullcap, or a turban or a burqa, or a 'full set,' or a dog collar, or a lapel badge or brooch, we may not even realise they subscribe to a cult way of thinking. But it can dawn on us, and quickly, if they ever, in a coffee break, say, are to offer some bizarre opinion, so non-mainstream that our suspicions are immediately aroused. On their own perfectly pleasant, like that Doberman or Rottweiler, but let loose in a pack...?

Then, in general, we are on our guard, once we know or suspect who and what we are dealing with, or in the company of someone who is either capable of, or has already committed to, a philosophy that is fundamentally at much variance with the mainstream thinking, which is often just plain 'not thinking,' but equally possibly just one at variance with our 'sect' or our 'cult' thinking.

Most cult thinking, like all sects, in wishing to deter opposing views, aims to win over everyone to 'their' way of thinking, because they believe they are right. So they become evangelical, missionary, as in 'on a mission.' Many see this as just plain 'bigotry.' Is someone with a firmly held belief that is refuted by our own belief, automatically a 'bigot?' Isn't it bigoted to brand the other person a 'bigot' because we refute their opinions? Surely to label anyone a bigot risks us being labelled a bigot also? It is a heavy label to place, so best use it carefully: the giving and taking of offence is a two-way thing. It takes two to tango. Best we don't fight with pigs – they enjoy it, and we get dirty.

If a salesperson wears some religious symbol to 'brand image' their cult-following, employers of today think customers of other or no 'faith' (as in sects or otherwise) will take offence. If we are walking down a street and see a sign for 'halal' meat, do we take offence, or just think how 'stupid', how illogical, how mindlessly ritualistic, or do we pop in and buy a big joint of lamb, but not pork, of course.

The company employing the 'naughty' salesperson wearing cult branding is afraid their business will be harmed so that another company will then steal their cows. The NHS takes a similar view; company branding is to be worn only, no labels of one's own, no individualistic, ideological thinking, no bigotry, nothing to denote you as a zealot or even a Christian. Keep your opinion out of work is what is demanded, and as they also say, keep religion out of politics (sic). Will robot-workers have opinions?

Political correctness, as it is termed, is nothing to do with politics – it is a pandemic that has spread like a prion throughout Western civilisation in recent times. The symptoms? The first symptoms appear in those of a certain disposition, having a too delicate sensibility and their innate uncertainty fosters an insecurity of theirs and everyone else's persona. Often it's the same people who have been given, inappropriately and with little or no proper training, the role of carrying out Health and Safety risk assessments. They see a risk in 'everything,' just as they see a potential for the giving and taking of offence in everything. They should 'cool it,' and some more of 'Be cool, man!' is needed.

Rabid zealots at the time of these writings have concerned themselves with the differentiation of the sexes, the labelling of either males as males or females as females, even now on a birth certificate. Up goes the battle cry, and all 'Rent-a-Mob' take this up as their cause, seeking to shake the foundations of millennia of civilisation of mankind, seeking to deny the biological physical facts, sense on a pretext that we can choose our sex when we grow up, irrespective of the various dangly bits we came anatomically 'endowed' with. 'Ah!' they say, or even, 'Ah-ha!' It's not those bits that count, it's how you feel, who you think you are, it's 'what' you think you are, inside, your body 'knows' if it's male or female irrespective of one's 'dangly bits,' one's external and internal genitalia. This is just so much perverse nonsense; those with any sense just breathe out heavily and think of something worthwhile like, 'Where have we all gone wrong? And what are the cruel, environmental influences that society has created to destroy the ordered thinking of an intelligent species, Homo sapiens?'

And here's the rub. The rub of all sects, cults, weirdo zealot groupings, and of individualistic various nutters. We can always choose what we think. That thinking is influenced by our subconscious, our emotions. But emotions are mostly based on our experiences of life, in particular, our formative years; like an unprogrammed computer, we are born with an operating system, a brain of massive, interneuronal connections with the built-in capacity to form, to develop many more; the more, the better, we could say, the more, the merrier. What we have learnt are the apps; the data being the events we experience.

We live a life, from young, and what we experience becomes stored in our memories, to be drawn upon as and when. Those memories can bring with them an emotional response, a neuronal-humoral response, a flush of hormones, like cortisone and mostly adrenaline, and the memories either 'pop up,' spontaneously, or when called upon by our intellect. The psychic response may bring along related physiological responses to our memories, such as a pulse that begins to race, a face that reddens, or even a stirring of the loins, but more likely 'the spleen.' Memories can be called up like an 'app' and others then may pop up, like a cookie message, and they can be irritating when not needed, not convenient. We learn, or should learn how to call up these apps, control their 'popping up,' but more particularly render most of the nuisance ones 'inactive.'

The point is that we get to choose, as a conscious choice, what we think, what we feel, how we feel, to research our options before deciding on our preferences and making any decisions especially on what sect or cult is good and worthy, to join or not. And we can only truly make prudent choices when we are on our own, there specifically in retreat, to mull over the well-researched options, listen to a variety of opinions, eschewing those who insisted on giving their advice and be especially wary of those demanding our money as a condition of joining or staying.

However, there is one huge snag here. It is undeniable that every major decision we make, in the end, deep down, is an emotional decision. Even, or especially, the toughest decisions are in the end made on a basis of one or more emotions. We can be rational and reason as much as we can, but if we truly look at our major decisions in our life they are made on an emotional basis; a basis that is in line with our self-image, or our self-concept, or a desire to seek peace of mind and freedom from a fear, a fear of something, perhaps one feared more over another fear. Certainly it is never easy. Or we can just join a sect and have the thinking done for us.

CHAPTER 26
A MAN OF WAR

A man-of-war was a term that used to apply to certain ships, ships 'of the line' with a certain number of guns. But these writings that follow are little about those fighting ships, although they have been and are still instruments of war, and so formed part of the extension of a nation's power and influence across the waters of this world.

Who can say why wars are fought? Are there common 'causes' running through history and still relevant today? Many will answer 'religion,' saying that religion has been the cause of all wars since the year dot. It is true that many wars have been attributed to attrition between opposing religious beliefs, but apart from the Crusades and some minor civil wars, it is not easy to go along with that sweeping generalisation.

It is tempting to say all that the average man in the street (at one time referred to as 'the man on the Clapham omnibus,' alias Mr Average), and all those through history, the serf, the forester, the farmer, the yeoman and artisan, all they wanted was a peaceful life in which to live, to raise a family, work and trade; the iron forged into ploughshares, not swords and cannon.

If we look at the composite types in any society, we see Mr Average and, of course, we mean Mrs Average, too. But apart from a few notable exceptions, including Boadicea and Joan of Arc, wars at the sharp end have been fought by the men, and mostly a nation's young men, brought to a state of war by older men. And it's to do with that general acceptance of an order in society that if we are to live under 'law and order,' and live in peace with each other, there has to be a hierarchy in society. The rulers and the ruled. The governors and the governed. The orders given and the orders to be obeyed. In this case, the call-up, the 'mobilisation' of manpower in the country to leave work, leave families, leave trade and go and fight for the cause that has been decided by the nation's rulers.

There's no choice once general mobilisation is declared. Mostly the rulers are exempt from fighting, no risk of injury or death for them, apart from a general insurrection by the people. So, the casus belli, the cause for war, must be seen in the country to be 'just,' and the general belief at the outset has to be and must be that it will be quickly resolved.

So, do the young believe more 'passionately' about things than the old? Fighting for existence and survival of one's family prompts passion, certainly, and in the old, too. But fighting for causes? Other people's causes, people unknown, in distant lands? Rulers tend to think in 'passionate' terms. In history they were mostly landed gentry and so had time to attend court or parliament. Today, someone, anyone, can interest themselves in affairs of state, developing influence, influence for their particular way of thinking, their own preferences for a set of outcomes and, like control freaks, they challenge the controlling influences of others.

To be prepared to go and fight for the survival of our homeland in a 'kill or be killed' situation may or may not be easy to understand. To volunteer to leave that peaceful life at home and go and fight, or to go willingly once 'called up' (as in ordered) to go and fight, readily, or even with enthusiasm, is a character trait found in very many men and these days even women.

Looking at the front-line troops, these are those who have chosen a career in the military, in peacetime, to be part of the defence of the nation and part of that extension of the nation's power that seeks to maintain conditions over seas and on the sea, for peaceful trade. They know that in opting for this career, they are putting their lives on the line. It's all a matter of chance, chances that they are prepared to take, and for that, the people, society, should reckon on supporting them with admiration, respect, courtesy and a decent living. The same, but perhaps to a lesser extent, meaning all of the above applies to the police, to the firefighters and the unpaid life-saving crews of the RNLI.

Wars don't just happen, as if by accident, although it is very conceivable today that in the era of the 'red button,' it only takes one idiot to press it and bingo there is war. And, yes, there are idiots in power, and idiotic enough, we fear, to press the button.

Blessed are the peacemakers, but many believe peace can only be obtained through having a balance of power; a balance in the number of tanks, of guns, of fighter planes, of bombers, of aircraft carriers, destroyers, fighters, ICBMs and nuclear warheads for the missiles, the 'Star Wars' anti-missile missile systems. And there's much money to be made by the defence procurement manufacturers. Who is to question this? Pacifists believe if we are weak and defenceless, adopt a pastoral economy with no influence at all on overseas trade, then no one will want to conquer us, and if someone did, well, too bad, we'd just have to go along with our new rulers as best we can. But Hitler was going to castrate all the English men if he won, and then to put his officers (note: not his ordinary troops, but his cream) on the English women, because he envied the English character and their way of life. To the victors go the spoils. As to pacifism, us go along, to get along? Ouch! No thanks.

Perhaps it might be better if it were to be decided that no MP or Lord in the House of Lords could be elected or take a seat until they have reached the age of 50. Today we have a whole host of young, seeking degrees straight from school, possibly after a 'gap year' studying PPE (Politics, Philosophy and Economics) as a speedy route to entering parliament, that most 'exclusive' club (aka 'sect') in the country. Certainly, the most privileged club and comes with its hardly optional 'gravy train.' Leaving the EU would somewhat 'shrink' their career opportunities, but that's no bad thing because a young 'greenhorn' clutching a downgraded, cheapened degree in PPE to almost 'Mickey Mouse' degree status, has no suitable qualification for becoming a 'control freak' of an MP. But then we hear, 'What about William Pitt the Younger, Prime Minister at 24?' Ah. Well, he was the King's favourite.

What, can we conjecture, makes someone want to become an MP? In Victorian times they were often referred to as 'legislators'; a very handy term for the basic function of MPs, to adopt laws and vary laws for the perceived betterment and fairness amongst the people. But then, as now, often due to their mistaken actions and party politicking shenanigans, MPs were the object of ridicule and satire. In those days only those in government office were actually paid; the rest were self-funded. Billy-oh!

When general mobilisation occurred, MPs were not conscripted, nor were farmers and miners. We needed the food and the coal. It is the MP's vote that in theory takes us into war, but in reality, the decision rests higher up their hierarchy, the rest of us are cannon fodder. Converting a peace-loving man, the man on the Clapham omnibus, into a fighting, killing machine is easier if he (or she) has undergone 'National Service' when younger.

Possibly the single most effective way of inculcating a young person with the reality that we live in a democracy is for them to be called up, to do one or two years in National Service. This may seem to be something of a paradox. To explain. When young, just left school and going to 'uni' or 'tech college' (do they still exist?), we think how ideal it is to live in a free country. We read about totalitarian states present and past, military dictatorships and the sheer despotism of Russia under Stalin, police states of East Germany etc. And we read of mindless aggression of some states aiming to make their ideological political system rule the world.

Suddenly we are called upon to give up two years of our youthful freedom to become one of the armed forces, and just as suddenly we realise, with a shattering reality that, our 'freedom-loving democracy' must be defended, prepared to be defended against all comers.

This 'call-up' comes with a great benefit of some discipline to the untutored, unco-ordinated youth of no discipline. Discipline in society's members is so much and so desperately needed, and needed to bring about an in-grained 'respect' for order and reason that finally becomes its own 'self-discipline.'

It is such a great pity that today there is no system such as National Service to evoke in youth an adult awareness of the reality of living in a peace-loving, orderly, respectful, democratic society. It is conjectured that should a general mobilisation, a 'call-up,' happen in the UK today, huge numbers would claim to be 'conscientious objectors,' especially if the reason for the call up came from a country or countries of the Islamic world. The UK, as a fighting, self-defending country, would be 'sunk.' Many non-Islamist UK soldiers, sailors and airmen and airwomen might be killed, leaving more Islamists per head of population than before. How would that degree of pleading pacifism be tolerated?

This question raises the spectre again that has bedevilled statesmen. How can, or does, a faith make a race of people? In general, the Arab states are regarded as Islamic, but there are people, smatterings of other faiths, living there. Are the Israelis all people of the same faith, and so all of the same 'race?' We can turn the 'problem' on its head and ask hypothetically if all the Jews accepted Christ, as in became Christians, would the Jewish 'race' no longer exist? (A question to ask the Messianic Jews.) That is to say, if enough people believed the same ideology, and only marry and bring up their children in the same ideology, then after a few generations, have they become a 'race' of people?

Sometimes we can see it as a curse to have an ideological 'cult' following, so ideological, an infectious ideology that they'd go to war to be allowed to live out their ideology. Is it never, ever going to be possible to live in peace, one country with another, going along, rubbing along with the differences in understanding, on priorities, preferences, even ideologies, whilst loving and respecting peace above all things? A nirvana. A man, a woman, accepting peace, accepting sharing, no greed, no malice, no hate, no envy, nothing coveted. As if. No men-of-war again.

Is there a streak of cruelty in all of us? Is there something that makes us, men mostly, ready for a fight, spoiling for a fight, keen to 'have a go' at someone? As seen nowadays, the mindless muggings, not for money, but for their own sake, and no-sense attacks. Look how many young men rushed to leave their peacetime occupations to sign up to fight the Germans, for an unclear clause, in the summer of 1914; keen to have a 'go' at them and be home for Christmas. Thousands and thousands like lemmings went to their death.

Consider the ghoulish gatherings to the 'thrill' of seeing humans boxing or wrestling, and animals fighting for their life, male animals usually, instinctively fighting for sexual dominance. Ghoulish as in watching even things like 'stoning' (and even taking part), crucifixions, gladiators, bull-fighting, dog fighting, cockfighting, boxing and wrestling (both supposed to be an approved regulated 'sport,' not the ghoulish spectacle of one inflicting pain and injury, forcing one or the other into submission, which in an extrapolated way is just the same as 'war,' beating the other into submission.

Male animals fight for sexual dominance, proving the greater in physical stature, strength, willpower and so the 'right' to be the one to spread his DNA for the betterment, strengthening of the herd, flock or whatever. In history, soldiers went raping the women of the conquered people for the same, 'albeit' subconscious, feral-like reasons.

The euphoria of the pathophysiology of fighting with its massive release of adrenaline, noradrenaline, cortisone and endorphins may possibly be an addiction created through experience, the experiences of the practised pugilist. Real injury, as from cuts, deep wounds, gaping or otherwise, lacerations opening body cavities, chest or abdomen, fractures, even simple, let alone compound fractures, can all become suddenly disabling through the onset of shock, 'traumatic' shock and 'surgical' shock and the near-simultaneous onset of psychic shock. "Good God, they've shot my leg off," said Lord Uxbridge at the Battle of Waterloo, and looking to see the C-in-C, Wellington, next to him, said, "Good God, so they have." It's not recorded, but then all the shock set in with the pain.

Torture has been something of a ghoulish spectacle through history and, of course, crucifixion was tortured death. The 'drink' of herbs is believed to have been an analgesic potion to 'string' out death. Just the nailing of hands and feet one would think could be enough to 'shock' a victim to death. Consider those who did the nailing, presumably a paid person or persons, like the medieval executioners paid to chop off someone's head. Even today, there are executioners and squads of 'soldiers' in those countries that retain 'death by execution,' by shooting to death, not forgetting the person who throws the switch to the electric chair, or administers the lethal injection.

The 'legalised' murders depend upon someone carrying out the murders. And there will always be someone with the 'stomach' for it. Those with the 'stomach' don't faint at the sight of blood, or bodies blown apart into bits. Somehow their emotions don't allow it. In war, soldiers become inured, and when peace comes, they come home and are silent; silent because once they start to talk, to relive what they have seen, they would 'go to pieces.' Some say that it 'helps' to 'let it all out.' Maybe for some, but to do that is very doubtfully a panacea. PTSD. It's a toughie.

Some are overcome by psychic shock and faint just on receiving terrible news of a loved one. The fainting is well depicted in dramas onstage and screen, usually by a young female, but surgical sights and smells do affect even the biggest and toughest-looking men. We should note here that animals do not faint through shock, psychic shock. That we humans do proves that we are ruled by our emotions, and in that ruling lies our humanity, and our sentience and our soul, not present in animals.

We none of us know how we will react when the test comes; to be involved in, or be a nearby witness to, terrible trauma and death to others; to be present in a terrorist bombing, for example. It is hardly something we can prepare for. Soldiers train and get used to the loud bangs and explosions, but cannot rehearse the 'blood and brains' being splattered 'everywhere.' Some suggest the extreme frankness depicted in violent scenes on-screen and TV these days would prepare us. Who knows? For others, being prepared by thinking dispassionately, 'If I am involved, this is how I will react,' as if some form of psychic preconditioning

339

were going on. Could work.

Is it worth thinking about how we would react when the police knock on our door and say, 'We are sorry, but we have some bad news about your husband/wife/partner.' How would we react? Let out a scream and faint? Would our knees buckle under us and we'd have to be 'grabbed' to stop us falling? Would we invite the police in and say we'll put the kettle on for a cup of tea? How would we react? Can we precondition ourselves?

The reaction of the body can depend upon things such as we have just eaten a meal when the psychic shock comes, and that then evokes a 'fight or flight' adrenaline response, the digestive process underway is aborted, and this may lead to our lovely meal being returned the way it came in, i.e. being vomited up. Psychic shock can lead to a loss of control over one's sphincters, bladder and anus. So embarrassing but, yes, a fact of life.

Perhaps for those of us who enjoy watching, even cheering on, the ghoulish spectacles of animals and mankind fighting for their life somehow 'harden' us, prepare us, for the shocking experiences that can occur in life. And yet, often we aim to protect our children from the harsh realities of 'man's inhumanity to man' for as long as possible, to let them enjoy their childhood innocence. Not much hope of that these days with all the violence in TV and computer 'games,' where death is not real, it's just a hologram, a holographic statistic.

The Prussian Chancellor Bismarck once described peace as that uncomfortable time between wars. In those days, actually in the closing days around that time, wars were fought as one or more battles where there was a clash of armies at a location, in a field. The winning army then advanced to the capital town or city where a peace treaty was concluded, money was handed over and some boundary changes were agreed. The conquerors then retreated, possibly leaving behind a 'puppet' ruler, King or Governor to see that the defeated 'behaved themselves' and, as said in the Latin caveat, 'quamdui se bene gesserint.' Otherwise, the civilians were hardly involved. WW1 saw an end to that, and war took on a new, totally dreadful aspect, wreaking death and destruction on armies and civilian populations alike, with the range of artillery extended almost indefinitely by air force bombings.

The term 'total war' was coined, and everyone knew it. Not just the older men creating the war, and the young fighting it, but everyone from aged grandparents to the latest infant arrival. Where is the sense in it? To prove a point? To get submission, to be forced to stop 'a country' (i.e. its leader or leaders) doing what they are doing; refusing to live in peace, to find the peaceful answer to nations living and trading together in peace? Too ready, too quick to pull the trigger; the pugilist in them coming out?

The armed forces in peacetime train and train; trying out new weapons, new strategies against possible aggression, always ready to go on the 'defensive,' as in, 'We don't intend, and won't start anything, we won't have war machines and mechanisms built for aggression, just defence.' But, apparently, that doesn't work; somehow just not practical. For a start, it breeds a weakened, dispirited type of solder, sitting and waiting and waiting, the thinking 'Our defensive positions are impregnable'; the Maginot Line, the Siegfried Line, Hadrian's Wall and the Great Wall of China and other similar lines drawn. Rehearsing for modern warfare attitudes on this notion is not very practical. Napoleon's highly regarded Imperial Guard, always kept in reserve in case things weren't going as he wished, but which they mostly did. This elite corps, so vainly proud and pompous at being Napoleon's chosen ones when finally launched into battle, were just about finishing off Wellington when the Prussians arrived to save the British skins, just in time so late in the day, and Napoleon's out of practice Imperial Guard turned and ran. Probably the best argument against relying on a 'defensive' philosophy.

The counterargument is that a pre-emptive strike against a preparing and posturing aggressor is more effective, more likely to 'cool' the situation, a show of strength, in preference to the more pacifist, defensive approach. The first punch a knock-out. To do this we have to be guided by and put our trust in the hands of the professionals, in the armed forces, at least in the early days of an outbreak of hostilities; put trust in those who have studied and rehearsed the art of modern warfare, strategies linked with diplomacies and the wielding of a 'balance of power.' Does this earn them the title of pugilist or peacemaker? Or even peacekeeper?

Is there any merit in treaties? Can they help keep the peace? Promising, on paper, to come to the aid of a friendly, small country if another country, small or big, invades. And then the invading country's own 'big friends' come to their aid, and before anyone knows it, we have the First World War all over again. Who does the signing? The head of state in traditional times, the elected head of government these days. The problem with treaties is that alignments of countries in treaties are seen as a 'ganging up' against one or more other countries, who then feel threatened. NATO made the USSR feel threatened. Oh, yes? Wasn't NATO formed in response to USSR's imperialism? The other problem is that, like nuclear bombs, the treaties are meant to be passive, as in meant to prevent aggression between countries, never really ever meant to be put into action. It's like threatening to sue someone. We should never threaten to sue, unless we would really mean to go ahead and sue. To have thought it all through, the justification of the expense, the publicity, the aligning of friends on either side, the embitterment that comes, and the smiling lawyers, as they chirrup, 'Yes, you have a good case!' (one that will line their pocket, whatever the outcome for the client, the poor mutt, rushing with his pounds so keen to be parted from). It's the same with treaties, so-called defensive pacts; we should always be prepared to enforce what we have promised, too. And that means always having the means to fight.

In the 19th century, Great Britain had a policy often applied of 'splendid isolation,' which eschewed treaties. Perhaps the UN could do something about treaties, and meanwhile, like the League of Nations that failed, work towards dealing with aggressors' territorial claims, claims seemingly always made by the impudent arrogance of the heads of state. Devolution and democratisation of localities surely are a better way forward into today's 'globalised' world.

So much hangs on trade, and tariffs have mostly been a bone of contention. Nowadays it seems most countries can make and produce anything they want and export it with competitive prices based on their labour, taxation and raw material costs. Countries (developed countries – one might think) that have well-established welfare benefit systems have much higher labour costs due to imposed taxation (the money the socialists thought would come from the rich, only it is never enough). Those same countries need tariffs to see their own industry is not harmed by cheap imports, from products made in 'poor' countries,' with 'sweatshops' turning out goods, sometimes cheap in quality, but also sometimes surprisingly good.

Trading blocs, like the EU, form to promote trade with each other, tariff-free, but this brings huge numbers of rules, regulations etc., to see fair 'competition,' and the process becomes bureaucratic, undemocratic, with federalisation; and bizarre outpourings, like the drafted legislation to sell only straight bananas, and must only sell in grams and kilograms, not the indigenous pounds and ounces.

There is no easy answer, no hope for a quick fix. Developed countries that can see themselves as democracies also feel that state welfare benefits are vital on moral and humanitarian grounds. Likewise trading with developing countries where workers have a much lower standard of living and no welfare benefit system, by trading with them, we help to raise their standards. So, in helping them, we may be harming ourselves. Our governments seek to strike a balance, but after two world wars and massive social change in Britain, the country's overall wealth has greatly diminished since the days of Queen Victoria's rule, when GB was 'top nation.'

Countries rely to a great extent on their natural resources, or should do, on the principle of 'Acres of Diamonds.' Coal was a great natural resource for Britain, now not wanted. Hydroelectric power is a great resource for some countries. More rare mineral deposits and oil come high on the list today, as does agriculture, as it always has. But what about the 'natural resource' of the county's people, its workforce? Isn't that one of its greatest resources? As with us all, each individual, our wealth depends on our own individual industriousness, and so the nation's collective wealth can depend upon the hard work of its people, industrious, orderly and skilled. Skills mostly come from education, so high-quality education of a country's young adds to its earning ability. The German national character and that of some other nations is known, and generally reckoned to be of a people organised and industrious. That makes the nations rich, whereas, for example, some Mediterranean nations, for example, do not enjoy that same enthusiasm for work, not in that climate, and so not so wealthy.

We know, we see, that keeping up to date with scientific and other innovations is vital, and so investing in Research and Development is important. Britain has many but less obvious wealth-earning opportunities via the 'City' that is a great source of business financing for much of the world. Few of us really understand the business that the City conducts; one almost has to be 'born' into it, but it is very successful for Britain, and a source of envy by some countries.

It seems we must have trade and trade at a profit, for the profit is someone's livelihood. Profit is not a dirty word, if it is honestly earned and even 'excess' profit if it can be gained by worthy effort. It's what is done with that profit that matters; that is to say, a fair and reasonable division of that profit, shared between the shareholders, the investors, and those who worked to create the profit. Chairmen (and -women) hogging a lion's share often seems disproportionate, but the matter ultimately rests with the shareholders, who too often are disorganised and so toothless to stop such gross payouts.

We need to trade because we are acquisitive, always wanting more, or better, or just new. The world's population is growing, all the time creating additional need for housing, clothing and food as well as energy, the energy to extract and transport raw materials, for building and manufacture. So, the demand will ever increase until world population growth stops.

Where there is trade, and where there are international agreements and sometimes disagreements, especially about trade, or about boundaries and land with raw materials, coal, gas, oil and chemicals, then there will be the need for a Navy to protect our trading ships, an air force to protect the Navy, and the ground troops protecting ports and warehouses and, ultimately, boundaries.

In general terms, the attitude to hostilities that would use only conventional weapons is one of being more ready to have resort to their use, but the fear of nuclear war is far more real. And yet, the world fears the spread of these terrible weapons into the hands of the more volatile nations, volatile in their readiness to negotiate their way in the world to get their way through aggression and their adopted stances of hate towards some. We fear that spread, big time. And so we continue to be on our guard, to spend vast sums in so doing, and must continue with our selecting and training 'men-of-war.'

Those servicemen and -women will need to be of high calibre, with that grit, 'true grit,' which means that special feature of strong, reserved, grim resolve and character, instinctive in our 'man-of-war,' that is within, and it is honed and fine-tuned by training, 'hardening up' to be ready for the magnitude and altitude of man's inhumanity to man. Not that which enjoys the ghoulish, illegal, cruel sports of fighting between animals, but as we have discussed earlier, boxing and wrestling.

A 'man-of-war' is something special. The man on the omnibus, with bowler hat (as was), sandwiches in his briefcase, goes off to work for the day, Monday to Friday, 9 to 5. Is it in him, is he capable of being 'a man-of-war?' Yes, but probably not the first in the line; we'll leave that to the professionals, and hope there's enough of them left to train the rest of us, if necessary.

CHAPTER 27
LEADERS AND HEROES

Do we often, if ever, stop to think where leaders come from? That is to say, how is it that they become a leader, as in the leader of a nation? We can see even as children that there are some, just a few, possibly only one in each 'year class' at school, who have the force of personality that begs others to sit up and take notice. He or she soon gathers around themselves a cadre of friends, supporters and even some admirers.

Once the budding leader recognises what's happening, he or she begins to flex their muscles in small ways; changing things to their liking, getting 'friends' to do things for them. And so it all develops from there. From the boy in the class, to the outspoken student as he develops a skill of oratory, reaching and rousing the people, then as a member of the workforce, he could even become eventually one of the most feared and dreaded leaders in recent history, like Adolf Hitler. But for his own, Hitler was also for a long time their hero, their most fêted and admired leader. He was so popular at the beginning (and even right up to the end for some) and successful of a kind, by hiding so much of the truth from the people, and he even begun to think he was 'Messianic.'

It seems to be the case that in the animal kingdom, the higher animals always have a leader, one of the herd, the pack, the flock, the skein of geese, or the tribe that assumes some authority usually by force of its physical, brute strength and also its personality by which all the others are subordinate. And yet, when mankind gets to 'shepherd' the animals, it's not the leader that comes forward as the first to be subjected to the will of man. No, the leader holds back, and the lesser ones are pushed forward to experience first what man has in mind for them. So, not really leading, then.

We in turn seem only to function if we have a leader; we start with a Sixer in the Cubs, a patrol leader in the Scouts, a school monitor, prefect, head boy and head girl, president of the students' union, Chancellor of the University, leader of the orchestra, the drum major, the inspector on the buses, the mayor, Chair of the Committee, Leader of the Opposition, the PM, Lord Chief Justice, a corporal over a few, a general over many more, an admiral, First Lord of the Admiralty, Marshal of the Air Force, and at the top, The Queen. It is riven throughout the whole of society, as a sort of natural order of 'events,' always a hierarchy.

Why is it we, as any large grouping of people living together with some sort of combined purpose, cannot seem to function without a leader, a chief to whom we look for some sort of permission by which we go about delivering on the purpose; a boss person to provide some sort of cohesion, some sort of orderliness to keep some sense of civilised conduct to the desired, decided and adopted pattern? In the same way, a country has to have a national leader, a Head of State, a King, an Emperor, a Czar, a Kaiser or President. It's the same for the faiths: most have an adopted leader, the Pope, the Archbishop of Canterbury, the Chief Rabbi, the President of the Methodist Church etc.

In the UK, of course, we have the Prime Minister. Apparently, it's a job they (the politicians) all want; the power, the fame, and for most, afterwards, a title and a fortune. Prime Ministers act increasingly as if they had Presidential powers and authority. They don't, but they are taking powers unto themselves, and we are not arguing, and our MPs are so pusillanimous, hoping for some crumbs from the table. They all want it, and yet all Prime Ministers fail, ultimately; and they fail because people get tired of waiting for the betterment in their lives and they blame the Prime Minister, the bigwig at the top. Some PMs are so big a disaster that, once out of office, they hide themselves away for a few years, so to give people time to forget their mistakes and their errors.

Some might think the best form of government is a 'benevolent' dictatorship. But that notion still allows nothing at all, in every imaginable way that is possible, that inevitably some people or even many people will be disgruntled and unhappy with their lot. They just can't seem to thrive, make their lives work under the current leader (or any leader, but they don't realise that). And so they voice dissension. In a democracy, enough dissenting can force a change of government. In a totalitarian state, you just disappear; like in Peru – 'les disparus'; just disappeared.

At the end of the 18th century in France, the people rose up in anger and killed all their 'ruling class,' and then those with some leadership qualities from their lower, once-humble class chaotically governed for several years. The crowned heads of Europe became afraid for their own heads and resolved to restore the monarchy, a Bourbon king again on the throne of France. The people's army were struggling to prevent those crowned heads of Europe from succeeding until a Corsican artillery officer named Napoleon began winning battles. The French peasantry made him their new hero and Napoleon, sensing the mood, snatched power, whereupon they made him their 'Emperor.' See: people just need a leader, preferably a pretty good 'smart alec' of a leader, who can command his 'troops' and command the respect and loyalty of enough of the people to hold onto power. Of course, it was not quite as just said, and Napoleon always had trouble with some French who could only just put up with him, until Napoleon, like all leaders, eventually made a mess of things, as he did at Waterloo.

We tend to forget that the popularity of leaders while in office waxes and wanes like the tide (not twice-daily, fortunately). Most are only in power for no more than about ten years. Despots like Mugabe and Putin, of course, stick around for longer.

But why do we place so much trust and faith in one person? Why should monumental decisions rest with one person? Historically, for the captain of the ship, his word was law, his decisions carried out as Master under God. Today, with so much at stake, a captain takes reports and advice from his/her 'heads of department' and then takes the orders from the 'strategic masters' safely tucked away at the home base. Also historically, victorious battle-hardened generals become heroes with the troops and the people, for deliverance from the enemies of the state. Time and time again through history, generals have gone on to become a ruler of their country. We can think here of Alexander the Great, Suleiman, Julius Caesar, Napoleon, Wellington (Prime Minister twice), and Eisenhower as President of the USA. Russian generals seem to be the exception.

So, is running the country in peacetime different to running it when at war? Certainly, there should be no urgency in running the country in peacetime, except for those domestic crises due to extreme weather or a riot. But the press and media seem always to expect the leader to have an immediate assessment and ready response to any and to every situation that arises; so immediate, one might think, it's all a plot to wrong-foot the leader and show up some incompetence.

But why do leaders themselves allow the burden to be heaped on one person, expecting that they can perform as some superhuman being, however much their ego is massaged by the power, the position, and their authority? If one PM said, 'I am going to delegate to my heads of department and we will have Cabinet government.' Would that PM be accused of wanting to 'cop out,' in an 'if you can't stand the heat, get out of the kitchen' situation?

We know they all, without exception, make a mess of things and have to go. Every dog has his day. A triumvirate would be better. Three people, three elected leaders. Oh yes. There are many jokey quips about 'committees'. A camel is a horse put together by a committee. The best number for a committee is an odd number, and three is too many! As we have said elsewhere in these chapters, we all have 'two minds,' the yay and the nay. With the triumvirate, we'd have six minds and three votes, where a majority of two out of three would carry the day. And we should bear in mind that that final arbiter over our earthly lives, the law of the land, is subject to an Appellate Bench of three judges, whose verdict is final. The value of the rule, the ruling, perhaps we should say, is understood.

We should back away from the modern 'Presidential' style of Prime Minister, back to the more power-sharing PMs of the 1860s. What keeps most people, more people, happy and happy for longer is 'middle of the road' political decisions. PMs should eschew rightism and leftism. Both lead to disaster for the people, the plain, uncomplicated, peace-loving people, the 'getting-on-with-their-lives' people.

And so where do leaders come from? We form an action group, a committee, we agree a chairperson (for Pete's sake, whoever Pete was, what was wrong with chairman? It's like a manhole in the road, it's a unisex term, the same as chairman). Committees form subcommittees, and these organisational structures then bud, blossom and multiply like hydras and so we have systems like the government, the military, the NHS and the Church, and hundreds and thousands of associations and companies. Each has to have a leader. We can have a King, a President, a Prime Minister, a Field Marshal, a Marshal of the Royal Air Force, the First Sea Lord, the First Lord of the Treasury, the leader of the Council, the Headmaster, the Chancellor of the University and the leader of the Clan.

To become a leader, does it take an instinctive character trait? Is it inbred in leaders, as in 'genetic,' to thrust themselves by force of character into leadership, or is it that we scan around to find a leader because we so crave to be led, be told what to do, how to be, how to organise ourselves, even perhaps how to think and even how to feel?'

The Romanovs ruled Russia for 300 years. Their dynasty began with a deputation of some nobles who asked a Romanov to be their Czar. The Romanov decided that God was acting via the deputation, and so he accepted their offered fate, to rule and deliver what they sought, someone to organise defence of their borders, and organise the sprawling wilderness of a country. And that mostly happened, but each 'Czar' in turn saw to it that any dissenting voices were effectively muzzled, just like Hitler did, and just like Stalin did. They're all the same. The Romanovs were called to power, to rule Russia in the mid-17th century because there was no firm management of the country, when 'every man Jack' was suiting himself and seeing that he's okay, Jack, except that it wasn't working out. Anarchy never does.

The Jews were looking for a warrior king, or so we are taught, a hero who would remove the burden and tyranny of the Roman yoke. Jesus was popular for the healing He performed, and His words made them think and think hard, but also confused at the same time. He was mocked on the cross with the title – King of the Jews. He was not the kind of king they were hoping for, and deliverance from sin through His death on the cross and resurrection was not something they could understand, as many today still can't understand, especially, so it seems, the Jews. What kind of Messiah are they hoping for now? Or it is just that kind of successful association with rules, enough dosh and the right sort of support that means it can keep going and doesn't have to close?

The Caesars were leaders of character and skill at first until the principle of inherited titles supervened. It was likewise for Napoleon, who tried and failed to set up a familial dynasty, but the monarchs of England, the kings of Europe and Czars of Russia have long since been accepted as inherited rulers. They may have no leadership qualities at all, and the last rulers of Europe who lost their thrones in WW1 most certainly led their countries into disaster, meaning the Czar, the Kaiser and the Dual-Monarchy 'King-Emperor' of Austria-Hungary as well as the King of Denmark, but in fairness most of the monarchs were intimidated by their pugnacious generals.

Presidents can be expected to be those with some good degree of natural leadership; if not natural, then acquired leadership and statesmanship. And besides that, a great skill at political manoeuvring, for such is the 'dirty' game of politics, like cockerels fighting over who gets to crow on top of the dung heap each morning. Presidents and the system that sets them up, a sort of democracy, are elected. So, we delegate the business of running the country, including its defence, to them and other elected bodies, parliaments, and senates so we can leave the dirty work, the hard, really important work, the decisions (big ones) like the economy, to the state.

We have to assume they will be competent in office. In the USA many Presidents come up through the ranks of State Governor and Senator. But when a rich, vocal person thrusts himself or herself forward and they are compelling with words and have the right looks, and then get voted into power, what comes out of that just has to be tolerated if it's not popular. It's the same in France and in the UK: we can end up with a PM who has never held office as a government Minister. Such antics would never be allowed to happen in commerce or industry. Chief Execs always have some track record, of a sort.

The armed forces, the welfare state, any health services, the secret service, our state pensions and care in old age, all are left to supposedly elected bodies, ostensibly led by one person, and then we can grumble when we don't like what's served up; we don't know and can't find out who that one person is, and all the while we suspect snouts are in rich troughs! It's anthropological.

When things don't work out for us, and when things do – we 'blame' fate, only too ready to believe there is a force greater even than our King or President, shaping our lives, fate pushing all the buttons and pulling all the levers controlling everything going on in the world! But what about natural phenomena: storms, earthquakes and volcanoes, causing large losses of life?

We believe that in the origins of ancient and anthropological societies, the rule of the jungle applied to the early species of mankind. The strongest, fittest, most intelligent and fiercest would have become the tribal hero and leader. He may even have had an early 'droit du seigneur,' a tribal mating right with the females as happens in other mammalian species, to be sure those with the worthiest genes get to breed.

And so it is likely that these leaders became the early kings and all sorts of obeisance and privileges would be accorded to them, their champion fighter and leader. Yes, fighter, for the early kings were warrior kings. The last king to lead his army and die as a result was Richard III at Bosworth Field – a warrior leader. Privileges: yes, that, too, because we all like a spot of comfort and luxury, but most of us, and most of them, too, in those days couldn't rise to luxury, but the tribal leader could have the little luxury there was, and so privilege was born.

There is something of the 'sheep' in most of us. We are garrulous and gregarious. From the soup of human masses comes one with sense and the gift of a strong personality. If popular in some way, such as achieving defeat of the enemy tribe in the next valley or across the river, who came to fight us to steal our cows and womenfolk, then that leader gets a good dose of mass hero worship. It's one of the many outcomes of successful battle, the adulation coming from the relief at survival, possibly with some gain of territory and its assets, extra room to live, Lebensraum. There may be no comparison with animal herds and flocks, where their leadership means nothing more than that afore-mentioned 'droit du seigneur,' using their physical strength to fight and overcome all young pretenders in the herd or flock to be the most powerful and so have their one privilege, the right to mate all the females.

Hero worship and adulation led to certain leaders being thought to have 'blue blood' (possibly their blood was only seen when dying or dead; by which time it would have been blue – deoxygenated) and that they were destined by some birthright to rule as King or Queen; waiting only for an event, a death, or perhaps in battle or a revolution to put them on the throne. They came to be called and they called themselves 'princes of royal blood,' said to be chosen by God, giving them their 'Divine Right' and were not to be harmed, short of incurring God's wrath. And, when captured, they were not killed, but instead they were held to demand a ransom, and mostly the host peoples paid up, a king's ransom. Another privilege.

Many medieval kings believed seriously in their Divine Right, not only to be King, but also that all their decisions were divinely inspired and so could do no wrong. Probably the last to so deceive himself like this was Czar Nicholas II in 1914, which is pretty recent for this kind of psychology, this kind of highly imaginative and uninformed thinking. No hero he.

It was acknowledged that God anointed this Kingship, this person, with his sons and daughters as God's chosen on earth and so the myth of 'blue-blooded' royal princes, who were by common acceptance to be treated as hardly human by their subjects, but more as 'God ruling here on earth through this King.' Blue Blood and Divine Right gave rise to the law of primogeniture, which is to say they believed that if they were chosen by God then it followed that their son, or failing that, a daughter, would become King or Queen after them; so preserving the rights and privileges that the 'family' had assumed to, and would continue to

351

be accorded to them, as long as enough of the citizens accepted their 'right' to be there. The Romanovs' extended family lasted in power for 300 years.

Napoleon rose from a middle-class Corsican to be offered kingship over France some years later: his sense was to decline Kingship and accept the status of Emperor instead. He did his best to arrange matters so that his offspring would follow in his footsteps, but without any real success. His son died at the age of 21 and his nephew became the first President of the Republic of France for 4 years. Presidents don't command a king's ransom but it would cost as much in armed rapprochement (sic) if a country did 'entertain' a President or a Prime Minister beyond his or her invited duration.

It is commonplace for republicans and others to question the inherited monarchy, and many did so in Britain in the run-up to and during the only civil war England has ever had. Out of that unhappy chaos a republican leader emerged, as leaders do, one Cromwell, Oliver that is, not Thomas. He was made Lord Protector, a name chosen over any other pretentious title.

After the First World War the losses of autocratic monarchies led to young democracies most notably in Germany, Austria-Hungary, and an oligarchy in Russia. From that, 'natural leaders' have been elected either democratically (hopefully by a legal process such as monitored by the Electoral Reform Society) or by corrupted election processes. Those so-called 'elected' and despotic presidencies, such as the suspiciously re-elected Stalin, Mao Tse-tung, Mugabe, Kim Jong-un, and perhaps even Putin, having found themselves elected, by fair or foul means, their next steps are to consolidate their position and to seize more power, which they do by undermining the democratic bastions such as the free press, then free speech especially at the universities. They set up a secret police, and a not-so-secret police, as in Iran, the NAJA, and then we have another Hitler and his Nazi Gestapo, another Stalin's NKVD and another Honecker's Stasi.

We see in many societies such groups as boyhood and youth gangs, as were seen in Sheffield and Glasgow in the decades of brief peace between the two world wars. For some, for a while, there is a certain safety in a gang, especially if there is a fundamentally 'good' gang leader; whereas the 'bad' gang leader, the pugnacious bully, is set to become a thug, like the Kray brothers.

With any strong section of society, and not necessarily a majority, but with most of them ready and willing to adopt a leader, a consolidated leadership then brings a sense of cohesion to the people, the malcontents stop jostling for power by the threat of violence and disruption, and settled government brings order to the people and security within its borders, and usually prosperity.

Self-government is the natural state; people still prefer and want 'self-government,' e.g. Scotland, even though that nation state, if it seceded, would be worse off as an independent country. We might think that such causes in these cases are often led and driven by a bunch of nationalistic zealots, obsessed with their declared target and blinded to the reality and munificence of its parent and its remote, often very remote government. This situation has parallels with Brexit.

So, we form groups of like-minded people – at least like-minded in a few or enough issues or principles to get together for a purpose. A leader is then elected to become the chairman (sic) or president of the club, the society, a political party with the potential to include whole swathes of the country. Scary though it might be, taking that concept to its ultimate and historic extension, the tribal leader comes to be seen as a king-to-be, who then leads the people into battle, the battle of wills, is successful in battle, and takes all the 'riches' that accrue to the victors. The leader, the king-to-be that was, is now set well on his way to full 'kingship' for himself and his heirs, if they play their cards right. We'd best watch out, or there will be another Hitler.

That natural leadership somehow evokes a certain obeisance from the supporters, and in a sense of reciprocation, the leader, sensing the mood of the people, the supporters, recognises that for what it is, and so he assumes 'kingship,' to great roars of approval. In history, this often meant deposing his predecessor. Mostly by incarceration.

There must be many causes of wars, those 'casi belli,' and potentially a 'casus foederis,' (that implementation of a promised alliance), no doubt very complex in reality, but if we were to attempt to simplify matters, but by looking at some instances, we can 'see' or at least imagine that the decision for the nation's people to take up arms was often 'decided' by a nation's leader or leaders and was down to imperialism. It could well start with a desire to extend their home nation's borders, and so to secure land with its natural resources or to settle border squabbles with its irritating neighbour, e.g. Serbia in early in the 20th century always irritating Austria, and now Spain over Gibraltar. Or a desperate nation may seek to take for itself and to gain and hold its own seaport, to advance its trade.

353

And then there's colonialism, that policy of empire building – to 'own' remote lands which produce raw materials and goods needed in the homeland, that pays 'peanuts' for, yes, peanuts and many other commodities, and to sell to the colony's peoples the home nation's products. All this involves governing the new land and often with suppression of the native people, who rise up, sooner or later, however well governed, to get 'self-government.'

Other wars came about because of a treaty, an agreement between two or more nations' rulers (an agreement for the time being only, as it mostly turned out), and they were thought a good idea, at the time, for peace and trade. It says, in effect, 'If a gang attacks your gang, let us know and we'll come and help you fight off that gang, because we think we are just about the strongest gang around.' Such boasts were made with bluster and chest-puffing, typically such as the national pride and vanity of the French, who thought no one would dare put to the test any treaty they had put their name to. It still goes on today with such claims made by President Trump in 2017 (on the subject of Syria versus Russia). Vaingloriousness all.

Prior to the First World War, Europe was affected largely by the treaties that had been made many years earlier. The various alliances between 'fearful' countries, fearful of federal Germany, who, being very naturally frightened of those treaties saw them as a 'ganging up' against her and being still a fairly new nation state (less than 50 years) feared for its survival. France had already tried to prevent the formation of Germany in 1871, and had lost, big time, with the Germans crowning their first Kaiser in the Palace of Versailles. A sense of vengeance was still lurking with them, the French, especially over the loss of Alsace and Lorraine and the reparations the Germans made France pay.

Treaties are supposed to maintain peace and perhaps they mostly do. It is generally thought that NATO held back the threat of communism spread from Russia across Europe in the second half of 20th century, and possibly SEATO had similar effects against communism in that part of the world.

Or is it the threat of nuclear war? Not all countries in treaties may have nuclear weapons, but so long as at least one in the treaty, the most peaceful country, is nuclear-capable, peace may be held. Nuclear nations try to stop the spread of nuclear weapon capability because some 'rogue' nations are regarded as too unreliable to have such a weapon at its command. Totalitarian regimes, e.g. North Korea, and possibly Iran, have been regarded as 'crazy enough' to set off a nuclear holocaust. And that is the fear we have to live with. It's like people who choose to live at the foot of an occasionally active volcano: you never know when the balloon is going to go up and then you have to run like hell, leaving all behind you. No chance in a nuclear holocaust.

So why don't the 'good' countries invade and depose these leaders of 'bad' countries, set up a democratic government and take the fear away? Regard Afghanistan – in recent times – the home of Al Qaeda terrorist training camps and poppy growing to supply and intoxicate the world with opium and heroin. 'We' (the good guys) went in, fought for years with much loss of life, and eventually set up a government who may be strong enough to survive, if the people support it. But the 'bad guys' are still there, re-emerging from their hideouts with their same philosophy, unaltered, hardened even. You just can't kill an idea, even by killing the person, whose off-spring will then pick up the baton and run in their parents' place. We can't kill a notion in someone's head if they're determined to believe they are right in their thinking, a stubbornness redolent of Mrs May and her Brexit 'deal.' Even when pointed out how others are living a better, more peaceful life, contented, at least in part and prosperous, they are blind to it.

So, the question remains. Do we vest too much power and authority in our leaders? They are put in power by enough supporters and then kept in power by a closer cabal of supporters, sycophants and cronies, any one of whom would stab their leader in the back if they thought that they could take his or her place as leader. And why would they want to be the leader? They lust after it like a morphine addict, prepared to lie and cheat, deceive and indulge in all sorts of duplicity as they wait for the day to come; the day when their leader stumbles and falls to be trampled underfoot by the one-time followers, now turning their face elsewhere.

Why would anyone want to be the Prime Minister, the President of America, President of almost any country? It's the most awful job in the world; well, it is at least the way they have all taken the job for what it is, rather than seeing that the job is just that, for a few years. The job to a very great extent has become what the leaders have made it become, under pressure from the media and free press, who drive their expectations of the leaders to be as omniscient and as omnipotent to a degree that is humanly impossible. And the leaders try to be the impossible. The strain is significant. If matters go well, for a while they tell themselves they are a wonderful leader. When a job doesn't go well, they look for a scapegoat, but ultimately, they are 'responsible.' But who takes 'taking responsibility' responsibly these days? Aren't we 'response-able?' That is to say, if we agree to 'take responsibility' we have to make a response. That may be to put matters right. Or if we can't do that, we resign. That's what taking responsibility means. So few in power anywhere these days understand that. And if we insist on taking too much upon our self as top dog, leader over all, Prime Minister, too much, when delegation should have been the 'modus operandi,' and things go wrong, we resign. They say so often, 'I take full responsibility' which means, or should mean, in most cases, 'I'll go.' But most don't go.

They want to cling onto their job, their glory of some power, pay and status. And is that the point of wanting the awful job in the first place? For the power, as in an 'I'll show 'em,' a chance to do things their way, which, of course, is perceived as better, and for the status the job brings. That status gives them such addictive trappings that they become absorbed in their exalted position, to be able to go almost anywhere they want at anytime, on a whim, no travel problems, no queuing, best seats, everywhere he/she goes, crowds part like the Red Sea for the Israelites. Wonderful. Yes. Wonderful but it's temporary, very temporary and like a good book, it has an ending. Enjoy it while it lasts.

That power can mean that, to a much greater degree than we often think possible, really huge decisions of long-lasting effect and impact upon us, the people, we ordinary people that make up the nation, the decisions are taken, in the end, by that one person, the leader. We daren't argue with their decision because we have, over time, ceded to them that authority. Like the 'third runway' issue for Heathrow Airport, and so very many others. And that is the way power and authority have evolved. A leader of strong personality takes the power unto themself – like Hitler did. No one dared argue with him, because his sycophantic followers would carry out the worst and the final punishments to ensure there would be no more arguing with their leader.

We hear the term 'statesmanship' from time to time but less so these days. Why is that? we wonder. We can define statesmanship as that quality that drives a political leader to make judgements as worthy as a Solomon and also of having a long-term policy for his/her country that stands up to scrutiny by the consensus of the populace. Statesmanship hardly lets anything deviate him, or her, even a temporary loss of office in an election, from their aim of the implementation of that policy. As opposed to a career politician, who indulges in short-term policy decisions for popularity and a fervent desire to retain their position and income, at least for the time being. Their colleagues are often of the same ilk.

The statesman is rather more like the captain on a ship. The captain is aware of and made aware by his 'heads of departments' of an issue, a matter to be resolved that is big enough to affect the ship, its passage towards a destination and its survival. The captain, unlike the heroes of novels, films, TV and history, does not make an instant, swift decision as if driven by an internal, omnipotent automaton. No, he or she consults with the heads of departments as their skills and wisdom are important to the captain, and then his HQ, and for all on-board ship, all their livelihoods depend on the captain. Having consulted, discussed and perhaps even debated, the captain makes his/her decision and that is carried out with discipline, because the captain is the ultimate responsible person on-board. He/she is response-able. He/she can make a fresh decision or reverse the previous one. And the crew do as they are told, because they know that at sea, only by acting as one under orders can the ship come through. They do as they are told, even if they don't agree or didn't agree with the decision, and that includes the department heads.

But politics and government are different. In the wider field there is no disciplined crew to do as they're told. We, the public, are free to think, do, say and act as we choose, and we can openly argue with the decisions of those in power. The job role of nation's leader is so huge that the responsibilities should be devolved, to 'response-able' Ministers. No one ever said the Prime Minister had to make all the decisions. That is what Cabinet is for; but the Cabinet is so big these days that it works better for the inner Cabinet to make the decisions. Still too big? Well, probably yes, but this is the way companies and other organisations are run, by committee decision. But here again we know that some very awful decisions come out of committees. They used to speak of a Cabinet responsibility. If Mrs May had listened to her Cabinet in 2017, she would not have called a snap election, seen as a huge mistake.

We do need more democracy to be returned by the leadership of nations, to reduce the power and autonomy of leaders somewhat. The burden is more than one person should have to bear. The Romans ruled their empire for some time by a triumvirate. Three potent leaders acting in unison. And when not quite in unison, then with two out of three, the problem comes when the dissenting vote of the three leaders one refuses to go along with the decision of the other two, throws his toys out of the pram and resigns, taking his supporters with him to try and destabilise the government and do away with the 'triumvirate' style of government.

And sadly, a triumvirate would almost certainly fail again if tried these days, but we could look at the High Court and the Appeal Court. Government has too many with too large egos, too much lust after power and 'glory' and status to accept a 'Cabinet responsibility,' a common acceptance of what had been agreed. Look at the Brexit versus the Remain position. Look at the Scottish Referendum. What on earth do they teach children in schools these days about the democratic principle? There are senior politicians who would seek to overthrow a democratic vote of the country. They are beavering away with all the conniving of a scoundrel seeking to overturn a democratic vote of the people. Banana republics all the time refuse to accept the result of their general elections, claiming fairly or unfairly that the vote was rigged. Are we to become a banana republic, too, that we refuse to accept the results of referendums? We should love democracy more; albeit its variant, a two-party parliamentary democracy. It's what we fought two world wars for, or rather our fathers, mothers, and grandparents fought for. Why have some people lost sight of that? Many are senior political figures whose minds have become fogged with the obfuscations that are the result of sitting in the House for too long. Their comfortable lifestyle in the House and constituency as an MP has dulled their reasoning, and certainly sank any qualities of statesmanship they ever had, if ever any at all. To those with a despotic tendency who may fancy themselves as a 'benevolent' dictator, we can say the old adage, 'Democracy is an awful way to run a country, but it is the best there is.'

There is this great mistake by so many who think that the answers to all or woes and ills can be laid at the foot of government, and the government is the only way of putting matters right. The biggest present the government can give the people is freedom, freedom to trade, to create jobs and wealth. Less government is better always than more. For example, both Brexiteers and Remainers think the answer lies in politicians making deals with the EU, and think if we don't get a good deal, we all end up in penury.

Rubbish. Rubbish, because what drives us is not the 'done deal' by governments, but the drive, initiative and skills of each and every one of us that, in needing to make a living, to earn a crust, we create wealth because of our hunger, hunger for ourselves and the need to provide for our family. And the same applies to the people of the EU. If we want to buy a German car, if it's the right price we will buy it. If we can't afford it, we will go elsewhere or go without until we can afford it. It is the innate need of people that will be the saving of the Brexit issue, not politicians and unelected 'officials' on either side, however much those 'stuffed shirts' may preen themselves into thinking how great they are.

Many may scoff at the notion of resurrecting a governing style that was rejected over 2,000 years ago, but if we stop to consider the Appeal Court with their trio of the top judges in the land, the best distillate of legal understanding and thinking to resolve and decide upon issues mostly for an individual but sometimes for a body such as a corporation, a company, why not apply the same principle to running the country?

It could work like this. We would still need Ministers, Ministers to run the departments as now. They would be appointed by the trio. The trio would be elected by all the MPs on the basis of the transferable vote choosing from members of the party winning the election. The general election would be run as now, mostly a two-party system with the third party of also-rans supported by those who don't want to choose either of the others, left and right, and which fortunately exists to give those a third option, doing their bit for the country rather than abstaining. Those Ministers, heads of departments, would have much more executive power than now, but available to consult the trio when tough policy decisions need to be made. Any one of the trio who resigns over a disagreement would be barred from office for ever – that should stop them throwing their toys out of the pram.

Throughout history there have been Kings Spiritual and Kings Temporal, just like today when we still have Lords Spiritual and Lords Temporal, with the only difference being that the Lords Spiritual are real enough physical specimens, being as they are representatives, nay, leaders of 'spiritual' organisations, the Church, the Episcopal Church, the Bishops and Archbishops.

Kings Spiritual then are the imagined kings of the heavens, the Greek Gods, for example, and, oh yes, there is a King of Kings, named Zeus, as top god, over all. That mankind has to imagine these Kings is something that amazes; but surely it tells us that we are conditioned, or perhaps programmed, to so arrange our lives as tribal beings, that one must have a leader, and if we must have gods, then there must be a leader of gods. And if we must have a God, and a leader here on earth, what are their respective roles and purposes? When reasoned out there

359

is much confluence of their (historic) roles and purposes – to protect, to deliver 'unto' us. And so hence the historic notion of the King being God's chosen servant here on earth, which just leaves God to deliver, if we deserve it, in the life hereafter, and to stand by in case any earthly thing happens to unseat our leader.

Each of the faiths in the world claims their God is the lord of all, the God of Gods. But many are careful, of course, 'not to decry the existence of others' Gods, in case one of those gods gets upset if we were to deny its existence totally,' but, 'Oh, by the way, we still rather think 'Our' God is tops.'

So, if there is any reality here, any at all, perhaps we should ask if this is a pyramidal arrangement, or circular, as in orbital, with the top god as the centre of the axis, and lesser gods in orbit. It's all so conjectural, but suffice it to say, we can liken things to the CEO, Chairman and his/her Presidents who, in effect, are the Heads of Departments in US-style companies, with their Vice-Presidents, like the angels doing the actual work at the sharp end, but in the hierarchy we are at the base of the pyramid.

Leaders come to have power. It is either granted to them by the people under them, by the 'rules of the organisation,' or in other places and at other times and in other ways, leadership and authority are assumed, as we have previously alluded to. It's taken, snatched, grabbed, as did Lenin, Stalin, Mugabe, Hitler and Napoleon. Snatched while good men are being 'weak' and 'honourable,' and undecided, dithering. Despots 'emerge' from the morass of disorganisation and chaos, but only if it is at the accepting will of their supporter-followers, who mostly have guns.

Often people speak of their leader's eyes as 'piercing' (probably unblinking). They 'outstare' anyone who questions their word, their authority. They 'stare people down' – not by looking into their challengers' eyes, but by staring at a point in the middle of their forehead and imagine drilling a bit into it; and keep looking there steadily until the challenger gives way, submits to the stronger personality and lowers their eyes and head, to walk away, defeated. Leaders exert their will and have their way through this means, this medium of willpower beaming through the ether and drilling into the mind of the person to be subdued to the leader's will. It's sort of mesmeric. Think on it.

Jesus also had special powers, imparted through His eyes; He must have. He must have been mesmeric, to the extent of being 'magical' and 'miraculous' in His power over people, but in a nice way, of course. He must have been mesmeric to persuade a Galilean fisherman to leave their means of earning a living for himself and wife and children (presumably most adult, healthy males were married, and marriage meant children, mostly) to go, unpaid, and follow Jesus trooping around the countryside.

And the tax collector (very unpleasant job) in risky (health and safety-wise) but paid employment, to pack it in, without working his notice, but presumably handing over to the Romans anything he had collected before upping sticks and following Jesus. How? What 'spell' was Jesus able to put them under in order to have His magical twelve, to do His work, to serve His purpose. And who looks after the abandoned family? 'Your father's gone off with another woman' is a phrase so frequently heard by children from their mother. Only on this occasion it's more a case of 'Your father's gone off with a mystic,' and if he has to go off, thank goodness it's a mystic and not another woman, 'there's a chance he'll come back!'

This is, of course, all so much conjecture, but the Gospels are like the 'newspapers' and women's bikinis. What they reveal is interesting, but what they hide is vital.

However, that mesmeric quality is not only in the eyes. Leaders have that knack of gathering around them an adoring, almost worshipping, cadre of supporters who would do anything, yes, anything for their leader, to please him, to be 'patted' on the head with some preferment. To those who do not show support, the leader is cruel, hard, vindictive and threatening. Oh yes, he knows what gets him results. And doubtless any female despot would behave just the same.

There are, of course, kindly, considerate and fair leaders, bosses, in work and elsewhere. Good leaders, as in managers who know how to get the best out of people. How to make their people feel worthy, and to feel good about themselves. They catch their staff 'doing something right' and praise their work. Not praise the person direct, that can be misinterpreted, but praise their work, their outputs, as to quality and quantity.

For that is what work is. Work is something we do, a voluntary activity to earn a living, where the quality and quantity of our outputs are subject to the scrutiny of our customers. Customers? Yes. We all have customers. In the business of our personal lives we all have customers. They are all the people we 'sell' our wares to; our skills, the products we make in part or in total, our services, our physical and mental efforts, our time. We 'sell' these outputs to our boss, the employer, or if self-employed, our clients, our 'direct' customers. And we flourish (or not) by the quality and quantity of those outputs, and also by the way we promote our personal business, us, ourselves, the way we 'promote' ourselves to our customers. The 'Me Co. Ltd.,' and 'me.com.' It doesn't matter if we are the smartest guy in the world, if we don't 'promote' ourselves we will probably never be noticed under the swarms promoting themselves. It's no good waiting for another bus; the bus waiting at the stop now is probably the last one, so get on it before it gets going.

Some bosses are not fit to be bosses. These are mostly labelled 'Type A' personalities. They tend to think they can goad people into better and more work by bullying, destructive criticism and humiliation. With despots, such people need the Army and police to keep them in place, to retain their power. Of course, they are as nice as pie to the Army and police, they need them both, but the Army and police aren't fools, they know what's going on.

However, even for the successful and admired leader, leadership is a lonely thing. When, ultimately, the decisions are down to us as leaders, often tough decisions, harming someone, disappointing some, pleasing others, leaders find that it doesn't work being too matey, too familiar with the staff, or even supporters. To maintain just that degree of aloofness is required. Staff and supporters know this, but still attempt to curry favour by trying to 'befriend,' to be the one with that 'special relationship' with the boss, to break down the boss's reserve so that the boss then loses some authority, some discretion of the decisions to be made. Beware the sycophants. Bosses relate to other bosses, not their staff, their underlings. Bosses can't run with the hare, and hunt with their hounds. It's the loneliness of command. The ship's captain dines alone.

When chosen to lead, it's certainly a boost to our morale, our self-esteem, and pride. But it can bring some anxieties. Are we up to it? Will we make a hash of it? Will I be liked! Is it necessary for me, now a leader, to be liked? Isn't just to be respected as leader enough? We can be called as Sixers in the Cubs, patrol leaders in the Scouts, class monitor at school, a prefect even, head boy or head girl: what an honour. Promoted to corporal to lead a platoon of men (or women); an officer (and we hope a gentleman – whatever that means today); an MP, or as a councillor or become an employer; all positions of some responsibility, more or less. Perhaps the best way to view that is as a general making a strategic decision, on which the lives of many of his men depend in battle. Get it right and he is fêted. Get it wrong and many die. Are we up to it? Or are we vaingloriously holding a position that should be held by someone better able. How do we know until we are tested?

One thing is for certain at least: we can't do without our leaders. Leaders are there solely to be 'of service' to those who appointed them, and to those in whose charge they are. Leaders are not there to pander to their personal whims and vanities. Mostly they are there to serve those for whom they are response-able (aka responsible). We are always required to be 'of service' to someone or some body of people, through our employment, and if not, then we are required to be 'of service' to ourselves, the business of our life, 'Me Incorporated.'

We all come up against the twin opposing issues of money versus ethics. These are two most persistent issues that are always in our lives. The third is sex. Money, ethics and sex. Most of us have trouble with these three 'principles' at some time in our lives. Society's leaders, the politicians, the so-called 'lawmakers', are constantly juggling issues for the country centring around money. So, too, are the business leaders and for both groups, ethics keeps bubbling up to require them to modify their greed, their favouritism, their need to be of service to both their shareholders and their customers, as well as see they look after themselves. Greed often holds sway with both politicians and businesspeople, sometimes even including the judiciary, some of whom become corrupted away from their duty to serve as a leader in society.

It is hard to lead a life governed entirely by ethics – that would be just too ideal. But it is an ideal to try to live by. Apart from money, its need and its greed, then it's sex that can break our ethical code, sometimes, even often, with such powerful, reckless motivations and urges us to risk a loving relationship, a loving family, a position in society, in business, in a profession, an income and wealth. All for some sex. We eschew temporarily, perhaps even permanently, all those achievements, all our bounds of 'civilised behaviour' and break what we hoped, and expected, what we thought were promises of fidelity, very solemnly made, not only to our spouse, but also to ourselves as our own chief executive. But there is another side. The side where the partnership made when young is simply just not working out, and the business of life is just not thriving; its intrinsic unhappiness is manifest. One may wait for an opportunity to draw a line and sever the partnership, with all its heartache, bitterness, loss of income and status. Seemingly unavoidable, it is a facet of life. We live with our shortcomings, our deficiencies, and we have to accept our human frailties, and forgive ourselves for the part we have played in the damaging of lives. What we do is for love, or to make up for the loss of it.

We would dearly like ethics always to 'hold sway,' so that when it comes to money, we will consider our adopted ethical guidelines, and when it comes to the temptation of 'illicit' sex, consider and then reject that fleeting moment of lustful pleasure that sets others on a pathway to unhappiness. We like to think we are 'as free as an indulgence,' and maybe we are, or at least happier thinking we are, but do indulgencies come free? Almost certainly not. Most indulgencies are addictive and too much of anything, of everything, either is illegal or immoral, or makes us fat, or rots our teeth. But seriously, being teleogenic creatures, ever wanting to move to a greater comfort zone of sybaritic pleasure, in which we want to indulge ourselves, we should also include, carry with us, a very large dose of ethics.

Both leaders and heroes become in their own way examples of what the young, the adolescents and later many adults come to look up to. Often sports personalities rapidly achieve hero status, worthily acquired, worthily granted by the followers of sport, winning something for themselves, for their country or for their club. They are inspiring. Leaders in other walks of life seldom achieve hero status, leaders such as captains of industry and Ministers of the Crown. But, like heroes, they have a certain fame, and they can enjoy that fame in the spotlight for a while at least. The public who follow the activities of the leaders, and the public who follow the sports heroes, are just the same as the public who welcomed Jesus on the pony entering Jerusalem on Palm Sunday. What a rapturous welcome. And yet just four days later they were calling for him to be crucified. But was it the same public? We'll never know. But what we do know is that if our modern-day heroes, and our modern-day leaders, breathless at their new success in life, are found to be lacking in any propriety as to conduct and to money, as to ethics and as to sex, then there is an equally fast fall from grace. As Evita and General Peron, once President and First Lady of Argentina, respectively, sing in Andrew Lloyd Webber's excellent historical musical, '*High-flying adored, did you believe in your wildest moments, all this would be yours; don't look down, it's a long, long way to fall.*'

There is in mankind, as in many large groupings of mammals of some intelligence, a natural order among us; an order of rank, with obeisance and deference of an automatic respect shown to a leader, and leaders to their leaders, however those leaders have come about. It happens as an inevitability, a predictability as certain as the sun will rise in the morning, although when revolution comes the sun can take some time to rise. Of course, there is jostling; sorting out the pecking order; and with back-stabbing; leaders fearing long knives in the night, and fearing swords rattling in their scabbards, as at Runnymede. And yet, a man is a man when a man is needed – else he remains a child; and leadership establishes for us, one way or the other, 'the mark of the man.' It is gratifying to see that Elisabeth Elliot, she, at least, recognises real women, as well as real men, and any real person of either sex will inevitably be a leader of some sort, somewhere, sometime.

Some idealistic malcontents dream of an equality among mankind. It is, of course, a sheer and utter nonsense that denies the biological and anthropological natures of our beings. The best we can and should strive for is an equality of opportunity, an equality of treatment under the law and for a general disposition of wealth that is comfortably accepted as fair to the less fortunate. That is fair in terms of their achievements in life; for no one expects the Prime Minister to be paid the same as the road sweeper, especially the road sweeper.

The disappointment for us, as for the leaders, too, in their eventual disillusionment, is that they all succumb to a certain kind of vanity, a misplaced sense of their own rightness, a sort of saying, 'I am the leader, I expect you to follow me.' But leaders are only held up above us in a human pyramid of authority as long as we will stand supporting the leader on our shoulders – from that height we expect the leader to see further and better and clearer. But when they ignore what they see and just to puff out their chest with pride as being 'up there,' then we will walk away and bring about their downfall. There is a tide in the affairs of leaders that taken at the flood leads on to success, but to confront the tide always fails, like Canute. All leaders fall foul of this deception of their exalted position. Leaders can only go with their supporters' tidal flow. Supporters will not be driven any more than Canute could drive back the tide. And if our leaders are brilliant and serve us well, then they will become to us, in a way, a certain kind of hero.

PART SIX

CAN WE SPARE A MOMENT?

CHAPTER 28
THE TRACTABLE MIND

We often say, 'I am minded to...' or 'I have it in mind to...' But also on occasion we say, 'I am in two minds whether to...' and at other times, 'My mind is made up.'

The mind is a complex, decision-making organ that in the end it seems as if it has, like a computer, just two options, yes or no. Some might say there is a third option, to abstain; abstain that is, from the decision or issue being faced, but as far as the mind is concerned that is as good as a 'No,' an acceptance of the status quo.

In another sense, we always have 'two minds,' two decision-influencing mechanisms in the brain and both influence our decision-making, for, let's face it, everything we do or say comes as the result of a decision made, a Yay or a Nay. In conversation, we say things following a decision made in a nanosecond. The radio presenter Anona Winn once said that is impossible to have an argument with a man who is smoking a pipe. This is because the pipe smoker puffs to keep his tobacco alight, because if too much time is taken away from puffing to speak, the tobacco goes out. So, he, the pipe smoker, takes time to think his response through, while puffing, and what is more, he keeps his answers short. Pipes are best smoked in solitude, even better than that, best in the cockpit of a yacht, in a pleasant anchorage, after a pleasant meal, on a balmy summer's evening. It's at these times we can have peace of mind, providing the clattering of dishes being washed up below decks isn't too disturbing.

Of those two minds, one is the 'seat of emotion,' our subconscious mind, the mind that looks after us, while the other mind, our higher mind is distracted or asleep. The first is where our infantile original fear is founded, the fear of falling, and fear of loud noises, and directs in an instinctive way how our bodies react to those stimuli. Its other functions are acquired, developed from those fears, and they are our emotions; how we feel about all sorts of things, things like what we see, hear, touch, smell, and even how we feel about our thoughts and ideas, that we have in our other higher mind. Emotions can make us feel either good or bad, positive or negative, happy or sad, calm or angry. Looked at, as these opposites, one would think we have a choice, but in practice, in life, we have little choice about how our 'emotions' will respond, because they are mostly instinctive and mostly so well entrenched and developed, they are difficult to train. But this doesn't mean we have to show what we are feeling. As we mature, grow up, far older, more experienced of life, and develop our personalities, and be 'what we are known for,' we either show our emotions or we 'hide them,' brave face, stiff upper lip, 'he's a cold one,' or 'still waters run deep,' and all that.

Too much 'emotion showing' can make us excitable, nervy, unreliable under pressure, voluble, garrulous and inconsistent. Too little 'emotion showing' may appear desirable, but it can lead to high blood pressure, indigestion, ulcers, eczema and a lack of demonstrated affection, when it was due. Our 'emotional' mind, that fear-of-falling mind, is the one that saves us as we leap out of the way of a fast, oncoming lorry when we went 'absent-mindedly,' and unthinkingly and stepped into the road.

To what extent is our 'emotional' mind, our emotional centre, the 'subconscious mind' at all tractable? Can we truly learn to control our feelings? Should we allow others to have an effect, to prey on our emotions? We feel hurt when we are not selected for promotion, or a pay rise, and we experience feelings of jealousy, hatred, resentment and a whole host of negative emotions. Can we accept and deal with the feelings of guilt for something said or done, and can we get to accept that with equanimity? Can we cope with being accused of something we have not done and deal with that with equanimity? Being innocent, how would we cope with being found guilty at law, on its balance of evidence and advocacy, found guilty of some misdemeanour or other. And if we are not innocent, how would we cope with the consequences, legal, social and otherwise? Even without the weight of the law, we can be held as guilty by an individual, or a group, like the golf club committee, who found us cheating, caught in the act, no doubt at all about that. At another time, an individual or a group may hold us guilty on some premise, but never 'proven,' as can happen in one of life's idiosyncratic irregularities. Only we know if we are guilty, and we may struggle with the reasoning behind the judgement; we may have a difficulty in seeing what we did, or said, that was so wrong in the first place. We have a certain reasoning that, on this occasion, at least, is obviously in conflict with the accusers, and those who sit in judgement on us. The complicity of others in whatever it was that brought us to accept some contributory guilt should not be set aside, but duly reckoned on.

No matter, whether truly guilty or not, in our mind, we can and should accept that judgement if we are ever to swim in water again and not mud, to go with the mainstream and not flog without any progress against the tide, the powerful tide of mainstream thinking; the thinking of judgements. And yet, like a prisoner who wipes the slate clean by serving a term in prison, all liberty denied, and even atoned, we can only hope we have to deal with the feeling of guilt. That feeling is the judgement that we impose on our self, no one can put it there but us, we, for or against ourselves. There are those in life who get a perverse kick out of throwing guilt, an everyday sort of French 'J'accuse.' We should have no truck with them, we should not 'catch' their thrown guilt, often thrown to detract us away from their own complicity. So we avoid 'guilt throwers' and 'guilt catchers,' both afflicted sadly with irrational thoughts and feelings. The justice system is cruel sometimes to the innocent and it seems totally wrong to admit guilt just to be granted probation or a shorter sentence.

Initially we accept some feelings of guilt, and yes, we do need to accept our 'done-wrongness,' but we don't have to live thereafter with that feeling, as it can destroy us. We can eschew the feelings of guilt, by a process of a self-taught, self-learned and oft-practised genuine self-forgiveness. Accepting comes first, and then some time living with the feeling of guilt, for a definite time period of our own choosing, and when ready, we forgive ourselves. Getting ready may involve some thoughts of apologies that we may or may not deliver, because to deliver is not always wise, for it depends so much on the person or persons we have offended, damaged, traumatised; those whom we are thinking of apologising to. We can never eradicate from the depths of our minds the feeling of guilt if it was ever a truly valid feeling. It's like we should put it deep down in the ship's hold and batten the hatch. We can no more eliminate them totally than one can erase history; but the point is that with our tractable mind we can know that we have dealt with this issue, truly dealt with it, years ago, and we know that it is there, settled and settled it right, so we get on with our life. No need to keep beating our self, bashing our head against a wall, because we know it hurts too much, and there's just no sense in it.

The same question applies to our positive emotions of joy, elation, pride, as in 'a just pride.' A false pride is an invention of the other so-called higher mind, but still based on our negative emotions. Can we have too much or too little of our positive emotions, ready to be switched on, when appropriate situations or events are conducive?

We know we are all neurotic, to a greater or lesser extent, for if we are not neurotic, then we must be psychotic, which is to say we are 'out of touch' with reality. We neurotics all have 'mood swings,' emotional ups and downs through the day, each week; feeling really good about something or feeling down, subsequent upon something; something happened or heard, or news read or told, or it's just naturally cyclical and we just don't recognise it as such.

If our mood swings are more usually, and as a general rule, modest in their extent, and not at all excessive, we would not be charmed to be called 'neurotic,' because the term neurotic is mostly, perhaps more correctly, deservedly reserved for those of us who have moods swings in the 'extreme'; very happy at times, ebullient, extrovert, bubbly, and then at other times morose, depressed, morbid and gloomy, despairing of self, of others and of the world at large.

And this is where our other mind comes in. The other mind is the mind of intellect, of reasoned thinking and reasoned judgement. It is the mind that can modify, suppress and trap and lock away thoughts and their associated feelings in an attempt to be lord over our emotions. This mind is mostly definitely tractable in a sense of a computer with spare capacity, waiting to be loaded, ideally with worthwhile, meaningful and 'high-minded' apps, useful to self and humanity at large or with apps that are not.

And like a puppy that desires to please its master, this other mind needs training if it's ever to be a pleasant, worthwhile pet to own, and not a disobedient, destructive, wilful creature that comes to 'rule the roost' in that house. An 'app' is short for 'application,' and is only a programme, a programme which is enabling, and for enabling ourselves, as in a training for anything we want to do, or be. We have to apply ourselves, apply our mind to the matter, to the question of learning to acquire that new facility, that new skill, new knowledge, and by so applying our mind, we are in effect downloading and installing and running a new application.

We educate our children, but also we often waste wonderful opportunities for those young, unprogrammed minds, blank as a blank sheet of paper, so eager and ready and quick to learn, so more really like blotting paper. We try as a society to educate them well, but sometimes only perfunctorily, and we also fill their minds with harmful dogma, from our own prejudices; such as faith schools and precocious sex education. All is aimed to make them compliant and inclusive adults, in a society that's so overcrowded we might as well be hens in battery cages or sardines in a tin. Don't all breathe in at the same time, there just isn't room. It's no wonder their emotions have to be so trimmed, curtailed and caged to become urbanised so that our wild, prehistoric ancestry is all but annihilated, driven out.

Our higher mind is capable of great intellect, reasoning and goal setting. It is capable of much influence, almost by persuasion over our subconscious 'emotional' centre, but never in complete control because to attempt to do so is rather like putting one's finger in a dam; if it stops that leak, another leak breaks out. If we can suppress one emotion, another starts to simmer and may boil. We can't close down our emotional centre just like that, and not even really put it on pause.

The two minds are mutually interactive in a way that can be complimentary or antagonistic. Their functions are different but with similarities. One has the 'sense' the other the 'sensibility,' or if you like, one has the pride, the other has prejudice. We can argue the rights of pride being a product of the upper mind until the cows come home, and some will never accept that. We can draw on Jane Austen's Elizabeth with her notion of Darcy's 'just and proper pride' and 'of no improper pride,' for example, and in 'a mind improved through reading.' It is what one does with that 'pride' that risks it becoming vanity, that is an emotion of the lower mind.

So, the higher mind is the trainable mind, malleable and ductile for mental health for better or for worse, by which we mean like any other organ of the body, it is vulnerable to malfunction. It is, or should be, our choice, under our control, to be the operator of the levers in the 'railway signal box.' We can ask ourselves, 'When did I last go into my mind's control box and throw a lever?' and 'What was the lever?' Was the lever to stop envying someone, or the lever to forgive myself for saying that stupid, angry rejoinder to my son? And so, on and on, indefinitely. We can train ourselves to go into the junction box and throw levers, preferably before we do or say something that our decision-making system, our conscious mind versus emotional mind indicates we may later regret this decision; so beware. There are many very worthwhile levers there, too, ones that give us our 'get up and go.'

Are there any factors that can heighten our awareness of our 'higher' mind, the conscious mind? There are outside influences, certainly. Good relationships, and choosing to avoid the other types of relationships, the not-so-good or even downright bad relationships; bad for us, that is. We need good relationships, be they at home or at work, good in that they promote not only our creativity, but also our peace of mind. And then there are things like our sensible choice of films, books and TV to watch, social media contacting, avoiding the crass and the trolls. Good things can stimulate the intellect, and we hope they do, given enough time in the day or night to meditate a little.

Another factor can be our 'inner strength,' achieved through training and practice, and that can be helped by a suitable diet, relaxation, rest and exercise, with nothing excessive, no obsessions, no vast excess of work, no intolerable pressures on us. That is to say that the benefit to the 'tractable mind' comes when we provide the right conditions, the right environment for it to grow and thrive.

The going is never going to be easy for most of us. Yes, there are undeniably some, a few, born with a happy, non-discriminating and non-judgemental disposition, probably from birth, even genetic, who, despite adverse parenting and negative experiences at school, enter life with a sunny disposition. But not so for most of us. Our emotional mind has developed and has powerful influences over our daily lives, ploughing the crooked furrow as we upset and apologise seemingly again and again, rather like a ball buffeting its way down a bagatelle board.

We may have only two types of sensibilities, only two types of feelings. Pain feelings and emotional feelings – two sensibilities – challenged sensibilities, that are directly analogous to the instinctive neonate's fear of loud noise and the fear of falling. There are times of such extreme shock and sadness, usually after some major traumatic incident leading to the loss of loved ones, that our feelings can freeze, like a computer that's gone into 'sis,' or seized and has to be switched off and rebooted.

Pain we know we have to move away from; away from the source of pain and rest that part to reduce the pain. And it is our negative emotional feelings that makes us want to cause pain in others. That may be by word of mouth, spoken or written, or by indirect action to cause emotional pain, as in creating a loss of something to them valued or loved. We may also want to cause real pain, real physical pain, by causing injury, through fighting in some way, as an individual, or sadly the travesty of being in a group. But in war, in the armed forces fighting for our country, the positive reluctant emotion and purpose is to inflict pain, even unto death.

All of this causing of pain comes either from us as aggressors or as defenders, including the aggressive actions of the defender, fighting back, even including the 'pre-emptive' strike, knowing that if we don't act pre-emptively, we know or suspect we know, we have no other way to withstand the oncoming aggression. Aggressors want to cause pain, either to gain what they want, what they covet, or to inflict revenge for some hurt felt, justified or unjustified, even unto avenging their parents and their parents' parents; a doctrine of some cults, masquerading as faiths, masquerading as religions, all misguided by their Holy book, their book of instructions, that 'Policies and Procedures' doc., and their 'Statement of Purpose,' needing an update.

As adults, the aggressors, should know exactly what they are doing, and mostly they don't care as long as they can have what they want. We can't always move away from pain, or rest the painful part, for fear of some loss; and that means we respond, as in we feel we are bound to, to minimise our hurt, and that of our loved ones. In this sense, we are overruling our emotional centre with a sense of duty.

To get along with people and peoples of other nations, which means in essence their leaders, is a worthy ideal to the politicians, diplomats and statesmen (and stateswomen). The problem is often the national leaders, the politicians, are people who, by their natures, are restless malcontents, dissatisfied do-gooders, who often make matters worse: in their arrogant thinking theirs is the right way, so they seek to have control over all things. Their mindsets only become anything like malleable once they have resigned or been kicked out of office.

Too much governing is like too many changes in course steered, and the progress is less than the straight line. It's like a city with too many traffic signs, traffic controls, and where the experiment was to remove the traffic lights, traffic actually went much better without them. The freely acting drivers use their common sense, and their sense of decency. Unlearning traffic-signed discipline did not take long to be dispensed with and not long for the new self-responsibility to take over again.

In society today, in this early start to the 21st century, mental health has become the biggest concern of humankind, along with population growth, population densities and so much migration. By mental health here is meant not those unfortunates who develop psychoses, but the rest of us, the neurotic rest, durst we say so?

Our modern education is now showing as disadvantageous to the progress of democracy and diplomacy. For those intractable minds there is or should be much concern. We need to beware the schooling that raises a child to show false pride and arrogance as an adult. Let the young mind be as it should be, for survival, flexible, tractable and malleable yet always seeking. People of all walks of life have developed in such a way as to be intransigent and dogmatic in their thinking, in their attitudes and beliefs. A referendum was held and yet the disappointed kept fighting against its implementation. And they meant it. It's not just a whim they indulge in, for a few moments spare in their day. No! It becomes an obsession. Democracy can go hang. They are disruptive to society, anti-democratic, disloyal, even treasonable in certain lights (but the law of treason is not at all straightforward); but certainly disgustingly egregious, and yet they are proudly arrogant. And they have no peace of mind. Watch the eyes of union leaders when engaged in an unjustifiable battle of wills with employers. Over the days and weeks, the strain of their unworthy fighting shows and shows as the strain bears. And the same applies sometimes to the other side, their unreasonable obduracy telling on them, too. They know who they are, and they have no peace of mind, no just cause, just their prejudice. At football, would they accept a 'we lost' result? No, they wouldn't, they'd say all sorts of rubbish about fouls and unfair practices and demand a rematch, and then another rematch, again and again until we, GB, gave in. Just like the Germans in the early 1930s with so many elections in a year, that when they gave in, and they let Hitler become Chancellor, and the first thing he did was to ban all future elections. Such madness.

It is often said we cannot help the way we look, those features that we were born with, inherited from our parents and grandparents, atavism at work. It is not necessarily true, but indeed, probably always partly true. Our thoughts, our feelings, our prejudices, even our hopes do become reflected in our physiognomy. We can look at some of society's leaders, and these days we can look really closely, due to the marvels of large-screen TV close-ups, and also on the internet. We can see eye movements, lips, nostrils, foreheads and eyebrows a-twitching, and body language. All these reflect who we are, who we are becoming, and, in their way, we can form some kind of idea of their motives, what secretly they are about. But not if we are talking to a burqa.

Most top politicians want to be the leader, have that view to the top job, President or Prime Minister. Some politicians more than others will beaver away, cunningly, in a disguised way to undermine their leader, until he or she fails or falls. Worthy conduct? Hardly. We see it in their eyes, their face. Can anyone see it coming? Certainly, and it's egregious to the extreme. They cannot know any peace of mind. And what will it profit them? Well, if they didn't attempt to get the job, another might succeed in their place, but who would have been the better leader? It's just a pity that such foul conduct exists and if it didn't, we can justifiably conjecture the result could turn out to be just the same. It is likely that politicians work hard on their emotions and work hard at submerging their fears and perhaps even their emotions, whenever they happen to surface. They aim to keep a brave face, and a straight face at most times. The strain on them, maintaining their façade, will always be telling.

For most of us, we can see the law, the law of the land, as a good thing. From young, we become increasingly aware of the law: whilst being abstract and intangible in concept, its effects are real enough, as the law, the guiding principles behind the law are brought about, by a compliant people, the willingly compliant general public, and then by the officers of the law, the police and the judiciary system, the attorneys, solicitors, barristers and judges. And then we become aware of the physical restraints of handcuffs and prison cells and the financial constraints of fines, the taking away of our money and sometime even our property. And these restraints and constraints may even lead to the shrinking or perhaps the loss of a love, a once-cherished loving relationship. But do we ever think of that, as a possibility, when we were so errant as to suffer under the law? It is an experience to learn from. Or we should do. Most do. But there are some who are so intractable, blaming always others for their being found guilty. Despite counselling to help them see the way to look at becoming a law-complying member of society, they are unable to shed their negative emotions that led to them turning to crime, and then blame law-abiding others for their getting caught. And then, so they think, the law not punishing the right person. They have no tractable mind, blocked by some form of prejudgement, as a prejudice.

Then there are some, of reasonable intelligence, who just shut their eyes and ears to the facts of life. Like the student cleric who, given some information for health, said with some pride that he just didn't want to know about how his body worked: 'It works and that's okay. If it stops working, I'll go to the doc to get it working again.' A simple example of a real obduracy of mind, declining, positively declining, nay, outright refusing to be tractable of mind. Fortunately, most young minds soak up any and all information on almost every subject possible, not to learn as an academic study, but when freely ranging around as the day goes through. It's probably best to say that these young minds are impressionable, because that introduces the idea that not all impressions are good. We, as a society, have to be, or should be, so careful what impressions we give the young. We know that young children understand very much of what they overhear their parents and others are talking about. We don't usually credit those young minds with so much perspicacity, but we really should.

And being so impressionable, we find that their preferences and their allegiances tend to go with those whom they like and approve of most. Being young and naïve, they are vulnerable to those smarmy, persuasive individuals, men and women, boys and girls, with hidden but malevolent agendas, or with boys and girls, initially at first, perhaps, just out for some adolescent mischief, that gets out of hand and the younger vulnerable child is abused. The seeds of the obsessive, fanatical zealots are sown in the young mind. If only we could have an 'awareness app' to activate beforehand. Such innocence, angelic even, but we just have to try and educate them into avoiding situations where they could get to be abused. Happily, their young and malleable, comprehending minds, when all is explained, can be astounding.

That most of us are prepared to be compliant shows that our minds are malleable, ductile even, and mostly wish to avoid restraints and constraints. The law in all its forms is constantly being varied and upgraded, and the wise among us will be alert to those changes, then being of a mind, a certain mind will either accept so as to learn a modification of some new required conduct of our life, or perhaps we'll tire of being compliant, and decide to 'slip' under the net, under the radar of the law and its officers, to demonstrate that we wish to be free to do what we want, and the law-abiders can 'go hang' (but not literally).

It has often been said that the criminal mind is the more intelligent of the two, the criminals and the police. It can only be true of the successful criminals, the ones who are not caught. But it shows a certain contempt for the law and for all those who operate its mechanisms. They even have their own range of disgusting, derogatory terms for the police, too vulgar to bother repeating here (just go and watch a BBC1 police drama: they pull no punches on anything these days). But the cunning, devious, calculating mind of the successful criminal, artful at studying human nature and the way most of us behave in living out our lives, leaves a certain perverse admiration in us for them, but we only get to marvel at that when they are caught, and all is made news.

And so the question becomes: how well do we want to understand all that goes on in our minds? How much do we want to be able to think constructively, to move progressively to live our lives as teleological, goal-seeking lives, of love and with peace of mind?

How tractable should we allow our minds to become, when beset by ideologies that are capable of bringing about a reversal of all that we were brought up to think, to understand and love what is reckoned to be worthy and good? Here we refer to some faiths and creeds, down to the most obscure cults, so cranky as to defy our reasoning, to sets of behaviour patterns that can become obsessive, that can so ordain our lives that we are set apart, but not apart from the other handful of followers of the cult, the fanatical believers elsewhere in the world.

There are the brain- and personality-adjusting procedures that are known as 'brainwashing.' It is supposed that we are all vulnerable to the process. There is an 'intense short-course' version, that suits the very frightened, the very gullible and the extremely naïve; otherwise we tend to get it in unrecognisably subtle, small doses, drip-fed out of the media daily, as feature writers and TV producers set about delivering their own agendas. Should we believe them? Don't we crave just the 'bare' facts, so we can make up our own minds? Isn't this what people accuse the BBC of trying to do – so much subtle, subliminal left-wing slant on all things, especially the news, so to turn us all into straitjacketed, placard-toting socialists chanting for a republic and a United States of Europe or of the World? So what? What does it matter as long as we are always aware of our options, knowledgeable and understanding so to be capable of reining in our emotions, and so to allow our minds to be as malleable and tractable as our well-balanced cognitive intelligence can reasonably live with?

It is the minds of the young, the adolescents and bored young adults that can give cause for a concern arising from the distractions of the plethora of advertisements on TV, the internet and social media. We are all inundated by advertisements, constantly, almost inescapably, and they work by persuasion of the naïve, receptive and impressionable mind. There are at least two media issues. One is that our minds are being constantly distracted away from our primary objective of the moment, from whatever it was that we are wanting to concentrate on. The young can find it hard to learn to focus their attention, and to reason and rationalise on any single issue that may be an important matter in the planning of their life. The second issue is that a whole series of fast-delivered advertisements of a wide and varying type can have an effect on our subconscious and be emotionally unsettling. All advertisements evoke in us some kind of emotional response, but to be effective, we are not given the time needed evaluate their messages. An advertisement in one breath that evokes thoughts of a peaceful, relaxing and romantic holiday followed only a nanosecond later by a film advertisement depicting scenes of violence, murder, death and destruction by fire and explosion is to our emotional centre very unwelcome news. We are not designed to cope. Will we, society, or HMG ever learn that?

To what extent do we copy behaviour patterns we witness on the TV? The language, the tantrums and bigotry seen and heard in soaps. And the many unknown, laying flowers at a certain site when someone has died, in an act of an expression of sorrow for someone known of, but not known. This practice has become huge. And like certain other 'crowd' features, it seems to be a sort of fashion, turning into a custom, a set of conducts that have become popular as a way of identifying with others, the many others, so we can be comfortably, in our mind, one of their set; of their mindset. And, on the many issues of today, are we, the crowd, like lemmings, brushing aside centuries of social conventions for well-argued but fashionable whims of vocal but misguided quasi-intellectuals?

Oh. Yes. Our minds are malleable and ductile. Is that wrong? Do we have any degree of control over those two minds that sometimes we say we are in?

CHAPTER 29
LOGIC AND REASONING

This chapter could just as easily have been headed Logic, Reasoning, Vanity and Pride, or even all that plus Nationality.

Logic and reasoning can be viewed as synonymous to a degree but are really quite different in essentials. Logic is best viewed as binary, an algorithm of only yes and no answers to a sequence of relevant questions. The skill lies in setting the questions, and then by understanding the issue to be resolved by logic. Reasoning is more the being involved in setting the questions, but logic can be resolved by computers, whereas reasoning involves more, such as the third answer to a question, loved by humans that is yes, no and neither. The 'neithers' vote is to abstain, or not to vote at all.

Logic can go down entirely false trails when the questions put are misleading, distracting or just plain irrelevant, questions either innocently put, or mischievously or malevolently put. So, relevance is all-important and the rationaliser needs to exercise his or her intelligence to see no false trail is being led. Rather like a game of chess, we have to make every effort to see where our questioner thinks he or she is trying to take us.

Mr Spock of *Star Trek* fame exercised always his non-human variety of logic as a Vulcan can only do, and without humour, cynicism or spite. Just facts – well, his 'reasoned' facts, his QED. In other words, what the scriptwriter of the series was trying to demonstrate was the idea of a simple logic, simple and straightforward in its reasoning, but as ever, it still requires a close examination of the issue, 'the question' that arises in applying logic to solve an issue.

We might argue that a certain depth of experience of life is first necessary to be able to be logical, knowing what outcomes are either possible, likely or inevitable. Alternatively, we can use logic just to identify scenarios, alternatives that any issue that is being questioned could thus resolve into.

The concept of logic as an abstract and academic concept to a philosopher is one thing. But to the 'man' in the street, he or she is more interested in what is 'common sense,' an acquired innate 'streetwise' awareness of a likely, indeed most likely, outcome, based on experience and knowledge that will be the result of the question in hand. *Well, it's logical, ain't it? It's common sense, ain't it? Makes sense, don't it?* Yes, yes and yes, but only if the factors fed into the equation truly apply, truly belong. It's like tough decision-making, we need to review all the factors we can possibly identify that bring to bear on the decision to be made. And so it is with logic, all those factors bringing to bear.

How do we go about identifying those factors? That's where reasoning comes in: good, thorough, sensible reasoning comes out of many aspects that we resort to.

Certainly we can draw on our education and our experience of life with all its nuances, all its exigencies, but somehow our reasoning uses more than that, because we condition our thinking by what is stored, by what comes up from our subconscious, where our emotions are sealed.

Such things constitute our self-esteem, made up of our self-image and self-concept, which helps or hinders our reasoning of a situation, either because we fear a detrimental outcome, or because we have ambitions for ourselves of some gain. And in doing this, we may hardly know we are doing it, being selfish, rather than dispassionate, impartial or altruistic. For true logic, derived from sound, fair, impartial reasoning is just that: true logic. Not faulty logic as is so frequently presented to us as palatable logic or reasoning by politicians, who so often seek to persuade us to their particular line of thinking that appears for many of us more as obfuscations.

For very many years Latin was taught in schools, but many seemed never to recognise its benefits, its worth. Their reasoning would say, 'Hang on a minute, why are we being taught this dead language that no one speaks anymore? There is no sense in it, and a waste of my time at school if I have to sit and learn this nonsense: hic, haec and hoc. And the teachers and the leaders in education say, 'Yeah! Yer right, we could be teaching you all about LGBTQ, equality, and diversity, and sex education, instead.' But what they failed to appreciate, whilst perhaps cumbersome as a language, those who studied and learned from Latin classes gained an understanding of the application of reasoning that leads to logic. Tussling with those sentences in Latin scripts, translating them was the exercise and training of the mind, for reasoning and logic. It is doubtful that

Google Translate would get it right any more than a second-year pupil studying at school. It's a pity the acquisition of that skill was or had to be dropped from the syllabus, that is now so crowded, as the needs base of education has expanded.

Vanity, otherwise called false pride, is a corrupt form of logic, derived from twisted reasoning that arises out of ignorance and self-deception and detachment from a certain sense of the reality of the world to what's going on in the vain person's little world. It can be born out of insecurity and from being thrust, often thrust by a birthright, into a position of rank, with fawning by sycophantic servants and followers. But many can become vain through no good reason other than having made a study of his or her own image in the mirror, daily, several times daily, never passing a mirror without a quick glance to admire oneself. Such nonsense, not logical, no reasoning, unless it is our image that earns our living such as a film star or a model.

There are differences in reasoning and logic that occur between peoples of different nations. Sadly, these differences in understanding can cause the breakdown of international relations, trade talks and loss of peace.

In the UK we know full well that our reasoning is different to that of the French or the Germans, and if different to their way of thinking, then it's likely all nations bring to bear their own 'national psyche' when international matters are being discussed. Why is this so? Why should it not be so? For a nation's 'psyche', read its 'leaders' psyche'; and for its leaders, just read 'the man off the street.'

Vanity and pride come into it very largely, for they know they have to come out of international negotiations and go back to their own people as a champion, having 'won' the battle to secure the best deal for their country. But when sides can't agree, the talks fail, leaders return, as in a 'feign knights' situation until the battle of words recommences. Their fear of failing is great. Fear of loss of face, giving in, fearing the wrath of their people, who fear being worse off while other nations prosper at their expense.

And this is their reasoning. Not all can do well, so they think they must stand firm until the weaker side gives in. The reasoning should be surely that all can do well enough. It's only logical that a solution must be reached if trade is to happen (assuming trade and not boundaries are the issue between nations) and if a solution is to be reached then all sides should work together to achieve that abstract goal of success in international relations, not leaving one side or the other with a bitter taste and a brewing sense of resentment to boil over, first at home, and then the breakdown of the agreement struck. Statesmanship is the wanting of the success more than the return of an all-conquering hero; wanting good international relations more than a temporary vainglorious return from battle. And the logic of that is that it will need to be sold at home to the bloody-minded, blood-seeking zealots in their own country. It's tough.

The national characteristic of pride is very well exemplified by the French; we may mock them for it, and secretly we admire them for it. They put their country first, first and foremost. Not that the country has all that much to shout about, apart from its cooking, wine and topography, as well as a charmingly romantic language. But their collectivism in reasoning leads them to be cohesive, especially in such matters as going on strike. But they can be so vain. In 1940, the French Admiral François Darlan at Mers-el-Kébir was so proud as to reject all logic in addressing choices put to him by Churchill in WW2 to avoid the French fleet falling into the hands of the Nazis. Not wanting to suborn his authority to the Churchill (GB Ltd), and also not to receive orders from the new Vichy French government, which had done a deal with the Nazis to run the rest of France, he, the French admiral, said instead he would 'sink' his fleet. Only he didn't sink them, battleships and the like that Britain badly needed. And so, then, when Churchill opened fire and killed 1,000 French sailors, Admiral Darlan blamed Churchill for their deaths. Such false logic, no real reasoning, all driven through the fog of French vanity and false pride.

So, we do better if we are fair and reasonable, objective even, in examining our motives, if we are ever going to be truly logical and of sound reasoning. To help we need good self-awareness.

Is it reasoned logic to put to the electorate of the UK that if we come out of the customs union with the EU we will be worse off because trade tariffs will be an impediment? Why ask if it is anything to do with logic? It stands to reason! No, it doesn't. We can sell, with someone buying. We can't buy without someone selling. It's like oxidation and reduction; if something becomes oxidised, something else becomes reduced. We cannot give without someone receiving. They go together. So, if we fear being unable to afford through tariffs to buy German cars and other goods or French cars and other goods, it means the German and French manufacturers will not be able to sell their wares to UK/GB Ltd. The politicians, especially on the EU side, are behaving oddly in a way that does not smack of ethics, nor can it be money, but more out of vanity and pride of the constraint. They know the dreary, unseemly history of their countries and how the 'Perfidious Albion' has had to come and bring peace assisted by the other great English-speaking nations, mostly the Americans, but also the Canadians, Australians, New Zealanders and others. And yet, in their collusion with each other, Germany and France seek to 'put one over' on GB for deigning to divest itself of the shackles of their questionably democratic, monolithic EU Commission. Any why? Why walk away? Because their logic is not our logic, and their reasoning is not our reasoning. How did we ever 'get into bed' with a system of faux-democracy, a style of simulated democracy that is better described as an oligarchical bureaucracy? Does the 'average' man or woman even know if in the EU decisions, all brewed and fomented in the bosom of the EU Commission, are made on the basis of a true partnership, one country one vote, or a country's vote that's proportional to its population? One could almost guess at the answer and see how Turkey's 80 million entry into the EU would upset the apple cart in more ways than one.

Finally, on this subject of logic and reasoning. The French are proud of their regicide, and their 'Liberté, Égalité and Fraternité,' most especially when it suits them, but the philosophers of this world, well, at least some of them, argue that the French can only have any two of those three at any one time because to have all three at the same time makes them incompatible. We can think about this, and perhaps the French have as well, and this could account for some of their own special brand of logic, of reasoning, to apply any two of these 'principles' to a question, but not all three.

For example, the French say they won the Battle of Waterloo. How so, say we? Well, they say, it was fought over three days. They won two out of three battles and so being in the majority, they won. What marvellous, with a certain logic, comme vous voulez, but oh, such misguided reasoning.

But equally our reasoning is at fault also. Wellington didn't win the Battle of Waterloo at all. He was about to be beaten after so many hours when Blücher, the Prussian General arrived with his army, got stuck in, saved the English (er, sorry, British) from defeat and routed the French, whose 'Oh-so famous' Imperial Guard, always held back in case, so smart in their uniforms all unsoiled, preening and strutting, saying look at us, we are the Imperial guys, we guard the Emperor, and in the process 'got soft,' saw Blücher's gang and promptly did a bunk. That was their logic; save their own skins, the white flag brigade, and Napoleon just sat there on his cushion, nursing his piles, before also jumping into his carriage and also doing a logical, rapid debunk from the field of battle, to Paris, with some hope-filled explaining to do.

But for some totally illogical and unreasonable reason, Wellington was fêted big time as the conqueror of the dreaded Napoleon, and Wellington's head got very big, given big estates, the position of Prime Minister twice, but he wasn't all that good at that either. Understandable, maybe, but not logical. We can reason why he was so 'worshipped', why the 'truth' became so distanced and remote, but any ethics were buried on the battlefield, and then when he went to bed with Napoleon's mistress. That he succumbed to vanity was probably a logical conclusion.

Sometimes, indeed all too frequently, no amount of reasoning, no amount of applied logic will convince some people to change the views, albeit only recently adopted views as well as long held views. They aver not to change or alter their thinking, their habits and their character one jot, one iota. They find the argument interesting, even tempted to like, but something in them, something rises up and says, 'I know what I like, like to think, like to identify with, who and what I am, what I stand for, and what is more important, for peace at home, I need to hold to the same beliefs as my partner.' And this can go to the extreme of being seen as being 'unreasonable' in the fullest sense that we simply just cannot 'reason' with them.

The problem is we have dared to challenge their cherished opinions, their cherished beliefs. We have unwittingly challenged their self-image and their self-concept, those two subconscious frameworks of who they think they are and who they think they are becoming and have risked denting their self-esteem. Rather like the way we should never criticise a woman's fashion choices or a man's driving – Heaven forbid; else we risk wrath and rejection. Both these dearly held concepts we should never openly challenge, especially anyone like unthinking, clumsy, arrogant oafs.

And we, in turn, can find ourselves challenged by the rejection of our logic, our reasoned logic, which of course, as sine qua non, is so superior, so well considered to be worthy of acceptance by all, n'est-ce pas? And so, the exchange of feelings can be reciprocal – if we are not careful. Does the bus driver care if they don't get on the bus when it stops at the stop? After all he is not on commission, or is he? But we do care if they don't get on the good bus, 'In Omnibus Deum,' that signals its destination as 'A God for All,' and that frequently stops to let new passengers alight.

Sometimes in international negotiations the gap is too wide, due to cultural differences, which amounts to differences in upbringing, the custom and habit that are comfortable at home, no 'foreign' ways, not foreign thinking, and this is sad because no one culture has the monopoly of the best ideas, and the best opinions. At other times it can be put down to a mulish, wilful character, determined to be 'right' in all they think and feel, to a clash of personalities, and to reject any sound reasoning solely down to a dislike of the other person, a distrust and disapproval to the point of being ready to walk away, or just because they smell.

If we think about the Brexit negotiations and ask ourselves: were personalities being brought to bear here, between the parties? It is very rare that our personalities do not come into negotiations. Is it easy or very hard to set aside the initial impressions we have automatically formed on that first occasion? Those first impressions that always count. It is easier, with practice, to set aside the unease we feel at someone's unfortunate physiognomy, or a disrespectful, inappropriate style of dress for the occasion or even their exuberant overfamiliarity on a first meeting, with coarse dialect and an effeminate whiff of too strong aftershave.

Knowledge and understanding are partners and in co-operation lead us to show a sensible, mindful cognisance, which in turn helps us towards a witting judiciousness. In so doing we can apply that degree of logic that enables worthy, solid deductions to be reached by sound reckoning and reasoning, reached via our chosen route of clear and valid thinking to our arrived-at logical conclusions.

And they in turn incite in us some sagacity, some wisdom that shows a far-sighted penetration and the judgement of discernment. In short we can be said to be sapient, and in so doing we can be true to our species title name, 'Homo sapiens.'

If we do twice as much listening as talking in respect to our two ears and only one mouth, and read plenty of useful books, we will be doing well. It has been said and this applies to woman, too: 'Give instruction to a wise man and he will yet be the wiser.' Quite so. Would that we could be so, too.

———•———

CHAPTER 30
THEIR CAUSES

There was a character called Sir Humphrey Appleby who was the Cabinet Secretary to the PM in the TV series, *Yes Prime Minister*. Sir Humphrey was a through and through career 'keep-your-copy-book clean' civil servant and was once suspected of being a spy for Cold War Russia; he was quick to hotly deny any such suggestion by protesting very emphatically that he'd never believed in any cause in his life, let alone believe passionately.

What a sensible man. Why is it we take up 'causes,' become convinced of the 'wrongness' of some issue, and 'gird our loins,' take up our 'sword and buckler' and go to battle to gather supporters amongst the like-minded, would-be zealots looking for some cause or other that then takes over their life. And it needn't be a 'wrongness,' waiting only to be corrected; it could equally be a 'rightness,' a rightness that is hardly recognised as such, not sufficiently 'head above the parapet' for society to take notice.

Causes. In other words, beliefs. We come to believe something is and shouldn't be, or isn't and should be. Rather like politicians, that esoteric coterie of chronic malcontents. Malcontent? Yes, well, the cudgel they've taken up is a 'sine qua non' (but we will say it anyway here): their role is to 'make laws' that are their ideas, to change and modify the way we live our lives, ostensibly for the better. For the better for some, or even for many, is the aim, and of course, to keep the country at peace, both intrinsically and extrinsically, while staving off bankruptcy of the nation by the levying of painful taxes. They are ever seeking to put things that in their view, the currently elected MPs' view, they are now making things better for as many of society as possible and so they are generally perceived to be right, in righting a wrong. Some just see it as meddlesome.

They are the malcontents. Couldn't do the job, if they were not. That is their cause, then, apart from getting themselves a livelihood, and there's little wrong in that, as long as they use no unfair tactics in doing so.

For politicians, like most causes, that basic philosophy, that basic aim, becomes dichotomous, and each branch often dichotomous, too, and so we land up with two basic beliefs in politics. Capitalism versus socialism, which both hide their fundamentalism under the protective skirts of the brand image names Tory or Labour, Republican versus Democrat. Each country has its own brand image name, names that often become despised by dogmatists of the alternative cause.

If we get on a bus, we need to know where it's going, and why it's going there. It's no good getting on because it's a nice colour, or arrived at your stop at a convenient moment, or because you see some of your friends already on-board. Perhaps we get on because it's the only other bus that comes along but it is just plain, unappealing in some way, because its passengers seem grim-faced, one bus all wearing dungarees or another with them all in suits. Perhaps we get on because this is the bus our parents always took. So, where is it going and why?

The fundamental ideologies of the two opposing systems are very inadequately spelled out, even in the 'hustings,' when, at election time, the only time we ever have a say, we are asked to make a choice. Does any real clear water ever exist between the façades of the two camps? Sometimes we wonder if the smiling canvassers, asking for your vote on the actual day, are ever sure, could ever articulate the fundamental principles behind their political party.

Capitalism is the party that believes in private enterprise, from the man who scraped together enough to put down the deposit on the 'corner shop' he has yearned after for so long. His shop. His business. His capital invested in it and working for him as he works for his customers to make his shop, his business, his life successful. And if he fails, his business fails, it's his loss and he learns from his mistakes and starts all over again.

But he doesn't fail, he goes on to start a second shop, and a third, and so on. In ten years his shops are all over the country. His company has 'gone public' and individuals can now buy shares in his chain of shops, so the chain can grow and even open shops abroad. The dividends come unto the investors and the share value rises. But they don't always rise, and like the original small corner shop that failed, sometimes the big company fails and the value of the shares plummets to zilch. Ouch. Private enterprise. Pick ourselves up, dust ourselves off and start all over again. That is capitalism. And it works, mostly, because it is born of man's natural instincts, a method, a system, a lifestyle that comes and suits so naturally mankind all over the world. The feeling is there, even in deep-seated, blankety-blank, rampant communist countries.

As for socialism, it's not so easy to boil down to its essence, so it's hardly surprising its supporters identify themselves by saying what they don't want, don't like, get to hate even, and that the Tories are especially not wanted in 'power.'

They take up against the excesses of capitalism and perhaps rightly so. The Tories could do much more to regulate the obscene excesses of some aspects of capitalism. That there are excesses is, of course, all down to the self-greed of some capitalists, who give the rest a bad name. Does 'the other side,' the socialists, suffer in the same way? Oh! Yes! There are sinecures and nepotism and the illegal taking of bribes to favour someone with a fat, juicy government contract. But then does the whole system, the whole political party, and all it stands for, become vilified for those excesses? No, it does not. The guilty individuals do, but not their party; in contradistinction to the Tories who, to a man, are at once brandished as 'filthy capitalists.' As said, the socialists don't really seem to know what they stand for, but they most definitely know what they don't stand for, and stand against the evil Tories.

Seeking to get to the socialist's bedrock beliefs, it seems to be a system whereby the state will look after us, through money raised through taxes. Taxes that leave us little to save for a corner shop deposit, but we can get benefits that include 'the dole' if out of work. Enough dole to get by, without work. No more getting up at 5.30am to go to work, we can lie in bed until, until anytime we like, almost – except that we may have to go and 'sign on' if we are to get the dole.

After the Second World War there was a massive swing to socialism and whole industries were nationalised, taken into state ownership. Those industries became inefficient, uncompetitive, lazy and corrupt, all with 'the people's money'. Well, the government has no money of its own, only that which it takes from the people. Unless we are thinking communism, where the state owns everything and, in its munificence, hands out goodies to the people as and when it, the government, sees fit. And in the government there are those few individuals who happen to have found their way to the honey pot.

So in effect, are socialists 'closet' communists? If so, and if their secret were let out, would that cause their party to 'implode,' so, they, knowing the communists' first aim is towards anarchy, an overthrowing of capitalism, greedy, evil capitalism, to replace it with good, kindly goodies for all and fair to everyone communism. And on the road, the long journey, like the works bus with no destination shown, it's a case of 'let's all be socialists, we know we have to go along with a mixed economy, as we work to nationalise industries again, and legislate against big cheating, swindling multinationals until they evaporate.'

But is all this fair? No, it most certainly isn't. The Labour Party is in effect the party of the trade unions, and whether we like it or not, the trade unions have broken the iron fist of the Victorian mill and factory owners and their like, whose aim was to keep the people working in their factories as humble and poor and uneducated as possible, so to have more riches for themselves. In breaking that grip the unions did a magnificent thing, and they have done much since to strike a better balance between the fair return for the savings of the thrifty, and the needs of the 'working people.' Sadly, very sadly, the unions came to be taken over by people smitten with causes, and their biggest but undeclared cause was the bringing about of a communist state, breaking for ever the natural system of mankind's ingenuity and enterprise, the capitalist system. If only capitalism had a 'nicer' name.

What of the other parties? They have causes, too. What a waste of effort. Any party in power has to have sorted out its 'beliefs,' its policies on every possible identifiable need in society as a cause and their proposed solutions. 'Single-issue parties? A waste of effort. But the system allows it. But they may lose their deposit.

There is nothing wrong with the dream of a communist state – as long as it remains a dream. A dream in which everyone has the same things, no one with more than any other, where everyone is kind, generous and hard-working, conscientious on behalf of the state and on behalf of everyone else, who are also kind and generous and hard-working. A fair society. A very fair society. Wonderful. But why, when reality strikes, does the government of that communist state muzzle the 'free press' (free as in to say what it likes) and have a secret police to arrest any agitators, never to be seen again? Why are the people so grey and glum-looking? Are they not living in a nirvana realised? We need to wake up to this, this fantasy lurking in the shadows of socialism. What is the socialist truly thinking, if thinking anything constructive at all, and not just thinking we don't want capitalism, certainly not the Tories idea of capitalism? Ah! So! Is that the way forward? Find capitalism without the nasty Tories. Now there's an idea that could become a 'cause;' 'une cause célèbre, peut-être, n'est-ce pas?'

The recent and ongoing 'ad nauseam' issue of Brexit versus Remain presents two causes, one each only for the followers. Neither camp is really clear what is the fundamental thinking, the fundamental ideology, behind their cause. At the time of the 2016 Referendum and since, there has not been a single politician, a single legislator, elected and paid by the state to represent the people in the constituency, who has been able to enunciate to the media exactly and simply what the issue of Brexit was and still is. Not quite true. There was a previous PM who spoke so briefly and arrogantly of his summary of the issue by saying, to no one in particular – which was useful, because no one in particular was listening – that the issue of how we are governed doesn't matter, what matters is how well off we are, and that will be if we 'Remain'. He's still hoping, they say, to be the first President of the United States of Europe. Please, no, not he, he with so little regard for honest statesmanship and due democratic process.

And that is the point, the issue, the cause. How do we want to be governed? The two-party parliamentary democracy that evolved in Britain evolved over hundreds of years. Europe has never been able to be at peace with itself, and finally, hopefully, finally after the Second World War enough people felt 'enough is enough,' we must evolve a system of living together in trade, and in peace. First to arrive was the Coal and Steel Federation based in the Ruhr, between the then West Germany and France, with Italy looking through the window, expectantly. From this grew the Common Market, a trading association of five countries, and France in the name of General de Gaulle, that 'cross' Churchill had to bear all through the war, persistently vetoed any idea of Britain (then of 44 million souls) joining in. Such 'gratitude.' We were able as an empire to stand out against German aggression for long enough until the American (240 million souls) came to our help (again) and together freed Europe from the rampant evils of Nazism. He, de Gaulle, said, 'No, you can't join our trading club, go away.' Gets back to his own country, had to be first to re-enter Paris after the Allies kicked the Nazis out, puffs his chest out on assuming the Presidency and says, 'Non,' no GB in the EC. Such ingratitude. Such arrogance. So normal human behaviour. And then in 2016, it turns out he had been doing us a favour all along. He just knew oil and water don't mix. Residing in the UK all those war years, in exile, he got to know us, as Churchill got to know him. Which is why Churchill said, and he knew a thing or two, that we, GB, should be 'of Europe' but not 'in Europe.' Wise, old buffer.

The Common Market grew in the number of willing entrants and became known as the European Economic Community. Like any organisation of any size it needs its administrative structures, and as a 'political' reality it needed its politically minded and politically capable people at the top. They arrived, in due course, were appointed by the individual nations' leaders, appointed to 'run the show – and told to 'just get on with it.' This is the European Commission, a bunch of European idealists, not elected, but given, at first, powers that soon became more, and other powers they just 'took' for themselves: governing roles, unelected, unaccountable, and a massive budget of the public's money. Oh! Yes? So, what about the European Parliament? So what? A set-up. A smokescreen, like a demulcent carminative, a huge sinecure, a gravy train. No governing is done in reality. It's an allegory, an illusion.

Should we be happy to go along as members of such a set-up as we have now for 40 years since France finally relented and let us join the Common Market? Since the UK and other countries have ceded tranche after tranche of sovereignty, by our sovereign government over to the Commission. We, governing with our parliamentary democracy that was the envy of the world, give up democratic government for an oligarchic bureaucracy? Yes, we did, as it seems, because enough of us believed we were entering a trading group that could keep the peace in Europe, and peace would bring prosperity. Well, it didn't happen. Well, the peace did, sort of, but we lost control of our world trading links, and our borders. GB has become poorer and poorer as a result, just as General de Gaulle predicted. Not poorer than the Italians, as he said, not yet, because we are getting out. Out of bondage. Brexit.

But can we now make a go of it? Like a man used to crutches, can he suddenly find the strength and skill to stand 'on his own two feet'? That we have the innovative skills badly needed to go on and develop and create is accepted. The concern is that we have lost our diplomatic and self-governing skills. GB, and for England in particular, is not at all the same country, as it was 100 years ago. It was then at the core of the great Empire on which the sun never set, and the then core British, of stout heart and purpose, were trying to heal the near-fatal wounds received from the German aggression of the First World War. The travesty of the Treaty of Versailles should have been a lesson, a lesson against random carving up of national boundaries and the demanding of reparations. France, almost childlike, said to Germany, 'You made us pay you reparations in 1871, and took Alsace-Lorraine away. And how dare you come to Versailles, crown your first King, your Kaiser, of your new united nation state of Germany, here, in our Palace of Versailles? Bloody cheek! Well, we beat you this time. We'll make you pay, and pay and pay us reparations until the 'pips squeak.' Well, they did squeak with the result that 20 years later Hitler was parading down the Champs-Élysées.

What is the point of this rant? Well, one point is that we have lost the art of negotiation and it is negotiation that is needed to bring about diplomacy, which is the practice of foreign policy short of military action. The French have their own style of negotiation. It is almost unique. To them the word 'negotiate' means to keep demanding what they want until the other side, in exasperation, desperation and exhaustion, gives way, either totally submissive or partially so. Look at the farce of the EU Commission decamping from Brussels (Belgium) each month for a couple of days or so to Strasbourg (France), just so the French can have their way and say that the HQ of the EU is in France. And this is the way they are, unless there's a fire in the 'white flag' factory, and then some unbending occurs.

So, do we in GB have the governing and diplomatic skills needed to make a success of Brexit? We know that there are many in this country now who possess great intellectual potential. The classic indigenous English and Scottish 'upper' class of privately educated, so typical of those Victorian and Edwardian times, have all 'disappeared' to be replaced by something else: no one is quite sure as there seems to be no pattern. The once highly regarded civil service has struggled to live alongside edicts from Brussels. Why do we still have 600 MPs and a tottering number of civil servants, who now cheat the taxman by getting their pay paid into their 'single person' limited company, ostensibly supplying services to its single customer, the HMG. What a travesty that is. Is there no one politician who hates 'cheating' of the system enough to sort this misdemeanour out? Make it a cause? Get all those tax-fiddling civil servants back on the employee payroll, with so-called employee benefits, including their pensions, that, even though notionally as yet 'self-employed,' they still assume they can take all the benefits. We could sack the lot, no fear of an employment tribunal, because they are not employees, their working relationship with HMG is as a subcontractor, as a firm, a 'one-man' firm. Oh. How those civil servants would squeal if we gave them the sack. We won't, of course; no stomach for it really.

Few now deny the cause of caring better for the environment, global warming and environmental pollution, as large chunks of ice as big as the Isle of Wight crumble into the Southern Ocean from the South Pole ice pack. As glaciers visibly shrink before our eyes. As we splutter along, the diesels spray exhaust aerosols and fumigate pavements in our cities. Yes, we'd do anything and everything to stop polluting our planet, except stop breeding. Stop breeding? What's that got to do with it? Simple. We, each of us, every man jack of us, in the modern society of today have a desperate need for energy, the use of energy. Energy to provide us with food, shelter and warmth, and energy for work: the work, that funds our pleasure.

Also, each us gives off heat, and masses of carbon dioxide. Multiply that by the millions of people on earth, and millions more each year, more childbirth, more and more of us living longer; the energy demand, ever and ever growing.

So far, we have only skimmed on the surface of producing non-polluting energy. Those systems themselves, the manufacture of solar panels and so on, take energy to fabricate. It is possible, in time, that the world will become more proficient at 'renewable' green energy, but can it 'allow' more and more humans on earth? How many is too many? By the time we have too many, will we be able to colonise the moon, or Mars? Where are 'we' all going to live? Under the sea, in submerged cities? Green, then, is definitely a justifiable cause, for us all. It's a mindset, a cause.

Causes come from beliefs and convictions, and these came from ideas and notions. Causes can be to serve real situations such as the hard-enduring grind of real poverty, or the bewildering distraction and wretchedness of illness. We can see these things with our own eyes and other senses. We can empathise, and we can do our bit to help.

But there are other causes based around abstract ideas, imaginings, things and thoughts we cannot see, hear, feel, taste or smell. But the idea lingers and, in lingering, appeals and grows as a notion, then a conviction to become a cause. And we can act; act to follow some creed, as to our conduct, our behaviour as in the arrangement of our day, our week, our year, as to how we dress and eat.

There are at least two major categories of these abstract constructions of the mind. It is thought Homo sapiens evolved from Homo erectus because of his newly acquired ability to imagine, and with that imagining, to be able to communicate those thoughts.

Our forebears developed to leave us an ability to create abstract concepts that seem real enough. If we consider a car manufacturing company. It has a factory filled with machinery. It has a workforce. It has directors who govern, it has shareholders who have 'bought shares' as in paid some money and in return received a piece of paper. It has cash in the bank, and probably international bank debts. If we remove any one part of these components, the physical aspects would still exist as a fact, a physical fact. If we removed the factory and contents, the people and the cash, in real terms as in banknotes, returned the shareholders' investment, what would be left of the company? A list on a register at Companies House? The 'company' itself is an abstract creation of the human mind, the mindset of society that has been recognised and registered by another abstraction, another creation of human society, the 'law.' The written-down, set-in-print-on-paper Memorandum and Articles are the physical embodiment of the concept of the company. Something tangible, the first tangible thing that represents 'the company.'

The other type of abstract construction is a construction of the mind that cannot be proven, seen, felt, touched or realised because it is ethereal, made of nothing more than a set of ideas, but based on superstition. Those ideas can mount up to be known as a religion, or a political party or some other ideological grouping. The notion doesn't need buildings, but they are often brought about due to a perceived need, due to that custom, tramline, orthodox thinking of human behaviour; it doesn't need a workforce and yet humans like to engage teams, evangelical troops, to engage and spread their 'mission' as believing theirs is the best, the only message worth it. It doesn't actually need money or shareholders, but because they have gone for buildings and teams, the 'troops,' money is needed. Some of these beliefs bring about such a fervour that they 'overtake' someone's life, their whole existence, just because an idea, a notion, becomes a conviction and they can't help themselves but move from the endearing innocence and naïvety of children and early teenhood into the rabid 'soldier' of the cause; not free in the mind anymore to reason, to debate and chew over life's debatables, but only to strive, to churn and stir up the lives of others and to distil from the morass of their own lives a fervour for their way, the zealots and the dogmatists' way of thinking.

So, this power of imagination can be creative or destructive. In creative mode it harnesses the power of good, the power of goodness that is the power of God.

It can bring about the creation of things that improve people's lives, not just for a few, but potentially everyone, things that people can appreciate, welcome and even love. It can be from anything practical as in medical developments, to useful practical institutions, machinery and equipment, through to something useful, like Velcro, or things we can just see or hear as items of beauty, to love.

But in destructive mode our imagination works to evoke hate, rather than love. Deep within some, the thoughts, the ideas, the twisted thinking processes of the like-minded, sick and sad people, they simmer and bubble with hate – hatred of other people's ideas and their creations. And that hate turns to an all-consuming drive to destroy, to kill and maim other people who become quite randomly victims of another's hate. This is the imagination in the absence of goodness. No such thing, no such intangible concept called evil at work, just no goodness there, a denial of goodness. In the shade, a dark place.

There is the potential to love and to hate in all of us. To some, to love life, people, animals and all life around them comes easily, even often without thinking; it seems instinctive to them. Even if they have experienced negative events in their life, they remain positive, outgoing, happy people; good, kind and loving. They are fortunate in that disposition.

Can we learn to be like them? The answer is most definitely yes, but sadly, just as those with their inborn goodliness, there seems to be the opposite, people whose minds work to see dislike, disapproval, distrust, disbelief, disrespect, disgust, reason to disregard and just about every other 'dis' anyone can think of. They are branded a negative person. Some make it their cause in life to reduce and suppress negative thinking where it exists. They join the Church, may become an evangelist, it becomes their cause. They mean well, but as we have seen elsewhere in these chapters, their thinking and their imagining can be faulty or incomplete and so develop mistaken beliefs, as in the case of Jehovah's Witnesses; well-meaning but so, oh, so mistaken.

Many of mankind's scientific advances bring about benefits for humanity, once the advance is adopted; we think here of the benefits of radio, of television, of the internet, of atomic power. And yet these same beneficial discoveries can also be used against us, in negative ways, to harm, to disrupt, and worse, to maim, or kill. The television is a wonderful invention, which can educate, inform and entertain us, and even bring out the best in us. And yet it can also bring out 'the worst' in us, leading by bad examples into crude vulgarity, to show us how to ridicule and denigrate, to indulge in false 'emotions,' letting them run rampant in our minds, so that we can even begin to overdo empathy. TV programmes also demonstrate scheming and plotting with deviousness and they can provoke an obsession with sex, sexual deviations and perversions, not to mention violence and unspeakable cruelty, all on the pretext of entertainment.

Similarly atomic power has such great advantages for us, although undeniably bringing with it some inconveniences. And yet mankind is fascinated and willing to create a tool to use its inherent destructive power, the atomic bomb. National leaders, with a fear of aggression from other countries, a fear that breeds a kind of hatred in their millions of minions, just want to acquire this ultimate tool to return hatred, gain revenge, but could bring about the destruction of life on earth.

Or does it all stem from fear? Is it the desire to have tools of war the other side don't yet have, or perhaps already have and to have it on both sides creates a balance of power and so a 'threatening' peace supervenes. Why can't nations live in peace and contentment with other nations? Oh, they can, or rather they could, but only if their leaders seek that path and those of other nations, mostly neighbouring nations, nearby, will let them live in peace. In the end Napoleon begged to be allowed to rule just France, for peace, but the ancient European monarchies, fearful of an uprising in their own country wanted their own people to be shown that the 'rightful' monarch had to be restored at the head of France. Those monarchs refused to trust Napoleon, and that was hardly a surprise; which leopard ever changes its spots?

But they don't and they won't, even today, trust and live in peace, for we are just not made that way. They, the leaders, those grown-up children, are racked with the fears and weaknesses they had as children. The Brexit negotiations are a fine example of this. Proud, arrogant, hollow leaders, posturing, because they are in a position of some power. Upset because their clone, their EU family and their dream of federation is clearly in danger of falling apart, and because they have failed to devise systems that bind people. They want an almost enforced stay, enforced in making the leaving process almost too hard to bear. They overlook the fundamental feral nature of that primordial man still within us, instinctively being tribal, the family, the village; the village elders we know, trust and love, not some remote unelected bureaucratic dogmatist building his empire or own 'super-village' where all individuality of thought, of preference, of determination has been taken away and placed in the hands of strangers, all in the name of … of what? Of peace? Living in peace with each other? That was the idea, the ideal.

But just like TV and atomic power, the idea has become thwarted, deprived and depraved, because the implementation of the ideal has been too little understood, too little thought through, too little honest frankness, statesmanship with integrity, too disregarding of who we are, as highly intelligent, imaginative creatures, as animals. So, like the Treaty of Versailles, created by ignorant people, ignorant of who and how we are. The childlike squabbling over land and money, who has what 'toys' to play with. They should be ashamed of themselves. Negotiate? Most couldn't negotiate the skin off a rice pudding.

Frequently taught negotiating skills orientate to what you can get off the other person while giving away as little as you can get away with. That may be fine in business, but also in business, it is well known, repeat business is the best. Too smart, too clever negotiating leaves one or the other feeling cheated, 'done over' in some way, 'bested.' Repeat business? No chance. And so it is with international negotiations; it's not about what you can get, it should be about what you can give, about what good relationships we can create. Can we create enough jobs, yielding enough income to each, to enjoy a life with peace of mind? We know that all the goodies, the consumables, are mostly things that we can do without, and yet, indulging in them creates a demand, and that demand translates into employment, and those employees spend their pay, amongst other things, vital things, but also on the consumables they don't really need. It's a merry-go-round that needs a better answer: a cause.

In Brexit, the European side simmers and seethes with resentment that GB, a key player, but one who has always been a thorn in the side of the federalists, GB, always fighting to bring about a more democratic organisation, less of an oligarchic bureaucracy. On leaving, the resentment could be replaced by a mood of valete, 'bon voyage' and please continue to trade with us because trade, fair trade, brings friendship, trust and peace. Do the European negotiators know this? No, they are playing 'hard school,' and using unfair and unjust negotiating tactics attempting to do us (GB) down: so wrong, so mistaken, so childlike. If they have an ounce (or 28.5 grams) of decency in them. They may very well come to be ashamed of themselves in time, but we doubt it.

And yet that is their cause, their belief, federalism, the slow, steady march, slow, steady abrasion of village mentality, but also adversely creating the eruption of 'seeds' seeking independence, the Spanish Basque, Catalonia, Scotland, where next? Self-rule versus a federal Europe? Those two ideas in anyone's mind at the same time can only cause the computer of our mind to crash! Those ideas are as immiscible as oil and water, as Nazi and Jew, as capitalist and communist. A total no-go. And yet, for example, while some of Scotland's activists seek independence, they say they will seek to be part of the EU. Two conflicting aims, not once understood, it seems, in their minds; their mood is, 'Let's dump London, but, oh, gosh, we need financial support. Ah. Yes, let's get it from Brussels, they'd help us, wouldn't they, help us do London one in the eye?' But few seem to see the way the EU has gone, and is going, and so are quite keen on snubbing distant London with its rule, and opt for Brussels with an even more distant rule; but Brussels comes with strings, big time. So, they, those Scots, are being illogical; and perhaps need to take more water with one wee dram at a time, and only once a day.

For the Eurocrats, federalism is their cause, their belief, then 'casus belli,' obsessive zealots. Will it come about? Will it ever work? If the cause can become something clear, something the vast majority will see as good, as fair, fair in all things as much as is ever possible, at least striving in that way, of peace, of trade, within and with the rest of the world, then it will work, but only if we have sound, stout-hearted, good people at the top, not self-seeking, pocket-lining, self-serving autocrats. If France, for example, would turn round and say, 'Oh! It's okay, folks, there's no longer a need to move from Brussels to Strasbourg every month, you can cancel the gravy train, and only every now and then, in a blue moon to appease France's vanity,' we'll insist the EU indulges in the expensive farce once again.

Everything in life resolves down to a matter of money, or ethics or a mixture between the two. Let's look at France, because they, above all, love to wear their hearts on their sleeves. Now, when their fishermen go on strike and block the ports, and when their farmers go on strike and block the motorways with their tractors, that is for money. It's an issue, it's their cause, as it's their livelihoods, as they see it. Then their air traffic controllers go on strike, as they do every summer on the pretext of wanting more money, and Heaven knows they are well enough paid in the first place, but nonetheless, they want more, on a pretext that it's an issue of money, when more truly it's a matter of ethics because they know they have to work harder each summer transiting all those hundreds of British holiday planes over their airspace, and they get a kick out of annoying the British every summer by going on strike. They are as predictable as the seasons, and it's their ethic in France to stand together – fraternity.

However, when the French vegans start a rampage and destroy the charcuteries, and boucheries, France's butchers serving the meat-loving, meat-eating French and any other soul who enjoys a pavé de boeuf, or a boeuf bourguignon, frogs' legs or even a coq au vin, then they, the vegans have taken up a cause to put the meat eaters right and go vegan. That's pure ethics, their ethics, not money, not for money at all, just ethics. Have they never heard a lettuce scream when it's pulled up out of the ground? It's as if they, being vegan, have developed some amino acid deficiency, like tryptophan; developed through avoiding meat, it has made them turn into a crazed zealot to thrash about in an holier-than-thou stance and to go on a crusade. The nutters. Causes; of the sort of gripe that overtook the French when hungry, from having no bread to eat, were told to eat cake instead, and so they rose up as one, and chopped the heads off the cake eaters, and then breaking into the Bastille prison to do some good and release thousands of political prisoners believed stowed there, only to find a small band of 40 hardened criminals who, they agreed, should really be there or be beheaded, for the villains they were. Those hungry bread eaters could have been more wary of their assumptions, as indeed so should we, at all times, and we are not just speaking about being hungry here, either for money or for pursuing some ethics.

Causes can be our making or undoing, but mostly they are our undoing. Best seek a 'worthy cause', one of Godliness and God's single-minded goodness

CHAPTER 31
THE NOES AND THE DON'T KNOWS

In the Middle Ages, ignorance and superstition held sway. For most ordinary folk, life was pretty wretched and must have seemed very pointless until one reckoned that there had to be an afterlife, a better life. But how to get there, to be assured, at least through hope, that they would get there? Many world religions are based on the expectation of an afterlife, and most promised that, but only after a life of certain requirements of conduct here on earth had been consistently met. All of those 'afterlives' revolved around a central concept, a figurehead, a God.

Atheists and agnostics have looked at those 'requirements of conduct' and have seen many involve a style of worship with each religion's concept of God, and have seen cruel, mindless hate, and brutality, fighting, murder and even wars carried on under the banner of religion. They have very reasonably concluded that religion is a load of tosh and therefore there is no such thing as God, or in the case of the 'don't knows,' the agnostics say there probably isn't a God.

And if there is no God, then there probably isn't an afterlife, and whether there is or there isn't, what's the point of worrying about it, you're going there, or somewhere anyway; but probably nowhere. If there is no God to sit in judgement as to our conduct here on earth, then our conduct here on earth is immaterial, and so we can behave as badly as we like.

Well, actually, we probably wouldn't behave all that badly because our innate self tells us we reap what we sow, mostly, here on earth and this leads to a 'Do as you would be done by' approach to life. We get to know what thoughts bring about the best actions, the better to make us feel good about ourselves and loved by people. That is unless we are a total screwball like Hitler and other total jerks in history, with brains fogged with screwed-up thinking. But the average atheist is probably a very decent, straight-thinking, level-headed person who has decided he or she has no time for, no love for, religion. And this is the strange thing, that committed Christians both young through to elderly, believing in Heaven as their afterlife, mostly do not want to die, as if they are having too good a time here on earth, or as if they have some mission they haven't yet completed. Do anything, almost, not to die, except the very old, the very unhappy and the terminal ill, the dying – the living dead. If Heaven is so wonderful, wouldn't it be logical to feel that we should be ready to go at anytime, when called: 'Come in number ten, your time is up,' calls the boatman on the council's artificial boating lake. Or do we never feel ready to be called and hope for some more time in which to improve?

As for agnostics, like any election, any vote, even directors around the boardroom being paid to vote, there are the 'don't knows'; often very decent people, but who just can't seem to work out in their mind the basic issue, the principles of the argument, even after the erudite have discoursed, have brilliantly coruscated in the most recondite way, they still dither, and this almost certainly is because they are allowing other less obvious factors to hinder their decision; such as prejudices, constraints of vested loyalties and clashes from deep within, such as self-concept, self-image, and even self-worth.

Even if Jesus were to appear in front of them and demonstrate the stomata in his hands and feet, the agnostic would probably worry if this vision before him or her was not just a trick, a hologram of some kind, by religious zealots. Whilst some may think it unfortunate, or even disreputable that agnostics can't seem to come off the fence, one side or the other, haven't the ability to perceive and grasp the concepts being explained to them, even argued very convincingly, and is just down to some people's character make-up, their intelligence perhaps, although in many other spheres regarded as bright, there is something missing or lacking in their perspicacity, but perhaps down to an inactive gene. They may be a brilliant research biochemist, or clever sculptor or surgeon, but when it comes to these philosophical arguments they are left like a whale on a beach, grounded, flapping in a forlorn effort.

If we were to succumb to the temptation of being judgemental (Ha, ha), we may ask ourselves, which is worse: an atheist who denies God, or a Jew or a Muslim, both denying Jesus as the Son of God, yet share the same concept of God, Jehovah, after a fashion? Both of those followers of Jehovah, who to the

Muslims is called Allah, seem to demonstrate a misunderstanding of what is God and so by misanthropomorphisation of the deity, effectively deny God as well.

The corruption and conceptual thinking in the Roman Catholic Church in the Middle Ages have left a legacy of distaste, of which the worst was probably the attitude it bred in people whose self-styled philosophy became: 'I can do just as I want in the week because I can just go to confessional, get 'forgiveness' that may cost me something, but it's worth it!'

And sadly, today, the churches come under fire repeatedly as the 'wrongdoing' of priests and vicars, and choirmasters who turned out to be child molesters and other vices.

This book presents a case for God being undeniable as the evidence is irrefutable. We all grow up to realise what is good, good for us as sentient beings, comfort-seeking and hedonistic (albeit in different ways and different degrees). That which is good derives from goodness that is the power, a force of goodness. It is a force for and a power of goodness, that life force in all living things, that is of God, giving each the potential of godliness that thrives on the goodness around. Atheists may argue, as may biochemists, that life is just a phenomenon, derived over billions of millennia by the initial coming together of certain chemicals on earth, in the air and sea at the time, sulphurous fumes from volcanoes spewing gases and larva into a nutrient soup of the sea acted upon by the wide array of radiations from the sun, eventually developing that all life-giving molecule we call 'chlorophyll.' Let's face it, we'd be nowhere without chlorophyll. All plant life depends on it and all animals depend on plants either directly or indirectly; just as animals in turn rely on haemoglobin, in some form or other, or some related variant of haemoglobin. Without the haemoglobins, animal life would be nothing.

So, if we want, it's okay to believe chlorophyll and haemoglobin have derived from pure 'chance' coming together of the necessary chemicals to undergo a chemical reaction, involving sunlight for chlorophyll. These two molecules are actually elaborated as we have known now for many decades, in specialised cells, chloroplasts in the plant leaf and stem, and erythroblasts in animals, where the erythroblasts derive from stem cells, which carry the DNA profiling to bring about the body in toto.

Physicists may even come into the argument on the atheists' side, with their special understanding of quantum physics, with electrons 'jumping' from one orbit around a nucleus to another orbit within an atom, within a molecule, either absorbing or yielding 'energy' in the process, and this energy driving on the chemical reactions of life. Without knowing it, perhaps not even thinking daringly enough, that that energy is the life force, or part of the life force, let's say 'an aspect' of the life force that is the force for life, the force for goodness, stirring in many to be present as goodliness, that all-powerful force for good, that is God. This can disprove the atheists thinking that eventually science will destroy religion, which it may well do, but it will not destroy faith in God. There is a huge difference.

Of course, to believe something, we have to 'want' to believe something, generally, that is until the obvious is so undeniably shown or demonstrated to us, like Thomas putting his finger into the stoma in Jesus's side. But, generally, we tend to believe what we want to believe, and atheists and agnostics may be very comfortable in their lives with the positional thinking they have come to. They may even be prepared and willing to try to convince others with the rightness of their thinking. It can make 'good sport' testing their reasoning, but, like puppies playing, at first, play then getting rougher, until they or someone stops the fight. When someone disputes and then refutes our opinion, we are tempted to think of prejudice and bigotry. But they may be thinking that of us. Oo-err.

The selfish feelings that go with the 'closed' mind may be best left alone. Brow beating someone with one's own philosophies can be very unpalatable, and it's better to think, 'Do I want to be liked, or do I want to be right?' Go for friendship every time. Influencing the thinking of others is never easy. And as it's said about dinner parties, best avoid religion and politics.

Books have been the media for spreading and disseminating ideas for centuries, and still represent a very assured way of making one's point. Some books become so revered that they become almost idolised, sanctified even, as in the case of the Bible and the Koran. People get to believe, seriously believe, every word written, which is sad. Sad because they have blinded themselves to the obvious conclusions. Both were written by man. Neither is a contemporaneously written record of events that are vicariously assumed to have taken place. The Koran's original scripts, like the writing of the Bible, had to be interpreted into their modern-day language using words as best that could be found to represent what was thought by the religious scholars to be the meaning meant when the words were originally written. And there is scope for fallibility. As a consequence, it is never safe to believe implicitly in what is said in the Bible or Koran. It is more sensible and realistic to read the message, to look for the underlying message to determine for our self what the message is. Bear in mind it was written for a generation now nearly two millennia ago, when much of life was ignorant of scientific understanding, superstition was rife, and so very different, primitive even, by the standards of today.

Often there are contradictory passages, which the devotees of 'the Book' are keen to gloss over or dismiss, and whilst the Bible is interesting and inspiring, it can be helpful, like a crash course, just to draw nothing from the Old Testament except the Ten Commandments, and from the New Testament just draw the Beatitudes of Christ, and the story of the disciples, who became the Apostles and the Lord's Prayer. Hopefully, even atheists as well as agnostics have taken time to consider these 'Key Features' of the 'Policy' before adopting their preferred philosophy on God.

Many of us spend our working life following a set of written rules, the 'rule book,' the firm's written 'Policies and Procedures.' It's so staff know what they should and shouldn't do, can and can't do, for and on behalf of their employer, who, in the last resort is responsible for the torts of their staff. Civil servants have their 'rule book' and aim always not to 'blot' it and risk harming their pension. Their pension used to be almost their sole aim in life, their 'raison d'être,' being poorly paid, slaving for a good pension in the end. These days they are relatively well paid in the middle and upper echelons and notwithstanding are still fighting to hang onto their exceptionally good pension.

But why let our real life, the real us, 'who we are when we're not at work,' be dictated to by another 'rule book', especially a book of policies and procedures that has not been updated for centuries? Companies and HMG update their 'rule books' continuously. But to live a life by an archaic rule book that should be referred to only for historical referencing seems hardly right, hardly relevant or sensible.

Referencing, yes. We draw strength from referencing, and today let's call it 'filtering,' as we do when shopping on the net for our preferences. Filtering for the relevant, to underscore our searchful thinking, or just to see we have a wider scope to our thinking. No, we don't need a book of rules, but, like a dictionary, when we want to check on the meaning of a word, it's good to have it on the shelf – for referencing.

There is nothing too fundamentally at variance with the thinking of atheists and agnostics, at least those who have thought the issues well through. It's just that their thinking has not been extrapolated sufficiently towards a worthy conclusion. It's like they are driving a car, driving extremely well, proficiently, down a motorway, and not yet realising they are on the motorway going in the wrong direction. It is a case of, 'Yes, I am on the M4, I know I am on the M4; look the blue sign says M4.' And our reply is that yes, you are on the M4 but going towards Wales, not London.

They can leave at the next junction and rejoin the motorway and go in the right direction, or they can turn on and believe their in-car navigator, always assuming they have entered the correct destination!

If we are at the bus stop, and the bus comes along with the destination we really should choose, and the bus stops, opens its doors, we should get on, ignore those getting off, if any, and don't worry about the cost of the journey, because the money, just enough for the trip, will come. What we are saying here is that having thought through as best as we can, researched, referenced all the best of the world's philosophies on the meaning and purpose of life, do we have to believe, or should we believe in a spiritual existence?

Some merit exists in getting as far as agnostics and atheists have gone, in that they have at least rejected the 'cranky' obsessional beliefs of the many world religions that have irrational, completely irrational beliefs. Irrational because reading their basic tenets alone is so potentially exasperating.

Is there any hope for mankind? Why do we have to live our lives depending upon believing in some external fate-imposing, ultra-intelligent, purposeful, all-powerful deity who 'has given' us a book of rules 1500-2000-5000 years ago to obey? Is it the book that makes us dress differently, including the wearing of odd hats; eat differently as in selectively, grow beards, turn to some geographic point on the compass and 'pray' with a regularity almost of a heartbeat, and in doing so prostrate ourselves, and ultimately at some time in our life make a pilgrimage there. Oh! We are so governed by our beliefs, beliefs adopted or inculcated in us from young, most of it coming from someone's interpretation of the book. Surely, we should be educated, as in trained, how to think, to research, to philosophise and then to make our own choices. Schools should teach about the 'great religions' (there's not time enough for the small ones) not just the one 'faith,' that particular religion that funds the school's existence.

How many agnostics and atheists ever use the words so popular as an exclamation, or even as an expletive, 'Oh my God,' the OMG phrase, or even 'Good God!' Such phrases are in common parlance, used without thinking, unfortunately. We should, but we don't think before speaking, before uttering those phrases. We should only ever say what we mean and mean what we say. Which is to say, as the Irish comedian used to finish his programme with, 'May your god go with you,' an evocative choice of words, implying that we all have a different god, be that god a deity, or that earthly sybaritic oasis in our life.

It is very possible that atheists choose not to believe in God because to them, they see, as almost everyone does, that if you believe in God, you are inevitably religious and worship according to one of the great religions that have the existence of their understanding of God as their fundamental belief. And it is those religions that the atheists are 'kicking against,' they see God and the religions together as 'the deal,' and particularly the 'organised' religions, not the alternative, minor, weird and cranky religions. And they see the major 'organised' religions split into denominations, factions and sects from which they conclude that the thinking of those factions must be muddled; and so from that they conclude there is inadequate logic to hold the thesis together. And they'd be pretty much right.

Meanwhile, the agnostics, half of their mind thinking like an atheist, the other half 'minded' to a kind of guilt for not accepting or answering the siren call of the Sunday bell or the muezzin's call to prayer. It's like someone not voting on General Election day because they can't decide who to vote for; can't decide because they've not done the research, and very understandably cannot discern the differences from the 'blurb' the political parties spew out in the hustings, the foam on the broth, not the raw ingredients.

It is indeed very possible, very acceptable to say when asked, as one is from time to time, 'Do you believe in God?' and answer, 'Yes, I believe in God,' but quietly add, to dispel the questioners' preconceptions, 'But I don't suppose for a moment that my understanding of God is the same as yours, or the same as many peoples, and I am not religious.' If the questioner is at all a thinking person, that should give them something to think about.

Books are sets of ideas set down in print, and this can include non-fiction as well, because even these books, whilst aiming always and only to present facts as they have been researched from any records and others' writings, or as generally seen through a camera lens, the facts are presented as the author or authors see them. But books, those sets of ideas, thoughts occurring, rising and nurtured enough to be set in print, as this book is, are capable of carrying messages and conclusions, true or false through the ages, through history. Some ideological zealots think they can suppress ideas in books by burning them, but that would only work if they found them all, which often they can't. At other times they just have a ritualistic burning, a symbolic rejection of those ideas and principles the book hosts. Well, we all love a bonfire, but most emphatically seldom go along with the burning of books.

Consequently, it behoves us, before jumping unthinkingly onto any ideological bandwagon that turns up, to use our God-driven intelligence to work out simply, benignly and lovingly what in the reading of the book makes sense; for if it doesn't, it must be nonsense, and then we should have 'none of it.' And so, it makes the book just an allegory, but if any attention to the book is to be paid at all, as a serious work, perhaps it'd be better if we made it be part of a wider and personal research project.

If we can accept that there is a life force that drives the metabolism of plants and animals, is it not reasonable to argue that that life force is the power of god, the power of all goodness or some aspect, some variant, version or derivative of that power which is argued here in this book is synonymous with God, the concept of God as here propounded? And yet, as we have to admit, all life on earth is dependent entirely on the life-giving qualities of the sun, our sun, one of very many stars in the universe.

All forces, at least here on earth but probably universal, can be thought of as having a direction, towards an outcome. The forces, being there, are they randomly spread out, as in deployed purposelessly? Or are they directional? Gravity and magnetism certainly are directional. Gravity is non-influenceable except to other gravitational forces, but can be overcome by enough kinetic energy. Electricity is by way of being directional, ever seeking to flow to a lower potential difference. The light energy and associated 'radiations' from the sun are omnidirectional like the force of goodness, omnidirectional unless refracted or even polarised by some means or another.

It may be helpful here to put forward an explanation or two of certain phenomena that can be attributed to this force of goodness. Consider the open wind blowing at a steady 20 knots coming up against a row of houses with narrow gaps in between. The wind 'funnels' through gaps and the speed and so the force of the wind at that point is increased. Consider rays of sunlight falling on a lens and passing through but diffracted by the shape of the lens and the rays becoming focused on a point of such energy that it will ignite any combustible material at the focal point, and just about every material we know is combustible if the igniting temperature is high enough and if oxygen is present. In a similar way magnetism can be increased in its power, its effect, as in electromagnetism in dynamos and electric motors to produce kinetic energy. It is heat and kinetic energy that bring about all sorts of change in our world, in industry, in commerce, in pretty much all of life. Likewise, it is so with the force of goodness. Under some circumstances it becomes so focused, diffracted into a more concentrated force, and physical changes can be brought about; it is so with the Power of God. Think about healing of the sick; and think about intellectual inspirations, and changes of heart; think about the Virgin Mary and the Immaculate Conception, all seen as miracles in one way or another, now with a physical explanation, or at least metaphysical for those preferring their perception of metaphysics.

Why do we have to have beliefs? Why not just stick with what we can see, feel and hear (yes, and smell, too) as the facts of life. Why do our excellent powers of imagination, by which we have created so much in our evolution, our societies, now over thousands of years since the change of the period of Homo erectus to the supremacy of Homo sapiens, insist, as it were, in coming up with notions or beliefs that we can only imagine, like suspicions, and not prove? Are such thoughts appropriate conduct at all, just because we have the gift, the power of imagination?

All imagination is based on superstition. We conjure up abstract things like companies, that, then having buildings – they're real; staff – they're real; and shares, not real, they are imagined. The money that changes hands for an exchange of shares is in a way not quite real, but the shares are abstract, even though represented on paper like monies, are the product of imagination, of superstition. And so it is with God, with Gods, the Gods of Jews, of Muslims and of Christians; taken and then feared as products of our imagination. It seems true enough that a man called Jesus existed, and so did His disciples, the Apostles. They've been documented and accepted as authentic. But who was Jesus and who were his disciples? It's pretty certain that Mohammed existed: it's so well documented. Many Islamic males are given the name of their prophet, their Mohammed. Oddly, by comparison, few Christians would be comfortable being named Jesus.

It's their supposed teachings, rules and requirements that enter the world of superstition – How much of what is in the Bible and Koran is 'for real,' is true? And if not true, as in provable, then surely it must all be superstition. We have a choice, to believe it as true or not. Those three religions can all argue certainly that their versions are true, and we can make it four religions if we include those followers of Messianic Judaism. Well, they would all argue their corner, wouldn't they? But we don't have to believe what they say, their argument, their reasoning unless we want to, or we just can't help ourselves.

And there's the rub, we tend to believe, to accept, only that which we want to believe, 'minded' to believe, as they say, and as a result that's what we become: a Yay, and not a Nay, a No, or just another Don't Know. Then if a Yay, and so very convinced, much too convinced, we can become a zealot, a fanatic, even a terrorist. Shame.

CHAPTER 32
THE DIVINE TRUTH

Many brains, much greater brains that this author's, which would be seen as feeble by comparison, have allotted their time to ponder and to discern, maybe divine even, the meaning of truth. However deep into the depths of philosophy one may ever wish to go, the rest of us have to get by with what is best reckoned and assumed, and that is that we have a child's understanding of what truth is. And that is 'whatever is known, recognised and accepted as a fact and is or was known to be a reality.' Yes, there was an earthquake in Peru on such and such a day because a hundred people, named people, died. We can accept such things as true.

When it comes to the witnessed truth some challenges arrive. We may attest to what we saw, or think we saw. Think we saw from the angle we were at. The physical phenomenon of parallax can deceive us. Sometimes we are surprised at how mistaken we have been in the conclusion we drew from what we 'saw,' and later often shockingly to have to accept it as what we 'thought' we saw. And what we thought we saw was for that event, to us, the truth, until other, more accurate evidence showed our belief in what we saw was mistaken. 'I promise to tell the truth, the whole truth, and nothing but the truth, so help me, God.' Let's look at 'nothing but the truth.' Sometimes we are so keen to establish what we are saying as a truth worthy of being accepted as such, that we tend to embellish, embroider the truth we are elaborating upon, to be more convincing. Bad practice, especially in a court of law.

About the whole truth we can imagine there are occasions when we kid ourselves we are being of service to justice and probity if we impart just enough truth to feel that we, ourselves, are being honest, at least honest enough to be seen and heard as an honest person.

Sometimes we don't want to impart the whole truth, the whole knowledge, but knowledge is power, and with money to hand, very much more power or enough power to gain some money, as in bribery, blackmail or plain inducement!

There is a spectrum, a cascade, with truth at one end and lies at the other, with graduations in between, in the middle sits ignorance. So, we can know the whole truth about a situation and tell the truth or we can lie about a situation, telling it, the lie or, as the in-between to two 'extremes,' we can find we are ignorant on the matter. This can be blissful, but can leave us ponderous.

As said elsewhere in these chapters, we first learn to lie, probably from siblings or even from listening to our untruthful 'at times' parents. Kids can know when their parents are telling the supermarket delivery man a 'whopper.' Often children watch and listen to us, the adults, much more and earlier in their little lives than we give them credit for. Children lie to avoid some withdrawal, seemingly, of unconditional love or approval, or merely to gain something even as simple as another cookie. 'No, Mum, I've only had one cookie today!' Liar, she's had two.

Detectives, fictional and real, have the ability to beaver away at a witness or an 'accessory to the fact' but especially at the 'perp,' who's not yet exposed, not yet proven. They beaver away until the façade of half-truths is broken down to reveal the whole truth. They have used their special, almost intuitive skills to 'divine the truth,' like a water diviner with his hazel branch going over the ground until the rod in his hand twitches, where, after digging, a supply of water is found. And it is likewise with the truth being divined. The truth diviner uses his or her intellect and experience to closely watch the eyes, the face and facial movements, eyelids, eyebrows, nostril and head movements, hands, fingers, leg movements. In all these, the detective can scent the lies, whilst divining truth.

The oath in the court of law finishes for those who accept the God-fearing position, will say, 'So help me, God!' What a curious notion, derived from yonks ago, back in history when most in this country (England) were Christian, God-fearing people; people for whom survival meant if life gave away as any successes, believed they were derived from God, who would then deliver retribution to one or one's kith and kin in return for any ungodly behaviour, or a 'plague on both their houses.' God's Truth was required of all underlings. The lord of the manor could lie his head off, until it actually did come off after he had made a quick confession to God in mind and heart before the axe fell under the King's order.

So, the oath is either saying, 'God help me tell the truth,' which could mean that by telling the truth, if I tell the truth, will the villain I am condemning have me maimed or killed in revenge and may God please not let that happen? Or is the oath saying, 'If I don't tell the truth and tell a whopping porkie, will God please forgive me? I am only human and if I told the truth I would lose something I want to keep or value – like my life, or those of my wife and children?'

Going back to the spectrum span of 'truth through to lies,' there are recognised to be some people, some delusional people, whose grasp of the truth is poor; the very concept of truth seems to have passed them by, completely. They lie easily, so easily and out of habit, especially when business affairs are involved; totally deceiving, misconstruing, misrepresenting, lying, cheating tradespeople and dissembling. Telling these porkies are biggies, and they matter: of consequence for someone, sometime, somewhere.

Lying can come from 'storytelling' often about their past lives, or more likely how they wished their past lives had been, the exaggerating to look big, more important than the reality. Harmless lying possibly, no 'biggie,' as they say, but there is always the lie that is deceptive, deceitful, hurtful even, and they come from the lips of those 'Billy liars' so easily that they believe, or almost believe, the lie they are telling. We'd best avoid them or humour them. To confront them could mean the end of a 'friendship', an acquaintance, but if it's a family member? Who wants rows? Only if it's a 'biggie.'

God's Truth is the Divine Truth. The truth of God that is godly, containing only godliness. Pure, simple honesty. It's the meaning of the expletive, 'Cor, strewth!' This derives from the expression, 'God's Truth,' but today that slang is rarely used in any situation where the need to say 'In God's Truth' would apply. It's just an expletive used by some. People often say in discussion, 'To be honest …' which could be taken too literally as that they have not been honest so far, or that they have decided against embarking on, and were just about to tell a lie. The phrase we should use instead of 'To be honest…' is to say what we really mean, and that is, 'To be explicit…' or 'To be more precise…' Or simply, 'To be frank.'

God's Truth is taken to mean the absolute truth, the absolute undeniable reality. We instinctively know and believe that God cannot lie, so God's Truth is incontrovertible. It follows, then, that to lie is ungodly, which we all knew anyway. So we use the phrase 'God's Truth' to underscore what we are telling, saying it's not only our truth, but God's Truth, too. If we are ever to convince someone of an incontrovertible truth then there had better be others who can be a witness to that truth, because it is so unnerving when we are disbelieved.

The absolute truth is genuinely what we believe to be so, unshakably believe to be true. We tell and resolutely believe in what we saw, read or heard, albeit now sometime ago, but we trust our memory implicitly, and we then are telling with no ulterior motive, no negative schemes or 'unfair weapons,' the plain, simple, unvarnished truth as we know it. We can do no more. It is sad and frustrating, a travesty even, if our truth is not accepted, just not believed. If they don't want to get on the bus, it's their lookout.

It is what we understood to be true, even if subsequently shown up to have been mistaken in what we saw, even what we heard, smelled or felt. It's what our human senses told us, how we interpreted them, those sense organ-derived impressions on our mind, to enter our memory banks, to become lodged in our minds as true.

And that which comes from our heart is believed. From our heart, that seat of all love and emotion, and believed to be true and told, should only ever be told, poor humans that we are, as others seek to divine the truth. 'So help me, God,' the truth, a divine truth; the Divine Truth.

CHAPTER 33
AN EPISCOPAL LITURGY –
YES, YOUR WORSHIP

The First Commandment, as stated in Church of England communion service, goes: 'Thou shalt love the Lord thy God with all thy soul, with all thy strength, and with all thy might.' From the earlier chapter we have seen that in essence we are embracing, nourishing and willing ourselves to be continuously mindful and aware of living a life full of feeling and giving out that sense of the good in life, whenever we can. We have argued that God is all goodness and is all that is good in life. So, the Commandment is to strive to recognise all that is good, especially the good in people, which is mostly far from our minds when meeting people in our daily lives. It could be a business meeting, with a first-time meeting with someone new, or someone we have done business with before. Because of the business being conducted, providing it is fair business and not crooked business, any thoughts of our business associates' innate goodness are likely to be far from our mind. But both parties, if striving for a fair business agreement, and only ever wanting a fair business agreement, will be 'embracing' the goodness that is of God.

The same goes for personal relationships. 'God chooses our relations, thank God we can choose our friends,' as the saying goes. But if we are 'to love one another as we love ourselves,' as the Commandments require, then we will have to do better than to write off our relations as the saying above implies.

A reasonably good 'self-esteem,' a worthy self-esteem that gives us a healthy contribution to our peace of mind seems an essential prerequisite to 'loving' other people. We all use the term 'love' to have so many applications. 'I love that painting' or 'I love your new kitchen;' it's just a term of general or hearty approval. The same goes for loving a character in a film, or even the actor playing the part. And the local cake shop blazing across its bows, 'Made with Love.'

We are introduced to someone, say the local Mayor, and most would not say they 'loved the Mayor,' loved meeting the Mayor maybe, the meeting being a happy interaction between two people who had not met before. So, what does it mean to love one another? It simply means to show them all goodness, all the goodness at all times that we have; in other words, not to speak in negative terms, to deal fairly with them always, even perhaps at our own expense in both material and spiritual terms. 'They may dissemble (be untruthful) but you will not find me so,' is a good motto. (Yes, and 'Thank you, Lady Catherine de Bourgh.') And so, 'For the love of God,' all the other Commandments fall into place.

What does it take to be a good Christian or even just good, a good person as in the case of a humanist, an atheist? Many devoutly practising Christians will always include 'going to church.' This is open to question, and if not question, then certainly open to discussion.

We use the term 'church' generally to mean a building, a place of worship. It can also refer to the abstract concept of that body of followers of the faith, who work towards keeping their faith alive, serving its precepts. It seems from the very earliest days that all the major faiths emerged feeling there was a need to build an edifice dedicated to their beliefs. Mainly simple edifices at first, a place to gather, to worship, to reflect, to gain inspiration, to make Holy, and out of the rain and bitter wind. It has been more or less so since pre-Christian times, with many churches becoming the predominant building in the community, especially as the wealth of the 'Church' increased.

Buildings became steadily ever bigger; cathedrals taking 100 years to build, and taller, more complex 'temples' to their God. Taller to help their prayers get to God faster, it being then a shorter distance to Heaven, or so they thought; which is rubbish, because we are still building taller and taller successively as the challenge to be the tallest, for a while at least, in the country or the world, and all are secular, but the top floor could always be rented out for prayer.

Many cathedrals have since become admired features of architectural splendour and nowadays cost an enormous amount to keep from deteriorating and crumbling, falling down. And yet we ask, 'Are these buildings necessary?' – don't they just represent how the carrying out of religious practices, the robes and candles, the bowing and genuflecting, have all become part of the building, and veering towards 'cult' practices rather than worship, simple worship? It is natural to take shelter from the cold and rain, although we do expect our troops in the field to contend with such things, open-air services will have little appeal unless the content is sufficiently uplifting to become truly satisfying of our spiritualistic needs and comforting to the soul. But would we stand and listen in the rain? Men might, but not many women. And yet crowds of both sexes will stand in the pouring rain to watch Wales beat Ireland in the Six Nations. At the open-air service, there'd be no collection, would there? (There being no building to maintain.)

Great preachers often look to deliver their message in the open. The point being that buildings intrinsically cost, plus they need organisational talent to operate and maintain. There is much beauty in simplicity, and a place of worship needs to be no more than that. And yet, once a building or a room has been dedicated for worship, it behoves us to keep it solely for that purpose, so that at anytime one can go and visit, and meditate, contemplate and pray, encouraged by the atmosphere of solemnity that the room or building acquires. Too often these days trendy vicars and the like have started using churches for social functions, even semi-commercial, like the temple in Jesus's time in Jerusalem, when he questionably 'lost his cool.' Do we never learn?

It is virtually impossible to sing when in a foul or grumpy mood, including hymns. So, joining in the singing can help shake off that mood. Inconveniently, some tunes, some words in hymns and chants can enrage some of us as just too preposterous, and why do we have to endure the 'endless' grinding on verse after verse as we wade through the excesses of the hymn writer's enthusiasm for 'prattling' on in his/her own chosen words of musical praise?

So why have hymns? Many groups gathered for some social reason find the need to 'burst into song'; as in football crowds, club groups such as nautical types and many other groups on a rally and generally after a meal and drink, fireside 'Ging-Gang-Gooly etc., and in the stadia 'Abide with me.' And then there's the specialist groups called choirs, who get together just to have a jolly good sing-song and often 'compete' whilst somebody has been chosen to judge and rate their performance. It's bonding for all for that moment, and 'bonds' congregations in church – fleetingly for the while, but when Monday morning comes?

Originally, probably well 'Before Common Era' (aka BC) began, a secular pagan midwinter feast was held, and it was a rare opportunity for the masses to eat some first-class protein, that the general peasantry were very short of in their daily lives, unless they 'got lucky' with a rabbit or a pigeon! That midwinter festival was adopted by Christians as 'their festival of the birth of Christ' (reckoned and believed to be somewhere about the time of Dec 21 – Jan 9th) depending on which calendar was used or believed and by the reckoning of the stars in the cosmos.

The issue for many is whether Jesus Christ was and/or is the 'Son' of God – whatever that means. That He was 'of God' should never be disputed, the story of His life and His message confirm that. Was He born of a virgin? Even today our still simple understanding of the cellular processes that take place in reproduction – the meeting of two haploid gametes (with a single set of chromosomes – egg and sperm) to form the diploid foetus (double set of chromosomes) – this is sexual reproduction. The queen bees reproduce the worker bees by parthenogenesis (reproduction asexually) as in 'Dolly the sheep' cloning, and the queen bee only every now and then mates with a drone bee (male) to produce another queen.

It is entirely possible one day for a child to be born without sexual reproduction – in fact a clone – but Jesus was a male born to a woman and therefore somehow the male Y chromosome must have been introduced. But did Mary produce a diploid egg with a Y chromosome to give birth asexually to a boy? The appearance of the Y chromosome in an otherwise XX chromosome being takes some imagining, but a mutation is not impossible to imagine in biochemistry and genetics. We now know in 2018 that certain wavelengths emitted from LED street lights can bring about genetic changes, mutations in humans with DNA, alterations such as triggering cells to cancerous cell divisions and multiplication.

The point is – does it really matter? – Christmas celebrates the birth of a boy who was 'of God,' bringing goodness into the world – it is right to celebrate such a birth. But how to celebrate it? There is really only one way – with love, the peace and goodwill message. Sadly, commercialisation has overtaken this message, but on the plus side, the boost to commerce 'oils' the wheels of the economy giving employment and so a livelihood for many. But perhaps only the well off can afford high ideals, which is odd, because often the poor and needy respect and value principles and ideals at least as much as the better off in society, or so it is often said. And why should it not be so?

To many, 'Church' signifies grand, old buildings, but not always old and not particularly grand. It's good to have a cover from the elements where like-minded people all meet, like a clubhouse. Church also signifies men and now women in robes with solemn countenance, the singing of hymns to organ music (where else is organ music heard these days, no longer adorning cinemas but only in church and the odd town hall?). And there's candles, as if expecting a power cut. Why the candles? What would you answer a child asking that question? Why sing hymns? How would you answer that? Or even, why the funny robes, and hats and strange sticks or rods? Don't even think about bicycle bells and sweet-smelling smoking, swinging things on a chain!

And this is what humans do. We get together in smallish groups, coteries really, and follow a set of custom behaviours, because it's traditional, i.e. gone on for centuries, for so long, in fact, we wouldn't dare change it, or even question it. And that is mostly because almost all of it is either symbolic or originally purposeful, but the reason or the purpose lost to history in these modern times. It seems only politicians dare change traditional things, often for change's sake, as they are restless souls, always thinking they can make a difference. Well, yes, they do, but mostly things turn out not quite as expected. So what? They are not on performance-related pay.

Going back to candles, so symbolic of God's light, 'Let your light so shine forth in the world,' as we have seen in a previous chapter, the analogy, the commonality, and the comparison between the physical properties light and the force of goodness, of that inner soul we are born with, like a flame wanting, yearning, needing to be fed, nurtured by loving relationships, else it is snuffed out.

Is it necessary to go to church to be a good Christian or even a plain, simple, faith-holding Christian? Let's look at what going to church can mean. As alluded to earlier, Church is like a clubhouse: what goes on in the clubhouse is 'worship.' It used to be just worship, but churches nowadays are opened as meeting places to drink coffee (e.g. as in Hereford). Quite what Jesus would say is open to conjecture. But churches are so desperate to find a means of appealing to the populace, they are coming up with all sorts of ideas, mostly any idea, so long as it doesn't question what it is about the services, the modes of worship, that are not so appealing.

Although likened to a clubhouse, a chain of clubhouses would be more appropriate. And as in any large organisation with a chain of 'outlets' there has to be some uniformity, indeed conformity to the procedures, the brand of product, that go on in each clubhouse. That way if, or when, local priests get tempted with bizarre ideas or when people move about the country, there is a 'guarantee' as to the quality of the product on offer, else there'd be, 'We do this here, but they do that there,' and then the squabbling would start. And the chain requires some central administration and control.

Not mentioned so far about what goes on in church, is the reading (out loud by someone) from 'the Book;' the revered book, which is the core facet of the faith. Each faith has its book, like a book of rules, like a company's written 'Policies and Procedures' on how we should do things, in case we can't work it out for ourselves, and let's face it, most of us can't. We need those written goals; those lists to work to. But for most faiths their book was written so many centuries ago that some are following the practices as 'ordered' by their book that are very grossly out of date and manifestly and provably unnecessary and inappropriate today. For example, Jewish ritual slaughter of animals for meat, and Islamic 'halal' meat. There is no sound reason for it today, for, however much and however well they argue their corner, any reasoning intellect will know that both are cruel practices, even with prior stunning of the animal to be slaughtered. We can guess at their feeling of superior exclusivity and of their feelings of their grander ideology as kings in the slaughterhouses, as if the rest of us are inferior in habit and inferior in thinking; we, the rest of the populace, who eat meat without the ritualistic slaughter. It's like, 'Oh. I always get my food from Fortnum's (meaning how superior my predilections are, and as if the food is better),' and 'Oh. I always eat kosher meat; I think it tastes better.' But in fairness, there's much sense in only eating plain meat and not meat containing 'processed' meat products. It has been found again and again that we just cannot be sure what we are eating. That meat pie: it said it was beef, but was it beef? How often is it shown up that the meat-processing industry is either corrupt or hopelessly incompetent, or possibly both?

So, wherein lies the cruelty? It varies around the world. Without thinking about the prior gathering and penning of these 'dumb' but noisy creatures, the ruminants, with their rumen full to the brim with gallons of rich broth of semi-digested grass and grain food, in many cases are placed into a rotating drum and turned upside down. This is the most unnatural and terrifying position for these particular creatures, and then their throat is cut. Anyone doubting cruelty should go to visit a halal or Jewish slaughterhouse. Even with pre-stunning, the delivery of the electric shock to 'stun' them first has little in the way of valid appeasement. The ancient rules require a kosher or halal 'priest' to see the animal chosen for their meat is alive and so assumed to be healthy, to bless and cut its throat to kill it and so it will 'bleed out' to help the meat to stay fresher longer. Whereas we non-believers already have ante-mortem and post-mortem 'meat inspection' to see the animal and its carcase are healthy for human consumption, and the animals are electrically stunned into anaesthesia while standing, and bled out when stunned. The bleeding out is what brings death to the animal. There is no need for priests, uttered sayings, prior inversion of the live animal, stunned or otherwise, but their archaic rule book says they must. The methods the rest of us to be sure our meat is healthy to eat are very adequate for the purpose.

If a large company, indeed any company is to survive, it will regularly update its policies and procedures to keep them relevant to its customers of today. What can a church do to 'update' its mode of worship, for its customers? If we could imagine going back to the life of Christ and becoming one of His followers, one wonders what Jesus had intended would happen to the new faith He had created, now two millennia later.

Already established in Israel of the day there were synagogues and temples, men in fine robes, and readings from the Book, the Torah, and the giving of money. Yes, and candles, too, in all probability.

Quite why did that birth happen to be one of the race of the Jews? And why there, in the land of the Jews, those formerly meandering twelve tribes of Israel. And why at that particular time, that age or era were they blessed with the giving of birth among them of one whom has since been called the 'Son of Man.' These are the questions. Of all the world, why there? Why not in ancient civilised China? Or ancient civilised Egypt or England with the warring factions all painted in woad? Or with the Aztecs in South America, or among the Sioux in what has since become 'the States?' Was it that in the 'Middle-earth' there was a certain stage of enlightenment, as in a spiritual not a scientific enlightenment? Spiritual as of Moses and the prophets, so close to God. And yet, is scientific enlightenment not of God, too? Think of all those who have enlightened the world, such as Newton, Stephenson, Edison, Curie, Pasteur, Hawking, Dawkins, Hoyle, Whittle, and Tim Berners-Lee, the inventor of the internet. And why choose then, that time, that era to send Jesus? Could it not just as well have been a hundred years earlier, for example, or a thousand years later when perhaps the Crusades might have been unnecessary?

And why then also, some hundreds of years later after Christ, there's another birth, this time an unheralded birth, the birth of a man whose philosophy and actions were to form the basis for one of the most powerful dynastic religions to rise and challenge Christianity, to form a warlike evangelism spreading to nearly all the countries bordering the Mediterranean Sea, with a battle cry that in effect said, be one of us or suffer an unpleasant death. A philosophy, a company policy quite 'foreign' to the thinking of the world of Christendom, which then had to take up arms to defend itself against this newer creed. If Christ had come a thousand years later, would there ever have been Islam? Would there have been Christianity?

And so it seems that there was already an established 'protocol' for worship since early times, robes, bells, candles, buildings and chanting, and the Christian Church has followed suit, which was a pity, and a pretty unimaginative pity at the time. Oh! But haven't we always wanted to build temples? Then various groups formed breakaway churches adopting variants of styles of worship, and with differing views of the interpretation of the words in the Book, the Bible and now the New Testament.

Seeing that many faiths seem to be there just to prepare us for death as a transient phase we go through to reach the afterlife, and if Christians have Jesus as their raison d'être, as their means of entry in the 'afterlife', what do the other religions have? What do they have to support the idea, that product of their imaginations, that there is an afterlife? Is it just because their Book says so, where someone once wrote down an idea, a thought, a dream or just an imagining that there just has to be an afterlife, if only we knew how to get there. 'Ah. Yes. I know. Let's build a temple, with an altar, and we will make sacrifices, sometimes sacrifice little children to show how obedient we are of the instructions, as we read them, in the Book. And candles, and scents and chanting. That should please our God, and we must do this regularly, every week, or come to that every day, and even several times every day.' And never let a chance to turn to face the east, from whence comes the sun, our source of life, and say a few prayers, asking to be admitted when the time comes to that afterlife (and some will turn up there, knock on the gates asking for endless virgins, no doubt).

We can question if communal worship, as practised, is a necessary part of being a Christian, a follower of the teachings of Jesus. Jesus was a Jew and so will readily have endorsed those Ten Commandments that purport to have come from God to Moses, on the top of Mount Sinai. There's no denying they are of

God, but whether Moses chiselled them himself or they miraculously were given to Moses, as cast in stone or clay, and some with many words, they must have been heavy and not easy to carry down a mountainside without dropping. Just a thought, but it's probably been asked before, and many times, questioning in such detail. These days, one could come down from Mount Sinai with all Ten Commandments on one tablet, no doubt bearing the illuminated emblem of the forbidden fruit, symbol of Eve's recalcitrance that started 'all the trouble of the world' (if we can Adam and Eve it).

The breakaway groups have become the denominations of Christ's Church today. Imagine a young person, drawn somehow to a feeling of perhaps he or she might like to 'go to church,' and not having had a religious upbringing, ponders which of the several denominations he/she best attend. Each is sincere in their religious practices, and in the past, different denominations have argued against each other, e.g. Roman Catholic (the 'first' and original 'Church of Christ') against nonconformists. And so finding a mode of worship that suits one becomes a matter of trial and error. One can go from very high Church with lots of formalities, 'bells and smells', statues and banners, to very low Church with plain and simple décor and usually a reputation for 'Bible-thumping' sermons, and with prayers as long as sermons, and sermons as long as books. Oh, the knees will suffer so.

But the point here is, 'What,' we wonder, 'would have pleased Jesus?' Of course, He would have known man's love of making 'rules' and 'clubs' with observance of their customs and practices. His injunction that says, 'Where two or three are gathered together, there I am in the midst of them,' could well have become dented or even thwarted in seeing today's modes of worshipping spread over so many denominations.

The Gospels refer to Jesus talking of 'Man's Rules' and 'God's Rules.' Man's Rules say that only a qualified celebrant can administer the sacrament of Holy Communion and this is probably very wise, so that the reputation of the celebration of the Last Supper continues to be a solemn and revered act. It strikes as odd that when dining out, at most good, 'classy' dining establishments and houses, we are offered bread in the form of a roll at the beginning of the meal and at formal occasions especially, we can have the choice a glass of port (or Madeira) at the end. The bread and the wine. Often at the start, grace is said and at the end the wine decanter is passed to the left. A sort of communion. So, at the start, the senior, usually the head of the table, could say in the grace that as we break the bread it is in remembrance of Christ's broken, sacrificed body, or, if preferred, 'With bread we honour the Body of Christ's Church.' And later, before sipping the port say, a toast: 'With this wine we honour Christ's Covenant.' These days there need be no reference to eating Christ's flesh and drinking His blood – so misguided an interpretation of the significance of the Last Supper and so off-putting to many. In those days there was a great belief that each of the emotions was seated in the various organs of the body. The liver for fear and cowardice, the spleen for hate, spite and venom, the heart for love and passion, the womb for hysteria (this gave rise to 'hysterectomy') and so on. The body, 'the soma' from which 'somatic' is derived, was the strength, the power to do things, get things done, the organisational framework, the broad, powerful back, from which hangs 'the splanchna', meaning all the organs, our soft underbelly. The blood was the source of life, the spirit that flowed around the body and the organs, and kept each part alive, and they understood that when blood flowed freely, i.e. it was spilt, life drained away and death supervened.

And so, when the bread is blessed, as in it is consecrated, it represents the body, the strength and the power to get things done, the framework that holds the emotions, the bodywork of His Church, the Church of His followers, not stone or bricks and mortar, but the grouping of His disciples, all of us now, who follow His word, His teachings, to get things done, or at best, all that our feeble attempts can achieve. The bond, but not in bondage, the esprit de corps.

And then, when the wine, the port is blessed, consecrated, it represents the spirit of the new covenant, the new promise of God through Jesus that sins can be forgiven and there is life hereafter; that is to say as Jesus said, 'No man can come unto the Father, except through me.' That is the promise, the covenant, and Jesus is the propitiation for our sins, or to put it another way, Jesus will be our advocate in Heaven on the Day of Judgement. What, all of us, all who have ever lived, judged on the same day, all dead, er... I mean, all the 'quick and the dead,' judged all on one day? Are there days in Heaven? Surely not. Surely the day just goes on and on. No night (night-time, when on earth bad things tend to happen). None shall sleep. Our bodies need sleep. No body, just the spirit, no sleep needed. Nessun dorma. Or each soul has its own Day of Judgement, soon on arrival. Saves that big queue, waiting. Everyone wants and will get their 'day in court'.

This communing, this communion, with the spirit, the emotion, the passion, the faith. Yes, it is all symbolic, but what is important is the common thought that goes with it. The common thought, the belief that Christ lived and died for a purpose, for our good. How so? By being subjected to Man's Rules, and found innocent, and even so, Man's Rules lead Him to be crucified, and in retaliation, it was demonstrated just as the 'Book' predicted, He rose from the dead, just as He had healed the sick, made the paralysed walk and the dead to wake up, He rose from the dead, and showed Himself to His closest followers. Why not to everyone? The Romans included? How much better that would have been; then we'd all have the absolute, incontrovertible proof we all thirst after: how easy it would make it for us, to have that proof. No more wondering, hesitating, doubting, disbelieving, no need for factions and other faiths, that absolute proof. We'd all know we just had to be good, or else. For sure, no choice.

Too easy, my friend; we can't walk into Heaven that way. How would we ever get to be worthy, as we should, under our own steam, worthy of the goodness of Heaven in our afterlife? Got it? The covenant. The promise. Let's not forget it, in the daily hurly-burly of our lives, God's promise to us, 'Follow the ways of Jesus, believe in Him, and the way to Heaven will be made open to us.'

'Drink ye all of this' is the phrase reported as used, meaning this symbolic representation of blood, His blood' (and 'all' means as in 'everyone' and not all as in drink the whole glassful, goblet-ful or even 'Holy Grail-full'). The most we are allowed is a sip of the consecrated wine, never clear why – surely even one good mouthful wouldn't hurt, would it? What strange practices these religious ceremonies have. It's not that His blood was to be drained away as in that He died as a result of blood loss, as in an ex-sanguination, but that His life was taken, sacrificed, and the life-giving, life-sustaining medium that flowed freely round His body under pressure from the heart, the seat of all love, stopped.

And that thought might stay with us in our daily lives until we are fortunate enough to re-create the symbolic gesture next. For many churches that seems to be weekly now, but in the mid-1850s even quarterly was considered enough, even by some clerics. In the Church of England, an institution ordered by the Episcopate and the Synod, almost every service now is a communion service, and for some, this is just too much, especially for newcomers, seeking a form of worship, a simple form of worship, of 'going to church' as too much to swallow, too intense for them to swallow. Whatever happened to Matins, a beautiful service? It was virtually wiped out and disappeared, as it were, overnight, some years ago. When asked why, a cleric answered that the congregation, the snowflake generation, preferred the communion service. Stuff and nonsense. If that were so, why the increasingly empty seats?

Why not keep it simple and save the more severe form of worship for those devout and for those new, only when they feel ready. It's hardly surprising church numbers are falling. Even with symbols clashing and drums and shouts of 'Hallelujah!' they aren't winning congregations. How about the informal gatherings as Jesus did, on a hillside, to hear Him preach? No bells, no candles, no fine robes, no roof over our heads, Well, there's always an umbrella, for the rain falls on the just and the unjust (but mostly on the just, if their umbrella was stolen by the unjust).

Has anyone ever noticed how few men sing hymns in church? When asked, they will often say, 'It's too high for me,' and all the women are singing like gusto. If men knew how to sing the harmony, the bass line, they could join in. But they don't, so hymn singing becomes the painful part of the service as hymns drone on verse after verse (well, the hour has to be filled somehow). No hymn should be more than three verses and that's one too many. At Prince Harry's wedding the hymns were only two verses. Now there's a chap who knows a thing or two. How to keep the troops interested and alert.

Then the sermon. So often quite unrelated to our daily lives, even our whole lives, going some way back and so often are boring, didactic and an insult to our intelligence. Mostly purporting to be an interpretation of the Book from a priest inculcated into the 'right' way of thinking in his or her three or four years of training. They deserve sympathy and it's no small wonder many go into furlough to rest and recover from their arduous, seemingly unrewarding work, their sincere fight against Mammon with one hand tied behind their back by the restraints of the rules of their denomination, the Episcopalian Liturgy. Each is in effect a sort of trained counsellor, which is good, but the strain of that, coupled with the perception of how they want to come across to their congregation and others, is hard and telling. How often does the service include prayers for the clergy, to pray for their sanity, their level-headedness, their comprehension of the impossible task they have taken on, shepherding a flock of sheep that has only limited understanding of the nature of God, and are much happier with their anthropomorphisation of the deity. And what happened to prayers for The

Queen and her family and HMG, that they may govern with humble probity?

Not all clergy feel it so, of course, but certainly a fair few. If married, then once in post as the vicar or rector (he who once received tithes from the villagers) it will soon show if he has made a good choice of spouse, for so much will depend on her (or him), how she (or he) can skilfully get into the part of the vicar's wife (or husband) and keep her husband (or wife) content and happy as he (she) daily goes into battle with birds of smaller or just different brains, that can be so exhausting. [Now, if we read the previous sentence again omitting the words in parentheses (brackets) – it then reads as it should, naturally, as it has done for hundreds and hundreds of years, innocently; surely only a few would get shirty, then uppity and want to burn a book written as of yore. Female activists would even like to take the 'man' out of 'woman' if only they could. But if they did that would just leave 'wo' and woe unto them and their crass nonsense.]

It is in the common parlance that we use the word 'God' so unthinkingly: it comes out as an expression of surprise, pleasant and unpleasant, it's even shortened by some to the 'OMG' phrase. The TV 'garden makeover' shows, the 'room makeover' shows, have the beneficiary led in blindfold so that when lifted the sudden revelation of the new look garden or room, the gasp, the covering of the gaping mouth, and then after taking a breath, the universal instinctive exclamation, 'Oh. My God.' Little do they realise what they are saying.

The word 'God' has been used to refer to the chosen 'Gods' of populations through history as in Greek gods, Roman gods, Egyptian gods etc., and one star on TV saying, 'May your God go with you.' So, it seems that mere usage of the word itself does not mean it is taken in vain, it's more a case of how the word 'God' is used.

The Jews' and the Christians' God has 'delivered' Commandments which are the essential tenets of the faith. Whether we believe Moses came down from Mount Sinai with ten tablets of stone or not is not really material to the issue. The point is that each of the Ten Commandments is a very powerful statement as to how we should lead our lives. And why should we lead our lives that way? Is it just to get us into Heaven? Or is it because it's the right and decent thing to do? But hang on a minute! An atheist would say, 'Hey, look; the first four of the Ten Commandments require you, or at least assume you believe in God, so I need only observe the final six to be a decent person.' But we say, to observe the other six and in so endeavouring to be a decent person, you are in fact loving that which is good, all that is good, and God is all goodness, and goodness and goodliness are God. That force of goodness, and the love of all that in life is good, is the love of God. Stop thinking of the anthropomorphised God, that avuncular powerful being sitting up there in the clouds with all those buttons controlling everything, at His fingertips, and think instead of the metaphysical power state, that force, that invisible, immeasurable but undeniable force that goodness is. Think of it as an ethereal plasma, ever present, but unseen, if that helps. And, knowing what an undeniable force that goodness is, we can only ever revere the name of God, soberly, admiringly and humbly as the power of goodness. No sane person would ever mock or denigrate that which is good. Always recognising that which is good, as opposed to that which is not good, and so possibly deserving the tag of 'evil,' is not always easy. And because it is not always easy, we need to recognise, accept and endeavour to observe the first four Commandments as our help and guide. QED, Mr Atheist.

In the First World War the German soldiers had on the buckle of their belts the words, '*Gott mitt uns*', translated as 'God is with us.' Obviously, someone in the upper echelons of the state thought this would inspire the soldiers and the public at large in Germany, and later in any occupied countries. It is certainly thought-provoking, although one little French girl, having seen it and on being told that the German phrase on the soldier's buckle meant that 'God was on the side of the Germans,' she replied, '*C'est-ne rien, nous avons les Anglais!* So, was the decision to imprint the buckles a cynical ploy of an uncertain nation, or did it spring from a sense of injustice that Germany was being forced to fight for its survival again? Again? Did it have to? In 1871 Prussia brutishly bullied the local princedoms into forming the new powerful Germany, and that frightened the French, who then piled in against this new upstart, united states of Germany. And now again, in the First World War, the French, aided by the British and for a while the Russians, and the Americans eventually and latterly, which finally tipped the balance after four weary years threw their hat in the ring as well. It's clear the Germans started it; their paranoia, their fear of encirclement by treaties, and was God on their side? How can the power of goodness take sides?

On an intrapersonal basis, we know a great deal more about what makes us tick as individuals, and so how we can elicit the best in someone, in the sense of how to have a good relationship with someone by recognising their fears and their ambitions? But at a national level, at the diplomatic level, are we any more advanced in our strategic thinking, and so our diplomatic thinking, which becomes the front we present to other nations? Are we still keen only to appear as an uncompromising swashbuckling Sir Galahad, ready to do battle if we can't get our own way? Or should we just be totally horrid and send agents to smear Novichok around the place while claiming to view a cathedral, and not a very special one at that. How about Peterborough next time, Vladimir?

Certainly, the use of God's name on the side of a conflict is an attempt to grab the moral high ground, but the Christian countries opposing the Germans (e.g. France, Russia, Great Britain and USA) would surely have seen it as taking God's name in vain. God doesn't take sides even when Christian is fighting non-Christian – fighting is not of God, but it is necessary sometimes, just to survive and to bring about peace as soon as possible, again by means of our armed forces – our 'blessed are the peacemakers.' And when our nation goes to war, those left behind fill the churches, suddenly devout, get out of bed on a Sunday morning, no brunch, and go to church and pray like hell that we will win.

The people have suddenly 'found their faith' and as an instinctive reflex, a knee-jerk reaction, turn up at the Sunday service to pray for just two things. Firstly, that husband Tommy in the Army will survive, and son Jack in the Navy will survive, and then add that no nasty bombs will land on our house and flatten us all. Yes, we are praying for ourselves that God in His Heaven will hear our prayer, and so direct the hand of fate away from my loved ones and from me. We go to pray, and it's 'Okay, well, I will sing those hymns and the droning chants I never know the tune to, and listen to the general prayers, to save everyone and the country from the evil of the Devil, the enemy, but honestly, I am just here, really thinking, hoping and praying for me and mine. I promise to be good for the rest of my life, never ever steal again from the greengrocer, and certainly never ever let the milkman do that to me again, I'd rather pay his bill in actual money; I promise, if only you, er, sorry, thou, will save me and mine.'

Many churches and chapels have been closed in recent times due to insufficient use, and too costly to keep open. Each is deconsecrated and then tuned into a bijou residence, but the Gothic windows are retained as the planning authorities reckon everyone must know that you are now living in what used to be a church. When war comes again, many will have no local church to turn to and the villagers desperate to pray will knock on the door of the old chapel and ask if they can come in and pray. The owner, being a non-believer, looks at the motley crew and tells them to sod off, he's not having that scruffy bunch spoiling his feng shui, and anyway, I have a houseful already, but then adds as an afterthought, there is a stable at the bottom of my garden, you can use that, and also just beyond and through the bottom gate there is a green hill, not far away, from where you can see the city walls.

There has to be an advantage to the Episcopal Liturgy, but it doesn't jump out at one. Every Church of England church in the land is following the same format up to a certain point in the service must mean something. The unregulated second half, as it were, gives the vicar or whoever some free rein, within his or her training, and it includes the sermon. In general, they keep their sermons ready to deliver again many years later when hopefully no one in the congregation will come up to the vicar after the service and say, 'I enjoyed that sermon today, and also enjoyed it the last time you gave it.' Like TV repeats.

Each sermon carries its intellectual property rights. They may publish some of their better ones, years down the line, like the sermons of John Donne. Perhaps they swap them around to save the resorting to an uninspiring effort at the end of a tiring week. 'He's working on his sermon and doesn't want to be disturbed as he (or she) grabs a well-earned break from the bleating of the sheep.

The good sermon can make a great impression on the congregation. It's a splendid part of the service where the congregation can sit back, and nothing is asked of them for 20 minutes other than to stay awake, or if unable to stay awake, at least not to snore. Some will listen, some may comprehend, some may be cynically dismissive of the vicar's notions, and others will let their minds wander and range over anything that happens to be going on in their lives, or some random fancy such as the fine features of the young woman, or man in the opposite pew, that, with just a furtive glance every now and then to stoke up the admiration and perhaps the worst of our imaginations, bounding into a fanciful world of ecstasy. Dream on, lover boy.

The same question keeps popping up. What would Jesus think if He came back to see our Episcopal Liturgy? Would He take to the nearest hillside and preach His Word in the open air? No costly building to maintain. No statues of saints, no hassocks, cassocks, surplices, no altar, so no sacrifices and no hymns, definitely no hymns and definitely no collection. But hopefully some loaves and fishes though, afterwards, for the undernourished, but that shouldn't be what we came for.

A certain kind of worship? Yes, Your Worship.

CHAPTER 34
THE LORD'S PRAYER

Known and loved throughout the Christian world and yet, do we ever stop to think, 'What do the words and phrases in the Lord's Prayer actually mean?' By the philosophy expounded in this work we are here to use the power of goodness in us, and in the world, to work out such answers for ourselves.

The Bible records that Jesus replied to the question 'How should we pray?' with this prayer, which is given to us as the most powerful of all prayers. When we pray, we set our busy, hectic, sometimes frantic lives on hold, press the pause button so we can open the app that enables our conscious mind to 'sync' with our soul, that burning flame flickering with the spirit that is the essence of life within us, and for those moments, we know who we really are, no shamming, no acting up, our personalities naked and as vulnerable as the day we were born, and yet so ready to go on from where we are, right now.

We should understand that prayers are forms of affirmations, positive statements made in the present tense of what we are aspiring to as if already achieved. The shy person's affirmation, 'I enjoy and am confident in company.' At our prayers, it is likely we will be considering our frailties, how we would like to be, how we aim to be and more importantly what we would like to have or to see brought about, for someone or for ourselves.

It is not at all easy to bear in mind that prayers are affirmations considering what the words in the Lord's Prayer mean. It is not a begging plea to a godly personage ordaining our lives, which would be that poor result of a simple-minded anthropomorphisation of God. It is the traditional lay view that a prayer is a plea, a request, giving 'someone else' the job, somehow to answer the call, the call to satisfy a need.

It will be seen in the Lord's Prayer as most commonly presented, is in three parts. Firstly, there's the acknowledgement of the existence and magnificence of

God. Then there are the supplications where we say to God, 'Give us this day our daily bread and forgive us our trespasses and deliver us from evil'. Then there's the closing phrases of further recognition and adulation of God's power. These last closing phrases were not in Jesus's originally reported prayer in the New Testament but were added by the early or medieval Church and have become accepted today as an integral part of the prayer.

This addition seems to follow the often practised literary teaching practice of essay writing: in three parts, an introduction, the message itself, and then 'closing' summary. In personnel management, it resembles the 'Tuesday sandwich' of staff motivation and improvement, where the message delivered by the manager is to praise the employees for what they do well, then tell them what they are not doing well, how that has had what a detrimental effect for the company and how you want them to do it better. Then, because this is, in effect, a criticism of them and their performance, finish off by praising them again for what they do do well. A sandwich, these days probably symbolically called a hamburger, a programme, a menu, like the settings, delivered on Tuesday as the best day of the week. Mondays are too phrenetic and staff often still in a dream from their weekend's indulgences. Thursdays and Fridays are too near the weekend because if a staff person is left feeling reprimanded and undervalued, he can brood all weekend and hand in their notice on Monday. Wednesday could be the day, but Tuesday is the best day. Believe it. We have time to revisit the matter in the week if there are any repercussions, anything misunderstood, time for more moral support from the manager or colleagues before the weekend.

But let's get back and go to the gospel version of just two parts, which is, as far as we know, the more accurate definitive version of Jesus's words. And let us remember always, if it is right, as is thought, that he spoke in Aramaic, and what he said was written down later, much later, and certainly not contemporaneously (would that it had been). Today it would be captured in a mobile phone video clip and on YouTube in a flash. The point is that we need to assume that in the time interval between Jesus uttering these words and their being recorded in writing, there will almost inevitably be some inaccuracies. There will be some differences, some loss of detail, a loss of meaning, especially in local translation, perhaps just due to local accent or vernacular, as in a man from deep olde Cornwall, writing down what he thought he heard spoken in Newcastle. Never Glasgow, please, he couldn't get a word down, could he, eh,

Jimmy? And so, some errors inevitably have been made, albeit hopefully only small ones; hopefully of not too great a significance.

And then there's the loss of complete accuracy in meaning, of understanding or the sentiment behind Jesus's original spoken words due to the loss in translation from language to language, for example from Aramaic to ancient Greek to Latin, through to Gallic French and so to modern English and other European languages.

Having said that and given acknowledgement to all that above, we can now start to look at what we can work out as the meanings for us of the words in the Lord's Prayer, using our understanding of God as the 'power of goodness.'

We start with the words *'Our Father.'* Why not Dear God, or Oh God, or Oh my God, or any mode of address, of initial calling up, as it were, or other rhetorical questions; the international code flag letter 'K' (Spoken as, 'Kay,' or 'Kilo,' signifying, 'I wish to communicate with you'). As far as we can tell Jesus chose these words, 'Our Father.'

Why 'Our?' 'Our' implies some collectivism with 'our' fellow worshippers who use the prayer. Consider a new person being introduced into using this prayer. Immediately he or she will have a sense of togetherness, of collectivism with those who use the prayer, of belonging, even being a part of a collective and thus a sense of being in community of those who acknowledge it as 'the Lord's Prayer.' A sense of collective 'ownership,' or more likely a collective common root or origin of the people. No one claims ownership of the sun or the moon, or even the sky, or magnetism or gravity, yet we, being of the world, could say that it's ours, our world. Villagers living next to a forest will often say to outsiders referring to 'our forest.' If you visit the Isle of Wight, locals will often ask, 'How do you like our island?' indicating most assuredly that they, the residents, are committed to where they live, it's their life and their philosophy. And it's the same with 'Our' in our Father. We are part of the collective, and committed, and it's our belief.

The term 'Father' brings with it so much. Why use the word 'Father?' Thinking away from the literal everyday use and understanding of the word, but more to its deeper meaning, primarily 'father' means the progenitor, the giver of life, and so-and-so was the father of modern medicine, but our parliament is the 'mother' of democracy. Odd that; but then a lot of talking is done there. Well, we can suppose it gave birth to other democracies in the world.

Father also means in the historic context, from early times, of Biblical times

433

through to the modern era, the provider of all we need to grow and thrive, 'the breadwinner.' It also means the one, the head of the family whose 'word is law,' and in a manner of speaking, both loved and feared, as well as respected for the retribution a father could bring.

So those two words, 'Our Father,' alone conjure up and set the scene of our calm, respectful and humble opening thoughts and words, as we seek to address within ourselves the spirit of goodness, of God. We could equally start by saying, 'We recognise, value and appreciate the power of goodness, which is complete love.' It's a positive statement, in the present tense, as an affirmation. Thinking of that, focusing on it, is the same as, or should be the same as saying, 'Our Father.'

Within recent times the leaders of the Church of England decided to change **'Which art in Heaven'** to 'Who is in Heaven.' This comes as a completely mistaken decision in the concepts of this book, seeing that here we are trying to get away from the presentation, the concept, the idea of God up there in the clouds, as a person, a sentient being, an avuncular munificent, with power over all our lives, every breath and every movement. No, in short it was very unhelpful. It was gratifying to hear at the Cenotaph service for 100 years since the end of WW1, a reversion to 'which art …' just for the older servicemen and -women. How kind. No trendiness there, then, on that occasion. Thank you.

The significance of the difference between 'which' and 'who' may be lost on many who received the education in the last quarter of the 20th century, when so little Latin was taught with the concomitant dropping of English language study, a language in which to be grammatically correct 'who' is applied to humans and 'which' to the inanimate objectives and animals. So, we say 'which' art in Heaven. Art is just an archaic version of the verb 'to be. 'Art' is retained as traditional, and reminds us that we are using the same words that have been used by Christians for centuries, and with whom we can identify, even though we are only as a grain of sand on the shore. 'Art' comfortably gets over the need for a more 'wordy' phrase. But it also leads us to deal with the more important phrase 'in Heaven.' Do those leaders of the modern Church really think that to 'get modern' and say 'who is in Heaven' that the pews would suddenly fill up? 'Big mistake,' that wonderful put-down used in the film *Pretty Woman*. 'Big mistake.'

Simply put, the words 'in Heaven' could apply to some a place, a location, but here, Heaven more appropriately implies a 'state' of existence, a metaphysical state of existence for a soul, like a phase of existence as in the 'seed' phase of the life of a plant, or the 'nymph' phase of the life cycle of a tick.

And this is the way we here hope we should look at 'in Heaven.' It is that state that exists of pure goodness, ever present and all-prevailing. No nasties at all, lurking in dark corners, because there are no corners, nothing tangible in Heaven, at all.

And so, we have in mind so far, Our Father which art in Heaven as that empowering force of total goodness that we acknowledge, love and respect. In itself, just taking a second or two to think before moving on in the prayer, it is a prayer in itself, like a simple thought in meditation, stepping off the whirling roundabout of life to acknowledge the existence and the power of goodness, that goodliness, and godliness, and that is what love is.

Also, we could say instead of which art in Heaven: 'We are focusing our awareness on that state of perfect goodness that is love.'

'Hallowed be thy name.' Hallowed – revered as Holy and always to be kept as such. It is a pity that so many people 'bandy about' the word 'God' in their everyday speaking, in particular the exclamation "Oh my God!" used with so little or no thought at all to what they are saying.

The state of perfect goodness is so beautiful, so immaculate, so desirable, so loved, that it should only ever be most highly regarded, respected and admired. And feared, yes, even in its perfection, because we are so lacking, so found wanting, by comparison and we are so in awe and smitten with the thought of our failure. Even the gods of ancient times were spoken of with reverence and respect. Today with all the other beliefs in the world, everyone should instinctively be respectful of those beliefs of others and their chosen understanding of their God.

There are many expressions, mostly exclamations that include the word 'God,' and these should be eschewed with all the same vigour we have been persuaded to find and to ignore all those 'politically incorrect' (non-PC) phrases. Samples are 'Good God, man' and 'Oh my God,' and 'Strewth,' short for 'God's Truth,' 'blimey,' short for 'God blind me,' and 'Good God in Heaven' (as in whatever next?). The American's hallow their flag, the 'Stars and Stripes' and the Muslims hallow their Koran. We ask that the word 'God,' when spoken or written as to refer to God in contradistinction to the generic word 'god,' and God is only ever used in a sense that would hallow God. It is the sense in which the word is used that is important. We, they, anyone, shouldn't use the word in any sense that does not revere.

435

'*Thy name*' reinforces that the name is specific and therefore should not be misappropriated or adopted by for anyone or anything else. Thus, when we think we might want to use the word 'God,' we need think very carefully about the appropriateness of its use, because as we have acknowledged it is 'hallowed.' The same applies to the name of Jesus, and Jesus Christ. It's saddening so much profanity is carelessly, unthinkingly and ignorantly spoken, and even written.

'*Thy kingdom come.*' What was a kingdom, and what is a kingdom these days? As tribal creatures, we are only too ready to accept a social hierarchy of organisational arrangements that have come about, evolved, by which our society has become ordered and orderly.

He, or she, King or Queen, reaches the pinnacle of that social hierarchy. This has come about, mostly as accepted by the mass of the 'tribe,' through acclaim, out of some sense of need of leadership, and so by common consent and acceptance, at least for the time being, or, and in most cases, by the enforcement of and legal use of strength. That strength is loyal, at least for now, to the leadership. And not forgetting, of course, kingship also by an accepted birthright, so far, and for now.

So, throughout history, kings and lords and kingships become associated with a structure of the society that resembles some form of orderliness in and around the lives of ordinary folk. It's accepted as the way it is, the way things are, and the alternative is anarchy, which is generally regarded as the unwelcome, undesirable and physically dangerous chaos.

So, in the words used in the Lord's Prayer, 'kingdom' was used to convey some specific sense of a desirable state of orderliness, the peaceful passage of our time, of living and stolid stability. Or the meaning may have been lost in translation, and 'kingdom' is the nearest and best available at the time of the original writings, and then translations, and the word 'kingdom' has stuck! But people were and still are obsessed with kings and kingdoms. Can't live without one. Who will be our King? Look how the Romanovs came into existence, in history. So, with that meaning we can say kingdoms are part and parcel of life, be they good ones or bad, we simply must have one. Well, that was how it was, and is, but within the old sense, mostly yonks ago.

'*Come*' implies the future, what will come about in the most affirmative sense, and when used here in the prayer, we become aware that that kingdom has not yet come about, at least for us, on earth.

Is this referring to the 'Day of Reckoning' sounded by 'The last trump' or what? The concept of the day of reckoning is enough to put the 'fear of God' (so to speak) into all of us. The word for 'the bill' in a restaurant and elsewhere in the Netherlands for other purchases, is 'de rekening.' Interesting, that.

That Armageddon is inevitably something that many come to believe in, or are encouraged to believe in. The physical universe in which earth lives is capable of producing, or bringing about the end of the world – the collision with massive meteorites, and ultimately the dimming of our sun, many moons hence (pardon the pun), or we all die in a mutual nuclear annihilation. All this is rather uncertain, circumspect. Rather more certain is one thing that will come and that is our death. And it is more likely that this is the notion that applies in 'Thy kingdom come.'

So that that state of Heaven, that state of perfect love and goodness is the 'Kingdom' that is there for us when we die – but with provisos, implications for us – as partly and possibly mostly achieved via the Lord's Prayer, that inestimable gift from Jesus.

Before moving on, it's worth noting something about lords and kings, how adulation comes about, particularly in early history, especially about the time of Caesar. The concept of 'gods' in their 'heavens,' even then, brought about the notion of a 'chief god,' a god of gods, king of kings, lord of the lords, and we have set such ideas as praiseworthy into strident music, which can be all very moving, so thank you, Mr Handel, for your Messiah and its Hallelujah Chorus.

The problem with the notion is that someone, somewhere, adopts a faith with a god who they claim is superior to all other 'gods.' Many faiths deny the existence of other gods; Islam, Jewry and Christians seem to share but hardly accept or acknowledge as the same God, Jehovah, perhaps all very well in origin, in theory, but hardly in practice. The religion of Oahspe accepts that there are other gods, but says that theirs is Jehovih, which is their worshipped god of gods, and is not the same as Jehovah. And so on. It all makes no sense, so it's nonsense. All through misanthropomorphisation, the mistaken attribution of human characteristics to a metaphysical, out of this world, all-powerful 'being,' like a sort of munificent Darth Vader? Why is it our wide imaginations are so narrow-minded?

'*Thy Will be done, on earth as it is in Heaven.*' Notice the use of 'thy' and not 'your.' Again, that implication of possession, of propriety over something, in this case 'will' as in an instruction, an order of God. We are left to work out what that will, that wish, that instruction or expectation is, but it is easy to see that it is to replicate Heaven on earth. 'Will' is a bit archaic these days. The genie asks, 'What is your will, O master?' Not at all the last 'will' and testament. Or is it not? Surely, our Will is our last 'please do what I want with my goods and chattels, it's what I will you to do, according to what I attest below.' And the executor sees this Will is carried out and be done. Be done, then. That you be? Right, then.

We can hardly understand what the word 'will' is meaning when we say the prayer without some prior awareness of what the Christian faith and beliefs are. Very simply put, God's will is that we believe in Jesus and his message of love, so that, in time, we can enter Heaven. As worded, Thy Will be done is possibly a statement certifying that something will happen, or an implied subjunctive, as in 'May Thy Will be done,' which is more likely, seeing that this is a prayer, a supplication, but it is also an affirmation; effectively stating in the positive and present tense, 'Thy will is being done.' Here the affirmation is similar to an affirmation that is so often encouraged and that is to say to ourselves to boost our self-esteem from a low state, 'I like myself, I like myself, I like myself; I really like myself,' so making it as come true now, as any affirmation can do. 'Thy will is being done. Thy will is being done. They will is really being done.' And lo, as we go, we go and do it better. God's will, that is.

'Give us this day our daily bread.' On the face of it, this part of the Lord's Prayer seems incongruous, with a surprising inconsistency, as the rest of the prayer is all 'spiritual' whilst this, superficially, appears physical, materialistic and 'of the body,' not the mind, the spirit.

'This day' can be taken to mean every day, daily, any day, on each day we say the prayer, and if we say the prayer at bedtime, when the day is over, we are clearly not meant to interpret the words literally, more like tomorrow.

Likewise, if we are to take 'bread' literally, we are acknowledging that our food comes as a gift of God, His, of the fertile earth, by the sun and the rain. And that acknowledgement is good, and is as good as saying that from the power of goodness that is God comes the life force by which plants live and grow and seed, and it is that life force that sustains us, and so also all animals on earth, directly or indirectly.

But Jesus seldom spoke completely literally. His words came as something for us to marvel at, and to ponder on as we seek to come to a better understanding of God. At the Last Supper, as recorded, or at least as later written, at the start of the meal, Jesus said as he broke the bread, 'This is my body which is given for you'. Elsewhere in these chapters we have pondered on the possible, even probable reason Jesus chose these words, what was probably understood by the disciples in those days. Now, His telling this to the disciples at 'the Last Supper,' His use of the word 'bread,' may have the literal meaning but rather more likely a wider meaning as well.

The conjecture here is that this invocation set in the middle of an otherwise 'all-spiritual' prayer, is likely also to have been meant to be taken spiritually. The word 'give' may best be taken to mean to 'send us' or 'Grant that we may be with' or 'Grant that we may find ourselves among' and in the context of His body, the source, the strength, that comes from being with other goodly people, of God's goodness, and in today's parlance, 'The body of His Church', His followers, those who love God. We gain spiritual love from the Beatitudes and obey the Ten Commandments. Good people, not perfect by any means, but trying to love God, and all that is good.

So 'Give us our daily bread' becomes 'send us those who love thee to give us spiritual nourishment.' But equally, it could just mean, 'please keep the world turning while we are on this life, so the seasons will still happen, the sun will shine to give life, and the earth with its rain will make it bountiful that we won't starve.' But this is unlikely, said where it comes in the prayer. Incongruous.

Either could be right and theologians with more erudition than this author may one day guide us in the light of a new discovery. Until then, the words, the phrase, is best taken as an acknowledgement of the power of goodness, as being that force for life and giver of all goodliness; it can only bring forth that which is good.

'*Forgive us our trespasses.*' Recently, on the internet, a Christian website has interpreted the original words to translate as 'forgive us our debts.' Whoever wrote and sanctioned this must be a monetarist. Was it written by a follower of J M Keynes? It's a nonsense. It cannot be so, as it is far too narrow, and is even so unrealistic as to be impractical; 'As we forgive our debtors,' it goes on. Right, anyone who lends money or any supplier of goods and services who later hears of hardship of the customer or the borrower, says, 'So you can't pay? That's okay, let's forget it.' Hardly. Something very misleading here! However, suffice it to say, those who 'have,' should – nay, must – consider a clemency towards those debtors who, simply, have not.

'Trespasses' is the time-honoured, time-served interpretation of the original Greek, from the Aramaic is far more comprehensible, as meaningful. By 'trespass' here is taken to mean quite simply 'to go where we shouldn't, as to a dark place' (to use modern parlance). In other words, not to do, say or think so as to dwell on, in our mind, anything that is not of God, not good, goodly or of godliness, and of goodliness, that which is not born of love for one another, as in not loving to thy neighbour – is to trespass. Or in other words, 'to stray.'

After all, there is a whole range of transgressions one can list, that one can commit against another. They're listed in the Ten Commandments (Old Testament) and in the Seven Deadly Sins, but murder, adultery, theft and coveting will do nicely for a start. Real 'trespasses,' and there are more that we can 'trespasses' against our neighbour, or more appropriate here, that our neighbour can transgress against us. And we are expected to forgive, truly forgive, in our hearts, then we gain from it. We gain so much, we can even forgive for the 'selfish' reason that we know we will feel better, healed somehow, by forgiving those who have transgressed against us.

As said elsewhere, by forgiveness we do not have to expect any reparation, no accord to be created or re-created with the transgressor. Just to forgive in our heart is all that is required, and 'Heaven knows' that is hard enough. So, as we pray that our trespasses are forgiven, we are acknowledging that the forgiveness will, can only ever be, to the exact degree, the proportional amount, that we can forgive others. 'Tit for tat,' so to speak, because we need also to learn the art of self-forgiveness, because it is so good.

Being loving and forgiving of others, to others, engenders, or so we pray, that we in turn will be treated likewise. And it can shake our faith, if we aren't forgiven by others, for like as not, on this earth, we may well not be.

'And lead us not into temptation.' Temptation can be a 'flash' thought, that comes suddenly on us most unexpectedly, perhaps most inconveniently, suddenly 'naughtily' as a 'Do this' and 'Do it now' as in 'Take it, do it, no one will know.' It is a thought, a choice offered by the mind, another of the thousand decisions we are expected to make daily, what to wear, whether to shower etc. etc. Simple routine decisions and then the day starts and presents much more detached, 'difficult' decisions, requiring more thought.

Temptation can also be a slow, long, 'festering' series of thoughts, planning something not good, not of God, one of the Seven Deadly Sins, or a transgression of any of the last six of the Ten Commandments.

Our minds are programmed rather like computers as in a 'binary way,' we narrow our decisions down to a 'yes' or 'no' option. Temptations are perceptions or reactions to situations we have put ourselves in, or, if we choose to look at it the other way, situations that others have put us in. The former is to be preferred, because wherever we are, at anytime, whatever situation we find ourselves in, is our responsibility. It was our choice to be there (excepting children, who are 'put' into school). And just because that situation presented a temptation it is our 'fault,' no one else's, and if we succumb to that temptation, it is 'our fault' and our fault alone.

To be tempted, to have a moment or two of temptation is very 'normal,' very usual, and natural. Those tempting thoughts do not mean one is a 'bad' person. But to allow those thoughts to keep recurring, to ponder them, to savour them, is not so good. For example, giving way in the mind to lusting after someone's wife, or husband, especially if he or she tempts us. Rejection of a recognised temptation is often hard, very hard. As Jesus said (as it is written), when in the wilderness 'get thee behind me, Satan.' Of course, no one was there to witness this, and it is unlikely Jesus told anyone what happened in the wilderness, but the message is a good one. Of course, too, there is no Satan, no 'Prince of Darkness', no Devil. This is just a fabrication, a personification made up to fire the imaginations of the fallible and gullible. As we have said elsewhere in these chapters, there is no force for evil, no force of evil, only the absence of goodness, of goodliness; the absence of God's goodness becomes the shade and darkness, just as in the absence of light, and in the absence of goodness is 'disorganisation' and disarray and chaos.

'Lead us not' is the active phrase here with temptation and there is good reason to doubt strongly the translation from the ancient scripts. It is no part, never was and never will be part of the love of God to 'lead us into temptation.' There's enough temptation around without that. But a loving force for good does not tempt us, not test us. Otherwise it demonstrates a disappointing lack of understanding. The Prayer really means to say, 'may we be drawn towards the good, good situations, where we can be at one with the godly. And the force of goodness will draw us only towards a life of goodliness.' No, it's not, 'Do not lead us into badness.' It's the classic situation of the double negative, as in 'There ain't no tea left' or, 'Don't you do no wrong now,' and by not doing it, you'll be good.

441

Well, certainly not bad, but a little more love may be required to sway us more to the good in us. 'With enough love of God, we will not give in to temptation' is the meaning here.

'But deliver us from evil' were the last words of the Lord's Prayer as recorded in the Gospels, i.e. the prayer ended there. *For thine is the kingdom, the power and the glory, for ever and ever Amen* were added by early medieval Christians to finish with a magnificent accolade and acknowledgement of the power and glory of God, so that the prayer finishes as it started, with awe, wonder, acknowledgement and a kind of worship of God.

'But deliver us from evil' reinforces the invocation to draw us towards the good and the godly. The phrase recognises that inevitably we will get entangled with people and situations who and which are not godly and so described as evil, and of 'evil intent' and as a result we will suffer physically and mentally sooner or later, either here on earth or at the last reckoning. And that result brings pain, the pain that which we fear we will suffer.

And so we hope, as we pray, as we affirm that we are being sustained by this, our emboldenment in making this affirmation. And as we do, we are giving ourselves the ability to endure and survive through the strength of God's love, that power of goodness to deliver ourselves from the corrupt, unholy, depraved, wicked, vile, iniquitous, evil badness of this world. We are affirming by stating we have the grit, that strength of willpower, squaring our shoulders, tucking our chin in, bracing ourselves with a determination for single-mindedness, to 'endure,' to 'deliver us from evil.' Amen.

PART SEVEN

WOULD THAT WE WERE

CHAPTER 35
ON A SIMPLE LIFE,
FOR THE POCKET

It is helpful, beneficially helpful, in life to have a clear idea what it is, in essence, that makes us happy. Many will start with money, and then launch into a list of material objects and self-indulgencies such as a holiday on a cruise ship. Sadly, these things do not in themselves make us happy, and the sooner we learn that, the better.

On the other hand, we could come up with the following things such as good health, good friends, a good job, loving relationships and last, but not by any means least, good attitude, that leads to our peace of mind. These are things we can dwell on, and value them, for they have an intrinsic importance to us and to those with whom we live.

Remarkably, none of these things cost a penny, but they are helped by freedom from financial worries, i.e. not in debt, and with some job security, whilst helped by a stable love, adequate food, clothes and shelter. But these last items do require money and, so it follows that all our spending needs to be focused on getting to have adequate but not excessive food, adequate but not excessive clothes, and adequate but not excessive shelter. And to prioritise towards settling any debts.

As to freedom from financial worries, this means a building a reserve for emergency spending, e.g. house repairs and a steadily accumulating pot for our pension – for the time when we are no longer able to work, and knowing the mortgage is steadily being reduced as planned all those years ago when we took it out, or, that we can see our investment assets, our savings steadily piling up to match the outstanding mortgage. The best time to start saving? The Greek saying that sounds like (and they are fond of it) 'Avrio, methavrio,' tomorrow, or the next day. No, no and no. Start today, even if it's only a pound a week, into an account, not a piggy bank, preferably, as it's just too easy to raid when the 'apparent' need arises. Saving is a habit, one we can savour and get really good at, like turning off needless lights and heating. It's an attitude, thrift.

We live in a conditioned society – conditioned to think we work hard: so we must have a holiday. Why is work always accompanied by the word 'hard,' as if no one ever considered the concept that work is work, on the one hand, and hard work is working harder, on the other? Politicians in parliament only ever use the cliché 'hard-working families,' as if work is fine, but hard work is a social injustice and so must be corrected, or if not corrected, then rewarded. But who are the hard-working families and who are those in work, who work but could possibly be seen by some HMG yardstick as not hard-working, just skiving? What stuff and nonsense. For many all work is hard, if they'd rather be lying in bed.

So we are conditioned to think by our 'hard work' we have earned a holiday, and holidays can mean hotels, cruise liners, away from the home, preferably in the sun. But this is not the best way to view a life, as if it's an equation that has to be balanced; I need my holidays because I work hard, or because I work hard, long hours – I must have my holidays. Work is that aspect of our life by which we earn a livelihood so that we can enjoy our time when not working. Fortunately over the last 100-150 years, working hours have become less, and so give a better balance to a working life. The balance is between sleep, work and leisure. We should not resent having to work, if it affords us a better time in leisure. We don't or shouldn't generally resent our time in sleep; we know it's vital, but it's part of the balance. Like all things, too much is bad, and not enough is bad, so we adjust the balance.

And there is a balance on the matter of how we spend our leisure time. Shall we 'scrimp and save' all year round to blow it all in ten days of lazy self-indulgence with the family in the sunshine?' Or shall we go for a less expensive 'break' and invest more in our leisure throughout the year? Hopefully spouses, partners and family will come to an agreement on that issue. But we are not conditioned to cope with an expense, nor the deprivation imposed by our saving, nor the impact of our one or two holiday weeks of hedonistic pleasure being so fleeting, so brief, on looking back. Holidays of that sort? It's all a matter of affordability.

Can we truly afford that expensive holiday, that expensive car, those ultra-expensive clothes, theatre, a weekend away? Have we truly valued these things as things that will make us happy and do they give us peace of mind? Well, 'The Jones always go away, every year, get a tan and come back and boast of their wonderful time. And tell us we should go, really should go, as they cruelly scheme and guess we can't really afford it. (Drat them.)

A good job is a valued thing and what constitutes a good job should come down to a matter of attitude. Avoiding stress at work is important. Remember that it is the person who finds the job stressful, it is not necessarily the job itself that is 'stressful.' People react in different ways and differently at different times. One may find the job stressful, another not so. 'Oh, so he's off again with stress, can't think why.' If a job is repetitive and unstimulating then it can be endured or tolerated while always thinking how it could be made less so, or how we might like to acquire new skills to move on, get a more interesting job. Attitude is the thing here, and attitude is something that can be learned, acquired or adopted and it usually takes practice, but it doesn't come easily.

A family can feed reasonably well on a low income. For example, in a family, the wife, a mother, may choose to remain in the home bringing up her young children rather than go out to paid work, and the same applies to the father or one of a couple of the same sex, who are married or just together, with a child or children. For these, it takes only a small skill set to find out how to avoid more expensive food shopping and focus on fresh, cheaper cuts of meat, fish, and on fresh, loose vegetables and fruit, to make cakes and biscuits, avoiding all the costly pre-packaged foodstuffs. This solution may not be for many, but it is something that can ease the pain of expense.

Our non-working time, our leisure time, should be spent creatively as far as possible, as well as some lazing, and learning is also included in the creative time. There needs to be, for most of us, a period in each day spent totally relaxing, probably in front of the TV, but we should try to choose programmes that stimulate thought, even if it's only valid criticism. In many ways the radio is still more intellectually stimulating than TV and it's so much easier to switch off.

Children of all ages need to be severely restricted in the amount of screen time done and a broadband computer in their bedrooms can be detrimental to their development. Likewise goes for smartphones and tablets. Networking with friends is a complex modern development that is almost impossible for parents to control, as even switching the Wi-Fi router off may not be sufficient to control overzealous use of networking by a child, with 4G and 5G around. As with all potential vices, prevention is best; by persuading the child, educating the child to make reasoned, rational decisions to limit the usage to just enough to obtain and retain friends. Good luck to that, as children are wilful, determined to show their independence, and their collective connectivity, supporting and scheming with others of the same age. Beware social networking. How do we, as parents, appeal to the child's inner sense of who they are to become? Sadly, we have no training in parenthood, and it's the only time in life where there's an exception to the law that says we can't get worse at anything for practice, because with more children, more practice, we can tire as we get older and then the younger children may get away with 'murder' (in a manner of speaking).

* * *

At some stage in our life we should consider our values. It's most unlikely we could live a life and never stop to consider the values we choose to live our life by; or is it? It may be we only considered one or two values when faced with some choice to make, a decision to be made, probably to resolve a dilemma.

Politicians talk about values, family values in an abstract way. People inexperienced in character assessment, especially their own character, might say, 'Well, what are values? What exactly do you mean by values? Does it mean I have to value a big house, big bank balance, a flash car?' No. Those are all material goals that many people wish to achieve in the course of their lives. We mean the course we want to steer, who we want to be, what we want to be, and what we want to be seen and known as. Values are usually certain characteristics which, once adopted and then used in our daily lives, give us a good feeling, a feeling of self-esteem, of being in some control of our lives, not of other people's, and us not floundering, wondering about our self, because we know instinctively, having thought about it first, that we are doing what is right, and right for us. It is how we have chosen and prepared ourselves to act when presented with life's situations.

When helping people to choose their values, many will say they would like to be known as a person of integrity. When adopted as a value, it is one of the highest ideals we can possibly choose to live up to. It means being honest, never deceitful. There is an attitude amongst some that to be honest, one has to declare all, to blurt it all out, to make a clean breast of it all no matter whom the truth upsets, ruins and wrecks their trust or faith in us, or someone. It's best not to subscribe to that view, but if it's a biggie that presents itself, then we are bound to disclose our part.

To lie is clearly wrong. But if we err and then know it, and determine to do better in future, then it's often best to keep it to our self. But if we are asked, then a person of integrity will be honest and endeavour to salvage the situation as best as possible, a damage-limiting exercise. When applying integrity as a value to one's life in business, there are many options to reject integrity in our worldly lives. Deliberately making errors of over-invoicing in otherwise profitable business deals, and backhanders are just some of the issues daily facing us in our work. Some might question the integrity of the fat cats of former public companies.

A big problem is someone taking advantage of us because we are trying to act with integrity and our work colleagues are not. In the last resort, compromises may have to be made. Compromises such as moving our job or risking physical harm to self or family when threatened by those indulging in malpractices and we won't join in. Many famous people through history have died for their principles; let's hope it doesn't come to that.

Usually integrity means much simpler matters, fortunately. Matters like paying our bills promptly and not walking out of the pub without paying for the food, or telling suppliers when they've undercharged us on our invoice. It's doing what's decent, right and honest, even, and especially when it costs you money, possibly money you can ill afford to part with.

Sadly, many feel politics and integrity are uncomfortable bedfellows, being mutually incompatible due to the need to survive and even thrive in that particularly savage jungle.

On the matter of politeness and courtesy, we know we all like to be liked. Why? Because 'I am the most important person in my life.' You are the most important person in your life. When someone is rude to us, it tends to offend, and we think the worst of them – at least for that moment, or if we are unforgiving, for longer. If we are polite we feel good, in line with our values. We are acknowledging the other person is the most important person in their lives! They should feel good. If not, then they have an attitude problem and it's their problem, not ours. Politeness recognises the other person has an importance to the world, at least, even if not to us.

Politeness and courtesy are skills which need to be learned and practised; but they can be ingrained by our upbringing to last a lifetime. To be polite at all times takes concentration and a genuine wish to make the object of our politeness feel good or at least notice our courtesy. We can consider if there is anyone to whom we should strive to show politeness, possibly to correct an unfortunate previous error on our part, an ill-mannered contact.

Many men still wish to treat women with courtesy, and not only those they may wish to court one day! Generally, women seem more feminine and gracious when treated with a courtesy that is arguably due to them. However, with some women these days they are offended if a man opens the car door for them. If men are rebuffed, they can just apologise and say they'll respect their wishes in future. For a man to open a door for a lady is good, but if she walks to the door and doesn't pause for him to open it, he could show his intentions faster, earlier, to open it.

Some people don't make it easy for us to be polite. An example of this is keeping people waiting. For example, having a good old gossip in the toilet room knowing our partner is politely waiting outside for you. It's not good to have to wait to start eating at table while our hostess mindlessly chats on and on, while everyone's food gets cold! The hostess has a duty of courtesy to her guests!

So, politeness and courtesy are double-edged weapons and in a marriage each partner needs to learn how to treat the other with courtesy. For example, we should never ever embarrass our partner in public, even teasing in jest. So much teasing is actually having 'a dig' with a smile on your face. To embarrass our partner in public is to criticise our partner, which is forbidden by these rules.

We should know that we should never criticise anyone as a person. We can focus on saying 'fix the problem, not the blame.' We can say, 'That was not the correct way to do that,' or 'There is a better way to do that.' Not, 'You stupid fool, what did you do it that way for?' So, even in the privacy of a one-to-one encounter, politeness should rule.

Maybe the boss needs to correct an employee. Best by a long chalk not do this in front of his or her workmates, remembering the employee is the most important person in his or her life. So, we don't challenge that. Accept it. We best start by acknowledging the good work the person is already doing, or if a new employee, praise their efforts for the amount of work, however small, which has been done correctly. Then point out factually but kindly what has been done incorrectly and what effect that has on the product or service. Then we can instruct, or arrange instruction, how to avoid that problem in future and finish our meeting with eye contact, and reassure the employee we have confidence that he or she will continue to do a good job.

Basically, politeness and courtesy are just reasonable considerations of the sensibilities and aesthetic senses of others. For example, in someone's house, no matter whoever we are, one of the family by birth or marriage, or an old or new acquaintance we should always refrain from arguing with the owners of the home we are in. Just out of respect for that status. Having invited someone into our home, only for them to be argumentative, is rude. Equally as hosts, when callers arrive, expected or unexpected, then if it's appropriate, we should ask them in, offer to take their coat, offer a seat and then some liquid refreshment. Standard practice, Mr Sulu. Make it so.

Table manners may become slovenly when eating on our own. But if anyone has ever watched pigs at feeding time, then they'll well understand why higher standards in table manners are necessary in company. Speaking with your mouth full of food is so disgusting to watch! It fills us with disgust. Smaller mouthfuls at each bite would make a good start.

People are often instinctively polite when talking to young children belonging to other people. It's because they want to be thought of as 'nice.' Unfortunately, there is little natural deference these days to our seniors. Youngsters seem brought up to act, 'Jack is as good as his master.' Well, so he might be someday, but he's not there yet. For a young pup to stick out and offer his/her hand for a handshake to one very much more senior in rank in society is impertinent. Wait for the senior to proffer.

We should instinctively be polite to anyone our senior in age and social rank. It's not good to be rude to our boss, but it's not wise to be sycophantic either. Older people are generally more sensitive to politeness and often only too ready to take up defensive attitudes. Unfortunately, elderly people can often be difficult to treat with politeness. It costs nothing to be courteous and polite, yet the dividends are truly great. Remember two wrongs don't make a right, and if we are on the receiving end of rudeness, don't retaliate. We will probably get upset, angry and generally feel negative and a temporary lowering of our self-esteem, but we can 'get over' it. If we take a deep breath, be mindful of our adopted value of politeness and calmly deal with the issue, either just sticking to the known facts or apologise, if appropriate, and correct the problem, if possible, as far as we can. Hopefully the person we are apologising to is actually listening. Many people in work are excellent at 'taking it on the chin' from the rude customers from the public. Well done, them. We can genuinely admire such restraint. These types of situation may arise at work, or even on the pavement when there is a 'collision' between pedestrians.

Courtesy while driving tends to be a rare thing. Pausing in progressing along the road to allow someone coming from a side road is something most of us could do more often, especially in rush hour when we all want to get to work. But a sense of proportion is very much needed to avoid a rear end shunt with the driver behind. Courtesy in parking is important, too. Often it's a case of snatch what you can and feel triumphant in denying the place another was already squaring up for. But this will leave us with a dirty feeling, a hollow triumph. However, if we never have a courteous thought in our head at all, it's hardly likely we'll be aware at all of the 'cheeky' cheat we are seen as.

What has been said in all of the above may serve as a fast-track summary on what could be for some a simpler life. And yes, possibly, but hopefully, a simpler life with some inner sense of satisfaction and some movement towards a greater peace of mind and one that just might be a bit kinder on the pocket.

CHAPTER 36
HONOUR

Honour. What is it? – What is it about? What was it about? Where has it gone, or indeed, has it gone?

Honour was a very frequently used word in the 19th century, rather less in the 20th, and so far, heard little of in the 21st century. The term appears way, way back in history, most noticeably in the Ten Commandments: 'Honour thy father and thy mother.'

It seems to have many usages, complex usages, but it is a good word, with a good sound when spoken, and immediately when heard evokes something better in us, appeals to our sense of the right, the proper and the worthy. 'Upon my honour,' said so often in Georgian and Victorian times, and today, phrases with the word honour are used so glibly as to dishonour the term. In parliament they refer to 'this honourable House' and 'the honourable gentleman,' but sadly, there are very many times in the past when the House and the gentlemen and gentle ladies have not behaved honourably. The recent 'expenses scandal,' with some other known examples of misconduct, make a mockery of them referring to each other as 'the honourable member for …' and 'this honourable House.'

Is honour a virtue that one should aim to adopt? The term seems to embody other virtues. An honourable person, at least in concept, would be someone who is regarded as always conducting himself (or herself) with honour. So that seems to mean, honesty, reliability, of worthy ideals, of probity, clean-minded (as in the Boy Scouts' dictum, 'A Scout is clean in thought, word and deed.') – and an upright person. A rector, being an ecclesiastic, has the title derived from Latin – rectus, meaning upright. In short – of integrity. In the courts of justice, a judge may be called 'Your Honour' or a magistrate called 'Your Worship;' both citizens appointed because of their 'supposed' and reckoned worthiness to administer the law of the land. It's a pity some judges seem so out of touch, barking.

There were times, mostly when we were younger, when we were being put 'on our honour.' This was a concept that we may well have experienced quite often, as children growing up. Our parents may have granted us consent, trusting us to behave correctly, to go and do what we promised, and the parent put us 'on our honour.' But do today's parents ever say it to their offspring?

Later, when grown up, we often find ourselves in a position where we have a choice to behave 'On our honour' or not. For example, we regularly read of teachers who have compromised their reputation and livelihoods 'by inappropriate behaviour' with a child or children in their charge. Also, of policeman (or policewoman) who have taken advantage of their position and behaved dishonourably with a vulnerable or gullible person.

It is possible to view all sources of dishonourable conduct as boiling down to just two issues, money and ethics, and with ethics we include sex. Money, as in the need of, probably a desperate need, or just greed, by which greed is to say someone who has money, but just wants more and more. As to sex, it seems such a powerfully distracting driving force, that many high-ranking persons in our society, throughout history, have risked and continue to risk and lose all that they have hoped for, worked for, and enjoyed the high regard of family, friends and colleagues, all lost by dishonourable, inappropriate sexual conduct.

So, clearly it is not easy to be always honourable. We are human; we err. But how? And how can we avoid falling, falling from grace, the honourable grace? Dukes are referred to when being addressed as 'Your Grace.' This is ponderable, like the Honourable Member for ...? Grace and Honour; both very ponderable, we should say 'virtues,' we'd like to say, 'virtues' and mean it. Yes, definitely virtues, only despoiled by mankind's wayward ways.

It helps to have in mind our adopted values, but possibly more helpful if we practise the art and make a skill of working out in advance the possible outcome of our decisions, our choices made. Like a good chess player. Some are better at working out the consequences, possibly people who are wiser, less trusting of human nature, and understanding people's motives better. Like the single girl who manages to refuse all urges to tangle with a married man. Others may find it easier just to rely on a sense, a simple sense of what's right and wrong, of being 'on their honour.'

But today honour seems an old-fashioned concept and a child using the term in the company of his/her peers may be laughed at, and no mean degree of fortitude will be required of the child to stand firm in the stormy winds and rain that may prevail, before the sun shines again. It is because honour is something more than plain honesty, plain fairness, a sense of 'fair play' of probity. It denotes character, who the person is, and who the person comes to be known as. Then 'upon my honour' carries meaning and weight. We still say, 'I will honour our agreement.' A shake of hands is a symbolic gesture when an agreement is made: 'Let's shake on it.' There's no need to spit on your hand first!

'Honour thy father and thy mother' is the Commandment when the term 'honour' shows another of its meanings. It seems to command unconditionally, too. Supposing a parent is a convicted thief, or a drug addict, a bully, an unloving vicious person towards you, their child. How can the command be valid? That we love our parents should never be questioned; it is instinctive, automatic, even if we cannot admit it, even if it is not demonstrable for any one of a variety of reasons.

If, unfortunately, a parent's behaviour makes that honour hard work, or seem false, we nonetheless should strive to recognise and accept that there almost certainly must have once been worth there, in their early lives, and that there is still that latent goodness existing in us all. But, if honouring a parent is still too tough a job, then we can just avoid dishonouring them. So, to honour them means in this case here more a situation of not dishonouring the parent, which is to say we would do nothing to harm them physically or financially, or do or say nothing to anyone to denigrate them.

Their disreputable behaviour almost certainly comes about through life's unfortunate consequences: a lack of love along the way, a lack of education, a deprived upbringing, the misfortune of poor health, and any one or more of life's sad exigencies. And in the case of an alcoholic, a drug addict, the parent's mind and personality have been chemically altered, either temporarily or permanently, and so, like an elderly with Alzheimer's disease, they are effectively not the same whole person they were originally, and any misdemeanours on their part are entirely forgivable but may well be beyond the help of their offspring. But they are still our parents and so should still be 'honoured' as the Commandment requires.

When looking back into 'honouring' our parents, and indeed others we consider worthy in our lives, it means we can respect and show our approval and approbation. An honourable person will always speak in positive terms of his or her self and other people (with the notable exception of a judge when passing judgement on a villain or murderer). It is so easy to slip into being judgemental or critical of others. The important word here is 'speak' (which for practical purposes includes to 'write'), i.e. always to speak and write in positive terms about a person or persons. If we cannot say anything positive because we don't want to be false, then say nothing. We may not agree with someone's actions or point of view but if we are to be fair, to be adversarial, we would wish to hear and perhaps acknowledge their reasons for their actions or opinions. In doing so, we can speak in positive terms about those things, those actions done. But if we are to speak in positive terms, we would not say, 'You are wrong,' or, 'You are foolish,' or say even worse of them, as a person, and avoid our being so very judgemental. We can criticise the deed, if that would be valid; we can argue with their opinion, but we should not criticise the person.

When we criticise the person, we challenge them as a person, their persona, their self-concept and their self-image and their self-esteem. That is the person they see themselves as, and the person they are aspiring to be and in that, they have their pride, which may or may not be a worthy pride or possibly a false pride, but in either case it is not our job to challenge someone that way. A neutral position demonstrates a positive decision to avoid negative feelings that can be and often are so self-destructive.

An aggressive young tyke may challenge us with a 'what are you looking at?' (meaning why are you looking at me that way?) and we can think we are looking at nothing much, but it would be too challenging to the young tyke's persona to say, 'Nothing much,' unless we were looking for real trouble, a punch-up, a head-butt and a stabbing. We don't fight with pigs: they enjoy it and we get dirty.

Even as late as the mid-19th century, there were, until outlawed, duels fought for 'honour.' And also, most incredibly, for the honour of their friend, the seconds fought a duel as well. Imagine, maybe two totally unknown to each other, fighting for their 'friend' whose 'honour' has been challenged, and often fighting to the death or serious maiming. It's all such uncivilised nonsense, all of the flesh, nothing of the Spirit of God at all, no understanding of the love of the power of goodness. Instead, just a stupid interpretation of the sense of one's honour, turned into vanity, even to the extent of proving one's honour to society as news of the duel leaks out. All so wrong, but this is why vanity is the worst of the Seven Deadly Sins. It seems redolent of stags fighting in the breeding season.

And finally, and let's be absolutely understood – there is no such thing as an 'honour killing.' Such a notion is clear ignorance of honour and a gross disreputable distortion of a word, as a sense of all that is good. We may be honoured for our conduct in battle, killing lots of the enemy, so helping ultimately to bring restoration of peace; but that honour is a recognition of our skill, or courage or for carrying out our duty, not for the deaths brought about, for the sadness of the relatives of the killed in action.

Of course, there are several other forms of honour. For example, there is the honours system where 'honours' are given by The Queen to those who have served the country in some special way. They may be ennobled as the highest honour down to the OBE (Order of the British Empire – such as it is, the Empire, what's left, that is, in 2019). There are honours degrees in university, awards that are one up on a general or ordinary degree, which may have been granted just for being there, however thick the graduate might be, just for the simple fact of paying their fees to attend the course and help keep the university afloat and the Vice-Chancellor in some luxury.

But a foremost interesting meaning is the near-archaic use of honour when applied to women. For example, a woman's virginity was referred to as her honour, in the sense that loss of virginity outside of marriage meant that she had 'lost her honour.' If known about, because the servants somehow always seemed to know or find out, and they couldn't button up, she was regarded as 'spoiled goods' and this seriously meant a loss of almost any chance of making a 'good' marriage. The term was also applied to a married woman, and in this case it referred to a woman who went outside of her marriage for a bedmate. Again, she had lost any sense of honour and respect. As many would note, the term was not applied to a straying husband. In marriage we agree to 'love and honour' – so important. An offer for her honour translated in those days into a proposal (of marriage?). Such a married woman knew her loss of honour in her heart and mind well before it ever became public knowledge, but to the philandering husband?

Almost everything that is not honourable comes with an alternative, optional word beginning with the letter 'D'; as in deceitful, distrustful, defrauding, disobedient, delinquent, disreputable, disgusting disingenuous, and so on. 'Dis' words are readily demonstrable as aligning with and synonymous with the negative state, which state, as we have said elsewhere, is where there is little of the power of goodness, of God, and of godliness.

Honour as a concept is an all-embracing term for many ideals of conduct.

It wraps up just about all other worthy ideals so that honour can be taught as a preferred and desirable, useful conduct, and worthy of being taught to our children. Every single day, never a day goes by without us coming up against dishonourable conduct, mostly read about in the newspapers or on the news media. It's as if we can talk about honour at the dinner table, or at home and answer yes, Mama, or yes, Papa, and then go out and forget all about any notion that to act honourably should apply to us, or be expected of us; only of other people.

Often for gain, as in money or fame, some dishonourable conduct is practised, as in the cricketers who hide their scratching of the ball from the viewers, in a vague hope that it will help their team win, by cheating. Shouldn't they use their imagination and 'go to the end-of-the-cinema-film feeling' and anticipate how they will really and truly feel on winning; the cheers and congratulations gained, only by cheating? But we know their win will go sour in their minds, and even the money gained will go sour, as it is frittered away, disrespectfully, in their shame.

Honour and rectitude are worth striving for.

———•———

CHAPTER 37
TRUST ME

How often do we hear 'Trust me, I am a ...' this, that or the other, as if to say we should grant our trust on the slightest of pretexts, but probably a claim to some authenticated skill or other? There is an old Chinese proverb of very much an individualistic interpretation that said, 'Though a woman bear you thirteen children, trust her not.'

It's funny, as in odd, how we use words frequently but seldom stop to think what we really mean by them. 'I trusted him,' the betrayed wives and girlfriends cry. 'I trusted you with my money,' the investor says to his broker. 'I put my trust in you,' says the anxious parent with the erring teenage offspring the parent is trying to train. But it can just be a simple reliance on someone carrying out an action as agreed, or promised, such as putting out the refuse bin while we are away on holiday. It's where concepts of trust and reliability overlap.

Trust would seem to be a placing of faith, a reliance on someone to do or not to do, to perform something or be something. It's a reliance on any other person. In placing that reliance, we are expecting something of that other person, or maybe faceless persons if establishments are concerned.

So, the decision to trust is a choice we make. When it comes to the affairs of the heart we usually make the decision to trust as a matter of instinct. After all, when we're in love, who listens to the voice of reason? What has reason got to do with it? Everything, unless we are prepared to risk getting hurt, after which we will probably feel like never trusting anyone again.

So, if we are going to make a decision, even when head over heels in love, our conscious mind must ask the question, 'Why should I trust this person?' and 'What do I know about this person?' How open a personality has this person got, what do the eyes say? What does the body language say? Have I explored the values by which this person lives his/her life? Are there any values at all? In other words, what is this person's character? Has this person any identifiable ideals?

If we decide not to trust this person, that is always a good decision. Good because we can always review it in light of further experiences. Good because we will have no unrealistic expectations to bring us disappointment. It doesn't mean we don't or needn't like that person. Only a very few special people in our life will ever be worthy of our trust. And when we have placed that trust, is all then well? No, it's not. On two counts at least. One is that our reasoned, entrusted person may still let us down. Our assessment may have been wrong. The entrusted person may change in themselves as they go through their life, and, despite their adopted values, they err occasionally, as all we humans do. We may not always have behaved ourselves in a way that encourages or enforces a trusted person's character. It is impossible to have any form of relationship with another person without the other person being influenced by that relationship. If we take a suit into the dry-cleaners, the contact with the counter person is minimal, but even that brief contact can influence, even if only temporarily, the feelings of the counter person. But when we live year in, and year out with someone, the influence we have over the other person's life is so great it can be terrifying, if we truly stop and think about it.

True companionship can be likened to the potter's hands moulding the clay, but with the clay also outstretching a pair of clay hands and simultaneously moulding the potter! Surreal, perhaps, but truly frightening, too! We can live with someone, so closely, in good regard or with disdain, that each has an effect on the other, so chronically and imperceptibly that each changes as a personality, over the years, to become someone almost quite different from the person and their character 25 years ago. 'You're not the man I married' syndrome, to which anyone can guess the response and it is this concept, the concept of being deserving of the trust placed by another person, the concept of reciprocity and of mutuality, that aligns with honour. Did the betrayed wife change so much in her ways that the husband came to realise his wife was no longer a worthy, deserving person to place her trust in him, and so why should he feel he should keep that trust?

Trust and truth seem to go hand in hand. Is there anyone who has never told a lie, except for Christ? Should we ever trust someone who we know is a liar? If we are all liars, are we not, then should we ever trust anyone, ever? Can we say, well, it depends on the lies? Surely there are lies that we have all told almost of

459

simple innocence, to ease a situation and where we reckon there should be no comeback. Little lies, otherwise called 'white lies.'

Why lie? It starts when we are children. Lying to a parent to avoid being told off – risking a withdrawal of approval, of love, even if only temporarily, or wanting too much to have our own way. Lying to a sibling to retain something of theirs we have coveted, nay, stolen, and then have to hide it away. Older, lying to impress, to create an impression of someone of character we'd like to be, but we know we aren't. Lying to gain a position or pecuniary advantage, as in business. Bigger lies. And then even bigger ones when cornered under questioning, until the lie bubble bursts. Telling lies can become so ingrained, so habitual, we get to see nothing wrong in it. We even convince ourselves sometimes that what we have told as a lie, a fantasy, has, with time, now become, for us, the truth.

So, it seems very clear that we would be well advised to consider very carefully where we place our trust. We can always respond to the question, 'Can I trust Fred?' with the answer, 'Trust Fred to what?' Let's not rush to endorse someone unthinkingly, however much we like and approve of a person. Being totally trustworthy is a rare commodity, and for most of us, we can be trustworthy in so many things, but with the caveat, trustworthiness with money, especially when big sums and in cash are involved: that resolve to be worthy of trust tests some to the limit.

So, it's trust to what? Do we ever know someone well enough to be able to give them a positive answer? And yet, if we hesitate, if we hold back, if we say, we are not sure, those words alone can tarnish an otherwise spotless reputation. So, it's still best to ask, 'Trust to what?' And then answer something conditional, such as, 'I have no reason to think you cannot trust Fred.' Or 'I believe him to be a trustworthy person,' in preference to saying, 'Oh, yes. You can trust Fred.'

The danger, the risk, of not trusting someone is that we can grow into a situation where we mistrust people, like the police. They mistrust everyone; it's their default position. They couldn't do their job properly if they didn't begin from the starting point of mistrusting simply everyone. How on earth someone in the police force ever manages to switch off their mistrusts enough to fall in love and marry someone is nothing short of a miracle of the human mind. A policeman by day, and a lover by night. Clever, that.

So, mistrusting is not the same as not being prepared to be trusting. Ignoring the remarks about the police, mistrust implies some prior assessment of someone that may or may not be a valid assessment, as in 'I wouldn't trust him an inch.' It is a fine line between being prepared to place a trust in someone after a fulsome assessment on the one hand, and on the other hand, a 'bind trust' that is given with no prior character assessment at all. In adopting an overall attitude of mistrust, we'd probably only rarely say what we are thinking, 'Okay, then, prove to me that you are worthy of my trust; I've so far formed the opinion that you are likely to prove unreliable, especially when under pressure, or always just too relaxed, and I know you frequently divulge things when you shouldn't.'

And isn't that the point? Most of us can be completely trustworthy when the going is smooth. But when conditions change, we, say, get overtired, have just a bit too much to drink, or we can get to feel so badly wanting to share the information we were given trustingly. And then at times we are subconsciously too keen to befriend, to gain another we can, in turn, place our trust in, and so doing, shattering our trustworthiness. We need to beware when interrogated by a very inquisitive, artful person who is best-guessing but making out they already know, and, in so doing, we then admit that fact, confirming what we have been given to hold in trust. Then we realise too late that we have been tricked.

Why is it we lead our lives in such a way, as an obligation on matters of trust to do with information? Why can't we always be open and above board? We can work out quite easily one reason why we cannot be open and that is that we need to be a commercial success with our first-in-the-field patented product so that we can earn our livelihood, and our shareholders can have a due return on their investment. And then there are national secrets, on which our security and defence rely.

But there are many other human character traits where some scurrilous conduct is expected to be held secret. Oh yes? Why? Well, it probably is none of our business, and it's hardly our job to go 'tomtitting,' but what about when the husband, the cuckolded husband, says, 'Why am I the last person to know my wife was cheating on me?' Life is just like that, and if we have a trust specifically given to us, we should honour that, but if it is a dishonourable matter, and having already been told, we can hardly decline the trust, but we can say we must be relieved of that trust at the earliest opportunity, that is to say that the other person should be told either to agree to 'come clean' or to promise and undertake to cease the unworthy conduct, forthwith.

Trust, truth and lying are complex issues and can only be looked at in the context of our total understanding of our thoughts, our feelings, our adopted values and so our understanding of what love really is. And it may be handy to remember the words of the song, 'No one is with you constantly, no one is completely on your side...' We so desire to place trust, as almost a desperate need, that need that sometimes some of us give into too readily. For everything we do, we do for love, or to make up for the lack of it. Placing trust, appropriately and inappropriately, has much to do with that.

While there is a gradation in trust in that we can trust someone to certain things, perhaps simple, uncomplicated matters and certainly not vital matters, especially to do with money, or commercial or national secrets, there is no true, easy, neutral position. There is no position where we can say we neither trust nor mistrust a person, because to fail to say we trust a person, in effect, whether we like it or not, we are saying there may be grounds for mistrust. Shouldn't we either endorse someone we might consider as trustworthy on a particular point or not? This is always a gamble, as explained earlier, or we stray into the realms of implying we mistrust a person. We could adopt a position and admit, 'I have no grounds for saying I believe "so-and-so" can or cannot be trusted to or with such and such.'

And that's about the measure of it. Trusting is a dodgy business: we become trustworthy only once and when we have proved we are. And hopefully we will always, from then on, be reliably trustworthy. It is not an easy merit to bear. And it's also like it used to be landing an aircraft at RAF Gibraltar. Pilots were not allowed to land an aircraft there until they had done it before (i.e. accompanied and witnessed). It's doubtful that many gain the rank of trustworthiness by being on an accompanied and witnessed training run.

—•—

CHAPTER 38
IN FOR A PENNY –
IN FOR A POUND

A wonderful maxim so often heard was, 'Look after the pennies and the pounds will look after themselves.' Oh, so true, but is it said much these days, to the young in particular, who always leap out of babyhood thinking money grows on trees?

When we start earning from leaving school, that reward from our effort in getting out of bed seems a worthwhile increase over our pocket money, which we are no longer going to receive. Years ago, wages were mostly paid in cash, but not so far back as when we were paid partly in salt that gave rise to the term 'salary.'

What a joy it is being young with no responsibilities, other than the amount to be handed over to our mother as the amount now demanded on payday for our keep. If no keep was demanded, then our parents were doing us no favours at all, because the sooner we realised our true cost of living, the better. But we need dosh to go and have a jar with our mates down the local of an evening.

Then we want to buy a car, get a set of wheels, probably an old banger, our first car love. Soon we want something with kerb appeal, which means borrowing or hire purchase or some such finance deal, with the repayments that have to be met or they, the moneylenders, will take our car away from us. We find we are no longer so flush with cash, after exorbitant car insurance and tax, even for an old banger, that the car and those planned treats out with our girlfriend, showing off, like they do in the films, buying her a candlelit dinner, with hopes of being generously rewarded on the back seat of our car on the way home: now all gone. We are growing up, getting wiser.

Slowly we can learn about 'eking' out the money through to the next payday, and then comes the responsibilities of renting a flat, with a chum or two, or even a girlfriend/boyfriend. What years ago, for us, was at first the free pleasure of our pay packet has now become a business, the business of living; so much for food, so much for gas and electricity, the rent, the car, the rates and oops, 'crikey,' there's nothing left for fun.

So, we get a better-paid job, the extra is a delightful prospect; we plan all the great things we are going to do with the extra cash each month. And then we see on the payslip, an amount, a staggering amount taken in tax. We feel this is unjust. We blame our employer, those rich bosses with their smart clothes, and posh, powerful cars. Oh! Yes! We've seen them, we noticed them, but they haven't noticed us. How did they get to be so rich? Are they crooked, getting some of our so-called tax-take?

Our new colleague at work seems a calm, sensible sort, and he/she explains the tax system to us, and we calm down, but still angry inside about how much has been taken in taxes and NI. We realise we are not going to be so much better off after all, but we are not prepared to be frank and honest with our 'partner,' as this would be just too 'humbling' and we can't quite manage those earlier plans. So, we get a credit card and start spending. And so on, until the card is 'maxed' out, and so we get another card, and spend until that's maxed out and so on, until the day of calamity happens, and real trouble comes, the law, the companies are going to sue you for payment. Help! We want to do 'a runner,' but there's no real place to hide because everything, just everything needs money. We may even then be tempted to crime, to take from the 'haves' to give to us, 'the have-nots.'

If we are fortunate, we will have a friend or a relative, possibly a parent, who, to save us from prison, will pay off the debts for us on the promise we will get real, get in 'control of our life,' and budget and track our income and expenditure. Salvation: how will we ever repay such kindness? We can, if made of the right stuff, and start a low-level savings account to drip-feed in, for years if need be, to build up a sum to return to our benefactor, if he/she is still alive by then. But it's the moral principle that counts, the moral obligation.

'Neither a borrower nor a lender be' used to be the mantra of so many in Victorian and Edwardian times. It's not a bad mantra, but it only applies to private borrowing and lending, between private people, and not in business. The business principle is to borrow money, to get to know how to use that money to make money; meaning, at first, to earn a living, and make more money later. All businesses need funding, either by borrowing, from a bank in the high street, or a commercial bank in the city, or even go to private equity firms. If they think your business worth it, and you have a matching collateral, that bit of worth, your home, that you dare to risk in the business, or if the business is already established, then borrow from the shareholders.

If we do wish to borrow or lend privately then, here is the caveat; there should be at least three realisations; one, to have the agreement and all relevant terms for its repayment written and signed and dated, with a copy each. Two, that the lender has to accept that they may never get their money back, in full or in part. Thirdly, that we may lose a friend if we choose, or he or she chooses to 'fall out' over this 'business' arrangement, or we may even lose a family member over our lending of money and expecting it to be repaid. Never mix business with pleasure, i.e. with friends. Never. Relatives, yes, but only with the huge risk of never seeing the money again; but friends, never, if you want to stay friends of any sort of high mutual regard.

Some enjoy budgeting and tracking their finances, 'The King was in his country house, counting out his money, The Queen was in her parlour, eating bread and honey' (and getting fat!). Such truth in this old nursery rhyme. For others, care of their financial resources is a chore and a bore, but, like the waste bin, if it's not attended to by our putting it out for the council, its contents will rot and stink, and the same goes for our finances. They need looking after, like the garden, like our car, like our house even. They may not be as 'real' to us as the garden, or our car, but, by George, they are real enough, and will jump up and bite us if not attended to with a modicum of skill and regularity.

Looking after our finances is being responsible – we will be response-'able,' as we track and see trends. It helps unrealistic expectations being avoided, and this brings a fair degree of contentment, some peace of mind. More free from headaches, like those real headaches that only deep finger massage to the base of the skull downwards to the nape of the neck would relieve and done repeatedly until the headache has gone; better than paracetamol alone.

Through budgeting we make for ourselves a smoother pathway to our goals. Goals for intellectual or educational gain may involve some financial commitment, such as the cost of training courses, books and certification. Goals for acquisition of material objects and property cost much more so, and this can involve additional effort at work, and additional effort in budgeting, making savings. We may be able to enjoin our partner in this, but our partner may not be equally committed and compliant, may be half-hearted, or even begrudging, for we cannot, or should never make goals for other people. When weakening in resolve of achieving a worthy goal, we can always resort to imagining that end-of-the-movie feeling, that good feeling we get at seeing the story end well, and so imagine how what we have worked and saved for will turn out to be worthwhile, a treat, and a satisfying acquisition, a comfort achieved. Enjoy. Budgeting and goals are worth it.

It seems an odd matter to ponder upon, but there are very many people in life who haven't the foggiest idea of how businesses function, what they are all about, other than a notion that they are all about profit. Teachers and lecturers, especially, minds full of academia, may be able to fit into the curriculum of history and media studies, some down-to-earth, practical knowledge in this respect, if they have it themselves. But many do not, cannot, pass that on to their eager and not so eager students who really do need a boost, a kick-start into the life of reality waiting for them at sixteen or eighteen, or even 21, depending on when the parental and educational umbilical cord is finally cut.

In dealing with our own finances we will in time come up against or be introduced to the structure and function of the various aspects, the component parts of a business. All businesses have the same basic component parts, and we can even see the same essential elements in our own private affairs that, if copied and adopted, can make our handing and understanding of our finances and some other aspects of our life become so much easier, worthwhile and orderly, more businesslike.

There are only two overall aspects of a business. The one, called here 'Business Promotion,' and the other 'Resource Management.' Let's look at Resource Management first, for without any resources there can be no business to promote.

A business needs a physical resource from which to work, as in from where to operate its business. However much we fight the idea, we have to accept that the corner of a bedroom with a sort of worktop, a computer and a broadband link is the physical resource, as is the garden shed which is given over to running the business up until we have the huge edifices of vainglory of the mega-international companies. Their physical resources, 'gotten' so gross, that in themselves have to be managed. That physical resource can be owned, perhaps on a mortgage or a business loan, or formally rented, but should never be 'borrowed' as in rented informally with no security, where a 'landlord,' once a good friend perhaps, boots us out, often precipitately. Most of the physical resources, the building, the fixtures, fittings and equipment all depreciate with age, use and obsolescence.

The business also needs a financial resource. In the first instance this means the capital, the chunk of money that sets us up. It could mean the cost of the new garden shed for an office, and with it a desk, the light, telephone and broadband installation, a computer or laptop, some stationery; all 'set-up costs.' And what we buy in the setting up is then shown at a value later in our accounts that have to be drawn up for taxation purposes, and for valuing the business in case we offer it for sale. The price we bought the physical resources at may be reflected in the account, but so will a revised value written down and in the accounts to reflect the depreciated value those 'assets' now represent. The business van, now at one cost, immediately written down as we leave the showroom. That written-down sum is shown in the accounts, as depreciation, and may affect any tax liable later.

As well as the set-up chunk of cash, we will need a sum left over as working capital. The whole object of a business is to sell goods and services or just goods or just services, for profit. First, we sell the product, and then we wait to be paid. If it's a cash-only business like a barber, or hairdresser, or fish and chips shop, when we are paid cash on the nail, allowing no customers any credit, everything we get in is 'turnover' or more precisely gross turnover. But most businesses realise they have to wait for the money to come in, and their invoices sent out for goods or services supplied expecting to be paid within their stated terms of seven days, fourteen days or 28 days. However, in the meanwhile, we will have bills coming in from the suppliers to us of their 'raw' materials that we have then sold on, modified or not in some way. Those intrinsic costs have to be paid for promptly, or should be promptly. If we are supplying some big businesses they may keep us, their suppliers, waiting 90 or even 120 days to improve their cash flow, or so weaken us, their suppliers to negotiate a cheaper rate, or weaken us, then, so that the big business can then buy us out, the small supplier. It's rather like a grown-up game of Monopoly, all based on our fears of failure; fear that the business may fail due the success of its competitors or through inadequate businesslike conduct of its owners or its directors. The directors are there being employed by the shareholders who, in reality, are the nominal owners of the business, like sleeping partners, and employ the directors to run the business for them.

After paying for our supplies, the raw materials, the amount left from the gross turnover, the sales, then becomes the net turnover – which some erroneously refer to as profit, or profit on sales or even gross profit. This is not the figure to rely upon, and not that which is wanted for the owner to get carried away with and go and buy a yacht. The reason is because the true profit figure can only be arrived at after overheads and dealing with the wretchedly cumbersome acronym EBITDA. Overheads are all those other costs of having the physical resources, the financial resources, e.g. the costs such as bank interest etc., the human resources (not yet discussed), and the costs of promoting the business such as advertising, websites, stationery etc., as well as any costs of governance (sets of procedures to do with compliance with the law, such as Health and Safety). EBITDA is that uncomfortable collection of ponderables and imponderables the government's fiscal agent, HMRC, apply to those in business.

EBITDA means 'Earnings Before Interest, Tax, Depreciation and Amortisation and can be taken as an indicator of the performance of a business, but it should be borne in mind that a set of accounts reveals only a 'pulse take' on the business within that given time frame only, and the worth of the business can be perhaps better taken from the balance sheet which records the situation with respect to all the business's physical and financial resources and so the total worth of the business as reckoned on that day, the date on the set of accounts. Some balance sheets include a variable imponderable called 'goodwill.' And thereby hangs a tale, beyond the scope of these humble writings; suffice it to say, it is an added amount taken as an imagined or standard reckoned sum, for that trade or profession, to represent the potential worth of enjoying the profits of that business for the foreseeable future.

One can easily see that the list of charges, costs, against all the sales income achieved is considerable and can be quite off-putting. It's frankly a wonder some businesses make any profit at all. Only when all the imponderables have been calculated and taken into account can we then decide if it is reasonable and safe to go and buy a yacht. And this is the point. To run a business, one has to be focused. To own and run a yacht, one needs focus. No man (or woman, however smart) can serve two masters. That is to say, it is unwise to buy a yacht ever, if running a business, but many do, or would if they could, because they are simply so much fun, so much pleasure, except perhaps in a gale, or when the keel falls off. And the lesson we should learn is the same lesson we should learn from business. It's better to rent a facility than to own it. Or more precisely, for the business to own it. If we start out and buy the physical asset, the building the business is in, we might very well be advised to 'take if off the balance sheet' and rent it back to the business. If the business goes bust, it doesn't take the asset of the property, and we can keep the asset as a reserve for rebirth of another business or retain for our retirement to enjoy a rental income. So, we'll charter that yacht and buy when we retire, so we can focus on the business while working and focus on the yacht in retirement. Good plan.

After all, what is retirement? Is it when we have a sufficiently large pile of nuts to see us right through the autumn and winter of our life? Well, yes, in a way. But there's another way. In Jane Austen's *Sense and Sensibility* Sir John asks a young lady about her beau, 'What is his profession?' She replies, 'He has no profession.' Upon which news Sir John pronounces, 'So he's a gentleman, then.' The point being that, back then, a gentleman was someone with a large enough pile of nuts, or received a regular and handsomely large supply annually of nuts, that he need not work, and that is where we are at today in retirement. We are all now gentlemen, then, and ladies, too, by today's reckoning, once retired, at least by Jane Austen's definition; that life of only two facets, the self time of recreation and sleeping.

And so, to the final of the three essential Business Resources that have to be managed and that is Human Resources. Many hate the phrase, likening people to inert objects such as property or pounds and pence, balance sheets. Whatever term is preferred, hopefully nicer for the understanding of people and their sensibilities being well taken into account, as to make some sense, there is no getting away from the fact that we need people. Even the one-man business has a human resource, it's him, or her. And being human, are subject to all the vagaries that humans are subject to. Humans can work well, learn and improve, become expert, can slope off early, or stay late, perhaps at no charge to the boss, can accidentally damage machinery, can fall sick, need holidays, pay rises, need a pension fund contribution, need Health and Safety policies and procedures, all sorts of operating procedures, including anti-theft and anti-abuse policies and can go on strike. Oh. Yes. Human Resources, they are always a headache. Employees have masses of legal rights. The employer seemingly has none where employees are concerned. Employment law forces bad employers to be better. It does not force bad employees to behave better; if anything, it facilitates any badness on their part. We need people, for our business depends on them. If we ever managed entirely with robots, whatever would our view on business and life in general then be? Would we all become 'gentlemen' (and ladies) any the sooner?

So, let's be clear. There are only two reasons for owning a business worth thinking about – to provide a livelihood and to sell one day. The business has two parts only, its promotion and its resources. Meerkat simple? Hardly, but worth the effort, usually.

Arguably, it's the promotion of business that provides a third reason to own a business, and that is that it can be, or perhaps should be, fun. Not juvenile frolicking fun. Not that wicked sort of fun doing down our competitor through unjust practices. No, we mean the fun of success. It can be so gratifying and also rewarding as new procedures and new equipment are developed to make business life easier and contribute to the success of the business. Of course, there are great and heavy responsibilities mostly due to the vagaries of people in the business or in other businesses or even clients, but overall, it should be fun. This is the attitude we should have, to go to work each day believing we are going to enjoy our work, even the stiff bits. Seriously: enjoy. For attitude plus aptitude equals altitude.

While concentrating on the pounds piling up from our saved pennies, we should not neglect another aspect of our finances that is linked to our self-esteem. This is to do with generosity. Our budgeting ideally could include an element of generosity to others, who can be loved ones, as in our family (no one likes a skinflint), but we should beware children getting to expect money from grandparents and uncles and aunts as the parents should be consulted and saving anything given can be learned as a good habit. Beware also grandparents 'competing for affection' by giving more than another relative.

There are aspects of income and wealth, generosity and meanness we can consider. We may not always feel like being generous, and on occasion we want to withhold from donating without feeling mean-spirited. If we know we are generally generous then we should take comfort from that, and often we may regard it as being sensible on occasion. Some are so generous, even 'to a fault' as in 'the widow's mite' – for those who can remember what that Biblical story was – it certainly is a story that tugs on the heartstrings. And yet, there are those who are so mean it is breathtaking.

It's probably to do with our desire for gold, and to accumulate a pile of nuts that will see us through. That may be the innocent explanation, but it is just as likely that meanness and generosity are either 'in the genes,' as in our nature, possibly from our training and examples set in childhood, especially a childhood with other siblings, or it can just as well be a learned habit. Why, how, for example, would anyone learn such a habit of generosity or meanness? Well, we know that we are influenced by people we admire or have a respect for; people who for us can be a subconscious role model, to align with our self-concept. From them we can learn to be either generous or mean. For example, if the role model is mean, he or she might say, 'I never leave tips in a restaurant; the waiters have their wages.' Or he or she might say, 'I never give to charities, they're all a bunch of scroungers, and if you give to one they all want you to give something.' A real hard man, we may think, who knows what's what, I want to be like him! Whereas the role model who gives, just gives and makes no song and dance about it, he or she does it quietly and with respect for the recipient. The recipient may modestly accept his or her gratuity, or, rather like the attendant on the Spanish beach given a tip for reserving a sun lounger, shouting a mighty 'Gracias,' just to let everyone else on the beach know they should be tipping him, too. Jesus gave good health back to the sick and told them not to tell anyone what He had done, but of course, they all told. The principle is the same.

The Church of England has tried to 'impose' guidance from the Bible on how much of our annual income we should give to the Church; it's in the region of 10%. Of course, with the Church being so rich up to the middle of the 19th century it has become progressively impoverished and few know the real facts of its situation. As the British people are following religion less and less, fewer are giving. Does anyone give who doesn't go to church? How well off or not are the other denominations: Roman Catholics, for example? That one may wish to give to the work of the Church is a matter for the individual, and doubtless the money is either well spent or well conserved. We know that the Church does a tremendous amount of benefit work for the sick and needy, whatever we may think of its teachings, its liturgy and the scandals. We may give to the British Heart Foundation as a worthy charity or any other humanitarian charity, and we give with a matter of trust in the expectation that the money will be well spent. Not to give on the premise that we don't know how well the money will be spent is a false pretext. Does one concern oneself with how a waiter will spend his or her tip?

There are others who give incredibly freely to their family, their children, even to the point of 'spoiling them' and to some, spoiling them 'rotten,' which is to say that the generosity is so great that the child loses all sense of value, and enters life as a damaged personality, sometimes permanently damaged.

The matter of generosity and meanness comes right back to not how well off we are, not to whether we reckon we have saved enough nuts for our retirement, but to how we choose to feel about ourselves. No one can give money they do not have and with those who are hard up we find that they are usually some of the most generous people we can ever have the pleasure of meeting. They give what they have. They give their time, they listen, empathise, they will make and mend things for us, they will go to the shops or other suppliers of goods and services for us. It is a matter of true generosity of spirit where we stand on giving or not. It's in the spirit that we see the nature of people. The sad thing about society today is that we are more insular, more inclined to be intent on what's on the telly than give our time to help a charity or some other needy organisation. We have become more insular, more selfish, more acquisitive, more desirous and so more ready to go on spoiling ourselves as we are told we must by the holiday advertisements, and because we deserve it. What rubbish. We need to be really sure about what it is we have done over and above earning a living before patting ourselves on the back and saying, 'Yes, I deserve to spend £5,000 on myself and go on a cruise,' and not for no good reason other than we got out of bed and went to work.

So, generosity and meanness are down to attitudes, and attitudes are malleable, that is to say open to influence and self-adjustment, and also open as to the choices we can make. And like so many of our choices, they are best if we research as many of the factors that have a bearing and then to make our decision, our choice, accordingly. And like all decisions, we can do our best by striving to see that they work for us; and if they don't, we can always review them.

Our money should be our servant; we should make it work for us, as in using it as wisely as possible. Not to get carried away with the pay rise into thinking suddenly we have entered the land of milk and honey. This is a trap that happens to those who are not fully aware or in control of their finances. Couples mostly usually share the finances as agreed between them. This is fine when things are tough. But both of a couple, whether both out to work or not, each should have something, however small, to set aside for their own personal use, absolutely at their discretion. So, in any one household, for example, there could be three accounts: the house account that bears all the money coming in, the income, and all the household outgoings. The household account is the business account for the business of running their life together, its promotion and its resource managements. Then another account for one partner of the couple, and then another account for the other partner, and these personal accounts are drip-fed from the household account by standing order each month with an amount as has been agreed between the couple. One could say these small amounts are the directors' drawings against the profits of the business. This respects their individuality as well as respecting their combined-ness, their joint venture of running the business of their life, the physical, financial and human resources (usually each other, with their entrepreneurial skills and the children) of their life. They can also work on the matter of promoting their business – further training and study for a career advancement, for example. To keep something of what we have earned for our self is so sensible.

One final thing about finances. Today, it is all too easy to fall into the trap of talking about personal money to friends, their and our money. Indeed, the whole subject of the cost of things is a bore, and very lacking in taste and offends other peoples' sensibilities. This is mostly because we all attach different values to things, things that people buy, or acquire, by a gift, or an inheritance. It's not long before we can be causing envy, or jealously or be thought reckless or hard or just plain obsessed with money. Better perhaps to talk politics or religion at dinner than money. But only just better!

CHAPTER 39
ON WITH EXERCISE

Some people seem to like exercise, and some don't. But whether we do or not, we all need exercise. Our bodies can be likened to a biological machine, which is not entirely very different to a mechanical machine. Our bodies thrive on being used and waste away if not. Generally speaking, man-made machinery lasts longer if 'not used' or used lightly. But with our bodies, the rule is 'use it or lose it' and that goes for our minds as well as our muscles and bones, heart and lungs. So, it's use it or lose it. And again, use it or lose it!

That threat may still not motivate us to exercise if we are the lazy, sedentary or just a 'too busy' type. Why doesn't the news of the middle-aged neighbour, who died suddenly from a heart attack, or the sight of weak, old and frail people frighten us into taking exercise and looking after our bodies better?

The reason is because we don't 'work' that way. It's a type of negative motivation: 'I'd better or I'll finish up like that.' Such thoughts only create 'fear' and fear is not a positive emotion. Only positive emotions can create a sustainable and achievable goal. Fundamentally, we have to want to take exercise before we can happily fit that into our busy daily routines, or happily give up slouching in front of the TV or being glued to the internet.

Let's identify the exercise that we do take subconsciously, by performing tasks, for example, like bringing the weekly shopping in from the car. Perhaps three or four trips with both hands full of carrier bags. Do we want to take this exercise? Some might say, 'No, it's a chore.' But we should look at it like this: we want to get the shopping in, if we don't, why buy it? It will do no good just heaped in the car. So, getting the shopping in is just part of a larger goal, that of wanting to restock the cupboards because we know we will want to eat next week. And eating is fun! So we take the exercise of carrying in the shopping because we want to eat. And there can be no better just reason than that.

The same goes for all our daily routine. So-called 'tasks' of getting up, going to work, working etc. We do these things because we want to. We want to have a pay packet at the end of the week as it is a major goal achievement to have the money to buy food, clothes, a roof over our heads, warmth and having fun once free of work. It's a sort of identifying cause and effect: the want is the cause and the movement, the exercise of our bodies is the effect.

We can consider some other goals that we can choose:

- We want good health,
- We want to feel good,
- We want to look good,
- We want lots of energy.

And there seems to be only one practical way to get these things we want… take exercise, not heaps of it, but an adequate amount. People less fortunate in health often deeply and earnestly desire to be healthy and may achieve it. We have said how we can identify, how we can simulate a 'want' to take exercise, but there's an even more motivating process than just reading that paragraph and thinking it through. The more motivating process is the creation of desire within us.

To do this we can click back to the basic principle of making a list by writing down what we value most. One of these will inevitably be 'good health.' Surely, we've never met anyone who, when questioned, didn't make 'good health' very high on their list of things to value in their life, except possibly the young who've never been ill. Writing it down 'reinforces' the idea, the concept in our mind. Then think, and think deep and wide, about what good health is, or imagine ourselves as someone already looking good, appropriate body weight, feeling fit, agile, alert, healthy complexion, healthy digestion and 'radiate' health.

This thinking it through is meditation; a useful constructive meditation in which we can imagine ourselves already having, being, those things, fit, agile, energetic. Yes, that is our self-ideal. This creates desire and the thought-processes to create the want, the want to take exercise and, as we do, we enjoy it a bit more as we feel better, feel good.

But what exercise? Pumping metal in the local gym or health club, or pounding the streets, mile after mile in expensive trainers? Yes, if we want, but it's not necessary. There are better more convenient ways, more 'tasteful' to those whose enjoyment of mass exercise in health clubs is not their thing!

We could usefully go through a set of exercises which take five minutes daily, plus 20 minutes three times a week. But before doing so, many believe it is important to know a little about our body and a little about the mechanism of exercise; possibly a recap of what we learned at school in biology.

Our skeleton is the structure which gives our body its shape and protects vital organs within it. The skeleton is made of bones which hinge together so we can move. Attached to the bones are muscles which are like hydraulic rams on a mechanical digger, and we have tendons which attach the muscles to the bones to be moved. Ligaments are the strong fibres which form the restraining bonds between the bones at the joints, keeping them acting like hinges. Joints allow only certain ranges of movement. So, when we take exercise the muscle contracts, the tendon transfers the force to the bone to be moved, and the joint (hinge) allows the bones to move.

For every muscle which moves the bone in one way, there is at least one other muscle which is attached to the opposite side of the bone to move the bone back again. These two opposing muscles are called 'agonist' and 'antagonist.' The agonist moves the bone from its usual position or resting position, and the antagonist brings it back again. Simple! Just like the arm on a mechanical digger with paired hydraulic rams!

Joints are best if they are put through a full range of their capable movement at least once a day. For example, doing ten 'frog squats' holding onto the back of a chair or other firm support will flex the hips, knees and ankles. Standing on tiptoe first as high as we can and then stretching and arching our back backwards as far as is comfortable will exercise the joints of the spine and neck, anteroposteriorly (front to back). Then with feet comfortably slightly apart we can gently swing our extended arms to the left and then to the right, increasing the amount of swinging round as is comfortable, turning the head to go with the swing. We can gradually see more of what's behind us as we rotate more, but we do need to go gently at it and not try to prove how wonderful we are immediately. This will exercise the lateral joints system of our spines from the neck under the skull down to the lower back. The owl has 21 neck bones that allow it to swivel its head right round to see behind it. We have only seven.

Still standing as we were, then lift one shoulder as in a unilateral shrug and then gently lower the shoulder. Repeat this with the other shoulder. Do it several times. Then carefully and slowly do it with both shoulders simultaneously, but only lower gently or we can damage the nerves of the brachial plexus underneath our shoulder blades. Do this a few times. Finally, with our arms at our sides, for the shoulders, rotate them several times in one direction and then in the reverse direction. That's good.

Finally, standing just the same, with hands on hips, consciously relax and then slowly bend just a little forward from the hips (to look at our feet with knees still straight) and then let our arms hang loosely down. At first that is all we should do. Bending down flexing our back is the most frequent cause of back trouble. Our evolution is from four-legged creatures whose backs do not usually have to carry the whole weight of their upper body, front legs, head and neck as we humans do. We could say our backs just were not designed well enough. The problem technically is that as we bend the discs between the vertebrae, the bones of the spine, like trucks on a goods train on a steep curve in the rails, when the inner buffers of each truck gets squeezed against the next truck, and a gap appears between the outer buffers of each truck. If we imagine a giant marshmallow between the trucks it will get squeezed on the inner aspect, it'll pop, and the marshmallow's inner gunk exudes between the outer aspects of each truck.

Similarly, when we bend our back, the joints between each bone of the spine narrows and this transfers pressure on the semi-solid gunk in the discs towards the back aspects of the discs, where the tissues are now stretched. And sometimes stretched to breaking point in many people's spines that are weak through being unfit and unused to bending much. The semi-solid gunk oozes out into the tunnel in the vertebrae (the vertebral canal aka neural canal) and presses onto thick bundles of nerves housed in the canal and between each bone of the spine, some nerve branches exit to go to the legs and various parts of the body. The gunk presses on the nerves, and bingo we have pain, big time.

Disc trouble is not the only cause of back trouble; for in bending and stretching the muscles of the back, being unused to stretching as in a bending down, our backs can suffer minor tears in the muscles themselves and so this damage to the muscle cells, leading to back pain, sometimes very severe and disabling, can take some long time to heal. One of the most common complaints at the doctors' surgeries on a Monday morning is men with back pain. Men, mostly office workers, who spent the weekend digging the garden. QED.

There is little need specifically to exercise our arms as most people, even the elderly are using their arms for lifting and carrying all the time. We are not talking pumping iron here. That can be gained elsewhere. However, lifting anything much above shoulder height is done much more rarely and so we can think about that. Our arms weigh a significant amount, without any weights: just lifting our arms vertically upwards as if reaching for something on a high shelf, so to be parallel alongside our heads, is a good exercise, repeated several times. We can keep our arms straight out sideways and stretched out wide, held for a few seconds feeing a pull on our shoulder, and then carry on upwards to the top alongside our head. And then we can slowly and in a controlled way lower the arms to be alongside our thighs. We can do this exercise sitting upright in a dining chair.

There are many other seemingly contortionist exercises such as yoga and the like, but these simple exercises, if done with patience until some strength and flexibility are built up, will serve us just fine. The point being that, while these things are so easy when young and flexible, as we age they are not. Our arms grow heavy and our thighs feel weak. Exercise can help slow this ageing process. Watch children playing, and lambs frolicking, It's the joie de vivre. When did we last feel like that?

The most important thing we should remember is that ligaments and tendons are rather like hemp ropes, but with use and with gradually increasing workload (but not meaning any form of weightlifting) from repeated correct exercise they will gradually become stronger to become more like nylon ropes and even in time, if done enough, come rather to resemble steel hawsers. Excessive strain of the hemp risks damage, called sprains, when the individual fibres of the ligament or tendon sever, causing some bleeding, perhaps bruising and certainly pain.

So, we need to get fitter slowly. It's no good thinking that exercises will help us lose weight, and if that is the objective then let's go on a diet. The exercising is for health and fitness, not weight loss – and so is just not a good worthwhile use of our time if slimming is the objective.

If sadly, someone who has joint pain, too much to exercise, they can help themselves to retain and regain muscle strength by a method called isometric exercises. There are exercises that use the muscles but do not move the joints. The system was developed firstly many years ago for Marines and the like, fit, strong, young men who found themselves laid up and temporarily incapacitated by their broken leg set in plaster of Paris. The isometric exercises developed meant that when the casts were removed the clinicians were amazed to find that there was no muscle loss, no wasting during the twelve weeks that a leg was in plaster, through inactivity, and in some, the muscle mass had grown somewhat.

The principle of isometric exercises is to identify some immoveable object and then endeavour to move it or to bend it in some way, and hold that muscular effort for a minimum of six seconds. There are, as said, agonist muscle groups and antagonist muscle groups, but isometric exercises use both groups simultaneously. More detail on these exercises is beyond the scope of this book but the information is available for free on the net and there is no need to buy any equipment. The equipment is there, in the house, in the office, in the car, always ready. For example, if stationary in the car, and engine not on, we are just sitting there, we can grasp the steering wheel and try to squeeze it, to bend it into the middle of the wheel, Of course, we can't do it, but we can feel the tension in our arms, shoulders, muscles at the base of the neck, in our wrists and fingers. Hold that tension whilst counting one thousand and one, one thousand and two, and so on to one thousand and six, then relax and let go. Then try to pull the wheel apart, in the opposite direction. There, we have a set of isometric exercises. And there are leg exercises as well. The only other fitness things to complement these are some cardio, but that's not much help to the person with joint pain. The easiest cardio to go with isometric exercises is to jog on the spot, lifting knees reasonably on the spot for three minutes. A five-minute fast-ish trot on the exercise bike will do just as well and may be possible to those with some joint pain.

Finally of this quick 'work-out' (if we must call it that) we should think about our heart and circulation. Whichever way we cut the cake, there's no getting away from the fact that we know by reasoning that prehistoric man got his exercise mostly by walking, except when running hell for leather away from a sabre-toothed tiger. Working people, through the centuries, walked long distances to and from work. Keats walked sixteen miles from Chichester to Bedhampton where he was staying, probably musing on some poetry while going along. Armies marched 30 miles a day – no problem – only then to fight an exhausting battle, although Napoleon tried to arrange his long marches so his men could rest overnight and fight the next day, but then he managed to get his armies to march further in the day than any other general had. He frequently 'stole a march' and in doing so surprised his enemy by turning up early and catching his foe unprepared. He was a good chap, really, but a bit misunderstood.

So, the message is, go for a walk. Where? Along a path with cars, lorries and buses pumping out diesel fumes? No. Any good by walking will be undone

479

by the fumes. This is the trouble with cities. There's little safe air for walking. 'Someone ought to do something about it,' they say, amongst other things. But it's certainly true. Even if only once a week, we need to find a safe air area for a walk, for a 20-minute brisk walk, not a stroll and back. Strolling does no one any good except young lovers. The brisk walk is the thing at a rate of at least 3½ miles per hour (5 kph).

But this is hardly enough. So, we can look indoors for some 'cardio' exercise. Bungalows hardly fit the bill. There's an attraction in them to many, but without stairs, some other cardio is needed. An exercise bike is good as it's good for the legs, no real wear to the joints like jogging on hard pavements. So many deluded will regret it, later, when arthritis sets in, even after buying the most expensive trainers. Our heart is a muscular pump, and a pump with valves that need to maintain their integrity. Too much stress on the heart can strain the muscle fibres just like muscle in our back and limbs. What the heart muscle needs to get 'fit' is progressive exercise, a progressive increase in pump workload, by longer cardio exercise at first and then asking more of the heart by going just that bit further, either walking or on the bike. Gradually, month by month, not day by day or even week by week. People are so impatient.

Why stairs? Going up and down stairs several times a day, carrying up the laundry and other trips, to make beds, to change clothes, to take a shower are all good for the cardio pump. If fit enough, we can try not holding onto the banister, let the legs do the levering uphill of the body, not relying on an arm helping pulling the body up.

So why no diagrams here to demonstrate? All writers of exercises draw diagrams. Well, if we read and stop to work out what each phrase refers to here, it should 'stick better' in the mind, and this should come from a better understanding of the nature of the tissues, not that much, but better than a diagram. By taking it gently at first the natural movements described should do us no harm if otherwise healthy, but if in doubt we should desist, and ask for competent help, preferably from someone who has read and agrees with the above paragraphs, or we can go on the net to learn more about our bodies and how to exercise them. It is usually the older person, who has neglected exercise, who gets into trouble going at sudden exercise too vigorously.

One last thought. Being overweight is the biggest strain and stress we can put on our bodies, legs, joints, especially hips and knees, our complex feet structures, and our hearts trying to pump when constricted by layers of fat that our gluttony (yes, gluttony) has caused masses of fatty tissue to be deposited around our heart. So, we can see there is a direct physical, causal link between being unfit and being overweight. And so are we eating so much because it makes us happy, feel good, because we feel we've earned it, as in deserve it, or are we so unhappy we take solace in the only proven thing in our lives that dependably gives us comfort, for a while at least?

Just that little bit too much eaten each day in excess of our calories being burnt off in just standing still and in any daily activity we can muster to, and in the end the waistband stretches, and we need a size of clothes one up. Next year another size up, and so on. Inevitability, so it seems. How can we avoid it and stay youthfully slim, but not youthfully skinny, please?

The whole subject of dieting is fraught with competing ideas, and most do not work, or if they work, they only work for a while. It is just as hard to get excess weight off obese dogs, but some have been successfully returned to a healthy size on an exclusive diet of beef broth, but that wouldn't be adequate for humans. Over-weight pet dogs frequently have over-weight owners. The best guaranteed way for us to lose weight is simply not to eat so much; drastically cut down, but maintain enough fibre, vitamins and some first-class protein each week. The fats and carbohydrates will take care of themselves for they are nearly impossible to avoid in food. Fibre means fresh vegetables which also yield vitamins (if not overcooked to a soggy mess) and some meat has the rest, as well as some fats, although a little oily fish is very helpful to maintaining health. We can weigh our food portions at first, so we then get to know roughly how much we are eating. If a vegetarian or vegan there's oodles of advice around on how to achieve that necessary balanced diet.

But why go to all this fuss? Isn't this book about learning as much from prehistoric 'man' as possible? They didn't slim, they ate all they could, as in 'could get.' And there's the rub: they couldn't get a lot; and apart from fruits and berries, any meat and fish were a very rare commodity.

No, we need to control our food intake because as a civilised society we have learned to produce foods in such abundance that there is a surfeit in our part of the world. And this is the morality of the issue; the ethics of the situation. Here we are, rich and fat, with an abundance of food, and yet in other parts of the world people are suffering from malnourishment and children dying for lack of

481

food and water. How can we bear it? We probably spend £5-10 more on food each week than we need to, and yet would we give that money to an Ethiopian charity? And if we did, can charities actually get the food to the needy peoples of the world, starving in the middle of a civil war that has been raging for years? Who was it who said charities are just there for the rich to absolve consciences? That's just too cynical.

We lose weight, that's good, and then we slip back into the old habits of eating too much. For why? Oh, yes. Eating is pleasurable enough, mostly a guaranteed pleasure. That certainty counts for something; there's no denying that. The certainty of a physical pleasure versus that of a psychological pleasure. For most of us, there's no competition. For actresses and TV presenters, their livelihood mostly depends on looking good and that mostly for the under-sixties means having a trim, balanced figure, to stay in work. It's odd that film and TV directors and producers focus on mostly having good-looking, slimmish people to perform for their audiences, who these days are mostly overweight. They believe, and they are probably right, that audiences like to see and admire good-looking, slimmish people. But do something about looking that way ourselves? It's a wonder.

So, the moral of all this is to try and set some of the records straight, to slay some weird dieting notions, that have come about as others make a profit out of fat people seeking an easy way to get slim. Fat chance. Isn't it incentive enough to be able to actually exit one's car in a supermarket car park. Even as 'slim-Jims' we have trouble with that. Or do some just buy skinnier cars?

If we are serious about losing weight, the only way is to eat less. Find a way. Learn about the essential nutrient requirements of our bodies and we will be surprised how small, how little are the amounts that we need to maintain health via an adequate supply of minerals, vitamins, essential fatty acids and essential amino acids. The details are beyond the scope of this book, but the information is out there, and no one should have to pay for the information. If asked to pay, look 'elsewhere,' as Mrs Proudie says, 'You are needed elsewhere, Mr Slope, elsewhere.'

We can forget about exercise as a main means of losing weight. We'd have to do so much exercise most of us don't have the time or even the energy. We are better saying to ourselves that exercise is good, really good at getting fit, toning up the muscles, all the muscle, legs especially, but arms as well, and that good old ticker, beating way faithfully day in – day out, on an average of 80 or so times a minute. Exercise will, besides toning up and strengthening ligaments and tendons, sinews, it adds strength to the bones; less likely to fracture, either in trauma or spontaneity, as with persons with osteoporosis.

Many of the body's structures are duplicated; eyes, ears, kidneys, gonads, even nostrils, if you like, but we only have one heart. Okay, yes, it's divided into two sides and each side divided into two chambers, but it works as a whole, so we only have one heart, and 'have a heart,' please, look after it. Let's not make it work harder by surrounding it in a cocoon of fat. And that fat takes on the nature of the fat we eat. For example, of our average fat or oil intake, if we ate mostly oils, such as olive oil or sunflower oil in our food, the fat surrounding our heart and elsewhere in our body, at body temperature, which it would be, we being alive, is in a liquid state, within each of the hundreds and thousands of fat cells, loading the work of the heart, but at least, with a degree of liquid flexibility for the struggling heart, as it swells and shrinks with each pump cycle. But, supposing we ate as a part of our normal meat intake, only lamb fat, and lamb fat is heavy and stiffer and harder even at our body temperature, which is lower than a lamb's. This heavy, harder fat 'embarrasses' the heart, loading its work, adding extra strain, but also clogging the arteries of the body with cholesterol plaque.

The mechanisms by which cholesterol is developed in our arteries are still being argued over by those who work on such biochemical pathologies, but it doesn't take an Einstein or an IQ of a Mensa to know that, on seeing an obese body of someone on the post-mortem table, the excess deposits of fat contrive to confound the organs and tissues from their designed and useful purposes. So, if we can as we slim, avoid fats and oils as much as is reasonable in our diet, then gradually the fat cocoon around the heart will be resorbed, and the heart will say thank you.

Eating is a transient pleasure. Hunger can be real enough, but most of us in Western civilisation do not know what true hunger is. We say we are hungry, but it is a false sensation. False because what we are sensing is the signal from our satiety centre in the brain saying it is our regular time for eating. Like an automaton we eat so regularly each day that the body gets to accept it as a habit, a habitual biorhythm. The pleasure of eating is just that, and little more. Oh, yes, we are taking in some essential nutrients to sustain life and blood glucose levels, but with sufficient determination we can retrain those biorhythms, those repetitive urges of our eating so habitually.

Eating only at mealtimes would be a good start, and never eat in public, any food, including ice creams, while walking or in public transport unless in a Pullman (restaurant) car on a train, or a ferry restaurant. We can make it an objective, like we are brought up not to pick our nose in public, never to eat in the street.

Since we must eat, and as it's a pleasure, why not make the pleasure last as long as we can make it? We can eat slowly, with smaller bite sizes, we can masticate each mouthful more slowly, more thoroughly before swallowing. Some eat as if they haven't eaten for a month, and won't 'talk at table,' and it would be easy to imagine them as a Labrador with a knife and fork.

So, it is clear that dieting loses us weight, exercise gets us fit. QED, a good job done.

CHAPTER 40
TIME LIKE AN EVER-ROLLING STREAM, BEARS ALL HER SONS (AND DAUGHTERS) AWAY

The ageing process seems defined in the genes of all living things. In its simplest terms, all living things are born, mostly of a seed that mostly, but by no means all, comes from a mixing of genes from the parent stock. Having been born, or 'sprouted,' then grows the 'adult' (i.e. finished growing) then to go about reproducing themselves; and having done so, then age, wither and die, leaving the next generation to go through the same process and so on and so on, until the day of the last trumpet. Simply put, this is the meaning and purpose of life, and if the philosophers read this, they'd all be redundant, on this subject, at least.

If living things didn't wither and die the world would just suffocate from overpopulation with living things. So, is it right that, as humans with all our science and ability, we should want to prolong human lives? Won't we just get to clog the planet up, with no air to breathe?

It is natural in virtually all humans to want to carry on living, and not to want to die, if we are healthy and reasonably happy. Disease and poverty can and do modify the urge to survive. What can be done to stay as healthy as possible, with a mind that is contented, and our physical needs provided for (a roof over our head, a shirt on our back, and food in our stomach)?

Disease is the most self-limiting thing. Can it be avoided? Yes, it can but only to a limited degree. What is disease? The word comes from 'dis' and 'ease' i.e. we are no longer at 'ease' with ourselves and our environment, no longer at ease with life or with someone in particular. Whether we are at ease or not stems from our attitude to life, and that's not always within our control. 'Dis' merely means 'not' or 'no longer,' and creates the opposite meaning to words.

So how is disease defined in biological terms? Let's first look at health. Health is defined as 'living well within the limits of adaptation,' To explain 'limits of adaptation;' living things are created (born) with the ability to adapt to their environment. As the genetic complement mix from the parents works out, some offspring are better suited to survive in the environment than the parents, but some of the offspring are less well suited.

Those less well suited fail to thrive (unless it is a human who is born into a caring society). The environment contains all sorts of threats to living things. These can be infectious agents wanting to attack and invade living things. Just think of plants in the garden being attacked by greenfly, moulds, slugs and even humans.

Humans are also challenged by moulds, viruses, bacteria and parasites. Being challenged doesn't mean we succumb, because we have our defence mechanisms, such as our skin, our mucous membranes and our immune system, with its reticuloendothelial system of 'white cells' and such things as humoral antibodies and complement proteins, in constant circulation in the blood and tissue fluids, as well as other mechanisms, notably the intrinsic cellular defence mechanisms.

To stand the best chance of not succumbing, we need to keep those defence mechanisms as healthy as possible. The other part of staying healthy, other than succumbing to infectious agents, is the loss of ease arising out of trauma to our bodies. Not enough is known yet about the causes of the genetic diseases of man, but there is hope that that will come. Likewise, for cancer, it is slowly being defeated as knowledge grows. There is some evidence or at least some likelihood that cancer can be avoided or lessened by being 'at ease,' i.e. following a healthy lifestyle with good attitude, especially to stress, recognising it and dealing with it. But our environments of today are toxic, mutagenic, teratogenic and carcinogenic. Wow!

So, while health is defined as living well within the limits of adaptation, disease is defined as 'living at the limits of adaptation.' That is to say that if we go to those limits, find ourselves at those limits, our bodies have failed to adapt, to cope, and illness supervenes. And if we go even further beyond those limits of adaptation, more disease ensues, leading to death.

Much is written about how to keep healthy in old age; good diet, regular, adequate, gentle exercise, an occupation or an occupied mind. Much more is known these days about the effect of certain vitamins and trace elements on our immune system, but by far and away the most significant aid is the adoption of a positive mental attitude (PMA).

It seems very likely that we are born with a positive mental attitude as from birth babies only have two fears – as already well noted, a fear of falling and fear of loud noises – but PMA is just as likely to develop early in life from receiving unconditional love that also somehow brings about a sensible, intelligent child. It is just as likely that it is down to genes as well, as there are some who go through life, with whatever life throws at them, maintaining a positive mental attitude.

Learning and practising this attitude is seldom easy. We can start by accepting responsibility for our decisions; those thousands of decisions we make, most of them subconsciously every day from the moment we wake up each morning. When to get up, whether to shave or shower, what to wear, what to eat for breakfast, whether to go to work or phone in sick, whether we are going to tell the boss what we think of him or her! All of these things we need to accept the outcomes for, and that is taking responsibility. But if we are that boss, and our employee decides to tell us what he or she thinks of us, are we responsible for that? Most likely yes, through our decision to employ that person (who may just be an unpleasant person), or we may deserve the criticism through our management style. None of us likes to be criticised, and it's natural to be offended, but on reflection, we often find either that it was deserved, or that we can see that others are entitled to their point of view, even if we don't accept that. No need to be offended.

So, PMA becomes a habit after practising, to look into each downside situation to see where and how we contributed to the outcome that has gone wrong. Once that responsibility is acknowledged, however big or small our part in causing the damage that is the outcome, we feel less negative about the other contributor or contributors, and that is a maturing process.

It is impossible to go through life getting everything right. Human relationships are so complex that we are bound to make a gaff sometimes. To err is human, and to forgive is divine. The real challenge with forgiveness and accepting responsibility is the ability to forgive our self. We cannot like our self if we are carrying a load of guilt about our previous actions, and we cannot have a positive mental attitude if we cannot honestly say we like our self. And it's so hard really liking others we meet if we can't really like our self. And we are not talking vanity here either.

Coupled with the concept of responsibility and forgiveness is the concept of guilt, and guilt throwers and guilt catchers. There are some whose focus in life seems to be that of the 'blame culture,' throwing guilt at people, accusingly, or keen to identify guilty parties or persons, whether this is fairly and justifiably done or not. Others may be and often are only too ready to accept that guilt thrown at them, again often unjustifiably and erroneously. It is not good to be a guilt thrower and not good to be a guilt catcher. Accepting responsibility for our erroneous actions or words, and then dealing with them is one thing, but persisting with a feeling of guilt is not desirable and often harmful to moving on. Guilt throwers and catchers are best avoided. They are not forgiving types of people.

In particular we should never accept responsibility for another person's actions. Everything we do should be our choosing – despite the influences and input from others, it's always our choice, our decision. That input from others includes advice received. The world is full of people only too ready to give us advice, to tell us what we should or should not do. Don't go down that road. 'Advice is often given, seldom taken,' as the saying goes, and that may or may not be a good thing. We have the concepts of good advice and bad advice – it all depends if the advice was taken and how it turned out.

Be very wary of giving or taking advice. Instead, go for the help that facilitates our identifying all the factors that bear upon or relate to the decision to be made, i.e. all the 'pros' and 'cons'; identifying and evaluating these is the art of the practised decision-taker. Having said that, there will be occasions when the decision taken is simply, in the end, based on an emotion we have in our subconscious and playing on our upper mind, our conscious mind.

There are many factors that dictate the speed at which we age, but most influential is likely to be the genetic make-up we inherited from our parents. The rest, the unquantifiable balance of factors we believe we can actually influence, such as PMA, a sensible diet, comfortable environment, by which one can mean a good supporting mattress to sleep upon, and a sensible supporting armchair. As well we need to avoid situations where injury is just too likely, e.g. reckless skiing or horse riding or risky weather yachting, without proper precautions. Avoiding too much alcohol, poor diet, too rich in sugar or fats or too high in salt, instead going for freshly cooked food, especially fresh, lightly cooked green vegetables, so that the vitamin content is retained, not stewed 'veg' that has been sitting around on a servery waiting to be eaten. There are foods that are considered particularly good for our immune systems, foods like broccoli and blueberries and tomatoes.

As to exercise, so many young and older people go jogging and then have to give it up due to arthritic joints. Prehistoric man seldom ran or even jogged unless hunting to either keep up with a prey or run like blazes to escape a predator or from a forest fire started by a volcano. Generally, he had no other motivation to run, but would walk and walk plenty, to seek out water, or follow a prey or to go to a new area of vegetation to pick fruit, or climb over the ridge to the next valley where a pretty blonde maiden has been seen (Why blonde? Ah. There's a story, perhaps even a book.)

Walking with a fair degree of briskness is as good an exercise as most of the elderly need for healthy muscles and joints, heart and lungs. Jogging should only be done when the going underfoot is semi-soft or semi-firm; the sort of terrain our prehistoric man would have trod. Not tarmac or concrete, however expensive our trainers were! It can be a problem for those who have no pleasant walks nearby. Walking amongst traffic noise and exhaust pollution can hardly be therapeutic and so some excursion is necessary to reach an area for a pleasant walk and this adds to the time, and cost (but what price do we put on our health?).

But we should invest time in our health. So often we can't see what's around the corner in life. We feel good and fit and strong and subconsciously we think this will go on for ever. But, like our teeth, with hidden 'forces' slowly causing degradation, our bodies are slowly degrading due to ageing. The aim is to slow up these processes, but we can't stop them, and, just as we can look after our teeth, we can look after our bodies. Reasonable exercise is good also for the mind. The uplifting effect of exercise is well known. But besides that, if we are feeling downcast for some non-identifiable reason or a reason we just cannot rationalise, some good help that for some can come from taking St John's wort, the only other recognised 'over-the-counter' natural product accepted by the medical profession as having a therapeutic benefit besides echinacea. Exercise is a great help towards those needing some form of antidepressant in their life. The beneficial effect is also a contributor to the health of our immune system, so vital in the wish to minimise the effect of life on our slowly ageing bodies and minds.

The last offering here towards slowing the ageing process is to occupy the mind with a worthwhile activity, an enthusiasm that involves action, movement, getting out and about. By far the most helpful action, if not the most popular, is to get involved in a voluntary or even paid work with an organisation. It could be to do with a sport or a commercial activity, but nearly all charities need additional help, mostly unskilled help, but just an ounce of common sense (but sadly, as it's often said, it's not so common!) and a genuine desire and practical ability to do what is asked of us (and not what we think we should do, and so try to take over the organisation). Oh! Yes, it happens! It is truly pleasant helping others, but be careful about accepting responsibility in retirement. Some thrive, at least mentally, but all responsibility requires us to be 'response-able,' and in retirement we're taking care of our health, especially our mental health, our peace of mind and so our immune system. Avoid worry, concern and stress.

It something truly wonderful to see more and more elderly people 'looking' less than their age, deceiving us to the fact they already have 80 or even 90 years under their belt. One wonders why this should be so. That they have been able to steer the course of their life so to avoid serious trouble, have been fortunate enough to stay free from serious grief, worry and concern all help. That there is something in their genes can be well reasonably concluded since a mother or father also lived happily to a 'ripe old age.' Most are people with a pleasant, positive and accepting disposition. Not always feeling the weight of the world on their shoulders, they seem to take an interest in what's going on in the world at arm's length, and revel more in what's going on in their local community. They are wise enough not to think they can influence the politicians and local government councillors by fretting all the time that 'That shouldn't be so.'

The day we retire we go immediately, as immediate as saying, 'Snap,' from being someone, someone of position, rank, power and authority, of making decisions that carry, and also known as someone for what we are, of repute and reputation at work, someone to be reckoned with. We go to being no one, as in a no one, no one in particular, and we can feel like a fish out of water, a craft adrift, as in not under power, aimless, like a prisoner suddenly set free into the bright shining sunshine that temporarily blinds us as we blink and fumble for some dark glasses, some dark glasses behind which no one will recognise us, hopefully.

It can all feel rather as we imagine a 'knock-down' in a yacht that the ballast keel, which we have drawn the analogy as the loving partner in our lives, helps bring the yacht upright again, and in so doing sheds tons of water, like tears, to leave being a tangled mess of ropes and equipment on the deck and even worse mess below decks. The mess that has to be immediately tackled and straightened out before we can continue the cruise of our life, and no little time needs to be allowed for this.

But for even the most cool, calm and collected individual, however much he or she may feel prepared and have already imagined what their retirement will be like, nothing beats the real experience. That is not to say that preparation in the mind and in one's life is anything other than a very worthwhile exercise; and the sooner the preparation of attitude and finances is made, the better.

Stress is just a reaction by an individual to a stressor. One individual may react with or without signs of stress showing, but perhaps feeling it internally. The other, no reaction at all and wonders what the fuss is about. 'What stress?' Having said that, there are situations whereby many will acknowledge that a particular situation was 'stressful' but the point to hold to is that stress is the reaction, not the situation. That is to say that some with enough 'metal,' enough 'grit' and PMA, and their health will not react and go down with 'stress.' For the elderly, with our mind still feeling as we did when younger, we think we can carry on as we did, as we always did, only to find we cannot; we haven't the strength, the stamina or even the grit, the metal we had when younger. It's wisest in these situations to accept and protect ourselves and avoid 'stressing' our bodies' and 'or minds.' In short, 'Take care!'

Often 'taking care' can mean we need help with certain things and that means bothering someone else, which we hate doing, hate showing our weakness or inability, our feebleness, even frailness. Helpers come mainly in two types, paid and unpaid. The unpaid come in two types, those ready, willing and able with good grace, and those who help with a sense of obligation or duty as in help from the family, for whom having to help Mum or Dad can turn into an inconvenient burden. Try to trouble the children, now adults, as little as possible but bear in mind to 'take care' at the same time. It is most likely that the family are happy to help, but always seem to prefer bags of notice and find it irksome to have to upend their life at a moment's notice to go and sort out something for a parent that could have been given rather more notice.

'Getting old is not much fun' has been said time and again. Let's hope for as little 'inconvenience' as possible, but more importantly let's hope for the strength, determination and willpower to bear our lot as bravely as possible. Life is sprouting up anew all around while the life that was, that has been, is fading, with entropy all around us, and affecting us, too. As we wither, and shrink (but not our earlobes, for they just keep growing – all the better to hear with – some hope) we should have nothing to fear. But we do fear pain. Medicine does what it can to relieve pain, and we always hope for better pain relief to be discovered. Is there anything wrong in a 90-year-old receiving morphine and becoming addicted to it? If it is the only thing that relieves the pain, may she or he not have it? What if they lived to 103 years as morphine addicts, would that be wrong? Isn't this where ageism can be allowed? Is it only because it is addictive that some doctors hesitate before taking a really positive step and act to relieve pain in some of their elderly patients? Do some doctors feel that at 90 you've had a good innings and he or she needs to concentrate their delivery of their version of medical care on younger patients? Isn't that a sort of reverse ageism? The doctor needs to reflect on that; they, too, will be old one day. That goes for politicians, too.

Apart from fearing pain, the elderly fear going 'gaga,' 'losing it,' going 'DLT' (Do-lally-tap – will that Google?) and in other words suffer from dementia. Suffer? Who does the suffering? Some say it is the carers who suffer – those with dementia don't mind. That remains to be seen.

Old age is a social concern, a burden, as so many are living so much longer, but not necessarily a healthy, active, longer life, but an inactive life, just eating and sitting; without care, getting dim-witted, slovenly and smelly. Finding enough young to care, to be trained to care and to enjoy this kind of work is an issue. It is an issue to find the resources to pay them enough so as not to be overburdened by the sheer weight of workload for minimal wages. Unfortunately, we have to look to the young, those who are still in work, to fund the care of the elderly via taxation, for they in turn will be elderly, too, one day.

Why should it be the responsibility of the state? Without one's own resources, no one else has the 'readies,' the 'wherewithal,' not even the charities, and the state has no money of its own, only that which it takes from the population. If too much is taken in tax, personal spending stops, businesses don't thrive, and their tax contribution falls, too. So, it's a fine balancing act that any government has to do. To get into power, political parties promise all sorts of things, but the sensible among us will know they will have to fund it either by borrowing or by cutting down on other avenues of spending. They are rarely honest, because the truth of the situation is just too brutal to all for it to be publicly acknowledged. The veneer of our civilisation is very thin. It is so artificial, based on acquisition and hedonism. But what else could it be based on? We are comfort- and pleasure-seeking organisms.

Our society is so complex that no individual has to cope with the self-support of the basic life prehistoric man had to, foraging for food every day, scraping skins for clothes, gathering wood to keep the fire going as once created; it's easier to keep it going than struggle Boy Scout-like to create fire by rubbing two sticks together.

No; we can earn a wage and buy in all those things we need to sustain life. And in fact, so efficient is our society compared to our atavistic ancestors that we have enough cash left over for some comfort and pleasure – such things as a new three-piece suite, a new bigger, clearer, all-singing, all-dancing TV, and a football match to watch; or even go on a cruise. All nicely provided for us by leisure-orientated businesses that can only survive as a result of our pleasure-seeking.

Caring for the elderly doesn't create a great deal of business demand, but if more funds from the tax on our incomes were allocated to paying the carers, that would re-enter the economy and would turn out to be good.

But sometimes, in a fit of pique, a son or daughter may shout at its 'demanding-of-care' elderly and sickly parents, 'I didn't ask to be born!' to which the only answer can be, 'No, you didn't, and you won't ask to get old, either!'

EPILOGUE

These 40 chapters represent a journey not only for the reader, but also for the author. Together we have travelled from a state of 'deus incognitus' to knowing there is a God for all, about which there can seem to be little to brook by way of an argument, even from staunch atheists, whose acceptance of 'In Omnibus Deum,' a 'God for all,' will probably still not see their way through the fog to accept there is an afterlife, but there is a hope that some might, if they could just develop something like that of an uncanny perception.

We go to our highest mountains, indeed to all our mountains. We plumb the deepest depths of our oceans and intrude into the most remote parts of our planet, deepest forests, wild, endless deserts. We go to the moon. Done that; Mars next? Why? Why do we go to these places? Because they are there. And that's why we also go to the dark places, dark in the sense that there's no goodness, no godliness there. And some get lost there, so lost as to take up residence there, not like Dr Livingstone in Africa, but in this case more like Hitler, Stalin and others of that ilk, ruling in the dark, dark place, where there's never any peace of mind because they have to struggle with a 'continually revising agenda,' as their fight against the power of goodness gradually goes against them. We are all tempted to go, but if we do, there is this guidebook to help us find the way back, out of the darkness.

Towards more peace of mind is the desired message here, and the means by which this might be achieved. Hopefully, how we look at fate has been enlightened, and how we think about things that affect us in general, well enough, we hope, to be able better to temper our feelings. How we bond with another and make the bond strong and stay strong; especially how a marriage bond could, nay, should begin with a detailed business contract that spells out what happens if the contract is broken, just like any business contract. Less romance attached, more codicils, to include the children.

Will we ever think of the uniform of our armed services as representing, not a warmonger, but a peacemaker? These are brave people who have volunteered to be in the front line of restoring peace and, in doing so, have taken a job that they know could cost them their life. We can only hope and do our best to see that the politicians who pull the strings of the armed forces will themselves be of sound integrity and probity. And can there be any doubt as to what that is, what that means? Our perception can show the way towards any common agreement of what is right, what is good, and towards a greater understanding of what truth is, and reach both those merits.

These chapters can come at any stage in life to be a set of references; a set to refresh ourselves of the ideas, the challenges to accustomed thinking, and of the questioning of the reasoning behind our habits and rituals. If the revelation of 'In Omnibus Deum' has come across, then the message has achieved its objective. We now know that prayers are actually affirmations, not just a means, albeit desperate at times, but a form of self-programming, goal setting, for our capabilities that are always set in a sea where all else is down to chance. Those affirmations are the means by which we get in touch, awaken and stimulate our interaction with the great universal intelligence, the power of goodness that is God. That self-programming can include the downloadable apps, the numbers game, when a complete set has editions 3,5,7,8,10 and 12. These give us the tools we need to get on with the job, and if floundering with too much, too many numbers, too many 'editions' of the numbers game, then the inner Cabinet, that inner cabal of 5,7 and 10 will serve almost as well, until we call for the rest.

Some may feel here that the particular group that they identify with, a group that embraces a common thinking and common rituals, has been chided. If they are comfortable in their way of life, then so be it, but a chiding does no harm, providing the group is doing no harm to any other. Life is so diverse, so complex, it is always going to be difficult, very hard even, to get along with a fair understanding of each other, but 'going along to get along' can only work with a genuine goodwill in place, and in place enough to override any missing understanding. Healthy self-criticism stimulated by the fair and reasonable on the outside, and that can beg some introspection, surely is always a sensible, worthwhile exercise for any group, organisation or even a cult?

The journey has been to lay out an encouragement to consider, to reflect upon and to form a conclusion, nay, even to judge the thinking and the contained conclusions reached here in these lines drawn by this graduate from the school of life and the university of experience. Words, sentences and paragraphs have been included that are hoped to be found thought-provoking, of deep thought even, if the reader will only make, and then take the time. There is a dividend yield from accepting the philosophy of In Omnibus Deum that begins immediately, from day one of investing, and if we don't reach pension age for some reason, then nice things will be genuinely said and meant at our funeral.

If we are to take anything from here, it is this. It is best if we say there is Heaven and even Heaven on earth, that at rare times, we can experience with all our senses; and there is God in all, in all that is good, wherever there is goodliness. And it is best if we say there is no such thing as fate; we plough our own furrow, driven by goodliness towards our own Heaven. Let's not, therefore, argue the semantics of Heaven and fate existing. For just as a doctor, a surgeon, and as vets divine their clinical judgements based on training and experience, so we just come to know some things with an uncanny certainty to be true. And then we can be true to ourselves and to others and reach towards 'a peace of mind that passes all understanding' and with the sunny uplands well in sight.

And when all is said and done, and the umbilical is just about to be cut, as our offspring are about to launch themselves onto the sea, the often cruel sea of life, what can we give them for the journey? A copy of *Auspicious Thoughts, Propitious Mind*? Or just the advice to, 'Look after your teeth, and look after your feet; you'll need them both and always, always guard your tongue; it's the rudder that steers your course through life.'

Ω